about the author....

Frank Cusack was born in Glasgow in 1947. The eldest of three children, his family lived in the Gorbals area of the City.

He saw his first game at Parkhead as a 10-year-old and has been a loyal Celtic supporter ever since.

He went to Holyrood Senior Secondary School and later attended the University of Strathclyde to begin his training towards becoming a chartered civil engineer. In 1968 he married Margaret Kerr who had also attended Holyrood.

The couple moved to Guernsey in 1975 when Frank took employment with States Technical Services. He played football in the lower leagues for Rangers before injury forced his retirement in 1982.

In 1986 he accepted an offer to coach Rovers' youth one side and in the years since has served the club in a number of roles and can currently be seen taking the gate money at home Priaulx matches. He has written a comprehensive history of Rovers but this has not been published.

A keen supporter of junior football, he also served on The Guernsey Football Association's youth development committee for a number of years.

Frank and Margaret have four children, Jeremy, Raymond, Jackie, David and a grandson Oakley who lives in New Zealand with his parents Raymond and Chell.

Frank is currently the Professional Development and Training Manager for Guernsey Technical Services.

CONTENTS

ISBN 1-869833-53-8
Published by Tony Williams Publications Ltd

Printed by Latimer Trend & Company Ltd

Front cover:
1. Les Collins (Guernsey) with Graeme Le Maistre (Jersey) along with G.W. Pullin (referee).
2. The Muratti Vase. 3. Jersey 1913. 4. Alderney 1906. 5. Guernsey 1905.

A Message from the FIFA President

For the last 100 years, the football communities of Alderney, Guernsey and Jersey have held a remarkable competition, the Muratti Vase, which has, through the powerful bond that only football can create, brought together the people of the Channel Islands year after year in the spirit of fair play and competition.

As a testament to the pride and passion of the fans, players and officials involved in the Muratti Vase - past, present and future - this book revisits the first century of the competition with wit and intelligence, as it prepares to embark on the next century and fulfil its important role in the grass roots development of the game in the region.

I am certain that the readers of this book will enjoy it immensely and have no doubt that it will also help to promote the positive values that are at the very core of the beautiful game. This is particularly important in this time and age because sport - and especially football - has the unique ability to use its unifying power to combat social ills such as racism and violence. These principles must be advocated from local communities all the way up to the world governing body for football.

Together, we have developed the game and brought it to the world - with your help, let us all take the next step together and help make the world a better place through football! I thank you for your support because every single person counts - our collective effort can truly make a difference.

For the Good of the Game

Joseph S. Blatter
FIFA President

Credit Suisse Private Banking Millennium Foundation & the Guernsey Football Association

The Guernsey Football Association is extremely fortunate to enjoy an excellent partnership with the Credit Suisse Private Banking Millennium Foundation : a partnership which has made an immense contribution to the development of our young footballers from Under 16 through to Under 18.

The Foundation recognised that its objectives of developing young people could be achieved by exposing them to challenging off-island experiences through its involvement with the GFA. This helps to prepare our youngsters for the responsibilities of adult life.

Since entering our first agreement with the Foundation in 2002, the improvement in the performances of our youth representative squads has been evident for all to see. Commencing with the 2004-05 season, the Foundation has extended their support to assist our Association with the development of girls' football. Whilst this is in its very early stages, our Football Development Officer will no doubt benefit greatly from the additional financial support as he seeks to introduce girls' football in Guernsey.

The Guernsey Under 18s have shown a marked improvement during their three years competing in the South West Counties Youth Championship, and in the FA County Youth Cup. During the 2004-05 season, the squad achieved second place in their six team SWCC group, winning three of their five fixtures, and losing just one. Our Under 16s returned victorious from the 2003 Haarlem Cup competition in Holland, and fell only at the final hurdle when defending their crown in 2004.

Participation in both competitions would not be possible without the generous financial support received from the Credit Suisse Private Banking Millennium Foundation. All in Guernsey football have many reasons to be grateful for the partnership we enjoy with our friends at Credit Suisse.

Dave Dorey
President, Guernsey Football Association

Proud sponsors of the Muratti Vase Centenary Celebration book

Credit Suisse (Guernsey) Limited is delighted to sponsor this book about the history of The Muratti Vase.

Football is one of the world's most popular sports, uniting communities behind their teams and providing enormous enjoyment to both players and supporters. It is as popular in Switzerland (where Credit Suisse sponsor the Swiss national team) as it is here in the Channel Islands.

All three islands have a long and proud tradition of amateur football, the pinnacle of which is this competition. For the past 100 years the Muratti has ignited the imagination of local people and there is no reason why it should not continue to be the premier competition for the next 100 years.

I hope that all readers and past, present and future players value this book as a memento of the wholehearted commitment and energy which continues to make The Muratti Vase such an exciting event in the sporting calendar.

Albert F Good
Chief Executive Officer
Credit Suisse (Guernsey) Limited
Guernsey and Jersey

Credit Suisse, supporting the 100th anniversary of the Channel Island Muratti and its associated values of strategy, teamwork and commitment, which always contribute to winning results.

Publisher's Foreword

By Tony Williams

To play for your country is every sportsperson's ambition and although the Channel Islands obviously have a far smaller population than senior world soccer powers such as Brazil, Italy or England, the thrill and pride that comes with selection is just as meaningful.

Jersey and Guernsey usually meet in the final of the Channel Island Championships played annually for the Muratti Vase and perhaps a unique aspect of this competition is the fact that most Islanders will actually know someone who has been involved in one of these inter island games.

As a resident in Guernsey for two years, I had the privilege of playing alongside patriotic Guernseymen in a 'Muratti' and also for an inter island league champions game for the Upton Park trophy. The passion of the crowds at both memorable occasions was staggering and I experienced the two extremes of victory and defeat while the visiting First Division referees from England had their hands full on both occasions.

My particular 'Muratti' at the Track in St Peter Port was interrupted by the Jersey supporters, who stormed onto the pitch and through the players to confront the home supporters at the other end. I had just managed to give Guernsey a 2-1 lead and we were on top and playing well so the interruption was a disaster.

The game was delayed by about ten minutes and when we returned to the fray our rhythm had gone and Jersey deservedly won 4-2. I didn't cover myself with glory by taking myself off for a meal on my own as I just couldn't cope with losing in such a frustrating situation and letting the locals down on their big day.

If it mattered to me, it certainly mattered even more to the Guernseymen who had been brought up to the local rivalry but I will never forget the thrill of actually walking out in front of thousands, and indeed the build up in the media for two weeks before the match.

The football talent in the Channel Islands is never ending and you will be reminded of so many Island heroes as you read Frank Cusack's excellent record of the Muratti competition. Just look at some of the attendances that the games have attracted and the reports of some of the great battles that will remain wonderful memories in the football folklore of the Channel Islands. Will Alderney ever forget their only triumph in 1920 and how did they achieve it?

I was privileged to play in a Muratti and will always be proud to have worn the green and white of Guernsey. I still have many football friends on the Islands, and of all the players I have ever played with or watched in non-league football I have always considered Colin Renouf the St Martins and Island captain at the time, to be the most complete.

Every single sporting Channel Islander, whether a player, spectator or official will surely have their own personal special memories of past Murattis, and we're greatful to Credit Suisse for sponsoring this wonderful book which will revive them all and give hours of enjoyment as they are relived over and over again.

Tony Williams, watched by his great friend 'Bonny' Eldridge (left) and Jersey's Harry Proffit, gives Guernsey a 2-1 lead in the 1965 Muratti.

1

In the beginning.
1905.

The Muratti Vase had its beginnings in the early days of January 1905 as football in the Channel Islands was becoming more organised with affiliation with the Football Association in England.

The Guernsey Football Association was founded in 1893 and affiliated to the Football Association in 1903, thus making it the senior football association in the Channel Islands. In January 1905 there was some talk of an inter-island football competition between Alderney, Guernsey and Jersey and on 9 January 1905 a short article by 'Onlooker' of the Guernsey Press stated: -

'As for a Channel Islands competition, I am informed that a cup would be available at any time for such a contest if a representative team from each of the Channel Islands could be got together.'

In Jersey they held the first Annual General Meeting of the newly instituted Jersey Football Association at the Beresford Café on 16 January 1905 with nine distinct clubs represented.

It was reported in the Guernsey Press for 30 January 1905: -
'A football challenge vase has been purchased in Alderney to be competed for between the local teams.

A league will shortly be started on the same lines as the Jersey Football League.'
So the climate seemed to be suitable in the three main islands for the idea of an inter-insular football competition to be pursued further.

An article in the Guernsey Press under the heading 'Proposed Inter-Insular Football Challenge Vase' appeared on Monday 27 February 1905 and read: -
'The Secretary of the GFA informs us that the prospect of an Inter-Insular Competition between Guernsey, Jersey and Alderney XI's is being more than talked about. He has had a personal interview (informal) with Mr. Lander, the Channel Islands' representative of a well-known tobacco firm and this firm seriously thinks of offering a £25 Challenge Vase for competition between the three islands. So far, no absolute conditions have been laid down, as the whole scheme is at present in the embryo stage. The probabilities are that arrangements would be made by representatives of the three islands meeting in Guernsey for the purpose of arranging dates, methods of competition, gates, medals, etc etc.

Mr Landers' only suggestion in the matter is that, if possible, the first match be played in Jersey, in order to give football in that island a substantial encouragement. This, however, is not a hard and fast condition, and Guernsey being affiliated to the F.A., and also being the senior Association, might have first claim.

Mr Lander, who is now in Jersey, intends putting the scheme before Mr T. Adderson the President of the Jersey F.A., and if arrangements can be effected in time a start may be made this season. So far nothing official has transpired, but with Jersey and Alderney rapidly improving in the game an Inter-Insular Competition may soon become un fait accompli.'

More information became available when an article appeared in the Star for Thursday 9 March 1905: -

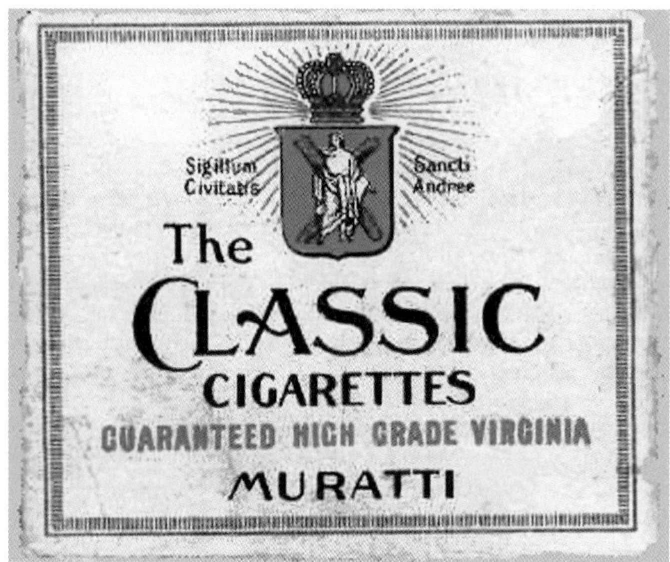

'We (Jersey Times) are informed by the Hon Sec. of the Jersey Football League that Messrs. Muratti and Co., Ltd., through the medium of Mr. E. Lander, their Channel Island agent, have offered a Challenge Vase, valued at £20, as a perpetual football trophy to be competed for by teams representing Jersey, Guernsey and Alderney, the conditions being that all players must be of three months standing in either Island, and that the first match must be played in Jersey. A meeting of the delegates of the various clubs will shortly take place in Guernsey as being the most central of the Islands, and it is hoped that the first match will be played during the month of April next. This generous offer by Messrs Muratti will, no doubt, be highly appreciated by lovers of football and, particularly, by footballers themselves. We (Star) gave similar information a week ago, with the exception of the name of the firm who were offering the challenge vase.'

The following day the Guernsey Press reported: -

'Negotiations have been proceeding recently for the inauguration of a Channel Islands football competition in which Mr. H.G. Bowden, the Secretary of the GFA has been taking an active part, and now appears likely to be brought to a successful issue. Mr. Bowden has received the following letter from Mr. E. Lander of Brook Street, Jersey: -

'Dear Sir – I have pleasure in informing you that the Directors of Messrs. B. Muratti, Sons and Co., Ltd., are open to give you a Challenge Vase, value 20 guineas, to the Channel Islands football club.

The only conditions are: -

1. The teams to represent Jersey, Guernsey and Alderney.
2. The players to be residents of not less than three months standing.
3. In order to give Jersey a start the first match to be played on their ground.

I am writing to the Jersey and Alderney Secretaries informing them of the conditions and will leave it to you to make the arrangements accordingly.'

'A point yet to be decided is whether the competition should be limited to civilians only, or whether military players should be admitted into the island teams. It would certainly be

a fairer test of inter-insular football to bar military players from this competition.
Arrangements are also being made for a conference here of football delegates of the three
islands with the object of starting the competition this season.
Mr Lander telegraphed today that it was not contemplated to place any restriction upon
military players.'
  On Thursday 16 March 1905 the Star reported on the Guernsey Football Association
Council Meeting. Item 7 of the agenda was concerned with the proposed inter-insular competition.
  'The Secretary brought forward the proposed Channel Islands' Competition for a silver
vase offered by Messrs. Muratti and Co. It was shown that owing to Rule 22 of the F.A.
permission to compete must first be obtained from the F.A. The Secretary was therefore
empowered to write to Mr. Wall, and also to make all necessary arrangements for a meeting of delegates from the three islands in Guernsey. Mr. H.E. Mauger was elected President
of this meeting of delegates; Messrs. Freckler and Bird were appointed as the Guernsey
delegates, with Mr. Bowden, Sec GFA, as Secretary of the competition pro tem. It is hoped
that the meeting will take place next Monday.'
  The Secretary of the GFA received the following communication from The Football
Association headquarters on 18 March 1905: -

'Dear Sir – I am in receipt of your letter with regard to the proposed competition. I cannot
venture an opinion until the application is before us.
I enclose form D and also send you for guidance in framing your rules a copy of a Report
recently presented by one of our Committees to which is annexed the heads of Rules for
Leagues and Competitions.
Yours faithfully,
F.J. Wall.

  Mr Bowden communicated with Alderney and Jersey, whose delegates will arrive on
Sunday and Monday respectively, in order to draw up rules and regulations governing the
competition,. The meeting was to be held on Monday evening at the Constables Office, and
the result will be forwarded to the F.A. for confirmation and permission.
  The Guernsey Press on 25 March 1905 reported: -
  'The Secretary of the GFA yesterday crossed to Jersey in order to interview Mr. E. Lander
in connection with admitting the Military into the inter-insular competition. Unfortunately,
Mr. Lander crossed to Guernsey by that morning's boat, not having received notice from
the Jersey Secretary that Mr. Bowden intended seeing him in Jersey. Mr. Bowden wired to
Mr. H.E. Mauger, President GFA, who during the day interviewed Mr. Lander here, and
after considerable discussion, the latter gentleman decided to agree to the unanimous decision of the Guernsey, Jersey and Alderney Delegates, viz, to confine the competition to
bona-fide civilian residents of not less than six months residence in the Island they represent.
  Mr. Bowden this morning received a communication from Mr. F.J. Wall, Secretary F.A.,
London, to the effect that the proposed competition was under consideration. An early
decision is expected.'
  The meeting of the inter-insular delegates on Monday 20 March 1905 was reported in the
Guernsey Press on Monday 27 March 1905: -
  'At last Monday's meeting of Delegates from Guernsey, Jersey and Alderney, Mr. H.E.

Mauger, President GFA, was unanimously elected President of the Committee of Management governing the competition. Mr. H.le Quesne, Treasurer of the Jersey FA, was elected as Hon. Treasurer and Mr. H.G. Bowden, Secretary GFA, was chosen as Hon. Secretary. It was also decided that each island should be represented on all occasions if possible by two Delegates, but the voting should be – one island, one vote. The competition will be on the cup-tie system, Alderney meeting Guernsey here and the survivor playing at Jersey in the final. Mr. W. Hammond, Secretary Alderney FA, has suggested Monday evening, April 17th, for the first match and April 27th was fixed for the final in Jersey.'

As stated previously, the competition was confined to bona-fide civilians of not less than 6 months residence immediately before the match in which they play. Next year, matches will be arranged that either Guernsey or Alderney will obtain the 'bye' and the final will be held in Guernsey. At present, it is not intended to hold any matches in Alderney for financial reasons, but should the island ever obtain a ground on which gate money could be taken, matches may be held there.

It was also decided that the winning team should be awarded small gold medals, and all visiting players should receive reasonable travelling expenses.

The next general meeting of delegates will be held in Jersey not later than July 1st 1905, when all accounts will be passed and audited, and any profit or deficit equally divided, and dates etc. for the following years matches arranged.

Mr. H le Messurier was appointed referee in both this year's matches.

The Star for Thursday 30 March 1905 reported from the GFA Council meeting that permission from the F.A. had not arrived, but might be expected shortly. April 17th at 5pm was fixed for the Guernsey v Alderney match in Guernsey, at the Cycling Grounds.

The Star for Tuesday 4 April 1905 reported on the unveiling of the Muratti Vase: -
'The Challenge Vase presented by Messrs. B. Muratti, Sons and Co., Ltd., of London, for inter-insular football, was received in Jersey on Saturday morning by Mr. Ed Lander, the firm's Channel Island representative, and will be on view in Mr. W. Lander's establishment, Bath Street next week, after which it will be on view in Guernsey about a week, and in Alderney for a similar period.

The trophy is a handsome one, and a fine specimen of the silversmith's art. The upper portion consists of a jardinière of a very fine pattern, and beneath it, standing at the foot, two miniature statues.

The Muratti Vase.

The whole stands on a large plinth. The trophy bears a suitable inscription, and is certainly one which any island should be proud to win. Jersey Evening Post.

There appeared to be some concern as the date for the first Muratti match approached, as there had been no confirmation from the F.A. a report of the GFA Council Meeting appearing in the Star of 13 April 1905 noted that the Secretary gave particulars of correspondence with the English F.A. in connection with the Muratti Vase. No permission had arrived although he had written several times and also telegraphed. The Press however had written on 12 April 1905: -

'The following telegram was received at noon today by Mr. Bowden re the above competition (the Muratti Vase.): - High Holborn. Provisional sanction given for insular competition. Football Association. Guernsey could now officially play Alderney on 17 April 1905.

MURATTI SEMI-FINAL.
17 April 1905, The Cycling Grounds, Guernsey.

Guernsey-6, Alderney-0.

Guernsey met Alderney at the Cycling Grounds, Track Lane on Monday 17 April 1905 watched by a crowd estimated to be in the region of 800. The Press report on 18 April for the match began: -

'The first match in the above competition was played at the Cycling Grounds yesterday afternoon before a large number of spectators. As might have been expected, this 'match of the season' brought many Jersey and Alderney officials and football supporters to the ground. Doubtless the Jersey folk were eager to witness the performance of the team which is to meet the Jersey team in Jersey on the 27 inst in the final. The Muratti Vase was exhibited on a table in front of the pavilion and was decorated with the colours of the three competing island teams. Mr. H. Le Messurier was the referee, his linesmen being Messrs. J.L. Le Maitre and J. Coward.'

Guernsey wore light blue shirts and Alderney were in yellow and black stripes. The wind was blowing across the Cycling Grounds as the President of the GFA, Mr. H.E. Mauger, kicked off this inaugural Muratti Vase match. In the opening moments Guernsey won their first corner and from the clearance Alderney won their first corner. The early stages of the match were fast and furious with Henson, the Alderney captain, making a spirited run down the visitors' left wing but the Guernsey defence held firm. Although the first quarter of the game was very even the home forwards were beginning to put some pressure on the Alderney goal with their short passing game. After 15 minutes Guernsey scored the first goal when, following some fine play on the left wing by Stranger, Heaume received the ball and sent it past Gaudion. Alderney's reply was swift and once again Henson was causing problems and Aubert had to be alert to save his fine dropping shot. The visitors continued to press forward and, following a scrimmage in front of the Guernsey goal, the ball was headed just over. E. Le Maitre then came close for Alderney but his low shot was just wide. Following an even first half the score was Guernsey-1, Alderney-0.

Guernsey switched their full backs round for the second half with Benstead taking Waterman's place as the home side started to gain the upper hand. A swift passing move between the Guernsey forwards resulted in a second goal with Heaume sending the ball to Jackson who fed Crews and he quickly scored past Gaudion. The Alderney keeper was again called into action and he saved well from a fine long range shot from Thorne but his clearance found Crews who scored number three. Although Alderney responded with Henson forcing Aubert into a save it was the home side that now had the upper hand. A further goal was scored when Heaume passed to Jackson and he fired in a strong shot from the wing for the fourth goal. Heaume was again involved when he took a pass from Jackson and he fired in a shot that Gaudion got to but could not hold and the ball entered the net. Moments later Heaume scored again to make the final score Guernsey-6, Alderney-0.

Alderney: T. Gaudion; J. Catts and H. Cleale; T. Allen, J. Le Maitre and
H. Le Vallee; W.J. Le Vallee, E. Le Maitre, J. Le Maitre, J. Petite and
A. Henson (capt.).

Guernsey: J. Aubert; T. Waterman; A. Benstead; R. Podger, J. Newberry and
S. Hands; S. Jackson, W. Crews, G. Heaume (c), F. Stranger and
E. Thorne.
Goalscorers: Heaume (3), Crews (2), Jackson.

James Henry Le Maitre (Alderney).

Following this match the Alderney team and other visitors from Alderney and Jersey were entertained at a 'smoker' at the Channel Islands Hotel. Mr. H.E. Mauger (President GFA) made an ideal chairman and was supported by Messrs. H.G. Bowden (Sec GFA), W. Freckler (Treasurer GFA), A. Henson (Capt. Alderney team), W. Hammond (Secretary Alderney FA), E. Dupre (vice-President Jersey Wanderers FC) and Mr. le Quesne (Treasurer of the Jersey Football League). The attendance also included many Jersey and Alderney football enthusiasts, who had come to Guernsey to watch the match. The Guernsey team and local supporters also attended as well as representatives of the Manchester Regiment. The Muratti Vase was placed on the Chairman's table.

The Chairman proposed a toast to the donors of the Vase, Messrs Muratti & Sons along with the name of Mr. Lander, who was instrumental in the trophy being presented.

Mr. Bowden (Secretary GFA) announced that he had received a note that afternoon which was not opened until after the match had begun. The note stated that Mr. J.W. Spiller had presented a silver medal with a gold centre to be awarded to the player who scored the first goal in the new competition. This medal had been won by Mr. G. 'Kitten' Heaume the Guernsey centre forward and was presented to him by Mr. Mauger.

Mr. H.G. Bowden received the following telegram on 18 April 1905 from Jersey: - 'Bowden, Secretary Football Association, Guernsey. - Heartily congratulate Guernsey on their success, much regret absence, but hope to be present on the 27th. - LANDER.'

Following the semi-final match, preparations were being completed for the final which was to be held in Jersey on 27 April 1905. There was some concern expressed over the football ground where this match was to be played. It was understood that the ground at the Royal Agricultural Grounds was only 100 yards long and 50 yards wide and that a portion of it was gravelled. The Press on 27 April reported:

'A Guernsey visitor to Jersey for the above match writes that the above ground is very small and at one corner there is no grass at all, simply a gravel walk. Our correspondent expressed the opinion that it is doubtful whether the Guernsey forwards could do good work under such cramped conditions, and adds that a good throw-in from touch near the corner flag would nicely land the ball in front of goal, and that the penalty area nearly reaches the touch-lines.'

The Jersey Evening Post on 26 April 1905 reported on the forthcoming match:

'We are now within measurable distance of the big struggle in the local football world. The match is to take place to-morrow afternoon between teams representative of Jersey and Guernsey Islands, and will decide the championship of the Channel Islands and the holder for 1905 of the Muratti Challenge Vase, which is being competed for for the first time.'

The Jersey team was selected and the Evening Post reported:

'In finally selecting the team to do duty for Jersey, the Selection Committee realised the important responsibility which was imposed on them, and also felt that it was not their business to consider private susceptibilities or the personal feelings of any individual club, but to carefully consider the merits and demerits of each player, irrespective of the club to which he belonged to, and to choose a team which would do the most credit to the whole Island.'

The Guernsey team arrived on the GWR steamer on the morning of 27 April and stayed at the Grasshoppers Hotel. They had a short practice in the morning at the Springfield Grounds.

MURATTI FINAL.
27 April 1905, Royal Agricultural Ground, Springfield, Jersey.

Jersey-0, Guernsey-1.

There was an animated scene on the Victoria Pier in the morning on the arrival of the London and South-Western Railway steamer 'Alberta', which brought a large number of Guernsey and Alderney supporters for the afternoon's final match in the Muratti Vase Inter-Insular Competition. The members of the Guernsey team, who arrived in Jersey yesterday, were on the quay sporting pale blue favours, whilst the Jersey adherents, wearing red and white, were also present in strong force.

In the morning the Guernsey Island selection committee met at the Grasshopper Hotel where the team for this afternoon's match was finally decided upon.

The final match for the Muratti Vase took place at the Royal Agricultural Ground, Jersey and, according to official figures, the attendance was about 2,000. The Guernsey team with its supporters, who had been driven round the Island in an excursion car in the morning, arrived at the Grounds at about 4.45, and after having their photographs taken, they appeared on the field receiving loud applause from the spectators. The Jersey team met with a similar reception. Mr. H. Le Messurier, HFA, was the referee, and the linesmen Messrs. A. Reed (Jersey) and J. Le Quesne (Guernsey).

The Council of the Jersey League met on 26 April where several delegates drew attention to the fact a number of tradesmen and shop assistants in the town were very anxious to see the match, but owing to the kick-off being timed for 4 o'clock, these folk would be prevented from seeing the greater proportion of the game. After considerable discussion it was decided, with one dissention, to change the kick-off from 4 o'clock to 4,45pm sharp. Mr A. Reed (Caesareans) was unanimously appointed as the Jersey linesman. Mr Reed has only been in the Island for four months and, due to the six months residential rule, was not eligible to play for Jersey.

The teams were led out by Mulholland (Jersey) and Heaume (Guernsey) in front of a crowd of around 1,500. The field of play was not in good condition and it also appeared too small. Mulholland won the toss and Heaume kicked off at seven minutes to five. From the kick-off Guernsey went on the attack but the move broke down as Renouf cleared well up-field for Jersey. Guernsey continued to exert the early pressure and after five minutes Thorne put his shot over and, following the goal-kick, Crews collected the ball and passed to Stranger who sent in a beautiful shot that beat Mulholland in the Jersey goal to put Guernsey 1-0 ahead. From the restart Honeycombe put in a centre that was well cleared by Waterman and then De La Cour hit Jersey's first shot at goal but he was ruled offside.

The game was swinging from end to end with Mulholland saving from Rihoy and moments later he cleared a long shot from Benstead. Aubert was then brought into action and he saved a shot by Boomer at the expense of a corner, followed by him saving a good shot from the wing by Honeycombe. Guernsey replied when a fine shot by Thorne skimmed the Jersey bar. Jersey then had a period of sustained pressure when successive shots by Golding, Honeycombe and De La Cour were cleared by Aubert. The play was going from end to end with Jersey now having more of the play but the size and condition of the playing surface was proving a handicap to both sides. The ball was often in touch and the game was littered with numerous goal kicks. Jersey continued to push on in search of the equalising goal and felt that they had scored it when Honeycombe put in a centre that was met by Chapman who fired it home, but the celebrations were cut short when the referee, Le Massurier, ruled the score out for offside amidst loud hissing from the Jersey supporters. Half Time arrived with the score Jersey-0, Guernsey-1.

Jersey started the second half well but were finding Benstead and Waterman in fine form

R. Stevens. (Jersey)

G. Le Page. (Jersey)

and they were ably supported by Aubert in the Guernsey goal. Jersey came close to scoring when Boomer sent in a superb shot that was well saved by Aubert, and as the home side kept up this pressure Aubert again brought off a series of remarkable saves. The unsuitability of the Agricultural Grounds as a football pitch was highlighted when Thorn had to run through a crowd of spectators who were encroaching the area, knocking down a policeman in the process, to put in a shot which Mulholland saved. Crews rushed at Mulholland and, with the ball just clearing the goal, Rihoy forced a corner. Guernsey bombarded the Jersey goal, keeping the ball there for some time until Crews forced the ball home. Once again the celebrations were cut short as the score was cancelled for offside. Stranger then came close when he fired in two excellent shots that were well saved by Mulholland. Near the end of the game De La Cour fell and sustained a fractured collar-bone. After medical examination he was taken home in a

cab, and will probably be incapacitated from work for three or four weeks. Just before time Jersey were pressurising the Guernsey defence and Aubert saved from Renouf but he took more than three steps and a free-kick was awarded. Guernsey lined up their wall in front of the goalmouth and kept the ball clear from danger until the final whistle sounded leaving the score Jersey-0, Guernsey-1.

Jersey: T.F. Mulholland (c), R.R. Stevens, G.M. Le Page, E. Pettiquin, D. Renouf H. Weir, S. De La Cour, P.H. Boomer, W. Golding, W.G. Chapman, A.H. Honeycombe.

Guernsey: J. Aubert, A. Benstead and T. Waterman; J. Rihoy, J. Newberry and S. Hands; S. Jackson, W. Crews, G. Heaume (c), F. Stranger, E. Thorne.
Goalscorer: Stranger.

Directly after the match was over a mob of youths assembled outside the dressing shed and threatened to injure the referee. On leaving the dressing shed the referee was surrounded by a noisy mob and to preserve him from harm two policemen escorted Mr. Le Messurier to a side exit. As he left on his wagonette he was followed by the howling mob who spoke in uncomplimentary terms of his decision about the 'offside' goal. It was a rather unpleasant end to a hard fought but fair contest.

That evening the Guernsey team and visitors to Jersey were entertained by a concert at the West Park Pavilion. It was estimated that there was around 1,2000 people inside the pavilion when the Cosmopolitan Orchestra Band (under Mr. A.B. Gulliver) took to the platform. In attendance were Colonel P. Robin, Mr. H.E. Mauger (President GFA), Mr. T. Adderton (President JFL), Mr. H.G. Bowden (Secretary GFA) and Mr. N. Gaudion (Alderney). Deputy E.B. Renouf began the presentation ceremony by welcoming the Guernsey team and congratulating all concerned with today's final. He said that following this game he was sure that although the day belonged to Guernsey, football would thrive in

Tom Waterman. (Guernsey).

Jersey and also in the other islands. The Muratti Vase was then presented to the Guernsey captain, Mr. G. Heaume, by Deputy E.B. Renouf. The proceedings concluded with three hearty cheers for Mr. Renouf, called by the Hon. Sec. of the Jersey Football League, followed by three cheers for Guernsey, called for by the Hon. Treasurer of the JFL. The proceedings terminated at 11.10pm with the National Anthem.

The Jersey Evening Post on Friday 28 April 1905 had some harsh words to say about the outcome of the Muratti Vase final:

'Chapman who had the whole time been on the right side of the Guernsey backs and of Honeycombe, rushed up as Honeycombe centred, and practically nipped the ball from the Guernsey right back. He got clean away, and with a nicely-judged shot found the net, out of reach of the goalkeeper. To the surprise of everyone in a position to form an accurate judgement the referee gave the goal off-side, a decision which, under the circumstances, was strongly resented by the spectators. Referees are not infallible, but it is as well to point out that Mr. Le Messurier was nearer the opposite goal when he blew his whistle, and further, he did not blow his whistle when Chapman secured, but waited until this player got clear away, and was in the act of shooting. We have no desire to dwell on this point. The refereeing difficulty for future matches is to be easily overcome, but speaking of yesterday's refereeing generally, it was not of cup-tie standard. There were many technical offences on both sides, which were not checked, and at one period it almost looked as if the players could indulge in anything bar outrageous fouling, without being pulled up.

Some of the subsequent rulings of the referee regarding free kicks were received with further demonstrations of disapproval from the crowd.

We strongly reiterate what was stated in these columns some time back when this competition was first mooted – that an English referee should certainly have been engaged for the matches. Without saying a word against Mr. Le Messurier, who has up to the present enjoyed a good reputation as a whistle blower, there is no going against the fact that he is a Guernseyman, and this alone makes it imperative, that in all future inter-insular competitions, a totally disinterested referee must be specially engaged.'

The Jersey Times reported also on 28 April 1905:

'The teams were very evenly matched; a draw would have fairly represented the play. Unfortunately a regrettable scene occurred immediately after the close with a great many of the spectators mobbing the referee, and the services of the police had to be requisitioned in his defence.'

The proposed first AGM of the Inter-Insular

Mr. Herbert Le Messurier.

1905 Guernsey Muratti squad. The first winners of the Muratti Vase.
Waterman, Aubert, Benstead.
Podger, Rihoy, Newberry, Hands.
Jackson, Crews, Heaume (captain), Stranger, Thorne.

Committee was reported by the Star on 11 May 1905: -

'The first annual general meeting of delegates from each of the Channel Islands in connection with the Muratti Vase Inter-Insular Football Competition to take place in Jersey on Thursday June 1st. At this meeting the tenders for the supply of gold medals to the winning team each year, and, which have been sent in by Channel Islands jewellers, will be considered, and arrangements made for the competition next year. - Jersey Evening Post.'

This historic meeting was reported by the Star of 3 June 1905. Item 3 read: -

'The selection of a standard pattern medal to be presented to the winning team was next proceeded with. The Secretary exhibited 23 gold medals from Jersey jewellers, 2 gold medals and 7 designs from Guernsey and 3 designs from Alderney. No delegate knew whose medals or designs were being tendered. After slight discussion as to price, the delegates eventually unanimously selected a design bearing the arms of the three islands. This design is composed of a plain gold circle engraved 'Channel Islands Football Cup' enclosing the three island shields arranged trefoil fashion, and is of unique design. After the decision of the delegates the Secretary announced that the winning design had been submitted by Messrs. Bachman & Co., of Guernsey, who thus secure the perpetual tender.'

The Star for 27 June 1905 reported: -

'The medals intended for the Guernsey team who won the Muratti Channel Islands Trophy at Jersey last April are now ready and will be on view at Messrs. Bachman & Co.'s stall at the Electrical Exhibition (St. Julian's Hall.). The medals which are about the size of a two-franc piece are of gold and of a very neat pattern. The centre of the medal is in three

Muratti Medal

a two-franc piece are of gold and of a very neat pattern. The centre of the medal is in three panels, on each of which respectively is engraved the Guernsey, Jersey and Alderney coat of arms. These pretty medals have been supplied by Messrs. Bachman & Co.

It was interesting to note in the Press of 26 May 1905 a report on the GFA Council Meeting. Item 8 read:

A vote of thanks was accorded Mr. Miller-Davis for gratuitously providing a four-horse car to meet the winners of the Muratti Vase on their return from Jersey on April 28th.'

The first year of Muratti football was considered a great success by all the Associations and the two games appeared to set the tone for the next hundred years with a mixture of hard fought matches, totally committed supporters and the added ingredient of controversy. The local newspapers in both islands covered the events with relish with their views on the matches being tainted with an island bias, which remains to this day.

Great Western 'Ibex' with the victorious Guernsey Muratti team and spectators return to St. Peter Port. 28 April 1905.

CIGARETTE SMOKERS!
ORDER YOUR EASTER GIFTS AND REQUIREMENTS OF
MURATTI'S High-Class
CIGARETTES
AT ONCE.

Virginia Cigarettes.		From 1/4 per ½lb. box to 3/9 „ 100.
Turkish	„	From 1/8 per ½lb. box to 8/- „ 100.
Egyptian	„	From 1/8 per ½lb. box to 6/6 „ 100.

"LITTLE JAPS" still going ahead. Keep buying and
PARTICIPATE IN SCHEME. Particulars late

The victorious Guernsey team aboard the four-horse cart.
28 April 1905.

2

The early years. 1906-1914.

1 9 0 6

Following the success of the inaugural Muratti Vase competition the football fans on each of the islands waited eagerly to find out if Guernsey could repeat their 1905 achievement or if Jersey or Alderney would be victorious.

As the 1905 competition was completed the plans for the new season were under way.

MURATTI SEMI-FINAL.
29 March 1906, Springfield, Jersey.

Jersey -1, Guernsey -2. aet

St. Helier was en fete, and ribbons were freely worn. The referee, Mr. G. Wagstaffe Simmons, had arrived by the morning's boat. Jersey had to make two late changes to their starting line-up with Honeycombe (Rangers) and Scoones (Rangers) still not recovered from their injuries and they were replaced with Voisin (Caesareans) and Labey. Guernsey wore green and white for the first time and Jersey was in red and white. It was interesting to note that J. Aubert in the Guernsey goal is a native of Jersey and Jack Coppin in the Jersey goal was born in Guernsey.

The opening exchanges were very tight as both sides strove to gain an early advantage with Aubert being the first keeper called into action followed by Jersey's Coppin saving from young Maguire. Jersey began to assert themselves and Benstead had to save the situation for Guernsey on a number of occasions. Jones was beginning to cause Guernsey problems and he came close but put his shot over the bar and then Duquemin had to be quick to clear the ball from him at the expense of a corner. The play was very fast with each side in turn having the upper hand although both defences stood firm. The first breakthrough came after 35 minutes when Voisin opened the scoring with a low oblique shot into the corner past Aubert to give Jersey a 1-0 lead. The response from the Jersey support was incredible with hats, sticks etc being thrust into the air in a scene of indescribable enthusiasm. Guernsey responded by mounting their own attacks but the Jersey defence held firm and at half time the score was Jersey-1, Guernsey-0.

The second half saw Guernsey come into the game more as they went in search of an equaliser with Coppin and Crews prominent. Crews came very close on a number of occasions and a Podger free-kick was collected by him

R.R. Stevens (Jersey Captain).

and only a headed clearance by Thornton prevented him scoring. After 65 minutes Guernsey equalised when Cotton received the ball and dribbled through the Jersey defence and crashed in a shot that left Coppin helpless. Guernsey was now in control and, following some good play by the visiting forwards, Maguire put his shot wide. Play was held up for a short time following an injury to Guernsey's Jackson but he recovered after treatment. Jersey rallied and Aubert had to be smart to save a good shot from Poingdestre then Coppin brought off a marvellous save from a Guernsey counter attack only moments later. Jersey continued with their attacks and then a thunderous shot crashed against the Guernsey crossbar causing it to collapse. Again play was suspended as the crossbar was quickly repaired and play continued. In keeping with the earlier play, both teams had chances to score but, as before, found the defences well organised. There was no more scoring and the game ended Jersey-1, Guernsey-1.

It had been agreed previously that if the match ended in a draw there would be half an hour of extra time. In the first period of extra time Cotton once again collected the ball and attacked the Jersey defence and when he got into shooting distance he hit a swift ground shot that gave Coppin no chance and Guernsey went 2-1 ahead. The visitors came close on a number of occasions to increasing their lead but the Jersey defence held out and at half-time the score was Jersey-1, Guernsey-2.

The second half was full of excitement with Guernsey slightly on top as they strove for a further goal but found the Jersey defence and Le Page in particular, in fine form. A foul by Mahy gave Jersey a free-kick in a dangerous position but Aubert was up to the task. As the game neared its end Guernsey was on top but there was no more scoring and the game ended Jersey -1, Guernsey -2.

Jersey: J. Coppin, R.R. Stevens (c), T.J. Thornton, L. Labey, E. Pettiquin,
               G.M. Le Page, D.M. Jones, J.M. Poingdestre,W. Vardon, W. Golding,
               S. Voisin.
               Goalscorer: Voisin.

Guernsey: J. Aubert, J. Duquemin, A. Benstead, R.W. Podger, S. Cotton (c), J. Mahy,
               F. Maguire, S. Jackson, W. Crews, F. Stranger, E. Thorne.
               Goalscorer: S. Cotton (2).

This was a hard fought win for Guernsey although the general feeling was that the best team had won. In the evening a promenade concert was held at West Park Pavilion and a smoking concert was held at the Southampton Hotel (the Guernsey Headquarters) which commenced at 10.00pm. The Guernsey team left Jersey aboard the Lydia arriving at the White Rock on the morning of 30 March. The Guernsey flag, which was presented to the Council recently, had not arrived in time to be displayed, and therefore the colours of the captain of the Guernsey team (Mr. S. Cotton) were flown in its place on the mast-head. As the vessel entered the harbour cheers were raised by the onlookers and the captain of the Guernsey team was carried ashore to the char-a-banc, the remainder of the team receiving an ovation. The team, accompanied by several members of the GFA Council and friends were driven around the town, eventually ending at the Weighbridge.

The Guernsey Evening Press on Friday 30 March 1906 produced the first Muratti cartoon.

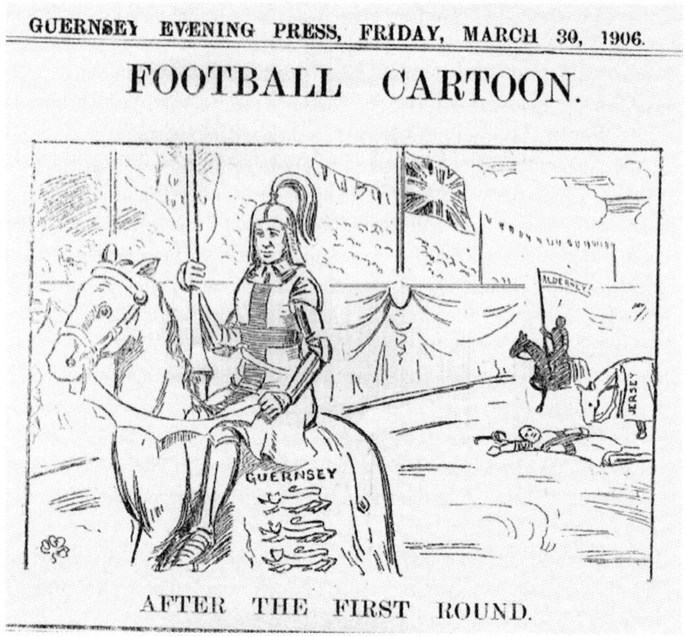

MURATTI FINAL.
2 April 1906, The Cycling Grounds, Guernsey.

Guernsey -1, Alderney -0.

In perfect weather conditions and in front of an excellent crowd, including the Lieut-Governor Captain Campbell, Guernsey entertained Alderney in the final of the Muratti Vase competition. The teams were led out by S. Cotton (Guernsey) and Arthur Henson (Alderney) amidst roars of applause from the spectators. The Alderney team were resplendent in their blue and white team strip. Henson won the toss and took advantage of the moderate breeze and immediately went on the attack but any danger was cleared up by Benstead and Podger in the Guernsey defence. There was an early scare for Alderney when Batiste needlessly came out of his goal and was relieved to see Stranger's shot go wide of the posts. The game became more even with half chances being created by both sides. Benstead cleared long and the ball was collected by Crews but Alderney's Cleale won the ball and the danger was cleared and a minute later Henson looked a certain scorer but Duquemin bundled him over and the ball broke to Quinain and he sent in a long range shot that appeared to be entering the net but Aubert, diving at the ball, brought off a sensational save. Although both defences were in control chances were still being created and when Thorne sent in a long dropping shot Catts went to clear, he was challenged by Maguire and he forced a corner from which Stranger headed over. It was an even first half which ended Guernsey-0, Alderney-0.

Alderney kicked off for the second half but Guernsey quickly regained the ball and Crews sent in a low shot that just missed the post. Once again both defences appeared on top with

Cleale clearing from Crews followed by Benstead foiling Henson. Eight minutes into the half Guernsey broke the deadlock when an Alderney attack broke down and Cotton received the ball and he sent in a beautiful shot that sped past Batiste. Moments later Batiste saved at the expense of a corner and Maguire's kick found Jackson but his effort was cleared by Catts. The Guernsey pressure was now mounting with shots by Thorne and Cotton going just wide and when Quinain lost the ball to Crews Batiste had to save twice from the Guernsey player. Alderney retaliated and penned Guernsey in their own half for a time and Petit came close with a fine oblique shot. As the game neared its end Cotton sent in a fast curving shot that Batiste managed to fist clear and the final result was Guernsey-1, Alderney-0.

Guernsey: J. Aubert, J. Duquemin, A. Benstead, R.W. Podger, S. Cotton (c), J. Mahy, F. Maguire, S. Jackson, W. Crews, F. Stranger, E. Thorne.
Goalscorer: Cotton.

Alderney: C. Batiste, H. Cleale, J. Catts, J. Le Maitre, L. Jacques, J. Petite, J. Allen, E. Le Maitre, Jas. Le Maitre, F. Quinain, A. Henson (c).

Alderney Muratti team.
Harry Cleal, Charlie Batiste, Joe Catts.
Joey Allen, Ernie Le Maitre, Fred Quinain, Jimmy Le Maitre, Arthur Henson.
Jack Le Maitre, Leonard Jaques, Jack Petit.

The Muratti Vase was presented to Cotton, the Guernsey captain, by the Lieut-Governor Captain Campbell.

Although Guernsey deserved their narrow victory the result could easily have been different had Alderney used the wind to their advantage in the first half and had Aubert not brilliantly saved the shot by Quinain. The visitors were well served by Catts and Cleale with Batiste playing well in goal. Guernsey's best were Benstead and Cotton and as the game wore on they could have won by more than one goal.

The Alderney team returned home on 3 April aboard the S.S. Courier. Shortly before 9 o'clock they drove down to the White Rock from the Channel Islands Hotel and went on board. Amongst the large assembly of people to see them off was Mr. E. Wagstaffe Simmons, the referee, and Mr. H.G. Bowden, Sec of the GFA. As the steamer left her berth at the White Rock Mr. H. Shirvell, proprietor of the Channel Islands Hotel, called for three cheers for the visitors. This was answered from on board, and the men could be heard cheering until the steamer was well out.

The Jersey Evening Post on Saturday 7 April 1906 reported that a protest had been entered by the Alderney Football Association against the Guernsey centre half and captain, Cotton, who had apparently not been registered for a sufficient period. If this protest was upheld there was every likelihood of the Muratti contest being re-played. This report was quickly replied to by H. le Quesne, the Secretary of the Jersey FA, who stated that he had received a wire from Alderney to say that they knew of no grounds whatsoever for protesting and expressed their surprise at the rumour.

So the second Muratti season ended with a little controversy.

The 'Courier' arrives in Alderney.

1 9 0 7

MURATTI SEMI-FINAL.
21 March 1907, The Cycling Grounds, Guernsey.

Alderney -1, Jersey -2. aet.

Alderney began their preparation for the 1907 Muratti Vase by arranging two matches against the 2nd Manchesters who were stationed in Alderney. The games allowed Alderney to give their Muratti team practice prior to their match against Jersey. The first match for the Alderney Cup took place on Butes on Saturday 9 March 1907 and resulted in a 4-2 victory for the 2nd Manchesters over the Alderney Muratti XI. The report in the Guernsey Press referred to the trophy as the Alderney Muratti Cup. The second match between Alderney and the 2nd Manchesters ended with Alderney loosing 2-0 and so the 2nd Manchesters won the 1907 Alderney Muratti Cup. Despite this defeat Alderney's preparation left them in good heart for their Muratti Vase match against Jersey.

Some 50 Jersey supporters, the majority of whom were sporting the Jersey colours, and including Col. Philip Robin, a prominent Jersey sportsman, arrived from Jersey by the s.s. 'Ibex' this morning for the Alderney v Jersey Muratti match. Mr. Mellanby, the referee, arrived from England and was welcomed on arrival by Mr. H.G. Bowden, Hon Sec of the Inter-Insular Committee and Sec of the Guernsey Football Association. There was a good crowd at the Cycling Grounds for the Muratti Vase semi-final between Alderney and Jersey. The Lieut-Governor, Major-General B.B.D. Campbell should have been present but was unavoidably absent through his motor breaking down. In attendance, however, was the Bailiff, Sir H.A. Giffard and Mr N. Barbeson, Judge of Alderney. Mr. G.H. Muir, one of the leading English referees, had been invited to officiate in both Inter-Insular games. Mr. Muir, however, cannot get away for the Alderney v Guernsey game which will therefore be in charge of Mr. T. Mellanby, HFA and Isle of Wight.

The weather was ideal for football as there was no wind and the sun was high enough not to prove to be a handicap. Jacques won the toss for Alderney and he elected to face into the sun. The game started at a rapid pace with Alderney leading the attack and, although the early play was exciting, the football was very erratic. Early in the game Millow was penalised for holding and from the free-kick Alderney came close when E. Le Maitre fired his shot over the bar. Following a period of Alderney pressure, Alexander broke clean away but could not convert an excellent chance for Jersey. He again found himself in a fine position when full-back Cleale was on the ground but Catts came across to clear. For the first 20 minutes both goalkeepers only had to deal with some long range shots with the defences in control. After 22 minutes Alderney won a corner and as the ball came over it was met by Quinain who put Alderney 1-0 ahead with a crisp shot that went in under the bar, although Coppin got his fingers to it, he could not stop it. Alderney nearly increased their lead when Coppin saved from J. Le Maitre at the expense of a corner. The play was beginning to open up and Alderney's Brooks brilliantly save from Alexander and Le Page. Jersey almost equalised when a fine cross-shot from the left by Voisin landed on the top of the net and Alexander came close but could only fire his shot over the bar leaving the half time score Alderney-1, Jersey-0.

Alderney was first into the attack in the second half and from a free-kick Catts forced Coppin into a good save. Jersey responded and Alexander made a clear opening and shot for goal causing Brooks in the Alderney goal to produce a fine save. Jersey won a free-kick and the ball was sent to Potier who fired in a close range shot that was saved by Brooks but the ball broke free and Le Page looked a certain scorer in the melee when Potier, from an offside position, collected the ball and netted. Referee Mellanby had no hesitation, however, in calling for a free-kick to Alderney. Jersey then began to exert some sustained pressure and Alderney was penned-in in their own half. Alderney was quick to counter-attack and Price missed an excellent chance from close in followed by a Henson shot that was saved by Coppin. E. Le Maitre then broke through for Alderney and Coppin had to rush out to clear the danger. E. Le Maitre again raced through the Jersey defence and put the ball into the net only to have the score ruled out by referee Mellanby for offside on the half way line. Jersey survived this scare and after 76 minutes they equalised when Poiter scored with a fast shot. Both goals came under some pressure but with no more scoring the game ended Alderney-1, Jersey-1.

Jersey now forced matters in extra-time and Brooks had to fist away Voisin's effort only to see the ball hit Catts; Alexander slipped in but put his shot over the bar. A fine shot by J. Le Maitre just failed to give Alderney the lead then a minute later Quinain scored from a melee but the goal was disallowed for a foul. Jersey then went clear and Brooks produced an excellent save from Poiter and the ball broke to Thornton who dribbled half way down the pitch before passing to De La Cour who in turn crossed to Alexander, but his shot went over the bar. The score at half-time remained Alderney -1, Jersey-1.

Early in the second half the play was suspended following an injury to Labey but he resumed after treatment. Price then came close for Alderney but Coppin managed to get his fist to his high effort. The deadlock was not broken until 8 minutes into the second period when Poiter beat Cleale and set the ball up for Le Page to score Jersey's second goal.

E. Alexander. (Jersey).

There was no more scoring and this exiting match ended Alderney-1, Jersey-2.

Jersey: J. Coppin, R.S. Stevens (c), T. Thornton,
            W. Millow, E. Alexander, L. Labey,
            S. De La Cour, G. Le Page, P. Poiter,
            J. Cole, S. Voisin.
            Goalscorers: Poiter, Le Page.

Alderney: C. Brookes, J. Catts, H. Cleale,
            H. Le Maitre, L. Jacques, J. Allen,
            E. Le Maitre, A. Price, F. Quinain,
            J.H. Le Maitre, A. Henson.
            Goalscorer: Quinain.

This match was described as a typical cup-tie with plenty of excitement and incident and in the main both defences were on top. Alderney could consider themselves unfortunate to finish up losers having put up an excellent display; however, it was Jersey who progressed to meet Guernsey in the Final.

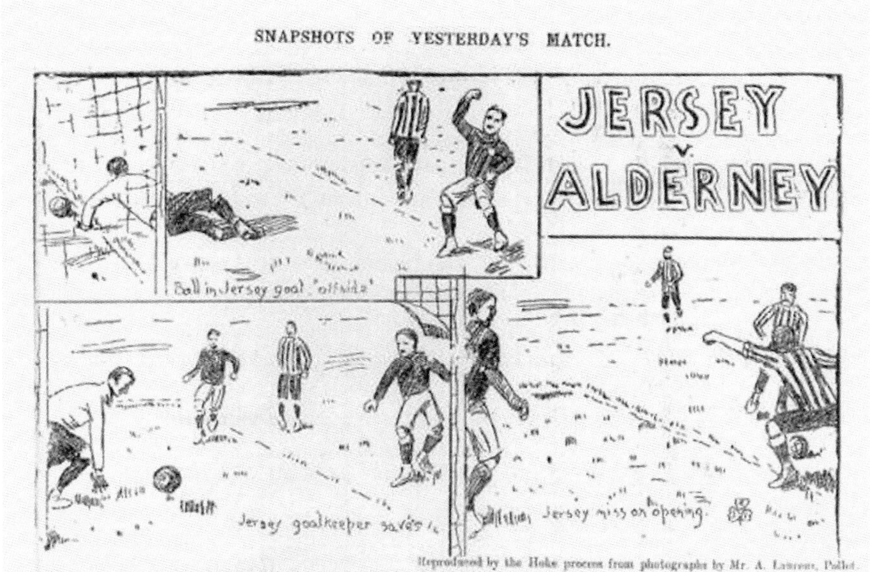

A report in the Star for 26 March 1907 stated:

'That a Press representative has the power to give a wrong impression will be readily admitted by those present at the Jersey-Alderney football match on Thursday last and who read the appended paragraph – taken verbatim from the JERSEY TIMES of Friday: -

Hostile Reception in Guernsey.

'When the Jersey team arrived on the field in Guernsey yesterday its members were greeted by a hostile crowd which jeered and hooted. This also happened when the team left the ground. It is even asserted that stones were thrown, as well as ground and turf.

It is to be regretted some of the Guernsey football public are not imbued with that true sportsmanlike spirit which should exist, especially in inter-insular competitions.'

There is not the slightest foundation for this gross mis-statement which may have been penned from sheer imagination. Nevertheless it is most regrettable. The part of the reprinted paragraph referring to stones, ground and turf is not only unfair, but is decidedly untruthful. Therefore we trust that in fairness to the Guernsey public our contemporary, the JERSEY TIMES, will contradict the above statements, as we are perfectly sure that on enquiry it will ascertain it has been greatly deceived by its correspondent who commented on the match and afterwards.

The ADVERTISER, of Saturday, says both teams received a hearty reception as they appeared on the ground.'

An article appeared in the Guernsey Press that also refuted these allegations. It therefore appeared that even at this early stage of the Muratti history temperatures were inclined to rise.

Fortunately this unpleasantness was soon forgotten as Jersey and Guernsey prepared for the final of the Muratti Vase at Westmount on 4 April 1907.

MURATTI FINAL.
4 April 1907, Westmount, Jersey.

Jersey -2, Guernsey -3. aet.

The Guernsey team travelled to Jersey on Wednesday and had a welcome rest in preparation for the final on Thursday. On Wednesday evening one of the members of the Guernsey Selection Committee (Mr. J.S. Head) invited the Guernsey players and supporters who were staying at the 'Star' Hotel to witness a performance of 'The Dandy Doctor' at the Opera House and this offer was readily accepted. Jersey had a late change to their selected line-up with Millow withdrawing due to having a strained back and he is replaced by Fox (Western United). The Guernsey side included new caps in E. Parry (Rangers) along with V. Cooper, A. Yates and Mockler all of Athletics and J. Leadbeater and T. Holland of North. The referee for the match was Mr G.H. Muir (Southampton) and he is a schoolmaster by profession and headmaster of the Mount Pleasant Boy's Council School. He was one of the founders and first secretary of the Southampton Football Club then known as Southampton St. Mary's for whom for many years he played left back.

This was the first Muratti Vase match to be played at Westmount and after the usual photographs Stevens won the toss for Jersey and, rather surprisingly, chose to kick uphill. Holland kicked-off for Guernsey and they forced the play into the home defence for a few minutes. The first piece of exciting play came when a long hard shot by Cole crashed off the Guernsey post. Labey then broke down the field in brilliant fashion and slipped the ball to Cole and his shot was well saved by Aubert in the Guernsey goal. Guernsey replied when Leadbeater twice in rapid succession put the ball over the bar when in good positions and then Coppin saved two really good shots from Thorne. Jersey's Fox then took up the ball and fired in a shot that Aubert managed to hold but a trio of Jersey forwards were on him and he just managed to screw the ball round the post. It was Aubert in the Guernsey goal who again called into action when he stopped a straight drive by Poingdestre and in the melee that followed Jersey's Labey was slightly hurt. Guernsey came close moments later when Coppin saved from Yates and conceded a corner and from this kick Cooper sent the ball over the bar. Poingdestre then started a dangerous move when he beat three opponents and he looked certain to score when Waterman unceremoniously bundled him into touch. Leadbeater came close for Guernsey when he hit the post with a superb ground shot with Coppin beaten. Both keepers were then brought into play as chances were created at both ends and Holland actually thought that he had opened the scoring but the goal was disallowed for an earlier infringement. With 30 minutes played the deadlock was broken when Waterman sent the ball into the Jersey goalmouth where Holland directed it to young Mockler who opened the scoring. Jersey nearly pulled it back moments later when both Labey and then Poiter tested Aubert and then Cole hesitated when an equaliser seemed imminent and the danger was cleared. Coppin then had to make four saves in quick succession and as the half neared its end Aubert had to clear from Fox and at half time the score was Jersey-0, Guernsey-1.

The second half opened with Mockler being tripped and from the free-kick Parry only missed by inches. Once again there were chances at both ends but they were confidently dealt with by the respective defences. Fox then seemed certain to score when he was 12 yards out but Stranger came in and cleared the danger and then Leadbeater beat four opponents then saw his fine shot hit the bar and go over. Mahy was then penalised near the penalty area but Aubert brought off a magnificent save from the free-kick with the Jersey forwards swarming all round him. Jersey began to take control and they deservedly equalised after 65 minutes when Poingdestre crashed in a magnificent shot that left Aubert helpless. Guernsey then had to defend for long periods with Aubert, Parry and Waterman outstanding. Aubert did very well to fist the ball away with three Jersey forwards bustling him as the pressure continued. Leadbeater relieved the pressure when he fired in a terrific ground shot that just missed the post with Coppin diving low. The last few minutes were anxious ones for Guernsey and Jersey would have scored but for an extraordinary save by Aubert from Fox and the game ended Jersey-1, Guernsey-1.

In extra time Guernsey won the toss and elected to play down the slope and, almost immediately, Waterman skimmed the Jersey bar from a free-kick. After two minutes play Yates broke away and crossed for Leadbeater who put Guernsey ahead again with a terrific upward shot that hit the inside of the crossbar and rebounded into the net. This put Guernsey on top and it was Jersey's turn to defend in depth and after 10 minutes Mockler and Leadbeater combined to find Holland who sent in a long dropping shot into the corner of the net with Coppin falling as he tried to save. The first half of extra time finished Jersey-1, Guernsey-3.

Jersey began the second half with the slope in their favour and were quickly on the attack causing Aubert to save from Fox. Waterman and Parry were once again performing well as they blocked shots from Le Page and Chapman and then as Labey was preparing to shoot Parry swooped in to clear the danger. With only two minutes remaining an individual sprint by Poingdestre on Jersey's right set up Cole who scored for Jersey to make the final result of this pulsating match Jersey-2, Guernsey-3.

Jersey:	J. Coppin, R.S. Stevens (c), T. Thornton, E. Pettiquin, P. Poiter, L. Labey, W.J. Chapman, J. Poingdestre, W. Fox, J. Cole, G. Le Page. Goalscorers: Poingdestre, Cole.
Guernsey:	J. Aubert, T. Waterman, E. Parry (c), V. Cooper, F. Stranger, J. Mahy, A. Yates, F.G. Mockler, J. Leadbeater, T. Holland, E. Thorne. Goalscorers: Mockler, Leadbeater, Holland.

This was an excellent game which was in the balance until the first period of extra time when Guernsey established a two goal advantage.

The Jersey Football Association organised a presentation evening at the West Park Pavilion. The Guernsey players and supporters were applauded as they walked to the seats that were reserved for them. The Muratti Vase and medals were presented to the team by Mrs Gough, the wife of Major-General Gough the Lieut-Governor of Jersey.

The Guernsey team arrived at the White Rock on Friday 5 April on board the 'Vera' which had the green and white flag with the Guernsey coat of arms displayed over the steamer's side. As soon as the vessel moored the Guernsey captain, E. Parry, was borne shoulder high, carrying the Muratti Vase, to one of Mr. Miller-Davis' char-a-bancs that was waiting. All the team took their places on the conveyance and drove throughout town amidst great cheers. The victorious Guernsey team received many congratulations on their win, including messages from His Excellency the Lieut-Governor Major General B.B.D. Campbell CVO, CB and the Bailiff, Sir H.A. Giffard KC.

Photographs of the match were taken by Mr. A. Lauren (Pollet). A large size colour photograph of Mockler scoring the first goal for Guernsey was on display in his shop. The 'Jersey Evening Post' reported:

'A fine match, in which the Guernsey team was always the cleverer and possessed more dash than the homesters. Jersey might have scraped home with a little more luck, but no possible combination of available local men could possibly outshine the visitors. Guernsey's team was streets ahead of that of two years ago, notably forward. We have improved, but not in the same ratio as the sister island and Jersey must buck up to catch them.'

It was reported that the Guernsey football officials wished to express their appreciation of the manner the Guernsey football officials and spectators were received in Jersey. All were accorded an amiable and amicable reception. They wished to thank the Jersey officials and public for expressions of good feeling. The arrangements in Jersey were carried out excellently. The ground left a little to be desired as it was difficult for the entire crowd to see the match clearly. It was reported that the Westmount ground is not a full-size pitch, but it is contemplated turning the pitch at right angles so that the next football season the Westmount ground will be one of the finest football venues in the Channel Islands.

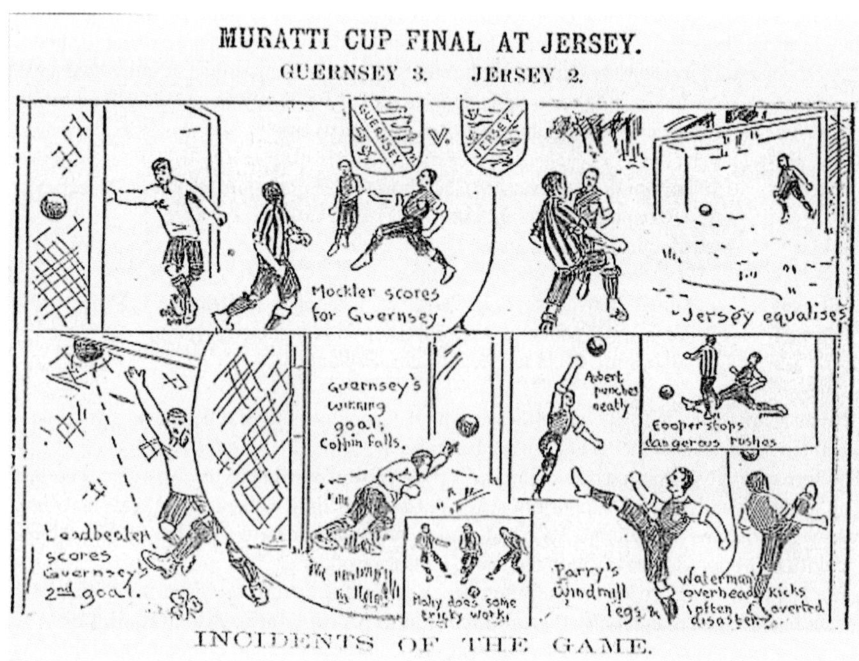

West Park Pavilion.

Guernsey.
Muratti Vase winners. 1907.

1 9 0 8

MURATTI SEMI-FINAL.
2 April 1908, Westmount, Jersey.

Alderney - 0, Guernsey - 3.

The Guernsey team travelled to Jersey by the GWR steamer 'Roebuck' and the Alderney team by s.s. 'Courier'. The Guernsey team were based at the Star Hotel and Alderney at Mr & Mrs Glenen's boarding establishment in St. John's Road. The Muratti Vase was displayed in the window of the Beresford Library (Messrs Labey and Blampied) bedecked in the red & white, green & white and dark blue & white of the competing teams. Alongside it was the Upton Park Trophy in the colours of Jersey Wanderers.

Jersey was a scene of excitement when the Muratti teams of Alderney and Guernsey visited along with the 'Guernsey Remainder' football team, the Guernsey Athletics hockey team and the Harriers. Prior to the Muratti match at Westmount a game between a Jersey XI and the 'Guernsey Remainder' was played with a 2.30pm kick-off and resulted in a 2-1 victory for Jersey.

The Alderney team were experiencing some difficulties prior to the match with Guernsey as two of their players, Jacques and Catts, being absent for six weeks due to injuries. Jacques suffered his due to an accident at a quarry and Catts during a cup-tie. Fortunately both were fit to play in the match. They had a new goalkeeper in Gamblin who was normally a half back.

The estimated crowd of 2000 heartily cheered the two teams onto the field of play led by the captains, E. Parry (Guernsey) and C.H.B. Jacques (Alderney).

Guernsey won the toss and were soon on the attack with Gamblin in the Alderney goal saving a long shot in the first minute and this was followed by Leadbeater putting a fine shot just over the bar. As Guernsey continued to press it was 10 minutes before Aubert in the Guernsey goal had his first kick. Although Guernsey were on top Alderney caused some problems with their counter-attacks and Mellanby came close but his shot was saved by Aubert. After 15 minutes Guernsey took the lead when Cooper sent in a fine shot that Gamblin caught but failed to hold and the ball hit the post and went into the goal. Alderney responded with a swift attack and Parry had to relieve the situation with a clearance that ended up in a tree. Guernsey then came close when an excellent shot by Zabiela came back off the crossbar. With 10 minutes remaining Leadbeater scored a lovely goal from 15 yards to put Guernsey 2-0 ahead. As half time approached Mockler sent in a good shot that appeared to slip through Gamblin's hands and ended up in the net. Alderney then put in some fine attacks and although Le Maitre put in some good attempts the half time score remained Alderney-0, Guernsey-3.

E. Parry. (Guernsey Captain)

C.H.B. Jacques. (Alderney Captain)

The second half opened with Zabiela sending in some excellent shots that were well saved by Gamblin. The game became very even with both goals coming under pressure when firstly a Mockler shot went over the bar then an Alderney attack was thwarted by Aubert. Mockler again came close when his free-kick was well saved by Gamblin and then a Leadbeater shot hit the crossbar and went over. Aubert was again called into action when he fisted out a long shot from an Alderney forward. Alderney were now in some control but could not make this pressure pay with their shots being either too high or too wide. There was no more scoring and the match ended Alderney-0, Guernsey-3.

Alderney: J. Gamblin, H. Cleale, J. Catts, H. Le Maitre, L. Jacques (c), J. Allen, Jas Le Maitre, F. Quinain, E. Le Maitre, P. McIlroy, C. Smith.

Guernsey: J. Aubert, A. Benstead, E. Parry (c), V. Cooper, F. Stranger, J. Mahy, F. Cleale, F.G. Mockler, J. Leadbeater, A.H.P. Davey, T. Zabiela.
Goalscorers: Cooper, Leadbeater, Mockler.

Following the game the two captains were interviewed and Edgar Parry, the Guernsey captain, believed that his side deserved to win. The Alderney captain, Jacques, felt that the first and third goals could have been avoided but believed that the Alderney team were handicapped due to the fact that they only had 15 men in Alderney who knew anything about football.

GUERNSEY : Hope you enjoyed the trip. I did.

MURATTI FINAL.
9 April 1908, The Cycling Grounds, Guernsey.

Guernsey -0, Jersey -4.

The scene on the New North Quay between the hours of 7 and 8 o'clock this morning was one of great animation. Long before 7.00am supporters began to arrive and by 7.45am a constant stream of people, resplendent in their bold red and white rosettes, was seen to be winding their way to the berth of the mail steamer 'Roebuck'. By the hour of departure the vessel's decks were crowded with around 500 on board as they sailed to Guernsey. Judge T. Brabenson, of Alderney, with some 80 supporters from that island arrived by the 'Courier' on the morning of the match.

The 'Guernsey Evening Press' reported that on arrival of the Jersey team in St. Peter Port they were confronted by a couple of cartoons in chalk one of them representing a scene from a match between the Alderney 'hogs' and the Guernsey 'donkeys'. The second cartoon represents a Jersey 'crapaud'; bag in hand, crossing the gangway from a South-Western boat. At the shore end is a Guernsey 'donkey' with the coveted Muratti Vase under his foreleg. The Guernsey streets were swarming with Jersey supporters wearing their red and white colours. Such was the great interest in this match seats in the pavilion were at a premium and they were being sold at a profit by those who had previously secured them. The electric trams from the Town Church were crowded from 2.00pm and along Glateny Esplanade vehicles of all descriptions were full of eager supporters making their way to the Cycling Grounds.

Prior to the match Jersey lost the services of Stevens, their popular captain, and he was replaced by Dennis Renouf. The Jersey team were based at the 'Bel Voir', Esplanade, St. Peter Port where they flew a flag representing the Jersey colours of red and white. The Muratti medals were on view in Mr J. Mourant's establishment in the High Street. A souvenir card was also produced for Mr Atkins on which was published the teams and past records, etc. On the day before the match Jersey visited the Cycling Grounds and had a 'kick about' practising at the nets. They afterwards took a drive around the island.

At the Cycling Grounds a special table was provided for the Press and a telephone line was laid by the States Telephone Department at short notice. This was the first time that a

NO. 1. MURRATTI CUP FINAL.
THE MEETING OF GUERNSEY AND JERSEY AT THE WHITE ROCK.

direct telephone wire to a newspaper had been fixed in Guernsey. The match was attended by Guernsey's new Lieut-Governor, Major-General R. Auld CB, this being his first appearance at a public function. The North United Band was specially engaged for the occasion and from 4.00 to 4.30pm occupied a position in the centre of the field and entertained the spectators with some lively music.

Parry won the toss and Guernsey played with the sun and a slight breeze at their backs. Although Jersey kicked off the early pressure came from the Guernsey attack with Leadbeater almost breaking through but he was stopped by Honeycombe who in turn initiated a Jersey attack. The first corner was taken by Cooper but his excellent cross was well saved by Stanley Le Blancq in the Jersey goal amidst tremendous cheering by the Jersey supporters in the pavilion. Guernsey came close to opening the scoring when Leadbeater saw his thunderous shot cannon off the Jersey post. The game settled and Grimster broke away for Jersey but he was halted by Mahy, and Stranger cleared the danger. Guernsey replied through Mockler but his chance was missed. Cleale set

Le Valliant (Jersey).

up a Guernsey attack and sent in a centre for Leadbeater but he was quickly closed down by the Jersey defence. Leadbeater then came close firstly with a fine overhead kick that went over the bar followed soon after by a shot that came back off the post. Jersey then began to take control and Guernsey's Benstead, and then Parry, had to clear up dangerous attacks by the visitors. G. Fox then came very close with a neat shot. The play became more even with both defences being called upon to clear and in one Jersey attack Aubert slipped as he went out for the ball but he was relieved to see it roll past the post to safety. Nine minutes before half time Jersey opened the scoring when, following an excellent bout of passing, 'Snatcher' Fox received the ball from a cross and passed to Grimster, who was well positioned, and he fired in a shot that beat Aubert all ends up. Guernsey responded immediately and forced a corner that was taken by Cleale but cleared by Le Valliant. Mockler then received the ball and shot, only to see the ball flash past the post to leave the half time score Guernsey-0, Jersey-1.

The opening exchanges in the second half were very even. The first breakthrough nearly came when G. Fox and Grimster combined well but Aubert saved Grimster's shot at the expense of a corner. Aubert again came to Guernsey's rescue when W. Fox brought the ball down and fired in a shot from close quarters only for the keeper to save. G.S. Fox then tested Aubert with a stiff shot that the keeper saved. The Guernsey forwards were trying to find an equaliser but were finding Dennis Renouf, the Jersey skipper, in superb form. Jersey continued to force the game and after 63 minutes they scored again when G.S. Fox sent the ball across the Guernsey goalmouth and W. 'Snatcher' Fox sent in a splendid shot to put Jersey 2 goals ahead. Jersey were now in complete control and two minutes later Grimster scored goal number three from a header following a corner kick. Guernsey came back with Holland, Leadbeater and Mockler combining well but the Jersey defence were now in command as they kept them out. Twelve minutes from the end Grimster scored Jersey's fourth when he dribbled the ball to the left, and swerved round, and he shot in from around 40 yards. The ball flew past the full backs and Aubert almost before the spectators could realise what was happening. This was a truly remarkable goal that was greeted by loud applause from all round the ground. As the game neared its end Reed sent in a shot that was well saved by Aubert and the match ended Guernsey-0, Jersey-4.

Guernsey: J. Aubert, A. Benstead, E. Parry (c), V. Cooper, F. Stranger, J. Mahy, F. Cleale, F.G. Mockler, J. Leadbeater, T. Holland, T. Zabiela.

Jersey: S.C. Le Blancq, T. Thornton, W.T. Le Valliant, W. Millow, D. Renouf (c), P.O. Dart, G.S. Fox, W. Fox, F. Grimster, A. Reed, A.H. Honeycombe.
Goalscorers: Grimster (3), W. Fox.

Dennis Renouf. (Jersey Captain.)

After the game the Muratti Vase was presented to Dennis Renouf, the Jersey captain, by the Lieut-Governor of Guernsey, Major-General R. Auld CB. In presenting the Vase to Renouf, His Excellency stated that after such skill displayed by the Jersey team no one would grudge them their victory. Mrs Auld afterwards presented each of the winning team with a Muratti medal and each player was enthusiastically applauded. A beautiful bouquet of carnations was presented to Mrs Auld by Miss Ruby Bird, daughter of Mr. W. Bird, the President of the Northerners FC.

The crowds which gathered around the 'Evening Post' offices in St. Helier from 5.00 to 7.00pm on Thursday evening spoke volumes of the interest which the game generated. The crowds were kept informed throughout with a series of telegrams and posters in the windows especially when a goal was scored. The enthusiasm which greeted the final score at 6.15pm was indescribable and the crowd was literally carried away with excitement.

Details of the game at the Cycling Grounds were relayed to the GPO offices in St. Peter Port by means of three express messengers with bicycles and the news was sent by wire to Jersey. Details of the goals that were scored were telephoned from the Cycling Grounds to St. Peter Port and relayed by the GPO to Jersey by wire.

Guernsey was a lively place on Thursday night and plenty of Jersey money was spent. Despite the fact that the 'Melmore' brought home about 200 Jersey supporters there did not appear to be any fewer Jersey folk in St. Peter Port. The High Street and Pollet were packed with people and the utmost good humour prevailed. The 'Roebuck' left for Jersey a few minutes after 8.00am on Friday morning and, following a happy voyage, as the vessel steamed between the pier heads in St. Helier, rousing cheers were raised for the Jersey captain, Dennis Renouf, who had to board the waiting boat to Southampton as he had to return immediately to London. As far as the Jersey supporters were concerned the journey back home was all too short but, on route, one local poet composed the following which was heartily sung to the tune of 'After the ball was over':

Through the courtesy of the "Guernsey Evening Press" we are able to reproduce the above sketches of incidents in Thursday's Muratti final match.

'After the ball was centred,
After the whistle blew.
Jersey lined out her forwards,
And up the field they flew.
Fox centred the ball to Grimster,
And Grimster netted the pill.
That's how Jersey won the cup,
By four goals to nil'.

It was a jubilant Jersey team that returned to St. Helier with the Muratti Vase bedecked in red and white colours.

The reception in Jersey was a fitting conclusion to a holiday that will long linger in the memory of all those who crossed to Guernsey. As the steamer entered St. Helier harbour those on board started singing their victory songs, Mr. McKee's band, which was on the landing stage, took up the chorus. The New North Quay, packed with people, was a sight from the deck of the steamer and as soon as the waiting crowd caught sight of the Muratti Vase held aloft by 'Father' Dupre, they cheered themselves hoarse.

In the excitement over the match, and possibly due to the fact that the majority of the JFA officials were out of the Island, no car had been ordered to meet the team but one of the passengers placed their car at the team's disposal. Flags were flying all over the town and all the people cheered as the car passed by with the precious Vase. The car was driven through a dense mass of people to the Halkett Hotel for a breakfast held in honour of their Island.

NO. 2. MURRATTI CUP FINAL. BURIAL OF GUERNSEY.

The effect that the 4-0 reverse had on Guernsey can be seen in a postcard that was issued after the match.

It was unfortunate for Jersey football that Grimster never played in another Muratti as soon after this match he signed professional forms for Reading. An interesting question was asked following the match as to the possibility of Sark entering a team in the competition. A couple of years previously an effort was made to promote the game in Sark.

1 9 0 9

It was announced in the local press that Mr. Mourant, Vice-President of the Guernsey Football Association, has presented an 'Island' flag to the Alderney FA. It is blue bunting with a lion rampart and 'Riduna' beneath.

MURATTI SEMI-FINAL.
18 March 1909, The Cycling Grounds, Guernsey.

Guernsey -3, Jersey -0.

The 1909 Muratti Vase competition began on 18 March at the Cycling Grounds and, as luck would have it, it was a re-run on the 1908 final with Guernsey meeting the Vase holders, Jersey, and the home side were still smarting following their 4-0 home defeat. An advertisement that appeared in the local press asked for 10,000 spectators to go to the Cycling Grounds to cheer the 'Green and Whites'. The advertisement also added 'but don't forget the Visitors'.

Jersey were the first to run on to the field to a fine reception from the large crowd of around 8,000. There was an even louder roar when the Guernsey team came out. Renouf won the toss for Jersey and chose to play with the wind at his back and it was Leadbeater who kicked-off for the home side. The first spell of excitement came after five minutes when some excellent interplay by Froome, Leadbeater and Davey ended with Davey missing his shot. Although playing against the wind the Guernsey forwards were adapting well and in one incident Le Valliant had to clear quickly in front of goal with Froome close by. The weather began to deteriorate after half an hour and soon the match was being played in a downpour. Soon after Guernsey opened the scoring when Leadbeater put in a stinging shot from a tight position which Le Blancq pushed out only for Zabiela to rush in and find the net. From the restart Jersey put the home defence under some pressure for a time but the Guernsey defence held out and as half time approached they broke away and as Cleale advanced on the Jersey goal he was fouled just outside the penalty area. Duquemin took the free-kick and scored number two for Guernsey. Immediately before the half time whistle W. Fox sent in a superb shot that beat Lanyon but went just outside the post and the score remained Guernsey-2, Jersey-0.

Jersey opened the second half in a more determined manner as they tried to get back into the game. Play was held up as Davey had to leave the field due to injury although he soon returned to the game. Guernsey came close to increasing their lead when a superb shot by Froome was well stopped by Le Blancq who dropped the ball near the post and in the scrimmage that ensued Guernsey won a corner. This kick was cleared in fine fashion by Le Blancq at the expense of a further corner and he was again prominent as Jersey finally cleared the danger. Jersey then produced a period of pressure on the home defence and Lanyon had to save in quick succession from Poingdestre and W. Fox. He then saved a fast ground shot from Carter by turning it away for a corner. Zabiela then sustained a cut under the eye from a kick and he had to leave the field for attention. After 78 minutes Guernsey broke out from this siege and Davey sped past Thornton and sent in a centre that was met by Cleale who scored goal number three. Zabiela returned with a well bandaged face but he soon had to leave the field and took no further part in the game. Jersey won a free-kick for a handling offence and W. Fox fired in a long-range shot that was well dealt with by Lanyon. Davey again got the better of Thornton in a race along the line where he crossed in for Cleale who hit his shot against Le Valliant for a corner. There were chances at both ends as the game drew to a close with the final score Guernsey-3, Jersey-0.

Guernsey: F. Lanyon, F. Duquemin, T. Waterman, P. Smith, W. Crews, J. Mahy,
             W. Froome, F. Cleale, J. Leadbeater, A.H.P. Davey (c), T. Zabiela.
             Goalscorers: Zabiela, Duquemin, Cleale.

Jersey: S.C. Le Blancq, T. Thornton, W. Le Valliant, G. Scoones, D. Renouf (c),
             R. Carter, J. Poingdestre, S. Carwright,. A. Yates, W. Fox, G.S. Fox.

The margin of the Guernsey victory was a great surprise against a fine Jersey side but with Duquemin and Waterman solid in defence the visiting forwards were denied many clear cut chances. With this 3-0 victory Guernsey were now looking forward with confidence to their match with Alderney. This match was due to be played at Westmount, Jersey on 25 March.

In the Jersey side was A. Yates (Caesareans) who played for Guernsey in the 1907 Muratti Vase final against Jersey at Westmount. He was formerly in the Manchester Regiment and afterwards played for Guernsey Athletics. He became the first player to play for two different islands in the Muratti Vase competition.

The reaction following Guernsey's victory could be seen in the postcard (right) that was produced shortly after the match reciting a poem entitled 'Death of Jersey's Gallant XI'.

MURATTI FINAL.
25 March 1909, Westmount, Jersey.

Alderney -0, Guernsey -2.

The Guernsey football team and their supporters arrived in Jersey on Wednesday morning and put up at the Star Hotel. On Wednesday afternoon the 'Courier' brought the Alderney team and a number of supporters including Judge Barbenson, Mr. Mitchell, President of the Alderney FA, and Mr. McLernon, Hon Secretary of the AFA. Despite the heavy downpour of rain at 6.30pm when the 'Courier' entered the harbour, a large crowd had assembled to welcome the 'blue and white', who were received with hearty cheers. The team were then driven to their headquarters in St. John's Road. Nearly three hundred people travelled from Guernsey by the 'Vera' in the morning for the Muratti Vase final in Jersey. Those on board included two members of the Guernsey team-E.H.P. Davey and F. Lanyon as well as referee Mr. A. Hambly, who had crossed from Southampton. Due to the fact that there was a high westerly wind and some rain, the 'Vera' had a fairly rough passage. The 'Devonia', which left St. Peter Port at 1.20pm with 150 passengers, had a much better voyage and arrived in St. Helier at 3.40pm.

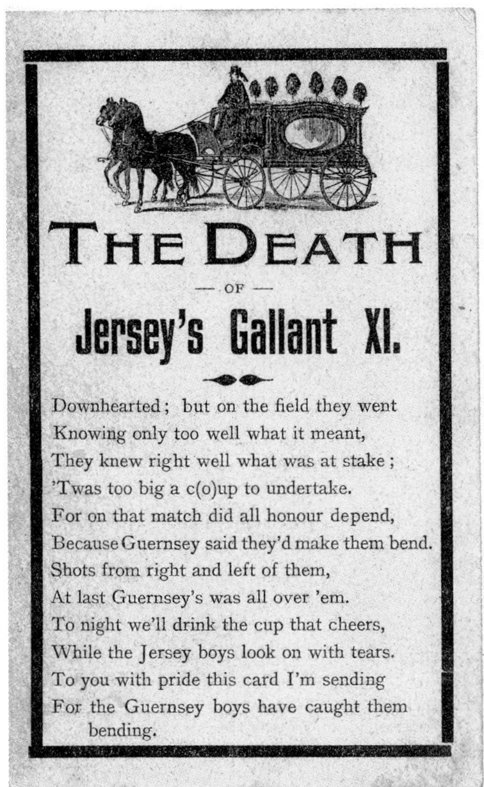

A football match was played prior to the Muratti Vase final between the 13th Co. Royal Garrison Artillery, of Guernsey and the 20th Co. Royal Garrison Artillery, of Jersey. After an exciting game the match finished with the Guernsey side winning 1-0.

There were around 4,500 spectators at Westmount for the final of the Muratti Vase competition as Jacques (Alderney) and Davey (Guernsey) led out their teams. There was a strong breeze blowing from the west and Davey took advantage of this when he won the toss. Rain began to fall as Henson kicked off for Alderney. Guernsey immediately gained possession and, after a free-kick, a fine move by the Guernsey forwards found Leadbeater in a good position and he beat Batiste in the Alderney goal from close quarters with only two minutes played. Alderney lost the ball from the kick-off and Davey and Zabiela combined in an attack that resulted in a Guernsey corner that was cleared by the Alderney defence. Le Vallee, the Alderney right winger, attempted to set up an attack but he was well tackled by Waterman. Cleale and Leadbeater received the ball and attacked the Alderney goal with Cleale scoring a second after four minutes. It appeared that Guernsey were going to gain a run-away victory but Alderney responded with some excellent defending with Caplain and Catts particularly effective. The Alderney attack was now pushing forward and Lanyon had to be alert to save a Henson shot. Guernsey again pushed on into the attack and Batiste did well to stop shots from Froome and Davey, both from close in. As the play swung from end to end Burgess and Smith were causing the Guernsey defence some con-defence some concern. Leadbeater then came close when his powerful shot hit the Alderney crossbar. Alderney replied by winning a corner and, from this kick, Henson fired in a great shot that was saved by Lanyon. The play was now very even as half time came with the score Alderney-0, Guernsey-2.

Alderney began the second half with the advantage of the stiff breeze and was immediately on the attack and Duquemin and Waterman were tested by their forwards. Although having the wind at their backs the Alderney forwards did not utilise the same close-passing of the Guernsey forwards preferring to use the long airborne ball that tended to overshoot. The Guernsey midfield was very busy in repelling the Alderney attacks and, following a scrimmage, the ball ended up in the Guernsey net only to be ruled out for offside. Due to the Alderney pressure Guernsey's attacks were confined to breakaways and from one of these they nearly scored when Davey, on receiving a pass from Froome, was shaping to shoot but was dispossessed by Caplain. As the match neared its end Lanyon saved from Gamblin and then Allen. This was followed by a shot by Burgess that went just wide and the final result was Alderney-0, Guernsey-2.

F. Duquemin, F. Lanyon, T. Waterman.
S. Davidson (reserve), W. Froome, F. Cleale, J. Leadbeater, A.H.P. Davey, T. Zabiela.
P. Smith, W. Crews, J. Mahy.

Alderney: C. Batiste, W. Caplain, J. Catts, J. Gamblin, L. Jacques, H. Cleale,
              W. Le Vallee, J. Allen, A. Henson, C. Smith, A. Burgess.

Guernsey: F. Lanyon, F. Duquemin, T. Waterman, P. Smith, W. Crews, J. Mahy,
              W. Froome, F. Cleale, J. Leadbeater, A.H.P. Davey, T. Zabiela.
              Goalscorers: Leadbeater, Cleale.

Following the game the respective captains were interviewed by the 'Star' and Mr Leonard Jacques of Alderney said that the game throughout was very fast and that his team was completely taken by surprise during the first half of the game. He felt that in winning the toss and by taking advantage of the wind when they were fresh, Guernsey took an early advantage. Davey of Guernsey conceded that the winning of the toss had a good deal to do with their winning of the game. He also felt that playing the ball low and under control was a better ploy to using a kick and rush style. It was a strenuous game with little to choose between the two teams.

The victorious Guernsey team were met by the Trinity Drum and Fife Band when they returned from Jersey on Friday morning. The team entered a four-in hand car and went by way of the Pollet, High Street, Fountain Street, Market Street, and back by way of the Quay to the Channel Islands Hotel with the Band leading the way.

The Council of the Guernsey Football Association gave a dinner at the Channel Islands Hotel for the Guernsey and Alderney team and officials on Friday 26 March. A limited number of tickets are to be sold, price 2s 1d. They may be obtained on Thursday evening at Mr. Rousseau's in the Pollet. Visitors will be welcome after the dinner, on presentation of their club membership cards.

1 9 1 0

MURATTI SEMI-FINAL.
7 April 1910, Westmount, Jersey.

Jersey -7, Alderney -1.

Included in the Jersey side for the match against Alderney was T.S. Mellanby who had refereed the Alderney v Jersey Muratti semi-final at the Cycling Grounds on 21 March 1907. He became the first player to have played in and refereed a Muratti match.

The two teams came out in front of around 2,000 spectators at Westmount that included the Lieut-Governor of Jersey and Judge Barbeson of Alderney. Stevens won the toss for Jersey and elected to play with the sun at his back. The pitch was dry and a little hard and soon the Alderney defence was put under pressure. Jersey had some early chances to score through Wheway and Chapman but the Alderney defence held out. Oselton began an attack for the visitors but the move broke down due mainly to a lack of understanding between the Alderney forwards. In a further Alderney attack Coppin, in the Jersey goal, rushed out to clear and injured his knee. He had to go off the field for treatment and was replaced in goal by Mellanby. Jersey reorganised their side and continued on the attack and Batiste had to save from a Chapman attack at the expense of a corner. Mellanby was then called upon came close when Cartwright headed over the crossbar and soon after it appeared as if he would score but put the ball over the bar. After 15 minutes absence Coppin returned to his goal and Jersey then began to bombard the Alderney goal but the shooting of their forwards was not very accurate and the game remained scoreless. The ball was then lost when it was kicked out of the ground and a replacement had to be found causing some delay. Chapman missed a fine opportunity from a Mellanby pass but soon after Jersey opened the scoring. Batiste saved a long range shot but the ball broke to Chapman who fired in the first goal. A minute later Wheway received a pass and ran in to score the second. There was no more scoring and half time arrived with the score Jersey-2, Alderney-0.

  Jersey began the second half by nearly increasing their lead when a shot by Poingdestre went wide. Jersey then laid siege to the Alderney goal with Cartwright scoring number three followed a minute later by him adding a fourth. Jersey were now playing with a lot of confidence but Alderney refused to concede and their defence was coping well with the almost continuous assault. Alderney was confined to breakaway attacks as Wheway came close for Jersey on a couple of occasions with Batiste in the Alderney goal saving well. Jersey scored again when, from a Poingdestre centre, Chapman scored a fifth goal. Quinain and Vagg set up an Alderney attack and Coppin had to save from the rush on his goal. Mellanby and Cartwright then combined well and Cartwright added a sixth goal followed almost immediately by a seventh goal from Wheway. Five minutes from the end Gamblin sent in a long shot that was saved by Coppin but the ball rolled across the goalmouth and Vagg nipped in to score a consolation goal for Alderney. The final whistle sounded later with the final score Jersey-7, Alderney-1.

Jersey: J. Coppin, R.R. Stevens (c), D. Renouf, W.C. Beasley, A. Reed,
                 G. Scoones, J. Poingdestre, S. Cartwright, Chapman, F. Wheway,
                 T.S. Mellanby.
                 Goalscorers: Chapman (2), Cartwright (3), Wheway (2).

Alderney: C. Batiste, Sebire, J. Lihou, J. Allen, Gamblin, Olliver, K. Oselton,
                 McLernon, F. Quinain, Vagg, A. Burgess.
                 Goalscorer: Vagg.

  This was a very impressive performance by Jersey. Their defence was sound and the mid-field pairing of Beasley and Reed controlled the game. Reed covered a lot of ground during the match and in the second half both he and Scoones' passes to Poingdestre were always useful. Wheway was the pick of an excellent forward line as he combined well with Mellanby. On this performance Jersey are stronger than they have ever been and Guernsey appear to have their work cut out when they meet on 21 April. The Alderney team never seemed to settle and their defence had great difficulty in dealing with the pressure exerted by the Jersey forwards. A fairly large contingent of Alderney and Guernsey spectators, including Judge Barbenson, returned to Guernsey on Friday morning and in the afternoon the Alderney team played a match against the Royal Artillery at the Cycling Grounds before returning home.

MURATTI FINAL.
21 April 1910, The Cycling Grounds, Guernsey.

Guernsey -2, Jersey -3.

The 'Courier' left Alderney about 6.00am and arrived in Guernsey at 8.30am with between 60 and 70 passengers on board, including Judge Brabenson, Mr. McLernon, Mr. C.R. Le Cocq and Mr. M. Baron. There were some 300 Jersey supporters on the 'Reindeer', which arrived at St. Peter Port on the morning of the game. Included were three of the Jersey team in Stevens, Reed and Poingdestre. Despite a somewhat choppy crossing the Jersey supporters were most enthusiastic as the vessel entered the harbour, and announced their arrival by the sounding of rattles, motor-horns etc. and the singing of popular songs. The 'Alberta', carrying some 534 passengers, arrived at 2.00pm and was gaily decorated with bunting and the passengers appeared very animated. A cinematographic picture of the arrival was taken on behalf of the 'Imperial Pictures Varieties'. The final of the 1910 Muratti Vase took place at the Cycling Grounds before a record crowd of over 7,600. The ends had been taken out of the pavilion and the seating extended. The Evening Press reported that the scene was a remarkable one with the complete area a sea of faces. They complemented the staff under the direction of Messrs. Bird, Freckler and Bowden for the way they managed the admission and seating of so huge a crowd.

The referee of the match was Mr. Pook who took charge when Jersey annexed the Vase in 1908 and the Jersey Press wondered if this was an omen. Jersey had to play the match without the influential Denis Renouf and it was thought that J. Whitworth (formerly of Guernsey Rangers) would take his place, however, in the end Scoones moved to full back and Bailey was brought in. It was noted that Jersey Wanderers supplied nine members of the Jersey team with only Chapman (Caesareans) and Scoones who do not play for Wanderers. Guernsey lost the services of their captain, Holland, just before the match due to the fact he was unable to obtain the necessary time off work and he was replaced by Purchas. The captaincy was given to P. Allen. Special green and white shirts had been ordered by the Guernsey team but they were damaged during manufacture and an emergency kit of green shirts and white shorts were used.

Guernsey won the toss and chose to play with the wind behind them. From the kick-off Jersey pushed into Guernsey territory but the play was quickly returned into the Jersey half and Cleale sent in a shot that came off of Scoones' legs and to safety. Stranger then sent a pass to Zabiela but his fine shot cleared the middle of the bar and this was followed by a break by Jersey which saw Chapman's shot go just wide. After 15 minutes play Guernsey were slightly on top and, following a throw in, Benstead shot for goal causing Coppin to

MURATTI CUP FINAL.

THURSDAY NEXT,
April 21.

GUERNSEY
v.
JERSEY

CYCLING GROUND.

Kick-off 4.30.

Presentation of Cup by T. MITCHELL, Esq., President I.I.C.

Plan of Reserved Seats at Mr. G. ROUSSEAU'S, Hairdresser, Pollet. Pavilion Seats (including admission to Ground), 1s. 3d. Juniors ditto, 10d. Advance Tickets admitting to Ground only, 5d. Juniors, 3d. Two hundred and forty extra chairs will be placed in front of Pavilion, if fine, at 10d. each, in addition to entrance charge; 200 seats on " Members' Stand," 5d. each.

Obtain your tickets early. Purchase Admission Tickets in advance to avoid rush at gates. All admission tickets will be collected at the Gates.

H. G. BOWDEN,
(6405) Hon. Sec. I.I.C.

F. Lanyon. (Guernsey).

Arty Reed. (Jersey).

fall to his knees to pull off a good save. Guernsey won a free kick on the half way line and the ball was sent towards the Jersey goal where Scoones cleared for a corner. The ball was cleared from this kick but returned by Duquemin and in a scramble in front of goal Stranger headed just over. With 20 minutes played Wheway put in a shot at goal that Lanyon could only parry and Chapman rushed in to crash it into the Guernsey net to give the visitors the lead. From the kick-off Guernsey forced a corner and the Jersey defence were having trouble clearing before Beasley put the ball out.

Jersey appeared to be playing better with their defence slightly on top but after 33 minutes Guernsey got the equaliser. Stranger and Chapple combined to pressurise the visiting defence and after they had attempted to clear a Jersey defender tried to kick the ball clear but it hit Chapple on the chest and into the net. Guernsey began to attack the Jersey defence but Reed and Scoones were putting in some cool defensive play to keep them at bay. Guernsey then produced some fine inter-play to set up Chapple who broke through again to score from six yards to put the home side 2-1 ahead. There were chances at both ends but the defences held out and at half time the score was Guernsey-2, Jersey-1.

  Jersey had the advantage of the wind in the second half but in the first minute it was Coppin who was called into action as he rushed out to clear up-field. The play was becoming more even as the action swung from end to end. Jersey then had a period of sustained pressure and Lanyon had to be quick to clear the ball into touch from a run by Beasley followed by Mahy cleverly dispossessing Poingdestre near the touchline. Ten minutes into the half Jersey equalised when, following an impressive attack, Chapman scored from close quarters. There was now nothing between the teams and in the midfield Allen and Stranger for Guernsey fought it out with Stevens and Beasley for Jersey. As this exciting game continued Guernsey won a free kick and Allen sent the ball into the Jersey penalty area and the ball appeared to be going into the net when it was handled by Scoones. Referee Pook pointed to the penalty spot and Benstead stepped up to take the kick but put his shot wide.

The Jersey goal is under pressure as the ball goes wide.

Chapple (centre, dark shirt) scoring Guernsey's second goal.

Minutes later Stranger came very close to scoring but his header went just past the post with the Guernsey crowd cheering as they thought that the ball had gone in. Lanyon was soon called into play again as he pulled off a sensational save from Mellanby. Jersey were now slightly gaining control of the game and Mellanby sent a header just past followed by a Poingdestre shot that hit the side netting. This pressure paid off when, following two corners, Wheway scored to put Jersey ahead with a few minutes to go. Guernsey nearly equalised following a scramble in front of the Jersey goal but Stevens cleared by sending the ball up-field. Guernsey were unable to close the gap and the final result was Guernsey-2, Jersey-3.

Guernsey: F. Lanyon, F. Duquemin, A. Benstead, E. Purchase, P. Allen (c), J. Mahy, G. West, F. Cleale, R. Chapple, F. Stranger, T. Zabiela.
Goalscorer: Chapple (2).

Jersey: J. Coppin, R.R. Stevens (c), G. Scoones, W.C. Beasley, A. Reed, Bailey, J. Poingdestre, S. Cartwright, Chapman, F. Wheway, T. Mellanby.
Goalscorers: Chapman (2), Wheway.

Immediately after the game a roped enclosure was formed in front of the pavilion. Mr. Mitchell (Alderney), the President of the Inter-Insular Committee, presented the Muratti Vase to R.R. Stevens, the Jersey captain. His wife then handed the Muratti medals to all of the winning team. Cheers were given to both teams and the officials after this presentation.

It was pointed out in the Press that it had been privately arranged that extra time would be played if the teams were level. There is apparently no rule on this point and the Press believed that there should be.

As the match progressed a description of the game was telephoned direct from the ground to the 'Evening Press' office and the description of the game was rapidly set up on the linotype machines. Three minutes after the game had finished the Football Edition was being printed and then passed through the folding machine. Two boys with bundles of Football Editions were hurried to a motor-car waiting in Smith Street and, as the final cheers were being raised after the presentation of the Muratti Vase, the motor-car started from Smith Street for the Cycling Grounds. A paperboy was dropped off at the end of Victoria Avenue so the spectators leaving the Cycling Grounds could buy a copy of a 'Football Edition' that had a full report of the match.

It was recorded in the Guernsey Evening Press (Friday 22 April) that sections of the game were recorded by the cinematography men. The pictures of the 1910 Muratti were to be shown at St. Julian's Hall the following week.. This was sponsored by the management of the 'Imperial Electric Pictures and Varieties.' The film begins with the Jersey supporters arriving at the White Rock on the 'Alberta' then moves on to the Cycling Grounds to show the teams taking the field then the toss up. All the goals have been captured; however, the light was not all that could be desired.

On the day of the game, the half-time and the result scores were telegraphed to Alderney. The scores telephoned from the Track to the 'Press' Office were telegraphed to Alderney with little delay. Sympathy in Alderney, as regards the waiting crowd, was on the side of Jersey. They were downcast when the score was 2-1 for Guernsey at half-time, but cheered for Jersey when the winning score came through at full-time.

A very large crowd assembled at the White Rock between 7 and 8 o'clock to witness the departures of the 'Alberta' for Jersey and the 'Courier' for Alderney. Naturally the Jersey supporters were jubilant and the scenes at No. 3 berth where the 'Alberta' lay ready for departure was an animated one. Rattles, motor-horns and other instruments of 'music' were sounded from all parts of the vessel, forming an accompaniment to the popular songs sung by the supporters. On Friday morning the Jersey team drove from the 'Bel Voir' boarding house to the boat in an excursion car and were obviously elated as they sang songs boarding the car to make their way to the 'Reindeer'.

The Press of Saturday 23 April reported on the return of the Jersey team:

'The Reindeer entered St. Helier's Harbour yesterday morning with all her flags flying, and the Jersey team and a number of returning football supporters on board. Ashore a crowd of some hundreds of people raised cheer on cheer as the vessel passed the pier-heads.

After landing, the team and the officials entered a char-a-banc with harness decorated with red-and-white ribbon, and several photographs were taken, by professional and amateur photographers. The car was then driven through the town, eventually stopping at the Beresford Café, where breakfast awaited the team.'

A happy ending to an excellent game for Jersey.

Preparations were well under way for Guernsey's Muratti semi-final against Alderney on 6 April. It had been agreed that the match would be preceded by a junior inter-insular game between Alderney and Guernsey. On the day before the match however severe weather prevented the 'Courier' leaving Alderney for Guernsey on Wednesday 5 April. Although the boat would leave on the Thursday it was felt that it would leave little time for the teams to reach the Cycling Grounds in time for the match. The weather forecast was not very encouraging and there was a good chance that there would be no football played in Guernsey. A decision was therefore taken to indefinitely postpone the match. The referee and Jersey officials were informed of the postponement. Later the games were re-scheduled for 20 April.

The Guernsey Muratti team played against South Bank (Bradford) on Monday 17 April and despite taking a first-half lead finally lost the match 5-2.

1 9 1 1

JUNIOR MATCH.
20 April 1911, The Cycling Grounds, Guernsey.

Guernsey -3, Alderney -2.

The 1911 Muratti match between Guernsey and Alderney was preceded by a junior inter-insular match between the islands. The hot weather of the Easter holidays had made the ground very hard but the showers that fell on the previous evening improved the conditions of the surface. The junior teams arrived shortly after 3.00pm, and the Guernsey team had their photograph taken.

Referee J. Duffey called the captains together and Guernsey having won the toss chose to defend the western goal and take advantage of the stiff breeze. Almost immediately Guernsey broke into the attack and Ellis slipped the ball to Chapple who scored past Hammond. Guernsey continued taking the ball to Alderney and Stranger came close but put his shot over the bar. Alderney held out well and began to attack the home goal without success. After 20 minutes Chapple once more found himself in front of goal but again he fired his shot over and he followed this with another shot that grazed the Alderney post. Hammond was again called into action when he held a fine shot from Milnes and seven minutes from half time Hammond save a good shot from Stranger. Alderney withstood this onslaught and as half-time approached broke away for Baker to score the equaliser. It looked as though this would finish the first half scoring but just on the whistle Milnes passed to the right and Stranger took the ball down and scored to make the half-time Guernsey-2, Alderney-1.

The opening minutes of the second half were very even, then after five minutes Guernsey were awarded a penalty. Chapple took the kick and Hammond saved, but Chapple collected the rebound and scored to put Guernsey 3-1 ahead. Alderney responded well and began to pressurise the Guernsey defence giving them and Langlois some anxious moments. With ten minutes remaining Milnes turned the ball back to his goalkeeper but the Alderney forwards quickly gained control and the ball eventually fell to Catts who scored to reduce the arrears. The last minutes of the game was quite even and the whistle went with the score Guernsey-3, Alderney-2.

Guernsey: Langlois, P. Butler, W. Priest, A. Robilliard, P. Milnes, J. Beech, F. Toms, J. Stranger, W. Ellis, H. Chapple, A.S. Blicq.
Goalscorers: Chapple (2), Stranger.

Alderney: J. Hammond, T. Oliver, C. Cooley, Maskell, J. Buckle, J. Sykes, Grier, W. McLernon, T. Baker, J. Catts, E. Thomson.
Goalscorers: Baker, Catts.

MURATTI SEMI-FINAL.
20 April 1911, The Cycling Grounds, Guernsey.

Guernsey -2, Alderney -1.

There was a fairly large crowd to witness the Junior inter-insular which preceded the Muratti semi-final. Needless to say, however, the crowd was augmented as 5'o'clock approached until the north side of the ground was well-lined and the whole of the wall was occupied by the green and white supporters. The German band was in attendance entertaining the waiting crowd as did a performance by a Scottish bagpiper. In the Pavilion were representatives of Alderney and Jersey including Judge Barbenson, Jurat N. Gaudion, Mr. McLernon (in charge of the Alderney team), Mr. Baron and Mr. Dupre, who is well-known in connection with Jersey football.

Guernsey. 1911.

J. Gamblin
(Alderney captain).

The main match between the senior teams of both islands was just as close and competitive. Alderney were first to run out wearing their blue and white shirts with white shorts followed by Guernsey in their new green and white shirts and dark shorts. Davey, the Guernsey captain, won the toss and chose to play with the wind and sun behind him. Alderney kicked off but Guernsey quickly gained possession and with only two minutes played Chapple sent in an excellent shot which flew past Brooks to put the home side 1-0 ahead. Guernsey again came close through efforts by Cooper and Chapple as they kept up the early pressure on Alderney. The Alderney attack was finding it difficult to breach the Guernsey defence in which Purdy was prominent but through Oselton and Allen they were gradually getting back into the game. Cooper then came close for Guernsey when he received a throw in and, from just outside the penalty area, sent his shot over the bar. A few moments later Waterman nearly scored when he sent a free-kick skimming over the bar. With five minutes remaining in the half Alderney broke away and Burgess nearly equalised when Lanyon could only kick his shot away. At half time the score in this tight match was Guernsey-1, Alderney-0.

Alderney began the second half with the sun and wind in their favour and within five minutes they equalised when they gained a corner that Oselton drove in across goal and it was headed in by an Alderney forward. Guernsey began to force the game and T. Zabiela sent a fine pass to Chapple who closed in on the Alderney goal but Brooks came out and booted the ball up-field to safety. After 65 minutes Guernsey regained the lead when Chapple scored from a Tommy Zabiela centre. Alderney responded immediately when Oselton got possession and drove his shot straight at Lanyon who fell whilst saving. He made strenuous efforts to clear the ball but in the melee which ensued Alderney gained a corner which came to nought. Cleale then sent in an excellent free-kick that was well saved by Lanyon and Guernsey had a worrying few minutes as Alderney strove for an equaliser. As the game neared its end Holland and then Chapple nearly scored but the final result was Guernsey-2, Alderney-1.

Guernsey: F. Lanyon, A. Benstead, T. Waterman, T. Holland, E. Zabiela, C. Purdy, F. Dorey, Cooper, R. Chapple, A.H.P. Davey (c), T. Zabiela.
Goalscorer: Chapple (2).

Alderney: C. Brookes, W. Caplain, J. Lihou, Jacques, J. Gamblin (c), H. Cleale, K. Oselton, J. Allen, C. Vague, A. Henson, A. Burgess.
Goalscorer: Oselton.

MURATTI FINAL.
27 April 1911, Westmount, Jersey.

Jersey -4, Guernsey -1.

The London & South-Western and the Great-Western Railway Companies prepared for the Muratti Vase final in Jersey by offering cheap ticket priced at 4/- second class return. The Great Western Steamer will leave for Jersey on Wednesday 26 April at 7am. And the London and South-Western Steamer will leave at 7am on Thursday. The returns will be by Mail Steamers Friday 28 April and Saturday 29 April.

Guernsey's team had to be rearranged when H. Stranger could not play as he was unable to get away due to pressure of business at the bank where he was employed at Southampton. Guernsey had hoped that Cleale might arrive by the 'Sarnia' in the morning and proceed to Jersey with the team to play in the match. This was not possible as his ship was expected to arrive at Plymouth at 5.30 in the morning. Only five of the Guernsey players crossed to Jersey on the 26th April, the remainder arriving on the 27th. The weather forecast was not good for the trip on the 27th with 'High winds, rough sea, squally and showery', not the ideal preparation for a Muratti Vase final. The 'Jersey Evening Post' noted that interest in the Muratti contest is not only confined to these islands. The Jersey colony at Gaspe, Canada, have clubbed together for the result of the match to be cabled from Jersey.

The Guernsey team together with the Committee and supporters left the British Hotel for Westmount in four wagonettes. The procession was headed by a donkey ridden by a boy, both wearing the Guernsey colours. The atmosphere at Westmount was electric. Motor horns, rattles, whistles, bells etc. were all in evidence and the roads leading to the ground were all packed with fans sporting red and white and green and white. Prior to the match the donkey bedecked in green and white was paraded round the park. Apparently the

Jack Coppin. (Jersey Captain)

A.H.P. Davey. (Guernsey Captain)

appearance of the donkey took the Jersey people by surprise, for some argument was necessary before the animal was allowed to walk round the field, although there was ample time. The followers, however, forced their mascot through and the parade came off. The boy enjoyed his ride from town and back. Further investigation revealed that the Guernsey hockey team had sent a wire to Jersey on Wednesday so that they could engage a donkey for the day so that it could be paraded through St. Helier decorated with the Guernsey colours.

It was a very windy day and it was thought that whoever won the toss would begin with an advantage. Guernsey were first to make their appearance to a loud reception and moments later Jack Coppin lead out the Jersey team to an excited round of applause. Coppin and Davey met in the middle to choose ends and the referee had to toss the coin twice (the first time the coin did not land flat enough to decide) Coppin guessed correctly and took advantage of the very strong wind. Jersey started quickly and in the first 30 seconds Lanyon had to pull off a fine save. The wind was playing havoc with the play but the pressure on Lanyon's goal was tremendous and Waterman and Mahy had to work very hard to keep the home side out. It only seemed a matter of time before Jersey scored and the first goal came after 25 minutes. Wheway collected the ball well out and, after beating Mahy, drove a magnificent shot under the bar from fully 25 yards out. The second Jersey goal followed five minutes later and was a disaster for the Guernsey defence when, following a mix-up in the penalty area, Sonnen had no difficulty in scoring. Jersey continued to use the elements to their advantage and were rather unfortunate to have two further scores cancelled by referee Ross. The third goal was not long in coming, however, as Chapman set up Wheway to score. Guernsey were very relieved when the referee blew for half time with the score Jersey-3, Guernsey-0.

Guernsey began the second half with what was described as a gale behind them. It was felt that the visitors would use the wind to their advantage and shoot at every opportunity but instead they appeared to want to make sure of their position before shooting and the chances were lost. They missed an early opportunity after 10 minutes to reduce the arrears but Bird missed this chance. More chances were missed by the visitors and it was a Jersey error that presented them with a goal when Coppin fell when clearing and Bird scored from 2 yards.

Guernsey's joy was short lived when a wonderful shot by Honeycombe from about 6 yards from the corner flag was caught by the wind and it curled past a despairing Lanyon and landed just inside the post. Guernsey tried to pull the game round but as the match wore on they became more erratic and the Jersey defence were very able at breaking up these attacks. About five minutes of extra time was allowed by the referee owing to the ball being so often out of touch in the second half. The whistle finally sounded and the score was Jersey-4, Guernsey-1.

Bird, scorer of Guernsey's only goal.

Jersey: J. Coppin (c), W.C. Beasley, J. Whitworth, Bailey, A. Reed, G. Scoones,
            A. Honeycombe, Sonnen, Chapman, F. Wheway, T. Mellanby.
            Goalscorers: Wheway (2), Sonnen, Honeycombe.

Guernsey: F. Lanyon, A. Benstead, T. Waterman, T. Holland, Mahy, E. Zabiela,
            F. Dorey, W. Bird, R. Chapple, A.H.P. Davey (c), T. Zabiela.
            Goalscorer: Bird.

This was Jersey's first Muratti Vase triumph on home soil. Best for the victors were Beasley, Reed, Wheway and Chapman in what was an excellent team performance. Guernsey were a little under par with Lanyon, who performed excellently, and Mahy the best for them.

Following the match both captains agreed that Jersey were the better team and thoroughly merited their fine victory. They had adapted to the very windy conditions well in each half. In the evening reception that was held at 'Olympia' the Muratti Vase and medals were presented to the Jersey team by Dr. Max Le Cronier. Dr. Cronier congratulated both teams on their display. Mr. Stanley Hope having extended a free invitation to the players and others staying at the British Hotel, the party retraced their steps and took reserved seats at the Opera House. Here the best parts of the programme were witnessed and thoroughly enjoyed. The proceedings closed with that portion of film taken by Mr. Clements showing incidents of the match. The film was to be shown on Friday 28 April at St. Julian's Hall and it would show the difficult conditions, and the excellent play of Lanyon. The Guernsey party left Jersey on Friday morning aboard the mailboat, 'Sarnia'.

Honeycombe, scorer of Jersey's fourth goal.

It was announced that the SS 'Roebuck' had been wrecked off Jersey on 19 July 1911. The 'Roebuck', built in 1897, was one of the boats that used to ferry Muratti spectators to the matches.

1 9 1 2

MURATTI SEMI-FINAL.
18 April 1912, Westmount, Jersey.

Jersey -3, Guernsey -3. aet.

Both islands began their preparation for the Muratti match early by arranging a series of practice matches. Jersey Probables played against a civilian/military side whereas Guernsey took part in three Whites v Colours matches as well as two matches between the Guernsey

Probables and the Garrison. Jersey were investigating the possibility of selecting E. Sonnen who was playing in France. Sonnen and Bailey (formerly of Jersey Wanderers) were playing for St. Servan along with Jones the one time member of the Rangers team. Besides being champions of Brittany the team eventually hope to become champions of France. The Jersey Football Association are petitioning for permission to play Sonnen in the Muratti. A special JFA Council meeting was held on Saturday 6 April to consider an application from Mr. E. Sonnen to be re-instated under the JFA rules. In his application Mr. Sonnen stated that he had been employed for several months in Saint Servan, France and had been playing under an Association which was not recognised by the English FA. He had, however, returned home permanently and requested to be re-instated under JFA rules. He also gave a promise not to again take part in any football outwith the jurisdiction of the FA. Under the circumstances the Council unanimously decided to grant the request.

Guernsey also had problems with their selected line-up when it was found that John Tostevin, the centre forward, was not on the list of registered players for the Muratti Competition and therefore would have to be replaced. The rule stated that the names had to be registered 26 weeks in advance of the first match. The Selection Committee decided to meet on Saturday 13 April to decide whether to replace Tostevin with Cleal. Cleal had apparently expressed an unwillingness to play except at centre forward. At this meeting it was pointed out that, according to Rule 12, Tostevin being a native of Guernsey was eligible to play as the 26 week rule was applicable only to non-residents. There was therefore no need to make an alteration to the selected team.

For the day of the match Jersey was bathed in sunshine with a cloudless sky. The mailboat brought in 220 supporters from Guernsey and they were wearing the customary green and white rosettes. A further 200 more arrived at 3.30pm on the 'Devonia'. St. Helier was very quiet during the earlier part of the morning but as time went on things livened up a great deal. At 3.00pm the spectators were taking their places and by 4.00pm the roads leading to Westmount were thronged and hooters and bells were being sounded in all directions. The Guernsey team and supporters left the Star Hotel at 4.30pm in brakes. Among the spectators were General Rochfort, Lieut-Governor of Jersey, and Colonel Kellett. Before the match started the Jersey team came out for a preliminary practice and their supporters paraded their mascot, a tame fox held on a chain, around the field.

Mahy won the toss for Guernsey and decided to defend the First Tower end with the sun at their backs. Jersey were first on the attack and Waterman had to clear from a shot by Sonnen and Hebdon was called on early when he had to save two dangerous shots. Guernsey responded and Zabiela tested Coppin in the Jersey goal followed by Tostevin sending in some low shots that the goalkeeper cleared. There was a period of even play as both sides fought for superiority then Fox broke through for Jersey and his shot missed the Guernsey goal by mere inches. When the game was 30 minutes old Cleal had to leave the field due to an ankle injury and he was carried off. Jersey came close when Stent drove down the field and centred for Wheway who collected the ball and fired in a shot that Hebdon saved well and cleared. Cleal returned to the game after a 10 minute absence and was greeted with enthusiastic cheers. Jersey were now gaining some control of the match and Stent sent in a shot that Hebdon managed to clear. The Guernsey defence was under some pressure but Jersey found Tooley in fine form. Just before half-time Wheway created a good opening for Jersey but put his shot over. The half time score was Jersey-0, Guernsey-0.

Guernsey began the second half by forcing two quick corners and from the first Dorey crossed in for Purdy to head over and from the second Joe Whitworth cleared the danger. Hebdon was then called into play when he saved a straight shot by Fox and then prevented what looked like a certain goal when a superb save. In the 65th minute Jersey opened the scoring when, following a melee in the Guernsey area, Stratford scored. Guernsey immediately pressed forward but Stranger was pulled up for a foul and the move broke down. Play was then held up for a time due to an injury to John Tostevin who had been playing out on the wing. Guernsey broke away with Dorey and he sent the ball to Zabiela but, as he tried to put in his shot, he fell in front of the goal and the chance was gone. Five minutes later a beautiful centre by Dorey was met by Cleal and he fired in his header to give Guernsey the equaliser. Two minutes later Jersey regained the lead when a low ground shot from close in by Stratford left Hebdon well beaten for 2-1, Jersey continued to press and only a fine piece of anticipation by Hebdon cut out a centre by Sonnen. Nine minutes from time Stranger's knee gave out and as Jersey pressed on Hebdon stopped an offside shot. As the game neared its end Guernsey exerted some pressure forcing two late corners and from the second Cleale scored a dramatic equaliser making the score, after the regulation 90 minutes, Jersey-2, Guernsey-2.

In extra time Jersey regained the initiative and again took the lead through Sonnen. It looked as if Jersey would triumph but Stranger scored a magnificent goal to equalise. Shortly afterwards referee, Mr. G.L. Miller of Norfolk, stopped the game owing to poor light leaving the score Jersey-3, Guernsey-3.

Jersey: J. Coppin, D. Renouf (c), J. Whitworth, W.C. Beasley, W. Millow, G. Scoones, E. Sonnen, Stratford, G.S. Fox, F. Wheway, H. Stent.
Goalscorers: Stratford (2), Sonnen.

Guernsey: J. Hebdon, A.E. Tooley, T. Waterman, C. Purdy, R. Chapple, J. Mahy (c), F. Dorey, H. Stranger, J. Tostevin, F. Cleale, T. Zabiela.
Goalscorers: Cleale (2), Stranger.

This remarkable match was the first Muratti game to end in a draw and it was decided that the replay should take place the following day at the same venue.

MURATTI SEMI-FINAL REPLAY.
19 April 1912, Westmount, Jersey.

Jersey -2, Guernsey -5.

Due to injury Jersey replaced J. Coppin (Wanderers), D. Renouf (Wanderers) and Sonnen by T. Garnier, Arty Reed (Wanderers) and J. Newson and the feeling was that this in no way weakened their side. Guernsey's only change was A. Yates (Athletics) replacing J. Tostevin (Progressives). Prior to the match commencing Jersey paraded their mascot, a tame fox, around the field as they did the day before and Guernsey produced their own mascot in the form of a toy pelican wearing the green and white colours.

The teams took the field at 4.35pm and were greeted with a round of cheers. Reed won the toss for Jersey and elected to play towards the town, Guernsey having the sun in their eyes. Straight from the kick off Guernsey went into the attack and Stranger sent his shot well over the bar. Jersey responded with Fox sending his header just past the post. The opening play was very even with Zabiela coming close for Guernsey by sending a shot wide followed by a near thing for Stent as he was just off target with a fine drive after collecting a pass from Wheway. Guernsey were getting the upper hand with Zabiela prominent, however, it was Yates who came the closest in the 10th minute when he missed an excellent chance to put Guernsey ahead. Stranger then had two good chances only to put his shots over but then after 19 minutes Yates sent a pass through to Stranger who put in a fine shot and, although Garnier made a great attempt to save, the referee adjudged that the ball had crossed the line. The loss of this goal seemed to deflate Jersey for a while but they regrouped and both Wheway and Millow went close. Jersey continued in this vein with Stent beating Tooley to send in a splendid high cross that was well met by Fox but his quick hard shot was superbly saved by Hebdon who followed this up by saving a dropping shot from Arty Reed. Eight minutes before half time Yates collected a fine centre from Cleal to score Guernsey's second with a terrific drive that gave Garnier no chance. Guernsey were now in complete control and Dorey came close but Joe Whitworth did well to clear the danger. A minute before the interval Cleale scored a third goal with a stiff shot that entered the net a foot inside the near post to give Garnier no chance. The score at half time was Jersey-0, Guernsey-3.

Jersey began the second half with Wheway badly injured and playing on the wing. The match was swinging from end to end with chances for both sides. As Jersey tried to reduce the arrears they won a series of corners that Guernsey managed to clear but not without a lot of difficulty. Their defence was under a lot of pressure but Tooley, Chapple and Hebdon all stood firm. A number of good scoring chances were created by Jersey but Newson was not having too much luck with his shooting as he shot wide from an excellent position. Jersey finally reduced the arrears after 20 minutes when Fox headed in from a Millow free kick. Hardly had the Jersey cheers died away when Guernsey were three up again. Following a corner, Stranger was well positioned and sent a well-placed shot through a group of players into the net with Garnier unsighted. Both goalkeepers were then called into action with Garnier saving a fast ground shot from Stranger followed by Hebdon tipping a splendid rising shot from Fox over the bar. Eight minutes from time Cleal scored with an excellent shot to make the score 5-1 and almost immediately Stent scored for Jersey to make the final score Jersey-2, Guernsey-5.

Jersey: T. Garnier, J. Whitworth, Scoones, W.C. Beasley, A. Reed (c), W. Millow,
               J. Newson, Stratford, G.S. Fox, F. Wheway, H. Stent.
               Goalscorers: Stent, Fox,

Guernsey: J. Hebdon, A.E. Tooley, T. Waterman, C. Purdy, R. Chapple, J. Mahy (c),
               F. Dorey, H. Stranger, A.M. Yates, F. Cleale, T. Zabiela.
               Goalscorers: Stranger (2), Yates, Cleale (3).

There were jubilant scenes at the end of the match with the Guernsey team being carried off the field by their supporters. In the evening at dinner in the Star Hotel, Mr. W. Stranger, President of the Guernsey Football Association presided and read out a number of congratulatory telegrams. He thanked the team for the way they had played and this was responded to by Mr. J. Mahy. The captain of the team, who thanked the Selection Committee for the way they had handled the team in Jersey. Almost all of the team and their supporters afterwards visited the Opera House. In the victorious Guernsey side was A. Yates who played for Jersey against Guernsey in the 1909 Muratti Vase semi-final. This was his second cap for Guernsey.

The Guernsey team and their supporters returned from Jersey on Saturday morning. As the 'Reindeer' neared the pier heads the joyous shouts of the Guernsey supporters could be heard. At 9.40am she berthed alongside No. 1 Landing and the drum and fife bands of the Royal Irish Regiment were playing. The crowd on the White Rock to witness the arrival was enormous and included several of the Guernsey Football Association officials who had been unable to remain in Jersey and Colonel Kellett, 2nd Battalion R.R. Regiment. As the players came ashore they were congratulated by Colonel Kellett, who shook hands with each of them. Mahy, the captain of the team, was carried off the boat shoulder high, and after shaking hands with Colonel Kellett and the Guernsey officials he was again carried to the excursion car, which was in waiting. The team got into the car as the bands headed them and marched up the White Rock playing alternately as far as the Weighbridge where three cheers for the bands were called for by Mr. Stranger. The bands then returned to the Fort by way of the Quay and the team, followed by many supporters in motor cars, drove through the town and dispersed near the Town Church.

It is sad to note that the report of this match appeared on the front page of the Jersey Evening Post of Friday 19 April 1912 alongside the tragic report of the sinking of the Titanic.

MURATTI FINAL.
25 April 1912, The Cycling Grounds, Guernsey.

Guernsey -4, Alderney -0.

Guernsey was very confident of victory following their excellent performances in Jersey as they lined up to face Alderney at the Cycling Grounds in front of a crowd of nearly 4,500. The colours of both teams were freely worn, green and white, of course, predominating. Bells, rattles and trumpets were much in evidence and Guernsey had a mascot in a donkey with green and white colours for harness. The rider was dressed as an old Guernsey woman in green and white, while a red and white ornament with the words 'In loving memory' served to remind how Guernsey won the right to play in the final. In attendance at the match was Sir E.O.F. Hamilton KCB, Lieut-Governor of Guernsey, Colonel Kellett, Mr. O. Priaulx, Constable, and Mrs Priaulx.

Guernsey won the toss and played with the sun at their backs. The opening stages of the match were very fast with Alderney opening the better side. Cleale nearly opened the scoring for Guernsey from a cross by Stranger but he put his shot wide. Zabiela looked dangerous as he took the ball down the line but was well shepherded out by Catts. Dorey almost opened the scoring for Guernsey but his excellent shot hit a defenders leg and went clear with Batiste beaten. After 11 minutes Zabiela scored with a terrific low shot that Batiste in the Alderney goal, touched but could not stop. Alderney replied through a fine shot by

Quinain that Hebdon touched on to the crossbar before finally clearing. They kept up the pressure with Attewell shooting wide and later the Guernsey defender, Tooley, was winded stopping a goal bound shot. Alderney were more than holding their own and once again Hebdon cleared a shot from Quinain. The play then moved quickly to the other goalmouth and Batiste saved brilliantly from Cleale and Dorey before Zabiela drove a fast shot just wide of the post. The half time came with the score Guernsey-1, Alderney-0.

The second half began with Burgess just failing to equalise for Alderney. The Guernsey defence were holding firm against the Alderney onslaught with Tooley and Waterman prominent. Zabiela then raced away towards the corner flag and put in a magnificent centre that found Yates who scored a second Guernsey goal. Straight from the kick-off Burgess missed a great chance for Alderney then Quinain sent in a shot from close range which Hebdon misjudged only to see it come off the post to safety. Some clever forward play by the home forwards resulted in Zabiela nearly scoring with a low shot. With 15 minutes remaining Cleale scored a third goal followed quickly by a fourth from Zabiela who dribbled the ball past Batiste to end the scoring to give a rather flattering score of Guernsey-4, Alderney-0.

Guernsey: J. Hebdon, A.E. Tooley, T. Waterman, J. Mahy (c), R. Chapple, C. Purdy, F. Dorey, H. Stranger, A.M. Yates, F. Cleale, T. Zabiela.
     Goalscorers: Zabiela (2), Yates, Cleale.

Alderney: C. Batiste, J. Catts, J. Lihou, J. Gamblin, H. Attewell, L. Jacques (c), K. Oselton, H. Cleale, F. Quinain, Baker, A. Burgess.

It was agreed by all that Alderney were unlucky to loose by 4-0 in what was an entertaining game. They made a great number of chances and, on another day, may have converted some of them. In Lihou they had the best defender on the park and also received excellent performances from Attewell and Quinain. It was arranged before the game that in case of a draw extra-time would be played, and, if still a draw, play would continue to a finish. During the game a unique situation arose when T.S. Mellanby acted as a linesman and this gave him the distinction of being the only former Muratti player (for Jersey) to referee and act as linesman in a Muratti match.

There was a very large audience at St. Georges Hall for the presentation of the Muratti Vase and medals. The audience included the officials of the Muratti competition, the Alderney and Guernsey teams and members of the Royal Irish band. The evening's entertainment was provided by the 'Mad Hatters' which included songs, monologues, concerted pieces etc. During the interval the presentations began and following the introductory speeches the Muratti Vase was presented to J. Mahy by Colonel Kellett and the medals presented to the players by Mrs Kellett. Following this presentation the Secretary of the Inter-Insular Committee, Mr. H.G. Bowden, announced that a collection in aid of the Titanic fund had amounted to over £25. The film of the Jersey v Guernsey match was to be shown at St. Julian's Theatre all week from Wednesday 24 April. A film was also taken of the Guernsey v Alderney match.

At a GFA Council meeting on 8 May 1912 a question was raised as to whether John Tostevin, who played in the first Muratti match in Jersey, but not in the subsequent games, should be presented with a medal of standard design by the local Association. Rule 21, which deals with this matter, stated that 'gold medals shall be presented to the winning team' therefore the Council reluctantly could not see their way clear to grant a medal. It was decided, however, that Tostevin should receive an Island Cap. The winning Guernsey Muratti team (pictured) were to be invited to a Banquet in their honour at the Royal Hotel on Wednesday 15 May. It was decided that the GFA should purchase 11 photographs of the winning team which would then be presented to the players on the night of the Banquet.

1 9 1 3

MURATTI SEMI-FINAL.
3 April 1913, The Cycling Grounds, Guernsey.

Alderney-2, Jersey-5. aet.

Alderney began the 1913 Muratti Vase match against Jersey at the Cycling Grounds with much confidence following their excellent display the previous year against Guernsey. The opening minutes of the match saw Jersey slightly on top as they attacked the Alderney goal with the advantage of the wind at their backs. The match started quietly and the first shot of note came from Wheway but Batiste, the Alderney goalkeeper, saved at the expense of a corner. Jersey won a series of corners but the resolute Alderney defence held firm. Alderney nearly took the lead when a mistake by Beasley almost let McLernon in but the Alderney player missed the chance when he fell and lost control of the ball. Jersey began to put some fine play together and, from a free kick, Wheway hit the post with Batiste beaten. Alderney replied with Quinain but Bourke in the Jersey goal cleared with some dif-

Alderney 1913.

ficulty. Moyse and Wheway broke away for Jersey but Attewell made an important goal
line clearance. Alderney were causing the Jersey defence a great deal of worry with
Attewell shooting over the bar and Bourke stopping a good shot from Quinain. Alderney
then suffered a major blow when the influential Attewell was injured and play was held up
for a time as he was assisted off the field for attention. Jersey tried to take full advantage of
their numerical superiority but the Alderney defence held out vigorously and then began to
attack the Jersey goal. Burgess was causing problems in the Jersey defence and twice
Bourke had to clear from him as he rushed in to goal. Attewell returned to the field after a
ten minute absence for treatment for his injury. Following a poor clearance by Bourke he
was baffled by a fine dropping shot by Oselton but much to the goalkeepers relief the ball
went a few feet wide and the half ended Alderney-0, Jersey-0.

The second half began with Jersey playing much better with good interchanging play by
their forwards. Jersey opened the scoring after 9 minutes when Batiste saved a splendid
free kick from Joe Whitworth but could not hold the ball and Moyse scored an easy if fortunate goal. Alderney pushed on to the attack and after 12 minutes had equalised when
Bourke could not hold a fine Quinain shot and the ball slipped into the net. The game
became more of a cup-tie and Alderney came close when Quinain slipped the defenders
and sent Burgess away and only a quick interception by Bourke saved the day for Jersey.
With the game nearing its end Jersey won a corner and a melee ensued in the Alderney
area but the danger was cleared by Attewell. Cleale then sent in a superb shot that beat
Bourke but came crashing off the post and this was followed by two excellent saves by
Batiste to firstly save a hot shot from Le Page and then a low ground shot by Moyse. There
was no more scoring and the 90 minutes ended Alderney-1, Jersey-1.

Alderney won the toss and it appeared that they might gain the upper hand in the opening exchanges and a fine shot by Oselton was cleared away by Beasley followed by an excellent effort by Cleale. Jersey came into their own as Alderney seemed to be flagging and Wheway quickly put Jersey 2-1 up. McLernon just failed to equalise, putting his shot over the bar. Kennedy then scored a third for Jersey to make the half time score Alderney-1, Jersey-3.

Jersey continued on top in the second period of extra time and saw Beasley head in a fourth goal. Jersey were now in full flow and it was no surprise when Wheway added a fifth. Alderney kept on pressing and were rewarded when Cleale scored their second goal with a fine shot to make the final score Alderney-2, Jersey-5.

Alderney: C. Batiste, W. Caplain, J. Catts, L. Jacques, H. Attewell, H. Cleale (c), K. Oselton, W. McLernon, F. Quinain, Baker, A. Burgess.
Goalscorers: Quinain, Cleale.

Jersey: Bourke, W.C. Beasley, J. Whitworth, G. Kennedy, W. Millow (c), Romano, J. Newson, Moyse, F. Wheway, Stent, G. Le Page.
Goalscorers: Moyse, Wheway (2), Kennedy, Beasley.

The general opinion was that the 5-2 scoreline was a little hard on Alderney who were by no way disgraced by the performance. The referee, Mr. J.W. Haxell, thought that both teams played well and was rather surprised that Alderney lost four goals in extra time when considering how well their defence played for the initial 90 minutes. It was readily agreed that Joe Whitworth was Jersey's best player as he hardly put a foot wrong during the whole game. Time and again the ex-Guernsey Rangers player coolly broke up Alderney's attacks in a quiet and unassuming way and this went a long way in assuring Jersey's place in the Muratti Vase final.

Jersey's Muratti squad.

MURATTI FINAL.
17 April 1913, Westmount, Jersey.

Jersey -2, Guernsey -4.

'All roads lead to Westmount.' This was the announcement advertising the 1913 Muratti Vase final on 17 April. There was an air of excitement around St. Helier prior to the match and there were red and white flags everywhere. Flags and rosettes display the Jersey colours at every point, and the Island colours are even used in decorating pet dogs. Needless to say the green and white is also to be seen, for a large number of Guernsey supporters have made the journey to Jersey, and what they lack in numbers is made up with enthusiasm. This morning over 400 supporters boarded the 'Lydia' for Jersey. Among the numbers were Mr. W. Stranger, President of the GFA, and the Guernsey goalkeeper, Lanyon. On the arrival of the boat at Jersey this morning, a meeting of the Guernsey Island Selection Committee was held to chose the team to represent Guernsey. The 'London Queen' left the White Rock at one o' clock with another party of 85 supporters. The 'London Queen' is to return direct to St. Sampson's this evening.

The teams were led out by Millow for Jersey and Chapple for Guernsey. Chapple took advantage of the strong breeze, as the game got under way. The first chance fell to Guernsey when Stranger had a fine shot saved by Garnier in the Jersey goal, the ball broke to Cleale who, when faced with an open goal, shot weakly past the post. Guernsey were making full use of the wind at their backs but were unable to turn this superiority into goals. Goldsmith fouled Chapple and from the resultant free-kick Guernsey put the Jersey defence under severe pressure for around two minutes but Garnier and the home defence held out well. Jersey finally broke out with Newson receiving a pass from Wheway but the move broke down and Guernsey cleared the danger. In the 25th minute Wheway broke away down the left for Jersey and sent in a beautiful centre that was met by Goldsmith who gave Lanyon no chance with an excellent header. This lead was short lived as Cleale equalised with a brilliant shot from 10 yards that left Garnier helpless. The pace of the

Millow. (Captain of Jersey.)

Chapple. (Captain of Guernsey).

game increased as the match progressed, but neither team were gaining the upper hand. After 30 minutes play the players were glad of a little respite when the ball was kicked out of the field. Millow was then injured in a challenge and play was held up as he received treatment but he had to leave the field. Following some superb play from Stranger he sent Dorey through but his fine shot was well saved by Garnier. Things were beginning to get a little heated with Scoones and Stranger facing-up but referee Duncan quickly settled everything down and play continued. Millow reappeared but his effectiveness was minimal due to his injury. Goldsmith then beat Lanyon with a fine header only to see the ball flash past the post. As half time approached Stranger hit a speculative shot, which entered just inside the post giving Guernsey a slender 2-1 half time lead. The talk was of whether this lead would be enough against the stiff breeze. Half time score Jersey-1, Guernsey-2.

Joe Whitworth-scorer of Jersey's second goal.

During the half-time interval the crowd was encroaching onto the pitch and had to be pushed back before the second half could commence. The second half began with Jersey on the attack almost immediately as the strove for the important equaliser. Wheway tested Lanyon with a low shot and Wheway and Newton missed an open goal as they attempted to score an early goal. The pressure on the Guernsey defence continued But Jersey found that Lanyon and Tooley were holding firm. Wheway almost equalised from close range but Lanyon just managed to clear. An equaliser nearly came for Jersey when Mahy, under severe pressure, miskicked his clearance but Lanyon rescued the situation for Guernsey. After 12 minutes of the second half, a foul throw by Maunder was seized on by Chapple who fed the ball to Yates. Beasley mistimed his tackle and Yates had an easy chance in front of an open goal to put Guernsey 3-1 up. Jersey got a free kick some 40 yards out following a foul on Wheway that was taken by Whitworth. Lanyon completely misjudged the flight of the ball, which entered the top corner of the net.

This success inspired Jersey who was now playing hard for the equaliser with Lanyon again being called on to save. Goldsmith nearly got this goal but Lanyon saved miraculously when it appeared that he was beaten. Finally Stranger dribbled through, beat Beasley and, evading Garnier, scored a fourth goal for Guernsey. This completed the scoring and the final result was Jersey-2, Guernsey-4.

Jersey: T. Garnier, W.C. Beasley, J. Whitworth, G. Scoones, W. Millow (c), Romano, Sonnen, Moyse, Goldsmith, F. Wheway, J. Newson.
Goalscorers: Goldsmith, Whitworth.

Guernsey: F. Lanyon, F. Duquemin, R. Leale, A.W. Maunder, R. Chapple (c), J. Mahy, F. Dorey, H. Stranger, A. Yates, F. Cleale, F. Falla.
Goalscorers: Cleale, Stranger (2), Yates.

The Muratti Vase was presented to Chapple, the Guernsey captain, by Mr. J.E. Pinel, the Constable of St. Helier, amidst great cheers followed by each player stepping forward to

Guernsey.
Duquemin, Lanyon, Leale,
Dorey, Stranger, Yates, Cleale, Falla,
Maunder, Chapple, Mahy.

receive their Muratti gold medal when their name was called. When Stranger went up to collect his medal he received a tremendous ovation from the fans. Mr. Pinel said that although he would have been pleased to see Jersey win, he congratulated Guernsey on their victory. It had been a splendid game.

The White Rock on Friday morning was full of local fans waiting for the return of the 'Lydia' which arrived, bedecked with bunting, at 9.33am. The mood on board was made audible by the ringing of bells and visible by long paper ribbons in green and white. At the pier-head a huge crowd sent up a welcome cheer, and individual players were singled out for special celebrations; notably the goalscorers. The 'Lydia' docked at No. 2 berth and the large number of passengers began to file slowly ashore, having to pass through an avenue of spectators some 30 yards in length from the landing stage. As the passengers landed they were confronted at the top of the steps by two cartoons drawn by the White Rock artist, Mr. Geo. Gurney. The top picture bore the legend 'Well done boys,' and the bottom one depicted the Sarnian colours being hoisted at the masthead and a diminutive Sarnian 'David' sitting on a Caesarean 'Goliath.' The inscription was 'In doleful memory of Jersey, who fell bravely at Jersey, April 17, 1913.' Needless to add, as in former years, the cartoons excited much amused comment. As the players left the ship, the Muratti Vase was not visible as it was enclosed in a wooden box with wooden fibre covering. There was no triumphal progress through the town with the players being met by relatives and friends and making their own way home. The Trinity drum and fife band which played selections as the boat entered the harbour, formed up on landing, and marched to the town playing stirring airs.

Mr. J.E. Pinel, Constable of St. Helier, prepares to present the Muratti Vase to Guernsey.

Chapple (Guernsey captain)

1 9 1 4

MURATTI SEMI-FINAL.
2 April 1914, Westmount, Jersey.

Alderney -0, Guernsey -4.

Three quarters of the Guernsey team arrived in Jersey on 1st April so that they would not be affected by the voyage on the day of the match, with the remaining arriving on the morning of the 2nd. The Guernsey team and officials were based at Ford's Lodging House. Due to the sailing timetable the Alderney team had to arrive in Guernsey on the steamer 'Courier' on the Wednesday and sailed to Jersey this morning. The Guernsey passengers who travelled to Jersey on the morning of the match were a bit anxious as to what time the 'Alberta' would get to Jersey as thick fog was encountered; only half speed being the order. Soon the Great Western steamer from Jersey was heard blowing her whistle and the 'Alberta' was stopped and her siren was blown frequently. The GWR steamer seemed to be a quarter of a mile off, but she could not be seen and when it was known she had passed, the 'Alberta' steamed ahead, the fog lifted and Jersey was safely reached at 11.00am.

The Star report of 2 April highlighted the fact that Alderney had put up some plucky fights against their larger neighbours over the years but without much success in the way of victories. The match was due to be played at Westmount with a 4.00pm kick off. The Guernsey team were to be captained by Harry Stranger (Andover FC) and Alderney by Joseph Gamblin. At Westmount there was a predominance of blue and white which indicated that the Jersey fans were supporting Alderney. There were sporting cheers when Guernsey appeared on the field but there was a veritable ovation when Alderney appeared. Despite the fact that the Jersey team would not be playing there was an extremely large attendance at Westmount. The large Pavilion was filled to overflowing and additional seating was provided. There was a great Muratti feeling about and the noise was increased due to the use of megaphones and other 'musical' instruments.

Joseph Gamblin (Alderney captain).

The game began 15 minutes late in steady drizzling rain and almost at once Guernsey went on the attack. Blicq missed a chance from Falla's centre and then Batiste in the Alderney goal cleared well from Falla's own effort. Following some sustained Guernsey pressure Alderney broke away and Lanyon had to save from Quinain. A dangerous move was set up by Baker and McLernon but Lanyon was quickly out and cleared the situation. Guernsey thought that they had scored when Cleale released Stranger but the referee disallowed for offside. Alderney reacted to this well and Attewell shot wide and McLernon, who was having a great game, was giving Mahy a lot of trouble. Guernsey had the ball in the net again through Cleale but the goal was disallowed due to a foul on Batiste. Batiste was again called into action when he held a

Harry Stranger scoring the first goal.

great shot from Cleale. The Alderney defence was holding out well but as Stranger tried to break he was fouled. Duquemin took the free-kick which found Stranger but he headed over from close in. Guernsey had numerous attacks but they all came to nothing due to some weak finishing. As the half neared its end Guernsey went all out to score with Falla coming through and passing to Cleale who hit a superb shot that was brilliantly saved by Batiste for a corner. From this corner Stranger headed over, Batiste then had to pull off two great saves from shots by Cleale as the pressure continued. The fog began to come down and it became difficult to distinguish the players. Alderney finished the half the strongest but half time came with the score Alderney-0, Guernsey-0.

Guernsey began the second half in a more positive manner and took the lead after 2 minutes when Stranger dribbled through the Alderney defence to score with a grand shot.

Alderney came back at Guernsey and Quinain looked like equalising but Duquemin cleared the danger. After 7 minutes of the half, following a Guernsey free kick, Stranger headed onto Blicq who scored the second goal with a beautiful shot. Guernsey again came close when Falla slipped the ball to Stranger and his excellent shot just skimmed the crossbar. Alderney were now playing better with Gamblin getting the upper hand of Mahy. McLernon was also causing trouble and Lanyon had to save. The play swung from end to end and Batiste saved brilliantly from Stranger. Following some sustained attacking Guernsey scored a third when Stranger netted with a low shot from a Falla pass. Alderney were now mainly on the defensive but following a poor clearance Jacques missed a good opportunity to score when he fired his shot over the bar. This was followed by Lanyon having to save from a header and, after a free-kick was awarded very close to the Guernsey goal, Leale had to be very alert to clear the danger. Batiste then came to Alderney's rescue when after Cleale had raced past the defence he looked certain to score but the goalkeeper raced out and timed his clearance brilliantly. With seven minutes remaining Guernsey completed the scoring when Falla beat Gamblin and centred to Cleale who evaded Oselton to shoot neatly past Batiste. The final score being Guernsey-4, Alderney-0.

Alderney Muratti Team. 1914.

Alderney: C. Batiste, K. Oselton, J. Catts, J. Gamblin (c), H. Attewell, L. Jacques,
             W. McLernon, T. Baker, F. Quinain, B. Collenette, A. Burgess.

Guernsey: F. Lanyon, F. Duquemin, R. Leale, W. Searle, R. Chapple, J. Mahy,
             F. Dorey, H. Stranger (c), A.S. Blicq, F. Cleale, F. Falla.
             Goalscorers: Stranger (2), Blicq, Cleale.

Mr. Haxell, the referee, commented that there was not a great deal to choose between the teams in the first half. The turning point, he believed, was the first goal by Stranger who superbly beat four opponents and scored with a great shot.

The Guernsey Evening Press ran a Muratti Competition where the competitors had to give what they thought the scores would be at half-time, fifteen minutes from the end and at the final whistle. The prize was £3.00 and there were three winners each receiving £1.00:- E.C. Arnold of Rouge Huis, T.H. Torode of Pont Allaire, Vale and T. Priaulx of Oatlands, St. Sampson.

Careful arrangements had been made for the wiring of a special report to the 'GEP' which was published in the green Special Edition and was on sale in the streets within a few minutes of the final whistle. These papers were on sale long before those who had witnessed the match had reached the foot of Westmount Hill. Thanks were given to the officials of the Post Office in both Jersey and Guernsey for this service.

It was recorded in the Star for 26 April 1914 that the Alderney captain, Joseph Gamblin, had got married by special licence by Rev. S.H.N. Rawdon at the Town Church on Muratti afternoon. He married Miss Eva Catts, also of Alderney. The members of the wedding party crossed from Alderney on the morning of the match by the 'Courier, on her football special. After the wedding Mr. Gamblin and his wife went to the Track to see the Muratti Vase final.

MURATTI FINAL.
23 April 1914, The Cycling Grounds, Guernsey.

Guernsey -2, Jersey -1.

There was a big crowd at the White Rock on the morning of the game as the 'Alberta' arrived from Jersey and berthed at No. 2. The scene was one of considerable animation and the air was filled with snatches of songs, parodied to the one topic of the day, and hooters, bugles and whistles played a part in the general outburst of friendly rivalry with the improvised orchestra on the 'Alberta'. From early afternoon spectators wended their way towards the Cycling Grounds by every possible means of conveyance, or on foot, to such a degree that long before the gates opened there was a long line of people waiting. It was reported in the local press that everything pales in comparison with the great football final to be played at the Cycling Grounds when Guernsey entertain Jersey. The kick-off has been fixed at a convenient 4.30pm which allowed many of the granite and other firms closing for quarter of a day to allow their workers to attend as well as enabling all children attending the primary schools to attend. Guernsey's recently appointed Lieut-Governor, Major-General H.M. Lawson CB, would be attending the final.

The referee for the 1914 Muratti Vase final was Mr. L.J. Duncan (Bournemouth.) He started playing football at the age of 16, and figured at various times as outside right, centre forward and right back. He played for Shirley St. James' for three seasons and when in London played for the Camberwell Rovers FC. Several times he had figured in the Andover Wednesday team. After ceasing playing at the age of 21 he passed as a referee of the Hampshire Football Association.

Jersey was the first to appear led by their captain, Frank Wheway followed almost immediately by Harry Stranger leading out the Guernsey side. The conditions were well nigh perfect; with the brilliance of the sun being partially hidden by a thin film of cloud, while the great crowd densely packed over the ground sheltered the pitch from the full effect of a fairly strong westerly breeze. His Excellency the Lieut-Governor arrived shortly before kick-off, the official flag being broken at the mast-head. Two buglers signalled his arrival, the great crowd standing and cheering loudly.

Stranger won the toss and defended the western goal with the wind and light in his favour. Guernsey were immediately on the offensive and Stranger narrowly missed the upright with a shot from a free-kick. Cleale nearly beat Garnier in the Jersey goal, the ball just going over the bar. The Jersey defence was playing well and in a counter attack Sonnen beat the defence but Lanyon saved his shot. Guernsey were pressing well with Blicq breaking through to cause problems in the Jersey defence followed by a fine centre by Falla that was cleared with difficulty. Poingdestre then attacked for Jersey but he was thwarted by Lanyon. After 39 minutes Dorey centred and Cleale headed past an

Mr. L.J. Duncan.

Harry Stranger. (Guernsey captain.)

Frank Wheway. (Jersey captain.)

onrushing Garnier to put the home side 1-0 up. This goal seemed to affect what was a quiet crowd who now became very noisy in encouraging their favourites. Garnier then brought off a fine one handed save from Stranger as Guernsey pushed on for the second goal. Blicq continued the attack on the Jersey goal as he passed to Stranger who sent a fast shot just past the post and this was followed by a Dorey-Blicq-Cleale move that resulted in Garnier being tested with a high shot towards the top corner of the net. Guernsey ended the half well on top with the score Guernsey-1, Jersey-0.

The second half began in sensational style. Jersey, who had been defending for most of the first half, equalised in the first minute of the second half. Goldsmith scored with a long-range shot which went in under the bar giving Lanyon no chance. As the second half progressed the play became more even with each side having their share of the attacking. The flow of the match was interrupted for a time as the game was being continually stopped for a series of free-kicks. Jersey, now with the advantage of the wind, came close to taking the lead but Wheway missed a good chance by shooting over the bar with only Lanyon to beat. Guernsey then won a free-kick on the edge of Jersey's penalty area and Strangers shot was saved by Garnier, at the second attempt, at the expense of a corner. Seven minutes from the end Guernsey regained the lead when 'Ratter' Cleale burst through the Jersey defence and as he was tackled the ball broke to Stranger who fired in a shot that Garnier could only parry and Blicq following up shot high into the net. Guernsey competently played out the remaining minutes to leave the final score Guernsey-2, Jersey-1.

Guernsey: F. Lanyon, F. Duquemin, R. Leale, W. Searle, R. Chapple, J. Mahy, F. Dorey, H. Stranger (c), A.S. Blicq, F. Cleale, F. Falla.
Goalscorers: Cleale, Blicq.

Jersey: T. Garnier, W.C. Beasley, G. Scoones, W. Millow, Romano, Wellman, W. Poingdestre, Sonnen, Goldsmith, F. Wheway (c), H. Stent.
Goalscorer: Goldsmith.

The Muratti Vase was presented to Harry Stranger and the medals to the winning team by His Excellency Major-General H.M. Lawson CB, who in reply to the welcome expressed by Mr. H.H. Randell, President of the Guernsey Football Association, said he did not remember witnessing a better game. He could see that football was a strong feature in the sports in the Channel Islands. Cheers were then given for His Excellency and for both the Guernsey and Jersey teams.

At the end of the game the Jersey captain, Frank Wheway, entered the Guernsey dressing room and shook hands with all the players congratulating them on their success. For upwards of an hour the crowd streamed from the Cycling Grounds, and from the Salerie the sight was one seldom seen in Guernsey. Mr C. Ferguson, the Special Constable for the Salerie and neighbourhood, maintained splendid order as far as he was able, and checked any obstructions to a clear run of traffic.

As with the Muratti semi-final the local press ran a competition asking competitors to predict the half-time, 15 minutes from time and the final score of the match. There was no entry fee with six points being awarded for the correct score at each stage with one point deducted for every goal wrong. The prize was £3.00 Br. for a Correct Forecast or £1.00 Br. for the most Accurate Forecast.

As it turned out this was to be the last Muratti match until after the First World War and the competition would not resume until 1920.

The Muratti Vase competition had come a long way since that first match on 17 March 1905. The excitement of the games and the passion of the supporters quickly became the trademarks of these fixtures. Guernsey had been the most successful team in the competition winning the Vase on 7 occasions. They had played 18 matches, winning 14, loosing 3 and drawing 1. They had scored 48 goals and conceded 23. Jersey had won the Vase on 3 occasions. They have played 14 matches winning 6, loosing 7 and drawing 1. They had scored 36 goals and conceded 30. Alderney had played 10 matches but have yet to record a win. They had scored 5 goals and conceded 36.

It was to be some time before the Muratti Vase made an appearance but before the enforced break the competition had produced some stirring moments with the hope of more to come.

The Jersey defence under severe pressure just before Cleale opens the scoring.

A. Yates (Trainer), Duquemin, Lanyon, Leale, Mr. Torode, Mr. Stranger,
Mr. Coward, Dorey, Stranger (c), Blicq, Cleale, Falla,
Searle, Chapple, Mahy.

Special
MURATTI Forecast

"Guernsey Weekly Press,"
Saturday, April 18.

PRIZES:
£3 Br. for a Correct Forecast
or
£1 Br. for the most Accurate
Forecast.

In the event of a Tie or Ties, the
Prize will be divided.

No Entrance Fee.

Six points will be given for a correct score at each stage, and one
point deducted for every goal wrong.

If a competitor forecasts the correct scores, but wrong team, in any
stage, he will not score any points
in that stage.

Muratti Match
GUERNSEY v. JERSEY.

Score at Half-time.

Guernsey . . . . goals

Jersey . . . . goals

Score 15 minutes from time
(75 minutes play).

Guernsey . . . . goals

Jersey . . . . goals

Result.

Guernsey . . . . goals

Jersey . . . . goals

I agree to accept the published
decision as final and legally binding.

Name

Address

Envelopes must be addressed
"Muratti Competition, 'Press'
Office." .·. Closing Date:
Wednesday, April 22, at 6 p.m.

Competitors must cut out the
Coupon, it must not be torn out.

3

After the First World War.

Following the end of the First World War preparations were being made in the Islands for the return of representative football. On 25 February the press reported, briefly, on a match involving a Guernsey Garrison team and the Jersey RGA. The match ended 0-0 although Guernsey was the better team in the first half Jersey took control in the second and could have won but for Barnicott in the Guernsey goal saving well from a Gibson shot. There then followed a match between the Guernsey Garrison and a Jersey XI at Westmount.

FRIENDLY MATCH.
25 February 1919, Westmount, Jersey.

Jersey -2, Guernsey -3.

There was bright weather, with drizzling rain at intervals, at Westmount as the Guernsey Garrison met a Jersey XI under the auspices of the Jersey Football Association.

Jersey opened well and almost opened the scoring early on but their attack broke down and the ball was cleared, Garnier in the Jersey goal then saved a good shot by Stranger. After 20 minutes Jersey opened the scoring when Kemp fired in an excellent shot past Barnicott. As half-time approached there was a flurry of goals when C. Purdy equalised for Guernsey only for James to restore Jersey's lead. Guernsey responded and following some excellent play Hawkswood scored to make the half-time score Jersey-2, Guernsey-2.

The second half was very even with both teams going close but the defences held firm. With five minutes of the match remaining Garnier saved from a Guernsey attack but in the ensuing melee C. Purdy scored what proved to be the winning goal and when the match ended the score was Jersey-2, Guernsey-3.

Jersey: T. Garnier, Le Sueur, W.C. Beasley, Vibert, Romano, Poingdestre, Darnborough, Pool, Jones, Kemp, Heulin.
Goalscorers: Kemp, Jones.

Guernsey: A. Barnicott, McLernon, L. Purdy, Peel, Gibson, Dyer, Stranger, C. Purdy, Hawkswood, Hall, Channings.
Goalscorers: C. Purdy (2), Hawkswood.

The feeling at the end of this tight match was that Guernsey performed better as a team although Jersey appeared to have the better individuals. The match, however, whetted the appetite for more inter-insular matches.

A further match was arranged between the Guernsey Island and the Jersey RGA. This game promised to be of almost as much interest as the Muratti matches. The Jersey Artillery team are the strongest in that Island and were unbeaten.

FRIENDLY MATCH.
20 March 1919, the Cycling Grounds, Guernsey.

Guernsey -0, Jersey -1.

The eagerly awaited match rekindled memories of Muratti Day with a steady stream of spectators winding their way to the Cycling Grounds merrily ringing their handbells. At the last minute Brown (Green Howards) replaced Maunder in the Guernsey side. Guernsey was to be wearing orange and blue with Jersey in red and blue. The referee was to be Mr. H. Le Messurier of Guernsey and the linesmen were T. Zabiela (Guernsey) and J. Plasting (Jersey).

The Guernsey team was the first to appear, quickly followed by Jersey with both sides receiving great applause. Guernsey won the toss and decided to defend the west goal with a slight wind advantage. The home side opened the strongest with Falla and Chapple pushing the Jersey defence back to 10 yards from their goal-line. The first real chance fell to G. Attewell when he skimmed the Jersey crossbar with a quick shot. Jersey was defending well although their own attacks were being confined to breakaways. Guernsey again came close to opening the scoring when Zabiela passed to Hawkswood but his shot went over the bar. The play then became confined to the midfield with any attacks being ably dealt with by the respective defences. As Jersey stepped up their pace they forced a series of corners and keeper Lanyon was forced into pulling off a good save followed by some tidy defensive work by Beach and McLernon, Zabiela then provided Attewell with another good chance but he screwed his shot wide. The Guernsey goal then received a scare when Laurent crossed into the area; Lanyon seemed to have the ball covered but momentarily lost control. Still collected the ball and pushed it towards the empty goal but Lanyon quickly recovered and diverted it clear. Near the end of the half Chapple fired in a fine shot that Dingle saved, as well as managing to avoid the onrushing Hawkswood and at half-time the score was Guernsey-0, Jersey-0.

Two minutes into the second half Zabiela almost gave Guernsey the lead but Dingle quickly saved his effort at the foot of the post. Beasley then cleared up-field and Dyer collected the ball and his attempt came close followed quickly by a Still header that went just past the post. Jersey continued to press and after Lanyon had collected a long shot from Jones he sent the ball downfield. Dyer gained possession and put in a stiff angled shot which Lanyon came out to collect, he slipped and the ball found its way into the net to put Jersey 1-0 ahead. Guernsey then began to pressurise the Jersey defence and Hawkswood went within an ace of equalising and this was followed by a good run by Chapple and as he got into a good position he was fouled. The game was now moving from end to end but once again the defences were on top with Lanyon twice pulling off good saves followed by Dingle in the Jersey goal saving well from Chapple, Falla and then Hawkswood. Chapple, following some neat Guernsey play, nearly equalised when his shot beat Dingle but slipped past the post leaving the final result Guernsey-0, Jersey-1.

Guernsey: F. Lanyon, McLernon, Beach, Spiller, Brown, West, G. Attewell,
              E. Zabiela, Hawkswood,Chapple, Falla.

Jersey: Dingle, W.C. Beasley (c), Le Sueur, Kitcher, Jones, Mush,
              Lees. Lieut. Still, Laurent, Le Page, H.C. Dyer.
              Goalscorer: Dyer.

Of the 22 players who took part in the match only four of them featured in the last Muratti match in 1914 namely Beasley (Jersey) and Falla, Chapple and Lanyon of Guernsey. This was an excellent match with Jersey ably served by Beasley, who was superb, Dyer, Dingle and Still. Best for Guernsey were Spiller, McLernon and Lanyon.

By a curious coincidence one of the winner's of the Guernsey Press' forecast competition, Gnr. H.C. Dyer (Jersey), was the scorer of the winning goal. The four winners were:

1.   Miss N. Robin of 46 Pedvin Street,
2.   Gnr H.C, Dyer, RGA, Fort Regent, Jersey.
3.   Mr. H. Adams of 11 Smith Street,
4.   Mr. T. Morgan of 21 Truchot Street.

The £3.00 prize was divided equally and each winner received 15 shillings.

Matches were being arranged between the Islands over the Easter period with Guernsey playing Jersey at Westmount on Good Friday, 18 April 1919. Under the auspices of the Guernsey Amalgamated Football Committee, who were arranging the Easter football fixtures, the Guernsey Press Co. Ltd. had given a cup for annual competition between Guernsey and Alderney. In a letter dated 9 April 1919 the Guernsey Amalgamated Football Committee accepted the offer and the first match was arranged for Easter Monday at the Cycling Grounds. The cup is to be called the Guernsey Evening Press Peace Cup. The match was to be played in the morning followed by a Guernsey- Jersey Victory Cup game.

The Peace Cup. The Cup is made of silver and is 5 inches tall and 6 inches in diameter. The engraving on the cup shows the crests of both Guernsey and Alderney surrounded by the legend 'Guernsey Amalgamated Football Committee' above the crests with 'Guernsey Evening Press Peace Cup 1919' beneath.

John F. Mahy and the Croix de Guerre.

It was reported in the Guernsey Weekly Press of 12 April 1919 that Sergeant John F. Mahy RE was awarded the Croix de Guerre for exceptional gallantry and courage at Courlandon on the Vesle on 27 May 1918 He had won 15 Muratti caps between 1906-1914 while playing for North.

FRIENDLY MATCH.
18 April 1919, Westmount, Jersey.

Jersey -0, Guernsey -3.

Jersey had selected a team with only three players who had inter-insular experience in T. Garnier, A. Romano and W.C. Beasley. They also included Poingdestre who's older brother represented Jersey in previous Muratti matches.

Westmount was packed on the occasion of a representative match between Jersey and Guernsey and the weather was ideal. Jersey was first on to the field, led by Kemp, amid shouting and ringing of handbells and the blowing of whistles. Lanyon then led out the Guernsey team to similar applause.

Guernsey won the toss and elected to defend the west goal with the sun at their backs. Jersey kicked-off and almost immediately Courtes came close with a fine effort and then Jones, receiving a pass from Marett, forced Lanyon into a good save. Guernsey were rather slow getting into the game and were nearly caught out as skipper Kemp came close for Jersey but put his shot wide. The visitors then began to settle and Marriette nearly opened the scoring for them followed by a long range shot from Spiller that was saved by Garnier. After 20 minutes play a period of sustained pressure resulted in a fine move by Marriette and Chapple and as Garnier saved Chapple's shot Beasley had to clear for a corner. Zabiela took the kick and Garnier again saved but the ball fell to Brown who set up Chapple to open the scoring. Straight from the kick-off Guernsey regained possession and won a corner, Zabiela once again took the kick and Marriette headed just over. Near the interval Garnier again had to be alert as he saved a long shot from Cumber and at half-time the score was Jersey-0, Guernsey-1.

The second half began with Jersey coming close when Marett sent in a shot that had to be cleared by the Guernsey backs. Guernsey suffered a setback after 57 minutes when Marriette damaged his ankle and had to leave the field and took no further part in the match. As the visitors were re-organising Jersey nearly equalised but the ball was cleared to safety by Spiller. Guernsey responded and after 65 minutes they increased their lead when, following a free-kick, Courtes scored from a cross-shot from the right. Jersey pushed on and were nearly rewarded but Lanyon saved well from Romano and minutes later Marett found a good position but placed his shot wide. Chapple then scored goal number three when he rushed through the Jersey defence and crashed a fine shot past Garnier. Jersey continued to push forward and Beasley sent in a shot that Lanyon could only tip over the bar leaving the final score Jersey-0, Guernsey-3.

Jersey: T. Garnier, Kitcher, W.C. Beasley, Vibert, Denize, A. Romano, Poingdestre, O'Neill, D. Jones, Kemp (c), A. Marett.

Guernsey: F. Lanyon (c), Beach, L. Purdy, Spiller, Brown, West, Zabiela, Cumber, Marriette, R. Chapple, Courtes. Goalscorers: Courtes, Chapple (2).

In a very good match Jersey were best served by Beasley, Garnier, Kemp and Marett. It was reported that this would be Beasley's last season which would be a great loss to Jersey. Guernsey's best were Lanyon, Purdy, Beach and Zabiela.

The Guernsey Evening Press Peace Cup was on view at Mr. J. Mourant's establishment, London House, Alderney and the Victory Cup was on view at Maison Roger, Arcade.

PEACE CUP.
21 April 1919, The Cycling Grounds, Guernsey.

Guernsey -3, Alderney -1.

The Alderney team arrived in Guernsey with Lieutenant G. Osborne in charge. They unfortunately had to make a late change when their goalkeeper, Mesny, missed the Courier and was replaced by Batiste.

Alderney were first to appear led out by their captain followed by Guernsey and their captain, Videlo. Guernsey won the toss and decided to defend the east goal with the wind in their favour. After the opening exchanges the game was 10 minutes old when Stranger and Hawkswood combined well down the right

wing and won a corner from which Bird shot over the bar. Alderney responded and Le Feuvre tested Guernsey keeper Barnicott. In the 15th minute H. Marshall received a pass from Stranger and sent in a lovely shot that hit the underside of the bar and crossed the line to put Guernsey 1-0 ahead. Straight from the kick-off Alderney's Le Feuvre again found space for a shot but Barnicott saved easily. Three minutes later Stranger gained possession and fired in a cross-shot that beat Batiste in the Alderney goal to increase Guernsey's lead. From the re-start Le Feuvre was again causing problems in the Guernsey defence and on one occasion only a foul by Tostevin prevented him progressing. The game was now switching from end to end with at one stage Bird and then Hawkswood shooting over the bar followed by Butler losing the ball to Alderney's Thomson who centred for Le Feuvre but his attempt was saved by Barnicott. Bird then came close for Guernsey when he received a pass from Stranger but missed his chance from close-in. Batiste then saved well from a fast shot by Bird at the expense of a corner. As the half neared its end a Collonette effort was saved by Barnicott and at half-time the score was Guernsey-2, Alderney-0.

The second half began with Alderney looking more dangerous but a good move by them ended with an offside decision by referee H. Le Messurier. After 60 minutes play Alderney scored when Thomson broke away and centred for Le Feuvre to send the ball into the Guernsey net. From the kick-off Alderney regained possession and attacked through Le Feuvre but he was stopped by Tostevin for a corner. The game began to settle down and then Guernsey increased their lead in the 75th minute when from a free-kick just outside the penalty area Bird received the ball and scored the third goal. Alderney responded but the Guernsey defence held out and at the final whistle the score was Guernsey -3, Alderney -1.

Guernsey: A. Barnicott, Tostevin, Butler, R. McAvoy, Videlo (c), A.N. Marshall, R. Stranger, Hawkswood, H. Marshall, Collins, Bird.
Goalscorers: H. Marshall, Stranger, Bird.

Alderney: Batiste, W. McLernon, Chappelhow, Ring, Gadie, Thomson, Meener, Le Feuvre, Collonette, Baker.
Goalscorer: Le Feuvre.

Best for Guernsey were Lanyon, Beach, Purdy and Marshall. Their forwards also performed well in what was a good overall team performance. Alderney was well served by Chappelhow, Ring, Thomson, Le Feuvre and Baker.
The Peace Cup match was followed by the first Victory Cup game where Guernsey entertained Jersey.

VICTORY CUP.
21 April 1919, The Cycling Grounds, Guernsey.

Guernsey -2, Jersey -0.

The first Victory Cup match was to be refereed by H. Le Messurier assisted by Rawlinson (Guernsey) and Coombes (Jersey). Kemp kicked-off but Brown quickly gained possession for Guernsey and in the first few seconds Garnier cleared the ball with some difficulty as he was harassed by the home forwards. Two minutes after the start Guernsey won a corner following a Beasley clearance and from the kick Cumber judged the flight correctly and headed past a helpless Garnier to put Guernsey 1-0 ahead. Shortly after this Jersey was awarded a free-kick and Beasley fired in a ball that Lanyon could only punch away and the ball fell to Denize but he put his shot wide. Guernsey began to exert some pressure on the Jersey defence but found Beasley in his usual fine form as he marshalled his defence. After 15 minutes play Guernsey increased their lead when Cumber passed to Zabiela but his run towards goal was stopped by Beasley at the expense of a corner. Zabiela took the kick and found Chapple who scored Guernsey's second goal. The home team were now on top and Zabiela was only inches away from adding a third. Keyho then came close when he collected a throw-in and then Courtes put in an excellent cross that found Cumber but his effort went over

the bar. From the resulting goal-kick Brown received the ball and shot but it went inches wide of the Jersey post. Jersey weathered this storm and in the final minutes of the half Kemp nearly broke through but he was hustled off the ball and Lanyon cleared leaving the half-time score Guernsey-2, Jersey-0.

The second half began with Jersey having the advantage of the wind, which had freshened. Marett and Poingdestre worked a fine move but Kemp failed to control the pass that was aimed at him, Denize rushed up to collect and put his shot wide. The game was becoming more even and, from a free-kick, Beasley gave Lanyon a troublesome shot to clear and from this clearance Courtes broke away to beat the Jersey defence to put in Keyho who would have scored but for an excellent tackle by Jones. The game quickly switched to the other end and Lanyon had to be sharp to foil O'Neill. The Jersey defence were proving very stubborn and forced Guernsey to shoot from further out with Garnier easily dealing with these efforts. Similarly the Guernsey defence were containing the Jersey forwards and the match ended Guernsey-2, Jersey-0.

Guernsey: F. Lanyon (c), L. Purdy, Beach, Spiller, R. Brown, West, Zabiela, Cumber, Keyho, Chapple, Courtes.
Goalscorers: Cumber, Chapple.

Jersey: T. Garnier, W.C. Beasley, D. Jones, A. Romano, Denize, Kitcher, Etiemble, O'Neill, Kemp, Poingdestre, A. Marett.

Following this match the presentations to both winning teams was made. Before these presentations Miss Ruby Bird presented Lady Kiggell with a beautiful bouquet of carnations and tulips tied with the ribbons representing the three teams. Mr. H.C. Mauger in a brief speech stated that as there were no Muratti matches this year, the Amalgamated Committee had come to the rescue and had presented a cup (the Victory Cup) to be played for annually. The 'Evening Press' had also presented a Peace Cup which was to be

Guernsey.
Purdy, Lanyon, Beach,
Zabiela, Cumber, (Mr. J.E. Coward), Marriette, Courts,
Spiller, Brown, West. (Chapple was not available for this photograph)

Jersey.
Mr. Bowers, Mr. E.C. Turner, Etiemble, Jones, Garnier, Beasley, Mr. Dupre, Mr. Le Caudey,
O'Neill, Poingdestre, Kemp, Le Caudey, Marett,
Vibert, Denize, Kitcher, Romano.

competed for between teams representing Alderney and Guernsey, which everyone hoped Alderney would eventually win, which might be accomplished if Alderney had a better playing ground. Mr. Mauger then called on the Lieut-Governor Sir L. Kiggell to hand the Peace Cup and medals to the winners, the Cup being received by Videlo, the captain of the Guernsey team. Lady Kiggell then handed the Victory Cup and medals to the winners of the Guernsey-Jersey match and Lanyon received the Cup on behalf of the team.

There was a slight disturbance early in the first half just after Guernsey scored their second goal against Jersey. A soldier, who wanted to fight a Jerseyman, was taken in hand by the police and taken away and handcuffed but being pressed by a crowd of soldiers, they were obliged to let him go. Having got away, the soldier was afterwards knocked down by a motor car and taken to the Military Hospital, where his injuries were found to be slight.

The Jersey team were due to sail out on the morning of 22 April but unfortunately they missed the boat. It was then decided to arrange a further match between the islands at the Cycling Grounds later on that morning. The match was refereed by H. Le Messurier. The brief report in the Press of 23 April stated that towards the end of the first half Brown scored for Guernsey. The second half was very even and at the end of this close match the score was Guernsey-1, Jersey-0.

Guernsey: Barnicott, West, McAvoy, Spiller, Brown, Attewell, Zabiela, Cumber,
              A.N. Marshall, Bird.
              Goalscorer: Brown.

Jersey: T. Garnier, W.C. Beasley, Kitcher, Vibert, Denize, A. Romano, Etiemble,
              O'Neill, Kemp, Marett, Lecaudy.

There was a meeting of club secretaries on 15 September 1919 and they decided on league and other fixtures. The inter-insular (Muratti Vase Guernsey v Jersey) was fixed for 15 April 1920. A report in the Press of Monday 20 October reproduced an interesting article by 'Red and White' from the Jersey paper commenting on the Muratti.

'It is an open secret that Jersey tried hard last season to bring the (Muratti) match off but the Inter-Insular Committee, or some other body, did not seem willing, and now, reading between the lines, it is plain that the Guernsey Football Association have found the same apathy existing with one of the Muratti officials' the report went on 'Jersey envies the sister isle having the piece de resistance – Guernsey v Jersey this season'.

The Guernsey Football Association Council's meeting of Tuesday 4 November 1919 confirmed the Muratti dates as being Guernsey v Jersey on 15 April 1920 at the Cycling Grounds and the survivor v Alderney on 29 April 1920 at Westmount. The Islands could now look forward to the excitement, drama and controversy of the Muratti Vase competition once again.

4

Alderney

1920.

Following the end of the First World War plans were being made for the return of the Muratti. Football was beginning to return to the local scene in the islands.

The Guernsey Evening Press of Wednesday 25 February 1920 reported on an article that appeared in the Jersey Morning News. The article stated that as the result of an informal conference in Guernsey on Saturday (21 February) between a Jersey delegate of the Inter-Insular Competition and several Guernsey Delegates and officials it was decided, in principle, that it would be to the interest of this year's Muratti competition if the first round between Jersey and Guernsey, which according to sequence is this year fixed to be played in Guernsey, is instead played in Jersey. Alderney would then only have to travel to Guernsey for the final and it is held that Alderney v Guernsey or Jersey in the later Island would be a greater attraction than would be the case if Guernsey beat Jersey and then had to play Alderney in Jersey. The matter is being referred to Alderney, and as the Jersey and Guernsey Delegates are practically agreed, the matter looks like being un fait accompli.

A report in the Guernsey Press of Thursday 26 February 1920 stated that from official information the match between Guernsey and Jersey will be played in Guernsey on 15 April when the referee will be Mr L.J. Duncan. The match between the winning Island and Alderney will take place in Jersey on 29 April when Mr. R. Pook will be the referee.

Alderney and Guernsey were to meet for the second competition for the Peace Cup on Easter Monday (5 April 1920) at the Cycling Grounds with a 10.30 kick-off. This match was to be followed by the Victory Cup match between a second Guernsey team and Clapton, also at the Cycling Grounds, with a 3.15 kick-off. This was to be the first time that Guernsey had played an English team in a cup-tie.

PEACE CUP.
5 April 1920, The Cycling Grounds, Guernsey.

Guernsey -2, Alderney -6.

Around 50 Alderney supporters arrived on ss Courier at 8.30am on the day of the match bringing a mascot of an Alderney youth dressed as a Pierrot in the island colours of yellow and black. The match was attended by Guernsey's Lieut-Governor, Sir Launcelot E. Kiggell KCB, KCMG and his wife Lady Kiggell.

Guernsey's Chapple won the toss and selected to play with the sun and against a strong westerly breeze. Alderney immediately took advantage of this breeze and set up an attack with Baker shooting wide. After 6 minutes play Longhurst put Alderney ahead when he headed in just out of Lanyon's reach. Alderney was combining well and at times was out-playing the Guernsey side. Butler and Beach in the Guernsey defence were forced into some rushed clearances and following a corner Lanyon appeared to fumble the ball but the danger was cleared. In the 10th minute Alderney increased their lead when Le Brun crashed home a first-time shot. Guernsey responded but found the Alderney defence in excellent form and a clever move by Cumber and Rich was comprehensively cleared by McLernon. Lanyon was again put under pressure and had problems with a centre by Le Burn. Alderney scored again when Baker on receiving a pass from Butler easily beat Lanyon. Alderney continued to press and Lanyon had to pull off an excellent save as the Guernsey defence came under severe pressure. A further Alderney goal arrived when Le

Alderney, Peace Cup winners, with their mascot.

Burn fired in a swift drive to put them 4-0 ahead. Guernsey tried to respond and a good move involving Noel, Cumber and Rich ended with Rich heading just wide. In the 35th minute Alderney scored again when, following a corner, Baker hooked the ball out of Lanyon's reach. As the half neared its end Collins came close with an excellent chance but at half time the score was Guernsey-0, Alderney-5.

Guernsey began the second half with the advantage of the breeze and the Alderney goal had a series of escapes. In one attack Le Febvre sent Rich clear but he tripped over and the chance was lost and then, from a corner-kick, the ball hit the top of the crossbar. After 11 minutes of the half Guernsey scored when Martel set up Cumber who beat Jennings with a stiff shot. The Alderney defence were put under pressure but McLernon and Coxon stood firm and they were ably assisted by Oliver and Allen. Alderney responded and Lanyon had to save well from Le Burn and then Baker. In the 65th minute Noel crashed a shot against the crossbar and Rich pounced onto the re-bound to score past Jennings. Guernsey continued to press forward and Jennings was tested by R. Chapple and Martel but it was Alderney who scored when Baker outpaced Butler and then beat Lanyon with a superb shot. The closing minutes were very even and when the match ended the score was Guernsey-2, Alderney-6.

Guernsey: Lanyon, Butler, Beach, Duquemin, R. Chapple (c), Martel, Le Febvre, Rich, Cumber, S. Collins, S. Noel.
Goalscorers: Cumber, Rich.

Alderney: G. Jennings, W. McLernon (c), Coxon, Gadie, Oliver, Allen, Hammond, T. Baker, Longhurst, Tapsell, Le Burn.
Goalscorers: Longhurst, Le Burn (2), Baker (3),

Alderney.
W. McLernon, G. Jennings, Coxon, Gadie, Allen.
Oliver, Hammond, T. Baker, Longhurst, Tapnell, Le Burn.

The Peace Cup was presented to the Alderney captain, McLernon, by Lady Kiggell amidst applause which continued as each player received his medal. There were great celebrations as this was the first trophy that Alderney had ever won and was a tremendous boost to their Muratti preparations for 1920.

At a Guernsey Football Association Council Meeting held on 7 April 1920 the Secretary read a letter he had received from the Jersey Football Association in which it was stated that the representatives of Muratti's had offered two best quality footballs for this year's Muratti match and asked for Guernsey's acceptance of one for the match on 15 April. The Council gratefully accepted the offer. At this Council meeting it was decided that the charge for admission to the ground would be adults 10d (including tax) and juveniles under 16, 5d (including tax).

The Muratti Vase and medals would be on view in Mr. J. Mourant's outfitting window, High Street, St. Peter Port.

MURATTI SEMI-FINAL.
15 April 1920, The Cycling Grounds, Guernsey.

Guernsey -1, Jersey -0.

Guernsey Muratti preparations suffered a sever setback with their comprehensive 6-2 defeat at the hands of Alderney in the Peace Cup. They recovered slightly when they won the Victory Cup with a fine 3-0 victory against Clapton. They also lost the services of their captain J. Mahy (Northerners) and he was replaced in the team by R. Brown, also of the Northerners, who also took over the captaincy. Mahy, who received his first Muratti Cap in 1906, played for Guernsey until 1914. He served in the R.E's during the war and was awarded the Croix de Guerre. The Jersey side were captained by W.C. Beasley and it was reported that apparently an unnamed Guernsey team tried to obtain his signature.

The Guernsey goalkeeper for this Muratti semi-final was John Aubert (Belgrave Wanderers). John was in goal for Guernsey in their first Muratti match in 1905 against Alderney and gained his 7th cap in 1908. H. Chapell (Rangers) gained his first cap in this match. He served with the Royal Engineers Signal Section during the war and helped the Bedford Signals Depot to become Champions of the Bedford League.

The Jersey team, with the exception of Stent who travelled to Guernsey yesterday, arrived on Wednesday morning (14 April) by the Alberta with some 300 supporters and the vessel berthed alongside No. 3 Landing. An ingenious cartoonist of the L and SWR Company had drawn a cartoon of welcome to the Jersey team which was posted on the goods shed. The team were based in the Channel Islands Hotel. In the afternoon the Jersey team and officials and a few Guernsey friends, about 22 in all, drove in a 4 horse break to the Cycling Grounds, where they had a quarter of an hour practice. From there they drove to L'Eree Hotel via Vale Road, Baubigny Road, Cobo Bay along the coast to L'Eree where they had tea and a game of bowls. In the evening they were invited to the Lyric Picture House. The fans that travelled from Jersey on the paddle steamer Conqueror had a very rough passage. They left Jersey at 7.30 am but found the wind and huge seas off Noirmont to much for her, so that it was two hours before she could round the Point and make for Guernsey. She

W.C. Beasley (Jersey).

had to put into St. Aubin's Bay as there appeared to be a problem in the engine room. She was signalled at Castle Cornet at 11.00am but her progress was slow and it was 12.45pm before she berthed alongside No. 1 landing with 218 passengers. The first round between Jersey and Guernsey was a happy sign that peace and normality were returning to the Islands. The demand for tickets was great and it was announced that all pavilion tickets were sold a long time ago. Arrangements had been made to seat 1,000 people in the open on chairs. The price of admission to the Track was one franc. His Excellency the Lieut-Governor of Guernsey, Sir Launcelot E. Kiggell KCB, KCMG, was received by Mr. H.H. Randell, President of the GFA.

A crowd of nearly 6,000 keenly waited the start of the game. The Jersey team, to a great cheer, were the first to appear, led by their captain; W.C. Beasley and they had a short practice on the field. Guernsey followed three minutes later to a similar ovation. Jersey won the toss and chose to play against the wind on a pitch that was far from perfect. The first couple of minutes were very tentative as both sides tried to get used to the conditions. In a Jersey attack St. George was caught offside. From the resulting free kick the ball went towards the Jersey goal and Purdy showed a quick turn of pace only to be stopped by Garnier who ran out to clear, but Warr was handy and pounced on the ball to give Guernsey an early lead with the game 3 minutes old.

Almost immediately Jersey nearly equalised when Joe Blake, with an open goal, shot wide. Purdy then tested Garnier with a hot low drive but the goalkeeper saved. Jersey was being put on the defensive with Jones and Marshall holding their line together. A fine solo run by Purdy, who outpaced Marshall, Jones and Beasley, ended with him hitting the side netting. A further Guernsey attack, started by McAvoy, set Purdy and Warr into the Jersey half; Warr beat Jones only to see his shot hitting the bottom of the post with Garnier beaten. Jersey replied when a Jones free kick just went over the crossbar. Blake then fired in a low shot that Aubert saved well. As the half neared its end Blake went on a fine run to set himself up in a good position, but as he set to shoot with Aubert at his mercy, Le Cheminant came quickly across to clear the danger. The first half ended with the score Guernsey-1, Jersey-0.

The second half began with Jersey on the attack as they strove for an early equaliser with Blake taking the ball through and, following a miskick by Curtis, he passed to Marett but he placed his shot over the bar. Guernsey replied when Purdy passed to Warr and he almost beat Garnier with a long shot that flew over the bar. The game seemed to lose its shape as play went from end to end. After 10 minutes Purdy missed an open goal following a corner. The game was becoming a little scrappy and, following a typical scramble, Blicq raced clear and found himself well into the Jersey half but Garnier looked the favourite as he came out to collect only for Beasley to, for some reason, to take the ball from him and, under severe pressure from the Guernsey forwards, was lucky to see the ball go safely away. Jersey began to take control of the game and there was some anxiety in the Guernsey defence. Stent fired in a shot that Aubert punched away well and he was again tested by another stinging shot by Stent. Jersey followed this with four rapid corners as they increased the pressure in search of the elusive equalising goal. Stuart shot over the bar then Blake fired in another shot that was cleared. Aubert then prevented an almost certain goal with a superb save from Kemp. Guernsey almost increased their lead when McAvoy managed to get the ball through to Purdy and as he was challenged by Beasley and Jones he fired in a dangerous shot that produced the save of the match from Garnier as he flung himself full length to concede a corner. In the final stages of the game Jersey made desperate attempts to equalise but Guernsey managed to hold on with the final result Guernsey-1, Jersey-0. In the scramble for the ball on the sound of the final whistle Brown, the Guernsey skipper, was successful.

Guernsey: J. Aubert, A. Le Cheminant, B. Curtis, S. Chapple, R. McAvoy, R. Brown, A.S. Blicq, L. Purdy, W. Warr, H.C. Chapell, W. Dunn.
Goalscorer: Warr.

Jersey: T. Garnier, W.C. Beasley (c), D. Jones, P. Stuart, A.G. Marshall, R. Brown, P. Kemp, C. St George, J. Blake, A. Marett, E. Stent.

The Guernsey team were invited to the Lyric Hall on 16 April and were welcomed by the manager, Mr. Brienski.

Following the match the referee, Mr. Duncan, thought that it was a good robust game, fought out in a good sporting spirit. He thought that Brown was the best Guernsey player although he felt (rather harshly) that Purdy had no conception of the duties of a centre forward. Best for Jersey were Blake and St. George. He summed up the game by saying that he thought that a draw might have been a fairer result and that the standard of the play was not up to the usual pre-war standard.

It was reported in the Press of Monday 19 April 1920 that there had been discussions between Jersey and Guernsey on the possibility of a return match between the teams that played in the Muratti Semi-final on 15 April. The proposed venue was Westmount in Jersey. It was reported in the Jersey Evening Post that the Muratti Final would be switched to Guernsey. The reason for this

The Jersey defence repel a Guernsey attack.

Jersey Muratti Team.
1920.
Beasley (c), Garnier, Jones,
Kemp, St. George, Blake, Marrett, Stent,
Stuart, Marshall, Brown.

additional match was unclear although it may have been considered as a revenge match for Jersey who lost a close match 1-0 to Guernsey at the Cycling Grounds in the Muratti semi-final. It is believed that Alderney insisted that the Final be played in Jersey as originally arranged. The Guernsey Evening Press, in a report on 20 April, was concerned that any change of the venue for the forthcoming Muratti Vase Final in Jersey would seriously affect Alderney's chances. The report continued stating that, in the opinion of the Press, Guernsey should not have anything to do with this proposed change of venue even though there would be a financial incentive if the game was played in Guernsey. The original idea of the Muratti Vase Competition was to foster sport and fraternity in the islands and not to build up large bank accounts. The report continued stating that Alderney had a unique opportunity of registering her first win should the game be played in Jersey following their excellent win on Easter Monday. Alderney made a request to be allowed to include non-native soldiers in their Muratti team.

The correspondence between Guernsey and Alderney over the above matters was as follows:

Alderney's request to include soldiers who are members of the Northern Belles in their Muratti team.
1.   The reply was that the rules of the Muratti should be adhered to.
2.   The request from Guernsey that the Muratti Vase Final be played in Guernsey.
3.   The answer was that the rules of the Muratti be carried out and the Final be played in Jersey.
   The Alderney Council stated that they did not intend to enter into any public controversy on this subject as they wished to maintain the same good feeling as in the past. The game is sport, true sport with them and clean at that.
   The Muratti Vase Final was therefore to be played as originally scheduled and both teams began their preparations for their match at Westmount.

MURATTI FINAL.
29 April 1920, Westmount, Jersey.

Alderney -1, Guernsey -0.

The Guernsey team were based at the Star Hotel. There was concern over the fitness of Len Purdy as he was having trouble with his leg injury. In the end he was replaced by Rich in the Guernsey team. The Guernsey officials approached their Jersey counterparts with a view to re-opening negotiations on the suggested alteration of the kick-off time from 3.30pm to 4 or 4.30pm. It was explained that the decision on Monday 24th April was the result of careful consideration and was final. A strong argument against altering the start time was the number of people who bought tickets assuming the original kick-off time. The Alderney team arrived on the mail boat Reindeer and on disembarking went aboard a char-a banc to their headquarters at the Homesdale Boarding House in New St John's Road. Included in the party was Alderney's mascot Master Tom Smith.

The Alderney team and supporters arrive in Guernsey.

There was much talk of Alderney's chances as no one could gauge their strength. One should remember, however, that over the Easter period Alderney defeated Guernsey 6-2 to win the Peace Cup. Prior to the game it became known that J. Lihou and S. Allen were to emigrate to America but they agreed to represent Alderney in the Muratti final before they left. They would sail by mailboat to England the next morning. It speaks volumes about their commitment to Alderney's cause in this important match.

Guernsey and Alderney both travelled to Westmount, Jersey for the 1920 Muratti Vase final. There were around 4,500 spectators in the ground when Alderney came on to the pitch amidst tremendous cheering. Led by their captain, Guernsey came out to a rousing reception. The Guernsey team were captained by R. Brown and Alderney were led by W. McLernon. Alderney's mascot, Master Tom Smith, came out with the team and he was decked in blue and white as well as black and gold. The referee was Mr. Pook who had ref-ereed in two previous finals in 1908 and 1910. (Both of which Guernsey lost to Jersey.) General Wilson, the Lieut-Governor of Jersey, arrived just before the kick-off. McLernon won the toss and chose to play with the sun at their backs. Warr kicked off and passed to Chapell who sent it to brown who quickly gave it to Keyho. Keyho sent in a cross that Chapell breasted just wide. Guernsey started the stronger and quickly forced two corners but with no reward. Alderney hit back after 10 minutes when Aubert saved from Gadie. Alderney's Baker then missed a glorious opportunity from a yard out but put his shot tamely past. The game became more even and Pike broke into the Guernsey half but was well stopped by Le Cheminant. After 25 minutes Pike was taken off injured leaving Alderney with 10 men.

Alderney kept up the pressure and Baker sent in a shot that just went over the bar. Lihou then came close on the half-hour mark when his shot hit the side net-ting. McAvoy, joining up well with his forwards, responded by twice shooting over the Alderney bar. Guernsey again came close when the ball was slipped towards Chappell, but it was taken up by Warr instead but he put his shot wildly past the post. Rich then had a great chance to open the scoring for Guernsey but failed to hit the net with only Jennings to beat. The game was becoming fast and furious and as Lihou got the ball near the half way line he beat McAvoy and sent in a soft delivery between the full backs that

W. McLernon. (Alderney captain)

McLernon and Brown toss up as Alderney mascot, Tom Smith, looks on.

ended up in the net out of Aubert's reach to put Alderney 1-0 up. There was no more scoring and at half time it was Alderney -1, Guernsey-0.

Guernsey began the second half with a misunderstanding between Oliver and Gadie and this allowed Rich in to fire in a quick low shot that Jennings held. The Alderney defence were having anxious moments as Guernsey continued to press forward. Alderney broke out and Lihou fired in a fine shot that Aubert did well to save. Guernsey were beginning to find more space against the 10 man Alderney team and in quick succession Warr headed over the bar then Chapell shot over from a good position. Jennings brought applause from the crowd by saving a bouncing delivery from McAvoy. Guernsey was having more of the pressure with some excellent attacking play from Brown, but the Alderney defence held firm. Once again Alderney broke away dangerously when Gadie passed to Baker who sped away with Attewell in close attendance, but Aubert threw himself at his feet and the danger was averted. Play continued to move from end to end but with Alderney slightly on top, the match ended with the final score Alderney-1 Guernsey-0.

Alderney: Jennings, W. McLernon (c), Catts, S. Allen, Oliver, Gadie, Hammond, Baker, J. Lihou, Attewell, Pike.
Goalscorer: Lihou.

Guernsey: J. Aubert, A. Le Cheminant, B. Curtis, S. Chapple, R. McAvoy, R. Brown, A.S. Blicq, L. Rich, W. Warr, H.C. Chapell, H. Keyho.

When referee Pook blew the final whistle there was pandemonium in the ground and the spectators swarmed round the enclosure where the Lieut-Governor of Jersey was to present the Cup and medals. Jennings was carried shoulder high by his teammates. The win was a very popular one and even the Guernsey fans were heard to agree. The Cup was presented to Mr. W. McLernon, the President of the Alderney FA, by the Lieut-Governor OF Jersey,

The injured Pike being taken from the field.

H. Keyho (Guernsey).

Major-General Sir Alec Wilson KCB, who congratulated Alderney on winning with only 10 men. Pike, the injured player, was assisted to the enclosure by two men to receive his medal. Warr picked up the match ball when the game ended but at an officials request gave it up for presentation to the Alderney captain as an additional trophy.

A large crowd gathered outside the Press offices in Smith Street, Guernsey during the progress of the game. Immediately before the final result was displayed Mr H.G. Bowden, former Island Football official, made a brief speech and called on three cheers for the little Island, which needless to say were heartily given.

From a Press report it would seem that even Guernsey supporters were delighted by Alderney's win. On Friday 30 April a large group of supporters assembled at the White Rock to meet the incoming Guernsey and Alderney sides. At the top of the steps at Berth No. 3 was a patient donkey gazing rather dispassionately at the series of cartoons drawn by the White Rock artist, Mr. George Gurney. As the Reindeer approached there was a burst of cheers and a crack of rattles that continued till the time the Reindeer was moored. A cry went up from the shore 'Who won the cup?' and the Guernsey contingent enthusiastically shouted 'Alderney'. The teams disembarked and the Guernsey Captain mounted 'Neddy' surrounded by the team. The Alderney team received hearty congratulations en route to the Courier, which left at 10 o'clock, with the prospect of meeting the greatest welcome which has ever been accorded players from that island.

The Guernsey Evening Press wrote an article on 30 April 1920 under the heading:

''Well Played Alderney.''

'Yesterday Alderney reached the turning of the lane which she has trodden uncomplainingly for the past 15 years and in winning her first game in the Muratti Cup competition set the seal on an ambition created in 1905, when the famous firm of Muratti presented the trophy for inter-insular rivalry. It has been a long struggle, against tremendous odds, and we would be lacking in chivalry were we to entertain one single begrudging thought at Alderney's momentous victory.

It has been said that financial considerations have had a deciding influence in Alderney's willingness to compete against Guernsey and Jersey, sometimes on disadvantageous terms; but this fable has, we should imagine, been exploded once and for all. Alderney played on with the hope that one year they would be in a position to inflict a decisive defeat on her rivals, and that time has arrived. Playing ten men for two-thirds of the game, Alderney held her own and won!

As an example of dogged perseverance Alderney stands out prominently. Year after year our northern cousins have come up smiling to pit their puny strength against their, comparatively speaking, powerful sister islands, for population should reflect our football prowess, and when one compares the tiny community of Alderney with that of Guernsey and Jersey, it is a matter of wonderment and congratulation that the former island responds so gamely to the call. But the love of sport is so inherent in their blood that despite their numerical inferiority and no training facilities worth considering, they toe the line without comment as the seasons come round, and whilst defeat has become almost second nature to them, it has not dampened their enthusiasm one whit.

Of a verity, Alderney has been a dark horse this season. Her insular play has undoubtedly been on the upward grade throughout the season, and this improved form found a reflection in the Peace Cup game.'

The Channel Islands Football Champions met with a hearty reception on returning to Alderney with the much coveted trophy on Friday 30 April, hundreds of people turning out

W. McLernon (Capt.), Tom Smith, the Alderney mascot and R.J. McLernon (Secretary Alderney Football Club).

to welcome back their victorious team with the exception of J. Lihou and S. Allen who were on their way to America. The school children in Alderney were all given a special day's holiday.

The Courier, appropriately adorned with bunting in honour of the occasion, arrived in Alderney at about 12.30pm. After a warm interchange of greetings and congratulations from the crowd a procession, headed by a voluntary band and the team, in two wagonettes, was formed, and the beflagged town of St. Anne's was paraded amid exultant enthusiasm. Before the dispersal of the crowd the Muratti Vase was filled with lemonade and offered to the happy bystanders in celebration of the famous victory.

In this year Alderney set a record of being the first Island to hold the Muratti Vase and the Peace Cup in the same year. This was a fine postscript to an excellent and historic season for Alderney.

5

1921 - 1929

1 9 2 1 .

PEACE CUP.
28 March 1921, The Cycling Ground, Guernsey.

Guernsey -3, Alderney -0.

Sir John E. Capper KCB, the Lieut-Governor of Guernsey was among the spectators for both the Peace Cup match and the Victory Cup match. There was a strong contingent of Alderney supporters and when the Alderney team in their blue and white striped shirts ran on to the field they were greeted with a fine reception. Alderney was of course the holders of the Muratti Vase and the Peace Cup.

Referee J. Duffey called the captains together and Alderney won the toss choosing to play against the slight wind. The first dangerous attack came when Pike took up a long pass and sped down the wing and, after tricking Watson, sent in a cross that went just behind the Guernsey goal. Guernsey then gained a corner which Alderney partially cleared but the ball was collected by R. Chapple who quickly fired in a shot that was kicked away by Jennings. Guernsey continued this early pressure and after four minutes Noel sent in a good centre that was won by L. Rich just outside the Alderney penalty area and his first time shot rebounded off the crossbar but he swiftly followed up to crash the ball past Jennings to put Guernsey 1-0 ahead. Guernsey was on top with Alderney only attacking with an occasional break out. Jennings again saved well from L. Rich despite being strongly hustled by F. Rich. Alderney responded with a fine move that resulted in Hammond putting his shot wide of the post. After 25 minutes Guernsey went 2-0 up when Noel sent in a beautiful cross that was headed home by Down. Guernsey continued their pressure and a third goal followed when F. Rich sent in a shot that easily beat Jennings and at half time the score was Guernsey-3, Alderney-0.

Guernsey was again dominant at the beginning of the second half and Jennings had to save from F. Rich who shot in following a Robin pass. Chilcott in the Guernsey goal was called into action when he saved a 30-yard shot from Redhead and following a period on even play in the midfield Baker just missed from close range for Alderney. Guernsey then forced two successive corners with Jennings firstly turning a shot by F. Rich round the post and from the resultant corner he punched clear Robin's kick. The quality of play then deteriorated with only half chances occurring at each end and as the game neared its end Jennings did well to get to a fine drive by F. Rich. The final whistle went with the score Guernsey-3, Alderney-0.

Guernsey: Chilcott, Watson, Leadbeater, Spiller, R. Chapple, C. Purdy, Noel, L. Rich,
             F. Rich, Down, Robin.
             Goalscorers: L. Rich, Down, F. Rich.

Alderney: G. Jennings, W. McLernon, J. Newton, H. Newton, T. Oliver, Sebire,
             J. Hammond, Baker, Redhead, Vague, F. Pike.

Following the Guernsey v Clapton Victory Cup match the Lieut-Governor presented the Peace Cup and medals to the victorious Guernsey team. After the two cup presentations a special presentation of an inscribed leather dressing case was made by A.A. Allain, Chairman of the Guernsey Football Association, to F. Coughlan, one of the linesmen for the Peace Cup match, as he was leaving for Canada on Wednesday 30 March. The inscription on the dressing case read 'Presented to Mr. F. Coughlan by members of the Guernsey Referee's Association, March 23 1921'.

MURATTI SEMI-FINAL.
7 April 1921, Westmount, Jersey.

Jersey-2, Alderney-0. aet.

The Courier left Alderney at 4.00pm and reached St. Peter Port at 6.35pm on 6 April and after the team posed for a Press photographer they proceeded to the Channel Island Hotel. The team, under the charge of Mr. R.J. McLernon, then made their way to Jersey on 7 April. The weather was windy but by the time the match began it had risen to a gale that was blowing across the field into the pavilion. The general opinion among the fans of both sides was that there was little to choose between the teams although both sets of supporters were confident about their own side.

Alderney won the toss and at 3.30pm Davis kicked-off for Jersey. The game began with some fast exchanges providing an exciting spectacle for the 3,940 fans. In an early Jersey attack Davis lost the ball but Marett picked it up and as he prepared to shoot at goal McLernon cleared the danger. Marett was causing problems for the Alderney defence and scored what he thought was the opening goal, but he was adjudged offside. The Alderney goal seemed to have a narrow escape when Jennings, looking remarkably cool, watched the ball roll round the post when it seemed to be rolling in. After 15 minutes play Davis passed up what appeared to be an excellent scoring chance for Jersey when, rather than shoot, he passed to Huson who was in an inferior position and the danger was averted. Alderney then had a further escape when one of their defenders appeared to hit the ball with his arm but the referee waived play on. The tussle between Marett and Alderney's McLernon was becoming a feature of the match. Jersey began to gain the upper hand and repeatedly threatened the Alderney goalmouth but weak shooting kept the score at 0-0. Alderney broke out of defence and an excellent shot by J. Baker was well saved by Garnier. As Jersey continued to press they came close through Marett but Jennings did well to thwart his effort. The pressure continued and from a corner on Alderney's left the ball was switched to the other wing and following a melee in the Alderney penalty referee Rogers saw an infringement and awarded a penalty. Beasley took the kick and his fine shot was

Alderney.
McLernon, Jennings, Buckle.
Newton, Oliver, Catts.
Hammond, Baker, Attewell, Pike, Baker.

excellently saved by Jennings, and Marett pushed the rebound over the bar. Despite all this
Jersey pressure the half time score was Jersey-0, Alderney-0.
  Jersey made a change for the second half with Stuart and Davis changing places and they
continued to have the upper hand in the second half with Alderney's attacks coming from
breakaways. Jennings once again saved from Davis who sent in a dropping shot and Huson
set up Stent but his shot missed the post by inches. Once more Alderney broke away and T.
Baker fired in a shot that Garnier saved. Alderney then had a period of sustained pressure
where Garnier saved firstly from Baker then from a hard ground shot by Attewell. The
Jersey forwards continued their pressure but their finishing in the main was very poor,
however an excellent shot by Marett was saved by Jennings at the expense of a corner.
Jersey continued to make chances but their forwards could not make them count and the 90
minutes ended Jersey-0, Alderney-0.
  Jersey won the toss and played against the sun which had veered round sufficiently to
give one side the disadvantage. They continued to put pressure on the Alderney defence
during extra time and at last the deadlock was broken. Journeux swung a pass into the

goalmouth and Stent collected the ball and scored the opening goal of the tie. Alderney made a change with Oliver dropping to left back and Attewell to centre half but with very little change in their fortunes. Jennings prevented a second Jersey goal by brilliantly saving from O'Neil leaving the half-time score Jersey-1, Alderney-0.

Alderney now began to push forward in search of an equaliser and Garnier was called into play on a number of occasions to keep them out. As Alderney pushed on in search of an equaliser this allowed Stent some room to hit an excellent shot that was well saved by Jennings. In the last ten minutes of the game it was evident that both sets of players were feeling the strain and the quality of the football suffered as a result. Four minutes from time Stuart added a second goal for Jersey and at the final whistle the score was Jersey-2, Alderney-0.

Jersey: T. Garnier, W.C. Beasley (c), Kitcher, P. Stuart, Medder, Journeaux, O'Neill, G. Huson, Davies, A. Marett, E. Stent.
Goalscorers: Stent, Stuart.

Alderney: Jennings, W. McLernon (c), Buckle, Newton, T. Oliver, J. Catts, J. Hammond, T. Baker, H. Attewell, F. Pike, J. Baker.

Once again Alderney had produced a fine display in a Muratti match and proved that they were a match for either of the larger islands.

It was reported that this match had been filmed by the manager of the Lyric.

MURATTI FINAL
28 April 1921, The Cycling Grounds, Guernsey.

Guernsey -0, Jersey -1.

The Muratti Vase and medals were put on show in Mr. Mourant's outfitting window on Saturday 16 April.

There were close on 5,000 spectators for the final of the Muratti Vase at the Track on 28 April. The two teams appeared to be evenly matched and a close encounter was envisioned and the tension was building as the teams were led out by R. Chapple (Guernsey) and W. Beasley (Jersey). The match was being filmed by the manager of the Lyric and he was situated on the roof of the 'Press' box. Before the march commenced the Jersey team were lined out in front of their goal and they all ran towards the camera.

A section of the large crowd. In the top left corner is the Manager of the Lyric filming on the roof of the 'Press box.

Jersey won the toss and chose to play facing the sun, then sufficiently high not to be of any serious inconvenience. The early stages of the game were very nervous as each side tried asserting their authority and the play was very evenly balanced. Guernsey had a quick break and Lester Rich won an exciting race with Garnier, the Jersey goalkeeper, but shot inches wide of an open goal. However the referee had already blown for an offside. Jersey raised the pace and put Guernsey under some sustained pressure. Guernsey broke out and Rich raced through on his own and shot hard and true for the corner of the net only to see Garnier making a fine full length save. Stent was beginning to cause problems for the Guernsey defence first with a great drive that was well saved by Watson then he just pulled a shot a trifle wide of the goal. Jersey, however, were having problems containing the attacking skills of Rich. Guernsey nearly opened the scoring when Sid Chapple sent in the finest shot of the game that was superbly saved by Garnier. Five minutes from the interval Jersey were putting a lot of pressure on the Guernsey rearguard and Beach handled just inside the penalty box and referee Morris immediately pointed to the penalty spot. Kemp took the penalty and Watson saved but the ball spun upwards hitting the underside of the crossbar. Watson gathered the ball and sent it up field. However, the referee had decided that it had crossed the line and awarded a goal to Jersey. The half time came soon after with the score Guernsey-0, Jersey-1.

The second half was a very even affair with both sets of forwards coming near to scoring. Jersey's Kemp swung in a quick pass which Stent controlled and fired in a hard shot that came off the bar, Huson then put the rebound over much to Guernsey's relief. Jersey came the closest to increasing their lead when Huson, just ready to shoot, was prevented by L. Purdy. Guernsey broke away and R. Chapple saw his long range shot saved by Garnier. Warr then produced a powerful cross/shot that missed the far upright by a fraction. As the game progressed the defences appeared to be gaining the upper hand and clear scoring chances were few. Guernsey realising that time was running out pushed on for an equaliser and rained in shots at the Jersey goal. Warr fired a fine shot just past the post and the pressure continued with shots coming from all quarters but with no success. During a Guernsey attack it looked as though H. Chapell was going to break through only for an excellent tackle by Beasley to end the danger. With five minutes remaining Garnier produced some superb saves to successfully keep them out. In the last minute of the match Guernsey was awarded a free kick just outside the penalty area but H. Chapell's shot was well blocked and punted clear and immediately afterwards referee Morris blew his whistle and Jersey had triumphed to regain the Muratti Vase with the final score Guernsey-0, Jersey-1.

Guernsey: F. Watson, L. Purdy, J. Beach, S.C.Chapple, R. Chapple (c), C. Purdy, S.A. Noel, L. Rich, W. Warr, H.C. Chapple, C.M. Doutch.

Jersey: T. Garnier, W.C. Beasley (c), B. Smith, P. Stuart, Medder, Journeaux, P. Kemp, G. Huson, G. Davies, A. Marett, E. Stent.
Goalscorer: Kemp (pen).

Mr. H.H. Randell, President of the Guernsey Football Association, opened the presentation ceremony by expressing his thanks to His Excellency and Lady Capper for their presence, and regretted the absence of Mr. Gaudion, the Alderney President. He then asked His Excellency to present the Muratti Vase and medals to the winning team. Major-General Capper said he had great pleasure in seeing such a fine game and congratulated Jersey on winning. He called the Jersey team captain to accept the trophy. Beasley received a rousing reception as he stepped forward. Three cheers for Jersey were led by Mr. W. Bird and then Beasley led three cheers for Guernsey. His Excellency expressed sympathy for Marett, who had to be assisted forward on receiving his medal. At the end of the match Marett could not walk and had to be carried by his team-mates. A lovely floral bouquet was presented to Lady Capper on whose behalf His Excellency returned thanks. Proceedings closed with three cheers for the Lieut-Governor led by Mr. H.H. Randell.

The White Rock was a scene of great animation due to the enormous crowds who gathered to await the two boats that would return the Jersey team and their supporters back to Jersey. The first batch went by ss 'Fawn' at 8.00pm and the remaining supporters plus the victorious Jersey team left about an hour later on the 'Courier'. The Jersey 'Morning News' reported that the two excursions were expected to arrive at about 11.30pm, and from 10.00pm onwards people began to go down to the Albert Pier. At about 11.00pm the band of the Jersey Union passed through the town in a Paragon char-a-banc, playing on route. It was estimated that there was around 2,000 present when the boats rounded Noirmont Point. The 'Courier' entered the harbour around 12.10am and the cheering was deafening. The team was loudly cheered as they landed and took their places in the waiting char-a-banc proudly displaying the Muratti Vase. Then followed the grand procession. Some 300 people headed the cavalcade followed by the band and cheered as the team passed. The procession went via Conway Street, King Street, Halkett Place and Hill Street to the Continental Restaurant where the team and officials were entertained to supper. Mr. J. Marquis presided and the Muratti Vase had pride of place at the top table.

1 9 2 2

MURATTI SEMI-FINAL.
6 April 1922, The Cycling Grounds, Guernsey.

Guernsey -8, Alderney -0.

Some of the Alderney team and supporters arrived on 5 April by the Helper. The remainder were due to arrive on 6 April by the Courier.

As Alderney and Guernsey prepared for their Muratti first round contest at the Cycling Grounds on 6 April 1922 there was a feeling in the air that could only be described as a 'Muratti feeling.' Alderney's recent displays in the competition showed that they were now a force to command respect. As the crowds gathered for the contest they were entertained by the North United Silver Band. A collection was taken prior to the match in aid of the local blind of which there are 40 cases in the island. The collection raised £26.17s. The Guernsey Football Association allowed hoards of children in free. The teams came on to the pitch to a rousing reception and at kick off a massed roar of voices; bells and rattles could be heard. Guernsey started in a more positive manner, winning two corners that came to nothing. Alderney took some time to settle down and Jeffreys picked a short pass from Warr and shot a few inches wide of the post. Guernsey put in some fierce attacks on Alderney's goal and Martyn, the Alderney goalkeeper, was relieved to see two of the shots land safely on the roof of the net. Attewell also made an excellent clearance to prevent Guernsey scoring. Guernsey were playing the better football but found McLernon, Oliver and Attewell in fine form in the Alderney defence. Following a piece of sustained Guernsey pressure Alderney broke out and McLernon drove a fierce hard shot that Watson fisted clear. Watson once again punched clear from the resultant corner. Amidst a roar of jubilation from the Guernsey supporters Jeffreys scored the opening goal after 25 minutes.

This was followed almost immediately by Cumber who, receiving a pass from Warr, drove through the Alderney defence and beat Martyn with a low shot after 26 minutes. Alderney

Martyn retrieves the ball after Jeffreys opened the scoring for Guernsey.

started to put their game together with Attewell working hard in defence with Buckle and Pike adding some attacking moves that kept the Guernsey defence on their toes. Following an Alderney attack the ball was cleared from the home defence and picked up by Chapell who slipped it to Hickman who in turn crossed it over; Cumber ran through on the cross to score a third goal for Guernsey. Just before half time Guernsey lost Purdy with a dislocated ankle. Alderney finished the half when Baker fired in a fast high shot that was held by Watson. The half ended with the score Guernsey-3, Alderney-0.

Alderney nearly scored early in the second half when Chapell lost the ball in a tackle with Oliver, the ball broke to Baker who fed Pike and his high shot was well gathered by Watson and cleared. Alderney continued to press in the early minutes of the half but were unable to break down the far from secure home defence. Warr then set up Hickman who raced to the corner flag and sent in a cross that McLernon managed to clear before Chapell collected. Alderney responded with Buckle taking the ball down the wing and passing to Pike, he tried to take the ball round the defence but Hickman won the tackle and sent it up to Warr. He then touched the ball to Jeffreys who in turn fed Rich with a low pass, Rich then crossed in for Cumber but his drive was pushed away for a corner by Martyn. Pike then took the ball down the wing for Alderney and Buckle met his excellent cross only to see his well executed header go just behind. Guernsey weathered this storm and after 29 minutes of the half Rich made a fast and effective run down his wing and centred to Chapell who ran past the backs to drive the ball past Martyn for Guernsey's 4th goal. A minute later a Cumber goal was ruled offside. After 35 minutes Rich received a pass from Warr, took it down the wing and crossed for Cumber to score from 30 yards to register goal number 5. Rich added a 6th followed a minute later by Cumber who hit number 7. The scoring was complete when Rich centred for Chapell to score the 8th goal. At the end of the game Guernsey had won with a record victory with the score Guernsey-8, Alderney-0.

Guernsey: F. Watson, A. Le Cheminant, L. Purdy, S.C. Chapple, W. Warr,
             D. Martel, F. Rich, F. Jeffreys, H.C. Chapple (c), H. Cumber, J. Hickman.
             Goalscorers: Cumber (4), H.C. Chapple (2), Jeffreys, Rich.
Alderney: E. Martyn, W. McLernon, T. Oliver, J. Newton, H. Attewell, E. Pasquire,
             J. Hammond, T. Baker, J. Buckle, J. Catts, F. Pike.

The referee, Mr. S. Stollery, commented after the game that he felt that although Guernsey was by far the better team, the 8-0 scoreline flattered them a little. He felt that Guernsey's play was equal to the Hampshire County League and if they figured in that League they would assuredly give a good account of themselves, being far superior to many of the teams on the mainland.

Following the Muratti semi-final both Guernsey and Alderney prepared for the Peace Cup match to be held on 17 April 1922.

The Referees Fraternity.
C. Batiste (Alderney), H. Le Messurier, S. Stollery (Referee), A.A. Allain, Sid Collins (Guernsey).
T.H. Zabiela, J. Duffey.

PEACE CUP.
17 April 1922, the Cycling Grounds, Guernsey.

Guernsey -3, Alderney -1.

There were two changes in the Guernsey side that played on 6 April with Barnicott and J. Beach replacing F. Watson and L. Purdy. Alderney also made two changes with Machin and Gadie replacing A. Martyn and F. Pike. The game was to be refereed by J. Duffey and the linesmen were J. Chapple (Guernsey) and A. Henson (Alderney). This match was to be followed by the Victory Cup match between Cardiff Corinthians and Nunhead.

Alderney began the brightest and some fine wing play by Baker sent Hammond off on a fast run but Guernsey's Le Cheminant cleared. After 26 minutes Chappell sent the ball out to Rich and Cumber ran through on the left and put Guernsey 1-0 ahead. Alderney was quick to respond and Oliver won the ball from Cumber and ran through to force a corner and from this kick Attewell drove his shot over the bar. Vague was then dispossessed by S. Chapple who ran at the Alderney defence and passed to Rich and after his excellent centre Hickman sent in a fast low shot that Machin saved with some difficulty. Machin again did well to save a high effort by Chappell. After 26 minutes Alderney set up an attack and forced a corner, the corner was cleared and from this clearance Warr sent a low pass out to Rich who fired in a fine shot that Machin could only direct onto the crossbar and Chappell slipped in to score goal number two from the rebound. The game became more even and the half ended Guernsey-2, Alderney-0.

In the first minute of the second half Attewell broke up a Guernsey attack and headed on to Gadie who in turn passed to Buckle and his pass to Baker was driven into the net wide of Barnicott to make the score 2-1. Alderney were now playing with more confidence and made several openings but the Guernsey defence stood firm and Barnicott was well protected. In the 65th minute Chappell slipped past Attewell and sent a fine pass to Hickman and as his centre came in McLernon in the Alderney defence failed to clear and in the melee that followed Cumber put the ball back into the goalmouth for Chappell to force it into the net. As the game neared its end Alderney began to exert some late pressure with Buckle sending in a fast shot that Barnicott pushed over the bar for a corner and he was again called on to save from the visiting forwards from 3 yards and just on time he gathered a long effort from Catts. The final score was Guernsey-3, Alderney-1.

Guernsey: Barnicott, A. Le Cheminant, J. Beach, S.C. Chapple, W. Warr, J. Martel, F. Rich, F. Jeffreys, H.C. Chappel (c), H. Cumber, J. Hickman.
Goalscorers: Cumber Chappel (2).

Alderney: Machin, W. McLernon (c), T. Oliver, J. Catts, H. Attewell, Gadie, J. Hammond, T. Baker, J. Newton, Vague, J. Buckle.
Goalscorer: Baker.

This was a much improved performance by Alderney following their heavy defeat in the Muratti semi-final. The Victory Cup was presented to Cardiff Corinthians after their 2-1 win over Nunhead and then the Lieut-Governor of Guernsey, Sir John Capper, congratulated H.C. Chappell as he handed over the Peace Cup and medals.

MURATTI FINAL.
27 April 1922, Westmount, Jersey.

Jersey -1, Guernsey -2.

Guernsey was confident on their trip to Westmount for the Muratti final on 27 April. The weather was warm and sunny.

Guernsey received an enthusiastic welcome from their army of supporters (estimated at around 1,400) when they ran onto the pitch at 3.51pm. They were accompanied by their trainer, Tom Holland and his faithful attendant W. Luscombe. The referee, Capt. J. Prince-Cox, crossed from Guernsey aboard the 'Courier' and arrived at the ground only 20 minutes before the start. The match was delayed when the referee, Captain Prince-Cox, asked Watson in the Guernsey goal to change his black jersey. The opening exchanges in front of over 6,000 spectators were very even with both defences holding out well. Guernsey opened the scoring when Rich, following some neat play, fed Chapell who beat Garnier with a fast oblique shot after 8 minutes. This early goal gave Guernsey a lift and for a time they were in the ascendancy. Beech in the Jersey defence began to organise his teammates and they began to push forward. A sustained piece of attacking by the Jersey forwards resulted in three shots in succession being blocked by the Guernsey defence. Play became very scrappy for a while and neither team were able to maintain any sort of pressure. Jersey began to push on for an equaliser and a clever move from Riley and McDermott set up Beach who had his shot blocked by Le Cheminant. Stent then sent a shot over the bar then Watson saved from Beech. Watson then closed down a shot from Stent and was injured in the process. Jeffrey nearly added a second for Guernsey when his shot skimmed the whole length of the Jersey goal line with Garnier beaten. Beech and Stuart were causing the Guernsey defence a lot of problems as the pressure mounted. Watson was performing wonders in the Guernsey goal as he kept Jersey out. Five minutes before the interval Jersey's Stent sent in a fine cross that Warr handled in the penalty area and a penalty was awarded. Beech took the kick and beat Watson with a hard shot in the bottom corner to equalise for Jersey. Just before half time Garnier pulled off a miraculous save from Chapell to keep the score at half time Jersey-1, Guernsey-1.

The second half began with both sides pushing for the crucial opening but the defences held firm. Rich was beginning to cause the Jersey defence some problems, and, taking a pass from Jeffrey put his shot just over the bar. There were chances at both ends but they were dealt with by the goalkeepers. Le Cheminant sent in a high drive that Medder partially cleared only for Cumber to regain the ball and send a pass to Rich and, after cleverly keeping the ball in play, he swung a high centre that Garnier got away to Journeaux who in turn sent it to Beech who fired in a shot that hit the outside of the net. Jersey was beginning to exert some pressure on the Guernsey defence by forcing a series of corners. Guernsey responded and Warr forced a corner off Davis from which Chapple put them ahead after 25 minutes of the half. Play for a while was contained in the middle of the pitch with neither team settling down. Jersey then came close when, following a free-kick, Stent collected the ball and passed to Beech but he fired his shot wide and then Beasley sent in an accurate cross into the Guernsey area but it was cleared off the line by the defence. Two minutes from the end H. Chapell was carried off injured. Beech came very close to scoring an equaliser but his excellent shot was well saved by Watson. The final whistle blew and the final result was Jersey-1, Guernsey-2.

Jersey: Garnier, Beasley (c), Smith, Davis, Medder, Journeaux, McDermott, Riley, Beech, Poingdestre, Stent.
Goalscorer: Beech (pcn).

Guernsey: F. Watson, A. Le Cheminant, J. Beach, S. Chapple, W. Warr, D. Martel, F. Rich, F. Jeffreys, H.C. Chapple (c), H. Cumber, P. Stranger.
Goalscorer: H. Chapple (2).

Prior to presenting the Vase Sir Douglas Smith, K.C.B., K.C.V.O., Lieut-Governor of Jersey, said that he was delighted with the clean type of play, and he would be pleased if it were possible to form a Channel Islands XI to play in France.

Deprived during the last few minutes of receiving the trophy in what had essentially been his victory, H. Chapple, Island and Rangers captain, sustained an injury that the medical officer diagnosed as a possible fracture of the ankle, but later realised that the injury was a

Guernsey team and Officials with the Muratti Vase. 1922.

severe sprain. It was understood that Stranger's inclusion in the Muratti team was due to the fact that he was the only forward who in the event of an accident could drop back as a defender. Apart from a couple of mistakes he played fairly well and in some measure justified his inclusion.

Whilst the Senior side were winning the Muratti Vase at Westmount, the first Junior Inter-Insular between the islands was taking place at the Cycling Grounds where Guernsey entertained Jersey. The match was for the LCIS Cup, a handsome trophy of some 30 ounces given by the London Channel Islanders Society for the purpose of fostering junior football in the islands. The game was refereed by Mr. H. Le Messurier and the linesmen were Messrs Hutchings and Martin. In a fine and closely contested game the final result was Guernsey-4, Jersey-2.

The victorious Guernsey team, with Chapell carrying the Vase, return to St. Peter Port.   93

Guernsey: Underdown, Parkyn, Wallbridge, E. Down, A. Leadbeater (c), Joughning, Hudson, Wellington, Torode, V. Le Huray, C. Down.
Goalscorers:

Jersey: Wakeham, Potier, Harben, Carter, Godrich, de la Cour, Bell, Becker, Le Gresley, Poree, Sarre.
Goalscorers:

Early on the morning of Friday 28 April the 'Vera', in the command of Captain Holt, left for Guernsey, and the passage across was very enjoyable. Mr. Barns' fife and drum band provided selections on route and the Rangers' Jazz Band duly 'jazzed' musically.

1 9 2 3 .

PEACE CUP.
2 April 1923, The Cycling Grounds, Guernsey.

Guernsey -2, Alderney -1.

The Alderney team left for Guernsey on the 'Helper' at 9.40am on Sunday 1 April and arrived at St. Peter Port at 12 noon. The official party were based at the Channel Island Hotel.

In the first dangerous move of the match Guernsey's Down put too much pace on his final pass and Hickman was unable to reach the ball before it went for a throw-in. From this throw-in Newton swung a long high pass that found J. Baker, who firstly beat Symons, but put his centre too far behind the advancing Alderney attack and the chance was lost. The play became very tight for around 10 minutes before Noel collected a lofted pass from Chapell and was brought down inside the Alderney penalty area. Chappel stepped up and took the penalty confidently to put Guernsey 1-0 ahead after 12 minutes. Alderney responded well and forced a series of corners that resulted in a number of shots just clearing the Guernsey crossbar. After 28 minutes Jennings had to be quick to save a shot from R. Chapple and from his clearance Buckle sent the ball up to T. Baker. He sent in a low ball across the Guernsey goal and Smith ran on to equalise for Alderney. There were chances at both ends but at half-time the score was Guernsey-1, Alderney-1.

Guernsey opened the second half on top keeping Alderney in their own half for the first five minutes. Chapell sent in a high pass to Hickman who worked his way forward and sent in a low centre from which a fierce melee ensued and led to shots from Noel, Chapell and Collins being charged down by the Alderney defenders. Bideau broke away for Alderney and passed to J. Baker who lost the ball in a tackle by Down. He quickly passed to Noel but he failed to control the ball and Oliver cleared to Hammond and set up an Alderney counter-attack. Down tackled Hammond and won the ball for Guernsey and sent it across to Chapell for him to slip it through to Noel who tried to place his shot in the corner of the net but Jennings managed to save the situation. With 12 minutes remaining Guernsey won a corner and from the kick Down sent a fierce drive over the bar. Guernsey won the ball back from the goal-kick and Noel fed it to Chapell who scored past Jennings to give Guernsey the lead once more. As the match neared its end Guernsey were maintaining their supremacy and at full-time the result was Guernsey-2, Alderney-1.

Guernsey: Chilcott, Bachman, McAvoy, Symons, R. Chapple, W. Downs, S. Collins, Jeffrey, S.A. Noel, H. Chapell (c), Hickman.
Goalscorer: Chapell (2, 1 pen).

Alderney: G. Jennings, W. McLernon (c), T. Oliver, Gadie, Smith, Buckle, J. Hammond, T. Baker, J. Newton, E. Bideau, J. Baker.
Goalscorer: Smith.

MURATTI SEMI-FINAL.
12 April 1923, Westmount, Jersey.

Jersey -0, Guernsey -1.

'Muratti fever' was at its highest pitch at Westmount when Jersey played Guernsey. Rain fell heavily from 9.00am onwards but did nothing to damp the ardour of the supporters who arrived on the 'Ibex' from Guernsey. The rain ceased an hour before the match and the weather brightened. Green and white was predominant in the town and shopkeepers did a roaring trade in favours. Woolworths' was crowded as never before by a besieging army of Sarnian buyers of balloons, whistles and wheezers. There were long queues of fans that waited eagerly to gain entrance to the ground. One of these fans was Georgie Dunn, dressed in green and white, (son of J. Dunn, the groundsman at the Cycling Track) who was the Guernsey mascot.

Jersey had three new caps in Picot (YMCA), Holmes (St. Paul's) and Le Masurier (YMCA). Joe Blake (First Tower) captained the Jersey side and H. Chapell (Rangers) led the Guernsey team which included two players in W. Down and J. Smith, both of Rangers, who were gaining their first caps.

There was a total absence of wind when the game started and Chapell won the toss and chose to defend the Tower goal. Due to the earlier heavy rainfall the surface was treacherous in the immediate front of goal. Direct from the kick off a mistake by Medder allowed Chapell to feed Rich who put in a dangerous centre that was cleared by the Jersey defence. The opening exchanges were, as usual, very fast and furious with no one dwelling on the ball for long. The first save of note was by Watson from a shot by Le Masurier. For a time the play was confined to the midfield then gradually Jersey were gaining the upper hand with two good chances falling to Stuart, with the second one being well cleared by Guernsey's Beach near the post. Guernsey reacted well to this and following a series of free kicks, Cumber fired in a great shot that would have beaten most goalkeepers but was superbly held by Garnier. The play began to heat up and after a series of fouls by both sides Le Masurier was cautioned for a foul on Warr near the centre circle. The resulting free-kick was sent into the Jersey goal-

Georgie Dunn. (Guernsey mascot)

mouth and it was finally cleared as Barry Smith booted it away downfield. Possibly due to the numerous infringements during the game, the referee called the players together in the middle of the pitch and lectured them for nearly a minute. Jersey was then put under a lot of pressure and Garnier saved well from Chapell. For the next few minutes the Jersey goal was put under siege and once again the brilliance of Garnier prevented Cumber and then Chapell from scoring. The final minute of the half saw Jersey pushing on for an all impor-tant goal but the cool defending of Le Cheminant and Beach kept them out and when half-time arrived the score was Jersey-0, Guernsey-0.

The second half began with Jersey on the attack but this was broken up by Beach who sent the ball high towards the Jersey goal. The high ball confused the Jersey defence who hesitated and Cumber headed past Garnier to put Guernsey 1-0 up. Play was getting very tight and when Le Masurier won the ball off Chapell he fed Huson but he appeared off bal-ance when trying to control the ball and the chance was gone. The game was held up with half an hour to go due to an injury to Le Cheminant who resumed after attention. Smith and Chapell began a fine Guernsey move that resulted in Warr setting up Smith, but the Jersey defence cleared only for Cumber to run through on a pass to score what he thought was a second Guernsey goal but the whistle had already gone and the score was ruled out. Jersey reorganised their side with Riley moving up to the forwards and Stuart moving back. Riley then received a throw in from Stuart but missed a good chance when he put his shot wide. With fifteen minutes remaining Warr robbed Medder but Picot regained the ball and pushed it to Huson who clipped an excellent centre into the Guernsey defence which

Mr. J.C. Wildig

caused some panic but Riley could not take full advantage and put his final shot wide. Once again the two defences were on top and they reduced the chances to shoot in on goal. As the game was nearing its end Jersey forced the Guernsey defence back as they strove for an equaliser. Guernsey held out, however, and the final result was Jersey-0, Guernsey-1.

Jersey: T. Garnier, Picot, B. Smith, Riley, Medder, J. Blake (c), Holmes, G. Huson, P. Stuart, Le Massurier, W. Poingdestre.

Guernsey: F. Watson, A. Le Cheminant, J. Beach, S. Chapple, W. Warr, W.H. Down, F. Rich, L. Rich, H. Cumber, H.C. Chapple (c), J. Smith. Goalscorer: Cumber.

Mr. J.C. Wildig, the match referee, was interviewed after the match and said that the game was very nicely and keenly contested, though he had to call the players together. He expressed himself highly pleased with the isles and in particular with the admiral reception we meted out to him.

Once again Smith Street in St. Peter Port was awash with supporters looking for news from Westmount. This year the crowd exceeded the size of anything yet known. From the bottom to the top of Smith Street a sea of faces were upturned to the Secretarial and Editorial Offices of the Press waiting for news of the Muratti match. It was estimated that at its peak the crowd numbered around 1,700.

MURATTI FINAL.
26 April 1923, The Cycling Grounds, Guernsey.

Guernsey -3, Alderney -2.

Alderney and Guernsey met at the Cycling Grounds in the Muratti final on 26 April 1923. A crowd of 7,200 eagerly waited what promised to be a very close match with a legitimate probability that Alderney would win. There were three of the Alderney team who were resident in Guernsey, W. McLernon, T. Oliver and T. Baker. At the last moment Cumber was unable to play due to an injury. Warr was moved to centre forward and Symons brought in at centre half.

Guernsey won the toss and defended the west goal. Prior to the official start of the match Major-General Sir J.E. Capper, the Lieut-Governor of Guernsey, kicked-off. Guernsey were the first to threaten when Warr sent a pass to L. Rich and he in turn sent in a cross that F. Rich sent over the Alderney bar. Alderney was taking some time to settle into a pattern of play with the Guernsey defence clearing any danger quickly. A fine Alderney attack by T. Baker, B. Newton and Bideau resulted in T. Baker driving in a low shot that Watson in the Guernsey goal managed to clear. Alderney were then pushed into defence but broke out and a high pass from J. Newton was collected by Hammond who fired across goal. From the goal kick F. and L. Rich affected a breakaway that led towards the Alderney penalty area and Smith sent in a high cross and an exciting melee ensued when the ball was headed up against the bar, banged against the post and then Chapple forced the ball over the line to give Guernsey a 1-0 lead after 14 minutes. Alderney replied with a series of attacks that were contained by the home defence. From one of these attacks Guernsey won a throw in which went to Warr who centred for Chapell who sent in a fine header just over the bar. The resultant goal kick was returned by Down and L. Rich passed to Warr who scored Guernsey's second goal after 19 minutes.

The game seemed to be moving away from Alderney then Buckle passed to B. Newton who quickly sent it to Hammond. Hammond beat Le Cheminant and gave the ball to T. Baker who scored with a high drive over Watson's hands to make the score 2-1. This goal had a positive effect on Alderney and they began to pass the ball about with more precision. Guernsey, however, were beginning to take control of the game with their faster neater play. F, Rich sent a high centre into the Alderney penalty area and it dropped into a bunch of players and the ball just whizzed past the post. Guernsey was at this time playing the better attacking football but they were finding the Alderney defence in fine form. The game began to quieten down a little but the crowd became excited when Warr beat J. Newton and pushed the ball to Chapell for him to race in on the Alderney goal but

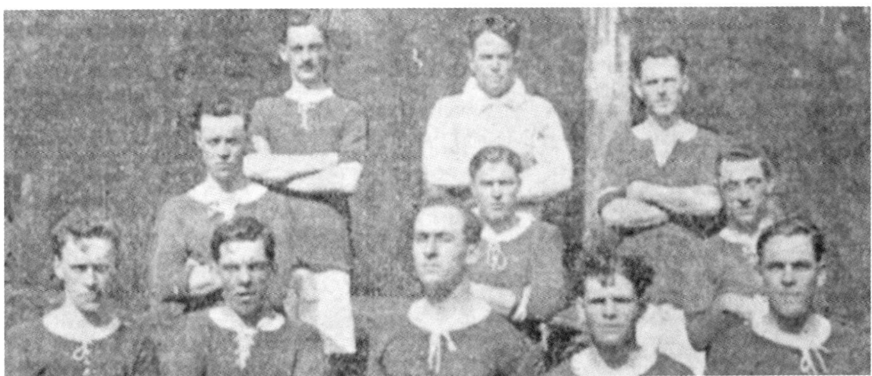

Alderney 1923.

Warr scores Guernsey's second goal.

Jennings was alert to the danger and rushed out to gather the ball and clear. Smith, on the left wing, sent a lovely centre into the goalmouth and F. Rich scored Guernsey's third goal low into the net. The half time ended with the score Guernsey-3, Alderney-1.

In the second half Alderney had the advantage of the wind behind them and this proved an asset in the long swinging game they were exploiting. They forced a couple of corners and within 2 minutes Watson saved a low drive from B. Newton. Guernsey broke out but were soon on the defensive with Watson saving a header from T. Baker. The Guernsey defence were feeling something of the intensity of the Alderney attack and their clearances were only too frequently straight and high into touch. An Alderney attack resulted in J. Baker sending in an excellent centre that was met by T. Baker but his fine header was well collected by Watson. Alderney were using the wind to their advantage and when J. Baker broke away from Chapple to receive a pass from Bideau, his centre into the Guernsey penalty area was only cleared after a lot of difficulty. A place kick was swung into the Guernsey area by T. Baker and as Watson saved the ball it was forced into the net by J. Baker to give Alderney their second goal. Guernsey pushed on to try and regain the initiative but found Jennings in excellent form. During the closing minutes Alderney forced three good corners and Watson saved a spectacular long shot from Oliver. The referee blew his whistle and Guernsey had won by the narrowest of margins, Guernsey-3, Alderney-2.

Guernsey: F. Watson, A. Le Cheminant, J. Beach, S. Chapple, G. Symons, W.H. Down, F. Rich, L. Rich, W. Warr, H.C. Chapell (c), J. Smith.
Goalscorers: H. Chapell, Warr, F. Rich.

Alderney: G. Jennings, Oliver, W. McLernon (c), Gadie, J. Newton, J. Buckle, J. Baker, Bideau, B. Newton, T. Baker, J. Hammond.
Goalscorers: T. Baker, J. Baker.

Sir Douglas Smith presenting the Muratti Vase to H. Chapell.

After the match little Miss Barbara Cox, daughter of C.S.M. Cox, and Miss Gwendoline Falla, daughter of Mr. Frank Falla, were escorted, respectively to Lady Capper and Lady Smith with beautiful bouquets which were graciously received and acknowledged. Mr. H.H. Randell, President of the Guernsey Football Association, expressed the great honour conferred by the two Lieut-Governors and their ladies through gracing the proceedings with their presence. This had been the first time that the Lieut-Governors of both islands had witnessed a Muratti Vase Final. The invitation to present the Cup was given to Sir John Capper, the Lieut-Governor of Guernsey, but this courtesy he had extended to his guest Sir Douglas Smith, the Lieut-Governor of Jersey. Sir Douglas said it had been a great honour and pleasure for him to be present. He then presented the Vase to Chapell, the Guernsey captain, amid applause and then the gold medals to the winning team. Advocate H.H. Randell led three cheers for the two Lieut-Governors,, who stood either side of him, and Mr. William Bird led three cheers for Alderney. The band of the Manchester Regiment then struck up the National Anthem.

There was a collection made during the game on behalf of charities and it realised £17.5.9. Two of the charities who were to benefit were the Royal Alfred Aged and the Local Blind Fund.

1 9 2 4 .

MURATTI SEMI-FINAL.
10 April 1924, The Cycling Grounds, Guernsey.

Alderney-0, Jersey-1.

Alderney's preparations for their match against Jersey went very well when they played three matches against the D Company of the Manchester's drawing the first 1-1 and winning the other two by 7-1 and 4-3. Their 7-1 victory was against a very much depleted Manchester side that had some of their players in action against Guernsey although their 4-3 victory was very well received.

Nearly 6,000 spectators were at the Cycling Grounds to witness the first round of the 1924 Muratti competition between Jersey and Alderney on 10 April.

A lively wind was blowing straight into the eastern goal. When W. McLernon (Alderney) and W. Riley (Jersey) tossed for ends the Jersey skipper won and decided to play with the wind for the first half.

As the match began the rain started and was heavy for a time. This affected the play as both sets of players found the slippery ball a disadvantage. Jersey was the first to create a chance when Le Cocq lifted a high shot that Parmentier saved with some difficulty. G. Davies was then put in possession by Journeaux who beat McLernon and set up Le Cocq but Parmentier was quick off his line and saved the danger. Jersey's goalkeeper, Garnier, was not looking steady when he sent out a weak clearance but a minute later he was given an ovation as he saved a fierce drive by T. Baker. Later on T. Baker fired in a fierce shot that Garnier managed to save. At this stage Jersey was slightly superior but Alderney was dangerous in breakaways. The deadlock was nearly broken when G. Davies broke clean through and ran on to smash a fast drive into a corner of the Alderney goal, Parmentier

Alderney 1924.

W. McLERNON

(Rangers F.C.)

Right Back.

W. RILEY

Centre Half.

bringing great applause by pulling off a spectacular save. From the resulting corner, taken by O'Neil, the Alderney defence was able to complete the clearance Jersey continued to have most of the play and after 35 minutes Le Masurier hit a low shot that evaded Parmentier and ended up in the far corner of the net to give Jersey the lead. Jersey then forced a couple of corners and from the second T. Baker cleared for Alderney and set up S. Newton in a swift counter attack. It was stopped as Parker intercepted Newton's centre and sent the ball to G. Davies who whipped in a high shot that Parmentier brilliantly tipped over the bar, As the half neared its end Garnier had to save from T. Baker to prevent Alderney gaining a late equaliser as they put some late pressure on the Jersey defence without success and at half time the score remained Jersey-1, Alderney-0.

Alderney began the second half with the advantage of the wind at their backs and early on J. Newton was running clean through when Mauger cleared for Jersey. Although Jersey was still playing the better of the two, the Alderney breaks were troubling the Jersey defence. Jersey was awarded a free-kick, which was taken by Riley, but he put his effort wide. From the resulting goal kick J. Newton was making for the Jersey goal when he was brought down just outside the penalty area. Oliver took the kick which was cleared, with some difficulty, for a corner by the Jersey defence. J. Baker put in a high cross that found the Jersey defence hesitating and J. Newton beat Parker to the ball and it went behind. Alderney again attacked and J. Newton beat Riley and crossed to T. Baker, he ran clean through and with only Garnier to beat lifted his shot over the bar. The Jersey defence was now under severe pressure with the ball clearing the crossbar and within 30 seconds it was driven just past the post. It was now looking very likely that Alderney would snatch an equaliser and the Jersey defence were tending to play the ball into touch at every opportunity. Garnier then pulled off a brilliant save from Oliver and then at the other end Poingdestre hit the bar with a short-range shot as the play swung from end to end. Jersey managed to hang on and it was considered that they were very lucky to win the game. Referee Winton blew the whistle with the final score being Jersey-1, Alderney-0.

Jersey: T. Garnier, C. Mauger, Parker, F. Davis, W. Riley (c), Journeaux, O'Neill, Le Massurier, F. Le Cocq, G. Davies, W. Poingdestre.
Goalscorer: Le Massurier.

Alderney: A. Parmentier, W. McLernon (c), B. Newton, Allen, Oliver, Gadie, S. Newton, J. Newton, J. Baker, T. Baker, Bideau.

When interviewed after the game the referee, Mr F.C. Winton of Sussex, said that the game was on a par with County football in the South of England. He was particularly impressed with the work of Alderney's J. Newton and Jersey's captain, J. Riley. He felt that Alderney lost because they could not take full advantage of the wind in the second half and wasted their opportunities.

On Saturday 12 April the Guernsey Football Press reported that W. McLernon (Alderney and Rangers) - right - had created a record when he captained the Guernsey team in their match against Rotherham Amateurs, which they lost 3-0. He is the only footballer who has had the honour of captaining two separate Island teams. At the time he was the captain of Alderney. Oliver, Tommy Baker and J. Baker from Alderney were also in the side.

Jersey. 1924.

PEACE CUP.
21 April 1924, The Cycling Grounds, Guernsey.

Guernsey -1, Alderney -2.

S. Chapple would miss the remainder of the season as he was suffering from pneumonia. The Guernsey side had to make a late change with F. Rich replacing Stan Collins. The Peace Cup match was being played in the morning with Guernsey playing Enfield in the Victory Cup in the afternoon.

Referee H. Le Messurier called the captains together and Richardson won the toss for Guernsey and selected to play with the high sun at his back. Guernsey started the quickest with Barnard shooting weakly past the post followed by F.C. Bird putting his shot just over the top left corner of the goal. After 6 minutes play Oliver sent the ball to J. Baker on the left and he fired into the goalmouth where J. Newton slipped his shot inches over the bar. For the next 15 minutes the play became very even as each side strove for the early break-through. Alderney then attacked through Tommy Baker and he set up Newton for a shot that Robinson in the Guernsey goal managed to hold but he carried it over the line for a corner. The Guernsey response was a sustained attack on the Alderney defence which resulted in Parmentier saving brilliantly from Bird, Collins and Barnard. With a minute remaining in the first-half Tommy Baker won the ball and put it out to Hammond who centred hard. The ball came back out and J. Baker centred it in again for Newton to hit a shot that was blocked only for Tommy Baker to crash it home through a group of players to make the half-time score Guernsey-0, Alderney-1.

Guernsey began the second half on top but found the Alderney defence in good form. The Alderney team settled and after 8 minutes increased their lead when a well placed centre found John Newton and from close in he scored a second goal. Guernsey then went on the attack and a fine shot by Stranger was well held by Parmentier and then Barnard got into a good position but sent his shot over the bar. As the pressure mounted W. McLernon and Oliver stood firm in the resolute Alderney defence. F. Rich then came very close for Guernsey but his excellent cross-shot curled just over the bar. Alderney broke out and a clearance by Oliver found T. Baker who sent a ball for his brother, J. Baker, and Newton to rush on for and Robinson brought off a great save from the right. With ten minutes remaining Guernsey reduced the arrears when Rich scored with a fine shot following a period of sustained attacking. Five minutes later Guernsey nearly equalised but Parmentier turned a dangerous ground shot away for a corner. Guernsey were pressurising until the end but Alderney held out leaving the final score Guernsey-1, Alderney-2.

W. McLernon, W. Parmentier, H. Newton,
S. Allen, T. Oliver, J. Gadie,
J. Hammond, T. Baker, J. Newton, Bideau. (J. Baker was unavailable for the photograph).

Peace Cup Winners – 1924.

Guernsey: Robinson, L. Purdy, Cox, Brehaut, J.J. Richardson (c), Bougourd, F. Rich,
                Collins, Barnard, F.C. Bird, Stranger.
                Goalscorer: Rich.
Alderney: A. Parmentier, W. McLernon (c), H. Newton, Allen, Oliver, Gadie,
                J. Hammond, T. Baker, J. Newton, Bideau, J. Baker.
                Goalscorers: T. Baker, J. Newton.

The Lieut-Governor of Guernsey presented the Peace Cup to McLernon, the Alderney captain. This was the second time that Alderney had won the Cup, their first success being in 1920. Mr. G.F. Peek, who represented the donors of the Peace Cup, voiced the thanks of the GFA towards the Lieut-Governor for his patronage and led three hearty cheers for the Lieut-Governor, Lady Capper and Miss Capper. In the Victory Cup match Guernsey lost 2-1 to Enfield after extra time. It was announced that the Muratti Vase final would be played on 1 May at Springfield and not at Westmount.

MURATTI FINAL.
1 May 1924, Springfield Stadium, Jersey.

Jersey -1, Guernsey -0.

The fans pack the 'Ardena' for the trip to Jersey.

For the first time the Muratti Vase final was played in May. The match between Jersey and Guernsey took place at Springfield on May 1 1924. The mailboat 'Alberta' left St. Peter Port on Thursday morning and took the Guernsey fans to St. Helier and very soon the town was awash with green and white. In the afternoon the 'Ardena' left St. Peter Port at noon with a very large contingent of football fans.Both teams were confident of victory and Guernsey was taken as very slight favourites. Earlier there had been some concern in the Jersey camp over the fitness of W. Poingdestre who had a slight limp, but he was declared fit to play.

W. Riley (Jersey) and G. Symons (Guernsey) lead out the teams along with Geordie Dunn the Guernsey mascot who was resplendent in his green and white attire. Symons won the toss and decided to play with the wind and defend St. Mark's end. Guernsey opened the quickest and Garnier had to save a fierce effort from Noel. Guernsey was sharper in attack but they found Mauger and Parker in good form. A Jersey attack broke down and Purdy passed on to Noel and after a fine run put his shot past the post. This was followed by W. Poingdestre crossing for G. Davies but his header was saved by Watson. Garnier then rescued Jersey by saving from Warr and then from Smith. Guernsey was playing very well and in an excellent move Rich passed to Warr who slipped it to Noel and he sent Rich through and as he bore in on goal the ball was well cleared by Mauger to the relief of the Jersey supporters. The majority of the play was around the Jersey goal but Garnier was up to the task and once again saved from Smith. Rich then lifted a high centre, Garnier ran out and missed the ball but Noel was unsuccessful with his header. Garnier was by far the busier of the two goalkeepers ably supported by his defence. Despite all their pressure Guernsey failed to score and the half ended Jersey-0, Guernsey-0.

It was felt that Guernsey were unlucky not to be in the lead but faced a second half against the wind all-square. Guernsey began the second half as they finished the first with a series of attacks on the Jersey defence. Garnier saved a great drive by Noel as the Jersey rearguard held out. Jersey then came close when Le Cheminant miskicked from a clearance from goalkeeper Watson and this allowed Poingdestre to gain control and send in a dangerous centre that F. Davis collected but could only shoot over the bar. The game became more even as play moved back and forth to each area. Guernsey's Le Cheminant miskicked again and almost conceded a corner but the ball went for a throw-in. From this throw-in, near the corner flag the ball was driven to Poingdestre and from his centre G. Davies missed a guilt-edged chance to put Jersey ahead. As the game wore on Jersey were shaping up better and after 24 minutes Le Masurier ran through to score for Jersey with a slow shot. This goal caused Guernsey to step up their attacks and a fight almost resulted when Le Masurier charged Purdy in a foul fashion and only the intervention of the referee prevented the situation from getting out of hand. Guernsey continued to press for an equaliser with Garnier saving from Warr. With eight minutes remaining Guernsey nearly scored with Garnier rolling on the ball but it was cleared. Noel then came very close when his fine shot rebounded off the crossbar and back into play and only a packed Jersey defence prevented a score. As Guernsey pushed on, Jersey hit them on the break and Le Cheminant had to be alert to hold up Poingdestre and in the final minute Watson saved a fast shot from the same player. There was no more scoring and the final result was Jersey-1, Guernsey-0.

Watson holds a shot from Poingdestre.

Jersey: T. Garnier, C. Mauger, Parker, F. Davis, W. Riley (c), Journeaux, O'Neill, Roberts, Le Masurier, G. Davies, W. Poingdestre.
Goalscorer: Le Massurier.

Guernsey: P. F. Watson, L. Purdy, J. Beach, A. Le Cheminant, G. Symons (c), W.H. Down, F. Rich, W. Warr, S.A. Noel, J. Smith, J. Hickman.

After the match Le Masurier was carried shoulder high by his admirers. It was one of, if not the best, Muratti matches ever played, though only one goal was scored, and the splendid defence put up by both sides was a real tribute to Channel Islands' football. The game was very well handled by referee Tolfree, who expressed himself as highly delighted with the game and fine sporting spirit shown by both sides. He noticed, however, that there was a slight inclination to take the man instead of playing the ball, and he advised on leaving such tactics alone. He was fully aware, however, that such infringements during the match were backed by good intentions only, and that there was not a single deliberate foul. It was a very good game indeed.

1 9 2 5 .

PEACE CUP.
12 March 1925, The Cycling Grounds, Guernsey.

Guernsey-3, Alderney-0.

Alderney was offered the chance to play this match at home but they declined and decided to play the game at the Cycling Grounds. They were handicapped by the fact that both Oliver and Baker were unable to play due to injury. The Alderney side travelled to Guernsey on the 'Courier' on 11 March and were based at the Channel Islands Hotel. Alderney was without the services of Oliver and Baker due to injuries.

Although the seating arrangements were admirable it was felt that the GFA could have improved matters if they had engaged a band to entertain the spectators before the match. There was a large crowd in the ground and Alderney received a rousing reception when they ran out onto the field. Guernsey was to be captained by W. Warr (North) and Alderney by W. McLernon (Rangers).

Straight from the kick-off Guernsey pressed and when Stan Collins sent in a cross Cumber collected the ball and passed to Chapell who smashed his drive just wide of the post. From the goalkick Alderney broke into the attack and Watson in the Guernsey goal had to rush out to clear away a chance by S. Newton. The opening ten minutes were very even with both goals coming under pressure. During a period of Guernsey pressure Chapple intercepted a pass from Smith to McLernon and sent the ball to Meagher who in turn gave it to Chapell. The ball was whipped into the centre for Noel to head goalwards only for H. Newton to clear. The ball fell to Collins who returned it into the Alderney goalmouth and after some close calls McLernon finally cleared the danger for Alderney. In the 11th minute Guernsey should have scored when a superb shot by skipper Warr struck the crossbar and the ball fell to Noel who sent in a fierce drive that cannoned off H. Newton to safety. A few minutes later Guernsey opened the scoring when a shot from Bougourd confused Parmentier and hit the inside of the post and in to the net. It took a few minutes for Alderney to recover from this setback but they were soon pushing in on Guernsey's goal and when Jones received a fine pass from S. Newton it took a good tackle by Meagher to clear the danger. Smith then had two good opportunities for Alderney but put his shots wide. With five minutes of the half remaining Bougourd received the ball from a throw-in and fired a low shot into the net for Guernsey's second goal. As the half ended Jones came very close for Alderney but at half-time the score was Guernsey-2, Alderney-0.

The second half began with Guernsey forcing two corners and came very close to increasing their lead. Alderney responded well and Watson had to be quick to clear a fine cross by L. McLernon. Watson again saved when he rushed out to kick the ball clear when under pressure by Jones, S. Newton and Smith. The Guernsey defence held out and the home side scored again when Noel took the ball into Alderney territory and, as Parmentier came out, slipped the ball calmly into the net. Alderney took this set-back well but were finding the Guernsey defence in fine form and it was nearly a fourth goal when, in a swift move, Warr slipped a pass to Cumber and he quickly beat Rose and sent in a cross for Collins. The ball dropped in front of the Alderney goal and Chapell ran in for it but the ball got jammed amid a bunch of players and was cleared. Guernsey were now in control and nearly scored again when, following a surging run by Meagher, Bougourd sent the ball to Noel who saw his shot come back off the crossbar with Parmentier well beaten. As the game was drawing to a close S. Newton found himself in front of the Guernsey goal but he shot weakly and the chance was lost. There was no more scoring and the final result was Guernsey-3, Alderney-0.

Guernsey: P.F. Watson, L. Purdy, S. Chapple, J.J. Richardson, W. Warr (c), J. Meagher, S. Collins, H. Cumber, S.A. Noel, P. Bougourd, H. Chapell.
Goalscorers: Bougourd (2), Noel.

Alderney: Parmentier, W. McLernon (c), Evans, J. Newton, Rose, J. Hammond, Jones, S. Newton, Smith, L. McLernon.

At the end of the game the crowd swarmed around the ropes as the officials prepared to present the Peace Cup and medals. It was announced by Mr. J.J. Eveson, Secretary to the Inter-Insular Committee, that Mr. Gervaise F. Peek was celebrating his 70th birthday, Mr Peek was due to present the Cup but he asked that Judge Mellish carry out this task and he duly handed the trophy and medals to the victorious Guernsey side. Mr. Peek stated that he hoped that Alderney would once again win the Peace Cup. After the presentation a vote of thanks was given to Mr. Peek and Judge Mellish amidst cheers.

In the Guernsey Football Press of Saturday 14 March it was reported that the referee for the Muratti Final between Jersey and Guernsey to be played at the Track on 30 April was to be Mr. J.T. Howcroft. This announcement, before the semi-final had been played, understandably upset the Alderney camp and a report in the Press of 21 March by 'Throw-in' commented that although Guernsey were the semi-final favourites for their match against Alderney the result should not be taken as a foregone conclusion. A letter from A.J.A. in the same paper echoed these sentiments.

The editor of the Press stated on 21 March that it regretted what was a printer's error and hoped that Alderney would forgive the paper. The editor added that if Alderney should win, the 'Football Press' would be the first to congratulate them.

MURATTI SEMI-FINAL.
2 April 1925, Westmount, Jersey.

Alderney -0, Guernsey -3.

As the 4,000 crowd waited for the first round of the 1925 Muratti between Alderney and Guernsey to commence they were entertained by the East Surrey' popular band who marched up and down the pitch resplendent in their bright red tunics. The two teams arrived at the ground from Hotel L'Europe where they were both staying.

Alderney. 1925.

The Alderney team were expected in Jersey on Wednesday. A bus was waiting at the quay to take them to their lodgings and evidently these people had received their orders from some authority and when all had landed would hardly believe that Alderney was not on board. One individual was seen to cross the gangway apparently bent on a feverish and fruitless search. It was the first of April.

The pitch was firm and dry and both teams got a rousing reception, but Alderney came in for the warmest cheer. Once again there was far too little room at each end for the men who had to take the corner kicks. Before the match commenced both teams were presented to Major-General Sir Francis R. Bingham, the Lieut-Governor of Jersey.

Guernsey won the toss and chose to defend the town end. The teams started in erratic style with Alderney doing all the attacking and J. Newton sent in a shot that went about 30 feet over the bar. Collenette and L. McLernon were causing problems in the Guernsey defence and Watson had to come to their rescue. Guernsey could not settle down and were put under a lot of pressure. Very gradually Guernsey began to assert themselves and push on to test Parmentier in the Alderney goal. After 14 minutes John Newton, the Alderney centre half, was in an accidental collision with Bougourd and broke his leg and he was carried off in a stretcher. Alderney had to reorganise their side following this major setback. Noel broke the deadlock after 22 minutes when he ran through on his right and scored with a fast drive. This goal settled Guernsey and they began to try and play their usual open fast game. Although Guernsey were not playing at their best, their defence was keeping Alderney at bay and after 31 minutes Noel added a second goal. As the half neared its end Bougourd latched on to a fine centre from Cumber but, with an open goal before him, shot wide with a weak shot. Guernsey's second goal seemed to affect Alderney and their play became very erratic but they managed to regain their composure and the half ended with the score Guernsey-2, Alderney-0.

John Newton. (Alderney.)

Guernsey started the second half in control and proceeded to put Parmentier's goal under pressure as he saved well from Bougourd and then Cumber. The pressure continued and a clever move by Noel and Bougourd caused Parmentier to rush out of his goal, but he missed the ball and Guernsey nearly scored. Baker broke out for Alderney on the right and shot at speed forcing Watson in the Guernsey goal to concede a corner. Alderney were fashioning a series of attacks and Watson had to deal with a slow drive from Hammond followed by a cross shot from Pasquire. Guernsey weathered this storm and Noel ran through and struck the crossbar with a brilliant shot that Parmentier did not see. Bougourd then smashed in a shot that Parmentier saved high up. Baker, then W. McLernon, both tried to ease the pressure on the Alderney defence by creating some attacking moves but with little success. In the last minute of the match Noel went through on his own and scored with the best shot of the match and the final result was Guernsey-3, Alderney-0.

Guernsey :   P. F. Watson, L. Purdy, G. Symons, J.J. Richardson, W. Warr (c), J. Meager, S. Collins, H. Cumber, S.A. Noel, H.C. Chapple, P. Bougourd.
Goalscorers: Noel (3).

Alderney: Parmentier, W. McLernon (c), H. Newton, Allen, J. Newton, L. McLernon, T. Baker, S. Newton, J. Hammond, P. Collenette, Pasquire.

Newton's injury was subjected to an X-ray investigation at 5.30pm. He received attention at the ground and was transferred to the General Hospital. His leg was broken in two places just above the ankle.

MURATTI FINAL.
30 April 1925, The Cycling Grounds, Guernsey.

Guernsey -2, Jersey -1.

It was estimated that over 1,400 Jersey supporters came over for the match and this was believed to be a record. The organisation at the gate was excellent and the marshalling to the seats was carried out well ensuring that everyone had a view of the game. Their Excellencies the Lieu-Governors of Jersey and of Guernsey arrived shortly before 4 o'clock and were warmly received by the Pavilion patrons in particular. The spectators had been arriving early at the Track for the 1925 Muratti final between Jersey and Guernsey. An hour before the game started a large crowd had assembled and they were being entertained by the band of the DCLI with a series of popular airs.

Jersey came on to the field led by A. Huson to a tumultuous welcome second only to that accorded the Guernsey team when they were led out by G. Symons. Jersey won the toss and defended the East goal. The rain started to come down heavily. Guernsey were first to attack through Collins but Parker cleared into touch. Huson sent Riley away towards the Guernsey goal but the ball was lost. Both midfields began to control the game as it swung from one end to the other. Jersey began to make aggressive raids on the Guernsey goal but they found Chapple and Purdy very steady. The rain, which started an hour before the kick off, was falling more heavily and began to have a treacherous effect on the ball. Jersey looked dangerous when Riley drove in a free kick that beat Watson and struck the crossbar, Garnett followed up and scored after 22 minutes. Guernsey replied to this goal with a

G. SYMONS
(GUERNSEY)

A. HUSON
(JERSEY)

Guernsey 1925.

Mr. J.T. Howcroft.

series of attacks but they were dealt with easily by the Jersey defence. Guernsey were in trouble again when Fenn put a centre plumb into the home goalmouth and Watson was injured in the face when clearing. At this stage Jersey's attackers were more dangerous than Guernsey's and the home team were much on the defensive. Guernsey won a throw in near the Jersey corner flag and this led to a sensational drive from Down right across the Jersey goal. Noel missed the ball, which cannoned off the post and Keyho shot behind. Jersey went on the attack and following a corner Watson pushed away a shot from Fenn. The half ended with Jersey on top and the Guernsey forwards unable to maintain any advantage. Half time Guernsey-0, Jersey-1.

Following their disappointing first half performance Guernsey began the second in a more positive manner. Noel was beginning to attack the Jersey defence and twice Parker had to clear to preserve Jersey's lead. Guernsey were now in command and were beginning to overrun Jersey but were unable to make a telling breakthrough. Garnier saved from Down, then there was a frenzy of excitement when a cross-shot from Meagher was nearly headed into the Jersey net by Parker. Noel then fired in a fine shot that just missed the post. The Guernsey pressure was so intense that the Jersey defenders were kicking the ball anywhere. A fine shot by Collins was saved by Garnier but he could not hold the ball and Noel sent the ball into the Jersey net for the equaliser. Jersey broke away and thought that they had scored but the goal was disallowed for a foul by Marett on Watson. Guernsey returned to the attack and Garnier turned his back as Noel shot but the ball hit his back and was cleared. Noel again worked an opening, ran through, and beat Garnier. His shot rolled towards the net off the goalkeeper and Keyho ran up, to make sure, by smashing the ball into the net with two minutes remaining of the game. When the final whistle blew, Guernsey had won an historic encounter with the score Guernsey-2, Jersey-1.

Guernsey: P. F. Watson, L. Purdy, S. Chapple, J.J. Richardson, G. Symons (c), J. Meager, S. Collins, H. Keyho, S.A. Noel, W.H. Down, H.C. Chapple.
Goalscorer: Noel (2).

Jersey: T. Garnier, A. Huson,(c) Parker, Riley, Folliot, White, Fenn, A.E. Garnett, Le Massurier, Marett, Barker.
Goalscorer: Garnett.

At the final whistle Noel was carried shoulder high and the injured Collins was assisted to the presentation ceremony. The Cup and medals were to be presented to the Guernsey team by Sir John Capper, the Lieut-Governor of Guernsey but he asked if General Bingham, the Lieut-Governor of Jersey, make the presentation and he said that he would be delighted to do so.

The referee, Mr. J.T. Howcroft was interviewed after the game and he said that he was very much surprised at the standard of play. He had not expected it to be so good. It was well up to the standard of anything he had seen on the Continent.

1 9 2 6 .

MURATTI SEMI-FINAL.
15 April 1926, The Cycling Grounds, Guernsey.

Guernsey-1, Jersey-5.

Guernsey's preparation for this match included two matches over the Easter period when they drew 4-4 with Clapton FC on Good Friday and lost 3-2 to St. Albans City on Easter Monday. Guernsey lost the services of W. Warr due to a leg injury and he was replaced by P.H. Bougourd. Jersey lost the services of Jack Le Gresley due to a knee injury as well as Garnett who broke a bone in the leg during the Wanderers v North Wheway Cup tie. The Jersey supporters arrived in St. Peter Port on the 'Reindeer' at 9.20am and by the 'Alberta' at 2.00pm, all smiles but all wet due to the inclement weather during their journey. There was an early deluge as the crowd, estimated between 7,000 and 8,000, made their way down Track lane to the Track for the first round Muratti tie between Guernsey and Jersey. The Band of the DCLI played a selection of music as the fans gathered.

The teams were led out by L. Purdy (Guernsey) and A. Marett (Jersey) and were present-ed to the Lieut-Governor by Mr. F.W. Mourant. (This short ceremony was filmed.) The turf

was on the heavy side following the rain but was in good condition. The opening five minutes saw both sides testing the goalkeepers but with no result. After 7 minutes, Noel lost the ball and from Davis' forward pass the Guernsey defence floundered. Garnett sent in a fast shot, Bird saving on the ground, but St. George followed up and put the ball high into the Guernsey net to put Jersey 1-0 up. Following this reversal, P. Bougourd, Noel and Chapell attacked the Jersey defence at lightening speed and Chapell fired home a great shot that gave Garnier no chance and Guernsey had equalised in 8 minutes. Guernsey maintained the pressure when P. Bougourd put in a centre and Chapell fired in a fast shot that Garnier saved on the goal line at full stretch and under pressure from Noel. As the game progressed Folliott passed the ball to the right and Owen, at the end of a short run, centred low. Purdy kicked out at the ball, mistimed it, and sent the ball into his own net to put Jersey 2-1 up after 16 minutes. Jersey were now in control and should have increased their lead when Marett put the ball past an open Guernsey goal. Chapple was injured after 21 minutes and had to leave the field of play. Folliott, then Garnett, went close for Jersey as they tried to further increase their lead. Chapple returned to the field but was limping badly. A further period of Jersey pressure saw Owen centring high and St. George heading in Jersey's third goal after 25 minutes. Jersey was continuing to have the upper hand but as the half drew to a close Noel and then Chapple came near to reducing the arrears. The first half ended Guernsey-1, Jersey-3.

Guernsey began the second half slightly better but very soon Jersey were once again on top. P. Bougourd took a Guernsey free kick and sent the ball in towards his forwards but they were quickly dispossessed and Folliott sent the ball through to St. George but he was halted by Down. The Guernsey forwards were finding the Jersey defence too sharp and when C. Bougourd sent in a centre Noel was unable to capitalise on a miskick by Huson and Owen cleared the ball. Marett broke through and the Guernsey defence faltered and before they could recover Marett had scored Jersey's fourth goal with an excellent shot that gave Bird no chance. Guernsey tried in vain to breach the Jersey defence with Garnier holding a high shot by C. Bougourd. Bird then had to be sharp to run out to clear and then in a counter attack Chapple was unable to collect a through ball from Spiller. With 9 minutes remaining St. George picked up a square centre to score a fifth Jersey goal. Jersey continued to press on and Bird had to concede a corner in saving from Marrett and as the match neared its end Owen centred and Garnett sent the ball over the bar. In the end Guernsey were routed with the final score being Guernsey-1, Jersey-5.

Guernsey: F.C. Bird, L. Purdy (c), S. Chapple, W.H. Down, Spiller, J. Meager, S. Collins, P. Bougourd, S.A. Noel, H.C. Chapple, C. Bougourd.
Goalscorer: H.C. Chapple.

Jersey: Garnier, A. Huson, Parker, Davis, Folliot, Marriot, Owen, A.E. Garnett, St. George, Marett (c), Barker.
Goalscorers: St. George (3), og, Marett.

This was the first time that Guernsey had suffered a first round defeat and it was a thoroughly deserved victory by a fine Jersey team. After the final whistle a party of Jersey supporters ran on to the field to shoulder their team off. This match was filmed by a cinema man.

There was a note in the 'Weekly Press' in Guernsey stating that Mr. H.G. Bowden had displayed some old photographs of the Muratti in the 'Press' shop window, which attracted an extraordinary amount of public interest.

MURATTI FINAL.
29 April 1926, Springfield Stadium, Jersey.

Jersey -7, Alderney -1.

The 1926 Muratti final was historic in a number of ways. It was the first time that Jersey had played Alderney in a final and it was the first final that did not include Guernsey. Jersey were firm favourites to win the Vase in front of their own Springfield crowd. The Alderney team suffered a blow before the kick off when it transpired that Chappelhow was unable to play as he was on the delayed 'Alberta' and would not arrive in time for the match. The Lieut-Governor of Jersey attended the match along with Sir William H.V. Vernon, the Bailiff of Jersey.

Alderney began the game well and forced two early corners that Jersey had difficulty in clearing. As the game progressed Jersey began to pass the ball more freely but found the Alderney defence resolute and well marshalled by W. McLernon. The Jersey forwards had plenty of possession in the Alderney half but their passing and shooting was weak. After 26 minutes Baker swung a cross in from the left that hit the crossbar and Garnett had a simple task to put the ball into the back of the net to put Jersey 1-0 ahead. Following a throw in Owen went away on a solo run and shot into the Alderney net for the second goal on 31 minutes. Two minutes later Barker sent in a cross that was met by St. George to score Jersey's third. These three goals took the wind out of Alderney's sails but they struggled on. As the rain began to fall Hammond had the misfortune to miss an open goal. Alderney

Alderney team and officials.

ended the half on top and missed another glorious opportunity when S. Newton and L. McLernon were right through. Within a minute Garnier had several shots to get away and from Redhead's centre, S. Newton smashed the ball an inch outside a post. The half ended with the score Jersey- 3, Alderney-0.

Alderney started the second half with the sun at their backs and although the rain had stopped the surface was treacherous. Alderney broke into attack but Davis cleared and within a minute of the re-start Garnett dribbled away on the left and Owen scored Jersey's fourth goal. Alderney replied with a number of attacks but these were dealt with by the Jersey defence. Tommy Baker then gained some applause for a clever dribble on the right and then centred to S. Newton who headed just over the bar. Jersey then increased the pressure with Davis putting his shot just a foot wide from a Garnett cross and then Marrett missed with a simple chance followed by St. George rushing through on a Davis pass only to send his centre round the post. Baker then had a couple of chances for Alderney when he put in a fast shot that went just wide and then Garnier had trouble clearing a further shot from him. Marriot broke away following an Alderney attack sent the ball to Folliott who passed to St. George to score the fifth goal. Jersey continued to press forward and a high St. George centre was put into the net by Owen for a sixth Jersey goal. Hammond scored a consolation goal for Alderney with a point blank shot and in the last minute Jersey completed the scoring when they hit a seventh from a corner. The final score was an emphatic 7-1 victory for Jersey.

Jersey: T. Garnier, Huson, Parker, Davis, Folliot, Marriot, Owen, A.E. Garnett, St. George, Marett (c), Barker.
Goalscorers: Garnett (3), Owen (3), St. George.

Alderney: W. Parmentier, W. McLernon, H. Newton, A. Pasquire, Gadie, Allen, J. Hammond, S. Newton, Redhead, T. Baker, L. McLernon.
Goalscorer: Hammond.

Mr. A.S. Donaldson.

The Cup and medals were presented to the victorious Jersey team by Sir William H.V. Vernon, the Bailiff of Jersey, who was attending his first Muratti. The Bailiff congratulated both teams on the very fine display and they hoped to see Alderney there again. The Lieut-Governor said that he wished to congratulate all on the cleanest and most sporting game he had ever seen. Jersey had completed a fine Muratti double by defeating Guernsey by 5-1 and Alderney by 7-1. They were a fine team and worthy winners of the 1926 Muratti Vase.

The Referee, Mr. A.S. Donaldson, thought that the football was of a very good order and that Jersey was the more polished side. He felt that Alderney did not make the best use of their opportunities but as Jersey were the better team they had the game well in hand.

1 9 2 7 .

MURATTI SEMI-FINAL.
7 April 1927, Westmount, Jersey.

Jersey -3, Alderney -0.

Jersey entertained Alderney at Westmount on 7 April in the first round of the 1927 Muratti Vase competition. Jersey were full of confidence following their superb perform-ances in annexing the trophy so convincingly in 1926 but Alderney were keen to erase the memory of that final.

T. Garnier had asked not to be selected for this match and he was replaced by Thornton in the Jersey goal. He was the son of T.J. Thornton who earned five caps between 1906 and 1909 for Jersey.

On a fairly good pitch and in a heavy wind, both teams had a rousing reception from the crowd of around 4,000. Alderney won the toss and played with the wind. From an early Jersey corner Pasquire nearly shot into his own goal but fortunately for him the ball went wide. The play was very scrappy with the tendency of both teams to play the ball in the air and the Jersey attacks were floundering against a strong Alderney defence. The play was going from end to end with Hurel being the most effective of the Jersey attackers and L. McLernon the pick of the Alderney forwards. Alderney began to gain the upper hand and when Barker went off injured Thornton, in the Jersey goal, had to save from Rose and had difficulty in getting the ball away when L. McLernon charged him off his feet. Alderney were doing all the pressing at this stage and L. McLernon shot just inches wide. Barker

Alderney team and officials. 1927.

returned as Alderney swarmed round the Jersey goal. Marett was the next casualty and, he too, was carried off. Jersey were finding their opponents pretty tough to tackle. Marett returned after 35 minutes. The Alderney attacks continued and the Jersey defence were not too confident in their clearances but still managed to prevent a score and the half ended Jersey-0, Alderney-0.

The second half began with Alderney continuing to play their aggressive style that upset the usual smooth play of the Jersey team. In the 48th minute, however, Garnett came through from a Marett pass, and from a bunch of players, fired the ball into the net to put Jersey 1-0 up. This goal gave Jersey the lift that they needed and after 51 minutes St. George scored a second goal. The game lost much of its pace after this goal although Alderney continued to push forward in an attempt to score with S. Newton prominent. Jersey came close again when Parmentier saved a hard cross drive from Hurel. With 15 minutes remaining Jersey's Barker had to leave the field. In the last minute Marett scored a third goal and the game ended Jersey-3, Alderney-0.

Jersey: Thornton, Freeman, Parker, Davis, Folliot, Troy, St. George, A.E. Garnett, Barker, Marett (c), Barker.
Goalscorers: St. George, Garnett, Marett.

Alderney: W. Parmentier, W. McLernon (c), H. Newton, A. Pasquire, E. Jones, J. Rose, J. Hammond, J. Ogden, S. Newton, L. McLernon, A. Newman.

A. MARETT
(Captain of the Jersey Team.)

MR. F. H. ROWLANDS, REFEREE.

W. McLERNON
(Captain of the Alderney Team.)

MURATTI FINAL.
28 April 1927, The Cycling Grounds, Guernsey.

Guernsey -1, Jersey -0.

A very large crowd was packed into the Track for the 1927 Muratti Vase final between Guernsey and Jersey and they looked forward to a tight struggle. Following Guernsey's 5-1 defeat the previous year there were wholesale changes in their side. It was noted that this was the youngest team to have appeared in the Muratti competition. Mauger, Leadbeater,

Noel (Guernsey) spun the coin and Marett (Jersey) guessed correctly and chose
to play into the west goal.

Dorey, Heulin, Barrassin and Solway all played for the Junior Muratti team in 1926. Prior
to the commencement of the game both teams were presented to Major-General the Hon.
Sir Francis Bingham (Lieut-Governor of Jersey) and Major-General the Hon. Sir Charles
Sackville-West (Lieut-Governor of Guernsey).Play was rather wild as both sides tried to
gain an early advantage. Guernsey seemed to settle quicker causing the Jersey defence to
hurry their clearances. The home side were soon on the attack and Warr sent a pass to
Barrassin who immediately transferred it to Solway who was charging through but Harben
cleared the danger. Goodrich picked up the ball and put St. George through but he put his
high shot just wide. The Guernsey defence were having trouble coping with the play of
Marett and Garnett but Bougourd was holding firm. After 11 minutes Dorey was brought
down by Mauger and from the centre Noel got within an ace of scoring. Guernsey continued to press and Leadbeater put in a fierce drive that scraped the crossbar. Jersey responded and from a clever free kick by Parker, Garnett headed the ball against the post. The play
was fast and furious but Guernsey seemed to be more in control although the Jersey
defence were holding firm with Harben outstanding. The first half ended Guernsey-0,
Jersey-0.

 The second half began at the same fierce pace. Guernsey started to pressurise the Jersey
goal, the move broke down and Goodrich fired in a high shot that Bird had to punch away.
The Jersey midfield was beginning to tighten up their game and were becoming more successful in thwarting the Guernsey advances. Guernsey set up an attack with Solway swinging the ball in, Mauger returned it to Barrassin who headed it into the Jersey net with 56

A Jersey throw-in from the stand side.

minutes having been played. There then followed some sustained Guernsey pressure with Solway shooting over and Thornton saving from Noel. Jersey survived this pressure and Bird had to save a low drive from St. George. This was followed by Folliott shooting high over from a free kick. The first corner of the match was won by Jersey after 61 minutes as Jersey pushed on for an equaliser. The game was becoming more even although Bird was having more to do than Thornton. Solway was putting in a lot of centres but most of these were well dealt with by the Jersey defence. Jersey thought that they had equalised when, following an attack that left Marett prostrate on the Guernsey goal line, the ball was rolling towards the Guernsey goal, Marett got up and blasted the ball in. The referee disallowed the goal for Marett being offside. The referee explained later that had Marett stayed on the ground and the ball had crossed the line, then a goal would have been awarded as Marett was deemed not to have been interfering with play. But as Marett got up and played the ball he was immediately in an offside position and the goal could not stand. As the game neared its end Garnett sent in a great drive that was tipped over by Bird. The final score in a close and hard fought match was Guernsey-1, Jersey-0.

Guernsey: F.C. Bird, P. Bougourd, W. Huelin, W.H. Down, W. Warr, A. Leadbeater, D. Mauger, S.A. Noel (c), H. Dorey, W. Barrasin, C. Solway.
Goalscorer: Barrasin.

Jersey: Thornton, Harben, Parker, Davis, Folliot, White, St. George, Godrich, A.E. Garnett, A. Marett (c), Hurel.

Introduced by Mr. H.H. Randell, President of the GFA, the Lieut-Governor of Jersey presented the Muratti Vase to Noel. His Excellency, who was popularly received, said he had seen a capital game. He eulogised the value of sport and after a brief commentary on the spirit of goodwill between the islands, presented the coveted vase and medals. The afternoon closed with a furore of cheering.

A simple but nevertheless an impressive little ceremony was enacted at the Island War Memorial at 2.30pm on Thursday afternoon, when the whole of the Jersey team with officials led by Mr. James Marquis, President of the Jersey FA, and A. Marett, captain of the team, formed in procession to place a beautiful wreath in memory of the Guernsey footballers who gave their lives in the war. The wreath, of a red, green and white colour scheme, which was supplied by Mr. A.E. Parsons, was laid by Mr. Marquis. The inscription was:-

'In remembrance from Jersey football teams and supporters, Muratti Day 1927.'

1 9 2 8 .

MURATTI SEMI-FINAL.
19 April 1928, The Cycling Grounds, Guernsey.

Guernsey -4, Alderney -0.

Guernsey and Alderney met in the Muratti first round at the Track on 19 April 1928. Guernsey had had an indifferent preparation for the competition whereas confidence was high with Alderney following their excellent displays against the Queen's Own in trial matches. The Guernsey team that was chosen has set a record when nine players from North were representing their island. The North players are L. Purdy, P. Bougourd, W.A. Warr (capt.), A.C. Leadbeater, H. Trustum, S.A. Noel, H. Dorey, W. Barrasin and C. Solway. This equalled the Channel Islands record.

The referee for this match was Stanley Rous and following the toss up Guernsey chose to play into the eastern goal. The 4,000 crowd prepared to cheer their favourites as the match began. Alderney started to bustle their opponents from the first moment and it was soon apparent that their policy was to hustle the Guernsey players out of their game. As usual the opening moments were a little erratic as the pace began to pick up. Guernsey were the first onto the attack from a throw in where Leadbeater crossed in high and Dorey headed goalwards where Parmentier, the Alderney goalkeeper, headed over. In a further attack Parmentier ran out to clear but Warr came up, driving from 30 yards to score Guernsey's first goal after 6 minutes. A free kick from Purdy found Dorey who scored a second with a flashing shot that gave Parmentier no chance. It was an unfortunate opening for Alderney as they were put under more pressure and Noel hit the crossbar with a fine shot. The game was 19 minutes old when Bevan in the Guernsey goal touched the ball. Guernsey were in total control with Dorey flashing a shot wide and Barrassin heading onto the crossbar from a Trustum corner. Alderney were trying hard to stem this tide but from a Solway centre, Dorey shot hard but Parmentier brought off a great save as the spectators applauded. Despite the almost continuous pressure, the Alderney defence doggedly survived the furious onslaught. The game was stopped when Dorey received a kick in the face, being knocked out and carried off in dead silence. Alderney attempted some attacks but they were repulsed and soon they were back in defence. Dorey returned with his head bandaged and received a tumultuous reception. The first half ended Guernsey-2, Alderney-0.

Alderney. 1928.

The second half was similar to the first with Guernsey pressing and Alderney counter attacking in breakaways. The pace of the game began to slow and the Alderney full backs, H. Newton and Chapelhow, began clearing long for their forwards to run on to but the home defence held. Chappelhow was called into action when he stopped a straight drive from Dorey and following a corner from the left Warr headed Solway's cross goalwards only for it to be kicked clear from the near post by H. Newton. Guernsey's third goal came after 62 minutes when Down scored with a cross shot. The Alderney goal had further scares and from a Dorey-Noel move Barrassin scored from close range after 72 minutes. The closing minutes of the game were spent round the Alderney goal but with no more scoring the game ended Guernsey-4, Alderney-0.

Guernsey: F.C. Bevan, L. Purdy, P. Bougourd,
             W.H. Down, W. Warr (c), A. Leadbeater,
             H. Trustum, S.A. Noel, H. Dorey, W. Barrasin,
             C. Solway.
             Goalscorers: Warr, Dorey, Down, Noel.

Alderney: Parmentier (c), H. Newton, Chappelhow,
             Pasquire, J. Rose, Caplain, Willey, Simon,
             J. Newton, S. Newton, Mesney.

It is interesting to note that the referee for this match, Mr. Stanley Rous, was in later years to become the Secretary to the Football Association and ultimately, as Sir Stanley Rous, the President of FIFA for a number of years. He became one of the world's most influential and respected administrators.

Stanley Rous.

MURATTI FINAL.
3 May 1928, Springfield Stadium, Jersey.

Jersey -2, Guernsey -1. aet.

On Wednesday 2 May the members of the Guernsey team marched to the Cenotaph in the Royal Parade and, on behalf of the Guernsey Football Association, placed a wreath at the foot of the Cenotaph. The wreath was composed of white flowers with green and white ribbons and the attached card bore the following inscription 'A tribute of admiration and respect from the Guernsey Football Association to Jersey's Glorious Dead. Their name liveth for evermore.'

The Guernsey team were reported fit and well. They took things easy in the morning, went out in cars in the country and played skittles. In the afternoon as the crowds made their way to Springfield a band led the procession into St. Helier with trumpets going, and causing a great stir.

The teams were led out by Davis (Jersey) and Warr (Guernsey) and the match was refereed by Mr. H.P. Morley. Once again North provided nine of the Guernsey team. Warr won the toss and decided to play into the east goal. The match started at a furious pace and both goals were soon under attack, as the early play swung from end to end. Solway nearly broke through the Jersey defence but was stopped by Harben and then Carter, in the Jersey goal, saved a shot from Dorey. Carter's clearance found J, De Gresley whose rush for goal was cleared by Leadbeater. As the pace continued, Noel flashed in a great shot from the right and Carter saved well. Barrassin then fired in two furious shots that were charged down by McAvoy. Bevan was then under pressure from a well placed McAvoy free kick

Guernsey supporters outside the British Hotel, St. Helier.

Match action at Springfield.

but he managed to punch the ball away. Guernsey were playing well when after 30 minutes Noel was right through and Harben pushed the ball with his hand and a penalty was awarded to Guernsey. Dorey miskicked on taking the penalty and the Jersey crowd went mad with delight. In a Jersey attack Bevan punched away from O'Neill's corner, then the crowd were vastly amused when Bougourd's clearance knocked out the referee. In defending a Jersey attack, Purdy miskicked, and with Bevan beaten, Folliott fired the ball towards the net but Down saved the day with a spectacular overhead kick. This pressure was maintained and following a great scramble in the Guernsey goalmouth, Folliott scored the opening goal for Jersey. The half time whistle came with the score Jersey-1, Guernsey-0.

Guernsey began fast in the second half as they went in pursuit of an equaliser. Carter fumbled Bougourd's free kick but cleared the danger and a fine drive by Down landed on the roof of the Jersey net. Carter was in action again when, on the goal line, he saved a shot from Solway. This pace continued with O'Neill finding H. le Gresley who fired his shot wide. Guernsey responded when Solway lobbed the ball over to Dorey who headed it into the net for the equaliser. The game if anything got faster as first Bevan and then Carter were pressurised by the forwards. Guernsey pushed on for the last few minutes of the game but it ended with the score Jersey-1, Guernsey-1.

In extra time the first chance fell to Solway but his shot was saved by Carter. Guernsey maintained this pressure and Carter was forced to punch away for a corner then Dorey shot just over the bar, and Garnett missed by inches with a fine shot. Solway then almost scored when Carter miskicked. There were chances at both ends but at the change over the score remained Jersey-1, Guernsey-1.

In the 3rd minute of the second period of extra time Folliott scored Jersey's second goal. The Guernsey team continued to press forward and Noel sent his header over as the home defence held out. There was no more scoring and the match ended Jersey-2, Guernsey-1

Jersey: Carter, Harben, McAvoy, Newington, Davis (c), White, O'Neill,
           A.E. Garnett, Folliot, H.F. Le Gresley, J.W. Le Gresley.
           Goalscorer: Folliot (2).

Guernsey: F.C. Bevan, L. Purdy, P. Bougourd, W.H. Down, W. Warr (c),
           A. Leadbeater, H. Trustum, S.A. Noel, H. Dorey, W. Barrasin, C. Solway.
           Goalscorer: Dorey.

It was pointed out after the game that Folliott had played for over an hour with a broken collarbone.

The Muratti Vase and gold medals were presented to the victorious Jersey side. Following the match the Jersey and Guernsey teams were the guests of the YMCA Football Club at a non-stop carnival dance at West's Ballroom.

1 9 2 9 .

MURATTI SEMI-FINAL.
18 April 1929, Westmount, Jersey.

Jersey -1, Guernsey -7.

Westmount was the scene of another tense struggle for football supremacy between Jersey and Guernsey, the meeting being the first round of the Muratti Vase competition. The match was played on 18 April under a hot Jersey sun. Guernsey caused a surprise when they played Len Purdy, usually a defender, as centre forward. North supplied seven players to the Guernsey side.

The two teams were soon testing each other during the opening minutes of the game and the first incident of note was when McAvoy conceded a corner when he diverted Solway's furious shot. Jersey replied when Folliott put the ball to Rouxin who passed to Benest and he fired in a shot that was saved by Helyar. Guernsey attacked and Purdy headed the ball over to Noel who scored after 9 minutes.

Jersey was playing a long kicking game but the Guernsey defence were holding firm. Following a corner by Mauger, Carter pushed the ball out; Solway lifted it back to Barrassin who scored Guernsey's second after 14 minutes.

The Jersey defence were under severe pressure with Barrassin heading against the bar, Purdy then shot against the goalkeeper and Carter conceded a corner with a wonderful save from a Noel shot. Jersey weathered this crisis and Rouxin scored a fine goal after 33 minutes. Barrassin restored Guernsey's two-goal lead when he headed in from a Mauger cross. The half time score was Jersey-1, Guernsey-3.

The second half began with both teams pressing for an early advantage. Carter was soon in action saving from Noel and Barrassin. The Guernsey full backs, Lewis and Heulin, were having splendid games and preventing the Jersey forwards from advancing too much. The Guernsey attacking continued and Mauger fired in a superb shot that Carter got his fingers to but could not keep out to put Guernsey 4-1 up after 62 minutes. Jersey rallied for a short time but again Guernsey broke away and Mauger centred for Noel to score the fifth

Guernsey supporters watch from the pavilion.

Carter (Jersey) clears a Mauger centre.

goal. Five minutes from the end Barrassin scored a 6th. Jersey began to put some pressure on the Guernsey defence as the game neared its end Noel picked the ball up on the edge of his penalty area and slipped it to Danny Mauger on the right wing. Mauger broke away on his own and as Noel raced up to support him, he received Mauger's pass and crashed an unstoppable shot from 25 yards that left Carter helpless in the Jersey goal to record His third and Guernsey' seventh goal. Jersey had gone to pieces and the game ended Jersey-1, Guernsey-7.

Barrasin scoring Guernsey's second goal.

Jersey: Carter, Harben, McAvoy, Newington, Folliot,
           White, O'Neill, A.E. Garnett, Rouxin,
           H.V. Benest, Hocquard (c).
           Goalscorer: Rouxin.

Guernsey: A. Helyar, J.A. Lewis, W. Huelin, W.H. Down,
           W. Warr (c), F.C. Bird, D. Mauger, S.A. Noel,
           L. Purdy,   W. Barrasin, C. Solway.
           Goalscorers: Mauger, Noel (3), Barrasin (3).

One of Guernsey's keenest supporters at the match was a well-known popular officer of
the RGLI Services Battalion who arrived from Canada in the morning. On being informed
by one of his old colleagues that it was Muratti Day, he at once made up his mind that he
must support the Guernsey team. After paying a short visit to his relatives, he joined the
happy band of excursionists on the 'Lorina' and to quote his own words, had one of the
days of his life.

MURATTI FINAL.
2 May 1929, The Cycling Grounds, Guernsey.

Guernsey -5, Alderney -0.

From early on Thursday afternoon on 2 May 1929 thousands were flooding up Track Lane to witness the Muratti final between Guernsey and Alderney. The majority of the 4,000 crowd were there to view the Guernsey team that so convincingly defeated Jersey at Westmount, but history has showed that you should never take Alderney lightly as 1920 proved.

Before the match the teams were presented to Lord Sackville, the Lieut-Governor of Guernsey.

A boisterous wind blew across the field but assisted the side playing into the west goal. Guernsey won the toss and Alderney kicked off with the wind behind them. Early on, from a throw in, Purdy collected the ball and hit a shot that struck the bar, Parmentier came out but Solway forced him off the ball. Before the defence could recover Solway sent the ball into the net, with a fast low shot to give Guernsey a 1-0 lead.

Alderney recovered from this start and began to push into the Guernsey half and gained a corner that the wind carried out. Guernsey returned to the Alderney area and Parmentier saved well from Purdy. Solway was causing a lot of problems with his excellent corner kicks and Chapelhow was having difficulty dealing with them. The second Guernsey goal

Lord Sackville meeting the Alderney players.

came in 18 minutes after some fine dribbling
from Solway, followed by a centre that
Parmentier tried to divert but Purdy raced in and
crashed a shot high into the net. Most of the play
was now taking place in the Alderney half with
an occasional breakaway that kept the Guernsey
defence on their toes. The half ended with
Barrassin scoring but the goal was disallowed
for offside. The half time score was Guernsey-2,
Alderney-0.

Solway. (Guernsey)

Guernsey had the wind behind them as they
started the second half and set up some good
attacking moves that were well defended by
Alderney. McLernon and Rose were prominent
as their midfield broke up the Guernsey moves.
The second half was proving to be more even as
Alderney pushed on in an attempt to reduce the arrears. However, after 57 minutes
Guernsey scored their 3rd goal when Mauger centred for Barrassin to score. Mauger
repeated this feat in the 62nd minute when he again centred for Barrassin to score goal
number four. Guernsey were now in complete control and they were containing Alderney's
attacks well. After 79 minutes Noel gathered a pass from Purdy, Parmentier came out and
Noel ran past him to score Guernsey's fifth goal. That completed the scoring and Guernsey
won the Muratti Vase with a final score of Guernsey-5, Alderney-0.

Guernsey: A. Helyar, J.A. Lewis, W. Huelin, W,H, Down, W. Warr (c), F.C. Bird,
             D. Mauger, S.A. Noel, L. Purdy, W. Barrasin, C. Solway.
             Goalscorers: Solway, Purdy, Barrasin (2), Noel.

Alderney: Parmentier, H. Newton, Chappelhow, J. Rose, McLernon, Pasquire,
             Hammond, Barker, S. Newton, J. Newton, Baker.

A few seconds after the end of the game the roped enclosure was thronged by thousands
to see the trophy presented. After the opening speeches Warr received the Vase from Lord
Sackville amid loud applause. Named individually by Mr. Eveson (Secretary of the Inter-
Insular Committee), each player came up to receive a medal as well as a due ovation. It
ended in sustained cheering – three for Alderney led by Warr; three for the winners led by
H. Newton (Alderney's captain), and three for Lord Sackville led by Mr. Randell (President
of the GFA).

The Muratti Vase Competition during the 1920's was very close between Jersey and
Guernsey. Jersey won 4 and Guernsey won 5 with Alderney winning in 1920. This made
the running totals Guernsey 12 wins, Jersey 7 wins and Alderney 1 win. This decade was
very successful for Alderney for not only did they win the Muratti Vase in 1920 they also
won the Peace Cup in 1920 and 1924.

Alderney attacks the Guernsey goal.

Guernsey. 1929.

6

1930 - 1939

1 9 3 0 .

It was reported that Sydney Charles Chapple (age 32) died tragically on 4 April 1930. He left a widow and five children. The ex-Muratti player played for both Belgrave Wanderers and Rangers during his career. Sid played nine times for Guernsey winning two Muratti medals. The Guernsey Football Association decided that the takings from the forthcoming Martinez Cup match would be set aside for his family.

MURATTI SEMI-FINAL.
10 April 1930, The Cycling Grounds, Guernsey.

Alderney -2, Jersey -3.

The Alderney team arrived in Guernsey on 9 April onboard the Riduna. They were accompanied by Mr. A. Depres and Mr. C.H. Richards. The team and the reserves travelled to their headquarters in the Channel Islands Hotel

Davis leads out the Jersey team.

Jennings (Alderney) under pressure.

Jersey selected E.F. Le Feuvre, the 17-year old Victoria College schoolboy, to lead their attack and gain his first Muratti cap. There was a large crowd in the ground that was continuing to swell as the teams came out. H. Newton (Alderney) and Davis (Jersey) lead their teams on to the field.

Alderney began the match quicker and more effectively than Jersey and very soon Allchin, the Jersey goalkeeper, was called into action when he saved from J. Newton. Alderney's bright start had the crowd on its toes as the early excitement grew. After 4 minutes S. Newton rushed in from the wing and the crowd burst into a deafening roar as he scored for Alderney. From the re-start J. Newton broke away and fired a shot into Allchin's arms. Jersey began to recover from Alderney's fine start and were soon attacking with young Le Feuvre putting in a high shot that Jennings saved. As the match became more even Le Feuvre scored the equaliser for Jersey after 9 minutes. Alderney set up a series of attacks and S. Newton centred low, and Hurel miskicked, Allchin stayed on his goal line and Randal fired in a low shot that Allchin could not stop to give Alderney a 2-1 lead after 16 minutes. This second goal unsettled Jersey for a while as Alderney took control. Jersey then came back into the game but found the Alderney defence in good form with Chapelhow and Baker prominent. As the game progressed both defences were getting on top and this was causing the forwards to rush their shots.

As half time approached Jersey forced an attack and during a scramble in front of the Alderney goal Le Feuvre scored the Jersey equaliser in the 41st minute. As the half ended Le Feuvre was injured and was carried off. After an excellent first half the score was Alderney-2, Jersey-2.

In the second half Jersey were relieved to have Le Feuvre back in the line up. The game continued in the same vein as the first half with both teams pushing for the crucial third goal. The deadlock was nearly broken when Jersey's Hefford went clear but saw his fine shot come back off the bar. The Jersey pressure began to increase and the Alderney defence came under an intense siege. In the 52nd minute Elliot and Le Feuvre forced the ball into the centre and Garnett met the ball from close in and put Jersey in the lead for the first time in the match. Jersey began to take more control of the game and was pushing Alderney back. Shots were raining into the Alderney goal with Jennings having to save twice in a short space of time followed by a Jersey shot hitting the post and a further three attempts being charged down by the Alderney defence. Despite this superiority Jersey were once again having trouble with the Alderney rearguard and could not build on their slender lead. As the game neared its end J. Newton nearly equalised and then Allchin was knocked out saving from Randal. Allchin resumed and had to save again from J. Newton and then Willey as Alderney put in a grandstand finish in search of the equaliser. Jersey held out to win a pulsating contest as the final score read Alderney-2, Jersey-3.

Alderney: Jennings, Chappelhow, Baker, Pasquire, H. Newton (c), J. Rose, S. Newton, Willey, J. Newton, McLernon, Randall.
Goalscorers: S. Newton, Randall.

Jersey: Alchin, Harben, Hurel, Boyd, Davis (c), Cummins, A.E. Garnett, Martin, E.F. Le Feuvre, Hefford, Elliot.
Goalscorers: Le Feuvre (2), Garnett.

Once again in this match Alderney proved that they were a match for both of the larger islands and could hold their own in this company. Jersey was fortunate to have included the young Le Feuvre in their side and he proved a match-winner with two goals.

MURATTI FINAL.
1 May 1930, Springfield Stadium, Jersey.

Jersey -2, Guernsey -3.

Following his two-goal performance against Alderney it was no surprise that the Jersey team once again included Le Feuvre, the Victoria College schoolboy to lead their attack and the team also had H.V. Benest, an ex-Victorian and now of Oxford, as outside left. The Guernsey team, Mr. E.C. Rich who was in charge of the Guernsey team, showed three changes to the side that defeated Jersey 7-1 at Westmount in 1929. The Guernsey team included three new caps in A. Toms in goal along with J.S. Brookes and W.C. Freeman both of Rangers. W.C. Freeman, appeared as a goalkeeper for Guernsey in the Star Trophy schoolboy match against Jersey in 1923 and 1924, he then played left back in the Junior Muratti's of 1926 and 1927.

W.C. Freeman.

Jersey was invaded on Thursday 1 May by a great throng of Guernseymen (and women) rallying around the Sarnians for their match with Jersey. The Guernsey team ran out to a good ovation, but there was a deafening roar from the thousands of Jerseymen when their favourites entered the field. Guernsey won the toss and played into the west goal. The game started at a furious pace with Jersey the first into their stride with some forceful runs from Benest down the wing. The Guernsey defence were, with some difficulty, holding the Jersey attacks thanks mainly to Down and Warr. For the first 10 minutes Jersey were the superior team but Guernsey started to get more into the game and W. Freeman soon tested Allchin, who saved well. Le Feuvre replied for Jersey with a fine shot that Toms saved magnificently as the game was becoming more even. Jersey were making good chances but their final shots were weak and they were to pay for this just after the half hour mark. Freeman swung in a clever pass to Mauger who put in a centre; Dorey saw the opening and fired in a shot to put Guernsey 1-0 up. Guernsey immediately returned to the attack and the Jersey defence crashed badly as Dorey dribbled through and passed to Brookes who scored Guernsey's second after 37 minutes. Warr then scored a third with a brilliant shot after 40 minutes. Jersey had completely gone to pieces as the Guernsey forwards rained in shots from all angles with Allchin performing heroics. It was a great relief for Jersey as the half time whistle sounded and although the score did not truly reflect the half, Guernsey had made the most of their chances whereas Jersey passed up similar opportunities. The half-time score was Jersey-0, Guernsey-3.

The second half began with Jersey facing an uphill task to get back into the game. The pace was slower than the first half as Benest and Garnett tried to work the ball down the wings, but the Guernsey defence held out. Jersey began to take the game to Guernsey and were finally successful after 67 minutes when Carpenter scored a splendid goal. Play was even for a while but with 14 minutes remaining, following a sustained period of Jersey pressure, Garnett went on a fine solo run and scored a second goal to once again reduce the arrears for Jersey. The game went on at a furious pace with Dorey and Down coming close for Guernsey followed by a shot from Le Feuvre that just went over the bar. This breathtaking match finally finished Jersey-2, Guernsey-3.

Jersey: Alchin, Harben, Freeman, O'Neill, Davis (c), White, A.E. Garnett, Martin, E.F. Le Feuvre, Carpenter, H.V. Benest.
              Goalscorers: Garnett, Carpenter.

Guernsey: A. Toms, P. Bougourd, W. Huelin, W.H. Down, W. Warr (c), F.C. Bird, D. Mauger, J.S. Brookes, H. Dorey, W.C. Freeman, C. Solway.
              Goalscorers: Brookes, Warr, Dorey.

The Vase was presented to Warr, the Guernsey captain, by Major-General E.H. Willis, Lieut-Governor of Jersey. The game was summed up as being packed with thrills and great excitement, providing a remarkable amount of good football that befitted the occasion. Guernsey's success was due to a temporary collapse of the Jersey defence about 8 minutes towards the end of the first half. The recovery after the interval was a wonderfully splendid achievement and in fairness it must be said that the losers deserved as much praise as the winners.

In Guernsey a large crowd had assembled in Smith Street where selected points of the match were being relayed and by 4.30pm the crowd had grown to around 2,000.

1 9 3 1 .

MURATTI SEMI-FINAL.
16 April 1931, Springfield Stadium, Jersey.

Alderney -0, Guernsey -1.

Guernsey met Alderney on 16 April 1931 at Springfield in the first round of the Muratti competition. On the evidence of last years match with Jersey, Alderney was going to be a difficult proposition for Guernsey.

Guernsey won the toss and Alderney kicked off and very quickly attacked the Guernsey defence, this was repulsed and Dorey and Barrassin set up a counter attack. Neither side were gaining the upper hand and although Guernsey was playing the more open football the Alderney defence easily coped. As the game progressed Barrassin put Solway clear and, from the wingers centre, Dorey headed just over. After 20 minutes Jennings pulled off a sensational save from Warren to keep the score 0-0 and following a Guernsey free-kick Dorey closed in only to see his header tipped over by the Alderney keeper. Helyer then proved his worth by catching a long drive from McLernon. The play was very ragged with the Alderney defence, with Jennings outstanding, breaking up most of the Guernsey attacks. Alderney then came close but Robins quickly cleared the danger before they could capitalise and this chance was followed by a cross drive from Alderney's Duplain that went just wide. Dorey then came very close when he fired in a header following a free-kick only

MURATTI SEMI-FINAL, 1931.

to see Jennings tip the ball over for a corner. Barrasin then fired in a fast low shot that just shaved the outside of the Alderney post for a goal-kick. Guernsey were settling down and their attacks had more rhythm and from one of them Dorey fired in a low shot that just went wide of the Alderney post. As the half neared its end Chapelhow fed Barker but his long-range drive went over and at half time the score was Guernsey-0, Alderney-0.

 For the second half Guernsey had the advantage of the wind behind them. They used this well and Barrassin centred for Dorey but his header went past the post. Dorey was injured in this attack and had to leave the field. The ten men Guernsey side kept up the pressure but were continually repulsed by a resolute Alderney defence. Jennings again produced a fine save from a quick shot but Chapelhow was injured during the clearance but resumed after treatment. Dorey later returned to the game but was limping. The game was now becoming a case of the Guernsey forwards against the Alderney defence with drives by Barrassin, Solway and Freeman being charged down. The pressure on the Alderney defence continued and from a Solway centre Mauger missed an open goal from 8 yards. The game was developing into a struggle between the Guernsey attack and the Alderney defence and in one of the attacks Guernsey's Barrasin was injured by heavy challenge but resumed after treatment. By this time Dorey was nothing more than a passenger and was contributing little to the Guernsey cause. As the pace of the game increased there was a further stoppage for an injury as Warren and an Alderney defender went down after a clash of heads but fortunately both were able to resume. The game seemed to be heading for a draw when Freeman scored for Guernsey with a shot that went in off a defender with only two minutes to go. The Guernsey team were very relieved and at the final whistle the score was Alderney-0, Guernsey-1.

Guernsey: A. Helyar, P.H. Bougourd, W. Huelin (c), F.E. Robins, E.J. Warren, F.C. Bird, D. Mauger, W. Barrasin, H. Dorey, W.C. Freeman, C. Solway. Goalscorer: Freeman (pictured)

Alderney: G. Jennings, G. Chappelhow, H. Newton (c), Catts, J. Newton, J. Rose, A. Duplain, W. Barker, S. Newton, L. McLernon, W. Randall.

This was a very hard fought Muratti with not a lot between the teams. Despite defending for much of the match Alderney equipped themselves very well. Once again there was a large crowd of at least 2,000 in Smith Street to listen to the highlights by Mr. George Keyho. As the game neared its end Mr Keyho announced 'Ladies and Gentlemen, we have something at last to announce to you.' A few voices cried 'Alderney has scored' But it was not so as the score Alderney -0, Guernsey-1 was read out amidst loud cheers.

C. Solway's Muratti Cap.

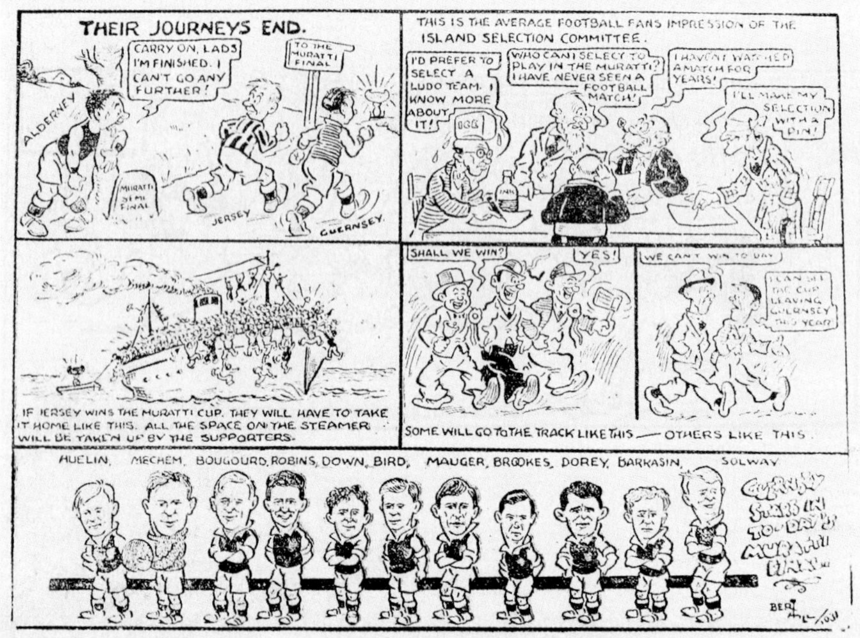

MURATTI FINAL.
30 April 1931, The Cycling Grounds, Guernsey.

Guernsey -2, Jersey -4.

There were lively scenes at the White Rock when the Lorina brought a contingent of Jersey supporters to Guernsey for the match. The fans were in great spirits and were singing and cheering as the steamer entered St. Peter Port Harbour. They speedily disembarked by the three gangways, though this was not quick enough for some of the more adventurous supporters who jumped over the side of the boat.

Guernsey's Lieut-Governor, the Lord Ruthvane and Lady Ruthvane were joined by Major-General E.H. Willis, the Lieut-Governor of Jersey, Mrs Willis and Judge R.W. Mellish OBE of Alderney at the Muratti Vase Final. Before the kick-off both teams were presented to the Lieut-Governors by Mr. H.H. Randell, President of the GFA. Among the spectators were T. Oliver and J. Hammond, former Muratti stars.

Before a record crowd, estimated at 12,000, Guernsey entertained Jersey at the Track for the Muratti Vase. The game started tentatively as the players edged their way into the game. In an early Guernsey attack Dorey went on a solo run and scored after 2 minutes. Guernsey almost scored again when Down fed Brookes who crossed in for Dorey but he spooned the ball over from close in. Jersey replied and Garnett almost scored but the ball was cleared by Heulin. As the play became faster Garnett sent a shot over the bar as Jersey chased an equaliser. Robins almost doubled Guernsey's lead when he sent in a terrific drive

Part of the large crowd awaits the beginning of the Muratti Vase Final.

that was saved by Burtenshaw. Jersey equalised after 22 minutes when Carpenter headed a goal from a left wing cross. Guernsey almost regained the lead when Mauger sent in a flying shot that produced a remarkable save from Burtenshaw. Jersey was holding out against a veritable bombardment from the Guernsey attack but their defence was magnificent. The remainder of the half was very even and it ended with the score Guernsey-1, Jersey-1.

Guernsey began the second half quickly in an attempt to score an early goal but although Brookes and Dorey both got their heads to a Mauger cross ball they could not convert. Jersey was then awarded a free-kick and Davis sent the ball into the Guernsey goal-mouth and Mauger cleared in the face of a dangerous rush of Jersey players. Mauger then created an opening following a clever dribble and he sent the ball to Solway, who in turn whipped in a centre that was met by the onrushing Mauger who had found an excellent position, but his attempt skimmed the crossbar. There were clearances at both ends before Garnett, in a solo breakaway, drew Mechem and scored Jersey's second goal after 53 minutes. Guernsey nearly equalised within a minute when Solway got away on the left and put in a fine centre into the Jersey goalmouth where, following a furious melee almost on the goal line, Jersey's White scooped the ball safely in to touch. Guernsey pushed on for the equaliser and Burtenshaw pushed over a magnificent free kick from Heulin. The pressure continued and Brookes broke away on the right and put in a centre that Dorey fired into the Jersey net after 58 minutes to equalise. This goal inspired Guernsey and they produced a sustained onslaught on the Jersey goal. Dorey again collected the ball and went on a solo run but, as he was tackled, the ball broke to Mauger and, as Hurel raced over to clear, the ball found Solway and he centred across the Jersey goal where Burtenshaw brilliantly fisted clear. Jersey weathered this storm and it was the Guernsey defence's turn to show their worth. There were clearances at both ends as Guernsey started to get the upper hand once more but Burtenshaw kept the forwards out as the home team forced a series of corners. Solway, again in the thick of the action, forced a corner off Freeman and he sent in his cross and Mauger missed an excellent chance to score by putting his effort over the bar. The game was then held up for a time as Guernsey's Bird was injured and had to be carried off the field. As the match was nearing its end Garnett scored a third goal for Jersey with one minute left of the game. This was followed quickly by Pincott who scored just on time to bring a remarkable end to a fine game with a final score of Guernsey-2, Jersey-4.

Guernsey: D. Mechem, P. Bougourd, W. Huelin, F.E. Robins, F.C. Bird, W.H. Down, D. Mauger, J.S. Brookes, H. Dorey, W. Barrasin, W.C. Freeman.
Goalscorer: Dorey (2).

Jersey: Burtenshaw, Freeman, Hurel, White, Davis (c), Cummins, Pincott, Carpenter, A.E. Garnett, Le Feuvre, Le Gresley.
Goalscorers: Carpenter, Le Feuvre, Garnett, Pincott.

At the end of this memorable match the Muratti Vase was presented to Davis, the Jersey captain by Lord Ruthvane, the Lieut-Governor of Guernsey. The referee, Mr. S.A Donaldson, who had refereed the Jersey v Alderney Muratti semi-final in 1926, said that the standard of play compared favourably with the best class of amateur football on the mainland. There was the traditional Muratti Ball on the evening of the match and it was held at St. George's Hall.

1 9 3 2 .

MURATTI SEMI-FINAL.
14 April 1932, The Cycling Grounds, Guernsey.

Guernsey -2, Jersey -0.

Guernsey fans on their way to the Track.

Once again the crowds came out for the Muratti with around 11,000 at the Track to witness the first round match between Guernsey and Jersey. Some Jersey supporters arrived on Wednesday morning and were further strengthen by some 300 on Thursday morning, and a further 735 on the afternoon's excursion steamer. A band, organised by Messrs. P.G. Landick and C. Noel, played on the 'Isle of Sark' during the trip from Jersey. Mr. F.T. Bennett's electrical amplifying equipment reproduced popular music at the ground before the game and during the interval. The referee was Mr. Stanley Rous who had refereed the Guernsey-Alderney Muratti match in 1928. He was one of the linesmen at Wembley in the England v Scotland match last Saturday.

The Jersey team were the first to come out, led by Davis, followed a couple of minutes later by Guernsey, led by Warr. The teams were presented to Colonel C.W. Carey, representing the Lieut-Governor.

C.F. Halstead (G), S.F. Rouse, Capt. Glover Price.

The Jersey defence deals with a Guernsey attack.

and forced two quick corners, from the second Carpenter drove hard against the post – a lucky let-off for Guernsey. Dorey led Guernsey's response as Burtenshaw had an uncomfortable few minutes in the visitor's goal. Down then sent a pass forward to Dorey who ran on and fired a shot low into the net to put Guernsey 1-0 up after 7 minutes. Jersey pushed on in search of an equaliser with Benest and Berry prominent. Garnett nearly equalised but his powerful drive hit the crossbar. A move by Mauger and Brassel created an opening that Mauger missed just 10 yards out. Jersey missed a similar opportunity when Benest centred to Berry who, with an open goal, put his shot wide. Play became very scrappy as both sides pushed on for the important goal. As the half ended Burtenshaw saved from Dorey and then Dorey put another drive over the bar. Half time arrived with the score Guernsey-1, Jersey-0.

The second half began in a similar vein with each side taking control but without the moves bringing a goal. Dorey and Garnett, however, came close for their teams. Jersey then set up a period of sustained pressure that brought out the best in the Guernsey defence and in a quick breakaway Freeman's shot landed on the top of the Jersey net. Garnett replied quickly for Jersey but put his shot over the bar. Burtenshaw then pulled off a remarkable save from an excellent shot by Freeman. Guernsey then had an escape when Mechem scrambled the ball away for a corner following a melee right on his goal-line as Jersey pushed on for an equaliser. The pressure remained on the Guernsey defence and Mechem had to save brilliantly from a fast running shot from Carpenter. In the 22nd minute Brassel raced along the line and centred into a swarm of players. Freeman got away with the ball and was making direct for goal and was tripped up in the penalty area. Referee Rouse had no hesitation in awarding a penalty and Warr took the kick scoring with a low drive. This goal relaxed Guernsey somewhat and they began to attack with more purpose and Dorey hit the side netting with a shot. Carpenter then attempted to break away for Jersey but he was dispossessed by Lewis at the expense of a corner and from this kick, Cummins could only head over. Jersey was on the defensive for the last few minutes and the match ended Guernsey-2, Jersey-0.

Guernsey: D. Mechem, J.A. Lewis, P. Bougourd, H. de Garis, W. Warr (c),
              W.H. Down, M. Brassel, D. Mauger, H. Dorey, W. Barrasin, W.C. Freeman.
              Goalscorers: Dorey, Warr (pen).

Jersey: Burtenshaw, Malzard, Harben, Haines, Davis (c), Cummins, Berry,
              Carpenter, A.E. Garnett, Stephens, H.V. Benest.

The referee, Mr. S.F. Rouse, in an interview with a 'Press' representative, said he was struck with the keen spirit displayed by both teams – and the crowd. He felt that the Guernsey defence had been grand and had undoubtedly saved the team and he could quite understand that by the sides' keen play they could defeat visiting English amateur sides. He was particularly pleased to referee again in the island after four years.

MURATTI FINAL.
28 April 1932, Springfield Stadium, Jersey.

Alderney -2, Guernsey -4.

The 'Lorina' (Capt. J.H. Swan) left St. Peter Port at 1.05pm with 365 excursionists. Although it was lunch hour there was quite a crowd to see her off, the Guernsey supporters cheering and being in obvious good humour as they departed. After a fine passage the fans arrived at Springfield at 3.20pm.
There were just under 5,000 spectators at Springfield for the Muratti final between Alderney and Guernsey. Along with the Alderney team was Peter Newton, son of Mr. & Mrs. H. Newton, who brought with him the Alderney mascot.
The referee, C.W. Durham was assisted by two former Muratti stars, L. Purdy (Guernsey) and W. Hammond (Alderney).
The Alderney team was lead out by H. Newton and Guernsey by W. Warr. Prior to the kick off both teams were presented to the Lieut-Governor of Jersey as well as the Bailiff of Jersey.
Alderney started sharper and Henson had a shot saved by Mechem early on. Odoir then sent the ball high into the Guernsey goal for S. Newton to place over the bar. Guernsey had difficulty in settling down due to the bustling tactics of their opponents. A neat Dorey-Mauger-Brassel move resulted in Freeman driving in hard and Jennings saving with a little trouble. Dorey drove in and Jennings miskicked for a corner. As Guernsey continued to press the Alderney defence, in particular Chapelhow and Allen defended with great spirit. With the game 20 minutes old Brassel raced past the defence but with Jennings helpless, put his drive wide. As the pressure continued Brookes passed to Mauger and he slipped it to Dorey who struck a magnificent drive that hit the underside of the crossbar and into the net with Jennings well beaten. Odoir came close for Alderney when his high drive ended on the roof of the net. Dorey scored again but was ruled offside. Guernsey scored a second

Peter Newton and mascot.

Guernsey being presented to Lieut-Governor and Bailiff of Jersey.

goal when Brookes passed to Mauger and he sent a high shot past Jennings. The half was nearing its end when Mechem had to turn a magnificent drive onto the bar. The half ended with the score Alderney-0, Guernsey-2.

Guernsey started the second half quickly and Dorey and Mauger nearly scored in early raids. Jennings was once again the busier of the two goalkeepers saving two drives from Brassel. The Alderney defence was holding out manfully as it was under almost constant pressure as Guernsey pressed on. Alderney nearly conceded an own-goal when Chapelhow put the ball inches over his own bar under severe pressure from Brassel. The Guernsey pressure was incessant with their full-backs operating from almost the half-way line. After 60 minutes Guernsey scored a third goal when Freeman crossed over to Brookes who in turn passed neatly to Dorey who crashed in a fast shot. Ten minutes later Brassel added a fourth Guernsey goal. Alderney replied quickly and J. Newton scored a fine goal after 72 minutes followed by a near thing when S. Newton put his shot just wide from 10 yards. With 5 minutes remaining McLernon scored goal number 2 for Alderney and the final result was Alderney-2, Guernsey-4.

Alderney: Jennings, Chappelhow, Allen, Catts, J. Newton, H. Newton (c), Odoire, Barker, S. Newton, McLernon, Henson.
Goalscorers: J. Newton, McLernon.

Guernsey: D. Mechem, J.A. Lewis, P. Bougourd, H. de Garis, W. Warr (c), W.H. Down, M. Brassel, D. Mauger, H. Dorey, J.S. Brookes, W.C. Freeman.
Goalscorers: Dorey (2), Mauger, Brassel.

The Muratti Vase was presented amid sustained cheers to Warr by the Lieut-Governor of Jersey after he had congratulated both teams on a fine game.

It was reported that details of the match at Springfield were relayed to Smith Street, St. Peter Port. The report came by telephone cabled from the playing field. In the Press offices Mr. F.T. Bennett had fitted up an electrical broadcasting unit and, with a microphone, Mr George Keyho, the well-known football referee, announced the salient features to the assembled crowd which had risen to around 1,500.

Part of the 1,500 crowd in Smith Street listening to the Muratti.

1 9 3 3 .

MURATTI SEMI-FINAL.
6 April 1933, Springfield Stadium, Jersey.

Jersey -6, Alderney -0.

At Springfield, Jersey on 6 April 1933 an attendance of 3,647 saw Jersey entertain Alderney in the first round of the Muratti competition. The Alderney team had made the journey to Jersey in the specially chartered 'New Fawn'. Among those who welcomed the Alderney team was Tom Smith, the 'lucky mascot' of 1920. Thick patches of fog were encountered and the dismal and intermittent hooting of fog sirens from other vessels was a feature of the journey. It was reported in the Jersey 'Morning News' that it was rumoured that E.F. Le Feuvre, the Oxford Blue selected to lead Jersey's line against Alderney might not be able to play due to injuries received in a Willis Cup match. He was undergoing treatment and he was hopeful that he would play but in the end he was replaced in the side by E. Cox (YMCA). Alderney also had problems and Mr. Depres and Capt. C.H. Richards (Council) stated as they announced their starting line-up that there had been three accidents in a trial match on Saturday afternoon and two of them involved some of this selection so the team may have to change. In the end there was only one change in their selected team with Henson replacing McLernon.

Alderney was the first to take the field and had a warm reception from the moderately sized crowd. Prior to the match commencing both teams were presented to the Lieut-Governor of Jersey.

From the kick off Jersey went immediately onto the attack and Anquetil in the Alderney goal faced an early barrage from the home forwards. Benest should have opened the scoring for Jersey but missed from 10 yards out. J. Newton and Allen were playing well and releasing the Alderney forwards with their long kicking and the Jersey defence was very shaky but managed to keep out the Alderney forwards. The Jersey forwards were finding it difficult to break down the Alderney defence in which Chapelhow was prominent and one of his strong clearances sent the ball right out of the ground. Alderney came close when Hanson met a well centred ball but sent it wide of the goalmouth. Anquetil was called into action when he turned a header from Cox over the bar followed quickly by an Alderney break that saw Duplain driving his shot over the bar. In 33 minutes, however, Jersey broke the deadlock when Carpenter deflected a free kick with his head past Anquetil and into the net. Two minutes later Carpenter shot through a melee of players past an unsighted Anquetil to make the score 2-0 in Jersey's favour. Alderney tried to respond but were nearly caught out when Cox missed a chance to increase Jersey's lead. Just before half time a mistake in the Alderney defence allowed Boyd to tap in to make the half time score Jersey-3, Alderney-0.

In the first minute of the second half Anquetil was injured in running out to clear from Benest but he resumed after some attention. The three-goal lead gave Jersey a lot of confidence and they were much on top. Their defence was now coping well with the thrusts of Randall, Barker and S. Newton. Alderney nearly capitalised on a mis-kick by Freeman that allowed Duplain through, Burtenshaw in the Jersey goal hesitated but Duplain's run was stopped by a fine interception by Malzard. Alderney again attacked and Barker drew Cummins out to put S. Newton clear and from the winger's centre Duplain scooped the ball behind. The play became more even with chances being made at both ends. Gamblin drove a free-kick from 35 yards into the Alderney goalmouth and Chapelhow cleared the ball around 100yards and found Randell who drove his shot hard into Burtenshaw's arms. Unfortunately for Alderney, Catts was taken off injured leaving Alderney with 10 men as they began to chase the game. After 25 minutes Burtenshaw had to race out of his goal to break up a fine Duplain and Henson move for Alderney. In the 71st minute, Cox met a centre from Benest to score Jersey's 4th goal. Six minutes later Carpenter diverted a free kick from Cummins into the net for goal number five. Catts then returned to the field for the last minutes of the game. Just on full time Cox scored a 6th goal for Jersey to make the final score Jersey-6, Alderney-0.

Jersey: Burtenshaw, Malzard (c), Freeman, Hitchcock, Cummins, Gamblin, Dingle, Carpenter, Cox, Boyd, H.V. Benest.
Goalscorers: Carpenter (3), Boyd (2), Cox.

Alderney: D. Anquetil, G. Chappelhow, H. Newton, Catts, J. Newton, Randall, Henson, Duplain, Barker, S. Newton, Allen.

 Despite the heavy defeat Alderney competed very well during the match but were unable to break through the Jersey defence. Chapelhow in defence and Duplain in attack were the best for Alderney. Jersey was worthy winners due mainly to their more clinical finishing and had excellent players in Cummins and Malzard.

 In the Guernsey Weekly Press for Saturday 8 April it was announced that the following players have been invited to go into training with a view to Muratti selection: Mechem, McLean (goal), Bougourd, Huelin, Lewis, Freeman (backs), de Garis, Leadbeater, Tozer, Down, Warren, McCarthy, Duquemin (halves), Brassel, H. Martel, Tett, Brookes, Allen, Smith, P. Barrasin, C. Solway (forwards). In addition the following non-residents are requested to hold themselves in readiness to assist if required: Dorey, Mauger, Robins and Le Maitre.

MURATTI FINAL.
4 May 1933, The Cycling Grounds, Guernsey.

Guernsey -4, Jersey -1. aet.

 Guernsey prepared for the Muratti Vase final by playing a match against Dulwich Hamlet at the Cycling Grounds on Monday 17 April for the Victory Cup, losing the game by 6-0. Guernsey made five changes for the final with P. Bougourd, A.C. Leadbeater, D. Mauger,

Muratti Final.

Jersey v. Guernsey

TO BE PLAYED AT THE

CYCLING GROUNDS
Thursday, May 4th.

KICK-OFF 4 p.m. ———— GATES OPEN 2.45 p.m.

Refe ee : Rev. C V. CLIBBON, M·A.
(Amateur Football Association).

TICKETS

Will be ON SALE on FRIDAY NEXT, April 28

PLAN OF NUMBERED AND RESERVED PAVILION AND OUTSIDE SEATS, AND ADVANCE ADMISSION TICKETS TO GROUND AT THE " STAR " OFFICE at 7.30 p.m.

Section of plan of Numbered and Reserved Pavilion Seats also on sale at PURDY BROS., Bridge, St. Sampson's, by Mr. H. F. Sallin (Treasurer, G.F.A.), at 6.45. Advance Admission to Ground and Outside Seats may be obtained from Messrs. W. J. Collins, Pollet; Bucktrout's Tobacco Shop (Arcade Corner); Le Riche's Stores (Tobacco Dept.); Stroobant and Symes, Market Hill; Purdy Bros., Boot Stores, Bridge and Banques; W. Elliott, near Old Post, St. Martin's.

PRICES (including Tax) :—
Entrance to Ground and Reserved and Numbered Pavilion Seat 2/6
" " " " " " Outside Seat 1/9
Advance Admission to Ground 1/-

Please Note——

THE SALE OF TICKETS FOR SEATS IS RESTRICTED TO TWO PER APPLICATION.
UNDER NO CIRCUMSTANCES WILL SEATS BE BOOKED BY TELEPHONE. TO GAIN ADMITTANCE TO THE GROUND EACH PERSON MUST BE IN POSSESSION OF AND SHOW HIS OR HER OWN TICKET.
SEAT HOLDERS ARE REQUESTED TO OCCUPY THEIR SEATS BY 3.30.

MUSICAL SELECTIONS by FAMOUS BANDS and ORCHESTRAS WILL BE BROADCAST by F. T. BENNETT'S SUPER-POWERFUL ELECTRICAL AMPLIFIER from 3 p.m.

Muratti Advertisment.

Isle of Jersey.

Some of the spectators at the Cycling Grounds.

Guernsey being presented to the Bailiff prior to the kick off.

Guernsey on the attack.

L. Smith and A. Le Maitre replacing Heulin, Duquemin, Martel, Allen and Solway. The previous Saturday Dulwich Hamlet had lost 5-2 to Jersey's YMCA with four of the goals coming from E.F. Le Feuvre.

The Jersey contingent at the Track must have numbered considerably more than 2,000, the large numbers which arrived on the 'St. Julien', being supplemented by the afternoon's 1,378 trippers by the 'Isle of Jersey'.

The Muratti final was played at the Cycling Grounds on 4 May in front of what was described as a record crowd. In attendance was Arthur W. Bell, the Bailiff of Guernsey.

It was estimated that there were more than 2,000 Jersey supporters in the ground when kick off time arrived. Guernsey were led out by Down and Jersey by O'Neill and both teams were presented to the Bailiff of Guernsey.

Jersey won the toss and Guernsey were set to kick into the eastern goal when it was discovered that there was no ball. There was an embarrassing delay of a minute or two while an official hastily ran to fetch one. When the game finally kicked off the early play was very scrappy and both sets of players appeared nervous. Mechem was the first goalkeeper in action when he punched away a dangerous ball from the Jersey captain, O'Neill. Mechem then produced an excellent save from a Carpenter shot as he broke through down the centre. The game settled into a pattern with Guernsey using a neat passing game with Jersey tending to favour a more open and direct style. Guernsey was dominating the early stages without being able to break down the Jersey defence. Guernsey came close when a huge drive by Dorey was charged down then Smith came through on the left and from his centre Burtenshaw could only partially save and from only 10 yards from goal Mauger hit the side netting. In a lighter moment during the game, C. Freeman ripped his shorts as he tackled Dorey and, to the great amusement of the crowd held onto the remnants as he left to change. He soon returned and reformed the excellent partnership he had with Malzard in the Jersey defence. As the game progressed it was Mechem once again who thwarted Jersey by saving well from a Carpenter header. The game was becoming more even with both defences on top. Midway through the first half Jersey's E.F. Le Feuvre (who was an Oxford Blue) dislocated his shoulder and was taken to the Victoria Hospital. Despite this handicap Jersey opened the scoring after 41 minutes. Gamblin passed to Boyd who beat De Garis and scored with a cross shot from close range. Guernsey replied with some fine attacks but could not break down the Jersey defence. During one of these attacks Gamblin and C. Freeman both rose to head the same ball and crashed their heads and both were knocked out for some minutes. Freeman recovered but Gamblin had to receive more attention behind the goal. Guernsey came close when Mauger broke away from C. Freeman and centred the ball. Le Maitre raced in from the left and met the ball in his stride only to put it wide of the goal; his momentum carried him on and he crashed into the side rigging and was temporarily laid out. At half time the score was Guernsey-0, Jersey-1.

Jersey began the second half well despite having a 1-man handicap as they strove to increase their lead through the forward runs of Benest, Boyd and Carpenter. Le Feuvre had not returned for Jersey although Gamblin resumed his position with his head bandaged. Guernsey's main threat was coming from Dorey although, in the main, the shooting of the Guernsey forwards was poor. Following a Jersey corner the home defence cleared up to Le Maitre who had found some space. He fired a fast shot that was well saved by Burtenshaw but his clearance was returned by Down, and Smith instantly shot for the far post when the Jersey keeper dived across and conceded a corner. Le Maitre's corner-kick bounced on the bar and went behind. The game was becoming very even with both goals coming under attack. Guernsey were unable to take advantage of their extra man By this time Hitchcock had to leave the field due to a strained muscle and with over 15 minutes remaining Jersey battled on with only 9 men as the pressure from Guernsey increased. With 7 minutes to go Guernsey equalised. Mauger sent in a high centre that the Jersey defence failed to clear and the ball was deflected into the net. Burtenshaw had a torrid time as he kept Guernsey out until the final whistle with the score Guernsey-1, Jersey-1.

Extra time saw Guernsey on the attack against a 9-man Jersey team and again Burtenshaw produced some fine saves to keep them out. Tempers were beginning to get a little frayed as Gamblin and Bougourd squared up and the spectators drew Gamblin away, and the situation calmed down and both players shook hands. It looked as though Jersey was going to take the lead again when they were awarded a penalty after Bougourd had handled in the box. Carpenter took the kick but put his shot wide of the goal, much to Guernsey's (and Bougourd's) relief. The Jersey goal was then put under severe pressure but they held out and the first period of extra-time ended Guernsey-1, Jersey-1.

The second half began with the Jersey defence under almost constant pressure as they packed their goalmouth although they were finding their two-man deficit difficult to cope with. Nine minutes from the end Dorey met a centre from Mauger and scored with a neat drive to put Guernsey 2-1 ahead. Two minutes later Le Maitre sent over a centre and once again Dorey scored with a low drive. Dorey them completed his hat trick by scoring from another Le Maitre centre to make the final score Guernsey-4, Jersey-1.

Guernsey: D. Mechem, P. Bougourd, W.C. Freeman, H. de Garis, A.C. Leadbeater,
W.C. Down (c), D. Mauger, J.S. Brookes, H. Dorey, L. Smith,
A. Le Maitre.
Goalscorers: Mauger, Dorey (3).

Jersey: Burtenshaw, Malzard, Freeman, Hitchcock, Cummins, Gamblin, O'Neill(c),
Carpenter, E.F. Le Feuvre, Boyd, H.V. Benest.
Goalscorer: Boyd.

Following the match the Bailiff presented the Muratti Vase to Down, the Guernsey captain. The final result of Guernsey-4, Jersey-1 was a little hard on the Jersey team who battled manfully for so long with firstly 10 men then ultimately 9 men as well as having Gamblin playing with a bandaged head. Burtenshaw was immense in an excellent Jersey defence. The Lieut-Governor of Guernsey sent a congratulatory telegram to the President of the GFA and it read:

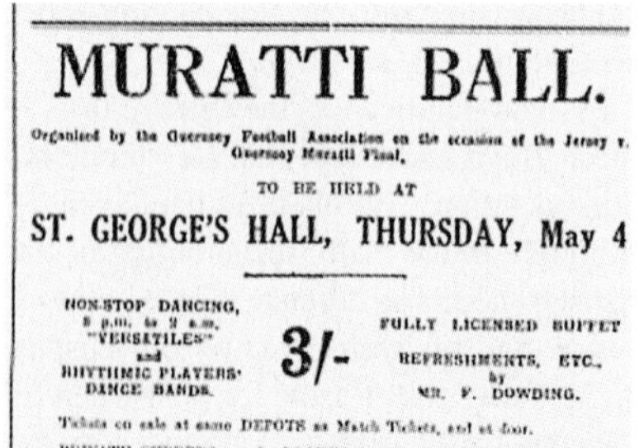

'Hearty congratulations to Guernsey team on again winning the Muratti'. Ruthvane.

E.F. Le Feuvre, one of the injured Jersey players, passed a comfortable night in Victoria Hospital and was well enough to return to Jersey on Friday. W. Hitchcock who was also injured with a fractured leg remained in Jersey's General Hospital until Wednesday 10 May.

1 9 3 4 .

MURATTI SEMI-FINAL.
12 April 1934, The Cycling Grounds, Guernsey.

Guernsey -3, Alderney -0.

It was reported that Jersey had played the French Army on 1 March losing to them by 9-4 and that leading the line for them was Guernsey's Harold Dorey (First Tower). Guernsey had four new caps in their side with H. Tozer, J.A. Martel and W.C. Freeman, all of Rangers, as well as W. Friess (North) making their debuts.

Alderney were preparing well for their match against Guernsey by staging three trial matches between their 'A' and 'B' teams and these games resulted in one win apiece, the final game being a 1-1 draw. Alderney had three new caps in their side with P. Allen, E. Picot and F. Odoir all making their Muratti debuts. Prior to the match commencing the crowd was entertained by the Band and Drums of the Royal Guernsey Militia. Guernsey was captained by Lewis (Rangers) and Alderney by Chapelhow.

Chapelhow won the toss and Guernsey kicked off. Alderney began the brightest with some fine wing play from the 15-year-old F. Odoir causing the home defence some concern. Chapelhow was marshalling his defence well and Simon and Picot pressuring an uneasy Guernsey defence. The home side replied when Freiss forced Jennings to make a

Chapelhow greets Lewis before the match.

Le Prevost (Guernsey) and Jennings (Alderney) go up for the ball.

fine save. Guernsey began to put more pressure on the Alderney defence with shots from Freiss and Le Prevost coming close. Jennings was certainly the busier of the two goalkeepers as he strove to keep Guernsey out.

Following a neat Guernsey raid down the centre, Le Prevost received the ball and drove a low fast shot into the net to put Guernsey 1-0 up after 19 minutes. Guernsey tried to increase this lead but found Chapelhow in uncompromising form as he repelled these attacks. Alderney broke away and Picot sent in a shot that Mechem saved well. The first half ended with slight chances at both ends but the score remained Guernsey-1, Alderney-0.

The second half began very well for Guernsey as they quickly doubled their lead. Freiss gathered a Le Prevost short pass and drove steadily into the corner of the Alderney net. Alderney replied when Picot passed to F. Odoir who fired in a fierce drive that Mechem saved well. Guernsey then applied some sustained pressure that was rewarded when Martel sent a fine shot into the net with Jennings helpless to put Guernsey 3-0 up. As the game progressed, Jennings, time and again, showed his worth with saves from Freeman, Mauger, Barrasin and Le Prevost. Near the end of the match Picot broke into the Guernsey defence and shot just wide leaving the final result Guernsey-3, Alderney-0.

Guernsey: D. Mechem, J.A. Lewis (c), W. Huelin, H. de Garis, W. Barrasin, H. Tozer, D. Mauger, J.A. Martel, T. Le Prevost, W. Freiss, W.C. Freeman.
Goalscorers: Le Prevost, Freiss, Martel.

Alderney: G. Jennings, G. Chappelhow (c), A.L. Allen, P. Allen, J. Newton, H. Pike, E. Odoir, S. Newton, E. Picot, T. Simon, F. Odoir.

There was a lot of praise for the performance of the 15-year-old F. Odoir of Alderney who was shaping up well during the game. Although Guernsey were worthy winners the score would have been higher but for the excellent display by the Alderney defence. Following the match a Muratti Ball was held at St. George's Hall with over 400 guests attending along with members of the Alderney and Guernsey sides.

There is apparently a section of Jersey opinion which calls for Harold Dorey to lead their attack. Dorey, who plays his club soccer in Jersey for First Tower, played for the Rest against the YMCA, who are the current Jersey champions. The match was for the Lady Bingham Cup and was played on Tuesday 19 April with the Rest winning by 4-0 and Dorey, who was in excellent form, scoring three goals with the other coming from Davis. As Guernsey had left Dorey out of the Muratti semi-final against Alderney there is a feeling in many Jersey quarters that they have every right to select him should Guernsey not have the vision to pick him and there is no reason why he should be at the match as a spectator.

MURATTI FINAL.
26 April 1934, Springfield Stadium, Jersey.

Jersey -0, Guernsey -1.

Jersey and Guernsey both played the same opposition in the matches over the Easter weekend with mixed results. Jersey drew 1-1 with Kingstonians whereas Guernsey defeated the same opponents by 2-1. In their second match Jersey lost 4-2 to Lovells and Guernsey lost 3-2 to them. The debate that surrounded Harold Dorey was silenced for this match as he could not play due to illness and he was replaced in the Guernsey side by A.E. Broadrib (North). Jersey had six players who were making their debuts in G. Le Riche in goal, P. O'Connor, Petra (Wanderers), Golding, Davenport (Wanderers) and Soudain. With the discussion in Jersey surrounding the possibility of Dorey playing for them it rather overshadowed the fact the G. Le Rich, in the Jersey goal, is in fact a Guernseyman. The excursionists sailed on the 'Isle of Jersey' (Capt. F.W. Holt), which left Guernsey at 12.30pm, numbered 737. Also on board were His Excellency Lord Ruthvane and Lady Ruthvane and His Excellency's flag was flown at the mainmast.

The 1934 Muratti final between Jersey and Guernsey was played at Springfield before a crowd of over 8,000 spectators including Major-General E.H. Willis C.B., C.M.G., the Lieut-Governors of Jersey, His Excellency Major-General the Lord Ruthvane, Lieut-Governor of Guernsey, and Mr. C.E.M. de Carteret, the Bailiff of Jersey. The two teams

The Officials and Jersey line up before the match.

were presented to the Lieut-Governors before the match. The Jersey team was captained by B. O'Neill (Wanderers) and Guernsey by J.A. Lewis (Rangers).

Broadrib, who replaced Dorey in the Guernsey side, was, incidentally, the leading goal scorer in the Priaulx League. Both teams were presented to the Lieut-Governors of both islands prior to the commencement of the game. The referee, Mr. G.D. Rudd, called both captains together and Lewis won the toss for Guernsey and Jersey kicked-off.
Guernsey began the sharpest and in the early minutes Jersey was entirely on the defensive with Broadrib having the first shot that went over the bar. Broadrib again came close when he headed in a cross from Mauger that went only a matter of inches wide. The game was only six minutes old when Broadrib saw an opening, ran clean through the Jersey defence and netted with a fine drive from close in to put Guernsey 1-0 up.

Guernsey continued to press and Martel then Freeman both went close. Jersey recovered from this start and Petra tested Mechem with a long drive. The game became more even with both sets of defences coping well with the attacks. Guernsey almost scored a second goal when Mauger put in a cross; Freeman drove in a high shot forcing Le Riche to pull off a good save. Le Riche was again called into action when he pulled off good saves from two flashing shots from Le Prevost. O'Connor then came to Jersey's rescue when he headed a Mauger cross away for a corner. Lewis then cleared when Jersey broke away through Boyd, the ball finding its way to Mauger. He passed on to Broadrib who immediately made for goal but Jersey's Freeman came in quickly and kicked the ball into touch. It looked as though Guernsey would get the second goal when Mauger sent in another fine cross that was met by Freeman who sent in a high shot that was well saved by Le Riche. Jersey then became an attacking force for a time but were finding the Guernsey defence very stubborn. Le Gresley nearly equalised for Jersey when his powerful shot cannoned off a Guernsey defender but Mechem managed to clear. As the half ended Jersey were beginning to get on top but the score remained Jersey-0, Guernsey-1.

The second half began with Guernsey having the advantage of the wind and early on Le Riche had to bring down a high drive from Martel. Guernsey continued to press and Le Prevost came close when he put his shot past the post. From the clearance O' Neill fed Boyd in a dangerous position and only an excellent tackle by Heulin prevented Jersey from scoring. An excellent de Garis-Martel-Broadrib-Freeman move set up Freeman but he put his shot over the bar. Jersey then broke away and Benest had a brilliant run along the touch-line and forced a corner and from the kick Le Gresley shot just over the Guernsey bar. Le Prevost was sent through by a defensive clearance and he passed to Broadrib and his fierce drive struck the bar with Le Riche beaten.

The ball cannoned back and was punted up field. Soudain and Boyd were quickly on the ball and from 12 yards Boyd smashed in a drive that only just went past the post. This was the pattern of play with attack and counter attack keeping the pressure on both defences. Soudain then broke through but Mechem saved his point blank shot. The closing stages of the game were played at an exhilarating pace but there was no more scoring and the match ended Jersey-0, Guernsey-1.

A.E. Broadrib.
(Guernsey)

Jersey kicks-off the 1934 Muratti Vase Final.

Broadrib sees his shot beat Le Riche only to come crashing off the bar.

Jersey: G. Le Riche, C.S. Freeman, P. O'Connor, B. O'Neill (c), Petra, Golding,
               Davenport, Le Gresley, Soudain,Boyd, H.V. Benest.

Guernsey: D. Mechem, J.A. Lewis (c), W. Huelin, H. de Garis, W. Barrasin,
               J. McCarthy, D. Mauger, J.A. Martel, A. Broadrib, T. Le Prevost,
               W.C. Freeman.
               Goalscorer: Broadrib.

  The Muratti Vase was presented to the Guernsey captain, J.A. Lewis, by the Lieut-
Governor of Jersey.
  A huge throng gathered in Smith Street, St. Peter Port to watch the state of the game posted up from the offices of the Guernsey Press. At intervals descriptions of the game were
given, the announcer being Capt. H. Brooks.

The Guernsey team and officials at their Jersey headquarters.

Part of the crowd outside the offices of the Guernsey Press.

1 9 3 5 .

MURATTI SEMI-FINAL.
11 April 1935, Springfield Stadium, Jersey.

Jersey -0, Guernsey -1.

The details of the Muratti match at Springfield were to be relayed to Smith Street by the Guernsey Press along with musical selections. Reports of the match were to be relayed to Guernsey by telephone.

In their preparation for the 1935 Muratti competition Jersey had employed the services of a professional coach. Jersey's hopes were high, as Guernsey's form up to this game had not been convincing. The Jersey side had four new caps with T. Hamon in goal and H.G.

The Press amplifier and gramophone and the Press telephone operator.

Presentation of the Jersey team.

Marie, N.T. Noel and A. Galway (Wanderers) making their debuts. The respective sides received warm ovations from the near 7,000 Springfield crowd as they entered the field. Both teams were presented to Major-General H. de Courcy Martelli, the Lieut-Governor of Jersey.

It was noted that Hurel, the Jersey inside right, was the third brother of that family to gain a Muratti cap.

Lewis, the Guernsey captain, won the toss and elected to defend the Springfield pavilion end. The first real thrill occurred when Wicks picked up a goal kick that eluded the Guernsey defence and fired in a shot that went past the post. Barrasin then came close for Guernsey when he broke through the Jersey defence but put his shot over the bar. Play went from end to end and the forwards were having difficulty in controlling a lively ball, consequently the two defences were on top. Le Prevost then took the ball clear and as he bore down on the Jersey goal, Hamon anticipated the danger and rushed out to clear. Guernsey then experienced a few anxious moments when Lewis had to charge down a good shot by Wicks and then Boyd put his shot over the bar. Play was end to end when Noel eluded the Guernsey defence and smashed his shot against the crossbar and then

Bougourd saved a situation by charging down a fierce drive by O'Connor. Guernsey suffered a severe loss after 22 minutes when Barrasin was injured in a collision and was carried from the field. Guernsey rearranged their defence and they were immediately put under pressure but held out and protected Mechem well. Barrasin returned after 30 minutes and immediately his return signalled a Guernsey goal. From a free kick Le Prevost, positioning himself perfectly, beat the defence and scored to put Guernsey into the lead. In the closing stages of this half terrific pressure was brought to bear on the Guernsey goal and Mechem had to produce some outstanding work to keep Jersey at bay. The first half was well up to Muratti standards and ended Jersey-0, Guernsey-1.

Both teams were given a warm reception as they returned to the field for the second half. As the half started and Brassel and Martel went on the attack but were well held by Morris and Marie. Brassel was the liveliest of the forwards and he came close on two occasions to increasing Guernsey's lead. Jersey's O'Connor latched on to a miskick by Lewis, and Mechem had to dash out to save. Mechem again had to be alert as he saved from Wicks. The Jersey pressure was mounting but the Guernsey defence was holding firm with Mechem particularly outstanding. Galway, the Jersey centre-half, was a tremendous worker and, as the half wore on, was becoming just as effective in assisting his forwards as he was in defence. He placed a free-kick right into the heart of the Guernsey defence and the ball was only cleared after a great scramble. Although Jersey was on top Guernsey came close when Bougourd sent in a shot that was saved by Hamon. Almost immediately Mechem saved well from Le Gresley, who was becoming Jersey's most dangerous forward. In another breakaway Brassel and Martel ran the ball cleverly through the Jersey defence but

Guernsey. 1935.

Galway quickly averted a dangerous situation. O'Connor again came close as Jersey mounted some furious attacks in am attempt to gain the equaliser but found Mechem in excellent form. De Garis was carried off injured but returned three minutes later following some treatment. Despite all the Jersey pressure in the second half Guernsey managed to hang on and the result was Jersey-0, Guernsey-1.

Jersey: T. Hamon, G.A. Malzard (c), H.G. Marie, N.T. Noel, A. Galway (c), G.E. Morris, H.F. Le Gresley, E. Hurel, P. O'Connor, H. Boyd, H. Watts.

Guernsey: D. Mechem, J.A. Lewis (c), P. Bougourd, H. de Garis, W. Barrasin, E.J. Warren, M.J. Brassel, J.A. Martel, T. Le Prevost, W.C. Freeman, A. Le Maitre.
Goalscorer: Le Prevost.

The referee, L.E. Gibbs (Reading), was very impressed with the standard of football which he felt was as high as many of the leading English amateur sides. Mr Gibbs was to officiate at that year's FA Cup final at Wembley as one of the linesmen.

The Press shop in Smith Street is besieged by a large crowd
waiting to buy copies of the green 'Muratti Press'.

MURATTI FINAL.
9 May 1935, The Cycling Grounds, Guernsey.

Guernsey -5, Alderney -0.

Following their sterling performance against Jersey, Guernsey were firm favourites to win the Muratti for the fourth successive time at the Cycling Grounds on 16 May 1935. As history has shown, Alderney was no respecter of reputations and would go all out to win the coveted trophy. Guernsey prepared for this match with a Victory Cup game against Ilford which they lost 3-0. Alderney arranged two 'A' v 'B' trial matches with the 'B' team winning both games by 2-1 and 5-1. Alderney unfortunately lost the services of G Burness, a first-class centre forward. He received an injury some 12 days ago that caused a bone to be misplaced and at Saturday's try-out match at the Track he was still troubled with the injury.

Alderney's Sidney Newton (Sylvans) fractured his leg for a second time in only eight months. Whilst motor-cycling he was involved in a collision with a motor-van and fractured his left leg below the knee. In one of the early matches this season Newton fractured a leg while playing centre-forward for Sylvans against North in a Priaulx League match at St. Peter's. He had only just recovered from that accident when the second mishap occured, and it meant he would definitely miss the Muratti Final against Guernsey. Sidney's brother, Bunny, also an Alderney Muratti and Sylvans player, claims to have broken nearly every bone in his body during his football career.

Alderney won the toss and played into the west goal with a gusty wind at their backs. This they used to their early advantage and Riou, with a short pass, put Picot through but Bougourd came across and cleared into touch. Martel began a Guernsey attack by passing to Brooke who in turn centred and Le Prevost raced onto the ball and smashed a high drive that Jennings cleared well. Guernsey was now in top gear but were finding the Alderney defence very resolute. Guernsey then broke up an Alderney attack and Bougourd cleared the ball up to Brookes and he sent a low pass to Freeman who was in space. He then sent in a fine cross to Brookes and as he raced in Jennings dashed from his goal and punched the ball clear. Although Guernsey was on top they were tending to overplay the ball allowing Alderney to put in some telling tackles. After some near misses Guernsey should have opened the scoring when Jennings mishandled the ball, ran from his goal, and a drive from Freeman landed on top of the net of an empty goal, a real let-off for Alderney. Pike then put in a long clearance and the ball found Riou, and he put a pass through to give a clear open field for E. Odoire. The winger raced in but missed the ball completely. Alderney then had a period where they pressurised the Guernsey defence and Bougourd headed away from Riou and then Warren had to clear as Picot and E. Odoire were combining well.

In 25 minutes Guernsey took the lead when Brookes collected a pass and drove a shot high into the net through a crowd of defenders with Jennings helpless. Despite this setback the Alderney defence were still holding out well and set up an attack when E. Odoir whipped the ball across the Guernsey goal and Mechem had to save first from Riou and then from Picot. Shortly before the interval Le Prevost beat the defence and drove the ball in, it hit a defender and went into the corner of the net for goal number two. Within a minute Guernsey nearly added another when Jennings brought down a cross-drive from Freeman; he was harried by Le Prevost, and as the ball went out to the right Brassel launched a flying drive just over the bar. After 42 minutes Barrasin lobbed a high pass over the Alderney defenders and Le Prevost took it in his stride and drove it in hard and low to make the half time score Guernsey-3, Alderney-0.

The second half began with Guernsey pushing on for more goals. The Alderney defence was holding up well but their forwards were making little headway when the opportunities arose although Riou shot over the bar from a cross from E. Odoir. Alderney were doing well in defence as Guernsey kept on the pressure although they had some breakaways where E. Odoire was their most effective attacker. In the 59th minute Martel sent in a fine centre and Le Prevost forced the ball past Jennings for a fourth goal. Although the game was fast moving away from Alderney, their defence and J. Newton, the Sylvans Priaulx player, in particular, was playing well. After 63 minutes Freeman put in a corner and Jennings fisted the ball away but Brassel raced in to net from close range for goal number five. Brassel was injured in scoring and was carried from the field but returned a little later. Alderney rallied for a time but were unable to get the better of Lewis and Bougourd. As the match neared its end a melee in the Alderney goal resulted in Barrasin driving his shot over leaving the final score as Guernsey-5, Alderney-0.

Guernsey: D. Mechem. J.A. Lewis, P. Bougourd, H. de Garis, W. Barrasin, E.J. Warren, M.J. Brassel, J.A. Martel,T. le Prevost, J.J. Brookes, W.C. Freeman.
Goalscorers: Brookes, le Prevost (3), Brassel.

Alderney: G. Jennings, N. Simon, A.L. Allen, H. Pike, J. Newton (c), T. Simon, E. Odoir, E. Picot, O. Riou, F. Odoir, W. Tarrant.

Guernsey had therefore set up a record of having won the Muratti Vase for a fourth successive year.

Major-General Broadbent, the Lieut-Governor of Guernsey, presented the Muratti Vase and medals to the Guernsey team and he congratulated both teams on a fine game. His final comment was that he hoped that Alderney would win next year. This was received with loud applause. The Muratti Ball was held at the St. George's Hall.

1 9 3 6 .

On 4 April the Guernsey Evening Press reported on an article that appeared in the Jersey 'Morning News' concerning Guernsey's Harold Dorey (pictured right). It reported that the recent fine performances by Harold Dorey in Jersey Senior football had brought forward the question of his Muratti qualifications. He had led Guernsey's attack from 1927-1933 and during that period only missed one Muratti match. Now, despite his native qualification for Guernsey, it was pointed out that he had a residential qualification for Jersey. The old squabble over Dorey continued. Apart for one year Guernsey had never failed to call upon Dorey, as a Sarnian born, to represent them in the Muratti. The 'Morning News' stated that it would be time to consider Dorey on his residential qualification when Guernsey decide that they no longer require him. To try and bring pressure on Dorey to play for Jersey against his native Island, whom he had represented on a number of occasions, is like asking a man to turn traitor to his native Island. The proper course, in the opinion of the 'Morning News' was to leave the choice to Dorey without pressure being brought to bear and if Guernsey wanted his services he should stick to his native Island where he learned and developed his skills.

The situation became even more complicated when both Jersey and Guernsey had arranged to play Wimbledon over the Easter period. Jersey played them on Good Friday and selected Dorey to lead their attack. He scored in a 4-1 defeat by the English side. Guernsey had selected him for their match against Wimbledon for the Victory Cup on Easter Monday and he led their attack in a 3-2 loss to the English team.

MURATTI SEMI-FINAL.
23 April 1936, Springfield Stadium, Jersey.

Jersey -9, Alderney -0.

Alderney were about to make Muratti history when they became the first side to travel to a Muratti match by plane. Nine players and officials flew into Jersey on a DH 86 of Jersey Airways on Wednesday 22 April landing in St. Ouen's Bay with a flight time of 15 minutes.

Jersey lost the services of C.S. Freeman (Wanderers) and he was replaced by J. Gamblin (St. Paul's).

Malzard, the Jersey captain, won the toss and chose to defend the Springfield Hall end. Jersey were the first to mount a telling attack when Berry put in a fine centre from the right and Galway tested Jennings with a fine shot, which the veteran goalkeeper saved in a manner that drew tremendous applause from the spectators. Alderney began the match well with Burness, Odoir and A. Barker causing problems. Jersey's first goal came after 24 minutes when Morris beat Jennings with a long-range drive. More pressure was exerted on the

The Alderney officials and players at St. Ouen's Bay.

Alderney defence and Jennings had to make a wonderful full length save from a shot by Benest. Jersey continued to have the better of the game and Jennings held shots from Berry and Noel. A few minutes later he fielded a high drive from Gamblin, but before he could make a clearance the ball was bundled out of his hands into the back of the net. As the pressure mounted an Alderney defender handled a shot from Davenport in the penalty area but Malzard put his kick yards wide. The half time score was Jersey-2, Alderney-0.

The second half was fast and furious with play going from end to end. Simon had a chance to open Alderney's account but he hesitated and the chance was lost. Alderney had changed their attack with Simon and Odoire swapping places and, for a time, seemed to give them an additional thrust and the Jersey defence was not too secure under the attacks. The Jersey side kept their shape, however, and in the 57th minute Davenport scored goal number three following a goalmouth scrummage. A minute later Galway met a centre from Smith to drive the ball past Jennings for goal number four. Almost from the kick-off Berry ran in to meet a beautiful pass from Benest to give Jennings no chance. The game was turning into a rout as Galway headed a 6th goal after 67 minutes. Alderney responded well and a good pass from A. Barker put W. Barker through and Le Riche had to be sharp to save the low shot. Galway increased the lead in the 80th minute to score number 7 with a simple lob into the net after Jennings was drawn out of position. The goals continued to flow and in the 82nd minute Benest put in a low centre to Galway, who missed the ball, and Allen put the ball in his own net. Benest completed the scoring by netting number 9. The bombardment continued and Jennings was eventually laid out by a terrific drive from Galway. He fortunately recovered and with no more scoring the final result was a resounding Jersey-9, Alderney-0.

Jersey: G. Le Riche, G.A. Malzard (c), J. Gamblin, A.F. Davenport, S.V. Nobes,
           G. Morris, J. Berry, E. Hurel, A. Galway, H.V. Benest, E. Smith.
           Goalscorers: Morris, Gamblin, Davenport, Galway (3), Berry, og, Benest.

Alderney: G. Jennings, N. Simon, A.L. Allen, Catts, A. Barker, Brehaut, R. Riou,
           R. Brehaut, E. Picot, G. Burness, F. Odoir.

This created a new Muratti scoring record beating the previous record set in 1922 when
Guernsey defeated Alderney 8-0.

MURATTI FINAL.
7 May 1936, The Cycling Grounds, Guernsey.

Guernsey -2, Jersey -1.

 The 'Isle of Sark' (Capt. R.J. Large) arrived at 2.35pm Thursday from Jersey with 1,325
Muratti supporters. The ship was crowded, the number being only 75 below her comple-
ment. Berthed at No. 2 Jetty, at 2.40pm, disembarkation by two gangways began and continued for 20 minutes till 3.00pm. The promenades were filled with onlookers, among
whom were many of the 600 who arrived in the morning. Many persons asked on landing
if the shops were open. They were not but the ice-cream men were busy. While the supporters marched to St. Julian's Weighbridge the whole area seemed to be given up to a
road-wide procession. Guernsey had to make a late change to their side when M. Brassel
was unable to play due to an injury to his spine and he was replaced by A.E. Le Maitre
(North). Guernsey met Jersey before a crowd of 11,005 at the Track in the final of the
Muratti competition. The scene was a colourful and picturesque one with Red and White
favours and Green and White favours everywhere. Prior to the match the crowd were entertained by the band and drums of the Royal Guernsey Militia. There was a rousing reception
for Major-General E.N. Broadbent C.B., C.M.G., D.S.O., Lieut-Governor of Guernsey
when he arrived at the ground, and before the match he was presented to both teams.
 Guernsey was led out by W. Heulin, and Jersey by G. Malzard. Guernsey won the toss

Presentation of the teams.

and defended the west goal. The opening encounters were very tentative with both defences clearing with ease. Jersey forced an attack and Berry swung in a high centre from the right and Benest crossed in to drive over the bar at short range. From the goal-kick Guernsey went on the attack and as Dorey ran in with the Jersey defence out of position Le Riche came out to thwart him by collecting the cross from Martel. The first goalmouth scare came after 5 minutes when Barrasin dropped the ball into the Jersey goalmouth and, with Le Riche beaten, it was entering the net when Nobes headed it behind for a corner. Jersey replied when Davenport put Hurel away, Syvret failed to get his cross in but Hurel smashed in a low drive that caused Mechem to produce a fine save. The game was quickly moving from end to end with both goalkeepers doing well to prevent a score. Jersey had an escape when, after 31 minutes, Freeman centred right across the Jersey goal; the ball cannoned off the defenders; Duquemin collected the ball and drove in a shot that came back off a defender before Davenport cleared the ball. Dorey nearly opened the scoring when, from a Barrasin pass, he fired in a shot that struck the goalkeeper and came out and was finally scrambled clear. In the last minute of the half Jersey won a corner, Berry took it and the ball was half-cleared but it fell to Syvret who crossed the ball back in and Hurel drove a high shot into the Guernsey net with Mechem out of position. As the half-time approached Dorey headed over the bar from a W.C. Freeman free-kick quickly followed by a running drive from Martel that just went over. At half time the score was Guernsey-0, Jersey-1.

The second half was as hard as the first but much of the play was ragged. Jersey had the advantage of the wind and sun at their backs and when Malzard broke up a Guernsey attack he set up C.S. Freeman but he put his centre far behind. Guernsey was pushing on to the attack but was finding C.S. Freeman and Malzard in the Jersey defence in fine form. They won a corner and from W.C. Freeman's kick there was a furious melee in front of the Jersey goalmouth but the ball was finally cleared. Guernsey had a lucky escape when Benest, with an open goal before him, miskicked and the chance was gone. The game was then played in the midfield for a time with occasional excursions into the goal areas. In a swift Guernsey attack Le Riche had to save at full stretch from an excellent effort from Le Maitre. After 79 minutes Duquemin, receiving a pass from the right, beat a defender and scored an equaliser for Guernsey with a beautifully placed shot. The game became even faster and Dorey came close with a shot followed a counter attack led by Berry. Duquemin and Dorey then combined well as they rushed through the Jersey defence in a move that ended when Dorey crashed a great drive just over the bar. Then only a great tackle by Huelin averted a Jersey goal when Galway was left 10 yards out with only Mechem to beat. The game had only four minutes to go when Dorey scored the winning goal for Guernsey, the final score in a pulsating game being Guernsey -2, Jersey-1.

Guernsey: D. Mechem, H. de Garis, W. Huelin (c), A.E. Broadrib, W. Barrasin, J. McCarthy, W.C. Freeman, J.A. Martel, H. Dorey, H. Duquemin, A.E. le Maitre.
Goalscorers: Duquemin, Dorey.

Jersey: G. le Riche, G.A. Malzard (c), C.S. Freeman, A.F. Davenport, S.V. Nobes, G. Morris, P. Berry, E. Hurel,A. Galway, H.V. Benest, A. Syvret.
Goalscorer: Hurel.

The Muratti Vase was presented to W. Heulin by the Lieut-Governor.

The referee, Capt. G. Hamilton-Jones, remarked that he had never seen a game played in a more glorious and sporting spirit. The Jersey and Guernsey teams were the guests of the GFA at the Muratti Ball that was held at St. Georges Hall. Many Jersey supporters were included in the 850 who attended. The music was provided by the Versatiles and Bert Williams' Bands.

1 9 3 7 .

In the Weekly Press for 4 February 1937 there appeared the following series of photographs showing a young footballer in action.

These are action photographs of four-year old Michael Brassel, son of M.J. Brassel, the

Rangers and Muratti outside-right, indulging in some 'footer' practice. Young Michael is beginning to show real ability even at his age. Watch him Rangers; this is a star player in the making.

The real significance of the last sentence of the caption would not become apparent until 6 May 1954.

MURATTI SEMI-FINAL.
15 April 1937, The Cycling Grounds, Guernsey.

Guernsey -4, Alderney -1.

Once again there were discussions about Harold Dorey prior to the Muratti match. Although Dorey was undoubtedly Guernsey's best centre-forward there was a strong feeling in favour of a leader who was playing in Guernsey football and if this feeling prevailed in the Selection Committee room then their choice could fall on T. Le Prevost (Rangers) who, in addition to scoring 8 times the previous week against Athletics, had led the Island forward line in fine style on Monday. Allen (North) also had a strong claim. For this match the Selectors chose Dorey, the First Tower centre-forward and captain, to lead their attack and this forced him to make a decision as to whether to play for Guernsey or for First Tower in the Lady Bingham Cup match against the 'Rest' which was on the same day. Dorey stated that he would play for Guernsey in the semi-final 'It is my Island', he explained 'and as they selected me I feel I ought to play for them'.

There was a large crowd at the Track to see Guernsey and Alderney contest the Muratti first round tie. Although it had been 17 years since Alderney's sole victory in the competition, they always gave of their best and were looking forward to the tussle. Guernsey had two new caps with D.B. Collenette (North) and W. Crocker (Rangers) making their debuts. There were five Alderney players making their debuts in P. Allen in goal along with H. Quinain, L. Bohan, N. Simon (Belgrave Wanderers) and R. Brehaut. Two of the Alderney players, P. Allen and E. Picot travelled over from England on the Wednesday and joined up with their team mates at their headquarters in the Hotel de Normandie.

H. De Garis led out Guernsey, and Alderney was led out by G. Burness. Alderney won the toss and elected to defend the west goal and play with the wind behind them.

Alderney started the sharpest and Mechem was tested by a long-range effort by Brehaut and an instant later when Riou centred cleverly, he dived full length to divert the ball, which would have found Picot with an open goal. Guernsey replied with a long range shot from Broadrib that went wide. Guernsey took the lead after 9 minutes when a move was worked by Martel and Collenette, who passed to Dorey, and he beat P. Allen with a fast shot from close range. As Guernsey pushed on Catts broke up an attack and later when Mauger, went through dangerously but was injured and had to leave the field. Picot and

G. Burness (Alderney) meets the referee, Dr. Barton.

Riou combined well in an attack but the final shot did not trouble Mechem. Mauger returned and almost immediately sent in a fine cross that found Crocker in space, but he put his shot wide. In 21 minutes Dorey rounded off a forceful attack by slipping between the Alderney full-backs and firing in a fierce drive for the second goal. Alderney fought back strongly and after 27 minutes reduced the arrears. Picot, when tackled by Huelin, passed to the unmarked Odoir, who shot and the ball was deflected by a defender into the net.

Picot (Alderney) following up as Odoir's shot is deflected into the net.

Alderney's Allen and Bohan combine to thwart Guernsey's Dorey.

This goal lifted Alderney and Bougourd had to produce a good tackle to stop Odoire progressing. Guernsey restored their two-goal lead in the 31st minute when Dorey and Mauger opened up the attack and Mauger scored with a great shot that went in off the base of the far post. As the game neared half time Crocker was causing a lot of problems for the Alderney defence but the first half ended Guernsey-3, Alderney-1.

Guernsey began the second half with the wind at their backs but without Mauger who was off injured and was being examined by Dr. Rose. Following a Guernsey attack, A.L. Allen miskicked, but goalkeeper P. Allen saw the danger and rushed out to collect the ball before Dorey could capitalise. Crocker again was causing problems but was well stopped by Quinain then Catts prevented De Garis from progressing. Dorey then broke through and looked a certain scorer but, from a few yards out, he drove his shot into the side netting. The game was hard and fast but much of the interest had gone out of the play and the crowd were strangely quiet. Alderney, however, were still dangerous in their breakaway attacks and Mechem had to be alert in saving a low shot from Picot and again when Odoire sent in a cross into a crowd of players he was happy to collect the ball safely. After 62 minutes Guernsey scored a fourth goal when Martel ran through cleverly and beat Allen from well out. Mauger returned to the field with a cracked rib and was quickly in the action when he crossed in for Dorey to send in a shot that was well held by P. Allen. The final minutes of the match were played out with Guernsey on the attack and, from a Bougourd clearance, Dorey sent a terrific drive wide leaving the final score Guernsey-4, Alderney-1.

Guernsey: D. Mechem, P. Bougourd, W. Huelin, H. de Garis (c), A.E. Broadrib,
              E.J. Warren, D. Mauger, J.A. Martel, H. Dorey, D.B. Collenette,
              W. Crocker.
              Goalscorers: Dorey (2), Mauger, Martel.

Alderney: P. Allen, H. Quinain, A.L. Allen, L. Bohan, N. Simon, P. Catts, R. Riou,
              R. Brehaut, E. Picot, G. Burness, F. Odoir.
              Goalscorer: Odoir.

Interviewed at half-time Dr. A.W. Barton, the referee, said that he thought the standard of play was very high. It was a very clean game and he was impressed by the fine spirit shown by both sides. This was regarded as one of Guernsey's poorest performances in years and a great improvement was needed for the Final against Jersey. Best for Alderney were N. Simon, P. Catts and F. Odoir.

MURATTI FINAL.
29 April 1937, Springfield Stadium, Jersey.

Jersey -2, Guernsey -2. aet.

Once again there was a large attendance to witness this Coronation Muratti final at Springfield between Jersey and Guernsey. Malzard (YMCA) captained the Jersey team and De Garis led the Guernsey side. There were no new caps in the Guernsey team but they lost the services of Brookes due to injury and his place was taken by H. Duquemin. W.

Excited fans make their way to Springfield Stadium.

The Guernsey supporters prepare to leave the ship.

A Jersey fan dressed for the match.

Freeman was pronounced fit and took his place in the team. Jersey had five players making their debuts: W. Dauny, E. Chevalier, C. Dale, G. Smith and F. Vardon. The last time Jersey won the Vase was in 1931 and only Chris Freeman remains from that team. Four of the Guernsey team on that day are on duty in this match. The mailboat 'Isle of Jersey' arrived with over 1,000 passengers on board and it took 20 minutes before the last passenger had disembarked with three gangplanks being utilised. Travelling to Jersey for the match was the Guernsey Brass Band (formerly the North Band).

Something of a raid was executed on a well-known store in St. Helier on the morning of the match and every available frying pan bought up by youths from Guernsey desirous of making as much noise as possible during the game. There was a big crowd at the ground with all the available space being occupied. The new concrete stand was used for the first time at a football match and accommodated 1,450; altogether there was seating for 3,200. The RMIJ band played before the game and a Guernsey accordion band also marched round the arena. For the first time the Jersey side met at the YMCA, where they changed, arriving at the ground shortly before kick-off.

Guernsey's W. Freeman had a try out last evening and was pronounced fit, however Brookes was unable to play due to an injury and was replaced by H. Duquemin. The Jersey

E. Chevalier (Jersey)

W. Crocker (Guernsey).

H. Duquemin (Guernsey).

Guernsey on the defensive at Springfield.

team were led out at 3.27pm followed by the Guernsey side five minutes later, or one minute after the game should have started. Before the match both teams lined up in front of the stand and shook hands with the Lieut-Governor of Jersey.

Malzard won the toss and decided to defend the Springfield Hall end. Jersey immediately went on the attack with Dale and Berry combining to give Berry a chance that hit the side netting. Guernsey replied with a fine move that ended with Le Riche saving a shot from Crocker.

Jersey was beginning to get on top and it came as no surprise when, after four minutes, a fine run by Dale and an excellent cross by Berry resulted in Chevalier driving low into the corner of the net out of Mechem's reach. Jersey continued to dominate with Nobes and Dauny shutting out any Guernsey attack and, protecting Le Riche Guernsey had a chance to equalise when, after Malzard had cleared weakly, Mauger found himself in a good position but could only shoot wide. An excellent series of fine touches saw Martel put Mauger away but he was well tackled by Nobes at the expense of a corner which was headed clear by Chris Freeman for Jersey. The game began to swing from end to end, and after De Garis had foiled Berry the ball broke to Dorey but Le Riche ran out to clear. Jersey nearly increased their lead when the ever dangerous Chevalier got through but Mechem was quickly off his line to fall on the ball. Mauger then collected a lose ball and put Duquemin into a good position but his shot was a poor one, resulting in a goal kick. Le Riche took the kick sending it down the middle where it found its way to Crocker and he fired in a shot that scrapped the crossbar. Guernsey was trying to bring Dorey more into the game but he was being well controlled by Nobes who was giving him very little space to operate As the first half neared its end, Duquemin gave away a free-kick which was quickly taken by

C. Dale (Jersey).

first half neared its end, Duquemin gave away a free-kick which was quickly taken by Nobes who saw his shot just go over the bar with Mechem in trouble. Mauger tried to force the pace but he was well contained and although there were minor skirmishes at either end, the half time whistle found the score Jersey-1, Guernsey-0.

The second half began with Varden, taking a pass from Chevalier, firing in a shot that Mechem saved well. Guernsey had a lucky escape in the 55th minute when a move by Varden and Berry resulted in Chevalier missing an open goal with Mechem out of position. When the game was an hour old Duquemin hit a fine shot that Le Riche could not hold and it dropped over the line for the Guernsey equaliser.

The game was now more even with both sides coming close. Dorey had to go off injured and he was soon followed by Warren who had to depart, leaving Guernsey with nine men. Warren quickly returned as Jersey tried to maintain an advantage and Chevalier drove over the bar from close in. Dorey returned to the fray after treatment as the game moved from end to end as both teams strove for an opening. Jersey increased the pace as they strove to regain the lead and Dale sent Berry away down the wing but his centre was too hard and Vardon sent his shot over the bar. The game was very open and in a Guernsey raid Mauger appeared to be brought down in the Jersey penalty area but the referee waved play on. Berry then missed a great chance for Jersey from 15 yards out by putting his shot over the top. With five minutes remaining Martel sent a fine ball into the Jersey area but Crocker could not convert. De Garis left the field near the end, being Guernsey's third casualty, and full time came with the score Jersey-1, Guernsey-1.

Guernsey started extra time without the services of De Garis but this handicap did not appear to have affected them. After three minutes, Broadrib took the ball from outside his own penalty area; he dribbled down the field beating man after man, and finally ended up crashing a magnificent shot inside of the upright leaving Le Riche helpless. This remarkable goal gave Guernsey a 2-1 lead. Guernsey's ten men were putting a lot of pressure on Jersey and their defence was having difficulty holding on. Jersey forced a corner a corner on the right and Berry sent in a cross that was met by Chevalier only to see it being headed to Mechem by Bougourd and the chance was lost. Smith and Dale were combining well but could not get the better of the Guernsey defence and as the game became more scrappy the first half ended Jersey -1, Guernsey -1.

De Garis returned to the field as the second period of extra time began and the game became more even. In the 112th minute Jersey equalised when, following a foul on Dauny by Mauger, Chris Freeman took the kick and Dale sent in a great header past Mechem.

In the last minute Jersey came close when Berry headed into the goal only for W.C. Freeman to hook the ball away for a corner. The Jersey players appealed strongly that the ball had gone over the line but the referee had no hesitation in not awarding a goal. There was no more scoring and the whistle sounded to end one of the most thrilling Muratti finals on record with the score Jersey -2, Guernsey -2.

Jersey: G. le Riche, G.A. Malzard (c), C.S. Freeman, A.F. Davenport, S.V. Nobes, W. Dauny, P. Berry, C.J. Dale, Le Chevalier, G.L. Smith, F. Vardon.
Goalscorers: Chevalier, Dale.

Guernsey: D. Mechem, P. Bougourd, H. de Garis (c), E.J. Warren, A.E. Broadrib, W.C. Freeman, D. Mauger, J.A. Martel, H. Dorey, H. Duquemin, W. Crocker.
Goalscorers: Duquemin, Broadrib.

This was only the second time in the history of the Muratti that a final required a replay; the first occasion was in 1912. The replay was scheduled for Whitson Bank Holiday, 17 May. The Muratti Day was brought to a fitting close at West Park Pavilion with a Muratti Ball that was held under the auspices of the Jersey FA.

MURATTI FINAL-REPLAY.
17 May 1937, The Cycling Grounds, Guernsey.

Guernsey -3, Jersey -3. aet.

For the second time in the history of the Muratti competition Guernsey and Jersey were engaged in a replay. This match was played at the Track on Whit Monday. Muratti excursionists were making their way to St. Helier harbour as early as 5.30am, and at 7.30am the principal street resembled the 1.00pm 'rush' hour. A small aeroplane circling over the harbour greeted the excursion boats as they arrived at St. Peter Port and also flew over the pitch during the game.

Before the game commenced Mr. W. Ph. Le Bas (President, CI Inter-Insular Committee) welcomed the Lieut-Governor of Jersey, Major-General H. de C. Martelli, KBE, CB, DSO,

Allen (out of the picture) scores Guernsey's first goal.

and the Lieut-Governor of Guernsey, Major-General E.H. Broadbent, KBE, CB, CMG to the Cycling Grounds. Both teams were presented to Major-General Broadbent, the Lieut-Governor of Guernsey. As he shook hands with the players the band of the Royal Guernsey Militia played 'For he's a jolly good fellow' with the crowd joining in - a pleasing gesture to Guernsey's popular Governor. Before the match the band played popular selections and during the interval gave a display of marching and counter-marching. Frying pans, saucepans and other household utensils were used by the Jersey supporters at the Track and they certainly created the necessary noise.

Bougourd won the toss for Guernsey and elected to defend the east goal. In the opening exchanges Lees attacked for the visitors but he was well intercepted by Bougourd and this was followed by a clever dribble by Martel who set up Crocker and he in turn was tackled by Malzard. From a corner by Crocker, H. Duquemin headed in but the ball was cleared by Nobes for a corner. Mauger took the kick and found Allen who drove it past Hamon to put Guernsey 1-0 up after four minutes.

This goal put Guernsey well on top and Martel, the best player on the field, made another of his clever runs and sent in a shot that Hamon did well to save. Benest was causing some problems for the Guernsey defence but Warren and Bougourd were managing to contain him. As Jersey continued to press Lees, and Chevalier combined well to try to set up Berry, he could not reach the ball and it went behind as Guernsey held out. Petra, Chevalier and Lees set up a promising move which ended with Lees sending in a superb ground shot that was well saved by Mechem at full stretch. Crocker came close to increasing Guernsey's lead but his point blank shot was saved by Hamon, and Bougourd hit the bar with the rebound. Jersey renewed the pressure and Bougourd cleared a certain goal when Berry collected a pass from Petra and had beaten Mechem. The pressure continued and Dale sent the ball to Berry who put in a fine centre that Mechem saved but could not hold, Chevalier raced in and breasted the ball into the net for the equaliser after 29 minutes. Mauger was injured in a collision with Jersey's Freeman and had to leave the field for treatment, returning after five minutes. No sooner had he returned when Dale had to go off injured but he too returned after treatment. The game was becoming fast and furious with both Hamon and Mechem making crucial saves to keep the score at half time Guernsey-1, Jersey-1.

The second half began in a similar vein with both sides coming close only to be denied by two excellent defences. Jersey cleared a Guernsey raid and Malzard gave the ball to Dale

W. Crocker (Guernsey).

George Malzard. (Jersey captain).

who quickly sent it to Davenport who put a shot into the goalmouth only for Mechem so save coolly. Jersey then had a close shave when Allen was put through by Martel and he sent in a fast ground shot from close in that was saved by Hamon's foot at the expense of a corner. Jersey then began to take control with their midfield dictating the play for long periods. They came close when Chevalier headed on to Lees, who beat two men cleverly and as he prepared to shoot from an excellent position, Bougourd raced across to clear the danger. Guernsey was under sustained pressure when, following some fine work by Martel, they won a corner. Mauger placed his kick perfectly, Crocker headed it back and Allen met it with his head to score a model goal after 73 minutes. Moments later Hamon had to rush out to prevent Allen scoring again. Jersey rallied and Mechem saved from Davenport and, Chevalier, in a further attack, drove just over. The breakthrough for Jersey came after 79 minutes when Benest headed in a clever goal from Berry's centre. Just before full-time Chevalier headed inches wide and then an excellent free-kick by Chris Freeman was well saved by Mechem leaving the final result, Guernsey-2, Jersey-2.

For the second time in this Muratti tie, extra time was played. Jersey began the sharpest and Dale sent the ball through to Chevalier who put his shot just wide. This was quickly followed by a Guernsey raid and Martel shot inches over the bar. After 12 minutes play Jersey had a fortunate escape when, with Hamon beaten, Martel saw his fine shot come off a defender for a corner. In the 103rd minute Guernsey took the lead again. Mauger put in a clever centre and Crocker headed past Hamon and at half-time the score was Guernsey -3, Jersey – 2.

For the second half of extra-time Lees and Chevalier switched positions in an attempt to vary the play. Jersey once again strove for the equaliser and in the 106th minute Petra sent a cross field pass to Dale. He in turn passed it on to Berry who sent in a fine centre that was met by Lees who headed it past a despairing Mechem. Both teams now pressed on for the winning goal and Mechem had to save twice from Benest. In the final minutes Benest headed into the goal and, as it looked like it might cross the line, Mechem flung up a hand and saved brilliantly. So after four hours the sides finished level – after one of the most gruelling matches on record. The final score was Guernsey-3, Jersey-3.

Guernsey: D. Mechem, P. Bougourd, W.C. Freeman, E.J. Warren, A.E. Broadrib,
              J.H. Duquemin, D. Mauger, J.A. Martel, W. Allen, H. Duquemin,
              W. Crocker.
              Goalscorers: Allen (2), Crocker.

Jersey: Hamon, G.A. Malzard (c), C.S. Freeman, A.F. Davenport, S.V. Nobes,
              A. Petra, P. Berry, C.J. Dale, E. Le Chevalier, J.E. Lees, H.V. Benest.
              Goalscorers: Chevalier, Benest, Lees.

Following the final whistle Lees was carried off the pitch to the pavilion shoulder high by a group of enthusiastic Jersey supporters.

The referee, Mr. Horwood, considered the game to have been remarkably even although he did not think that the combined work of either team had been as good as in the first game. He thought that the standard was something between the Surrey Senior League and the Isthmian League.

After the game Mr. W. Ph. Le Bas (President J.F.A.) addressed the crowd outside the Pavilion. He announced that the Inter-Insular Committee had decided that each side should hold the cup for six months, and that Jersey should hold the cup for the first six months as it had been in Guernsey for so long.

Mr. J.J. Eveson then called upon His Excellency the Lieutenant Governor of Jersey to present the cup to the Jersey captain and His Excellency the Lieutenant Governor of Guernsey to present the medals to the Guernsey team (Jersey would be awarded medals later).

The presentation closed with three cheers for their Excellencies.

Many Jersey football enthusiasts who were unable to cross to Guernsey for the match assembled outside the offices of the Jersey Evening Post to watch the scores being posted in the windows and so keep in touch with the progress of the play. With full-time approaching, the crowd was so great that the roadway was entirely blocked by a solid mass of people and police had to divert vehicular traffic into Charles Street.

When the Jersey team returned home aboard the ss St. Patrick they received a fine welcome from the large crowd gathered on the quay. George Malzard, the Jersey captain, who was carrying the Vase, was carried shoulder-high off the boat and followed by the rest of the side proceeded to an illuminated double-decker JMT bus (used in the Coronation procession) which was waiting. On arrival at the Corner House Restaurant the members were welcomed individually by Mr J.T. Ferguson, Constable of St. Helier, Patron of the JFA. He, on behalf of the people of Jersey, congratulated the captain and his team on their display and their spirit. They had gone behind on three occasions but had not lost heart and equalised three times and came close to actual victory. He added that this Coronation Muratti year would be remembered not only for the two games and the extra time but for the good sporting spirit displayed throughout. A buffet supper had been arranged as the players had to leave their dinner at the Hotel Normandie in Guernsey as the St. Patrick could not be delayed. An excellent ending to a memorable Muratti final.

1 9 3 8 .

MURATTI SEMI-FINAL.
28 April 1938, The Cycling Grounds, Guernsey.

Guernsey -4, Jersey -3.

The 'St. Helier' (Capt. R. Pitman) arrived on Thursday with 540 supporters for the Muratti match. They were, as usual loudly displaying their red and white colours. At the quayside red-and-white favours and hats of all descriptions were being sold. Also landing from Jersey were the Vauxbelets College Football teams and the party in charge of the Rev. Brother Donatian after their matches in Jersey the previous day, and the Jersey table tennis team. There were scenes of animation at the New Jetty when the 'Isle of Sark' arrived with more excursionists just before 3.00pm. A huge crowd had gathered to meet the vessel and as she drew near the Quay the clanging of frying pans, jingling of Muratti bells and roar upon roar of cheering greeted them, and were returned by the hundreds that thronged the ship's decks. Two gangways were inserted and for nearly 20 minutes the people swarmed from the vessel. Some supporters were in too much of a hurry to wait for their turn to pass

The Jersey team run out onto the field.

The Jersey defence clear a Guernsey attack.

Doug Mechem. (Guernsey)

down the gangway and preferred to jump from the vessel to the Quay. This number brought the total of Jersey supporters to around 1,500.

In the evening prior to match day the members of the Guernsey and Jersey Muratti teams were present at a dance organised by the Guernsey Rugby Football Club and held at the Duke of Normandie. The dance music was provided by Eric Paul Mahy's band and the function proved very popular and was well attended.

The joint holders of the Muratti Vase were now ready to meet at the Cycling Grounds in the first round of the 1938 Muratti competition. The teams were led by two very experienced players in W.C. Freeman for Guernsey and A. Galway for Jersey. The Jersey team included J. Drew who became the first ever player to be selected for the Senior and Junior Muratti matches in the same season. The Guernsey side included H. Duquemin who plays his football in Jersey for First Tower United.

Jersey won the toss and decided to defend the eastern goal with a fair north-easterly wind blowing. The opening play was very even, both sides were probing for an early lead with Jersey coming close when Hughes sent a pass through to Chevalier but Mechem saved his shot easily and cleared. Chevalier and Lees were shaping up well for Jersey and Duquemin and Le Prevost pushing on for Guernsey. The visiting forwards were combining well and when Chevalier set Lees away it took some fine defending by Broadrib and Freeman to clear the situation. Jersey was beginning to take control and Dale passed to Lees who was stopped by a dramatic interception by the home defence. Guernsey responded with a fine move by Duquemin and Le Prevost as they set up Crocker but his run was stopped by Kent in the Jersey defence. As Guernsey continued to press they were awarded a free kick against Chevalier, which Mahy pushed to Mauger, his fine cross was aimed at Duquemin

Jersey goalkeeper, Le Riche, saves bravely at the feet of Le Prevost.

who just failed to make contact. Jersey held out well and countered when Berry cut in from the right and centred neatly to Lees who beat Mechem with a high drive to give Jersey the lead after 20 minutes. Jersey was again dangerous and Mechem had to make a dramatic clearance as Lees shaped up for a shot. Guernsey could not make any headway against an excellent Jersey defence, in which Galway was particularly effective. Crocker, however, managed to burst through to send in a terrific shot that went past the Jersey post.

Jersey were again on the attack, Lees broke through the defence and, with the goal at his mercy, he drove hard but Mechem made a magnificent save at the expense of a corner. As half time approached an excellent Jersey move resulted in Lees scoring with a low shot out of Mechem's reach. Jersey was good value for the half time score of Guernsey-0, Jersey-2.

The hero of the first half was Mechem in the Guernsey goal who time and time again thwarted the rampaging Jersey forwards.

Guernsey started the second half in a positive mood and early on Le Riche had to save a Crocker shot. The home team continued to press and Crocker headed in a Mauger cross after 52 minutes to make the score 1-2. This early second half goal gave Guernsey more confidence and they moved on in search of an equaliser with a fine effort by Warren being headed away by Galway. After 57 minutes Guernsey attacked again and some excellent play resulted in Duquemin cleverly avoiding the challenges from the Jersey backs and driving in a fine shot past Le Riche to make the score 2-2. The play became very even with both goals having close shaves. Guernsey had a scare when Mechem fell heavily as he held up an attack by Drew but he recovered after treatment.

Guernsey rallied and Le Riche had to hold on to a high shot from Duquemin and before he could clear Le Prevost almost bundled him into the net. The Guernsey goal was nearly breached when Lees and Dale brought the ball through and as Mechem rushed out to clear Dale was left with an open goal, but Freeman managed to recover and managed to knock the ball clear. Jersey set up a fine move on their left which was expertly finished by Chevalier, who fired a beautifully placed shot into the net to give Jersey a 68th minute lead. Guernsey continued to press and four minutes later Duquemin and Martel set up Le Prevost who went through to beat Le Riche to make the score 3-3. Jersey replied with Chevalier twice setting up Drew who put one shot past and had the other saved by Mechem. The game swung to the other end and Duquemin raced through the defence, evaded Nobes, drew Le Riche and guided the ball past Le Riche and into the net to put Guernsey in front for the first time in the match. The home side now moved in to try and increase their lead and after having several good shots charged down the ball crashed against the Jersey bar and back into play only to be cleared. Le Prevost was then spoken to by referee H.N. Mee after he had rushed Le Riche. He immediately walked up and shook hands with the Jersey goalkeeper. There was no more scoring and this excellent game finished Guernsey-4, Jersey-3.

Guernsey: D. Mechem, H. de Garis, W.C. Freeman (c), H. Marley, A.E. Broadrib, E.J. Warren, D. Mauger, J.A. Martel, T.J. Le Prevost, H. Duquemin, W. Crocker.
Goalscorers: Crocker, Duquemin (2), Le Prevost.

Jersey: G. Le Riche, Kent, S.V. Nobes, A.F. Davenport, A. Galway (c), Hughes, P. Berry, C.J. Dale, J.E. Lees, E. Le Chevalier Drew.
Goalscorers: Lees (2), Le Chevalier.

Interviewed at half-time the referee, Mr. H.N. Mee, said that in his opinion Jersey were admittedly the better side. They used the ball to better advantage and Guernsey were rather lucky to be only two behind. Interviewed after the game the referee commented that there had been two complete phases in the game and Guernsey had played vastly superior football and Jersey had faded out. At the end he felt that Guernsey were slightly on top and deserved to win. Mr. Mee said that Martel was best for Guernsey with Chevalier and Galway the pick of the Jersey team.

Jersey and Guernsey fraternised in the evening at the Muratti Ball, which was held at St. Georges Hall and there were many football supporters from both islands present. The Ball was organised by the Guernsey Football Association and the music was supplied by two of Guernsey's foremost bands, the 'Versatiles' and the Sherwood Foresters.

MURATTI FINAL.
5 May 1938, Springfield Stadium, Jersey.

Alderney -1, Guernsey -3.

Alderney and Guernsey met for the ninth time in a Muratti final. The match was played at Springfield and Guernsey was confident of maintaining their unbeaten sequence in the competition, which has lasted since 1931. As the 2,500 spectators waited the start of the match they were entertained by the Band of the Jersey Militia. Among those present were His Excellency Sir Horace de Courcy Martelli, the Lieut-Governor of Jersey, the Bailiff of Jersey and the French Consul.

Guernsey won the toss and took advantage of the strong cross wind. The game was only 90 seconds old when, following a free kick, Marley beat P. Allen to score and put Guernsey 1-0 up.

Guernsey maintained the pressure and were able to prevent the Alderney forwards from troubling Mechem. The Alderney defence was also very tight with P. Allen in goal being

H. Marley.

John Martel.

Guernsey 1938.
H. De Garis, D. Mechem, A.E. Broadrib, W.C. Freeman (Capt.).
D. Mauger, J.A. Martel, T.J. Le Prevost, H. Duquemin, W. Crocker.
E.J. Warren, H. Marley.

well supported by Brehaut and Quinain. Play in the early minutes was fast but there was little constructive football. Guernsey went near to increasing their lead when Le Prevost was cleverly put through but his cross was kept out by the Alderney defence. Alderney then broke away with Simon passing to Riou only for him to put his shot just wide. Although Guernsey was on top the Alderney defence were able to ensure that any shots from the forwards were mainly from long range and these were well dealt with by P, Allen in the Alderney goal. Mechem in the Guernsey goal did not have much to do except for an occasional goalkick. After 33 minutes Martel finished off a fine move by scoring Guernsey's second goal as he placed his shot wide of Allen.

Two minutes later Mechem had his first shot to save as he collected a rather tame effort by Riou. The pressure was beginning to mount and although Brehaut and Quinain were continually breaking up Guernsey attacks, the shots were still raining in on the Alderney goal. The half ended with the score Alderney-0, Guernsey-2.

Alderney began the second half well and very quickly Odoir tested Mechem followed by Burness who swung in a terrific shot that hit the crossbar and rebounded into play. Guernsey survived this short onslaught and Le Prevost moving over to the left, received a good pass from Crocker, and sent a stiff shot that gave Allen no chance as it crashed into the corner of the net to register Guernsey's third goal. The game after this was fairly even and the Alderney forwards were beginning to make an impression on the Guernsey defence. Richards and Burness were combining well as they tried to reduce the arrears.

After a melee in the Guernsey goal the ball was cleared to H. Allen who sent in a fine shot that Mechem did very well to push away. P. Allen was becoming the hero of the match, for twice in five minutes he foiled the Guernsey forward line by saving almost certain goals from Le Prevost and Crocker. As the game neared its end Richards and Burness once again combined well and Burness fired in a great shot from 15 yards to score for Alderney with just three minutes remaining. The final score was Alderney-1, Guernsey-3.

Alderney: P. Allen, R. Brehaut, H. Quinain, H. Allen, N. Simon (c), R.J. O'Neill, C.J. Richards, G. Burness, G. Miller, F. Odoir, Duplain.
Goalscorer: Burness.

Guernsey: D. Mechem, H. de Garis, W.C. Freeman (c), H. Marley, A.E. Broadrib, E.J. Warren, D. Mauger, J.A. Martel, T.J. Le Prevost, H. Duquemin, W. Crocker.
Goalscorers: Marley, Martel, Le Prevost.

The Muratti Vase was presented to W.C. Freeman by HE Sir Horace de Courcy Martelli, the Lieut-Governor of Jersey.

1 9 3 9 .

MURATTI SEMI-FINAL.
20 April 1939, Springfield Stadium, Jersey.

Jersey -2, Alderney -1.

In preparation for their match against Alderney, Jersey called together 22 players for a training squad. The players chosen were J.C. Dale (First Tower), A.F. Davenport (YMCA), S.J. Davies (Wanderers), J. Drew (First Tower), E. Eloury (Magpies), P. Fosse (Old St. Pauls), C.S. Freeman (Wanderers), A. Galway (Wanderers), J. Gamblin (Old St. Pauls), E.R. Gould (Wanderers), C. Kent (First Tower), H.L. Hughes (Magpies), F. Leamon (Mertonians), J.E. Lees (Wanderers), E. Le Chevalier (Magpies), D.G. Le Riche (Magpies), K. Le Sueur (Wanderers), R.W. Lobb (Beeches), S.V. Nobes (First Tower), W.A. Pailot (Magpies), G.L. Smith (First Tower) and A.J. Syvret (Wanderers).

Jersey entertained Alderney in the first round of the 1939 Muratti competition. Alderney won the toss and chose to defend the Pavilion goal.

Jersey kicked off and was immediately on the attack with Gould feeding Le Chevalier who sent it to Drew. Just as he was about to shoot Quinain put in a superb tackle to save the situation. Jersey followed up and Drew sent in a high lob into the crowded Alderney goalmouth and Lee headed it wide. Gould then sent in a high drive that P. Allen in the Alderney goal tried to push over the bar, but the ball hit the crossbar and rebounded into play. In a hectic spell Allen once again saved from Gould and later cleared from Drew. The pressure on the Alderney defence continued, Allen once again saved from Gould and then he saw a shot from Le Chevalier hit the crossbar. Davenport then sent in a centre that was met by Le Chevalier who put it into the net in the 37th minute. Alderney responded by pushing onto the Jersey defence but with no success and in a Jersey breakout only a brilliant save by Allen prevented Davenport scoring a second goal. Half time arrived with the score Jersey-1, Alderney-0.

Alderney began the second half well with Richards then Simon both coming close. Jersey re-asserted themselves and almost scored through Davenport but his goal bound centre was headed clear by Brehaut. Some fine interpassing by Lees and Davenport set up Drew but his shot was saved by Allen. Simon nearly equalised for Alderney when he attempted an overhead kick that went just wide. The game was held up for a few moments when Gamblin was injured and had to be carried from the field. A fine passing move between Alderney's O'Neill and Allen forced them up the pitch and the ball was passed to Odoire. He sent a fine pass through on goal which caused Simon and Le Riche to race for the ball and, fortunately for Jersey; their goalkeeper reached the ball first and cleared the danger. Alderney continued their pressure when Duplain sent in a centre that was missed by both Simon and Nobes and was picked up by Richards who crashed a terrific drive against the crossbar with Le Riche completely beaten. Jersey produced a fast breakaway after 80 minutes resulting in Drew scoring Jersey's second goal. After 88 minutes Simon scored a deserved consolation goal for Alderney. The final result was Jersey-2, Alderney-1. Alderney had put up a gallant fight but Jersey ran out worthy winners.

Jersey: G. Le Riche, Kent, J. Gamblin, Davies, S.V. Nobes, M. Gamblin, A.F. Davenport, J.E. Lees, E.R. Gould, E. Le Chevalier, J. Drew. Goalscorers: Gould, Drew.

Alderney: P. Allen, R. Brehaut, H. Quinain, H. Allen, R.J. O'Neill, P. Catts, C.J. Richards, G. Miller, H. Simon, F. Odoir, Duplain. Goalscorer: Simon.

MURATTI FINAL.
4 May 1939, The Cycling Grounds, Guernsey.

Guernsey -0, Jersey -1.

Guernsey faced Jersey in the final of the Muratti competition at the Track. Lees, the Jersey captain, won the toss and chose to defend the eastern goal.

Guernsey opened the brightest with Duquemin prominent in their early attacks but Nobes was marshalling the Jersey defence well. The game began to even out but with no real threat to either goalkeeper. The first save of note came from Le Riche when he saved well from Crocker. Mechem's first save was from a tame effort from Leamon, however as the game progressed both defences remained on top. There was an interesting contest developing between Le Prevost and Nobes with the Jersey player having the slight edge. Most of the play was confined to the Jersey half but although on top, the final Guernsey pass, was poor and their attacks rarely troubled the solid Jersey defence. The play was hard but not a lot of good football was being played and the crowd was very quiet for a Muratti final. The first half ended Guernsey-0, Jersey-0.

Guernsey attacks the Jersey goal.

A rousing ovation greeted the teams as they came out after the interval, during which a collection was taken in aid of Lord Baldwin's Fund for refugees.

The opening stages of the second half saw Jersey slightly on top and Mechem had to make a fine save from Drew. The pressure continued and Gould found Le Chevalier with a pass, he then sent a fast ground shot through a crowd of players and into the net to put Jersey 1-0 up. Jersey were again on the attack with Drew going down the left wing and putting in a centre where Lees and Leamon were converging but Mechem managed to clear. Drew was causing a lot of problems for Guernsey as the pressure continued but Mechem remained firm. Leamon almost scored when he placed a ball past Mechem only to see Le Lievre kick it away from the empty goal. The play was now more even and there were incidents in both goalmouths.

As the game neared its end Guernsey forced a corner that was taken by Mauger. His perfect kick almost reached Le Prevost's head but was brilliantly fisted away by Le Riche. The game ended Guernsey-0, Jersey-1.

Guernsey: D. Mechem, E. Sauvage, W.C. Freeman (c), E.J. Warren, G. Taylor, S. Le Leivre, D. Mauger, J.A. Martel, T.J. Le Prevost, H. Duquemin, W. Crocker.

Jersey: G. Le Riche, Kent, J. Gamblin, A.F. Davenport, S.V. Nobes, Davies, E.R. Gould, J.E. Lees (c), F. Leamon, E. Le Chevalier, J. Drew. Goalscorer: Leamon.

The Muratti Vase was presented to Lees, the victorious Jersey captain, by HE Sir Edward Broadbent, the Lieut-Governor of Guernsey.

This was to be the last Muratti match until 1947 as the Channel Islands were about to endure many years of occupation.

Guernsey had won 7, and shared 1 of the 10 Muratti Vase Competitions in the thirties

Sir Edward Broadbent presents the
Muratti Vase to the Jersey captain Lees.

making the overall totals Guernsey 19 wins: Jersey 9 wins: Alderney 1 win.

As the year came to an end a proposition was put forward by the Jersey Football Association for some representative matches to be played over the Christmas period. It was hoped that a match between a pick of the Jersey team would play the pick of the Guernsey team, in Jersey, on Boxing Day as well as a match between the 'Rest of Jersey' team and the 'Rest of Guernsey', team in Guernsey. The fixtures would be reversed on New Years Day. These were virtually the Islands' first and second teams. There was a joint statement from the Jersey Football Association and the Guernsey Amalgamated Football Committee that these games would go ahead.

BOXING DAY.
26 December 1939, Westmount, Jersey.
Jersey -4, Guernsey -2.

The Lieut-Governor was among the 1,000 spectators at Westmount as referee J. Keyho called the captains together.

Guernsey opened the match the stronger and Barrasin thought that he had scored early on but he was correctly ruled offside. The game was very even for the opening 20 minutes with each goal experiencing narrow escapes. Midway through the half, however, Lees opened the scoring for Jersey. With 30 minutes played Guernsey equalised when Stan Le Lievre, Guernsey's best player, scored following a corner. Jersey began to take control of the game and when Sauvage miskicked, it let in Benest who sent in a centre that was met by Lees who put Jersey ahead. Jersey nearly increased their lead when, with 3 minutes of the half remaining, Mechem made a great save from Waite and at half time the score remained Jersey-2, Guernsey-1.

Seven minutes into the second half Lees completed his hat-trick for Jersey as they began to take control of the match and six minutes later he added a fourth goal. Guernsey began to fight back and with 15 minutes remaining Stevens ran through to score Guernsey's second goal. The game continued with Jersey in control and there was no more scoring leaving the final result Jersey-4, Guernsey-2.

Jersey: G. Le Riche, M. Freeman, J. Gamblin, Sgt. Stewart, Nobes, M. Gamblin, E.R. Gould, Sgt. Waite, J.E. Lees (c), A. Syvret, H.V. Benest. Goalscorer: Lees (4).
Guernsey: D. Mechem, E. Sauvage, W.C. Freeman, E.J. Warren, J. Hickman, S. Le Lievre, W. Stevens, Barrasin, T.J. Le Prevost, Smith, Radford. Goalscorers: Stevens, Le Lievre.

The star of the match was Jersey's Lees who rounded off a fine match with four well taken goals.

E.J. Warren.

Harry Finn.

26 December 1939, The Cycling Grounds, Guernsey.

Guernsey XI -3, Jersey XI -0.

The Jersey team included two Guernseymen in Harold Dorey (Magpies) and Harold Duquemin (First Tower). The referee was N.F. Ozard and the linesmen were M.L. Renouf and H.A. Martel.

There was not much between the sides in the opening minutes. The Guernsey forwards were not working well as a unit but still most of the early play was in the Jersey half. Marquand won an early corner on the right and from the kick McCarthy came close to opening the scoring for Guernsey. Jenkins in the Jersey goal was the busier of the two goalkeepers and he had to be alert as he came out to save well from shots by Young and then Robilliard. As he came out for a third time he fouled Allen resulting in a free-kick which caused a lively scrimmage in the Jersey goal before the ball was finally cleared. Jersey responded when Drew sent a pass to Dorey and he displayed excellent skill when he quickly spun round and sent in a glorious shot that came back off the crossbar. Dorey immediately latched onto the ball and fired in a second shot that was charged down by Le Poidevin. The Guernsey forwards were beginning to get on top and Allen broke through the Jersey defence to send in a terrific drive that Jenkins somehow pushed behind for a corner. Seconds later Jenkins pulled off an excellent save from a fast drive by Martel. Guernsey continued this pressure and they were rewarded when Marquand sent in a corner that was well met by Allen who headed it firmly into the net giving Jenkins no chance. There was no more scoring and half time arrived with the score Guernsey-1, Jersey-0.

Guernsey opened the second half on top and came close to increasing their lead but Jenkins was superb in saving two certain goals as Marquand, Allen and Young began to take control. Jersey broke out of defence and Dorey came very close but he was thwarted by a brilliant save by Harry Finn. Allen and Martel then fashioned a fine chance for Robilliard but he shot wide and this was followed by a fine shot by Marquand that skimmed the bar. Both goalkeepers were then quickly brought into play when Jenkins saved from Martel, followed by Finn saving a terrific drive by Drew. Although the excellent Jenkins was by far the busier goalkeeper, Finn in the Guernsey goal saved an almost certain equaliser when he turned a Duquemin effort over the bar. Guernsey increased their lead when Allen broke through to score with a ground shot that went in near the post. Guernsey was now well on top and twice in as many minutes they came close to increasing their lead. With five minutes remaining Guernsey scored again from a fine goal by Martel. With the game nearing its end Jersey were awarded a penalty. Duquemin took the kick but his shot was well saved by Finn and the final result was Guernsey-3, Jersey-0.

Guernsey: H. Finn, Le Poidevin, Simon, Marley (c), Wallace, McCarthy, Marquand, J.A. Martel, M.C. Allen, Robilliard, T. Young.
Goalscorers: Allen (2), Martel.

Jersey: H. Lloyd-Jenkins, R. Brehaut, E. Petra, Le Var, T. Noel (c), Jones, B. Esnouf, H. Duquemin, H. Dorey, C. St. George, J. Drew.

Although Harry Finn made some crucial saves, the star of the match was Lloyd-Jenkins (Wanderers) in the Jersey goal who brought off a series of remarkable saves throughout the match.

The two fixtures were due to be reversed on 1 January 1940 and supporters in both Islands looked forward to two more enthralling games.

7

Wartime 1940 - 1945

N e w   Y e a r s   D a y   1 9 4 0 .

1 January 1940, The Cycling Grounds, Guernsey.

Guernsey -2, Jersey -1.

There were around 2,000 spectators at the Track to witness this inter-insular match. The Jersey team had to make two late changes when Drew was not able to travel and Sid Nobes had left Jersey for the R.A.S.C. The Jersey side included Guernseyman Harold Duquemin in their forward line. The referee for the match was H.E. Trustum and the linesmen were L. Purdy and F.W. Prout.

The weather was fine for football if a little cold for the 1,500 spectators and there was a slight wind which, in the first half, Guernsey had in their favour. Guernsey began well but despite continual pressure their forwards never really tested the Jersey defence. The quality of football from both sides was not particularly good and the first half passed without any real incident and only some fine runs by Dick Stevens for Guernsey kept the game alive. Half-time arrived with the score Guernsey-0, Jersey-0.

The second half began a lot brighter with Jersey taking the early initiative with the wind at their backs and it was no surprise when they took the lead. Esnouf sent in a good centre that was met by Corporal Leamon who sent it past Mechem. For the start of the second half Guernsey had moved W.C. Allen to centre forward in an attempt to get more penetration and as the team settled after Jersey's goal they began to exert some pressure. The Jersey defence held out well with Le Riche playing very well in goal ably supported by Freeman and Smith. It was not until the 82nd minute that Guernsey made the breakthrough when Le Prevost, who had wandered out to the right, sent in a superb pass to Allen who quickly steadied himself and fired in a great shot that hit the underside of the crossbar and went into the net giving Le Riche no chance. Although Guernsey increased the pressure the Jersey defence ably dealt with the attacks and it looked as though the match would end in a draw. As Guernsey set up an attack with only 30 seconds remaining the ball rolled out from a group of players and Stan Le Lievre was on it in a flash and scored with a magnificent drive to make the final score Guernsey-2, Jersey-1.

Stan Le Lievre.

Guernsey: D. Mechem, E. Sauvage, W.C. Freeman, E.J. Warren, J. Hickman,
S. Le Lievre, W. Stevens, J.A. Martel, T.J. Le Prevost, M.C. Allen,
W. Crocker.
Goalscorers: Allen, Le Lievre.

Jersey: G. Le Riche, M. Freeman, J. Gamblin, Sgt. Stewart, E. Smith, M. Gamblin,
D. Esnouf, H. Duquemin,Cpl. F. Leamon, A. Syvret, Gould.
Goalscorer: Leamon.

The first half of the match was a disappointment for the fans but the second half livened
up a little. Best for Guernsey were Dick Stevens, Sauvage and Mechem. Jersey was well
served by Le Riche, who had an excellent game in goal, M. Freeman and E. Smith.
Collectively Jersey was the better side but could not make the most of their opportunities.
M. Freeman is the younger brother of Chris Freeman the ex-captain and full-back of
Jersey.

1 January 1940, Springfield, Jersey.

Jersey XI -4, Guernsey XI -3.

It was ideal football weather although the Springfield turf was a little on the slippery side
and the 1,000 crowd anticipated a fine contest. Jersey have included former North and
Guernsey star, Harold Dorey, in their line-up. The referee for the match was A.E. Marett.

Although both sides were evenly matched it was Guernsey that started the quickest. The
early part of the half lacked excitement but in the 18th minute Guernsey took the lead
when Young scored the opening goal. Jersey responded immediately and they scored
straight from the kick-off through St. George. The game then quietened down after these
goals and when half-time arrived the score was Jersey-1, Guernsey-1.

The second half started well and soon Harold Dorey found the net for Jersey but the score
was disallowed for a foul on goalkeeper Finn. Jersey then began to put the Guernsey
defence under extreme pressure but found Finn in excellent form. Guernsey withstood the
assault and Young managed to break free and as he drew Jenkins from his goal he centred
for Fallaize to score into an empty net. Jersey were stung by this goal and pushed on into
the attack and Waite sent an overhead pass to St. George for him to equalise. It was now
Guernsey's turn to attack the Jersey defence as they strove to regain the lead but after 67
minutes it was Jersey who scored when Waite fired home with a ground shot from the left.
The game was very tight but with six minutes remaining Fallaize scored again for
Guernsey. The game then swung back to Jersey as they pushed on for a winning goal and
with one minute remaining Harold Dorey found himself unmarked and he shot home the
final goal. The whistle went with the score Jersey-4, Guernsey-3.

Jersey: Lloyd-Jenkins, C. Freeman, Petra, Stone, Noel, Nicolle, Davenport, Waite,
H. Dorey, St. George, Benest.
Goalscorers: St. George (2), Waite, Dorey.

Guernsey: H. Finn, Simon, Le Poidevin, Marley, Wallace, Freiss, Falla, Radford,
Fallaize, Robilliard, Young.
Goalscorers: Young, Fallaize (2).

Following the successes of the matches over the Christmas period it was hoped that the Muratti would continue during wartime. It was conceded, however, that due to conscription both sides would be depleted. At that point no definite steps were taken to cancel the Muratti for that year. The general feeling in football circles was that the game should be played and it was hoped that this would be the case if conditions did not alter.

News was received that George William Scoones, former Wanderers and Muratti player, had died on active service in France. 'Skin', as he was popularly known among his friends, first came into prominence with Veneer FC, and his sterling play soon attracted the notice of Wanderers whom he played for afterwards. His consistency gained him further honours and, he was chosen to represent Jersey on eight occasions in the Muratti between 1909 and 1914 and winning two Muratti medals.

He subsequently went to France to play for Rennes FC and, after rendering them valuable service returned to Jersey. He returned to Rennes to act as coach to the team and when the Great War broke out he volunteered for, and saw service with, the Royal Field Artillery. In the Second World War he had three sons serving in the French Army, and despite his 53 years, again volunteered for service with the Royal Engineers.

He left Jersey on 1 January but died on 27 January in France.

At a Council Meeting of the GFA a letter was read from the JFA in which it was stated that it was decided not to consider the playing of the Muratti Vase match this season. The Chairman, Mr. H.H. Randell, thought that the GFA should do the same and this was supported by the Council. The Council also agreed to Jersey's suggestion to suspend the activities of the Channel Islands Inter-Insular Committee for the duration of the hostilities.

O c c u p a t i o n .

The Occupation of the Channel Islands which began in 1940 appeared to have put an end to the Muratti matches but in fact anywhere Guernsey and Jersey sportsmen were situated there appeared to be a need for such matches.

England.

28 February 1942, Chamber Hall, Bury, England.

Jersey -3, Guernsey -0.

There was a group of Jersey footballers based in the Bury area and they joined the Bury and District League for the 1941-42 season. They arranged a match against a Guernsey team at the Chamber Hall ground in Bury on Saturday 28 February 1942 with a 3.30pm kick-off. The Bury Times referred to the forthcoming game as a 'Novel Soccer match'.

Included in the Jersey squad was C. Coyde who was in fact a Guernseyman. The gentleman on the far left of the top row was J. Harrison who was also part of the Jersey squad. The weather was so bad, with snow and ice on the pitch, that it was said that this was the only game to take place in England on that day. The referee for the first match was Mr. H. Baxendale and he only allowed the match to go ahead because a coachload of Guernsey supporters who had arrived would have been bitterly disappointed.

Guernsey was represented by the following:

C.J. Brehaut, W.E. Lewis, L.J. Laine (c), R. Helman, F. Torode, P. Smith, R. Knight, T. Vidamour, W. Knight, J. Knight, S. Rabey (Oldham Athletic).

The reserves were C.E. Brehaut, S. Roberts and A.S. Maunder with H. Mauger acting as their linesman.

The game was a hard fought encounter on a frozen pitch with Jersey running out convincing winners by 3-0. After the match one of Jersey's players, C. Giot (the captain), offered to put up a cup that was to be played for annually. The first match for the Evacuees Cup would be played in Stockport.

C. Coyde, J. Barter, T. Noel, C. Cornick, E. Belhomme, B. Champion, J. Barry.
R. Le Signe, W. Sayce, C. Giot (c), L. De La Mare, H. Belhomme.
Jersey.

THE EVACUEES CUP.
28 March 1942, Hempslaw Lane, Stockport, England.

Guernsey -2, Jersey -5.

Guernsey started off very well in this match and very soon established a two goal lead. Le Cras opened the scoring and this was followed by an own goal from a Jersey defender. Jersey recovered well and Harrison scored two goals for them to make the half time score Guernsey-2, Jersey-2.

In the second half Jersey took control and H. Belhomme gave them the lead followed by goals from F. Belhomme and captain Giot to make the final score Guernsey-2, Jersey-5.

Jersey therefore became the first winners of the 'Evacuees Cup'.

G e r m a n y .

There were also three unofficial Muratti games held in the Laufen Internment Camp during 1943 and 1944.

The sports ground where the matches were played was situated just outside the confines of the camp. The ground was about one-third the size of a normal football pitch and had a step up around three of the sides and during wet weather the area became very waterlogged and muddy. Due to the fact that the area of the pitch was much smaller than a normal pitch the teams were reduced to seven-a-side and each goal measured about eight feet wide and seven feet high. As the match day approached the Muratti feeling increased and this was intensified by the fact that everyone was living in close proximity to each other.

1943, Laufen Internment Camp, Bavaria, Germany.

Guernsey -1, Jersey -1.

On the day of the match both teams were given a loud rousing welcome and, as the players warmed up, photographs were taken. Within minutes there was a torrential downpour and the pitch markings were soon washed out and the ground was left under several inches of water. Most of the water had to be cleared to the satisfaction of the referee and when this was done the match eventually started, although slightly late. The Muratti atmosphere was enhanced by the spectators making a lot of noise using any utensil they could find and both sets of supporters wore their team's colours.

The referee and linesmen were presented to both captains as they prepared for the toss-up. In goal for the Guernsey team was Frank Stroobant and he included an account of this match in his excellent book 'One Man's War'. The game was played like a typical Muratti match with noisy encouragement from both sets of partisan supporters and very quickly the muddy conditions made it very difficult to distinguish the different teams. When half-time arrived the score was Guernsey-0, Jersey-0.

As the second half began there was another downpour and the wet conditions had a great effect on the game with plenty of free-kicks being awarded and subsequently the play deteriorated. In a Jersey attack a penalty was awarded following a foul. The penalty spot had long been washed away so the ball was placed on a mound of mud. As the kick was taken the ball and the surrounding mud went towards Stroobant in the Guernsey goal and as he looked up towards the ball his face got covered in mud. As he lost sight of the ball it hit the crossbar, bounced down on his head and into the goal to put Jersey 1-0 ahead amid cheers from their jubilant supporters. In the dying minutes of the game one of the Guernsey half-backs dribbled the ball through the water to score an equalising goal. When the referee blew his whistle for full time it was agreed that, due to the appalling conditions, there would be no extra-time and the match ended Guernsey-1, Jersey-1.

Frank Stroobant.

When the match was replayed Guernsey won by 6-1. There was an impressive silver cup awarded for this match and it was made by enterprising craftsmen from silver paper. This trophy was presented to the captain of the victorious Guernsey team.

Midfield action.

Presentation of the trophy.

28 May 1944, Laufen Internment Camp, Bavaria, Germany.

Jersey -2, Guernsey -0.

Jersey played Guernsey on Whit Sunday, 28 May 1944 and a programme of events was as follows:

2.00pm	Players and officials meet on the island.
2.10pm	Introduction of players and officials to Mr. H. Gomperty (American Camp Senior) by Mr. Wynne Sayer (Chairman of Football Committee).
2.29pm.	The announcement of 'Surprise' sports item by C. Rose.
2.30pm	Kick-off.

The Guernsey team, wearing blue, were represented by F. Stroobant, R. Hurford, K. Berry, J. Campbell (c), J. White, W. Arrowsmith, D.A. Bisson.

The Jersey team, playing in red, were represented by C. Chapman, P. Garrett (c), M. Hill, D.A.D. Campbell, A. Le Main, J. Whitaker, V. Jarrett.

The Referee for the match was Mr. Chas. H. Daniel and his linesmen were J. Spera and W. Kolaowski.

The match was a close fought affair and was won by Jersey by 2-0. At the end of the match the cup was presented to P. Garrett, the Jersey captain, by Mr. H. Gomperty. A collection was taken for the Red Cross and YMCA Fund.

In a book entitled 'The Bird Cage' a small report appeared concerning the 'Muratti'.

The respective supporters of Muratti teams have, in spite of the oft-recurring 'lageritis' or 'feduptness', not neglected to create the atmosphere of the real thing, insofar as was possi-

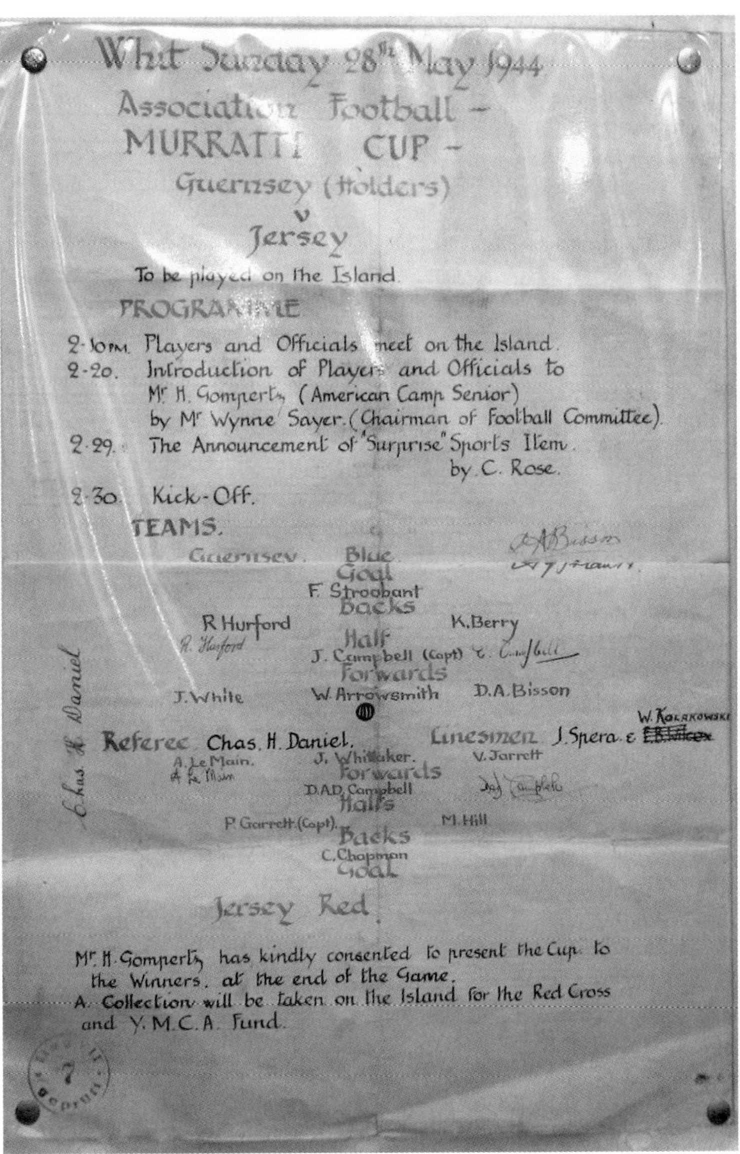

Matchday programme (signed by some of the players).

ble. Colours, rattles, fancy-dress, music (but nothing stronger than 'lager' beer and lemonade) have been in evidence on these occasions. Summing up for the two years shows Guernsey winners of the Soccer and Hockey in 1943 and Hockey and Rugby in 1944 – Jersey with the single triumph of Soccer in 1944 – but the latter put up a very strong fight in that latter season's Hockey and Rugger, which was anybody's game right up to the closing minutes. Impressive-looking (when seen from a distance) silver cups, in reality made by enterprising craftsmen from silver paper, were duly presented.

Ronald Hurford (Guernsey).
(Left) Guernsey Team..

(Below) Jersey Team.

The Guernsey Evening Press reported on Wednesday 12 July 1944 the death at the Emergency Hospital yesterday, of Mr. R. (Bob) Chapple. Mr. Chapple was 54 and he was a prominent footballer and he was a member of Belgrave Wanderers as well as representing Guernsey in the Muratti, gaining 9 caps from 1910 to 1914 and scoring three goals and winning three Muratti medals. He captained Guernsey against Jersey in the 1913 Muratti Vase final. He was a valued and skilled engineer of the Guernsey Railway Company Ltd and will be greatly missed. He entered the hospital for a serious throat operation. Unfortunately Mrs. Chapple and the family of two daughters and two sons are absent from the Island.

It was reported in the Guernsey Weekly Press on Wednesday 17 October 1945 that the Jersey Football Association have again assumed control of Jersey soccer and have approached the Guernsey Football Association with a view to

Mr. Chas. H. Daniel.

the resumption of the inter-insular games. But at present the Guernsey Football Association is dormant and nothing has materialised from Jersey's proposals. The Sarnian Football Association will approach the JFA with a view to staging two matches, one in Guernsey and one in Jersey. Should the present plans materialise it was anticipated that the first fixture will take place at Christmastide and the return next Easter.

Stroobant comes out to clear a Jersey raid.

Drawing from the book 'The Bird Cage'.

Guernsey-1945.

8

1946 - After the Occupation

In the early months of 1946 there was a strong feeling that a Charity match between Guernsey and Jersey representative sides would be arranged. On 1 February nothing concrete had been arranged but it was hoped that negotiations would be opened very soon between the Sarnian Football Association and the Jersey Football Association. One problem was the fact that the JFA may have considered the SFA to be a 'pirate body' but no news was forthcoming. There had been a lot of talk about the idea of the amalgamation of the Guernsey and Sarnian Football Associations and it was felt that this was a good opportunity for them to get together to decide what was happening next season. At the Guernsey Football Association meeting on 6 March 1946 it was announced that, subject to the approval of the Jersey Football Association, Guernsey would travel to Jersey for an inter-insular match on 11 April and host a return match at Cambridge Park on 2 May. The feeling in Guernsey was that due to the recent success of their clubs against Jersey opposition Guernsey would start favourites over the two games. The Guernsey team would be under the charge of Mr. A. Hunter, Hon Sec. of the Sarnian Football Association.

  As the preparations were being made for the forthcoming Peace Cup matches a report appeared in the Guernsey Evening Press on 25 March where it was pointed out that if Guernsey chose Guernseyman Len Duquemin (Tottenham Hotspur) for their team the Spurs management would not stand in his way. Duquemin himself was keen to play, but whether or not it would be wise for him to come over for the game is a debatable point. As it turned out he did not take part in either of the matches.

PEACE CUP
First Game.
11 April 1946,
F.B. Fields, Jersey

Jersey -7, Guernsey -0.

There was brilliant sunshine at the FB Fields where there were lorries parked on the touchline providing hundreds with grandstand accommodation. In attendance at the match were Sir Edward Grasnett KBE, CB, DSO, MC, (Lieut-Governor of Jersey, and Sir Alexander M. Coutanche, the Bailiff of Jersey. Rovers, strong favourites for the Sarnian Football League, had four players in the line-up in J. Loveridge, L. Robilliard, J.A. Martel and Les Collins as well as having Ted Chick as one of the reserves. The Guernsey football team, officials and

Len Duquemin.

some supporters left Guernsey Airport in relays in the morning to fly to Jersey.

Jersey came out first to loud cheers followed by Martel and the Guernsey team. Both teams were then presented to the Lieut-Governor and the Bailiff. The referee was E. Le Brocq and his linesmen were H.F. Faramus and C. Toy. The referee called the captains together, Guernsey won the toss and chose to play with the sun. There was a little breeze blowing across the pitch as Guernsey won the games first corner. The crowd had to be cleared from the touchline before Le Page could take the kick and when the cross came in Martel met it first time but placed it over the bar. The Guernsey goal was then put under severe pressure with Graeme Le Maistre getting into a good position but he put his shot just wide, followed a minute later by Loveridge being penalised for picking the ball up from outside his area. Loveridge did well to push out the free-kick but the ball fell to Drew, who was following up, and he hit the post with his effort. Loveridge then saved a point blank shot from White as the pressure continued. Guernsey held firm and, from a break-away, Martel set up a move and Taylor just missed connecting with a difficult dropping centre. Taylor then crossed to Collenette and Le Riche in the Jersey goal had to dive at his feet to save the situation. The attack then switched to Guernsey's goalmouth and Crowell drove the ball into the penalty area, Whare jumped to head it but handled the ball and referee Le Brocq had no hesitation in awarding a penalty. Graeme Le Maistre stepped up and scored with a hard ground shot. Jersey increased their lead after 30 minutes when Drew set up Le Maistre and he drove for goal, the ball spun out of Loveridge's hands and Olliver came in and crashed his shot into the top of the net. Loveridge then saved from Drew followed by Le Riche saving a header from Collenette as the half ended Jersey-2, Guernsey-0.

Guernsey was first into the attack in the second half but Le Riche saved easily from Le Page. After 11 minutes Jersey scored again when Smith beat Loveridge with a great left-foot drive from 20 yards. Jersey began to increase the pressure and Loveridge had to make a fine save from White, then Le Maistre beat him with a shot into the corner of the net. Moments later Froome parried a shot by Olliver but Le Maistre collected the rebound and scored goal number five. Guernsey nearly scored when a fine shot by Taylor seemed goalbound but it hit Collins in the face and was cleared. This was quickly followed by Loveridge pulling off a miraculous save at the feet of Drew. Four minutes later Loveridge was beat again, this time by Olliver, and in the final minute White received a pass from Le Maistre and crashed the ball into the net making the final score Jersey-7, Guernsey-0.

Jersey: G. Le Riche, D. Crowell, P. Poingdestre, J. Sherry, J. Layzell, G. Knight, J. Olliver, G. Smith, G. Le Maistre (c), W.G. White, J. Drew.
Goalscorers: Le Maistre (4, 1 pen), Olliver (2), Smith.

Guernsey: J. Loveridge, R.J. Mahy, Elliot, S. Whare, N. Froome, L. Robilliard, W.G. Le Page, J. Martel (c), L. Collinette, L. Collins, Taylor.

This was a resounding victory for Jersey whose excellent teamwork had Guernsey unnerved for most of the game. The Jersey team was too fast and organised for the Guernsey side. Guernsey had a lot to think about before the second match on 2 May.

An Island XI selected from the Sarnian Football League journeyed down on Good Friday (April 19) to meet a Jersey Football League side. No Rovers players were included as they had a game with the Jersey Saturday League on the Saturday.

PEACE CUP
Second Game.
2 May 1946, Cambridge Park, Guernsey.

Guernsey -0, Jersey -4.

Guernsey made four changes in their side with W. Freiss (Vale Rec), W. Warr (Vauxbelets Old Boys), A. Du Feu (Vale Rec) and L.L. McKane (Pessimists) replacing Elliot (Casuals), L. Robilliard (Rovers), L. Collins (Rovers) and Taylor (Vale Rec). Jersey, unsurprisingly, selected the same team. The referee was N.F. Ozard and his linesmen were H. Trustum and E. Field.

The Guernsey Football Association were making every effort to bring back the 'Muratti' atmosphere of the pre-war days for this match. The main factor against it was the unavailability of the Cycling Grounds. The match therefore went ahead at Cambridge Park. The grandstand consisted of parked lorries linning the touchline. Chairs were also available and tickets for them could be bought from Messrs Le Riche in High Street, St. Peter Port. Before the match both teams were presented to the Lieut-Governor of Guernsey, Lieut-General Philip Neame.

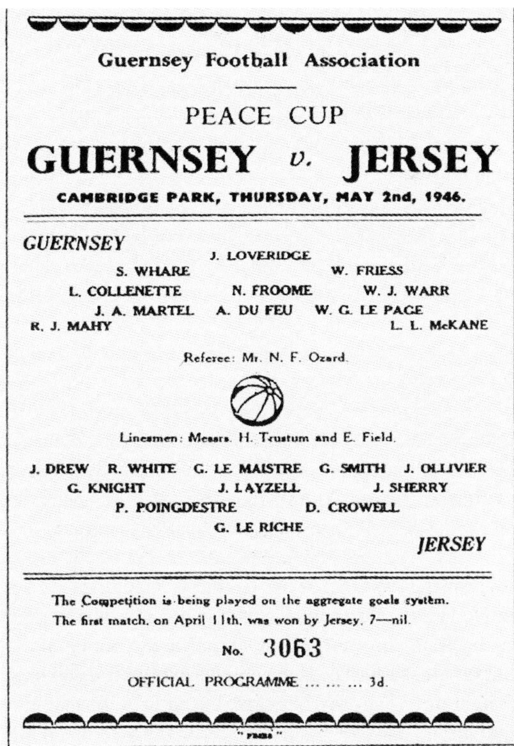

Guernsey Football Association

PEACE CUP

GUERNSEY *v.* JERSEY

CAMBRIDGE PARK, THURSDAY, MAY 2nd, 1946.

GUERNSEY

J. LOVERIDGE

S. WHARE   W. FRIESS

L. COLLENETTE   N. FROOME   W. J. WARR

J. A. MARTEL   A. DU FEU   W. G. LE PAGE

R. J. MAHY   L. L. McKANE

Referee: Mr. N. F. Ozard.

Linesmen: Messrs. H. Trustum and E. Field.

J. DREW   R. WHITE   G. LE MAISTRE   G. SMITH   J. OLLIVIER

G. KNIGHT   J. LAYZELL   J. SHERRY

P. POINGDESTRE   D. CROWELL

G. LE RICHE

JERSEY

The Competition is being played on the aggregate goals system.
The first match, on April 11th, was won by Jersey, 7—nil.

No. 3063

OFFICIAL PROGRAMME ... ... 3d.

The Lieut-Governor being presented to the teams.

Martel won the toss and Le Maistre kicked-off for Jersey and play moved to the left, Collenette miss-kicked, letting Drew in and the winger crossed the ball to Le Maistre who rounded Freiss and drove the ball into the net within 15 seconds of the start. No Guernsey player had touched the ball. Guernsey kicked-off and worked the ball upfield with McKane sending in a fine drive that was saved by Le Riche. There began a period of even play with both defences on top. Guernsey came close to equalising when De Feu was put clear but before he could shoot Crowell cleared into touch. Le Maistre was causing the Guernsey defence some concern when he just failed to connect with a cross by Drew and Loveridge had to be quick to close him down and cause him to hurry his shot which went wide. Whare then had difficulty in clearing a Jersey attack and Drew gained possession 20 yards out and flashed in a great left foot drive that went inches wide of the far post. Le Riche in the Jersey goal was then applauded when he saved well from McKane and cleared despite the close attention of three Guernsey forwards. Jersey then forced a corner which was taken by Drew and his excellent cross was headed goalwards by White but Loveridge saved when he tipped the ball over the bar. At half-time the score was Guernsey-0,   Jersey-1.

  Guernsey was soon on the defensive in the second half and very soon Le Maistre scored when his shot sped under Loveridge's body and into the net to put Jersey 2-0 ahead. Jersey continued their attacks and following a series of throw-ins Olliver set up Le Maistre but he blazed his shot over. De Feu then came close for Guernsey when he shot from a few yards out but the ball came back off the crossbar and was cleared. In the 57th minute Jersey scored again when a fine cross by Olliver seemed to deceive Loveridge and flew across the goal for White to head home. Guernsey responded with a De Feu shot being blocked and falling to Warr but he pushed his shot wide. Guernsey attacked again but Mahy's shot was saved by Le Riche, he cleared upfield and Froome handled in the penalty area. Referee Ozard awarded a penalty that Le Maitre took but saw his shot go wide. After 79 minutes Jersey went further ahead when Le Maistre swung the ball in from the right and it was collected by Drew who fired it into the net. The game became more even with the defences coming out on top again and the final score was Guernsey-0, Jersey-4.

Guernsey: J. Loveridge, S. Whare, W. Freiss, L. Collenette, N. Froome, W.J. Warr, R.J. Mahy, J.A. Martel (c), A. Du Feu, W.G. Le Page, L.L. McKane.

Jersey: G. Le Riche, D. Crowell, P. Poingdestre, J. Sherry, J. Layzell, G. Knight, J. Olliver, G. Smith, G. Le Maistre (c), R. White, J. Drew.
Goalscorers: Le Maistre (2), White, Drew.

This was another comprehensive Jersey victory with their superior teamwork and pace against a disappointing Guernsey team.

Jersey were worthy winners of the Peace Cup with an emphatic 11-0 aggregate victory. The stage was now set for the return of the Muratti Vase competition in 1947.

9
1947 - 1949

1 9 4 7 .

MURATTI FINAL.
1 May 1947, The Cycling Grounds, Guernsey.

Guernsey -1, Jersey -3.

A welcome sight in St. Peter Port with the return of the Jersey Muratti fans.

Following the end of the occupation the Channel Islands were beginning the process of returning to some sense of normality. The return of the Muratti Vase Competition was a welcome step as Guernsey and Jersey came together at the Track for the 1947 final. Alderney did not take part in this year's competition but were preparing to enter in 1948. Tottenham Hotspur manager, Mr. Joe Hume, sent a telegram to Mr Ted Zabiela wishing Guernsey all the best for this afternoon's match. Tottenham Hotspur has made two trips to Guernsey in 1932 and 1933.

The Jersey team included two players, Le Riche and J. Drew, who played in the Final of 1939 and the Guernsey side included three, Sauvage, Martel and le Prevost, from that match. Guernsey also included Bill Whare for his first cap. Bill was born in Alderney.

Five Muratti stars of the past were guests of the Guernsey Press and attended the match.
A. Benstead, W.H. Crews, J. Aubert, R.W. Podger and J. Dodd.

There were two new caps, one on each side, who would have an immense impact on the history of the Muratti Vase. For Jersey 26 year old Graeme le Maistre of St. Paul's began his Muratti career and receiving his first cap for Guernsey was Les Collins of Belgrave W. for his first cap. In future years both would have a significant impact on the destination of the Muratti Vase.

The contest was keenly anticipated with a large crowd, in the region of 11,500, gathering at the Cycling Grounds as the respective captains, Martel for Guernsey and Smith for Jersey led out their teams.

Jersey won the toss and Smith elected to kick into the western goal. Guernsey was the first to attack and in the first minute Collins hit the post with Le Riche beaten. Jersey's first opportunity came when Le Maistre collected a through pass and sent in a fine drive that Finn did well to turn away for a corner. Jersey began to take command and nearly took the lead after four minutes when Smith drove against the crossbar and, as it rebounded, Le Maistre headed over from three yards. The Guernsey defence were under some pressure but were well marshalled by Whare. After 13 minutes, Jersey took the lead. Drew made progress on the left, swung the ball into the middle and, as Finn lost the ball in trying to gain possession, Le Maistre had no difficulty in scoring from about five yards.

Ernie Sauvage.

Following some sustained Jersey pressure Guernsey broke away and won a free kick. Sauvage took the kick and sent it

Le Maistre opening the scoring for Jersey watched by Harry Finn.

Le Maistre fires in Jersey's third goal.

to Le Prevost. He passed first time to Martel who drove for goal but it was well saved by Le Riche. Crowell then broke up a Guernsey attack and sent Le Maistre away and he drove his shot high into the net past Finn to put Jersey 2-0 up after 28 minutes. Jersey continued to be the more effective team and it was no surprise when they scored a 3rd goal after 35 minutes. Jones' long pass found Le Maistre who played a one-two with White and finished by shooting past Finn to make the half time score Guernsey-0, Jersey-3.

 The second half began with an early chance for Guernsey as Martel's 25-yard shot brought Le Riche to his knees as he saved. Play became more open with both goalkeepers producing good saves as chances were made at both ends. Finn prevented a fourth Jersey goal when he dived at Smith's feet as he prepared to shoot. Guernsey reduced the arrears after 67 minutes when Mellanby sent in a cross that was headed past Le Riche by Le Prevost. The goal was initially disallowed but the referee changed his decision and awarded a goal. The Jersey players demonstrated over this but the goal stood. Play again was very even but with no further scoring the final result was Guernsey-1, Jersey-3.

Guernsey: H. Finn, E. Sauvage, W. Whare, L.J. Robilliard, N. Froome, J. Hartland, L. Perriam, J.A. Martel (c), T.J. Le Prevost, L. Collins, F. Mellanby.
Goalscorer: Le Prevost.

Jersey: Le Riche, Crowell, Layzell, Sherry, Gosling, R. Jones, White, Smith (c), G. Le Maistre, Knight, Drew.
Goalscorer: Le Maistre (3).

Finn prepares to gather the ball with Le Maistre in close attendance.

The two teams met at the Hotel Beaulieu following the match where they toasted each other.

When Jersey's victorious Muratti team arrived home on Friday a great welcome awaited them. A coach was put at the players' disposal and they went on a triumphant drive, which ended at the Town Hall where they were greeted by the Constables of St. Helier and were entertained at a vin d'honneur and civic reception. Congratulatory speeches were made by Mr. H.LeF Grant (Constable of St. Helier) and Mr. C.W. Duret Aubin, CBE, (ex-President of the GFA). Mr Philip Le Quesne proposed the toast to the team to which Mr. G.L. Smith, the captain, responded.

1 9 4 8 .

MURATTI SEMI-FINAL.
15 April 1948, The Cycling Grounds, Guernsey.

Guernsey -3, Alderney -0.

Guernsey entertained Alderney at the Track in the first round of the 1948 Muratti competition. This was Alderney's first appearance since the end of the occupation. Their last Muratti match was the 2-1 defeat by Jersey at Springfield in 1939. Three quarters of an hour before the kick off there were estimated to be well over 3,000 spectators in the ground with a steady stream pouring in from the Track Lane entrances. The crowd was entertained prior to the match by the Guernsey Brass Band and as kick off approached there were in excess of 6,000 waiting eagerly for the match. Guernsey had chosen Bill Farmer (Belgrave Wanderers) in goal for his first cap. Bill was actually born in St. Aubin, Jersey. The teams

Walter Cauvain, Alfred Mignot, Percy Allen, Norman Simon, Leonard MacLean. Raymond Mignot.
R. O'Neill, Buster Hammond, Fred Odoire, Noel Mignot, Joseph Harrington.
Alderney Muratti team.

Mr A.J. Sherwill is introduced to Mr. W. Ling.

and officials were presented to Mr. A.J. Sherwill, the Bailiff of Guernsey.

At four minutes to four a huge roar went up as Alderney came on to the pitch led by 'Butch', the dog, and Joe, his master. Seconds later a terrific welcome greeted the Guernsey team. At either end of the pitch police had to clear little boys away from the pitch. Marshall Carre, the Guernsey captain, spun the coin, won the toss, and decided to kick into the western goal.

 The early play was mainly in the midfield and the wind seemed to be troublesome to most of the players. The first chance came when Robilliard went on a fine individual dribble and set up Collins, but he could only put his shot wide. Allen, in the Alderney goal, was the first into action when he cleared from the feet of Carre and De La Mare. Though the football was not of the highest standard, Guernsey did most of the pressing in the first quarter of an hour and Alderney had their defence fully tested. Allen was in action again when he saved from Robilliard by scrambling the ball away and then, following a corner, he saved a header from R. Carre. The play was a bit scrappy at times and when Alderney won a free-kick, Mignot sent in a poor ball that was collected by Marshall Carre and he fired in a long drive which Allen misjudged. Rollie Carre attempted to force the ball into the net, but in doing so he fouled the goalkeeper. In the 23rd minute Guernsey took the lead with a very soft goal. A. Mignot failed to clear the ball away and Collins pushed it back into the centre, where De La Mare, after missing with a left foot drive, managed to get his right foot to the ball and pushed it very slowly goal wards. Allen seemed to have it covered but it trickled into the net. Alderney replied with a quick breakaway when Noel Mignot sent in a lovely cross to O'Neill but his shot went behind. This was followed by another fine move by Noel Mignot which sent Harrington bursting through past Carre and

The referee keeps a close eye on the action.

Alderney supporters.

'Butch' the Alderney mascot.

he crashed in a terrific drive that Farmer could only push out. O'Neill made a desperate effort to get to the ball but Farmer finally cleared.

Guernsey uneasily weathered this storm and in the 32nd minute Hunter disposed Simon and scored with a ground shot that gave Allen no chance to put the home side 2-0 up. Hunter nearly added another in the 37th minute but his hard shot was punched over the bar by Allen. As the half ended Allen had to save well from Collins and the half time score remained at Guernsey-2, Alderney-0.

The second half began with Guernsey doing most of the attacking with Alderney being restricted to breakaways. As the pressure continued both Collins and Hunter came close with fine shots. In the 57th minute Guernsey increased their lead when Rollie Carre sent a pass to Collins who beat three men to score goal number three. T Alderney continued to cause the Guernsey defence some concern and, following a corner, Noel Mignot put a hard rising shot over the bar. Guernsey should have increased their lead when Collins received a pass from Hunter and whipped in a good centre, de la Mare set up Rollie Carre, in an excellent position, but he headed over. Once again the Guernsey defence were in disarray when, from a high centre from the left, caused Farmer to fumble the ball and a goalmouth struggle ensued but no Alderney player could find a shot. The game became more open and although Collins came close for Guernsey and Mignot for Alderney the match ended Guernsey-3, Alderney-0.

Guernsey: W. Farmer, M. Carre (c), H. Le Poidevin, V. Tostevin, N. Froome
J.H. Hartland, S. De La Mare, R. Robilliard, R. Carre, A.M. Hunter,
L. Collins.
Goalscorers: De La Mare, Hunter, Collins.

Alderney: P. Allen, A. Mignot, L. McLean, W. Gauvain, N. Simon (c), R. Mignot,
R. O'Neill, W. Hammond, F. Odoir, N. Mignot, J. Harrington.

Although Guernsey won the match well their performance did not appear to impress Mr. Norman Sidey, the Jersey trainer, who must have returned home quietly confident of retaining the Muratti Vase.

The teams for the 1948 Muratti Vase Final.

MURATTI FINAL.
6 May 1948, Springfield Stadium, Jersey.

Jersey -6, Guernsey -3.

There was a crowd of almost 10,000 at Springfield to witness the Muratti final and the home supporters were very confident of a Jersey victory. The match was to be refereed by Mr. C.J. Barrick who refereed the Manchester United-Blackpool FA Cup Final two weeks before. The Guernsey team were based at the Merton Hotel and after a light lunch they travelled to Springfield, already changed for the match, and arrived about 15 minutes before the start.

The match had a sensational start, for within one minute Jersey was ahead. They attacked down the right wing and the ball was collected by Sherry who sent in a high centre that was lost by Farmer and dropped behind him. Sauvage kicked the ball out but the referee was right on the spot and awarded a goal. Guernsey tried to fight back but their attacks were easily dealt with by the Jersey defence. A high ball was sent down into the Guernsey half and Froome misjudged the flight but as Le Maistre raced through to collect it Le Poidevin whipped across and cleared the danger. Guernsey then came close when Hunter found some space and sent in a shot that went just past the post. Jersey responded and Farmer was very quick to take the ball off of Le Maistre's head. As the game progressed both Collins and Hunter came close for Guernsey but they went further behind when Jersey broke into attack and Hart scored in the top corner to put Jersey 2-0 up after 22 minutes. Jersey were the sharper of the two teams and were having more of the ball and Farmer saved a shot by Le Maistre followed by Le Poidevin clearing from Drew as the pressure mounted. A long pass by Sherry sent White away but Farmer saved well but a minute later Drew sent in a shot that skimmed the bar. Hunter tried to relieve the pressure but he saw his shot well saved by Arthur. Jersey scored again in the 35th. Minute when they raided down the right and Le Maistre took a pass beat Farmer to the ball to register goal number three and he followed this up a minute later by outpacing Froome down the middle to score goal number four. Within minutes another Jersey raid resulted in White sending in a glorious centre which Pamplin, headed just over the bar. Jones, the Jersey centre-half, who had been playing for quite a while with his face covered in blood, had to leave the pitch to receive attention. The half time whistle sounded soon after with the score Jersey-4, Guernsey-0.

When the teams came out for the second half, Jones had resumed in his customary position although his head was swathed in bandages. Although Guernsey started the half faster they soon found themselves 5-0 down after 49 minutes when Pamplin, receiving a pass from Le Maistre, scored with a lovely drive that went into the corner of the net. Jersey was in complete control and only fine saves by Farmer from Pamplin and then Le Maistre prevented them from increasing their substantial lead. Guernsey created a fine attack and Carre created some space and he sent in a shot that was speeding towards the far corner of the net but Arthur pulled off an excellent save Guernsey replied after 60 minutes when a centre by Collins was headed onto the bar by Hunter, and from the rebound Robilliard pushed the ball goalwards, although Arthur saved, the referee judged that the ball had crossed the line and awarded a goal. Guernsey had a short spell on top with Robilliard giving Harry Falla a chance but he was unable to control the pass and Arthur came in to clear. From this kick Jersey broke away on the right and White sent in a centre that Le Maistre,

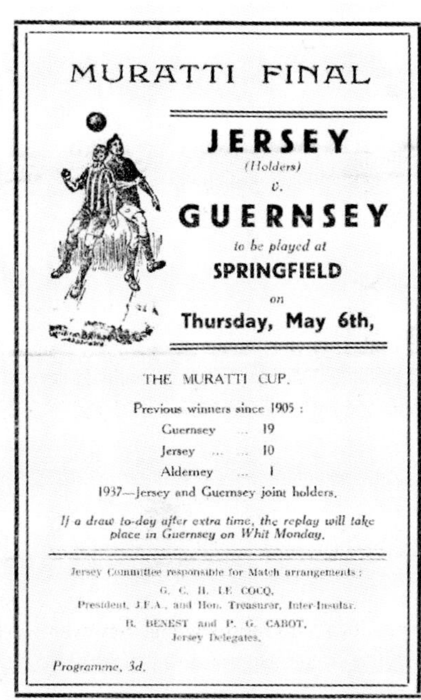

coming in at top speed, headed in Jersey's sixth goal after 65 minutes. The Jersey goal had a narrow escape when Robilliard put Collins away on the left and as he beat the full-back, he sent in a fast drive that Arthur deflected on to the post and Jones kicked clear. Guernsey was now combining better in attack and following some good play by Falla and Collins, Robilliard's shot went over the bar. In the 68th minute Guernsey reduced the arrears when Collins sent in a chest high centre and Falla headed in a fine goal. Guernsey continued to press and was rewarded when Tostevin sent in a hard drive from outside the penalty area that struck the crossbar and went in for their third goal. The game was now more even with Collins sending his shot just wide of the post with Arthur beaten followed by Drew crashing a grand shot against the Guernsey crossbar. The play was going from end to end but there was no more scoring and this pulsating match ended Jersey-6, Guernsey-3.

Graeme Le Maistre receiving the Muratti Vase.

View from the air of a packed Springfield on Muratti day.

Jersey: G. Arthurs, D. Crowell, P. Poingdestre, J. Sherry, R. Jones, D. Pitman,
R. White, R. Hart, G. Le Maistre (c), R. Pamplin, J. Drew.
Goalscorers: Sherry, Hart, Le Maistre (3), Pamplin.

Guernsey: W. Farmer, E. Sauvage (c), H. Le Poidevin, V. Tostevin, N. Froome,
J.F. Hartland, H. Falla, R. Robilliard, M. Carre, A.M. Hunter, L. Collins.
Goalscorers: Falla (2), Tostevin.

The nine goals were a record for a Muratti match as Jersey retained the Vase. Graeme Le Maistre scored a hat-trick against Guernsey in successive Muratti Vase Finals.

During the first-half of the match the spectators' attention was focussed on the Aerovan which flew over the ground with cameraman Dennis Hornsey taking photographs of the game for the Evening Press.

1 9 4 9
MURATTI SEMI-FINAL.
7 April 1949, Springfield Stadium, Jersey.

Jersey -9, Alderney -0.

There was little Muratti fervour in the streets of St. Helier during the morning, but some red and white and blue and white rosettes were seen. The Alderney team and officials arrived by air on Wednesday evening, and made their headquarters at the Ritz Hotel. Jersey began the defence of the Muratti Vase with one new cap in their side with Charlie St. George making his debut. Alderney included young Barry Venton, the junior who plays his football in Jersey, in their side for his first cap. Alderney's preparations were hampered when they lost the services of Noel Mignot, the Winchester City and former Southampton player, due to injury. The referee, Mr. A.W. Peacock, flew into Jersey on Wednesday morning.

Prior to the match the crowd were entertained by the Jersey Musical Union. When Alderney ran onto the field they were given a grand reception as they prepared for their first match on Jersey soil for 10 years. Prior to the match commencing both teams were presented to the Bailiff of Jersey, Sir Alexander Coutanche, and to the Lieut-Governor, Sir Edward Grasett.

Le Maistre won the toss for Jersey and chose to kick into the Pavilion goal with the advantage of the wind. The opening exchanges were fast and even with both sets of forwards having some success. New cap St. George went close when he tried to meet a corner-kick but the ball was cleared for another corner. This was crossed in and Sherry sent in a fast shot that Bond saved well on his knees. Jersey opened the scoring after 7 minutes when Davies scored with an excellent cross-shot that flew into the top corner of the net giving Bond little chance. Alderney replied quickly with Vague shooting just past the post following a corner. After a throw-in Le Maistre set up St. George but Odoire cleared the danger with a telling tackle. Jersey increased their lead after 15 minutes when a fine White-Le Maistre move resulted in Drew firing his shot off the opposite post and into the net. A minute later Drew squared the ball to St. George who scored easily. The pressure continued on the Alderney defence resulting Davies sending Drew away and he centred the ball in. The Alderney defence failed to clear the ball and it fell to Le Maistre and he headed the ball in and although Bond got his hand to the ball he could not prevent it from entering the net for goal number four. Two minutes later Pamplin gained possession on the edge of the penalty area and fired in goal number five. Jersey was proving to be a faster team and were moving into top gear. Alderney's first real dangerous move occurred in the 35th minute when Barker sent in a drive that Arthur saved comfortably. In the 38th minute Drew received a pass from St. George and fired in a shot that entered the net almost before Bond had time to move. The pressure on the Alderney defence continued and only a timely interception by Odoire prevented Le Maistre from adding to the score. There were more close things around the Alderney goal as half-time approached but the visitors held out leaving the half time score Jersey-6, Alderney-0.

  The second half began with Jersey on the attack and White shooting just wide but Alderney soon began to push forward and Vague passed to Roberts who saw his goal bound shot cleared over the bar for a corner by Layzell. After Odoire held up the Jersey attack again, Barker sent the ball down the middle, but Roberts' shot was deflected just wide. From the corner Vague headed goal wards but Arthur made a great full-length dive to push the ball away. Alderney was doing much better with the wind behind them and in a fine move Hammond flicked the ball over Sherry's head but Arthur saved from Venton's cross. N. Simon then saved Alderney when he kicked the ball off the goal-line after Le Maistre had beaten Bond to the ball and sent it goalwards. In the 67th minute Jersey increased their lead when Drew carried the ball upfield and passed to White and from his cross Le Maistre controlled the ball and smashed it past Bond. A minute later Sherry sent the ball to White who drove across the goal and into the net off the far post. Jersey was dealing with the spasmodic Alderney attacks very well but during one Roberts charged goalkeeper Arthur who went down injured but continued after treatment. Alderney continued to try and push forward and coming in from the right, Richards, tried to centre but sliced the ball behind. The ball travelled up towards the balcony of the pavilion, narrowly missed a spectator, and crashed into a window, smashing it. Six minutes from time White passed to Le Maistre who scored with a stiff drive to make the final score Jersey's ninth goal. Despite the heavy score Alderney continued to press and following a left wing raid Arthur had to save from young Venton and Sherry had to head away a cross-shot by Richards. As the game neared its end Jones cleared well upfield to St. George who slipped the ball to Le Maistre, but he drove his shot over the bar leaving the final result Jersey-9, Alderney-0.

Jersey: Arthurs, Layzell, Poingdestre, Sherry, R. Jones, Davies, White, Pamplin, G. Le Maistre (c), St. George, Drew.
Goalscorers: Davies, Drew (2), St. George, Le Maistre (3), Pamplin, White.

Alderney: F. Bond, W. Gauvain, J. Simon, Barker, F. Odoir, N. Simon, Richards, Vague, Roberts, W. Hammond, Venton.

Graeme Le Maistre had set a record by scoring hat-tricks in three successive Muratti Vase matches.

MURATTI FINAL.
5 May 1949, The Cycling Grounds, Guernsey.

Guernsey -1, Jersey -2.

A record breaking crowd of well over 12,000 turned up at the Track to witness the Muratti final between Guernsey and Jersey on 5 May. Prior to the match beginning the spectators were entertained by the Guernsey Brass Band. Both teams were introduced to the Lieut-Governors of both islands, the Bailiff, the President of the JFA, Mr. G.C.H. Le Cocq and the President of the GFA, Mr. C.J.H. Rawlinson.

Marshall Carre, the referee, Mr. Rae and Graeme le Maistre.

View of part of the massive crowd.

Marshall Carre tossed the coin and it was the Jersey skipper who won the toss and le Maistre chose to take advantage of the wind and kicked into the eastern goal. Both teams set up useful attacks but the rival goalkeepers, Ephgrave and Le Riche, coped well with the shots that came in. In the 4th minute Pamplin put White away and he sent in a great shot that Ephgrave did well to tip over for a corner. Ephgrave was again called into play and he saved well from Le Maistre. In the ninth minute Jersey was awarded a free-kick inside their own half and Jones sent in a high ball into Guernsey's penalty area, but Carre beat Le Maistre to the ball and headed it clear only for Pamplin to gain possession and shoot wide. Guernsey was finding that their attacks were being thwarted by a tight Jersey defence with Davies and Jones performing well. Jersey went close to taking the lead during a left-wing attack when St. George struck the base of the post with a fine shot with Ephgrave beaten and the ball rebounded clear. There was a slight panic in the Jersey defence when Falla centred right across and as Le Riche came out to save he dropped the ball but before Robilliard could take advantage he managed to push the ball away for a corner. Collins then had the crowd cheering as he went on an excellent 40 yard run that took him clear of Layzell and with Jones hesitating whether he would leave the centre, Collins crossed the ball and Poingdestre, in attempting to clear, sent the ball behind for a corner. Collins took the kick and Le Riche had to be on the alert to save R. Robilliard's smart header. A minute before the interval Jersey took the lead. Good interplay between Taffy Pamplin and St. George sent the ball to Drew; he beat two defenders and shot at goal. Ephgrave parried this shot but Drew followed up to score from the rebound. Right from the kick off Collins hooked in a shot that Le Riche fumbled but the ball was cleared by Layzell. The half time score was Guernsey-0, Jersey-1.

Guernsey began the second half with great purpose with Falla sending the ball over for Collins to whip in a shot that was saved by Le Riche and within two minutes of the re-start they were level. There was a tussle between Les Robilliard and Jones; Robilliard hooked the ball to Collins. Collins put it across the goalmouth and Buckingham running in drove it past Le Riche to equalise. Following this goal Guernsey raised their game and began to use the wind to their advantage. Layzell had to head clear a centre by Falla as Collins raced in. In a snap Jersey raid, Carre held up Le Maistre and his long punt into the Jersey half glanced off Jones' head for a corner. Collins took the kick and as Les Robilliard just failed to connect with his head the ball fell to Falla who blazed it high over the bar. Guernsey was now slightly on top and Collins again came close with a low drive. Although under some pressure the Jersey defence were coping well with Bram Le Riche being ably assisted by Jones and Sherry. Le Maitre began to wander out to the right in an effort to get more into his attack and in one such move he sent over a beautiful centre which seemed to catch the Guernsey defence out, but Ephgrave raced out at full speed to collect the ball. As he did so he collided with S. George and was hurt and as he dropped to the ground the ball ran loose. The referee instantly stopped play and allowed him to receive treatment and, fortunately, he was able to continue. Jersey were now coming more into the game and Sauvage twice held up attacking moves from Drew. As the game neared its end Guernsey forced an attack and following a mistake by the Jersey defence Les Robilliard collected the ball and sent in a stiff ground shot that Le Riche saved but could not hold but Falla drove his shot over the bar. The pace seemed to increase and Ephgrave saved well as St. George sent a high shot towards the top corner. Five minutes from the end Drew and St. George combined well and Drew sent in a cross that Ephgrave could not gather and the ball bounced at the feet of the unmarked and despite a despairing effort by Carter, White easily headed into an empty net to put Jersey ahead. There was no more scoring and when the final whistle blew with the score Guernsey-1, Jersey-2.

Guernsey: S. Ephgrave, E. Sauvage, K. Carter, G. Buckingham, M. Carre (c), W. Warr, H. Falla,R. Robilliard, L.J. Robilliard, W.G. Le Page, L. Collins.
Goalscorer: Buckingham.

Jersey: Arthurs, Layzell, Poingdestre, Sherry, R. Jones, Davies, White, Pamplin, G. Le Maistre (c), St. George, Drew.
Goalscorers: Drew, White.

The Muratti Vase was presented to Graeme Le Maistre by HE Sir Philip Neame, the Lieut-Governor of Guernsey.

With Jersey winning all three Muratti's this made the overall score Guernsey 19 wins, Jersey 12 wins and Alderney 1 win. The Vase was shared in 1937.

Graeme Le Maistre receives the Muratti Vase.

10

1950 - 1959

1 9 5 0

MURATTI SEMI-FINAL.
30 March 1950, The Cycling Grounds, Guernsey.

Guernsey -3, Alderney -1.

Guernsey and Alderney met at the Track in the first round of the Muratti competition. Once again Alderney suffered a blow before the game when their centre half, Odoir, sustained a cheekbone injury and was unable to play. Alderney had selected Barry Venton (St. Paul's) for his second Muratti cap. He was resident in Jersey and played for their Junior Muratti side against Guernsey later that year.

Both teams were presented to Sir Ambrose Sherwill, the Bailiff of Guernsey, prior to the match. Carre won the toss for Guernsey and the Alderney team kicked-off into the eastern goal.

The game nearly had a sensational start when in the first minute a faulty back pass by Oakley failed to reach Farmer and Hammond raced in to get in a shot. Farmer parried the ball which ran loose but Barry Venton could only shoot the rebound into the side netting. Moore and Bob Venton then carried the play into the Guernsey penalty area but Noel Mignot fired his shot wide. Guernsey responded when Collins slipped the ball across to Taylor who, moving into shooting range, drove the ball into the opposite corner of the net to give the home side a 1-0 lead after 9 minutes. The Alderney team were beginning to show some fine touches and Mignot and Hammond were setting up many telling raids and in one in particular Carre had to be quick to prevent Mignot getting in a shot. Alderney kept up this pressure and should have equalised. After two or three efforts had been blocked 'Buster' Hammond was given a through pass which put him clean away, but he lifted the ball over the bar and then held his head in disgust. After 25 minutes Hunter obtained the ball in midfield and weaved his way forward before giving it to Taylor who took the ball and switched it to Hunter who in turn crashed a beautifully timed shot past Bond to put Guernsey 2-0 up. Alderney responded well and within a minute returned to the attack. Hammond forced his way into the penalty area where the ball came off Oakley's hand and the referee awarded a penalty. After a slight interruption while a white dog serenely walked across the Guernsey goalmouth, Ron Fever calmly took the kick and drove it past Farmer to record Alderney's first post war Muratti goal.

Farmer is beaten by Fever's penalty kick.

In 31 minutes Alderney sustained a crippling blow when J. Simon, the Belgrave full-back, was severely injured in a clash with Falla. He was carried off holding his left arm and took no further part in the match. The remainder of the half was very even with Alderney making light of their one-man handicap. From an attack on the left Barry Venton cleverly tricked Sauvage before firing in a grand shot that was brilliantly saved by Bill Farmer, holding the ball to his body. Shortly afterwards after a period of short passing Reuben Robilliard tried to flick the ball under the bar but Bond cleverly tipped the ball over for a corner. In the dying minutes of the half Peter Moore and Bob Venton combined well on Alderney's right and Moore sent in a powerful shot that went just wide. Half time score Guernsey-2, Alderney-1.

The second half began with Guernsey more in control and an early Collins cross was headed just against the post by Taylor, the ball rolled right across the goalmouth but there was no one on hand to add the finishing touch.. This was followed by a brilliant save by Bond when he pushed away a high shot by Collins then saved the rebound shot by Falla. Carre had to leave the field with a bleeding nose following a collision with Venton. After 10 minutes of the half Guernsey

Bond clears from Robilliard.

should have increased their lead when, after some good approach work, Tayler had a great opportunity but he drove over when well placed. Carre returned to the game following treatment. In the 68th minute Guernsey raided on the right and a fast centre by Falla was forced goalwards by Robilliard. The ball was parried by Bond but as it fell loose Tayler headed into the net for a 3-1 score.

Alderney had further misfortune when Barker had to leave the field with 17 minutes remaining. Alderney were now forced back and Les Collins got in a thunderous drive from some 12 yards which was magnificently saved by Bond. Two minutes later they lost the services of Bob Venton although Barker could return leaving Alderney with nine players again. Both returned for the latter stages of the match. In the closing stages Guernsey missed another glorious opportunity when a cross-shot was stopped by Bond, but when the ball rolled loose with the goalkeeper beaten Hunter got his head to it; but instead of sending the ball into the unattended net he lifted it over the bar. Guernsey forced a few more corners but with no more scoring the match ended, Guernsey-3, Alderney-1.

Guernsey: W. Farmer, E. Sauvage, K. Carter, M. Carre (c), R. Oakley, L.J. Robilliard, H. Falla, R. Robilliard, K. Taylor, A.M. Hunter, L. Collins. Goalscorers: Taylor (2), Hunter.

Alderney: F. Bond, W. Gauvain, J. Simon, W. Hammond, F. Odoir, R. Fever, P. Moore, N. Simon (c), B. Venton, R. Venton, N. Mignot. Goalscorer: Fever (pen).

Players and officials of the Guernsey and Alderney teams were among the large attendance at the Muratti Ball at St. George's Hall. A highlight of the evening was the presentation of a silver Guernsey can to the visiting referee, Mr. A.C. Williams. The can was to be engraved with a medal representing the clubs concerned.

MURATTI FINAL.
4 May 1950, Springfield Stadium, Jersey.

Jersey -0, Guernsey -2.

Farmer saves from an onrushing Le Maistre.

Guernsey was fortunate to be able to call on the services of John Le Maitre (Marines and Rangers) for their match against Jersey giving him his first Muratti cap. John is the centre forward for the full Marine XI and has played for Devon County and for Combined Services in Malta. He has been selected by the Maltese FA to play for them against foreign teams, the only British serviceman to be chosen. He is expected to come out of the Marines next January.

Jersey met Guernsey at Springfield on 4 May in the Muratti final in front of HE Sir Edward Grasnett, the Lieut-Governor of Jersey and HE Sir Philip Neame, Lieut-Governor of Guernsey.

The opening exchanges were very even with both defences clearing any dangerous attacks. Collins thought he had opened the scoring for Guernsey but he was ruled offside. Graeme Le Maistre then had two good chances for Jersey but without success. As the play swung from end to end Doug Pitman in the Jersey defence and Marshal Carre in the Guernsey defence were outstanding as they continued to break up dangerous situations. Le Poidevin cleared up a Jersey attack and as he drove well upfield Le Maitre got possession and as he raced in for goal he collided with the goalkeeper. Arthur got the to the ball but both players went down injured and had to receive treatment. Both teams continued to attack but the respective defences were preventing any direct shots at goal. In a challenge between Drew and Sauvage, both kicked the ball at the same time and the ball burst; a new ball was quickly found. The standard of play was very good with each side mounting excellent attacks. From a Poingdestre free-kick the ball was

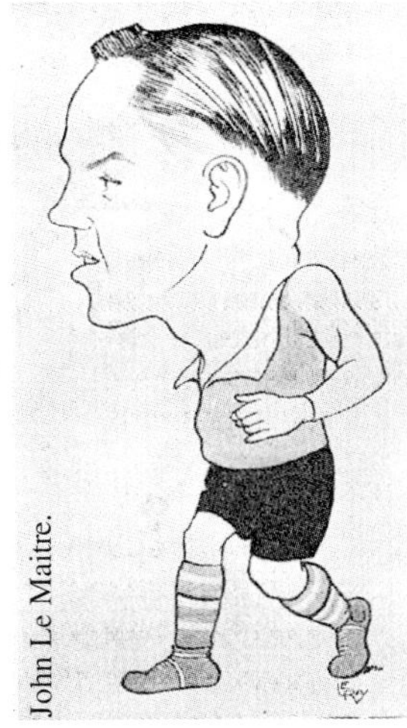
John Le Maitre.

played upfield. Le Maistre was on it in a flash and fired in a shot that Farmer did very well to save. As the ball went to the other end Le Maitre was penalised for a foul on Arthur. From the free-kick the ball was placed into the Guernsey area and although Sauvage beat Pamplin to the header the ball ran on to Tubby White, whose great drive just went over the bar. The game was developing into a typical Muratti Final and in a hard challenge between Jones and Hunter, the Guernsey player came out limping and the game was held up as he received attention. Guernsey began to gain the upper hand and Arthur's goal had a few escapes with the goalkeeper taking two attempts to stop a shot by Hunter.

In the 39th minute Robilliard passed to Hunter then received a return pass and, forcing his way through, fired in a great shot from 18 yards that flew past Arthur to put Guernsey 1-0 up. Jersey increased the pressure and Farmer was outstanding when, in a period of about 10 seconds, he saved from Le Maistre, Hart and White to keep Jersey out. Farmer was by then the busiest of the two goalkeepers when he firstly fisted out a threatening centre and then had to dive at the feet of Hart to prevent a score. As half-time approached white swept upfield for Jersey and centred the ball to Le Maistre, who sent the ball to Pamplin. The inside-forward was well placed inside the Guernsey penalty area, but put his shot high and wide of the goal. At half time the score was Jersey-0, Guernsey-1.

At the start of the second-half Guernsey had the sun in their faces and as it was setting it was no doubt going to be a source of some trouble for Jim Farmer in his goal. The second half carried on in the same vein as the first with both teams playing grand open football. Arthur came to Jersey's rescue when he produced an excellent save from a fine shot by Falla. Falla later sent in a centre, which went right through the Jersey defence, and Arthur made a great leap to get the ball but it flew past the post.

Jersey proceeded to increase their attacks and a good Hart-White move was stopped by Robilliard, who was having an excellent game. Later Drew and Pamplin combined but Carre cleared the danger. As the Jersey attacks continued Drew took the ball down the wing and sent in a perfect cross for White, but as he prepared to head it goalwards, Farmer managed to get a hand to it to get it clear. Although Jersey was on top they were finding it difficult to break down a Guernsey defence that was well controlled by Carre. With ten minutes remaining, Jones and Le Maitre tussled for the ball and Le Maitre tried to pass to Le Page but S. George blocked the pass. Freeman then bundled the ball away from Le Page

Geoff Arthur watches anxiously as the ball slips past the post.

and then as Arthur cleared it, it went to Hunter. He then clipped it over the goalkeeper's head and into the net to make the score 2-0. The final minutes were fast and furious with both goals coming under threat but Les Robilliard for Guernsey and S. George for Jersey kept things very tight. As the final whistle blew Sauvage won possession of the ball after a battle of words with referee Burgess and the final result was Jersey-0, Guernsey-2.

Marshall Carre with the Muratti Vase.

Jersey: G. Arthurs, Freeman, Poingdestre, D. Pitman, R. Jones, St George, White, Hart, G. Le Maistre (c), R. Pamplin Drew.

Guernsey: W. Farmer, E. Sauvage, H. Le Poidevin, V. Tostevin, M. Carre (c), L.J. Robilliard, H. Falla, W.G. Le Page, J. Le Maistre, A.M. Hunter, L. Collins.
            Goalscorers: Robilliard, Hunter.

This was Guernsey's first Muratti triumph since 1938. It was all the more memorable because this was reckoned to one of Jersey's finest teams who were very well trained under Vic Buckingham, a Tottenham Hotspur half-back and professional coach. It appeared that during the game Marshall Carre had broken his right arm when he had fallen awkwardly during the game. He did not realise how severe the injury was until the end of the game when people started to shake his hand and he flaked out.

Harry Falla, John Le Maistre, Bill Farmer, Bill Le Page, Alan Hunter, Les Collins.
Harold Le Poidevin, Vince Tostevin, Marshall Carre (c), Les Robilliard, Ernie Sauvage.

1 9 5 1

MURATTI SEMI-FINAL.
12 April 1951, Springfield Stadium, Jersey.

Jersey -8, Alderney -1.

The problems that Alderney experienced when preparing for the Muratti match were highlighted more so this year by the fact that half of their team normally lived outside the island. With the very limited range of players available, and the difficulties of getting together for practice etc., the odds were always against the northern isle. This year two players came into the team from the Southampton area; two were in the Royal Navy; and another lived in Guernsey. A further player who was under review of the selectors was unfortunately reported to be serving in Korea at the time.

Jersey entertained Alderney at Springfield on 12 April in the first round of the Muratti competition before a crowd estimated in the region of 4,500. Despite difficulties of transport the Alderney team had quite a group of supporters present when the game was due to start. Among Alderney FA officials present were Capt. C.H. Richards (President), Mr. W. Hammond and Mr. K. Duquemin (Vice-Presidents), Mr. G. Burns (Financial Secretary) and Mr. G. Chapman (team manager). Commander S.P. Herivel, President of the Alderney States, was unable to be present. Prior to the match the crowd were entertained by the Jersey Musical Union then the teams were presented to Sir Edward Grasett, the Lieut-Governor of Jersey.

Alderney kicked off towards the St. Mark's Road end, facing the sun. Alderney were immediately under pressure and after 3 minutes Jersey took the lead when White fed the ball to Pamplin and he squared it to Sherry who fired in a first-time shot that went in off the crossbar. In the 8th minute Le Maistre swung the ball out to Belhomme who beat Simon before shooting into the far corner of the net. Within two minutes Jersey increased their lead when Sherry swung the ball across the goalmouth and Barker was just unable to get the ball away. The ball fell to White who scored with a grand drive. The onslaught continued when Sherry scored from a Belhomme pass to make the score 4-0. As the game continued Bond, in the Alderney goal, was under severe pressure from Le Maistre and Pamplin, as Alderney tried to stem the tide.

After 30 minutes Jersey scored again when Belhomme fired in a shot that MacLean tried to head clear but he could not prevent it entering the net to make the half time score Jersey-5, Alderney-0.

For the second half Jersey had to reorganise their side due to the first half injury to the influential Reg Jones who had to be accommodated on the left wing. The second half was only two minutes old when, following a left wing corner, Bond lost the ball and Le Maistre tapped it home for 6-0. Alderney were still trying to push forward with Mignot and McLeod and won only their third corner of the match. This was followed by an awkward shot by Barker that was well saved by Arthur. Alderney reduced the arrears when Moore lobbed the ball down the middle and Mignot dashed in, controlled the ball, beat two defenders and then drove it beautifully into the net to score the goal of the match. A fine goal. This goal lifted Alderney for a time and Arthur had to save from Fever. In the 70th

Bond clears from Pamplin as Fever follows up.

minute Jersey scored when Pamplin tapped the ball in after a fine move and two minutes later White worked his way through the middle to score goal number 8. Mignot had two chances for Alderney near the end but the final score was Jersey-8, Alderney-1.

Jersey: G. Arthurs, Freeman, Poingdestre, D. Pitman, R. Jones, St George, F. Belhomme, Sherry, G. Le Maistre (c), R. Pamplin, White.
Goalscorers: Sherry (2), Belhomme (2), White (2), Le Maistre, Pamplin.

Alderney: F. Bond, W. Gauvain (c), J. Simon, A. Barker, L. McLean, R. Fever, P. Moore, R. Venton, W. Hammond, N. Mignot, D. McLeod.
Goalscorer: Mignot.

On the eve of the Muratti Vase final Mr. L.C. McLernon, speaking for the Alderney FA, created a sensation when he declared that under no circumstances would Alderney be 'driven out' of the Muratti competition and that, if necessary, they were prepared to go to Law. This frank declaration had come as a direct result of a speech made by Mr. G.H.C. Le Cocq, President of the Jersey FA, who publicly stated that it was now time for Alderney to quit the Muratti and suggested that a monetary grant to the northern Island would stand the game in better stead than Alderney's continued participation in the tourney. Mr. McLernon, one of Alderney's two delegates to the Channel Islands Inter-Insular committee, which controls the affaires of the Muratti competition, told the 'Guernsey Star' that the northern Island would resist this move to the bitter end.

MURATTI FINAL.
3 May 1951, The Cycling Grounds, Guernsey.

Guernsey -3, Jersey -1.

A record crowd of 12,692 witnessed the 1951 Muratti Vase final between Guernsey and Jersey at the Track on 3 May. The match was being relayed by the BBC by their radio commentator John Arlott.

Guernsey had an experienced line-up with Harold Le Poidevin as captain whereas Jersey had two new caps in R. Mauger (St. Paul's) and Graeme Mourant (Beeches) in their side. A close fought contest was forecast by both Ted Malpas, Guernsey coach, and Duggie Livingston the Jersey coach. Both coaches were confident about their own teams but believed that there would not be a lot in it. The referee for the match was Mr. Arthur Bond (London) who had recently refereed the Blackpool-Birmingham FA Cup semi-final. It was also noted that he would be the first one-armed referee to take charge of a Muratti match.

Harold Le Poidevin won the toss for Guernsey and chose to kick into the eastern goal with a slight wind advantage. The opening play was very even with neither side gaining the upper hand. Guernsey had an early scare when a Le Maistre lob from 20 yards was inadvertently headed to Pamplin by Warr just inside the home penalty area. Warr recovered quickly to thwart Pamplin. After 5 minutes play a through ball by Sherry was missed by both Le Maistre and Pamplin but ran on to Belhomme. He fired in a quick shot that was well saved by Farmer. Jersey came close on two occasions with Sherry shooting over the bar each time when put clear.

Guernsey replied with shots by Collins and Reuben Robilliard both going past the post. The Guernsey goal had a narrow escape when White sent in a low drive that beat Farmer but struck the post and was cleared by Carter. In a further attack Mourant won possession and fired in a shot that again beat Farmer but rebounded off the bottom of the post. The first half ended Guernsey-0, Jersey-0.

The second half began with chances at both ends but it was in the 54th minute that the deadlock was broken. Jersey were awarded a free kick just outside the Guernsey penalty area. Jones put in a terrific drive that Farmer lost and Jersey were 1-0 up. Guernsey pushed on for an equaliser and unsuccessfully appealed for a penalty when the ball appeared to

Crowell beats Robilliard with Mauger watching.

strike Poingdestre's hand. They continued to press and in the 65th minute Reuben
Robilliard beat the Jersey offside trap to fire in a shot that hit Mauger's body. From the
rebound Robilliard drove in an unstoppable shot for the equaliser. As the game progressed
Collins and Reuben Robilliard were combining well and troubling the Jersey defence, and
Sherry and Le Maistre were in turn causing problems in the home defence. With two minutes remaining, and the play going from end to end, White broke through and only a magnificent save by Farmer prevented Jersey from regaining the lead. At full time the score
was Guernsey-1, Jersey-1.

Hunter shooting past Mauger to give Guernsey the lead.

In extra time Guernsey started the quickest and after 94 minutes
Collins won possession and, although in a good position himself, passed
to Hunter who gave Mauger no chance with a strong low drive.

Jersey replied with Belhomme sending in a terrific drive that was well
saved by Farmer. With eight minutes remaining Collins received a forward pass from Reuben Robilliard and, running on, sent in a fine long-
range drive which entered under the bar with Mauger well beaten.
There was no more scoring and the result was Guernsey-3, Jersey-1.

Guernsey: W. Farmer, K. Carter, H. Le Poidevin (c), V. Tostevin,
W. Warr,

                 L.J. Robilliard, H. Falla, A.M. Hunter, J. Le Maitre, R. Robilliard,
L. Collins.
Goalscorers: R. Robilliard, Hunter, Collins.

Jersey: R. Mauger, D. Crowell, D. Poingdestre, D. Pitman, R. Jones (c),
G. Mourant, F. Belhomme, J. Sherry, G. Le Maistre, R. Pamplin, White.
Goalscorer: Jones.

This was Guernsey's 21st Muratti Vase success and it came after a hard fought and even
match. The game was a credit to both teams who performed in a sportsmanlike manner
throughout.

The Muratti Vase only stayed in Guernsey for a few days as, after a week, it made it's
way to England. The Vase went to London to stand beside the FA Cup and hundreds of
other National and Empire trophies at the National Sports Trophies Exhibition.

Le Prevost receives the Muratti Vase.

1952
MURATTI SEMI-FINAL.
3 April 1952, The Cycling Grounds, Guernsey.

Guernsey -7, Alderney -2.

Guernsey and Alderney met at the Track on 3 April in the first round of the Muratti. A crowd of over 5,000 were looking forward to a keenly fought match. Alderney had two new caps with A. Pasquire (VOBA) and H. Mesney (Alderney Athletics) making their debuts.

Guernsey were the first to mount a raid but this was easily repulsed by the Alderney defence. Alderney went on the attack and in the 4th minute, following a right wing corner, Bobby Venton fired in a stiff drive, which was deflected past Ephgrave by a defender to give Alderney an early lead.

Bobby Venton, scorer of Alderney's opening goal.

This was a shock for Guernsey, but in two minutes they were level. Le Maistre collected a clearance and put through a lovely pass, which Falla took in his stride, and, cutting in, he beat Pasquire with a low shot. Following this goal Collins came close on two occasions with his shots hitting the side netting. Alderney responded and were playing extremely well with Moore, Venton and Mignot putting the home defence under some severe pressure. Moore went close for Alderney when he fired past Ephgrave only to see his shot hit the side netting. Hunter then sent Le Maitre away and he beat two defenders to put Guernsey into the lead. Five minutes from half time Hunter centred the ball high into the middle and Le Page headed in between Pasquire and Harrington to make the half time score Guernsey-3, Alderney-1.

A minute after the restart Collins rounded off some good approach work by Le Page to score with a low cross shot. Guernsey increased their lead when Collins set up Le Page to score with a low shot. The home side continued to press and in the 64th minute Collins took a pass from Le Maitre to score goal number 6. In the 70th minute Collins was again on the score sheet when he added goal number 7. Alderney, however, stuck to their task and they were rewarded in the 75th minute when Mesney, resisting three tackles, centred to Mignot who half volleyed into the net to make the final score Guernsey-7, Alderney-2.

Guernsey: S. Ephgrave, E. Sauvage, G. Tolcher, R. Mahy, M. Carre, L. Robilliard, H. Falla, A.M. Hunter (c), J. Le Maistre, W.G. Le Page, L. Collins.
Goalscorers: Falla, Le Maitre, Le Page (2), Collins (3).

Alderney: A. Pasquire, W. Gauvain (c), J. Harrington, N. Mignot, L. McLean, J. Simon, P. Moore, R. Venton, W. Hammond, Vague, H. Mesney.
Goalscorers: Venton, Mignot.

Although Guernsey won well it was felt that the score flattered them and that Alderney had put up a grand performance. In the first half the home defence found the Alderney attackers a handful. It was felt that there had to be a big improvement for their visit to Springfield.

Missing from the Track flagpole during the match was the Alderney Football Association banner. The Alderney flag was found draped across the front of the bus that took players and officials to the game.

Harry Falla scores Guernsey's equalising goal.

Alderney. 1952.

MURATTI FINAL.
1 May 1952, Springfield Stadium, Jersey.

Jersey -1, Guernsey -3.

Guernsey's preparations for the Muratti Vase final went very well when on Good Friday they defeated Dulwich Hamlet 1-0 with a goal scored by Les Collins. During the match they unfortunately lost the services of centre-half 'Busty' Warr as he sustained a fracture of his right leg and this ruled him out of contention for a possible place in the team to face Jersey. They played Bishop Auckland, one of England's greatest amateur sides, in the Victory Cup on Easter Monday but went down 4-0. Jersey's youthful side was composed of seven new caps with F. Le Marquand (Wanderers), A. Browne (Magpies), Poree (First Tower), C. Dingle (Wanderers), Thomas (First Tower), Le Gallais (First Tower) and D. de Gruchy (Beeches) all making their Muratti debuts in what was seen as an experimental side. The stage was set as Jersey entertained Guernsey at Springfield on 1 May in front of over 10,500 fans and a keen contest was anticipated.

The opening stages were very even and for the first 15 minutes the game swayed to and fro. After 18 minutes Hunter sent over an excellent cross that caught the Jersey defence on the wrong foot and Le Page came in to give Le Marquand no chance with a fine header to put Guernsey 1-0 up. Guernsey kept up the pressure and Collins shot past an open goal followed by a good shot by Falla that produced a fine save from Le Marquand.

The game began to even out again although Guernsey appeared to have a slight edge. In the 30th minute Robilliard appeared to handle the ball but the referee allowed the play to continue. The ball broke to Collins who passed it to Le Maitre and he beat Le Marquand with a crashing shot. Jersey replied in the 39th minute when a loose clearance by Ephgrave went straight to Le Maistre and from 25 yards out he fired in a shot over two defenders and into the top corner of the net. A quite superb goal. The half time arrived with the score Jersey-1, Guernsey-2.

Jersey started the more dangerous of the two sides in the second half and the Guernsey goal had some close calls. Poree sent a free kick into the Guernsey area and Thomas' header went just over the bar. The match turned in the 64th minute when only a brilliant one-handed save from Ephgrave prevented White from equalising. Jersey switched their formation in an attempt to gain an equaliser but the Guernsey goal managed to withstand the onslaught. With 4 minutes remaining Guernsey won a corner, Le Page gained possession and he whipped the ball into the bottom right hand corner to make the final score Jersey-1, Guernsey-3.

Le Page heads home Guernsey's first goal from a Hunter cross.

Thomas heads over the Guernsey bar.

Jersey: Le Marquand, Browne,
            Freeman, Poree, R. Jones (c),
            C. Dingle, G. Le Maistre,
            Thomas, White, Le Gallais,
            D. De Gruchy.
            Goalscorer: Le Maistre

Guernsey: S. Ephgrave, E. Sauvage,
            K. Carter, V. Tostevin,
            M. Carre, L. Robilliard,
            H. Falla, W.G. Le Page,
            J. Le Maistre, A.M. Hunter,
            L. Collins.
            Goalscorers: Le Page (2),
            Le Maitre.

The Vase was presented to Ernie Sauvage,
the Guernsey captain, by the Lieut-Governor
of Jersey.

Sauvage receives the Muratti Vase from the Lieut-Governor of Jersey.

1 9 5 3
MURATTI SEMI-FINAL.
26 March 1953, Springfield Stadium, Jersey.

Jersey -4, Alderney -0.

The Coronation year Muratti Vase Competition began with Jersey entertaining Alderney at Springfield on 26 March 1953 in front of a crowd of over 3,500. Prior to this match commencing there was a two-minute silence in Memory of Queen Mary and both teams wore black armbands as a mark of respect.

Jersey has three new caps with G. Newton, H. Le Roux and M. Harben (all of Beeches) making their debuts. Alderney has included J. Mannion (Beeches), W. Birmingham (Northern Belles), K. Duquemin (Alderney Athletics) and W. Roberts their first caps.

Jersey was keen to begin proceedings and they were limbering up on the Springfield turf a good five minutes before Alderney ran onto the pitch.

Jersey won the toss and took advantage of a slightly following wind. Alderney began the quickest when Venton sent a dangerous cross into the Jersey goalmouth that Hammond collected, but lost the ball before he could get his shot in. Jersey replied when Pamplin passed to de Gruchy who beat Duquemin and fired in a shot that was well saved by Bond. Alderney were then pushed back with Jersey forcing the pace and in the 8th minute Le Roux had a goal rightly disallowed for pushing. Jersey continued to press and took the lead in 13 minutes when, from a corner, Pamplin drove in a great shot to make the score 1-0. The pressure on Alderney continued with Harrington in their defence in excellent form.

Alderney.

Bond had a fine save from Harben and then Pamplin headed just over the bar. After 35 minutes Venton caused some panic in the Jersey penalty area when he beat Newton and his cross was only cleared after a goalmouth struggle. This lifted Alderney and they had the upper hand for a five-minute spell. Jersey weathered this storm and in the 41st minute Simon attempted to clear a Jersey attack and miskicked the ball which fell to Le Maistre who coolly picked his spot to make the score 2-0. Alderney nearly scored in the last minute of the first half when Mignot passed to Birmingham who's shot was pushed away for a corner by Arthur leaving the half time score as Jersey-2, Alderney-0.

Le Maitre slots home Jersey's second goal.

The second half began with Jersey in control but they were finding it difficult to penetrate the Alderney defence with Bond performing well. Le Maistre broke through the Alderney defence but was brought down by Mignot and a free kick was awarded. Le Maistre took the kick himself and sent in a hard rising ball only to see Bond leaping high to punch over from just underneath the bar. Alderney were breaking up the Jersey attacks and forcing their forwards to shoot from long-range. The Alderney team did not lack spirit and in Venton they had a dangerous forward. It was one of his centres that put Birmingham into a good position but he was denied a scoring chance as Jones darted in to head away. It was only a matter of time, however, until Jersey scored again and in the 77th minute de Gruchy made progress down the right wing and sent in a cross that was met by Le Gallais but he missed his chance. A tussle ensued and Le Maistre, following in, slipped the ball past Bond. The loss of this goal seemed to demoralise Alderney and it was no surprise when, following a free kick for a foul on Le Gallais , Pitman lobbed the ball into the centre and winger Le Gallais headed home from close in to register Jersey's fourth goal to make the final score Jersey-4, Alderney-0.

Jersey: G. Arthurs, G. Newton, Poingdestre, D. Pitman, R. Jones (c), H. Le Roux, Le Gallais, G. Le Maistre, M. Harben, R. Pamplin, D. De Gruchy. Goalscorers: Pamplin, Le Maistre (2), Le Gallais.

Alderney: F. Bond, K. Duquemin, J. Simon, W. Hammond, J. Harrington, N. Mignot, P. Moore, J. Mannion, W. Roberts, B. Venton, W. Birmingham.

Jersey was a worthy winner over a stubborn Alderney side and could now look forward to the Muratti Vase Final against Guernsey at the Cycling Grounds.

MURATTI FINAL.
30 April 1953, The Cycling Grounds, Guernsey.

Guernsey -0, Jersey -2.

Confidence was high in the Guernsey camp as they selected an experienced side in an attempt to retain the Muratti Vase with only Roy Barrasin (North) and Les Howlett (Belgrave W.) being new caps. Guernsey were hoping to win the Vase for the fourth year in succession. The Jersey side had six of the Upton winning Beeches team included in their strong selection. Once again the match was being relayed through the BBC West of England Home Service by John Arlott.

The referee, Mr. A.W. Smith of Aldershot, was a Warrant Officer in the Royal Army Dental Corps. He was a linesman in the 1952 FA Cup Final when Newcastle United met Arsenal and refereed the FA Cup semi-final replay between Arsenal and Chelsea in 1950. He was also a linesman for the Coronation Cup Final in Glasgow on 20 May 1953 when Celtic played Hibernian in front of a crowd of over 117,000.

The conditions were far from ideal due to the persistent rain. It was falling steadily for the best part of the match and the pitch was very slippery. It certainly was a raincoat and umbrella Muratti. Prior to the match commencing both teams were presented to the Lieut-Governor of Jersey.

Jones won the toss for Jersey and decided to defend the eastern goal. The first shot of the match came after 4 minutes when Le Maistre latched on to a pass by Newton but his shot went wide. Although Jersey were having the better of the opening exchanges both goal-keepers were called into action. Ephgrave, however, was proving to be the busiest as he saved from Harben and then the ever dangerous Le Maistre. In the 25th minute a right wing cross into the middle by D. de Gruchy was bundled into the net by R. de Gruchy to make the score 1-0 in Jersey's favour. Three minutes later, with Howlett off the field receiving attention, D. de Gruchy sent in another dangerous curling cross that Ephgrave tipped on to the bar and saved. Guernsey replied when Falla put a low cross into the

Guernsey being presented to the Lieut-Governor of Jersey.

centre that was met by Collins. He quickly brought the ball under control and fired in a hard shot that was well saved by Arthur. Jersey continued to press forward with Harben causing the Guernsey defence a lot of trouble. Le Maistre then had two good chances to increase Jersey's lead, the first being saved by Ephgrave and the second when he sliced his shot wide when a goal seemed imminent. As half time approached Guernsey mounted some sustained pressure with Arthur saving a fine shot by Collins followed by a 30 yard shot by Robilliard going just inches wide. The half time score was Guernsey-0, Jersey-1.

The second half began with Ephgrave, who was having an excellent game, saving from Sherry. Guernsey began to force the issue with Collins, Le Maitre, Robilliard and Barrassin all coming close in a goalmouth scramble. Rueben Robilliard came close when he hit the underside of the Jersey crossbar as Guernsey strove for the all-important equaliser. Jersey held out well and in the 54th minute a move that began with Harben and Noel set up Le Maistre who scored with a hard shot into the roof of the net to put Jersey two goals up. Collins came close for Guernsey but his header was well saved by Arthur and, in the final minutes, Robilliard scooped a rolling ball over the crossbar. This was the final incident of note and the match ended Guernsey-0, Jersey-2.

Guernsey: S. Ephgrave, L. Howlett, K. Carter, V. Tostevin, M. Carre, L. Robilliard (c), H. Falla, R. Barrasin, J. Le Maitre, R. Robilliard, L. Collins.

Jersey: G. Arthur, G. Newton, R. Jones (c), J. Sherry, D. Pitman, H. Le Roux, D. De Gruchy, G. Le Maistre, M. Harben, T. Noel, R. De Gruchy. Goalscorers: R. De Gruchy, Le Maistre.

The feeling after the match was that Jersey had thoroughly merited their victory with the strength of their halfback line being crucial with the young Howard Le Roux being magnificent. The Guernsey Press reporter stated that the Caesarean triumph was, indeed, a most meritorious one and he offered his congratulations.

Jones, the Jersey Captain, receives the Muratti Vase from Guernsey's Lieut-Governor

Reg Jones is held high with the Muratti Vase. (1953)

1 9 5 4
MURATTI SEMI-FINAL.
1 April 1954, The Cycling Grounds, Guernsey.

Guernsey -2, Alderney -1.

The Alderney officials were confident of a close fought match with Guernsey at the Cycling Grounds as they were of the opinion that this was the best Alderney team since the war. Despite a rough crossing the previous evening when they travelled across the Channel by mail steamer, the three Alderney players- N. Mignot (Cowes, Isle of Wight), D. Jones (Burnley Highways) and R. Venton were ready for the match on 1 April. This was D. Jones' first cap. Guernsey had selected three new caps in Jim Murray (North), D. Vaudin (Rangers) and D. Mechem (North). F. Mellanby (Centrals) had been selected for his second cap, his first being in 1947.

Alderney's linesman was Jack Hammond, who was outside-right when Alderney won the Muratti Vase against Guernsey in 1920. The Guernsey linesman was W. 'Timmy' Allen who had also gained Muratti honours in the past. The referee was Mr. H. Ball (Worcester) and he arrived in Guernsey the day before and met with the Referee's Association at the Chamber of Commerce, Bordage in the evening. He had been a Class 1 referee since 1946 and had, in recent years, twice been in charge of derby matches between Bristol City and Bristol Rovers.

Both teams were presented to H.E the Lieut-Governor, Sir Thomas Elmhirst, prior to the match commencing. Hunter won the toss for Guernsey and chose to attack the eastern goal, which gave them the advantage of a stiff breeze. In the first minute of the match Murray in the Guernsey goal was forced to rush out after Mignot prompted a great move by the Alderney forwards. Guernsey then took control with Falla heading a Mellanby corner wide and then Mellanby himself shooting over the bar from a further attack. Alderney were being forced to defend but their tackling was effective and their clearances excellent. In the 20th minute Robilliard handled outside the penalty area and, with the Guernsey team

Billy Wright (Wolves & England) and Mr. Ball.

forming their defensive wall 10 yards away, Mignot drove for goal. The ball touched Hunter and bounced in front of Murray and entered the net near an upright. This was Alderney's 5th post war Muratti goal and was well received by their band of supporters. Guernsey responded with some excellent attacks by Collins and Hunter, however, Venton nearly increased Alderney's lead but Murray saved well. As half time approached Cauvain was injured as Guernsey forced an attack. Alderney held out and at half time the score was Guernsey-0, Alderney-1.

Frank Bond, the Alderney goalkeeper, fails to stop Hunter's winning header cross the line in the 88th minute of the game.

The second half began with Guernsey pushing on for an equaliser but Bond was equal to the task. After 58 minutes, however, Falla converged on the Alderney goal and fired in a grass-level shot that Bond was unable to hold and it travelled under his body and into the net for the equalising goal. The match became more even with Mellanby heading just wide for Guernsey followed by Moore shooting just wide for Alderney. As the game neared its last quarter it appeared as if Alderney were tiring but they responded well when Mannion put in a shot that was saved by Murray. With 10 minutes remaining one of Alderney's star men, Barry Venton, was injured and was carried from the pitch and did not return. The pressure on Alderney's defence was immense as Mechem came close with a header and Collins put a shot over the bar with only four minutes remaining. In the 88th minute Collins took a corner and Hunter, with a running leap, headed into the far corner of the net to put Guernsey into the lead. There was no more scoring and this pulsating contest ended with the score: Guernsey-2, Alderney-1.

Guernsey: J. Murray, D. Vaudin, E. Sauvage, V. Tostevin, M. Carre, L. Robilliard, D. Mechem, A.M. Hunter (c), H. Falla, L. Collins, F. Mellanby. Goalscorers: Falla, Hunter.

Alderney: F. Bond, W. Hammond, W. Gauvain, D. Jones, J. Harrington, J. Simon, P. Moore, R. Venton, N. Mignot, J. Mannion, B. Venton. Goalscorer: Mignot.

It was agreed by all that Alderney had put up a magnificent fight and were extremely unlucky to lose, especially as they lost the second goal when they were reduced to 10 men due to the injury to the influential Barry Venton. It was their best Muratti performance since they lost 2-1 to Jersey in 1939 at Springfield.

Young fans celebrate Guernsey's dramatic late winning goal.

MURATTI FINAL.
6 May 1954, Springfield Stadium, Jersey.

Jersey -3, Guernsey -5.

Guernsey had a lot of thinking to do following their narrow victory against Alderney as they prepared for the Muratti Vase Final against Jersey at Springfield. The selectors however retained faith with ten of the players who got them to this final. They made one change by bringing in Micky Brassel of Belgrave W. for his first cap. The defence remained the same but there were some positional changes in the forward line. Jersey's one doubt in their team was John Sherry of Beeches but he recovered from his wrist injury and took his place in the line-up.

It was also noted that it was six years since Guernsey lost a Muratti match at Springfield. Jersey last won there in 1948.

John Arlott, the BBC commentator, was to give a commentary on the second half of the match on the Home Service. He was stationed on a balcony at Springfield Theatre immediately above one of the goals.

Hunter won the toss for Guernsey and elected to take advantage of the wind and kick towards the theatre end. The opening exchanges were very even with both goalkeepers being brought into action. Jersey began to exert more pressure with Le Maistre and Eloury prominent. After 15 minutes Guernsey came more into the game with Collins firing his shot over following a free kick by Robilliard. Jones almost put into his own net but a clearance by Pitman saved the day for Jersey. This was followed by a brilliant save by Arthur from a Collins shot. The Jersey defence was holding out well but after 24 minutes a Newton back pass was intercepted by Brassel who drove the ball home to give Guernsey the lead. Falla came close to increasing the lead but after 27 minutes Jersey were level. White centred the ball and it was met by Le Maistre who beat Murray with a smart header. The tempo of the game rose but both defences remained on top. A minute from half time Collins rounded Newton and drove the ball against the crossbar. It rebounded into play and Brassel rushed in to head a perfect goal from the penalty spot. The half time score was Jersey-1, Guernsey-2.

Brassel turns away after heading in Guernsey's second goal.

Jersey began the second half in top gear with Murray being harried by the home forwards. Tostevin and Sauvage managed to clear a number of Jersey attacks as the pressure mounted. After a period of sustained Jersey pressure Guernsey broke away only for Tostevin to shoot over the bar. From the goal kick De Gruchy passed to Le Maistre who equalised from eight yards. Guernsey replied almost immediately when Hunter passed on to Brassel who scored the third goal for the visitors. Soon after, Arthur was beaten by a 30 yard shot by Hunter to give Guernsey a 4-2 advantage. This was followed two minutes later when Sherry put in a long pass to de Gruchy who fired in a superb shot over the heads of Carre and Murray to make the score 4-3. Jersey pushed on in search of an equaliser through shots by Eloury and Lempriere but the Guernsey defence held firm.

They managed to weather this storm and were rewarded in the 81st minute when Mechem latched on to a goal kick from Arthur and slipped the ball to Falla. He in turn sent it to Brassel who scored Guernsey's fifth goal to make the final score Jersey-3, Guernsey-5.

Murray saving from Jersey with Sauvage on the line.

Jersey: G. Arthur, G. Newton, R. Jones (c), Sherry, D. Pitman, D. Lempriere,
               O. Eloury, G. Le Maistre, D. De Gruchy, White, G. Mourant.
               Goalscorers: Le Maistre (2), De Gruchy.

Guernsey: J. Murray, D. Vaudin, E. Sauvage, V. Tostevin, M. Carre, L. Robilliard,
               H. Falla, D. Mechem, M. Brassel,
               A.M. Hunter (c), L. Collins.
               Goalscorers: Brassel (4), Hunter.

This brought to an end a quite remarkable Muratti. After the
final whistle a group of jubilant Guernsey supporters rushed
onto Springfield and carried 4-goal Brassel shoulder high to the
pavilion for the presentation ceremony. One of the first to congratulate Brassel was Pitman his immediate opponent during
the game. The trophy was handed to Hunter by His Excellency
the Lieutenant-Governor of Jersey, Admiral Sir Gresham
Nicholson.

Mickey Brassel left Jersey on board the excursion steamer Isle
of Sark at 6.30pm on Thursday along with His Excellency the
Lieutenant-Governor of Guernsey, Air Marshal Sir Thomas
Elmhirst and Lady Elmhirst. On arrival at St. Peter Port
Harbour there was one of the biggest crowds seen at the New
Jetty for some time to cheer for the hero, Mickey Brassel.

The Muratti Vase came back to Guernsey on the Isle of Jersey
on Friday morning, with most of the players and supporters

Four-goal hero,
Mickey Brassel.

returning on the vessel.also The Vase was carried ashore by centre-half Marshal Carre and
a burst of cheering broke out from the people gathered on the White Rock.

1 9 5 5
MURATTI SEMI-FINAL.
31 March 1955, Springfield Stadium, Jersey.

Jersey -3, Alderney -0.

The Jersey team to play Alderney at Springfield included three new caps Gerald Quarry (Beeches), Johnny Salsac (Magpies) and the 19-year old Roy Balston (St. Paul's). Alderney were confident following their narrow 2-1 defeat at the hands of Guernsey last year and the fact that Guernsey in turn beat Jersey 5-3 at Springfield. Alderney had two new caps in Albert Rose (Penguins) and Walter Cauvain (Northern Belles) as well as having the dangerous Barry Venton (First Tower) up front.

The two teams were introduced to the Lieut Governor of Jersey HE Sir Gresham Nicholson and the President of Alderney Comdr., S.P. Herivel, just before the kick off.

Reg Jones won the toss for Jersey in front of 3,000 supporters and took advantage of the wind. Alderney made the initial raids but the first incident of note came when Mourant crossed the ball, which bounced back into play off the top of the crossbar. Alderney defended well when Quarry had his shot blocked by Dennis Jones and then Pasquire had a brilliant save from de Gruchy. Mignot was the only Alderney forward who was consistently causing problems for the Jersey defence and a shot by him was saved by Mauger. Jersey

Dennis Jones, Walter Greenslade, Albert Rose, Jim Pasquire, Joe Harrington, John Simon.
Peter Moore, Johnny Mannion, Walter Cauvain, Noel Mignot (c), Barry Venton.
Alderney.

nearly opened the scoring but were thwarted when Greenslade threw himself across the goal to head clear a shot by Salsac. In 37 minutes a free kick by Lempriere found Le Maistre who outpaced the Alderney defence to open the scoring. As half time approached Alderney nearly equalised when Mauger was troubled by a Venton free kick and then he had to save at full stretch from Cauvain. In the last minute, however, Le Maistre came close to increasing the home side's lead. The half time score was Jersey-1, Alderney-0.

Early in the second half Alderney had the misfortune to sustain injuries to both Dennis Jones and Noel Mignot and this had the effect of disorganising the visitors' defence. Jones went off dazed but insisted upon being allowed to return to the field. Jersey tried to capitalise on this turn of events and put severe pressure on the Alderney defence who held out manfully. After 65 minutes, when Jones was off the field, Balston swung the ball across from the right and Noel scored into the corner to make the score 2-0. Five minutes later Noel centred the ball and Le Maistre fired in a shot to make the score 3-0. In the last five minutes Simon almost reduced the arrears but his superb shot was headed clear by Reg Jones leaving the final result Jersey-3, Alderney-0.

Jersey: Mauger, G. Newton, D. Lempiere, Quarry, R. Jones (c), Salsac, D. De Gruchy, Balstone, G. Le Maistre, Noel, G. Mourant.
Goalscorers: Le Maistre (2), Noel.

Alderney: J. Pasquire, A. Rose, W. Greenslade, D. Jones, J. Harrington, J. Simon, P. Moore, J. Mannion, W. Gauvain, N. Mignot, B. Venton.

Once again it was a case of what might have been for Alderney. Jersey, although winning well in the end, were unimpressive and the match was rather scrappy. However, it was Jersey who would travel to the Cycling Grounds to face Guernsey on 5 May.

MURATTI FINAL.
5 May 1955, The Cycling Grounds, Guernsey.

Guernsey -0, Jersey -0. aet.

There were no surprises in the Jersey Muratti team as they prepared to attempt to win back the Vase. The performances of Jones and Le Gallais in Magpie's Upton win against Rangers ensured their selection. It was thought that this would be a very close fought match with no outright favourites. It was anticipated that there would be a large Jersey contingent in the crowd to witness this enthralling contest.

Hunter won the toss and chose to attack the eastern goal and take advantage of the wind at their backs. The opening minutes were very tentative with neither side gaining the upper hand. The first real danger for the home defence was when Balston took a return pass from de Gruchy only to place his shot over the bar. This was followed seconds later when Collins fired his shot over the bar. The main action was taking place in the middle of the park but a move involving Froome, Brassel and Falla resulted in Le Marquand saving when the ball came off his chest and went to safety. Jersey's best chances in an even first half came when De Gruchy shot straight at Murray with the goalmouth beckoning, and Eloury shot over the bar. With seconds remaining in the first half, Falla saw his fine shot return off the Jersey crossbar leaving the half time score Guernsey-0, Jersey-0.

The second half began with Guernsey on top and only some good work by Le Marquand in the visitor's goal prevented a score. Collins, Brassel, Le Page and Falla, backed by Hunter, were testing the Jersey defence, which proved up to the task. Guernsey came close when Brassel just failed to connect with a cross by Collins. Guernsey continued to apply the pressure with Hunter shooting over the bar and then Le Marquand saved from Le Page and then stopped a point-blank shot from Collins to leave the full time score Guernsey-0, Jersey-0.

In the thirty minutes of extra time both sets of players appeared tired after a gruelling second half. During the second period of extra time, Falla hit the side netting and in the last minute Collins was only inches wide of the Jersey goal and the match ended Guernsey-0, Jersey-0.

Le Marquand making another wonderful save.

Guernsey: J. Murray, D. Vaudin, E. Sauvage, N. Froome, M. Carre, L. Robilliard, H. Falla, W.G. Le Page, M. Brassel, A.M. Hunter (c), L. Collins.

Jersey: F. Le Marquand, G. Newton, D.Lempiere, Quarry, R. Jones (c), D. Pitman, G. Le Maistre, Tredant, D. De Gruchy, Balstone, Le Gallais, G. Le Maistre, G. Mourant.

Although Guernsey might feel that they could, and should, have won this match credit must go to the sterling defensive work by the Jersey team and by Le Marquand in particular.

This was the first ever 0-0 draw in the Muratti Vase Competition and, although no official decision had been made, it was initially thought that the replay would take place on Whit Monday. It all depended on the availability of Springfield.

Jersey fans listen to the Muratti commentary in Bath Street, St. Helier.

MURATTI FINAL-REPLAY.
30 May 1955, Springfield Stadium Jersey.

Jersey -1, Guernsey -0.

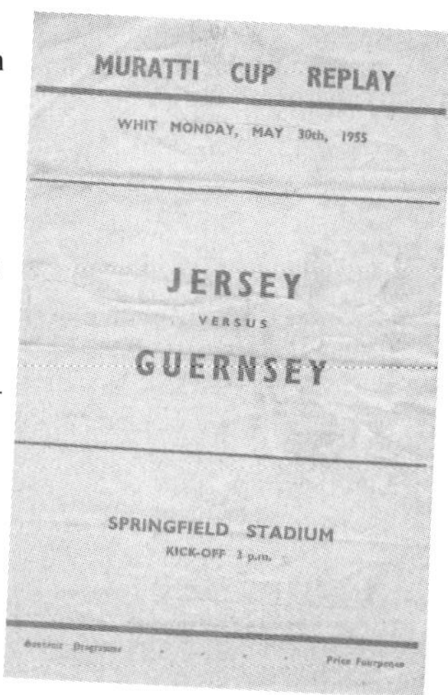

Guernsey made two changes for the replay with Tostevin and Mechem replacing Froome and Brassel. Jersey replaced le Gallais and Mourant with Le Roux and Ossie Eloury. The Jersey team strip was red and white quarters, white shorts and red and white stockings. Guernsey were in green and white shirts, blue shorts and green and white stockings.

The match was played on Whit Monday in front of a crowd of around 10,500 at Springfield and all were eagerly anticipating an exciting contest.

Jersey began the match in a more positive manner quickly putting pressure on the Guernsey defence. The match was a little edgy and there was a slight altercation between Robilliard and Balston which agitated the home supporters but the resultant free kick was unproductive. After five minutes play de Gruchy broke through but his shot was high of the target. The Guernsey forwards were finding it difficult to develop

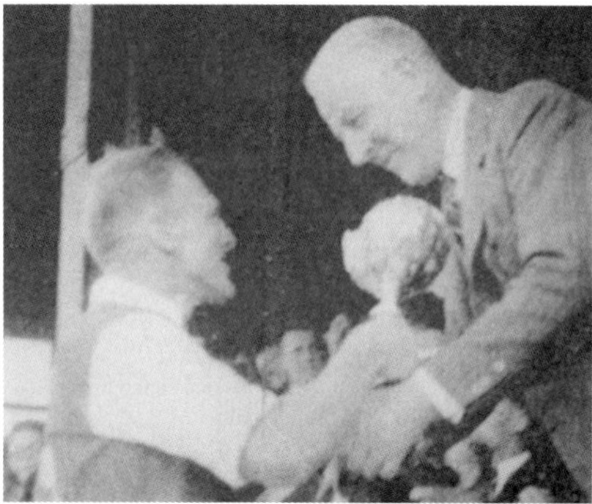

Jersey's Lieut-Governor, Admiral Sir Gresham Nicholson presents the Muratti Vase to Jersey's captain

any rhythm and the home defence were very rarely troubled. Eloury came close for Jersey when he skilfully kept in a pass from Le Roux, but his shot was well saved by Murray. As it was, Murray was proving to be the busiest player on the field as he brought off a series of fine saves from the Jersey forwards. Guernsey were being pinned back and were finding it difficult to produce any meaningful attacks. Balston and de Gruchy both had scoring chances and once again Murray was in action by punching clear a cross-shot from Eloury. A header by de Gruchy, from a Pitman cross, was well saved by Murray.

Jersey continued to play the more effective football and Le Roux came close but put his shot wide. It was not until the 36th minute that Guernsey had a worthwhile attempt at goal. Hunter passed to Collins and he in turn crossed in for Mechem to head in. Le Marquand easily caught the ball but, as he was challenged by Falla, he lost it. Mechem latched onto the loose ball but his shot just went over the bar. In the final minute of the half Jersey should have scored when Eloury beat Vaudin but he shot weakly and the danger was cleared. The half time came with the score Jersey-0,   Guernsey-0.

The second half began with the home side once more on the attack and although it was no surprise when they took the lead after 50 minutes the circumstances were rather unfortunate for the Guernsey goalkeeper. Balston swung the ball into the centre and de Gruchy, near the penalty spot, sent in a great header, which went just under the crossbar. Murray appeared to think that it was going over the bar, but instead it entered the net to give Jersey the lead. Guernsey replied by switching their forward line but with little effect as Jersey retained the initiative. Murray was again called into action and saved from Le Roux and then de Gruchy. As the game neared its end further good scoring chances were missed by Eloury and Le Roux but there were no more goals and the final score was Jersey-1, Guernsey-0.

Jersey:	F. Le Marquand, G. Newton, D. Lempiere, G. Quarry, R. Jones (c), D. Pitman, G. Le Maistre, R. Balstone, D. De Gruchy, H. Le Roux, O. Eloury.
	Goalscorer: De Gruchy.
Guernsey:	J. Murray, D. Vaudin, E. Sauvage, V. Tostevin, M. Carre, L. Robilliard, H. Falla, W.G. Le Page, D. Mechem, A.M. Hunter (c), L. Collins.

Jersey had thoroughly merited their victory and the margin would have been larger but for the performance of Murray. It was just unfortunate that the game hinged on a crucial misjudgement by him. The Jersey defence were always in control and were never really troubled by the ineffective Guernsey forwards.

1 9 5 6

MURATTI SEMI-FINAL.
22 March 1956, The Cycling Grounds, Guernsey.

Guernsey -4, Alderney -0.

The Guernsey team to face Alderney at the Cycling Grounds on 22 March included four new caps. They were Lloyd Duquemin (North), Johnny le Mesurier (Rangers) Richard Harvey (Vale Rec) and Ted Smith (St. Martins). The original Alderney selection also had four new caps. They were David Clark (Northern Belles), Charlie Dupont (Northern Belles), Charlie Dupont jnr. (Penguins) and George Bohan (Alderney Athletics). Following the selection of the Alderney team they suffered a blow when their captain, the experienced Cauvain, could not play and his replacement was young Michael Mapp (Alderney Athletics) who was playing in his first Muratti match.

The Guernsey team was regarded as one of the youngest ever to represent the Island in a Muratti match and Richard Harvey was one of the youngest players to play in a senior Muratti for them. As a 16 year old Richard had represented Guernsey in the Junior Muratti in 1955 and now as a 17 year old he was becoming the first Guernsey player to represent the Island in both Junior and Senior Muratti's in the same season.

Mr. Buckle was a Peterborough man and was an active footballer until 1931 when he had the misfortune to badly injure his left leg. He started as a referee in 1936 in the Peterborough League. In 1954 he refereed the Charity Shield match between Arsenal and Blackpool. Mr. Buckle thought that he must be the tallest referee in the League List, being 6 feet 3 inches in height.

The Guernsey and Alderney teams took to the field at the Cycling Grounds in front of a crowd of around 3,000 spectators. Prior to the match commencing both teams and officials were presented to the Lieut-Governor, HE Sir Thomas Elmhirst.

The game kicked off and Guernsey were immediately on the attack. The first shot of the match came from young Richard Harvey and it was well saved by Pasquire in the Alderney goal. Guernsey continued to push on and Hunter had a good opportunity but placed his shot over the bar, Harvey was having an excellent game but twice in three minutes he should have scored. Each time he outpaced the Alderney defence but missed with two good chances. Collins came close after 12 minutes when he deflected the ball with his chest but it was well saved by Pasquire. Although the Alderney goalkeeper was in fine form in preventing a goal, Guernsey were also finding it difficult to score through their own poor finishing. Half time came with the score Guernsey-0, Alderney-0.

Referee B.A. Buckle.

Alderney keeper, Jim Pasquire, clears up a Guernsey raid.

The second half was a repeat of the first with the home side pushing forward. Carre broke up a rare Alderney attack in the 54th minute and cleared, Harvey got the ball under control, beat Dupont and calmly placed it past Pasquire to put Guernsey 1-0 up. Having made this breakthrough it was expected that Guernsey would over-run Alderney but that was not the case. As it was, Alderney nearly scored when Dupont slipped the ball to Bohan only for Murray to rush out and clear. After 79 minutes Harvey headed a bouncing ball to Mechem who scored with a well-placed shot for goal number 2. Four minutes later Harvey passed to Mechem and his cross was turned in by Collins. A minute later Harvey completed the scoring from a pass by Hunter to make the final score Guernsey-4, Alderney-0.

Guernsey: J. Murray, L. Duquemin, D. Vaudin, V. Tostevin (c), M. Carre,
               J. Le Messurier, D. Mechem, A.M. Hunter, R. Harvey, E.J. Smith,
               L. Collins.
               Goalscorers: Harvey (2), Mechem, Collins.

Alderney: J. Pasquire, Mapp, D. Clark, D. Bate-Jones, C. Dupont, J. Simon (c) ,
               C. Dupont jnr., J. Mannion, G. Bohan, P. Moore, B. Venton.

Although Guernsey deserved to win, it was not considered to be a very good performance by them. Their poor finishing in front of goal had kept the score down to four with Harvey one of the few positive elements of the game for them. Pasquire, however, had an excellent game in the Alderney goal and could not be faulted over any of the goals. When asked following this game, what were Guernsey's chances against Jersey, Vince Tostevin put them at 50-50.

Alderney was pleased with their performance, with young teenager Michael Mapp having an excellent game against Guernsey's Les Collins. Alderney captain, John Simon said that the Alderney youngsters did very well for their first major game.

Following the match a dance was organised by the GFA in the St. George's Hall and was attended by a great many Alderney supporters. Bryn Timms and his band provided the music. Among those who attended were Mr. C.J.H. Rawlinson, president of the GFA, Mr. G. Burns, secretary of the Alderney FA; Mr. S.W. Tranfield, secretary of the Guernsey Referees Association and the referee Mr. B.A.E. Buckle.

It was agreed that a great improvement was required by Guernsey if they were to be successful against Jersey at Springfield on 3 May.

MURATTI FINAL.
3 May 1956, Springfield Stadium, Jersey.

Jersey -2, Guernsey -1.

Jersey's Lieutenant-Governor, Admiral Sir Gresham Nicholson, yesterday took the unprecedented step of inviting Jersey's captain, Reg Jones, to Government House to wish him the best of luck in the Muratti Vase Final. The Bishop of Winchester, who was staying with His Excellency, also expressed his best wishes to the Jersey captain. In a letter to the Sports Editor of the 'Press' this week, John Le Maitre, Guernsey's centre forward in five Murattis between 1950 and 1953, asks that his best wishes for success in today's game be passed to the Guernsey side. 'Get at Reg Jones and company and hit them hard.' He advises. He is currently serving with the Royal Marines in Malta and hopes to play against Leyton Orient when they visit the Island.

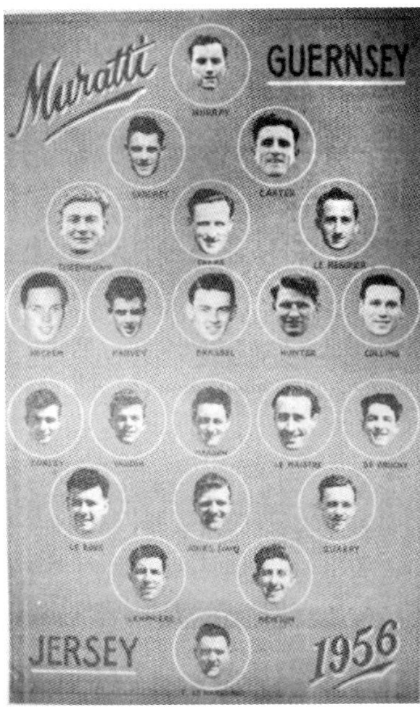

Hundreds of football fans waited round the States Airport on the morning of the match praying for the fog to lift. But they were unlucky and no planes left for Jersey. They all rushed down to the White Rock to travel to Jersey by the excursion steamer 'Isle of Jersey' which sailed at 12.30pm with a near full compliment of 1,000 aboard. There was a slight fright when one gangplank was up, it was discovered that Guernsey's left-back; Ken Carter was not on board. Just in time he arrived with reserves, Harry Falla and Johnny Hartland. Among the spectators will be Their Excellencies the Lieut-Governors of Guernsey and Jersey, Air Marshal Sir Thomas Elmhirst and Admiral Sir Gresham Nicholson respectively.

Jersey had two new caps in their team in Gordon Vaudin and Brian Corley as well as two players who had played in every post-war Muratti, skipper Reg Jones and Graeme Le Maistre. Guernsey had one new cap in Tony Sandrey (Rangers) as well as Les Collins who was winning his 16th successive cap, being capped in every post-war Muratti.

Pouring rain overnight softened the Springfield pitch and raised hopes that a good match would be seen. The previous night 54 lorries were moved into the ground to act as temporary grandstands. Islanders who were unable to see the match were able to hear a running commentary by BBC commentator, John Arlott. The commentary actually begins on the West of England Home Service at 3.34 (half-time) and continues until 5 o'clock.

Vince Tostevin won the toss for Guernsey and chose to attack the theatre end. From the kick-off Jersey attacked and maintained the pressure and when the Guernsey attack came into play it was well held by the home defence. The first corner of the match went to Guernsey following a Collins-Brassel move. Mechem's flag kick was scrambled clear and

Corley (Jersey) beats Murray to the ball but his header goes over the bar.

Graeme Le Maistre (8) scoring Jersey's second goal past Murray with Sandrey on the goal line.

Hunter fired in a shot that Le Marquand took easily. After six minutes play Guernsey missed a glorious chance when Hunter slipped the ball between two Jersey defenders to Harvey who, with the goal at his mercy, completely missed the ball. Jersey replied when Corley lobbed a high ball towards the goal line that was headed on by Harben and, with Murray caught out of position, it was left to Sandrey to clear the ball just on the line.

 The play swung from end to end with Mechem shooting for goal, then Murray had to save from Corley. The best early chance, however, fell to Jersey after 15 minutes when Vaudin found himself unmarked in front of goal but he fired his shot over the bar. Vaudin again missed a good chance when, from a Harben pass, he completely missed the ball. From the clearance Guernsey looked threatening when Newton and Jones had a misunderstanding after Collins had taken the ball down the right but Le Marquand was quick off his line to gather and clear. After 38 minutes Murray in the Guernsey goal punched the ball off an attackers head only for Le Maistre to swing the ball across again. Murray did well to save again from Corley's header and, in a counter attack, Mechem was dispossessed by Lempriere. The best attempt of the half came in the 44th minute after Brassel had been brought down by Lempriere a few yards outside the penalty area. Mechem took the free kick and placed it beautifully into the goalmouth for Brassel to beat Le Marquand with a fine header only to see Lempriere coming to Jersey's rescue and head off the line. The half time score was Jersey-0, Guernsey-0.

 After two minutes of the second half de Gruchy sped away on the right and crossed the ball, which was too high for Corley. The winger, however, was on it like a flash and centred it to le Maistre who scored with a great header to put Jersey 1-0 up. Murray got his fingers to the ball but could not stop it. As the game progressed the Jersey defence were beginning to get the better of the Guernsey forwards. The visitors were unlucky, however, when the linesman flagged for a handball by Newton in the penalty area but referee Williams refused to give a penalty. Guernsey came very close in the 57th minute when Vince Tostevin went through and crashed in a fine shot only to see it blocked by Reg Jones. As the ball ran loose Mechem then fired in a shot on the run that went just wide.

Mr. W. Bird.

Two minutes later Jersey increased their lead when le Maistre scored with a fine solo effort. He raced in from the right beating Marshall Carre and shot on the run, Murray fumbled as he slipped near the post and le Maistre, following up, side footed the ball home.

He nearly completed his hat trick when he beat Murray with a beautiful long drive but the ball rebounded off the crossbar. A third Jersey goal nearly arrived when in the 62nd minute Vaudin chased a shot that was going wide and turned it goalwards from about three yards. Murray was taken by surprise but quickly recovered to push the ball round the post with a superb one-handed save. In the 68th minute Brassel seemed to be through when he beat Jones after receiving from Hunter but as he prepared to shoot, Newton pushed him off the ball and Le Marquand cleared. Guernsey reduced the arrears when Brassel centred for Harvey to shoot. His shot hit the underside of the bar and rebounded out only to be met by Mechem who crashed it into the back of the net to make the score 2-1. Jersey nearly regained a two-goal lead through Harben but he was denied by an excellent save from Murray. As the minutes ticked away Tostevin averted danger for Guernsey when he just tipped a de Gruchy corner with his head to prevent Vaudin getting in a shot and a minute later Vaudin was put through by Le Maistre and lobbed the ball over the onrushing Murray but the ball just slipped past the post. The final whistle sounded and the final score was Jersey-2, Guernsey-1.

Jersey: Le Marquand, G. Newton, D. Lempiere, Quarry, R. Jones (c), H. Le Roux, D. De Gruchy, G. Le Maistre, M. Harben, Vaudin, Corley.
Goalscorer: Le Maistre (2).

Guernsey: J. Murray, A. Sandrey, K. Carter, V. Tostevin (c), M. Carre, J. Le Messurier, D. Mechem, R. Harvey, M. Brassel, A.M. Hunter, L. Collins.
Goalscorer: Mechem.

Jersey thoroughly deserved their victory as their forwards proved to be far more dangerous than the visitors. It was not a great game but there was plenty of excitement, especially in the second half. Referee, Mr Joe Williams, said that the standard was very high, comparable to that of many third-division games. He thought the linesmen were well up to the standard of English football league officials.

An interesting point was highlighted by the Press that at this match was 90-year-old Mr. W. Bird who was attending his 82nd Muratti match. He had seen every Muratti match since the competition began in 1905. Mr. Bird was one of the founders of North AC and was an ex-President and became Life Honorary President.

1 9 5 7

MURATTI SEMI-FINAL.
28 March 1957, Springfield Stadium, Jersey.

Jersey -7, Alderney -1.

There was some concern in the Jersey camp as it was reported that Graeme le Maistre might miss the Muratti match against Alderney due to him receiving an injury to the base of his spine during an Island trial game. Reg Jones also asked not to be considered for this game. Both players had played in every one of Jersey's post war Muratti matches. As it was Le Maistre was able to take his customary place in the Jersey line-up and also captained the side. Jersey had selected three new caps for their side in Denis Crenan (Magpies), David Parker (Wanderers) and Alan Venton (Oaklands). Parker played in the Junior Muratti last season and Alan Parker is the brother of the Alderney players Bobby and Barry. Although it was felt that Alderney had little chance of winning they could be expected to give their customary never-say die fight. They had included three new caps in their line-up in Carre, Randall and Waller, all of them Alderney club Penguins.

D. Lempriere, F. Le Marquand, H. Le Roux.
D, de Gruchy, G. Le Maistre (c), D. Parker, A. Venton, G. Mourant.
G. Quarry, P. Gosling, D. Crenan.
Jersey.

There was a late change in the referee for the match and Mr. Callaghan (Merthyr, Wales) would take charge. He replaced Mr. K. Howley (Middlesbrough) who was refereeing the FA Cup semi-final replay between Aston Villa and West Bromwich Albion.

The match at Springfield started very quietly with very little action during the first 15 minutes and it was after this opening spell that Jersey took control. In 17 minutes young David Parker flicked the ball over an opponent and left Pasquire helpless with a beautiful shot. A minute later Parker took a pass from de Gruchy and scored with a low drive as Pasquire advanced. Crenan and Nash both went close before Jersey increased their lead in 36 minutes. Parker beat two men on the left and squared the ball to de Gruchy who shot into the top of the net to make the score 3-0. Two minutes later Crenan placed a long ball into the Alderney goalmouth and Parker scored his third goal. As the half neared its end Le Roux set up de Gruchy to score to make the half time Jersey-5, Alderney-0.

The second half began and Jersey were soon off the mark when a pass by de Gruchy found Parker who made the score 6-0. The Alderney defence were under constant pressure and Parker nearly added to the total but put his shot wide. In the 69th minute a 'Nash' Venton long ball was met by Parker who scored his own 5th and Jersey's 7th goal. Alderney scored in the 81st minute when Moore received a pass from Bobby Venton and scored close in leaving Le Marquand helpless. Waller nearly added a second but shot over the bar. In the dying moments de Gruchy came close when his header came off the bar. The final score was Jersey-7, Alderney-1.

Jersey: F. Le Marquand, D. Lempriere, H. Le Roux, G. Quarry, D. Pitman, D. Crenan, D. De Gruchy, G. Le Maistre (c), D. Parker, A. Venton, G. Mourant.
Goalscorers: Parker (5), De Gruchy (2),

Alderney: J. Pasquire, M. Mapp, B. Venton, Jones, J. Harrington (c), Carre, P. Moore, J. Mannion, A. Randall, R. Venton, Waller.
Goalscorer: Moore.

The star of the match was undoubtedly 19-year-old David Parker who scored five goals and set up an individual scoring record for a Muratti match. Alderney's heroes were all in defence with Joe Harrington playing a real captain's game aided by left back Barry Venton and Mannion.

MURATTI FINAL.
2 May 1957, The Cycling Grounds, Guernsey.

Guernsey -6, Jersey -4.

Throughout the morning and early afternoon hundreds of Jersey supporters poured into the island, the Jersey team being afforded a warm welcome by an advance party on their arrival by air shortly before 9 o'clock. At the White Rock when the mid-morning steamer berthed from Jersey 457 fans landed and the swelling numbers of Jersey fans were joined by 719 more when the 'Isle de Sark' operated the day excursion from the sister isle. The steamer arrived prompt at 2.30pm leaving the supporters just enough time to reach the Track.

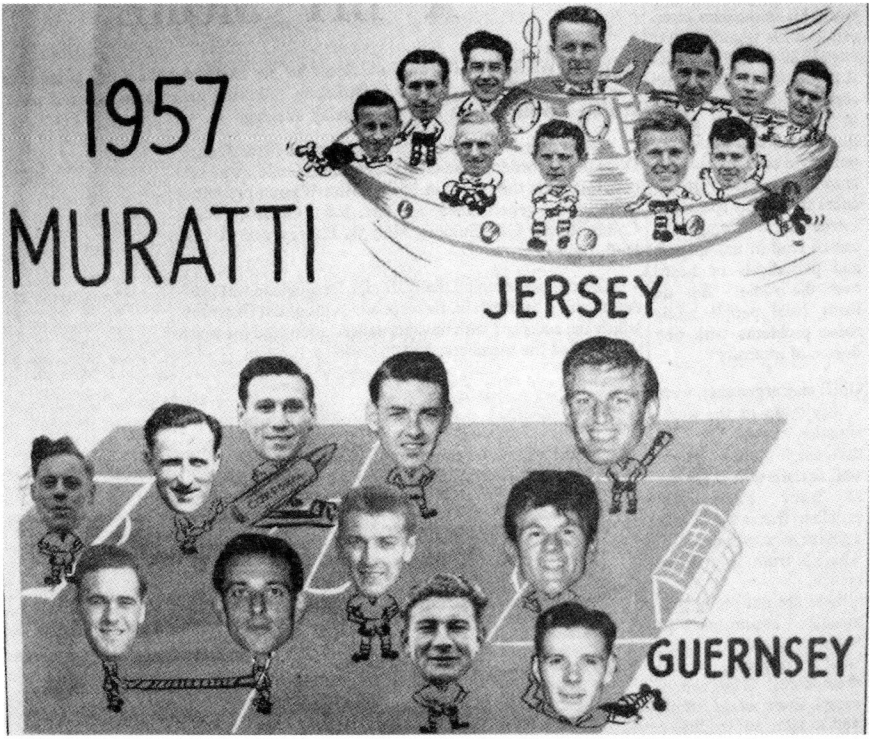

   The selection of the Guernsey team for their match against Jersey at the Cycling Grounds caused a stir in the local Press. There was surprise that Eker was selected at centre forward instead of Brassel (who played at inside left) and Marshal Carre at left half instead of left back. The team also included four new caps in Trustum (Vale Rec) in goal, Brehaut (Belgrave W.), Wilcocks (North) and Eker (North). The Guernsey team were coached by Bob Kelly. There was some concern in the Jersey team as David Parker passed a late fitness test to play in the match. The Jersey press, however, were confident of a Jersey victory. John Arlott sent greetings over the air to Mr. W. Bird who would miss seeing the game for the first time since the Muratti Vase competition started 52 years ago. Mr. Bird, one of the islands most colourful soccer personalities, was ill in bed.

   The Lieut-Governors, Air Marshal Sir Thomas Elmhirst (Guernsey) and Admiral Sir Gresham Nicholson (Jersey) should have been present at the game but illness prevented Air Marshall Sir Thomas Elmhirst from attending. Lady Elmhirst, however, attended the game.

The Guernsey side were led out by Marshal Carre and the Jersey team by Graeme le Maistre. The visitors were rightly installed as firm favourites to retain the Muratti Vase.

Guernsey started the quickest and were soon into their stride and took the lead after only 4 minutes. Brassel lobbed the ball into the centre and the bounce beat both Robilliard and Le Roux. Robilliard turned and was on the ball in a flash and shot first time into the top corner of the net. Jersey then took the initiative and began to look dangerous with 'Nash' Venton outstanding. After nine minutes the teams were level. Venton shot low across goal and de Gruchy ran in to smash it home. This proved to be Jersey's last meaningful shot of the half as Guernsey took control. Three minutes later Robilliard beat Le Roux on the right touchline and crossed a curling centre high over the Jersey defence for Collins to fire in a tremendous header into the net to restore Guernsey's lead. The play became more even although it was confined mainly to the midfield. Collins and Brassel both fired in shots that went wide then Jim Eker sent a 20 yard shot just over the bar. Guernsey was on top and the half time score was Guernsey-2, Jersey-1.

The second half was only four minutes old when Eker raced onto a Marshall Carre pass to beat Gosling and score Guernsey's third goal. As the game approached the hour mark a goal glut arrived. Les Collins ran in from the left and saw his left foot shot parried by 'Danny' Le Marquand. Collins shot again and once more it was blocked by the goalkeeper but Collins once more gained possession and slid the ball into the net. In the 65th minute Collins fed Brassel who fired a shot towards the top left hand corner of the net, it would have missed the target but Robilliard with a quick flick of his head sent it to the opposite corner to make the score 5-1. This was followed by a bustling attack by Vince Tostevin who forced his way passed two Jersey defenders and fired the ball into the roof of the net to amazingly put Guernsey 6-1 up. Jersey responded well to this major setback and in the 72nd minute le Maistre gathered the ball in the centre and went on to beat Trustum with a low shot. Three minutes later le Maistre rose to beat the keeper with a well timed header from a Venton cross to make the score 6-3. In between those two goals Brassel had been carried from the field still suffering from an injury he sustained shortly after the interval. He carried on but had to be taken off again after 80 minutes. Just after he was taken off Jersey hit their fourth goal when Parker, receiving a pass from le Gallais, scored. This remarkable match ended Guernsey-6, Jersey-4.

Guernsey: D. Trustum, L. Duquemin, D. Vaudin, V. Tostevin, R. Brehaut,
             M. Carre (c), L. Robilliard, F. Wilcocks, L. Eker, M. Brassel, L. Collins.
             Goalscorers: Robilliard (2), Collins (2), Eker, Tostevin.

Jersey: Le Marquand, D. Lempriere, H. Le Roux, Quarry, Gosling, D. Crenan,
             D. De Gruchy, G. Le Maistre (c), D. Parker, Le Gallais, A. Venton.
             Goalscorers: De Gruchy, Le Maistre (2), Parker.

A jubilant Marshall Carre received the Muratti Vase from the Lieut-Governor of Jersey after a magnificent victory.

The victorious Guernsey team joined over 1,000 dancers at the Muratti Ball in St. George's Hall following the match. They celebrated their fine victory to the music of Edgar Blampied and his orchestra. Guests-of honour included the president of the Guernsey Football Association, Mr. J.H. Rawlinson, referee E.S. Oxley and Guernsey coach Mr. Bob Kelly.

Marshall Carre receives the Muratti Vase from Admiral Sir Gresham Nicholson. (Inset) Marshall Care's Muratti Cap.

Guernsey 1957.
M. Brassel, V. Tostevin, D. Trustum, D. Vaudin, R. Brehaut, L. Duquemin,
L. Robilliard, J. Eker, M. Carre (c), F. Wilcox, L. Collins.

1 9 5 8

MURATTI SEMI-FINAL.
27 March 1958, The Cycling Grounds, Guernsey.

Guernsey -8, Alderney -2.

There was great uncertainty in the Alderney camp in the lead up to their Muratti match with Guernsey. The main cause for concern was the appearance of Johnny Mannion (Beeches Old Boys) as it appeared that he would not be allowed time off from his new job with British European Airways. He has been working for them for only a week. He believed that he would not be allowed time off and therefore withdrew from Alderney's squad but when BEA heard about his dilemma they informed him that he could play. As it turned out he did not play for Alderney in the match. Alderney will also be without the services of Barry Venton as he withdrew from the team because of injury. The preparations for the opening of Guernsey's defence of the Muratti Vase against Alderney were rather overshadowed by a report that appeared in the Press. It was reported that the Jersey inside forward, Alan 'Nash' Venton, currently rated their outstanding forward, was unlikely to play for Jersey in this year's Muratti Vase final on 1 May.

The rules of the Muratti competition state that a non-native cannot play for a particular island unless he has resided continuously in that island for 26 weeks immediately prior to the match.

Venton was, of course, a Guernseyman by birth but int the previous season he qualified for Jersey by having lived in that island continuously for 26 weeks before the final At the end of the previous year, however, he went to live in Southampton for 10 weeks, not returning to Jersey until just before Christmas. Therefore, when the Muratti Final came

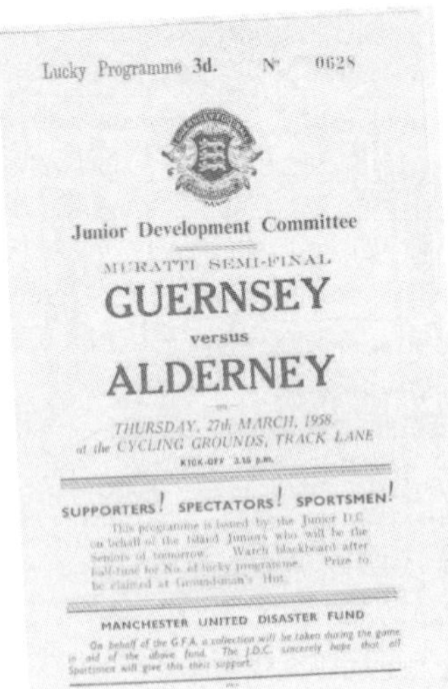

along, he would have been residing in Jersey for only four months and would not be eligible to play. A Jersey Football Association official said 'I have read the Muratti qualification rule very closely and I cannot see any loophole.'

Guernsey started the match against Alderney at the Cycling Grounds with two new caps Roy Martin and Les Pasquire.

The programme for the match stated that a collection was to be taken in aid of the Manchester United Disaster Fund. This Fund was set up following the Munich air disaster on 6 February 1958.

Guernsey set the tempo for the game very early on and Alderney, defending the eastern goal, encountered their first trouble after seven minutes when Derek Mechem crossed low to Collins who passed to Harvey whose shot into a packed goal-

Harvey (10) opens the scoring for Guernsey.

mouth was blocked by Clark. Two minutes later Guernsey should have scored when Collins was fouled by Jones in the penalty box. Collins took the resulting penalty kick himself but it was saved by Cartwright. Collins again came close in 18 minutes but his header was saved by the goalkeeper. Alderney broke away and Bobby Venton fired in a 25-yard shot that was well saved by Pasquire. In the 21st minute Guernsey took the lead when Collins moved in from the left with the ball and centred past Cartwright to Harvey who scored. Cartwright then saved from Harvey but in the 25th minute Collins broke through from a Mechem pass to crash a shot which went in off the underside of the bar to double Guernsey's advantage. The pressure continued and Cartwright did well when he tipped a Collins shot over the bar. Alderney unfortunately lost a third goal when, following a corner, John Dupont put into his own net. Cartwright was again called into action when he saved from Body following some good work by Collins. The half time score was Guernsey-3, Alderney-0.

In the second half Alderney made some positional changes but it was Guernsey that continued the scoring when a Vince Tostevin free kick found Harvey who headed in number four. Alderney replied a minute later when Hammond crossed in for Peter Moore to smash it in from close range. In 52 minutes Body found Collins and he shot in, Harrington partially blocked the shot but it spun away from Cartwright, who was helpless on the ground, and into the net. Harvey and Mechem then combined well to set up a scoring chance for Collins but he miskicked and the ball went to Body but he sent his shot over the bar. Harvey completed his hat trick after 58 minutes when he moved in from the left to smash in a great shot. A minute later a poor clearance gave Alan Hamon a chance and he scored with a superb 25 yard drive past a surprised Cartwright to make the score 7-1. The Alderney 'keeper was kept busy in the next minute as an unrelenting Guernsey attack maintained the pressure. He saved from Collins, then Harvey hit the bar and Collins had another shot that went over the bar. Alderney held out well and forced an attack in the 78th minute and when Lloyd Duquemin fouled Cauvain in the penalty area referee Hunt awarded a penalty. Moore stepped up and scored with a well-placed shot into the left hand corner. With six minutes remaining Harvey passed to Collins who turned smartly to lob the ball into the left hand corner to complete the scoring. The match ended Guernsey-8, Alderney-2.

Guernsey: L. Pasquire, L. Duquemin, D. Vaudin, V. Tostevin, R.O. Martin, B. Hill, A. Hamon, R. Body, L. Collins, R. Harvey, D. Mechem.
Goalscorers: Harvey (3), Mechem (2), Hamon, og (2).

Alderney: G. Cartwright, J. Dupont, D. Clark, D. Jones, J. Harrington, C. Dupont, G. Gauvain, W. Hammond, K. Duquemin, R. Venton, P. Moore.
Goalscorer: Moore (2, 1 pen).

Alderney were well beaten but, although he lost eight goals, George Cartwright had a fine game and made some good saves. Two-goal Peter Moore and Bill Hammond were the pick of the Alderney forwards. Peter Moore became the first Alderney player to score two goals in a Muratti match.

MURATTI FINAL.
1 May 1958, Springfield Stadium, Jersey.

Jersey -2, Guernsey -1.

The sunny weather put the soccer fans in the best possible mood and a great Muratti feeling was experienced as the trip boat 'Isle of Guernsey' left St. Peter Port Harbour. Hundreds of yards of green and white ribbon were seen as the 576 trippers joined the voyage to Jersey. In the lead up to Guernsey's match at Springfield there was some concern over Les Robilliard (Belgrave W.) who received a leg injury during the Jeremie Cup Final against Beeches. He had a fitness test on Wednesday and although he passed it he declared that he was not match-fit, but on the day of the match he informed the Island General Selection Committee that he would be able to play. Guernsey had one new cap in their side with Brian Mechem (North) making his debut. Jersey's team have all had Muratti experi-

ence. Admiral Sir Gresham Nicholson, Lieut-Governor of Jersey, summoned the Jersey captain, Graeme Le Maistre, to Government House on the morning of the match so that he could wish him and his team the best of luck in the Muratti Vase Final. There was a feeling in Jersey that interest in the Muratti was on the wane and this was reflected in the fewer number of applications for permission to use lorries as 'grandstands'. It was reported that the interest in Jersey was not as intense as in previous years and that, for the first time since the war, ground tickets would be on sale at the Springfield gates. The Lieut-Governor of Jersey, Admiral Sir Gresham Nicholson, and Lady Nicholson would be attending along with the Bailiff of Jersey, Sir Alexander Coutanche and other dignitaries. Mr. W. 'Billy' Bird, described as the 'grand old man of Channel Island football' would not see the match but would be anxiously awaiting the result from his home. Mr. Bird was 92 years old.

Arthur Kent and Frank Falla watch as John Arlott provides the commentary.

Once again the match was to be relayed by the BBC on the West of England Home service with John Arlott giving the commentary from Springfield. He would be assisted by Mr. A.G. Kent, sports editor of the Jersey Evening Post, and Mr. F.W. Falla of Guernsey.

It was reported that parts of the Springfield pitch had been returfed about three weeks before the final. The ground, however, was in excellent condition following the recent rainfall but the pitch may be on the hard side.

Guernsey captain, Dick Vaudin, won the toss and Jersey kicked off. They were the quickest into their stride and from the kick off forced a corner which Trustum punched over the bar. From the second corner he tipped a le Maistre attempt onto the woodwork before Mourant shot over. Guernsey tried to reply but Hill's good work came to nothing and Harben started a further Jersey attack when he set up de Gruchy but he put the ball wide as Trustum came out. By now Jersey were well on top and easily dealing with Guernsey's sporadic attacks. Tostevin had to be alert to take the ball of Parker's toe when a goal seemed certain. However, it was the visitors who took the lead in the 17th minute. Doug Pitman brought down Richard Harvey in the penalty area. Sandrey took the resulting penalty and crashed a rising shot into the net and although Mauger managed to get his hands to the ball he could not prevent it entering the net. Although 1-0 down Jersey were still the better team with Harben controlling play from the midfield. After 30 minutes Jersey drew level. De Gruchy and le Maistre worked the ball well and put in a centre. Harben miskicked the cross but regained control rounded Brehaut before smashing a low shot into the corner of the net well out of Trustum's reach. Jersey thoroughly deserved this goal, having been much faster on the ball and being in control of the game for long periods. There was no more scoring and the first half ended Jersey-1, Guernsey-1.

Jersey began the second half very slowly and Guernsey were on top for a time. The quality of the football deteriorated badly and neither team looked able to score. With ten minutes remaining Guernsey tried to force the issue and changed the team around. Duquemin was moved out of position and placed at centre forward with disastrous results as the rearranged Guernsey defence came under almost constant pressure without his steadying influence. Trustum was called on time and time again to produce brilliant saves to keep Jersey out. With seven minutes remaining Brehaut was accidentally put out of the action when the ball hit him in the face and the rest of the Guernsey defence was caught out of position when Le Maistre put de Gruchy away and as Trustum rushed out of his goal desperately to narrow the angle, de Gruchy shot low past him. The ball hit an upright but de Gruchy followed up unchallenged to drive the ball into the empty net for the winning goal. The result was Jersey-2, Guernsey-1.

Mauger, the Jersey goalkeeper, saves from Robilliard.

Jersey fans pack the main stand.

Jersey: Mauger, G. Newton, D. Lempriere, Quarry, D. Pitman, C. Dingle,
              D. De Gruchy, G. Le Maistre (c), M. Harben, D. Parker, G. Mourant.
              Goalscorers: Harben, De Gruchy.

Guernsey: D. Trustum, L. Duquemin, D. Vaudin, V. Tostevin, R. Brehaut, A. Sandrey,
              R. Harvey, B. Hill, L. Collins, B. Mechem, L. Robilliard.
              Goalscorer: Sandrey (pen).

Jersey had thoroughly merited their victory but it was a disastrous match for Guernsey. They were totally outplayed in attack, with Jersey's Parker, Le Maistre and Harben particularly dangerous. They went down to a better all round team. Credit should go to Trustum and his defence for restricting Jersey to only two goals.

1 9 5 9

MURATTI SEMI-FINAL.
9 April 1959, Springfield Stadium, Jersey.

Jersey -6, Alderney -0.

Six of last years Alderney Muratti team that lost 8-2 to Guernsey retained their places in the starting line-up. There were two new caps for their match against Jersey at Springfield and they were R. Mapp (Alderney Athletics) and A. Dupont (Penguins). The Alderney team left for Jersey on Wednesday 8 April and were based at the Merton Hotel until Friday afternoon. There were no new caps in the experienced Jersey team. Jersey drew with Dulwich Hamlet in their build-up for the Muratti and there was one change to that team with Micky Harben (Beeches) replacing G. Vowden (First Tower).

The referee for the match was John Martel (Guernsey), the first Channel Islander to be given control of a Muratti match for over 50 years. The only other Channel Islander to referee a Muratti match was Herbie Le Messurier (Guernsey) who took charge of both of the matches in the inaugural competition of 1905.

As the players were warming up for the match at Springfield a heavy hail shower five minutes before the start caused them to scatter. The shower did not last and when Johnny Mannion won the toss for Alderney the sun was shining. The visiting captain elected to defend the theatre end and robbing Jersey from the kick-off started two early moves that petered out because of poor finishing. Mannion then sent Alderney off again and when Peter Moore centred from the right Le Marquand had three or four desperate seconds as he tried to hold the ball when challenged by two Alderney forwards. Jersey weathered this storm and began to get on top and after 11 minutes went ahead when Parker scored. Soon after, Parker added a second when le Maistre slipped the ball through to him and he slammed it passed Cartwright. In 20 minutes the home team went 3-0 up when de Gruchy fired in from a Harben pass leaving the half time score Jersey-3, Alderney-0.

Jersey came out fighting in the second half and after two minutes scored goal number four. Harben passed to Parker who scored at the third attempt after Cartwright had blocked two of the shots. Alderney replied when, after 67 minutes, Venton hit a free kick into the Jersey area and Moore fired in a superb shot on the turn that was brilliantly saved by Le Marquand for a corner. From the corner Venton raced into the area only to have one shot blocked by a defender and a second saved, one handed, on the line by Le Marquand. Jersey continued their attacks and Cartwright made a spectacular diving save from Parker at the expense of a corner. 'Nash' Venton placed the corner accurately and Harben turned it in first time off the bar for goal number five. The scoring was completed by de Gruchy in 82 minutes with a rising left foot drive to make the final score Jersey-6, Alderney-0.

Jersey: F. Le Marquand, G. Newton, D. Lempiere, C. Dingle, D. Pitman, D. Crenan, G. Le Maistre (c), D. Parker, D. De Gruchy, M. Harben, A. Venton.
Goalscorers: Parker (3), De Gruchy (2), Harben.

Alderney: G. Cartwright, K. Duquemin, D. Clark, R. Mapp, J. Harrington, B. Venton, A. Dupont, J. Mannion, A. Randall, R. Venton, P. Moore.

This was a comprehensive victory for Jersey and they were on top for all but five minutes of the game. Alderney was slightly unlucky not to have scored a consolation goal.

On Friday evening the traditional Muratti Ball was held at Alserney's Grand Hotel, where the players were the guests.

'Tot' De Gruchy scores the final goal.

MURATTI FINAL.
30 April 1959, The Cycling Grounds, Guernsey.

Guernsey -2, Jersey -3.

It was pointed out that Roy Martin was probably the oldest player to be capped for the first time against Jersey and the first player to be honoured as skipper in his first final. There were three Guernsey players making their Muratti debuts and they were Don Batiste and Rex Diamond of Belgrave W. and Les Arnold. Although this was one of the oldest teams to represent the island it had only won 40 caps in previous games (Les Collins having won 19) with Jersey having a much more experienced side. Jersey was pleased to include 20-year old Alan Venton for his fourth cap. Guernsey born 'Nash' was unable to play in last year's final because he broke the qualification rule by living in Southampton and not returning to Jersey in time.

The referee for today's game was Mr. Jack Husband and he once refereed a match that started one day and finished the next. The game was between Brazil and Argentina, which took place in Sao Paulo, Cuppa Rocco, and started at 9.25pm. Extra time came, and it was five minutes after midnight when Mr Husband sounded the final whistle. In 1956 he refereed the Brazil-Italy match in Rio in front of a crowd of 193,000.

There was an excellent crowd of 10,566 at the Cycling Grounds on 30 April for the Muratti Vase final. The match was attended by the Lieut-Governor of Jersey, HE General Sir George Erskine and the Lieut-Governor of Guernsey, HE Vice-Admiral Sir Geoffrey Robson. Once again the match was being broadcast by John Arlott for the BBC. Roy Martin, in his first Muratti match against Jersey, was to captain the Guernsey side with Graeme le Maistre leading the Jersey team.

The game started with the unfancied Guernsey, having the benefit of a strong downfield wind, on top and being faster to the ball. They were keeping Jersey pinned back in their own half. Lloyd Duquemin, an experimental centre forward, was giving the Jersey defence

Lloyd Duquemin fails to connect with a Les Collins cross as Gordon Newton guards the Jersey goal.

a lot to think about as he chased down every ball that came close. It was a full time job for Pitman in the heart of the visiting defence. Despite this incessant pressure the Jersey team held out and, in their first meaningful attack, after 12 minutes they scored. Mourant crossed from the left to find Harben in a great scoring position but he shot weakly. Trustum fisted the shot away only to find le Maistre. He put it back into the middle to give de Gruchy an easy goal. Although le Maistre had been injured in a tackle with Collins, and not fully recovered, he was still mobile enough to cause danger to Guernsey. The Jersey goal survived a lucky escape when Pitman blocked a Duquemin shot with Le Marquand helpless.

Collins and Arnold were peppering the Jersey goal with crosses that the visitors managed to clear with some difficulty. Guernsey equalised when a Collins corner was fired towards the left of the goal by Batiste, Arnold returned it across goal for Duquemin to throw himself at the ball to equalise. Jersey almost restored their lead but Trustum made a great save from Venton. With 30 minutes gone John Mahy smashed the ball goal wards from the right. Duquemin could not reach the ball but a worried Newton had the misfortune to turn the ball into his own net with Le Marquand well out of position. The half time whistle went with the score Guernsey-2, Jersey-1.

The second half began with Jersey making full use of the strong wind and in the opening minutes came close with le Maistre missing a great chance. It was nearly disaster for Guernsey when Trustum slipped when taking a goal kick and fed the ball straight to Harben. He side stepped to gain a better position and fired in a shot that was cleared off the line by Sandrey. Chances came at both ends before Venton crossed in for the dangerous le Maistre to head past a surprised Trustum for the equaliser. Guernsey replied with shots by Harvey and Duquemin but they were easily cleared. The home team thought that they had regained the lead after 68 minutes through Arnold, but he was ruled offside. As the game continued a Batiste 'goal' was disallowed for offside as Guernsey strove for the winning goal. After 81 minutes Jersey won a corner and as the ball came in de Gruchy fired in a header that hit Vaudin on its way into the net to put the visitors into the lead. In the dying seconds Harvey almost rescued the game for Guernsey but he shot weakly from the edge of the area. The final result was Guernsey-2, Jersey-3.

Guernsey: D. Trustum, D. Vaudin, A. Sandrey, R. Diamond, R.O. Martin (c),
             R. Harvey, D. Batiste, L. Arnold, L. Duquemin, J. Mahy, L. Collins.
             Goalscorers: Duquemin, og.

Jersey: Le Marquand, G. Newton, D. Lempiere, C. Dingle, D. Pitman, D. Crenan,
             D. De Gruchy, G. Le Maistre (c), M. Harben, A. Venton, G. Mourant.
             Goalscorers: De Gruchy (2), Le Maistre.

It was agreed that this was an excellent Muratti match and the turning point appeared to be the extra big match experience of the Jersey team.

A proud Graeme le Maistre received the Muratti Vase from the Lieut-Governor of Guernsey, HE Sir Geoffrey Robson.

The fifties gave both Jersey and Guernsey five victories apiece making the overall score Guernsey 24 wins, Jersey 17 wins, Alderney 1, win with the Vase being shared once.

In the FA Cup Final at Wembley Manchester City defeated Luton Town by 2-1. In the Manchester City team was Bill Whare and he becomes the first Channel Islander to win an FA Cup medal. Bill won one Muratti cap for Guernsey v Jersey in the 3-1 defeat at the Track in 1947.

Graeme Le Maistre receiving the Muratti Vase.

11

1960 - 1969

1 9 6 0

MURATTI SEMI-FINAL.
31 March 1960, The Cycling Grounds, Guernsey.

Guernsey -5, Alderney -1.

Alderney announced that they would have two new caps for their match against Guernsey at the Cycling Grounds on 31 March. J. Coen (Penguins) who is from Jersey and Maurice Baker (Northern Belles). Guernsey's one new cap was Norman Le Cheminant (Sylvans). Norman is only the second Sylvans player to be capped and the first since Doug Mechem. During the lead up to this match Alderney were experiencing difficulties in reaching Guernsey on 29 March due to the airport being closed for at least 48 hours. They had to cancel their flight and were actually ferried to Guernsey in Nick Allen's motorboat in two trips on 30 March.

Guernsey squad.

Alderney keeper Peter Bond makes another thrilling save.

Alderney's preparations were further disrupted when at very late notice they lost the services of the experienced and influential Mannion due to illness. C. Dupont was called in as a late replacement with J. Dupont replacing Mannion in the forward line. Alderney's Maurice Baker was married at noon at St. Joseph's Church, St. Peter Port to Miss Joy Le Lievre on the day of the match and was due to fly to London at 4.00pm with his new wife but this departure was cancelled when he was selected for the Muratti match for his first cap. So three hours after he was married he was playing at the Cycling Grounds for Alderney. His new team mates attended the wedding.

The teams were led onto the pitch by Collins, who was winning his 21st cap for Guernsey, and Hammond of Alderney.

The game opened quietly with Alderney pressing first and their initial opportunity came from a Moore shot which was cleared by Martin in the Guernsey defence. In the third minute Guernsey flashed into the attack. Harvey switched play from right to left and found Collins. He brought the ball to his right foot and centred to Le Cheminant. The ball was just too high and a good chance was lost. Le Cheminant then fired in a shot from near the penalty spot but it was well saved by Bond. The game was very even with Harrington and Venton closing down the home forwards who were finding it difficult to make an impression. The opening goal came after 31 minutes. A long throw in by Harvey was headed into the centre by Arnold and Le Cheminant was on the spot to prod the ball home. Four minutes later Guernsey doubled their score. Collins flashed over a centre and Arnold glanced it to the right when trying for goal. Le Cheminant pounced on the ball and whipped a rising shot into the net from the narrowest of angles. Alderney replied when Venton saw his header catch Pasquier out of his goal but the ball rebounded off a post. Half time arrived with the score Guernsey-2, Alderney-0.

The second half started with Alderney having two good chances to score through Baker and then Randall but it was Guernsey who increased their lead. Good work by Harvey, Le Cheminant and Collins resulted in Arnold scoring goal number 3. Collins and Batiste then combined to present Arnold with a good chance but his fine header was brilliantly saved by

Bond. Collins, however, gave the Alderney keeper no chance in the 49th minute to fire in the fourth Guernsey goal. Alderney were again unlucky to see a Moore shot come back off the post. Collins and Arnold both came close but it was Alderney who scored. Hammond was fouled in the penalty area and Venton scored with the resulting penalty. Brassel then had a goal ruled out for offside as the game moved to a close. Arnold completed the scoring with a piledriver that fired into the top corner of the net. This made the final score Guernsey-5, Alderney-1.

Guernsey: L. Pasquire, D. Vaudin, A. Sandrey, R. Diamond, R.O. Martin, B. Mechem, D. Batiste, L. Arnold, N. Le Cheminant, R. Harvey, L. Collins (c).
Goalscorers: N. Le Cheminant (2), L. Arnold (2), L. Collins.

Alderney: P. Bond, D. Bate-Jones, J. Dupont, J. Coen, J. Harrington, B. Venton, M. Baker, J. Mannion, W. Hammond, P. Moore, A. Randall.
Goalscorer: B. Venton (pen).

It was not a very entertaining game although four of the goals were excellent. Alderney were severely handicapped by the loss of Mannion but Harrington and Venton stood out for the visitors. Peter Bond, the son of the former Alderney Muratti goalkeeper, Frank Bond, could not be faulted for any of the goals and had some great saves.

MURATTI FINAL.
5 May 1960 – Springfield Stadium, Jersey.

Jersey -5, Guernsey -1.

It was announced that neither of the islands Lieut-Governors would be present at the Muratti Final as they would be attending the Royal Wedding of Princess Margaret and Antony Armstrong-Jones. The Deputy Bailiff, C.S. Harrison, was sworn in as Deputy Lieut-Governor and would be present at the match. A large crowd was expected as some 225 Guernsey supporters travelled to Jersey by BEA and Jersey Airlines and another 600 or so by the early morning steamer and a further 700 on the excursions operated by the 'Isle of Sark'.

The Jersey team included two new caps in Bob Megaw (Oaklands) and Tim Browne (Beeches). The Guernsey team all had previous Muratti experience. The visitors suffered a blow when Les Pasquier was pronounced unfit, through a shoulder injury, at lunchtime and Barry Bishop (Athletics) replaced him.

The teams were led out on to Springfield by the captains Le Maistre for Jersey and Collins for Guernsey as the crowd of 6,750 anticipated a keen contest.

Les Collins welcomes Graeme Le Maistre before the match.

Jersey began the match in sensational fashion by taking the lead after 25 seconds. Graeme Mourant began the move as he took the ball along the centre line. He swung it to Le Maistre on the right wing; he in turn drove the ball to Parker who hit a magnificent first time shot that gave Bishop no chance. Before three minutes had elapsed Jersey's Denis Crenan left the field for treatment with blood pouring from his right temple. He was rushed to hospital for stitches before returning to the match. Nine minutes later Guernsey's Johnny Le Maitre had to leave the field following a head injury. Fortunately both players were able to return to the game. Jersey was by far the more menacing team but in the 21st minute Guernsey drew level. Hamon ran onto a loose ball out on the touchline and had plenty of time to swing in a centre that was met by Arnold who beat Le Marquand with a beautiful header. A minute later de Gruchy missed an excellent chance when, after receiving a fine pass from Parker, he shot straight at Bishop. After 27 minutes Mourant took a corner for Jersey and de Gruchy burst through the centre to chest the ball home to restore Jersey's lead. The home side nearly scored again when a de Gruchy shot beat Bishop, but Sandrey stopped the ball on the line. Guernsey replied when Hill beat two opponents and pushed the ball to Arnold. His first time shot seemed destined to enter the corner of the net but Le Marquand dived full length and pushed the ball around the post. In 35 minutes Jersey increased their lead. Crenan took a free kick in the midfield and Parker met the bouncing ball to head into the net to make the half time score Jersey-3, Guernsey-1.

Le Messurier and Sandrey cannot stop Jersey's fifth goal.

Guernsey made a promising start to the second half with Harvey laying on a good chance for Collins but he miskicked and lost a good opportunity. In Jersey's first attack, de Gruchy pulled down a Parker cross but as he was in the act of shooting, Martin rushed across to dispossess him. Guernsey continued the pressure and Le Marquand had to fist a Collins drive off Arnold's head. This was followed by Hill firing a shot that beat the home goal-keeper but Newton cleared. It was against the run of play when Jersey went further ahead in 61 minutes. Venton created a good position for himself and fired in a terrific shot from 18 yards which Bishop saved but was unable to hold. The ball broke to Le Maistre who dashed in to head goal number four for Jersey. Three minutes later de Gruchy gathered the ball from a throw in on the left and, moving in on goal, lobbed it over Bishop's head and into the net. Le Mesurier and Sandrey chased back in a desperate effort to clear off the line but were unsuccessful. Guernsey's attacks were becoming more sporadic but a long range shot from Sandrey forced Le Marquand to pull off a save from just under the bar. Jersey broke away again and it took a great tackle by Vaudin to prevent Parker racing through for another goal. Jersey were now in complete control and the match ended Jersey-5, Guernsey-1.

Jersey: Le Marquand, G. Newton, Megaw, Browne, D. Pitman, Crenan,
G. Le Maistre (c), D. Parker, D. De Gruchy, A. Venton, G. Mourant.
Goalscorers: Parker (2), de Gruchy (2), Le Maistre.

Guernsey: B. Bishop, D. Vaudin, A. Sandrey, B. Hill, R.O. Martin, J. Le Messurier,
A. Hamon, D. Batiste, L. Arnold, R. Harvey, L. Collins (c).
Goalscorer: Arnold.

The Muratti Vase was presented to Graeme Le Maistre by Mr. C.S. Harrison, Deputy
Lieut-Governor of Jersey.

Jersey fully deserved this emphatic victory in what was Graeme Le Maistre's last Muratti
appearance. He played like a man at the peak of his career and he was the number one
menace to Guernsey. Le Maistre's Muratti career was very impressive with 24 goals in 21
appearances as well as winning nine Muratti medals. He was not only one of Jersey's
greatest players but was one of the greatest Muratti players of all time.

Graeme Le Maistre and Les Collins. Two Muratti greats.

1 9 6 1

MURATTI SEMI-FINAL.
13 April 1961 Springfield Stadium, Jersey.

Jersey -4, Alderney -2.

The Alderney players flew into Jersey in a specially chartered aircraft as they prepared to take on Jersey. Included in their side was right half Alan Barker. He was first capped against Jersey in 1949 and again in 1951 and had been living in New Zealand for some years and whilst there played for the New Zealand Navy, Combined Services, and Auckland Province against Australian international sides. His Ellersie team mates included ex-Chelsea wing half Ken Armstrong; ex-Blackpool and Scotland left-back John Aird; and former Ireland forward Billy Walsh. In a match for Auckland Province against Australia Barker scored the second goal in a 2-1 victory. Also in the side was 16-year-old Billy Bohan (Alderney Athletics) who was winning his first cap in what was to become a remarkable Muratti career. Alderney's team manager was Mr. E.H. Levin (successor to the late Mr. George Burns as secretary to the Alderney FA) and their trainer was Mr. F. Bond. The party stayed at the Merton Hotel. Jersey had a moral boosting 2-0 victory against Hounslow Town on Good Friday as they prepared for their match against Alderney and they included one new cap, Gorin (First Tower) in their experienced side.

There was a crowd of 1,430 at Springfield confident of a Jersey victory. Alderney almost had a sensational start to the match, however, and they nearly snatched the lead after 15 seconds. The young right winger, Jock Dupont, received a pass from Clark and sent a lovely centre that Le Marquand just managed to sweep off Randall's head. There followed two fine shots by Clark and an overhead kick by Randall that were just wide and Le Marquand had to pull off a brilliant save from a fine shot by Clark. Alderney continued this period of pressure and a Barry Venton free kick went to Mannion and his left foot shot just cleared the bar. This whirlwind start staggered Jersey and it was not until half way through the half that they pulled it round. In the 28th minute Gorin slipped a fine through ball to Parker and he gave Peter Bond no chance with a searing shot to give Jersey the lead. This reverse did not seem to deter Alderney as they produced some of their best football in a Muratti. With five minutes of the half remaining Alderney suffered a blow when young Jock Dupont had to go off with a leg injury following a brush with Dennis Lempriere. The half time arrived with the score Jersey-1, Alderney-0.

The second half began with Alderney again attacking and Dupont, who had returned after treatment during half-time for his injured leg, was a touch slow in trying to convert a fine Barker pass into a goal. Jersey began to slowly exert themselves on the match and in the 58th minute they increased their lead. A Gorin through ball just beat Harrington and de Gruchy squared it to Nash Venton who hammered it home from close range. Within two minutes, however, Alderney reduced the arrears to the biggest roar of the afternoon. Le Marquand fumbled and dropped a drive by Barry Venton and A. Dupont was there to hit the ball over the line. Five minutes later Jersey regained their two goal advantage when Nash Venton found Parker who beat Bond with a beautiful low drive into the far corner. In the 69th minute Jersey appeared to have put the result beyond doubt when Mourant took a pass from Gorin to surprise Bond with a right foot shot into the opposite corner of the net. Jersey came near to further increasing their lead but Bond saved a rocket shot from de Gruchy followed by a Nash Venton shot that hit the bar. Alderney proved, however, that they were far from finished. Nine minutes from time a Mannion corner beat Le Marquand in the air and dropped by the far post. A scramble ensued and it was cleared, but Alderney appealed and referee Le Cheminant, after consulting with the Alderney linesman. Awarded a goal. This goal was later credited to Albert Randall. Alderney came close to scoring a third goal when in the closing moments Clark shot just wide and the match ended Jersey-4, Alderney-2.

Jersey: Le Marquand, G. Newton, D. Lempriere, C. Dingle, D. Pitman (c), Crenan, D. Parker, Gorin, D. De Gruchy, A. Venton, G. Mourant.
      Goalscorers: Parker (2), Venton, Mourant.

Alderney: P. Bond, D. Jones, C. Dupont, A. Barker, J. Harrington, B. Venton, A. Dupont, J. Mannion, A. Randall, D. Clark, W. Bohan.
      Goalscorers: A. Dupont, Randall.

Although the victory belonged to Jersey the glory was exclusively Alderney's and the cheers from the 1,430 crowd were all for the men in blue. This was their finest Muratti performance at Springfield, which saw them scoring two goals against Jersey for the first time since the war.

MURATTI FINAL.
4 May 1961, The Cycling Grounds, Guernsey.

Guernsey -1, Jersey -2.

It was announced that Guernsey's Lieu-Governor, HE Sir Geoffrey Robson as well as the Bailiff W.H. Arnold would be joined by Jersey's Lieu-Governor, Sir George Erskine for the Muratti at the Cycling Grounds on 4 May. Once again John Arlott would be providing the commentary for the BBC.

For only the second time in Muratti history Guernsey included a player who was winning his first Senior cap in the same season as he gained a Junior cap. Young Colin Renouf of St. Martins was to line up against Jersey. Guernsey had two other players gaining their first caps in 21-year-old Graham Brehaut and young Barry Mahy, both of Northerners. Guernsey were a little apprehensive as, in their build up, they had lost 2-0 to Hounslow Town whereas Jersey had defeated the same

G. Newton, F. Le Marquand, D. Lempriere,
D. Parker, D. Gorin, E. Vibert, A. Venton, G. Mourant,
C. Dingle, D. Pitman (c), D. Crenan.
Jersey.

opponents by 2-0. For the first time since the war, Jersey fielded a team without either Graeme Le Maistre or Dennis 'Tot' de Gruchy, although 'Tot' was named as one of the reserves. These two players had scored 24 of the 34 goals netted against Guernsey since the war. Included in the Jersey line-up for the first time was Ted Vibert (Georgetown), who that season had been playing in England for Leyton Orient's 'A' team and St. Alban's.

For the first time the weather severely interfered with the most important game in the Channel Islands. The game was threatened with postponement and the start was, in fact, delayed for 50 minutes. Half an hour before the scheduled kick-off time the referee, Mr. W. Clements, inspected the Marais side of the ground where a sheet of water covered the surface and agreed to a postponement of the kick-off time so that the CI football officials could make attempts to have the water cleared. Torrential rain which fell throughout the lunch period flooded the playing area up to three inches deep in parts and as the 5,845 spectators crammed into the ground, there were doubts that the match would even start. There were also concerns voiced by some Jersey supporters that if the match was delayed, started and finished late, would they be able to return home. The Guernsey Press contacted British Railways and the airline companies who agreed to delay their services as much as possible in an attempt to accommodate their passengers. The Fire Brigade were called to assist in the removal of the excess water and finally the match commenced.

The two captains, Dick Vaudin (Guernsey) and Doug Pitman (Jersey) led their teams onto a very wet pitch. Jersey adapted to the conditions quicker with the Guernsey defence very shaky. The sun came out for a while only to be replaced by torrential rain. Jersey opened the scoring when, in the 16th minute, Ted Vibert passed to David Parker who took the ball calmly past Murray and pushed the ball into the net. As the weather deteriorated there were genuine fears that the game would be abandoned but referee Clements decided to continue. Nine minutes later Gorin picked up a pass from Mourant to feed the ball past Murray for Jersey's second goal. For the first 30 minutes of the game Jersey were in complete control and only some great goalkeeping by Jim Murray and some large slices of luck restricted Jersey to two goals. Guernsey fought back from this setback and only the fine goalkeeping of Le Marquand prevented the home side from scoring and the first half ended Guernsey-0, Jersey-2.

The Fire Brigade help to clear the pitch.

The Jersey defence try to clear their lines.

Jersey began the second half the brightest but gradually Guernsey began to come more into it. Considering the appalling conditions, the quality of the play was excellent as both teams strived for supremacy. Colin Renouf and Barry Mahy began to come to terms with the conditions and started to pressurise the Jersey defence as the home came more into the game. Guernsey finally reduced the arrears when young Colin Renouf brilliantly headed a goal after 60 minutes. As Guernsey pressed there were thoughts that they may score again to take the match at least to extra time. The Jersey defence, with Le Marquand, Newton and Lempriere excellent, held to the final whistle with the score Guernsey-1, Jersey-2.

Guernsey: J. Murray, L. Duquemin, G. Brehaut, D. Vaudin, R. Brehaut, B. Mechem, J. Mahy, L. Arnold, D. Mechem, C. Renouf.
Goalscorer: Renouf.

Jersey: F. Le Marquand, G. Newton, D. Lempriere, C. Dingle, D. Pitman (c), D. Crenan, D. Parker, D. Gorin, E. Vibert, A. Venton, G. Mourant.
Goalscorers: Parker, Gorin.

It was agreed after the match that Jersey were worthy winners. They were stronger and more experienced and adapted to the conditions quicker and better than Guernsey. Dick Vaudin, the Guernsey captain, believed that Jersey had won the game in the first 20 minutes. Jersey skipper, Doug Pitman, said that this was one of the best Muratti he had ever played in and that both sides had played extremely well in terrible conditions. He also felt that Jersey had the greater experience and that this was a telling factor. It truly was 'Muratti a la Mer'.

Jersey skipper, Doug Pitman, receives the Muratti Vase from Sir Geoffrey Robson.

Hamon (Guernsey) on the far right threatens the Alderney goal.

1 9 6 2

MURATTI SEMI-FINAL.
29 March 1962, The Cycling Grounds, Guernsey.

Guernsey-6, Alderney-1.

The Alderney team showed two changes from last season with veteran 'Buster' Hammond and George Bohan coming into the attack for 'Jock' Dupont (a victim of a motor-cycle crash) and Billy Bohan. The official party of 18 made their headquarters at the Lansdowne Guest House, St. George's Esplanade, St. Peter Port. The party were led by the Alderney FA president, Mr. Frank Bond, and secretary Mr. E.H. Levin. Jersey Airlines put on two planes to bring the supporters. The Guernsey selectors had chosen two new caps, Mick Wylie (Athletics) and Johnny Brehaut (North) for their match against Alderney at the Cycling Grounds.

The two captains Duquemin (Guernsey) and Hammond (Alderney) led out the teams in front of the rather small crowd of 1,616. Guernsey took early control of the match. Alderney had to wait for ten minutes to have a shot at goal and Bishop easily saved this Randall effort. Earlier Guernsey had come close when Mick Wylie headed a John Mahy centre just wide. Guernsey took the lead after 14 minutes when the ball fell loose on the edge of the penalty area after John Mahy tried to break through and, as he fell, Wylie crashed a chest high shot past a helpless Peter Bond. Seconds later there were two near misses around the Alderney goal when Barry Mahy just failed to reach a John Brehaut cross and then Hamon headed a Harvey cross inches wide. The Alderney defence were under severe pressure and they were having difficulty in clearing their lines, too often they were caught in possession. Three of them tried unsuccessfully to clear a Brehaut cross and this gave Barry Mahy a chance that he scooped over the bar. After 21 minutes Bond failed to hold a Wylie shot and Hamon forced the ball into the net for goal number 2. Three minutes later Alderney nearly scored when Barker crossed to Clarke, who was unmarked a few yards from goal, but he blazed his shot over the bar. After half an hour's play Barry Mahy put in a shot which was deflected away from Bond by Harrington and Hamon had the easiest of chances to make it 3-0. Three minutes later Bond and Harrington got involved in a mix up over a short goal kick and Johnny Brehaut nipped in fast to gain possession and score at his second attempt. The biggest cheer of the afternoon came when Alderney scored after 35 minutes. Randall, beating Renouf, put in a centre that was guided home by Clarke. The half time score was Guernsey-4, Alderney-1.

The second half was very scrappy and it appeared as if Guernsey were happy with what they had. This allowed Alderney to come more into the game and with a bit more sharpness up front they might have added to their total. Guernsey could have increased their lead but they were let down by some indifferent finishing. The final scoring action came late in the match with John Mahy scoring in the 85th minute followed by Wylie in the 87th minute. In the final seconds of the game both Barry Mahy and Mick Wylie missed from clear positions to leave the final result Guernsey-6, Alderney-1.

Guernsey: B. Bishop, L. Duquemin, G. Brehaut, R. Harvey, C. Renouf, B. Mechem, J. Mahy, B. Mahy, A. Hamon, M. Wylie, J. Brehaut.
Goalscorers: Wylie (2), Hamon (2), Brehaut, J. Mahy.

Alderney: P. Bond, D. Jones, C. Dupont, A. Barker, J. Harrington, B. Venton, G. Bohan, J. Mannion, A. Randall, W. Hammond, D. Clarke.
Goalscorer: Clarke.

Overall it was not a very exciting Muratti although Guernsey ran out easy winners in the end. As usual the Alderney team fought to the last whistle, their heroes were veterans centre-half Harrington and inside left 'Buster' Hammond. Left-half Barry Venton was the hardest working player afield but alas he was also the game's roughest, and this earned him a caution from referee Troy just before the end.

It was announced that Mr. H.C. Chapell OBE, the President of the Guernsey Football Association, had died on 11 April 1962 at the age of 67. Mr. Chappel had played a progressively more important part in local football since before the First World War and had earned the respect and admiration of people interested in the sport. He started playing football as a junior with Guernsey Rangers Football and Athletic Club before the First World War and spent his entire playing career with the same club. He was a fine player and won ten Muratti caps between 1920 and 1926, captaining the Guernsey team five times. He won 3 winners medals and scored 6 goals. After his retirement as a player, Mr. Chapell took an active interest in the game, serving on Rangers' committee and finally being elected President of the club. Four years previously, he succeeded the late Mr. C.J.H. Rawlinson as President of the Guernsey Football Association.

MURATTI FINAL.
3 May 1962, Springfield Stadium, Jersey.

Jersey -2, Guernsey -1.

Jersey had three new caps in their side; David Rouille (Beeches), Dennis Henstridge (Wanderers) and Ralph Harben (Beeches). Guernsey had one new cap in goalkeeper Colin Gervaise-Brazier (St. Martins). It was thought that Guernsey's Vince Tostevin at 40 was one of the oldest players to be selected for a Muratti. Les Collins also returned to the side for his 23rd cap.

Guernsey won the toss at Springfield and began the better side playing fast open football. After only three minutes Collins fired in a brilliant cross for Brehaut to drive in only to see it superbly saved by Rouille. In eight minutes Collins again fed Brehaut but he put his shot wide and a few minutes later he again shot wide of Rouille's left hand post. After the panicky Jersey defence let him through. The pressure on the home defence continued and Barry Mahy headed a Collins cross inches over the bar. Two minutes later Barry Mahy received the ball from a long throw in from Harvey but he skied the ball over from almost underneath the crossbar. In the first 20 minutes Guernsey had three outstanding chances to score but failed to do so.

The opening goal came after 32 minutes when Derek Mechem passed to Collins and his cross was met by Barry Mahy who sent in a glorious header inches under the bar and into the net.

Five minutes later the lead was almost doubled when, following a Collins-John Mahy move, Brehaut gained possession near the far post but, although his shot beat Rouille, it crashed against the crossbar and to safety. It was just before half time that Jersey equalised. De Gruchy sent in a fine centre that was headed goal wards by Parker. It hit Brazier on the right shoulder and rebounded towards the line. The keeper recovered quickly to drop on the ball, however the Guernsey linesman, Les Smith, had seen the ball go over the line and signalled a goal. Half time Jersey-1, Guernsey-1.

Jersey started the second half in a much more positive manner and their attack was quickly in action. In the first five minutes Brazier was forced into making two brilliant saves. The first involved him diving at Parker's feet to save and the second involved him flicking a header over the bar. In the 55th minute Crenan was badly injured in a tackle and was forced to continue the game on the wing and this was followed shortly by Renouf also being handicapped by injury. Jersey won a free kick which was taken by Lempriere. He floated the ball beautifully to Parker who steered his header between Brazier and his left hand post and into the net.

Guernsey were unlucky not too have equalised a minute later when Barry Mahy dashed through only to be thwarted by a brilliant save by Rouille. In the 72nd minute Jersey nearly scored again when Parker got clean through following a Guernsey miskick but put his shot wide. There was no more scoring and the final result was Jersey-2, Guernsey-1.

Brazier knocks the ball over the bar from a Jersey raid.

Barry Mahy heads Guernsey into the lead after 32 minutes.

Jersey: D. Rouille, D. Henstridge,
D. Lempriere, T. Browne, R. Megaw,
D. Crenan, D. Parker, R. Harben,
D. De Gruchy, A. Venton, G. Mourant.
Goalscorer: Parker (2).

Guernsey: C. Brazier, L. Duquemin,
V. Tostevin, R. Harvey, C. Renouf, B. Mechem,
J. Mahy, B. Mahy, L. Collins, D. Mechem,
J. Brehaut.
Goalscorer: B. Mahy.

This was a game that Guernsey felt that they should have won but the fact was they lost due to the superior finishing of the Jersey side. Best for Guernsey was the great veteran, Vince Tostevin, who gave a flawless display by blotting out the Jersey right. His positional sense was uncanny and his interceptions perfectly timed. Guernsey was also well served by Colin Renouf and Colin Gervaise-Brazier, Jersey's best were two-goal David Parker, goalkeeper David Rouille, right-half Tim Browne and inside-left Alan Venton. The jubilant Jersey captain later admitted that his side was lucky to have won.

Brazier just fails to stop Parker's winning header for Jersey.

1 9 6 3

Muratti Semi-Final.
4 April 1963, Springfield Stadium, Jersey.

Jersey -6, Alderney -0.

Alderney's preparation for their match against Jersey was disrupted as their squad was ravaged by injuries. Their brilliant young goalkeeper, Peter Bond, was out due to injury and Billy Bohan, normally a forward, would be playing in goal. Their stalwart defender, Dennis Jones, will also be missing. Barry Venton (First Tower), one of Alderney's post war stars, and Michael Mapp would also be out due to injury. Michael had been selected to play at centre-forward but had to withdraw because of a rib injury sustained in a recent game against a visiting naval side. Venton suffered a recurrence of knee trouble that caused him to come off at half-time playing for Jersey Sylvans in a Saturday League game at the weekend. It was also felt that Johnny Mannion (Beeches Old Boys) was not 100% fit and he only rates his chances as 50-50. He had made his first appearance for Beeches for six weeks and although he lasted 90 minutes he was troubled by injury throughout. It was announced that this was to be 40 year old Harrington's last match for Alderney. The Alderney team included four new caps in John Cadoret, John Carpenter, Billy Bohan and Rex Audoir. Cadoret and Carpenter had learned their football in Guernsey with Elizabeth College and Belgrave W. juniors. The Jersey selectors had chosen four new caps in Robin Mahrer (Oaklands), 'Mo' Vowden (Wanderers), Geoff Ruellan (Georgetown) and 'Topsy' Cronin (Beeches).

 As the match began Jersey quickly imposed their authority and went ahead after nine minutes. Dave Parker broke away from Harrington on the halfway line and beat Clarke before scoring with a low drive. Alderney had a good chance to equalise after 17 minutes when Rouille failed to hold a shot from Alan Barker, the ball broke to Harrington but the Jersey keeper gathered well and pushed the shot away for a corner. Jersey's second in 22 minutes was a tragedy for the Alderney defence. A long low ball from Vowden appeared harmless and Bohan seemed to have it covered but at a crucial moment Dupont deflected the ball and it went into his own net. In the 35th minute an Alderney free kick was taken by Mannion and was well saved by Rouille. His clearance found Parker who raced away to score goal number 3. A minute later Hammond was unlucky when his header went narrow-ly past. The half time score read Jersey-3, Alderney-0.

 Alderney reorganised their team for the second half but Jersey remained in control. Twenty minutes into the second half they went four goals up. Ruellan sent in a good cross that was crashed into the top of the net by Cronin. Bohan then had to produce two good saves to prevent Jersey increasing their lead. Roger Mapp tried to reduce the arrears but his long range effort was saved by Rouille. In the 77th minute Cronin put in a centre that was met by Megaw. Bohan saved the first shot but had no chance with Megaw's second shot. With two minutes remaining Ruellan crossed in for Venton to complete the scoring. The result was Jersey-6, Alderney-0.

Jersey: Rouille, Henstridge, Mahrer, Vowden, Galway, D. Crenan (c), J. Ruellan, Megaw, D. Parker, A. Venton, Cronin.
Goalscorers: Parker (2), Cronin, Megaw, Venton, og.

Alderney: W. Bohan, D. Clarke, C. Dupont, R. Audoir, J. Harrington, R. Mapp, J. Cadoret, J. Mannion, A. Barker, W. Hammond, J. Carpenter.

 Although Alderney was well beaten it was not considered to be a vintage performance by the victorious Jersey team as they prepared to meet Guernsey on 2 May. Best for Alderney were Billy Bohan, who gave an outstanding display, veteran Joe Harrington, David Clarke and Johnny Mannion. The main successes for Jersey were their young wingers Geoff Ruellan and 'Topsy' Cronin with both Denis Crenan and Dennis Henstridge getting through some good work.

MURATTI FINAL.
2 May 1963, The Cycling Grounds, Guernsey.

Guernsey -1, Jersey -4.

The Guernsey team included two new caps in John Loveridge and Rodney Brache both of St. Martins. The Jersey team included Stan Le Cornu (Old Victorians) and Mickey Ryan (Wanderers) for their first caps. This was to be the first Muratti match to be televised. Most of the second half was to be televised live by the BBC with Tom Salmon providing the commentary.

The opening play at the Cycling Grounds was very scrappy with both teams taking a long time to settle down and it was not until the 11th minute that the game came to life. Jersey's Ryan broke away on the left and hit a cross shot that Brazier did well to hold. Cronin then blasted in a 35 yard drive that the keeper did well to clutch beneath the bar. Guernsey's first dangerous moment was in the 26th minute when Collins took a pass from Loveridge and fired in a shot that was well saved by Rouille. In the 28thminute Jersey went ahead when Cronin sent in a cross cum shot which seemed to catch the wind and deceive Brazier before ending up in the top corner of the net. Jersey increased their lead in the 34th minute when Ryan beat Renouf and then Brache to shoot low into the right hand corner of Brazier's net. Two minutes before half time Collins found Loveridge but his header was well saved by Rouille. Half time Guernsey-0, Jersey-2.

The second half began with Guernsey having the wind behind them but it was Jersey who started the quickest and came close through Venton and Cronin. Jersey continued the pressure and went 3-0 up after 53 minutes with a finely worked goal. A long ball up the centre beat Renouf and found Ryan who passed onto Cronin. Cronin crossed it in and Parker cut it back to Gorin who slipped it low past Brazier. Guernsey reorganised their team with Renouf moving to centre forward with Harvey taking his place at centre half. Before Guernsey could settle, Gorin capitalised on a defensive lapse to score Jersey's fourth goal. With three minutes remaining John Mahy crossed from the right and Collins threw himself at the ball to head home a consolation goal. The referee blew his whistle to end the game with the score Guernsey-1, Jersey-4.

Guernsey: C. Brazier, L. Duquemin (c), R. Brache, B. Hill, C. Renouf, R. Harvey, J. Mahy, B. Mahy, L. Eker, J. Loveridge, L. Collins.
Goalscorer: Collins.

Jersey: Rouille, Henstridge, Megaw, S. Le Cornu, Vowden, D. Crenan (c), D. Parker, D. Gorin, M. Ryan, A. Venton, D. Cronin.
Goalscorers: Cronin, Ryan, Gorin (2).

This was a very disappointing display by the home side and it was Jersey who ran out worthy winners. Duquemin, the Guernsey captain, conceded that they had lost to a much better side.

Dennis Crenan leads Jersey's Muratti celebrations.

1 9 6 4

MURATTI SEMI-FINAL.
11 April 1964, The Cycling Grounds, Guernsey.

Guernsey -3, Alderney -0.

As Guernsey prepared for their match against Alderney there was great disquiet amongst local football fans that the selectors had decided to drop Graham Brehaut. He was widely regarded as the best full back in the island. Guernsey had two new caps in Noel Jeffreys (Rangers) and Marcus Le Tissier (Belgrave Wanderers). Alderney announced that they would have two new caps in their side Dave Hogman, a Birmingham man who was now living and working in Alderney, and Billy Roberts. Joe Harrington had stated that this would definitely be his last Muratti. To add spice to the match it was rumoured that Mike Laing, the Guernsey coach, had informed his players that he would be satisfied with nothing less than a 10 goal victory against Alderney.

Richard Harvey had to withdraw from the team due to injury. The team was reorganised with Graham Brehaut taking his customary place at full back.
As the game got under way four of the Guernsey forwards changed from their original places and almost immediately put the Alderney defence under extreme pressure. Eldridge dropped back to act as a deep lying centre forward and began to conduct the proceedings. Despite all this early pressure Guernsey were finding it difficult to get the better of an inspired Bohan in the Alderney goal. It was not until the 21st minute that, following a misunderstanding in the visitors defence, Guernsey scored through a right foot shot by Renouf. Bohan continued to defy the Guernsey forwards and at half time the score was Guernsey-1, Alderney-0.

The second half was a carbon copy of the first with Guernsey on the attack and they increased their lead in the 53rd minute. John Brehaut sent in a cross that was well met by Renouf to leave Bohan helpless. In the 73rd minute some delightful interpassing down Guernsey's left culminated in Renouf crossing first time. Le Tissier seized possession and sweeping across the goalmouth suddenly swung right round and left the gallant Bohan well beaten with a flashing drive to make the final score Guernsey-3, Alderney-0.

Guernsey: C. Brazier, G. Brehaut, R. Brache, N. Jeffreys, R. Brehaut, J. Martel, M. Le Tissier, J. Loveridge, C. Renouf, A. Eldridge, J. Brehaut.
Goalscorers: Renouf (2), Le Tissier.

Alderney: W. Bohan, D. Jones, D. Clarke, R. Audoir, J. Harrington, C. Dupont (1), C. Dupont (2), J. Coenen, M. Mapp, D. Hugman, W, Roberts.

This was a rather patchy performance by Guernsey with Eldridge the best for the home side. For Alderney Bohan was outstanding in goal and Charlie Dupont the best of the outfield players.

MURATTI FINAL.
7 May 1964, Springfield Stadium, Jersey.

Jersey -1, Guernsey -0.

Jersey announced that they would have four new caps in goalkeeper Peter Osment (Wanderers), Dave Ferey (St. Paul's), Micky Keites (Georgetown) and Harry Proffitt (Oaklands) all making their debuts. Proffitt had played for Lancashire schoolboys from 1958-1960 and later became a professional apprentice with Everton. Guernsey's build up for their match at Springfield was given a boost due to their fine 5-1 victory against Stevenage Town. Richard Harvey (North) was ruled out of the game due to suffering from pulled tendons in his ankle and John Martel (St. Martins) came in at left half. Les Collins, at 38, announced that this would be his last Muratti as he gained his record breaking 25th cap.

Denis Crenan (Jersey) and Bob Brehaut (Guernsey) led out their sides in front of a crowd of 5,000 at Springfield. Jersey began the match the liveliest and during some early exchanges Guernsey suffered a blow when Le Tissier twisted his ankle and his early effectiveness was greatly reduced. The visitors' first real attempt at goal was in the 15th minute when Renouf fired in a header that Osment deflected onto the bar and over. Jersey began to put more pressure on the Guernsey defence but Bob Brehaut, Graham Brehaut and Rodney Brache were having excellent games and managed to keep them at bay. In the 31st minute there was a nasty clash of heads between Renouf and Megaw that resulted in the Guernsey player being taken to hospital for treatment to a gash on his head. Jersey continued to attack and in the 38th minute Henstringe sent in a long ball that was met near the penalty spot by Ruellan and he fired in a first time shot that was magnificently saved by Brazier to ensure that the half time score was Jersey-0, Guernsey-0.

As the second half began there was still no sign of Renouf and it was not until the 50th minute that he returned to the fray with his head in stitches but he was severely handicapped and could not head the ball. Seven minutes later Jersey scored. Osment received the ball from a free kick and his long clearance found Ruellan. Brache and Martel closed in

Guernsey
Bob Brehaut (capt.), Graeme Brehaut, Jeffreys, Brazier, Martel, Brache.
Le Tissier, Loveridge, Renouf, Eldridge, Collins.

Jersey.
Keites, Megaw, Ruellan, Venton, Cronin.
Proffitt, Vowden, Crenan (capt.).
Henstridge, Osment, Ferey.

on him but he cleverly eluded them and sent in a cross towards Venton. 'Nash' nodded the ball to his feet and closed in to give Brazier no chance to make the score 1-0. Guernsey responded positively to this reverse and began to mount a series of attacks on the Jersey goal but to no avail. In the 73rd minute, however, Guernsey thought that they had equalised. Jersey goalkeeper, Peter Osment, produced another thrilling save to turn a Marcus Le Tissier shot away for a corner. The ball was sent over and Collins flicked the ball into the net, following a hectic skirmish, but referee Crawford awarded a free kick to Jersey. The visitors continued to press but the Jersey defence stood firm and the final score was Jersey-1, Guernsey-0.

Jersey: P. Osment, D. Henstridge, D. Ferey, H. Proffitt, M. Vowden, D. Crenan (c), M. Keites, R. Megaw, J. Ruellan, A. Venton, D. Cronin.
Goalscorer: Venton.

Guernsey: C. Brazier, G. Brehaut, R. Brache, N. Jeffreys, R. Brehaut (c), J. Martel, M. Le Tissier, J. Loveridge, C. Renouf, A. Eldridge, L. Collins.

This was a close, hard fought match but Guernsey suffered from the early injuries to Le Tissier and Renouf. Guernsey coach, Mike Laing, although disappointed was proud of his team and the quality of the football that they played but it was Jersey who got the goal that mattered. Best for Guernsey were 'Bonny' Eldridge and John Loveridge. Jersey's star was goalkeeper Peter Osment who defied Guernsey with a series of superb saves. It was a happy and relieved Jersey captain who received the Muratti Vase from the Lieut-Governor of Guernsey, HE Sir Charles Coleman. This was Jersey's seventh successive victory.

 As this match ended, the Muratti career of Les Collins came to an end. Les gained a Channel Island record 25 caps the first being in 1947 and he will be remembered as one of Guernsey's greatest players. In his Muratti career he won five Muratti medals and scored 10 goals.

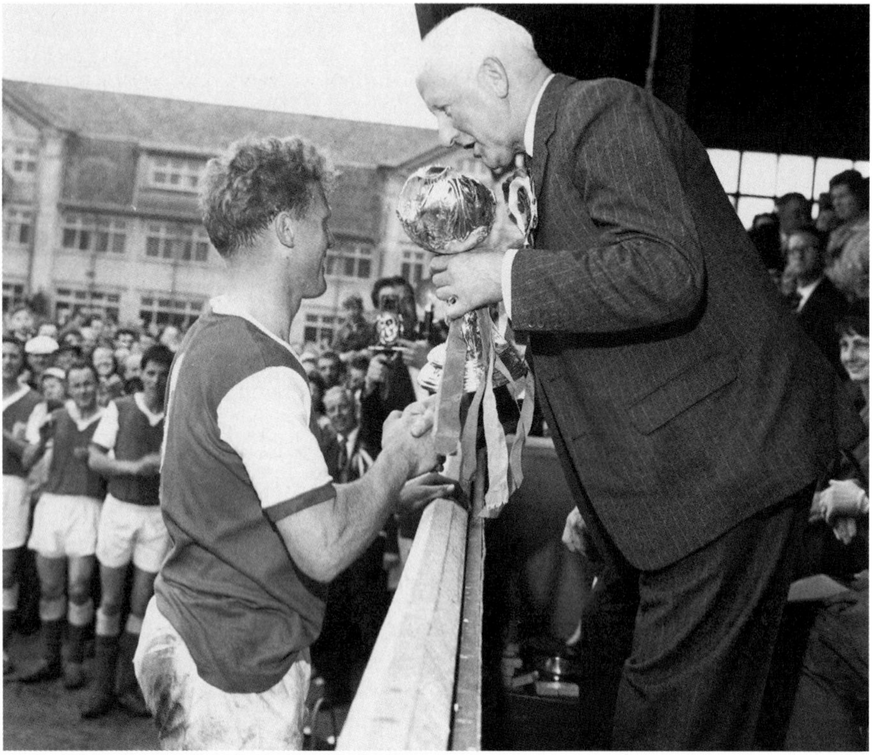

Denis Crenan, the Jersey captain, receives the Muratti Vase from the Lieut-Governor of Guernsey, Sir Charles Coleman.

Les Collins.

1 9 6 5

MURATTI SEMI-FINAL.
8 April 1965, Springfield Stadium, Jersey.

Jersey -8, Alderney -0.

In the build up for their Muratti Vase match against Jersey at Springfield Alderney were experiencing severe difficulties in preparing their 12 player squad. Their problems were compounded when John Cadonet could not travel to Jersey due to work commitments and during a training session they lost the services of the former North and Tics player, Charlie Dupont, due to injury.

Alderney contacted the ex-Beeches star, Johnny Mannion, and although he had not played any football for two years he agreed, although he had only half an hours notice. It looked at this stage as if veteran keeper Frank Bond, the 47-year-old former President of the Alderney FA, would have to make his first Muratti appearance for six years. He actually arrived at the ground wearing the yellow jersey. It was not until the game was 11 minutes old that Johnny Mannion actually entered the field of play, as his boots had to be fetched from another ground, and by that time Alderney were 1 goal behind.

This was not the best of preparations for a Muratti match and it was no surprise that Jersey took the early initiative. The Alderney heroes were mostly in defence with Joe Harrington excellent followed by goalkeeper Dupont, Rex Audoir and George Bohan. Although he had little prior notice of the match it was agreed that this had been one of Mannion's best Muratti's. In the first minute Jeff Ruellan crossed from the right and David Parker headed past John Dupont in the Alderney goal. This was Dupont's first game in goal for Alderney although he had previously been capped in other positions. Venton scored goal number two with a spectacular shot and Ruellan scored two more before half time to make the score at the interval: Jersey-4, Alderney-0.

Alderney's defence held out for the first 10 minutes of the second half before Ruellan scored goal number five with a 25-yard shot. There was no more scoring until the last five minutes when Ruellan, Cronin and Parker confirmed Jersey's superiority with three more goals. The match ended with the convincing scoreline Jersey-8, Alderney-0.

Jersey: P. Osment, M. Henstridge, R. Megaw, H. Proffitt, M. Vowden, D. Crenan (c), D. Parker, Craydon, J. Ruellan, A. Venton, D. Cronin.
Goalscorers: Parker (2), Ruellan (2), Venton, Cronin.

Alderney: J. Dupont, R. Audoir, D. Clark, G. Bohan, J. Harrington (c), J. Clark, C. Dupont, J. Mannion, M. Mapp, G. Rennel, J. Carpenter.

MURATTI FINAL.
6 May 1965, The Cycling Grounds, Guernsey.

Guernsey -2, Jersey -4.

Guernsey's preparations for their match against Jersey at the Cycling Grounds were not helped by a very poor performance when losing 5-0 to Welton Rovers; however, Coach Mike Laing was hopeful that there would be a marked improvement on 6 May. The general feeling was that some of the Guernsey players were being played out of their club positions without success .Guernsey had four new caps in Arthur Pugh, John Forsey and Tony Williams, all of St. Martins and R. Hemery of Belgrave Wanderers. 26-year-old Tony Williams has had an excellent career in the mainland and has been capped for England in an under-18 schoolboy side. He has played for the RAF and has also seen service with Reading's reserve side (playing 15 games and scoring 6 goals between 1957-1960) and for Kingstonians, Corinthian-Casuals as well as Redhill.

Tony Williams.

Guernsey also selected a further three members of the Upton winning St. Martins team in Brazier, Loveridge and Renouf. Jersey selected an experienced side with only M. Le Louarn (Georgetown) making his debut.

The teams were led out by Bob Brehaut (Guernsey) and Denis Crenan (Jersey) as the crowd of 5,141 eagerly waited for the start of the game.

Guernsey started the match unimpressively still, apparently unsure of the system they were being asked to play and Jersey were slightly on top. Despite this, however it was not until the 26th minute that Jersey took the lead. Cronin and Venton combined well to take the ball

Guernsey.
1965.

Renouf wins an aerial battle.

through the home defence, the move ended with Cronin hammering the ball home. After this reverse Guernsey took the initiative with Arthur Pugh being brought into play and the side reverting nearer to their club positions. In the 37th minute John Loveridge took a return pass from Pugh and fired the ball into the net from close in. Guernsey continued their pressure and should have gone ahead but a 30-yard shot by Roger Hemery was brilliantly saved by Osment making the half time score Guernsey-1, Jersey-1.

The second half began with Guernsey in complete control and from a Loveridge free kick Renouf glanced the ball to new cap Tony Williams who, with his back to goal, hooked it into the net to give the home team a 2-1 lead in the 51st minute. Guernsey continued to pound the Jersey goal but could not score the all-important third goal. They were in full cry when a large pitch invasion by the supporters caused referee Roper to take both teams off for their safety and the police were called to restore order and clear the pitch. It was some time before the match restarted but Guernsey had lost the impetus. Guernsey paid for this in the 63rd minute Parker beat Brazier to a Proffitt pass to bring Jersey level. Osment then had three excellent saves from Renouf, Noel Jeffreys and Eldridge before Jersey broke away to score. A pass from Ron Craydon found Ruellan completely on his own in front of goal and he had time to pick his spot to put Jersey 3-2 up. This goal seemed to take some of the heart out of the home team and a fourth Jersey goal followed when Parker crossed in for Venton to score. The final score was Guernsey-2, Jersey-4.

Guernsey: C. Brazier, L. Duquemin, J. Forsey, N. Jeffreys, R. Brehaut (c), R. Hemery, A. Pugh, J. Loveridge, C. Renouf, A. Eldridge, A. Williams.
          Goalscorers: Loveridge, Williams.

Jersey: P. Osment, M. Le Louarn, R. Megaw, H. Proffitt, M. Vowden, D. Crenan (c), D. Parker, Craydon, J. Ruellan, A. Venton, D. Cronin.
          Goalscorers: Cronin, Parker, Ruellan, Venton.

The Muratti Vase was presented to Denis Crenan, the Jersey captain, by the Lieut-Governor of Guernsey, HE Sir Charles Coleman.

Guernsey had performed above the pre-match expectations and had been in control for long sections of the game but could not finish the match off with a third goal when leading 2-1. Credit, however, should go to Jersey for the way that they weathered the storm and responded in a positive manner.

The one sad episode during the game was the second half disturbances by a section of the crowd. Some spectators encroached on to the pitch and the referee, Geoffrey Roper, had no alternative but to suspend play while the police were getting the situation under control.

1 9 6 6

MURATTI SEMI-FINAL.
2 April 1966, The Cycling Grounds, Guernsey.

Guernsey -10, Alderney -0.

Following last year's defeat Guernsey awarded four new caps for their match against Alderney at the Cycling Grounds. They were John Herpe, Micky Duncan and Wally Torode all of St. Martins and Alan Conway (Rangers). Alderney awarded first caps to three players in Brian Farnham (Rangers), Joe Goasdoue and 17 year old Tony Robilliard both from the UK.

Colin Renouf (Guernsey) and Joe Harrington (Alderney) led their teams on the pitch for this semi-final tie. Guernsey were very quickly into top gear and went ahead after only two minutes. Harvey sent a pass through to Loveridge who cut in and fired in a shot that Bohan touched but couldn't stop. Seven minutes later Guernsey went 2-0 up when Eldridge scored from a header after hooking against the bar. Alderney replied when Farnham came close with a free kick. The scoring continued in the 23rd minute when Torode found the net with a 30 yard drive just inside the diving Bohan's right hand post. The home side continued the onslaught and three minutes later Eldridge added a fourth goal. Two minutes later the Alderney defence failed to clear a Harvey pass and Loveridge chipped in goal number five.

Brazier collects the ball as Renouf holds off Michael Mapp.

The one way traffic continued when in the 34th minute Conway shot under Bohan for the 6th goal and a further two minutes later Arthur Pugh converted a cross from Torode to make the half time score Guernsey-7, Alderney-0.

Alderney came a little more into the game in the second half and Brazier had to be at his best to prevent a score.

In the 68th minute, however, Loveridge headed home a fine centre by Conway for the 8th goal and he also hit the 9th after 81 minutes after Bohan had failed to hold an Eldridge cross. A minute later Eldridge completed the scoring by adding a 10th goal. In the closing minutes Joe Goasdoue would have scored for Alderney but for the agility of Brazier and the match ended Guernsey-10, Alderney-0.

Guernsey: C. Brazier, N. Jeffreys, J. Herpe, M. Duncan, C. Renouf, R. Harvey, A. Pugh, J. Loveridge, A. Conway, A. Eldridge, W. Torode.
Goalscorers: Loveridge (4), Eldridge (3), Torode, Conway, Pugh.

Alderney: W. Bohan, Carre, C.J. Dupont, R. Audoir, J. Harrington, B. Farnham, Robilliard, J. Goasdue, M. Mapp,Cadoret, J. Carpenter.

This was a record score for the Muratti and the first time a team had reached double figures. Despite the score the young Alderney goalkeeper, Billy Bohan, had some brilliant saves. Harrington once again had stated that this would be his last Muratti as he was hoping to move to Australia.

MURATTI FINAL.
5 May 1966, Springfield Stadium, Jersey.

Jersey -1, Guernsey -1. aet.

Jersey had four new caps in their team to defend the Muratti Vase. Barry Breuilly and Brian Beckett from First Tower along with Pat McLaughlin and Johnnie Wilson from Magpies. Barry Breuilly was only the second Jersey player to be selected for both the Senior and Junior Muratti's in the same year. The first being J. Drew in 1938. Guernsey had one new cap in Ken Giles (Vale Rec). It was also announced that John Herpe was to immigrate to Australia. There were some injury concerns for Guernsey when Arthur Pugh passed a fitness test in the morning of the game.

Jersey got off to a great start with a goal in only four minutes. McLaughlin took a throw in and gave the ball to Ruellan who rounded Harvey and crossed for Wilson to head past Brazier. The early stages of the game had Jersey well in control and it was only after 10 minutes that Guernsey came into it in an attacking sense. Right back Hamon raced up the wing to fire in a low that Breuilly did well to hold. Parker brought the best out of Brazier after 17 minutes as he pushed his drive around the post. As Jersey kept up this pressure Ruellan headed just inches wide of the goal. Guernsey managed to keep the home side out and in the 27th minute equalised. Guernsey broke down the middle and as Pugh chipped the ball forward, Loveridge with great precision, put the ball over the head of Breuilly. This

Guernsey.
Hamon, Duncan, Harvey, Brazier, Renouf, Herpe,
Pugh, Loveridge, Eldridge, Giles, Torode.

'Bonny' Eldridge on the attack.

This goal seemed to lift the visitors and they could have gone ahead but for a great save by Breuilly from Eldridge. This pulsating first half ended Jersey-1, Guernsey-1.

The second half began well for Guernsey and in the 50th minute Pugh crashed a terrific 25 yard shot that was brilliantly saved by Breuilly. By this time the Guernsey forwards Harvey, Giles and Loveridge had picked up injuries and Jersey began to take command. McLaughlin and Cronin missed chances for the home side and they were denied when Brazier got down well to save from Parker in the 66th minute. Ruellan came close to putting Jersey back into the lead as the home side continued to press forward but the Guernsey defence were holding out. As the match ended David Parker crashed the ball past Brazier but referee Jennings had already blown to signal the end of the match a split second before so the match ended Jersey-1, Guernsey-1.

During the first period of extra-time both sides came close as the crippled Guernsey side held its own territorially. In the 100th minute Eldridge was carried from the field due to a damaged thigh and although he soon returned he could only hobble about and left the pitch for good soon afterwards. The half-time score was Jersey-1, Guernsey-1.

The second period of extra-time saw Jersey in control as they exerted continual pressure and this was met by defiant defensive work by Guernsey. The depleted Guernsey side held out with the final score Jersey-1, Guernsey-1.

Jersey: B. Breuilly, M. Le Louarn, D. Henstridge, McLaughlin, Beckett (c).
            M. Vowden, D. Parker, J. Wilson, J. Ruellan, A. Venton, D. Cronin.
            Goalscorer: Wilson.

Guernsey: C. Brazier, A. Hamon, J. Herpe, M. Duncan, C. Renouf, R. Harvey,
            A. Pugh, J. Loveridge, A. Eldridge, K. Giles, W. Torode.
            Goalscorer: Loveridge.

Guernsey's dressing room resembled a casualty clearing station with Giles, Loveridge and Harvey all nursing injuries that could keep them out of the replay. Eldridge had already been taken to hospital. The visitors were happy to be still in the tie following some sustained second half pressure from Jersey.

The replay was scheduled for the Cycling Grounds on 9 May. This was to be the first Muratti Vase Final to be played on Liberation Day.

Loveridge opens the scoring for Guernsey.

MURATTI FINAL REPLAY.
9 May 1966, The Cycling Grounds, Guernsey.

Guernsey -3, Jersey -1.

The Guernsey side showed three changes from the first game with Marcus Le Tissier, Henry Davey and John Martel replacing Pugh, Eldridge and Giles. This was a first cap for Davey (St. Martins). Jersey made one change with Megaw replacing Wilson.

Jersey won the toss and rather surprisingly decided to attack into the stiff wind. They were immediately put under pressure by Guernsey in the opening minutes. The home side nearly scored after four minutes when Loveridge won the ball from Beckett and crossed for Davey who nearly beat Breuilly with a header. Breuilly again was called into action by Hamon. In the 13th minute Davey had a first time hook brilliantly saved by Breuilly and as Jersey tried to defend Hamon dispossessed Cronin and passed through the middle to Davey who flicked it to Loveridge who rifled it past a despairing Breuilly to put Guernsey 1-0 up.

Jersey replied with Cronin heading a Parker cross just past followed by Brazier saving well from Venton. Guernsey returned to the attack and after 31 minutes Torode won the ball and fed Martel who cut a low cross into the goal and Loveridge crashed the ball first time into the net for 2-0. The home side came close just before the interval when Loveridge just failed to score from a Davey cross leaving the half time score Guernsey-2, Jersey-0.

The second half began with Guernsey once again in control with Breuilly performing heroics in the Jersey goal. He bravely cleared at Loveridge's feet as the pressure mounted. The game began to get a little heated as Ruellan was booked for a crunching tackle on Herpe and then Harvey received a nasty tackle from Megaw. The game was slowly drifting away from Jersey and in the 79th minute Vowden lost control when attempting to cut out a Le Tissier pass and Loveridge latched onto the ball and accelerated through from the left at tremendous speed. Breuilly rushed out but Loveridge calmly slipped the ball past him for goal number three. Breuilly once again came to Jersey's rescue when he saved firstly from Loveridge and then Davey. Jersey then broke away and forced a corner. Cronin took an in-swinging kick and it was deflected past Brazier by Hamon to make the score 3-1. With only seconds remaining Cronin blazed his shot over the bar making the final score Guernsey-3, Jersey-1.

Guernsey: C. Brazier, A. Hamon, J. Herpe, M. Duncan, C. Renouf, R. Harvey, M. Le Tissier, J. Loveridge, H. Davey, J. Martel, W. Torode.
Goalscorer: Loveridge (3).
Jersey: B. Breuilly, M. Le Louarn, D. Henstridge, McLaughlin, Beckett (c), M. Vowden, D. Parker, R. Megaw, J. Ruellan, A. Venton, D. Cronin.
Goalscorer: og.

This was an excellent performance by Guernsey and it was only the brilliance of Breuilly that kept the score down. Loveridge had the distinction of scoring all Guernsey's goals over the two games and he was well supported by the 19 year old Davey and the veteran Harvey. Best for Jersey was the inspirational Breuilly and Cronin.

For the first time in nine years a Guernsey captain went up to be presented with the Muratti Vase as Colin Renouf received the trophy from HE Vice-Admiral Sir Michael Villiers the Lieut- Governor of Jersey. This was Guernsey's 25th Muratti Vase.

The Guernsey Evening Press for Thursday 12 May reported on a serious dispute that arose before the Muratti replay. The Guernsey selectors had looked beyond the travelling reserves for Jersey and brought in three completely new players for the replay. Guernsey coach, Frank Mackwood, was upset at this and, in effect, resigned his position. He was not in charge on Monday and handed over to trainer Jack Loveridge when he heard what the selectors had done. Mr. Mackwood said 'I was very disturbed when I heard the team and found that none of the players who had been reserves in Jersey had been chosen. I did not wish to be associated with it and so I handed over to Mr. Loveridge.' Mr Mackwood made it clear that he felt that the selectors had not been fair to Noel Jeffreys, Alan Conway and Dave Lesbirel as they had been in training, whereas the replacements brought in had not. Mr. Les Smith, secretary of the Selection Committee, and Mr. R.G. Warr, secretary to the GFA, both refused to comment on what happened.

Renouf receives the Muratti Vase.

1 9 6 7

MURATTI SEMI-FINAL.
6 April 1967, Springfield Stadium, Jersey.

Jersey -3, Alderney -1.

Channel Island soccer history was made on 6 April when for the first time a Muratti match was played at night and, for part of this time, under floodlights. The game at Springfield started in daylight but ended under the grounds new £4,000 lighting system. It was thought that none of the Alderney team had ever played under lights.

Jersey started the match with four new caps Barry Thorp and Phil Rowan of Georgetown along with Ian Watts (St. Paul's) and Dave Cooper (First Tower).

Alderney were well fired up for their golden jubilee Muratti match at Springfield and were determined to put up a good show. Jersey, however, started the best and went a goal up after only five minutes. Henstridge fired a long ball into the Alderney area and Dave Cooper scored with a header. Alderney tried to contain Jersey with a tight defensive game and managed to hit them on the break much to the consternation of the home defence. Alderney held out until the 29th minute when Phil Rowan added a second goal for Jersey. Smith almost opened Alderney's account when Breuilly had to be at his best to save his fierce left foot drive just before half time. At the break the score was Jersey-2, Alderney-0.

The second half followed the same pattern as the first and it was not until the hour mark that Jersey scored their third goal from Cronin. Alderney continued to counter attack and they were rewarded in the 71st minute. A terrific shot by Maurice Baker came down off the bar and after another shot had been parried by Breuilly; Micky Smith hammered the ball into the net. As the game neared its end it was Alderney who was on top but they could not score again and the match ended Jersey-3, Alderney-1.

Jersey: B. Breuilly, D. Henstridge, M. Vowden, Thorp, M. Le Louarn, H. Proffitt, D. Cronin, P. Rowan, I. Watts, J. Ruellan, D. Cooper.
Goalscorers: Cooper, Rowan, Cronin.

Alderney: W. Bohan, P. Turner, C. Dupont, B. Farnham, J. Harrington, W. Roberts, M. Smith, J. Cadoret, D. Hugman,G. Goasdoue, J. Carpenter.
Goalscorer: Smith.

This was rightly considered to be one of Alderney's best ever games at Springfield and their performance certainly shook the favourites, Jersey.

MURATTI FINAL.
9 May 1967, The Cycling Grounds, Guernsey.

Guernsey -1, Jersey -3.

Guernsey's preparation for the Muratti suffered a setback when the Island team played a practice match against Belgrave W. The first half was goalless and in the second half the Island went 2-0 up through Renouf and Torode. Belgrave W. fought back, however, and scored through Maurice Hemery and Marcus Le Tissier to bring the scores level, then Hemery scored again to give Belgraves a stunning 3-2 victory. Not the best result for Trainer Frank Mackwood. Guernsey had one new cap in their team, J. Booth of St. Martins.

The two teams were introduced to the Lieut-Governor of Jersey, HE Sir Michael Villiers prior to the match. The crowd of 8,738, of which a large proportion were Jersey fans, prepared for the contest.

The first half of the match started very poorly with not a lot to get the fans excited. Jersey came close but Hemery cleared a Ruellan header off the line. Guernsey took a long time to perform as an attacking force and it was not until close to half time that Breuilly was called upon to show his worth. He made a hat trick of saves from Giles, Renouf and Loveridge to ensure that the half time score remained Guernsey-0, Jersey-0.

Guernsey opened the scoring just after half time when Giles fired in a shot that Breuilly and Thorp went up for- John Loveridge had tried unsuccessfully to get a head to it - and the ball was then deflected into the net. Jersey's equaliser came seven minutes later after Roger Hemery once again cleared of the line. He kicked from near the far post after young Ian Woods had shot past Brazier. The ball was not fully cleared and it was returned across goal where Phil Rowan sent it flashing into the top of the net for 1-1. Jersey continued this pressure and Ruellan came close when he missed an easy chance and a minute later had a 'goal' disallowed for offside. In the 80th minute Guernsey thought that they had won the game. Wally Torode sent in a cross and Loveridge fired in a superb header that had 'goal' written all over it but, with a cat like spring to his left, Breuilly miraculously clutched the ball. The regulation 90 minutes ended Guernsey-1, Jersey-1 and extra time was called for. As extra time began Guernsey decided to switch their team around. The game was still very even and in the 95th minute a low ball was swept into the Guernsey area, Harvey failed to intercept it and the ball rolled to Ruellan who fired it into the net out of Brazier's reach to give Jersey a 2-1 lead. With only seconds remaining of the first period of extra time a Guernsey attack broke down and the ball came off Renouf's head and found a Jersey player. The ball was quickly transferred to Dave Cooper who crashed it past a helpless Brazier. There was no more scoring and the game ended Guernsey-1, Jersey-3.

Guernsey: C. Brazier, G. Brehaut, R. Hemery, J. Booth, R. Harvey, M. Duncan, J. Martel, W. Torode, J. Loveridge, C. Renouf, K. Giles.
    Goalscorer: Giles.

Jersey: B. Breuilly, D. Henstridge, M. Le Louarn, D. Cronin (c), M. Vowden, Thorp, Rowan, D. Parker, J. Ruellan, D. Cooper, I. Watts.
    Goalscorers: Rowan, Ruellan, Cooper.

It was a game that could have gone either way but Jersey were worthy winners by being able to convert the chances that were offered.

1 9 6 8

MURATTI SEMI-FINAL.
30 March 1968, The Cycling Grounds, Guernsey.

Guernsey -2, Alderney -0.

The time for the start of the Muratti match between Guernsey and Alderney at the Cycling Grounds was put back from 3.00pm to 4.00pm due to the fact that the Grand National was being televised.

Guernsey had to rearrange their team when Richard Harvey had to withdraw due to tonsillitis. There were three new caps in the home side in Brian Gorvel, Art Le Page (Centrals) and Peter Mellor (Vale Rec). Alderney announced that Brian Farnham (Rangers) would captain their side.

The home side started quickest and were very soon on top with the Alderney defence, Bohan in particular, battling to prevent an early score. Guernsey continued to attack but some of their finishing was very poor. In the 30th minute Giles put in a shot that Bohan did well to save but he could not hold the ball and it fell to Micky Duncan who right footed it into the net for 1-0. Ten minutes later Duncan crossed from the left and Renouf headed in goal number 2. The home side continued to make the openings but could not find the net leaving the first half to end Guernsey-2, Alderney-0.

The second half began badly for Alderney when after only seven minutes Micky Smith received an ankle injury and had to be taken to hospital. He was replaced by Roy Stower, who became the first player to come on as a substitute in a Muratti match. The game continued as before with Guernsey missing a number of chances to increase their lead and the Alderney defence being well marshalled by Farnham. The final score was Guernsey-2, Alderney-0.

Micky Duncan beats Bohan for Guernsey's opening goal.

Guernsey: C. Brazier, B. Gorvel, C. Renouf, A. Le Page, R. Hemery, M. Duncan, P. Mellor, M. Le Tissier, W. Torode, J. Loveridge, K. Giles.
Goalscorers: Duncan, Renouf.

Alderney: W. Bohan, P. Turner, C. Dupont, B. Farnham, D. Clarke, W. Roberts, M. Smith, J. Cadoret, D. Hugman, G. Goasdoue, J. Carpenter.
Sub: R. Stower.

MURATTI FINAL.
9 May 1968, Springfield Stadium, Jersey.

Jersey -2, Guernsey -1.

Jersey named their team and it included two new caps in Les Selkirk (First Tower) and Phil Scott (Oaklands). Just hours before the match Guernsey were unable to name their side due to a series of injuries to Colin Renouf, Micky Duncan and Barry Tullier. The visitors were to be kitted out in a brand new strip of thin green and white stripes and white shorts, white socks with two green bands around the top.

The game was watched by a crowd of around 7,500 in warm sunshine with the Springfield pitch in good condition. Guernsey were first to come close when, in the third minute, Lesbirel cleverly beat his man only to see his shot go wide. In the 10th minute Jersey should have taken the lead through Phil Scott but Brazier brilliantly saved his shot from point blank range. Two minutes later Jersey won a free kick and Harry Proffitt drove it wide of Brazier's left hand post when Hemery headed it off the line. Denis Henstridge collected this clearance and pushed it through to Ruellan who fired it past Brazier to put Jersey 1-0 up. As the pace stepped up there were chances at both ends when Scott missed a chance for Jersey followed by a Loveridge header that Breuilly managed to hold at the second attempt. In the 26th minute Ruellan put Parker away, he crossed high over the Guernsey defence and it was met by Ruellan who cracked in a low shot past Brazier from the edge of the penalty area. The game was swinging from end to end and the visitors nearly scored in the 37th minute. Micky Duncan was involved in a good short- passing movement down the centre and he fired in a rising shot that Breuilly seemed to think was going over. It hit the bar and Lesbirel headed it back only for Breuilly to make a great save at the expense of a corner. As half time approached Parker cut in and shot past Brazier but Art Le Page got back and headed off the line leaving the half time score Jersey-2, Guernsey-0.

Early in the second half Guernsey had an escape when Watts hit a shot that came off of the foot of Brazier's left hand post and Scott missed with the rebound. Guernsey began to assert themselves but the service to their front players was not good. Ruellan again came close midway through the half when he fired his shot past following a pass from Parker. In the 75th minute Guernsey thought that they had scored when Torode cut the ball back to Hemery who hit it home but the whistle had already gone, the ball being over the line. The game was drifting away from Guernsey but in the 88th minute Tullier crossed a long high ball from the right and Loveridge leapt to head a spectacular goal just inside Breuilly's right hand post. This goal, however, came too late to affect the result, Jersey-2, Guernsey-1.

Jersey: B. Breuilly, D. Henstridge, M. Vowden, Thorp, Selkirk, H. Proffitt,
               D. Cronin (c), D. Parker, Scott, J. Ruellan, I. Watts.
               Sub: Golding.
               Goalscorer: Ruellan (2).

Guernsey: C. Brazier, A. Le Page, R. Harvey, B. Tullier, R. Hemery, M. Duncan,
               K. Giles, P. Mellor, D. Lesbirel, J. Loveridge, W. Torode.
               Goalscorer: Loveridge.

It was a double celebration for 2-goal Ruellan as he had become a father on the eve of this match. This Jersey victory meant that they were now level on Muratti Vase wins with Guernsey on 25 each.

Jersey team celebrate with the Muratti Vase.

1 9 6 9

MURATTI SEMI-FINAL.
27 March 1969, Springfield Stadium, Jersey.

Jersey -5, Alderney -0.

There were two new caps in the Jersey line-up for their match with Alderney. They were Tommy Bone (Magpies) and Paul Sands (First Tower). Alderney had five new caps in their side. They were Jim Dupont, A. Benfield, J. Baker, R. Chivers and John Simon of Rangers. Brian Farnham was due to captain the Alderney side but there were doubts whether he would play as his face was swollen due to a tooth extraction. In fact he did play but the captaincy was given to Billy Roberts.

Jersey began this match the quickest and were very soon into their stride putting pressure on the Alderney defence. The visitors' rearguard, however, held out with Bohan and Jim Dupont outstanding. It was not until the 21st minute that Jersey took the lead when Timmy Browne converted a cross from Sands to make the score 1-0. The Alderney defence did not falter following this setback with Farnham and Charlie Dupont putting in fine performances. Young John Simon caused the Jersey defence a lot of problems but Alderney could not capitalise due to the lack of forward support. The second Jersey goal did not arrive until four minutes before half time and it was an unfortunate own goal from Farnham making the half time score Jersey-2, Alderney-0.

Although the second half found Jersey once again pressuring the visitors' resolute defence it was Alderney who came the closest when Turner shot inches over the Jersey bar. The home side continued their attacking without success and it was not until the 75th minute that Bohan was beaten. Sands put in a cross that was met by Ruellan, but his header hit the bar and Proffitt sent the rebound past Bohan for goal number three. With five minutes remaining Ruellan scored a great goal from the angle and Bone completed the scoring just on time to make the final score Jersey-5, Alderney-0.

Jersey: B. Breuilly, M. Le Louarn, M. Vowden (c), Browne, Thorp, H. Proffitt, T. Bone, P. Sands, Craydon, J. Ruellan, A. Venton.
Goalscorers: Brown, og, Proffitt, Ruellan, Bone.

Alderney: W. Bohan, J. Dupont, B. Farnham (c), C.J. Dupont, R. Stower, W. Roberts, A. Benfield, J. Barker, J. Simon, R. Chivers, P. Turner.

This again was a gritty performance by Alderney with all their heroes in defence. Jersey thoroughly deserved their victory but found difficulty in converting all their territorial superiority into goals.

MURATTI FINAL.
9 May 1969, The Cycling Grounds, Guernsey.

Guernsey -2, Jersey -1.

The Guernsey side to entertain Jersey at the Cycling Grounds on Liberation Day included three new caps in Geoff Mahy (Vale Rec), Alan Bannister (St. Martins) and Micky Girard (North). The Jersey side was an experienced one with all players having Muratti experience. It was announced that attending the match would be Sir Stanley Rous, the President of FIFA. Sir Stanley had refereed two Muratti matches, the Guernsey v Alderney semi final in 1928 and the Guernsey v Jersey semi final in 1932.

Prior to the match both teams were presented to the Bailiff of Guernsey and Sir Stanley Rous. Jersey had the benefit of the breeze in the first half and territorially was on top. The first goal chance, however, came from Guernsey when Loveridge and Mahy combined to produce a shot that went just wide. In the 15th minute Torode received a pass from Loveridge and attacked the Jersey defence to force a corner. Torode, taking the corner, sent in a cross that Renouf met superbly to put Guernsey 1-0 up. Drama came into the game in the 35th minute. First, Guernsey had a penalty appeal turned down by referee Corbett when Davey was floored in the box, and then Micky Le Louarn went down when tackled by Noel Jeffreys and was carried off to be replaced by Les Selkirk. Jersey began to pressurise the Guernsey defence and in the last minute of the half they equalised. Barry Thorpe took a free kick and crossed in for Ruellan to beat Brazier with a fine header, the ball rebounded off the left hand post and was whipped into the net by Ian Walker to make the score Guernsey-1, Jersey-1.

Sir Stanley Rous.

The second half began with Guernsey on top with Barry Breuilly coming to Jersey's rescue with some excellent saves. In the 57th minute Duncan missed, with a great effort, the ball going past off the top of the post. In the closing minutes Loveridge was only a fraction wide with a left footed drive from 30 yards and he then just failed to connect with a long low ball struck into the goalmouth by substitute Giles. The regulation 90 minutes ended Guernsey-1, Jersey-1.

The first period of extra time again showed that, as in the previous 90 minutes, neither side was gaining control of the midfield. In the 100th minute of the match Mahy won the ball on the half way line and went on a run on the right wing, he cut past Thorpe and, inside the box; he was brought down by Browne. Referee Corbett had no hesitation in pointing to the spot. Girard stepped up and scored to the keeper's right as he dived to his left. There was no more scoring in this tight match and the final result was Guerney-2, Jersey-1.

Guernsey: C. Brazier, A. Le Page, M. Girard, C. Renouf, A. Bannister, M. Duncan,
N. Jeffreys, G. Mahy, H. Davey, J. Loveridge, W. Torode.
Sub: K. Giles.
Goalscorers: Girard (pen), Renouf.

Jersey: B. Breuilly, M. Le Louarn, M. Vowden (c), Browne, Thorp, H. Proffitt,
A. Venton, I. Watts, J. Ruellan, T. Bone, P. Sands.
Sub: Selkirk.
Goalscorer: Watts.

It was a hard fought match with little finesse but with a lot of determination and fighting
spirit from both sides.

During this decade Jersey had won 8 Muratti's to Guernsey's 2 making the overall score
Guernsey 26 wins, Jersey 25 wins and Alderney 1 win.

Girard scores the winning goal from the penalty spot.

Guernsey celebrate.

12

1970 - 1979

1 9 7 0

MURATTI SEMI-FINAL.
4 April 1970, The Cycling Grounds, Guernsey.

Guernsey -4, Alderney -0.

For the match against Alderney the Guernsey selectors had chosen one new cap in Colin Reeve (Belgrave W.) Alderney had four new caps in Brian Machon, John Barrett, John Maurice and the young schoolboy Colin Randall who played for the Rangers Junior team. This match was the 50th Anniversary of Alderney's famous Muratti Vase victory of 1920.

Guernsey had the ideal start to the game when they went one up after five minutes. Reeve swung in a fine cross over to the far post, Davey turned it past Bohan for Loveridge to score easily from close in. Guernsey tried to capitalise on this early lead but found Bohan and Peter Turner in the Alderney defence in superb form. Bohan had great saves firstly from Dave Lesbirel and then John Loveridge to deny the home side. As the first half neared its end Guernsey struck. Brazier had saved from an Alderney attack and set up Davey who broke away down the middle, beat two defenders, and cracked the ball past Bohan. Just on half time Loveridge passed to Torode who scored to make the half time score Guernsey-3, Alderney-0.

John Loveridge beats Bohan for Guernsey's first goal.

Alderney began the second half with the breeze behind them and started to mount some attacks. They came close when schoolboy, Colin Randall, had a clever run into the box and appeared to be brought down. Alderney's appeals for a penalty were turned down by referee Pyman. Guernsey maintained their control of the match and Brazier did not have a meaningful shot to handle. With eight minutes remaining full back Art Le Page entered the attack and scored from a Loveridge pass to make the final score Guernsey-4, Alderney-0.

Guernsey: C. Brazier, A. Le Page, M. Girard, C. Renouf, A. Bannister, M. Duncan, D. Lesbirel, W. Torode, C. Reeve, J. Loveridge, H. Davey.
Goalscorers: Loveridge, Davey, Torode, Le Page.

Alderney: W. Bohan, J. Dupont, P. Turner, C.J. Dupont, Machon, R. Stower, B. Farnham, Randall, Barrett, Maurice, Simon.
Sub: Barker.

This was a less than convincing display by Guernsey and even after an early goal it took them a long time to finish the game off. Bohan was the best for Alderney closely followed by Turner, both the Duponts and Farnham. Young Randall was the pick of Alderney's forwards.

MURATTI FINAL.
9 May 1970, Springfield Stadium, Jersey.

Jersey -2, Guernsey -0.

Jersey announced that they had one new cap for their match against Guernsey at Springfield and he was R. Spink. Guernsey fielded an experienced line-up with no new caps.

There were around 6,000 fans at Springfield as both teams were led out to contest the Muratti Vase. Jersey quickly established an early superiority in the midfield area through Harry Proffitt and 'Nash' Venton. Their wingers, Paul Sands and David Huson were causing a lot of problems to the Guernsey defence. After 18 minutes Jersey won a corner and as Huson sent it in it was only partially cleared by Brazier. An initial shot was cleared but Ruellan got hold of the rebound and struck it firmly low past Colin Renouf on the line. Guernsey tried to respond but found the home defence in fine and confident form with Breuilly performing particularly well. Colin Reeve tried to breech the Jersey defence with some good penetrating runs but to no avail and the first half ended Jersey-1, Guernsey-0.

Guernsey changed the team round in the second half with Renouf moving to centre forward. It was at this time that Guernsey had their only real chance when Reeve fired a shot that Breuilly saved brilliantly by swooping to the foot of his right hand post to send the ball round with one hand. Jersey soon regained the initiative and in the 52nd minute Ruellan picked up a misdirected pass by Davey and raced away from Lesbirel to fire in a low shot that came off Art Le Page to put Jersey 2-0 up. Ruellan was later injured in a clash with Micky Girard and had to be taken off. He was taken to hospital where X-rays revealed a hair line fracture of a shin bone. Guernsey tried to get themselves back into the game but Jersey were proving too strong in all positions and the final score remained Jersey-2, Guernsey-0.

Jersey: B. Breuilly, M. Le Louarn (c), Browne, Thorp, Selkirk, H. Proffitt, A. Venton, Sands, B. O'Boyle, J. Ruellan, Huson.
Sub: Spink.
Goalscorers: Ruellan, og.

Guernsey: C. Brazier, A. Le Page, M. Girard, C. Renouf, A. Bannister, M. Duncan, D. Lesbirel, A. Pugh, C. Reeve, J. Loveridge, H. Davey.
Sub: J. Herpe.

Jersey thoroughly merited this fine victory which was achieved through the excellent quality of their football. Both sides had now won the Muratti Vase 26 times.

1 9 7 1

As Alderney and Jersey prepared for their Muratti semi-final it was announced in the Guernsey Press that the Guernsey Football Association had agreed unanimously to invite the former Scottish international, Jimmy Gabriel (pictured), to coach the Guernsey Muratti team during the fortnight preceding the Muratti. Delegates at the GFA Meeting were informed that Ted Bates, the Southampton manager, had offered to send Gabriel and pay his wages for the two weeks with the GFA agreeing to pay his expenses. Gabriel played 300 games for Everton winning a Championship medal in season 1962-63 and an FA Cup winner's medal in 1966. He also won two Scotland caps. He later moved to Southampton.

MURATTI SEMI-FINAL.
March 1971, Springfield Stadium, Jersey.

Jersey -11, Alderney -0.

Alderney had a new goalkeeper for their match with Jersey. Phil Sowden won his first cap with Billy Bohan playing in midfield. Jersey included Roy Marett for his first cap.

The teams ran out at Springfield in front of a crowd of 818. The opening exchanges were very even with Alderney more than holding their own with David Hugman coming close on a couple of occasions. His second chance was a fine header from a Farnham free kick. In the 21st minute, however, Jersey opened the scoring. Venton took a pass from Dave Huson and crossed perfectly for Ruellan who dived and headed powerfully out of Sowden's reach. Sowden then had two spectacular saves from Ruellan and then Marett. Jersey continued to press and went further ahead after 29 minutes when Ruellan hooked the ball into the penalty area and O'Boyle anticipated the bounce beautifully to half volley it past the advancing goalkeeper. As the half neared its end Huson worked his way skilfully along the right touchline and crossed in a ball that went into the net off Sowden's shoulder to make the half time score Jersey-3, Alderney-0.

The second half began with Marett crashing the ball into the far side of the net for number four. Then the goals came at regular intervals as Jersey took complete control of the proceedings. O'Boyle scored the fifth when he headed in Marett's cross after 53 minutes and two minutes later Ruellan collected a ball from Marett, beat Turner and slammed in a low hard shot for goal number six. In the 59th minute another Marett cross was slammed in by O'Boyle for the seventh and Marett again supplied O'Boyle in the 65th minute to register Jersey's eighth goal in what was becoming a rout. O'Boyle turned provider when he took a left wing corner for Barry Thorp to score goal number nine. The Alderney defence, although under almost constant pressure, were sticking manfully to their daunting task. After 75 minutes Turner had the misfortune to hook the ball into his own net for the tenth goal. With nine minutes remaining Jersey made Muratti history by scoring an 11th goal when a chip by Ruellan hit Turner and left Sowden helpless. This remarkable match ended Jersey-11, Alderney-0.

Jersey: B. Breuilly, M. Le Louarn, B. Thorp, Spink, Blake, H. Proffitt, A. Venton, D. Huson, B. O'Boyle, J. Ruellan, R. Marett.
Goalscorers: Ruellan (2), O'Boyle (4), Thorpe, Marett, og (3).

Alderney: P. Sowden, C.A. Dupont, P. Turner, C.J. Dupont, J. Simon, W. Bohan, B. Farnham, M. Cauvain, Maurice, D. Hugman, Randall.
Sub: A. Benfield.

It was announced that Alderney had applied to host next years Muratti match against Guernsey. This application was considered by the Channel Islands Inter-Insular Committee Meeting in June. Guernsey's new coach, Jimmy Gabriel, watched his side go down 7-0 to Bristol Rovers of the English Third Division.

MURATTI FINAL.
15 May 1971, The Cycling Grounds, Guernsey.

Guernsey -0, Jersey -1.

Guernsey selected three new caps to face Jersey at the Cycling Grounds. They were Laurence Graham and Andy McMillan from Sylvans and Alan de Jersey from North. Prior to the start of the match Jersey suffered a setback when Brendan O'Boyle failed morning fitness test on a pulled thigh muscle and had to withdraw from the selected team. He was replaced by young Rory Crick who was gaining his first cap.

The game began as a very tight contest with both defences dealing well with any attacks. Most of the play was being confined to the midfield with neither team appearing to gain the upper hand. The Jersey defence was being well marshalled by Barry Thorp, and they were easily dealing with the Guernsey attacks. The only real effort of note came from Rory Crick who fired in a shot from just outside the penalty area and it took a good save from Brazier to prevent a score. As the first half ended it was plain that Breuilly was having a quiet time and in fact did not have a real shot to deal with during the opening 45 minutes. An uneventful first half ended Guernsey-0, Jersey-0.

The second half began a little livelier when in the first minute Giles broke through the Jersey defence and crossed for McMillan to dive in for a header that was blocked. Jersey replied with Ruellan coming close twice, then the impressive Crick went very near with his attempt. In an effort to gain the advantage Guernsey moved Renouf into the attack and

Andy McMillan, Alan de Jersey and Laurence Graham.

replaced Hemery with Bannister but to no avail. With the game in deadlock and looking as if it would end 0-0 Jersey took the initiative with 15 minutes remaining. Paul Sands came in from the right wing and was fouled by de Jersey. He took the free kick himself and it was cleared for a corner. Sands took an in-swinging corner from the left and it was cleared for another corner this time on the right. Huson took an in-swinging corner to the far post and found an unmarked Ruellan who headed it past Brazier. This goal caused a pitch invasion by the jubilant Jersey supporters. With five minutes remaining Loveridge thought that he had scored the equaliser but this 'goal' was disallowed by referee Burtenshaw as McMillan had already been given offside. This caused a section of Guernsey supporters to invade the pitch and damage the goal nets as they swung from the crossbar. The match was held up for 10 minutes as the pitch was cleared and the goal net replaced. There was no more scoring and the game ended Guernsey-0, Jersey-1.

Guernsey: C. Brazier, A. Le Page, J. Herpe, C. Renouf, A. de Jersey, L. Graham, K. Giles, R. Hemery, J. Loveridge, A. McMillan, W. Torode.
Sub: R. Bannister.

Jersey: B. Breuilly, M. Le Louarn, Spink, B. Thorp, Blake, H. Proffitt, A. Venton, P. Sands, R. Crick, J. Ruellan, D. Huson.
Goal scorer: Ruellan.

This hard earned victory put Jersey in the lead in Muratti Vase victories for the first time in the 66 year history of the competition by 27 wins to 26.

At the end of the match Mr Jack Dupre, Chairman of the Inter-Insular Committee, apologised to the distinguished guests for the crowd 'incidents' before calling on Sir Charles Mills, the Lieut-Governor of Guernsey, to present the Muratti Vase to Micky Le Louarn, the captain of the victorious Jersey team.

At the GFA Meeting on 25 May the President, Mr. W.H. Le Prevost, described the crowd troubles at the Muratti as hooliganism. The GFA wished to secure evidence so that those responsible for the unpleasant scenes at the Cycling Grounds could be convicted.

Alderney's application to stage the 1972 Muratti semi-final against Guernsey in Alderney was discussed at the Inter-Insular Meeting on Tuesday 15 June 1971. Under Muratti rules the team winning the semi-final would be guaranteed a place in the following years final. The GFA Council instructed the GFA's senior representative on the Inter-Insular Committee, Mr Bill Paul, to vote against the idea. As it was one island, one vote, the decision now rested with the Jersey delegate.

Following the meeting of 15 June it was announced that the 1972 Muratti semi-final between Guernsey and Alderney would take place at the Cycling Grounds so Alderney would have to wait a few years before hosting their first Muratti match.

1 9 7 2

MURATTI SEMI-FINAL.
3 April 1972, The Cycling Grounds, Guernsey.

Guernsey -5, Alderney -0.

Alderney were forced to make two changes to their selected side with goalkeeper Phil Sowden leaving the island to work in London and Charlie A. Dupont being on holiday. The selectors recalled Charlie J. Dupont ('Mulo') and Dave Hugman. Billy Bohan, initially chosen as a left back, returned to goal. Their team included three new caps in 'Podge' Greenslade (Rovers), Dave Coquelin (Centrals) and Trevor Pasquire who was a junior with Vale Rec. Guernsey had one new cap in Kevin Allen of St. Martins.

The teams were led out in front of a crowd of 900 at the Cycling Grounds by the respective captains, Loveridge (Guernsey) and Bohan (Alderney). The visitors made a bright start to the match and forced the first corner of the game. After five minutes Guernsey went ahead with a disputed goal. Reeve pushed the ball to Graham and, from the left he crossed high to the far post. Loveridge leapt in to head it goalwards, powered the ball against the woodwork and knocked the rebound over the line. The Alderney defenders claimed that he had hit the ball in with his arm but referee Ahier allowed the goal to stand. Guernsey should have made it 2-0 when Davey shot wide as Bohan advanced. In the 17th minute the home side increased their lead. Bohan was penalised for taking more than four steps after

Henry Davey follows the ball in for Guernsey's first goal as Charlie Dupont is down injured.

collecting a Graham drive. Loveridge cut the free kick to Reeve who scored off an Alderney defender. Keeping up the pressure Guernsey scored again three minutes later. Loveridge latched onto a Graham pass and shot for the left hand side of the net and Davey coming in made sure by turning it in just inside the post. Guernsey came close on three further occasions but Bohan made excellent saves from Loveridge (twice) and Dave Lesbirel to ensure that the half time score read Guernsey-3, Alderney-0.

Guernsey maintained their pressure in the second half and increased their lead in the 56th minute. Kevin Allen overlapped to take a pass from Lesbirel and his well-placed low centre was lashed into the net by Loveridge. Alderney replied with a long range drive from Hugman that curled just wide of Brazier's left hand post. Eight minutes from time Mick Girard took a free kick on Guernsey's right wing and Lesbirel left Bohan helpless with a superb flying header from just inside the penalty area to make the final score Guernsey-5, Alderney-0.

Guernsey: C. Brazier, K. Allen, M. Girard, J. Herpe, A. de Jersey, L. Graham, D. Lesbirel, R. Bannister, J. Loveridge (c), H. Davey, C. Reeve.
Sub: W. Torode.
Goalscorers: Loveridge (2), Reeve, Davey, Lesbirel.

Alderney: W. Bohan (c), J. Dupont, T. Pasquire, D. Coquelin, C.J. Dupont, Greenslade, Turner, D. Hugman, Randall, B. Farnham, Cunningham.
Sub: Baron.

Guernsey were worthy winners but they only played well in patches and at times their football was careless. They were well served by Graham and Reeve, and Allen and de Jersey impressed in the home defence. Bohan, as usual, had an excellent game for Alderney and was well supported by young Pasquire, Barron, Coquelin and Greenslade.

MURATTI FINAL.
9 May 1972, Springfield Stadium, Jersey.

Jersey -0, Guernsey -3. aet.

As part of their Muratti preparations Jersey had an excellent 3-3 draw with Wycombe Wanderers, and Benest, by scoring all three Jersey goals, confirmed his place in the final. Benest (Old Victorians) was one of four new caps in the Jersey line-up the other three being Vic Bourgoise (Army), Stuart Pirouet (First Tower) and Mo Mathews (First Tower). Benest was replacing 'Noddy' Ruellan who had moved to Australia. Guernsey's preparations included a 6-0 defeat at the hands of Fourth Division side Brentford.

Barry Thorp (Jersey) and Art Le Page (Guernsey) led out their teams in front of a 4,000 Springfield crowd. Guernsey nearly had a dream start by almost scoring after 7 minutes. Lesbirel latched onto a Graham free-kick and headed it past the advancing Barry Breuilly but, in attempting to make sure the ball went in, Micky Girard inexplicably hit it over the bar. Jersey responded with Richard Benest cracking a shot that had Brazier diving to his

Reeve (11) opens the scoring for Guernsey.

left to pull off a fine save. Reeve was beginning to cause the Jersey defence a lot of problems with his threatening runs. In the 40th minute Graham created the second real chance of the game when he capped a great run to put the ball across to Davey but he failed to get a head to the ball. The half time whistle went with the score Jersey-0, Guernsey-0.

Guernsey opened the second half promisingly and a move between Torode and Davey resulted in Davey firing in a drive that Breuilly did well to hold. Again Breuilly saved Jersey in the 62nd minute when Davey got his head to a Graham corner but, with magnificent reflexes, brought off a thrilling clutching save. Four minutes later Brazier did well to reach a Benest drive but he could only parry the ball to the feet of Huson, who drove over an open goal. The regulation 90 minutes ended Jersey-0, Guernsey-0.

Extra time had only been in progress for 90 seconds when Guernsey got the vital first goal. Torode came in from the right, beat Bourgoise and cut the ball into the goalmouth. Breuilly dived out and got his hands to the ball but failed to hold it and it was hooked into the net by Reeve for 1-0. Jersey hit back with Thorp thumping a tremendous shot that caused Brazier to leap across goal to his left to pull off a magnificent save. Jersey came close again when Allen headed off his line to deny Bourgoise an equalising goal. In the 9th minute of extra time Torode came in from the left and pushed the ball into the goalmouth where substitute Giles crashed it first time into the net to make the score 2-0. In the 117th minute Reeve beat his man and centred to Graham who should have scored. Barry Breuilly blocked the ball away but it ran to Torode who sent a right foot drive into the top left hand corner of the net to make the final score Jersey-0, Guernsey-3.

The victorious Guernsey team.

Jersey: B. Breuilly, Spink, Burgoise, B. Thorp (c), Blake, H. Proffitt, A. Venton, Pirouet, R. Crick, Benest, D. Huson.
Sub: Blacklock.

Guernsey: C. Brazier, K. Allen, M. Girard, J. Herpe, A. de Jersey, A. Le Page, D. Lesbirel, L. Graham, W. Torode, H. Davey, C. Reeve.
Sub: K. Giles.
Goalscorers: Torode (2), Giles.

This was a superb performance by the Guernsey team in an exciting match and it was Guernsey's first win on Jersey soil since 1954. The Vase was presented to skipper Art Le Page by the Lieut-Governor of Jersey, HE Air Chief Marshal Sir John Davies. The victorious Guernsey squad celebrated their triumph at the Muratti Ball that was held at West Park Pavilion.

1 9 7 3

MURATTI SEMI-FINAL.
29 March 1973, Springfield Stadium, Jersey.

Jersey -6, Alderney -1.

It was reported that Alderney were hoping to obtain the services of the veteran Jersey star 'Nash' Venton for their match with Jersey but they were unsuccessful. He qualified for them as he had an Alderney mother. Alderney included tree new caps in their line-up in Frank Keachie, Ricky Cook and D. Baron along with substitute P. Marriano. Billy Roberts had returned from Australia and was also included after a few years absence. Their team manager is Frank Bond, President of the Alderney FA, and trainer is John Dupont. Jersey, with eight First Tower players, included five new caps in Archie Baillie, Jeff Carter, Alan Pitman, Rowan and Mike Seater (Magpies).

The opening exchanges were very even and Farnham twice went close to giving Alderney the lead but it was Jersey who scored first after 18 minutes. Seater received a pass from Crick, turned on the ball, and scored with a great shot from 20 yards. Six minutes later Bohan failed to hold a header by Seater and Rory Crick swept in Jersey's second goal. The home side were proving quicker to the ball and went further ahead after 28 minutes. A fine long pass from Mo Mathews sent Stuart Pirouet racing away on the right wing and his cross was headed in by Seater. The fourth goal followed only three minutes later when Derek Huson took full advantage of a defensive lapse by Alderney to crash in another 20 yard shot past Bohan's right hand. The fifth goal came after 35 minutes when Huson headed home a cross by Pirouet. The half time score was Jersey-5, Alderney-0.

Alderney began the second half in a more determined manner and they scored after 51 minutes. The Jersey goalkeeper, Breuilly, conceded a free kick for carrying. Crook tapped the ball to Farnham who blazed the ball into the far side of the net giving the keeper no chance. Alderney nearly scored again but Breuilly foiled Crook with an excellent one-handed save round the post. The visitors were now on top and Crook again tested Breuilly. Jersey were having problems containing Crook's runs into their defence and in the 80th minute he raced away on the left and cut in for a drive which flashed only inches wide of the far post. Jersey weathered this storm and with three minutes remaining they increased their lead. Huson, breaking from the half way line, beat three men in a sparkling run to leave Bohan helpless with a great shot into the right hand corner of the net to make the final score Jersey-6, Alderney-1.

Jersey: B. Breuilly, Baillie, J. Carter, Pitman, A. Venton, M. Mathews, Rowan, Pirouet, R. Crick, Seater, D. Huson.
Goalscorers: Huson (3), Seater (2), Crick.

Alderney: W. Bohan, Baron, Pasquire, Coquelin, Turner, G. Greenslade, W. Roberts, F. Keachie, Randall, R. Crook, B. Farnham.
Sub: Maiorano.
Goalscorer: Farnham.

It was generally agreed that this was Alderney's best performance for years and they did not deserve to loose by five goals. They were by far the better team in the second half with Ricky Crook having an excellent game in his first Muratti match.

MURATTI FINAL.
9 May 1973, The Cycling Grounds, Guernsey.

Guernsey -1, Jersey -4.

Guernsey included five new caps in their starting line-up for their match against Jersey at the Cycling Grounds. Mick Falla (Vale Rec) in goal along with Peter Blondel (Vale Rec), Geoff Rowe (St. Martins), Colin Loveridge (North) and Brian Robson (Belgrave W.). Peter Blondel became only the third Guernsey player to represent his island in Junior and Senior Muratti matches in the same season. The Jersey selectors included three new caps in Dixie A' Court, John Robert and Joe Griffiths all Magpies. Guernsey showed six changes and Jersey seven changes from the teams that contested the 1972 Muratti Vase final.

The two captains, Art Le Page (Guernsey) and Jeff Carter (Jersey) led their teams out in front of 3,350 excited fans at the Cycling Grounds expecting a keenly fought contest. The weather was windy and the pitch appeared rather bumpy. Jersey started the brightest with Rory Crick proving to be their most dangerous player. As the game progressed both teams seemed to be cancelling each other out with neither producing any clear cut chances.

Guernsey.
Herpe, Blondel, Falla, Rowe, Allen, Le Page (c).
Robson, Loveridge, Graham, Lesbirel, Reeve.

Reeve equalises for Guernsey.

However in the 42nd minute, following a throw in, Griffiths played the ball through the Guernsey defence, Benest raced onto it and struck it low and firmly past the advancing Falla's right hand. This was the first genuine opportunity either side had created in what was a kick and rush first half. This was the only score and the half ended Guernsey-0, Jersey-1.

  Guernsey started well in the second half and began to spread the ball around well as they searched for an equaliser. It came finally when Rowe hit a long ball down the left and Colin Loveridge and Breuilly raced for it. The Guernsey player got there first and as he swept it past the keeper, Colin Reeve dashed in to shoot it past the stranded Breuilly into the left hand corner of the net. Five minutes later Guernsey almost took the lead when a good head flick by Robson sent Reeve away and, when he crossed, Breuilly only just beat Loveridge to it. This was quickly followed by Robson heading a Loveridge cross only inches wide. A minute later as Loveridge entered the Jersey penalty area he appeared to be bundled off the ball but referee Harold Hackney waived play on. Guernsey again claimed a penalty when Brian Robson was tackled from behind in the penalty area but the referee deemed the tackle fair and allowed play to continue. Jersey replied when Richard Benest picked up a through ball from Joe Griffiths. He knocked it past the onrushing Falla and as he went round the keeper he was brought down. To the consternation of the local fans the referee immediately awarded a penalty. Falla made a great effort to save Jeff Carter's spot kick but could only divert it on to the inside of his right hand post and it rebounded into the net to make the score 2-1 for Jersey. The visitors continued to press home their advantage and soon went 3-1 up. Benest worked his way into the box but lost control of the ball, Geoff Rowe tried to clear and hit the ball off Benest and it went over the luckless Falla into the net. Guernsey had two apparent penalty claims dismissed by referee Hackney but it was Jersey who were now in control. In the final minute Jersey completed the scoring when Paul Sands put the ball in from close range. The final score was Guernsey-1,   Jersey-4.

Jeff Carter receives the Muratti Vase from Vice-Admiral Charles Mills.

Guernsey: M. Falla, K. Allen, P. Blondel, J. Herpe, G. Rowe, A. Le Page, D. Lesbirel, L. Graham, C. Loveridge, B. Robson,C. Reeve.
Sub: A. Taylor.
Goalscorer: Reeve.

Jersey: B. Breuilly, D. A'Court, J. Carter (c), Pitman, Selkirk, R. Crick, J. Roberts, P. Sands, Benest, J. Griffiths, D. Huson.
Sub: A. Venton.
Goalscorers: Benest (2), Carter (pen), Sands.

Although this was a very disappointing home display by Guernsey it was a fully justified victory by Jersey. Guernsey's Lieut-Governor, Vice-Admiral Charles Mills presented the Muratti Vase to the proud Jersey skipper Jeff Carter. Guernsey captain, Art Le Page, conceded after the match that Jersey had deserved their victory because they had four chances and took them all.

Victorious Jersey team with the Muratti Vase.

Art Le Page takes the ball past goalkeeper Sowden.

1 9 7 4

MURATTI SEMI-FINAL.
1 April 1974, The Cycling Grounds, Guernsey.

Guernsey -6, Alderney -0.

The Guernsey team included 5 news caps for their match with Alderney at the Cycling Grounds. They were Ralph Anthony (Belgrave W.) along with Malcolm Marquand, Ray Blondel, Nigel Le Page and Kevin Gleeson all of Vale Rec. The Alderney team all had Muratti experience but they had lost the services of the experienced Roberts as he had returned to Australia. Once more goalkeeper Billy Bohan played in an outfield role for the side.

Guernsey took a little time to settle in this match but they soon took control and scored after 7 minutes. Kevin Allen fired in a cross that was met by Ray Blondel whose header came off the crossbar. The ball was cleared for a corner and Gleeson swung over the kick for Blondel to head past Sowden. This was the start that Guernsey were looking for and 8 minutes later they doubled their lead. Allen sent in a centre that Nigel Le Page turned back to Gleeson who hammered the ball against the bar. Dave Lesbirel collected the rebound and set up Blondel to score from the 18 yard line. Both Nigel Le Page and Art Le Page came close but both were thwarted by Sowden and the half ended Guernsey-2, Alderney-0.

The second half began with Ralph Anthony crashing a shot against the bar as Guernsey tried to get the all important third goal. Alderney replied quickly but John Barker failed to profit from a fine pass from Crook. Ray Blondel completed his hat-trick in the 59th minute with a superbly headed goal from a Gleeson cross. Four minutes later the roles were reversed when Blondel chipped the ball over the onrushing Sowden for Gleeson to head into an empty net. In the 67th minute Blondel went through the middle and took the ball round Sowden to score goal number five. In the final minute Gleeson lobbed the ball over the out of position keeper to make the final score Guernsey-6, Alderney-0.

Guernsey: M. Falla, K. Allen, P. Blondel, J. Herpe, G. Rowe, A. Le Page, D. Lesbirel, R. Anthony, R. Blondel, N. Le Page, K. Gleeson.
Sub: L. Graham.
Goalscorers: R. Blondel (4), Reeve (2).

Alderney: P. Sowden, D. Baron, P. Turner, Maurice, T. Pasquire, Randall, W. Bohan, Greenslade, J. Barker, R. Crook, B. Farnham.
Sub: Benfield, Smart.

Although heavily defeated the Alderney coach, Brian Mercer, said that he was happy with his team's performance especially that of Sowden and Crook. After many years Alderney once again awarded Muratti caps to its players. The presentation was made by the Alderney FA President Mr. Baron at a dance held at the Island Hall and during his speech he expressed the hope that Alderney would soon have the facilities for future Muratti semi-finals. The caps were made by Rita Gilmore. A presentation of a table lighter was made to Brian Mercer by the Alderney FA in recognition of all the hard work he had put in training the team and producing the Junior side.

The Alderney team with their Muratti caps.

Guernsey Squad
Millman, Hargreaves, Reeve, Brazier, Rowe, Renouf (c).
Marquand, Lesbirel, N. Le Page, Allen, A. Le Page, Gleeson.

MURATTI FINAL.
9 May 1974, Springfield Stadium, Jersey.

Jersey -1, Guernsey -2. aet.

The Jersey selectors had chosen four new caps in their starting line-up in David Jones (Wanderers) and Reg Coutanche, Ken Billot and Hellier Falle all of St. Paul's. The Guernsey team included one new cap 'Milko' Millman of Vale Rec. This ensured that Vale Rec supplied eight players in the starting line-up. The referee for the match was John Homewood (Sudbury-on-Thames) who had refereed the FA Challenge Trophy match at Wembley on Saturday 27 April.

The rival captains, Jeff Carter (Jersey) and Colin Renouf (Guernsey), led their teams onto Springfield in front of a rather small crowd of 2,600. Jersey made the more impressive start to the match and put the Guernsey defence under some early pressure. The visitors' centre pairing of Peter Blondel and Colin Renouf, however, were beginning to get the better of the Jersey strikers, O'Boyle and Seatter. As Jersey kept up the pressure they scored after 23 minutes. Hellier Falle took a corner kick and Rory Crick had his drive blocked, Falle ran on to the loose ball and scored in spectacular style with a searing 25 yard shot that flashed across Brazier into the top corner of the net. Guernsey equalised in the 37th minute when a Malcolm Marquand free kick found Ray Blondel ghosting in from the blind side and he calmly ran the ball round Breuilly before whipping it into the net. This goal seemed to act as a tonic for Guernsey and they took up the running for the remainder of the half which ended Jersey-1, Guernsey-1.

Guernsey remained on top for the early part of the second half and should have taken that lead in the 55th minute when Blondel broke clean only to see Breuilly save the ball, it went lose and Gleeson's attempt was cleared on the goal line by Dixie A' Court. Ten minutes later Jersey nearly scored when Seatter's shot came off Brazier's left hand post. In the last minute of regulation time a Kevin Allen cross beat the Jersey defence but Nigel Le Page got his foot under the ball and put it over the bar leaving the score Jersey-1, Guernsey-1.

In the 8th minute of extra time Nigel Le Page brought out a sensational save from Breuilly who pushed the drive round the post. The winning goal, which came in the 100th minute, was a disaster for the Jersey defence. Reg Coutanche foiled a Guernsey attack from the right and turned the ball back to Breuilly but the pass was under hit. Blondel was on it in a flash and swept the ball round the despairing keeper and cracked it into the wide open net to make the final score Jersey-1, Guernsey-2.

Jersey:	B. Breuilly, D. A'Court, J. Carter (c), Roberts, Coutanche, Jones, R. Crick, Billot, B. O'Boyle, Seater, H. Falle.
	Sub: Dolbel.
	Goalscorer: Falle.
Guernsey:	C. Brazier, K. Allen, P. Blondel, C. Renouf (c), M. Marquand, A. Le Page, D. Lesbirel, N, Millman, R. Blondel, N. Le Page, K. Gleeson.
	Sub: C. Reeve, G. Rowe.
	Goalscorer: R. Blondel (2).

This was a fine hard fought team performance from Guernsey and, following their equalising goal, a victory that they deserved. It was a jubilant Colin Renouf who received the coveted Muratti Vase from Jersey's Lieut-Governor after the match.

Colin Renouf receiving the Muratti Vase from Jersey's Lieut-Governor.

Guernsey team with the Muratti Vase - 1974.

1 9 7 5

MURATTI SEMI-FINAL.
18 March 1975, Springfield Stadium, Jersey.

Jersey -3, Alderney -1.

Alderney had two new caps for their match with Jersey in Alan Pasquire (Vale Rec.), in goal, and Paul Newton (Rovers). Jersey had four new caps in J. James, S. Harzo, R. Harbin and R. Pollock.

As the game started Alderney shocked the Springfield crowd by scoring within 20 seconds of the start. They kicked off and Farnham played the ball to Frank Keachie who passed back to him and ran on to receive the return pass and proceeded to lob in a 35 yard shot. Breuilly in the Jersey goal grabbed it but as he fell the ball bounced out of his hands and flew into the net. This was not only one of the fastest goals in the history of the Muratti; it was the fastest Muratti goal that Alderney have ever scored. This stunning start put Jersey on the back foot and they were struggling to make an impact on the match. Alderney kept up the pressure and came close to doubling their lead in the 26th minute when Benfield cracked in a shot that produced a great save from Breuilly to send it round the post. Jersey responded well to these setbacks and in the 31st minute they equalised. Ron Pollock swung the ball across from the left and it dipped past Alan Pasquire as Harben rose to meet it, ending up in the net. It was initially thought that Harben had headed it in but he later confirmed that he had not touched the ball and therefore it was credited to Pollock. Alderney were working tremendously hard to contain and then pressurise Jersey as they strove to regain the lead. This pulsating half ended Jersey-1, Alderney-1.

The second half began with Jersey gaining control of the match as they started to mount a series of attacks on the visitor's goal. Alderney responded with Stevens, Trevor Pasquire, Turner and Maurice contesting every ball as they continually repulsed the Jersey pressure. This pressure continued to mount and Jersey came close with a Steve Harzo shot in the 71st minute and a further one by Rory Crick in the 75th minute, both of which came back off the woodwork. In the 77th minute it was tragedy for the Alderney defence. Trevor Pasquire had the ball and his brother, Alan, in the Alderney goal called for it, but the back-pass fell short and Ralph Harben nipped in to push it into the net for 2-1 to Jersey. The game still remained in the balance, however, until two minutes from time when a long ball from Dixie A' Court found Harben and he sent Ron Pollock clear to score the all important third goal for Jersey. There was no more scoring and this remarkable match ended Jersey-3, Alderney-1.

Jersey: B. Breuilly, D. A'Court, J. James, A. Pitman, D. Blake, S. Harzo, K. Billot, M. Mathews, R. Crick, R. Harbin, R. Pollock.
Goalscorers: Pollock (2), Harbin.

Alderney: A. Pasquire, Stevens, Turner, Maurice, T. Pasquire, Greenslade, B. Farnham, Coquelin, Benfield, P. Newton, F. Keachie.
Sub: Baron.
Goalscorer: Keachie.

After the game the Jersey officials were full of praise for the Alderney performance and their coach, Harry Proffitt, described it as the most professional display he had ever seen from them.

MURATTI FINAL.
9 May 1975, The Cycling Grounds, Guernsey.

Guernsey -2, Jersey -2. aet.

The Guernsey selectors made whole-sale changes for the Muratti final against Jersey. They included six new caps in Roger Froome (St. Martins) in goal, along with Mick Cotter (Vale Rec), Drew Pollock (Belgrave W.), Ron Depres (Belgrave W.), Martyn Loveridge (St. Martins) and Colin Fallaize (North). Jersey began with a more experienced team with only two new caps in Dave Mathews (Georgetown) in goal and Eddie Appleyard (Oaklands).

Dave Mathews and Eddie Appleyard.

Noel Jeffreys (Coach), Brazier, Loveridge, Blondel, Froome, Robson, Le Page, Graham, Rowe, Jeffreys.
Fallaize, Reeve, Lesbirel, Depres (capt.), Marquand, Cotter, Pollock.
Guernsey Muratti Squad.- 1975.

They had unfortunately lost the services of Ron Pollock (Oaklands) due to an injury he sustained playing in a Touzel Cup semi-final. Ron was an experienced player who had spells with Glasgow Rangers, Fulham and Queen of the South before moving to Jersey. At the very last moment Jersey also lost the services of Rory Crick (First Tower). After training on Thursday night he reported to team coach Harry Proffitt at the Quayside at St. Helier on Friday morning that a knee had swelled up and he would be unable to play. He did not travel and he was replaced by Steve Harzo (Beeches).

Ron Depres (Guernsey) and Johnny James (Jersey) led out their teams onto the Cycling Grounds in front of a 3,000 crowd. Guernsey started the brightest with the young Colin Fallaize prominent. In the 11th minute the home side went ahead when following a determined run by Nigel Le Page, the ball was fed to Reeve who crossed to Fallaize. He darted in between A' Court and James to score an opportunist goal.

Guernsey felt that they had scored a second when Fallaize ran through the middle of the Jersey defence and sent a glorious right footed shot into the left hand side of the net. He was mobbed by his team-mates but the home celebrations were cut short, however, when referee Burns noticed that his linesman, Coppell, had flagged due to Reeve being in an offside position on the far side of the pitch. Although extremely disappointed at this decision Guernsey kept up this pressure but the visitors were beginning to settle. Four minutes after the disallowed goal Jersey felt that they should have had a penalty when Marquand used his arm to control the ball inside the area. The referee, however, awarded a free kick just outside the penalty box. This partial success seemed to inspire Jersey and they capitalised on a defensive lapse by the Guernsey defence in the 29th minute. A ball was pushed in from the Jersey right wing and Froome rushed out to the edge of the area and threw himself at the ball, but he failed to get hold of it cleanly. It bounced over him, and Eddie Appleyard coolly chipped it over Froome and into the empty net. Jersey nearly scored again but Marquand made a last ditch clearance from Harben. With a minute to half time Jersey went ahead when Bernie O'Boyle pushed a lovely ball through the centre and Harben swept majestically round Froome to clip it into the net from the most acute of angles to make the half time score Guernsey-1, Jersey-2.

Fallaize opens the scoring for Guernsey.

Mathews pulling off a brilliant save from a Reeve header.

The second half began with Guernsey gaining control as they strove for an equaliser. It almost came when, after taking a throw in, Fallaize received the ball back and lobbed it across to the far post. Reeve got up for a header that appeared to be heading for the net but Mathews pulled out the save of the match by clutching the ball on his left.

Fallaize nearly scored in the 75th minute but his first time drive went flashing over the bar. Guernsey equalised when Cotter sent in a beautiful cross for Reeve to out jump Mathews, and head in an excellent goal. There was no more scoring and the match ended Guernsey-2, Jersey-2.

In extra time Jersey brought on Alan Pitman (First Tower) for Paul Harzo and the match was even with close things at both ends although there were no goals. Half time Guernsey-2, Jersey-2.

There was more action in the second period when Mo Mathews cleared a Colin Reeve header off his line. With two minutes remaining the Jersey goal had a miraculous escape when Nigel Le Page saw his chip over Mathews slip over the bar. A minute later a shot by Ken Billot rebounded off Froome's right-hand post to Appleyard and only a tremendous save by the Guernsey keeper prevented a sensational Jersey winner. In the dying seconds Colin Fallaize broke through for Guernsey only to see his shot hit the side netting. Extra time produced no goals and the match ended Guernsey-2, Jersey-2.

Guernsey: R. Froome, M. Cotter, P. Blondel, A. Pollock, M. Marquand, D. Lesbirel, R. Depres (c), M. Loveridge, N. Le Page, C. Fallaize, C. Reeve.
Sub: G. Rowe, L. Graham.
Goalscorers: Fallaize, Reeve.

Jersey: D. Mathews, D. A'Court, M. Mathews, J. James, D. Blake, S. Harzo, R. Crick, S. Pirouet, B. O'Boyle, R. Harben, E. Appleyard.
Sub: A. Pitman, R. Dunford.
Goalscorers: Appleyard, Harbin.

Guernsey coach, Noel Jeffreys, said that after a great start they had a bad spell but fought back well. He was confident about his side's chances in the replay. Harry Proffitt, the Jersey coach, thought that his team had played well and was also confident about the second match in Jersey. The replay was scheduled for Springfield on Monday 26 May.

MURATTI FINAL-REPLAY.
26 May 1975, Springfield Stadium, Jersey.

Jersey -2, Guernsey -3. aet.

Both sides had to make changes due to injury, with Jersey losing the services of Ron Pollock as he had torn ligaments, and Guernsey's Peter Blondel failed a late fitness test and was replaced with Drew Pollock. Guernsey also had a new captain with goalkeeper Brazier replacing Depres.

Jersey opened the strongest and were looking very impressive and it was no surprise that they took the lead after 15 minutes. Jersey won a corner on the right and Appleyard crossed in to find Johnny James unmarked and he headed past Brazier. Jersey were now in control and pushing on for the second goal. Guernsey's chances were few although Mathews had to be smart to save from Le Page and then from Rowe. The play returned to the Guernsey end and Brazier had to be at his best to make two splendid saves from Ralph Harben just before the break. The half time score was Jersey-1, Guernsey-0.

 Five minutes into the second half Brazier was again called into action when he threw himself to the left to hold a 30 yard drive from Crick. In the 58th minute he saved what seemed a certain goal from a close range Crick header as the pressure mounted. Just as Guernsey thought that they had weathered the storm Jersey scored a second goal. Lesbirel tried to make a back-pass but the ball was picked up by O'Boyle who sent in a shot. Brazier did well to get a hand to the ball but it spun across the goalmouth to be knocked in by Harben for 2-0. Brazier was again lively when he stopped O'Boyle from adding a third and then he just managed to deflect an effort by Harben. Although the game seemed to be going away from them Guernsey kept on battling and they were rewarded in the 81st minute with a goal. Laurence Graham swung over a right wing corner and, as the ball came out to him after a brief skirmish, Le Page hammered it high into the net. Guernsey pushed on for an equaliser and came close when substitute Keith Jeffreys fired in a fine shot that Mathews did well to turn round the post. As the minutes ticked away Jeffreys came in from the right beat one man and was in the act of going round David Blake when he was brought down in the box. Referee Burns had no hesitation in pointing to the spot. Up stepped Dave Lesbirel who scored with a low shot that beat Mathews on his left for 2-2. Guernsey nearly won the match in regulation time when Reeve raced in from the right to latch onto a Jeffreys pass and fired a shot just past the post. The 90 minutes ended Jersey-2, Guernsey-2.

 In extra time Jersey replaced Stuart Pirouet and David Blake with Tony Guegan and Alan Pitman and immediately forced their way into attack, winning two corners in the first minute. Guernsey responded in the forth minute when, following a foul on Fallaize, Reeves and Jeffreys worked an excellent free kick. Reeve shaped to chip the ball into the centre but instead tapped it to Jeffreys. He took it round the Jersey wall and crossed to Lesbirel who flicked it to Fallaize in the centre of the goalmouth and he hit it first time out of Mathews' reach to put Guernsey 3-2 in front. Jersey reacted positively but they could not find the net and the final score was Jersey-2, Guernsey-3.

Jersey:	D. Mathews, D. A'Court, M. Mathews, J. James, D. Blake, S. Harzo, R. Crick, S. Pirouet, B .O'Boyle, R. Harbin, E. Appleyard.
	Subs: A. Pitman, A. Guegan.
	Goalscorers: James, Harbin.

Guernsey:	C. Brazier (c), M. Cotter, G. Rowe, A. Pollock, M. Marquand, D. Lesbirel, M. Loveridge, L. Graham, N. Le Page, C. Fallaize, C. Reeve.
	Subs: R. Depres, K. Jeffreys.
	Goalscorers: Le Page, Lesbirel (pen), Fallaize.

 This was a tremendous fight-back by Guernsey who were 2-0 down with nine minutes remaining. Guernsey were still in the game due mainly to the heroics of Gerve Brazier in goal with a string of superb saves and it was the delighted keeper who stepped up to receive the Muratti Vase from Jersey's Lieut-Governor, Lieut- General Sir Desmond Fitzpatrick after the game.

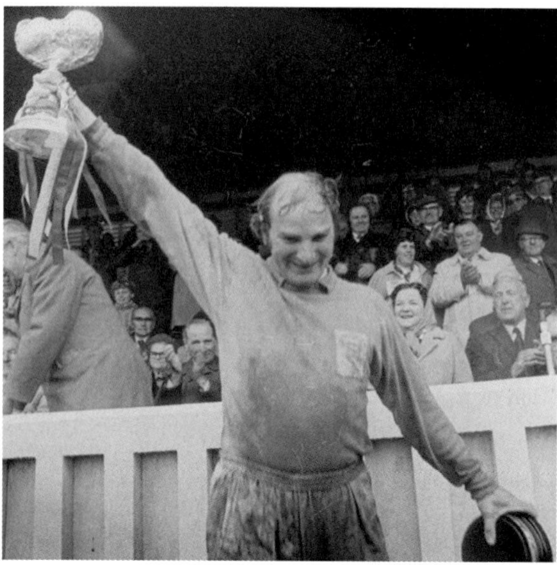

Jubilant Gerve Brazier with the Muratti Vase.

Brazier announced after the match that this was to be his last season and he was going to retire. Gerve played in 16 Muratti matches winning six medals along with a host of honours with his club St. Martins.

At the Annual General Meeting of the Inter-Insular Football Committee on 11 June it was decided that the semi-final for the Muratti Vase for 1976 would be held in Alderney. This outcome came about largely through the persistent efforts of the President of the Alderney FA, Maurice Gillmore, and it is news that was well received throughout the northern isle.

1 9 7 6

MURATTI SEMI-FINAL.
20 March 1976, Mount Hale, Alderney.

Alderney -0, Guernsey -5.

It was an historic occasion when Alderney hosted a Muratti match for the first time at Mount Hale on 20th March 1976. Alderney had selected one new cap for this match with Albert Greatbanks making his debut. Guernsey had selected what they believed to be the youngest ever Muratti player in 16 year old goalkeeper Chris Hamon of Belgrave W. It was pointed out in the Press, however, that Alderney had a player called Freddie Odoire who was aged 15 years and 9 months when he turned out against Guernsey in 1934.

The Muratti Vase was taken to Alderney by Guernsey and this was the first time it had been in the northern isle since 1920 when Alderney won the trophy following their 1-0 defeat of Guernsey at Westmount, Jersey. The significance of this first semi-final of the Muratti Vase competition ever to be played in Alderney – marked by the release of balloons – was not lost on the island's 1,800 population. Led by Alderney FA's President, Mr. Maurice Gillmore, their cheers could be heard at the top of the town.

Alderney were led out by Peter Turner and Guernsey by Colin Hargreaves onto the Mount Hale pitch in front of a crowd of around 500. It was a sunny afternoon but a cold wind was blowing. Guernsey had the advantage of this wind in the first half and put Alderney under

Alderney.

considerable pressure. Alderney defended powerfully with Alan Pasquire in the home goal dealing with everything confidently. It looked as though the first half was going to end goalless when Guernsey struck in the 39th minute. Lesbirel made a great run down Guernsey's left and crossed in for Le Page and his header was cleared for a corner. Reeve took the kick from the right and his in-swinger curled into the net for the first Muratti goal to be scored in Alderney. The half time score was Alderney-0, Guernsey-1.

The Muratti Vase in Alderney.

Reeve's inswinging corner entering Alderney's net.

Alderney began the second half with the breeze at their backs but it was the visitors who began the better and within two minutes they came close when a Reeve shot was cleared off the line by Dave Coquelin. As the pressure continued Reeve received a long cross-field ball from Blondel and he centred to Hargreaves who miskicked it. As luck would have it, it landed at Le Page's feet and he cracked in a fine rising shot past Pasquire. Fallaize thought that he had scored after 69 minutes but it was disallowed by referee Parker. Pollock substituted for the injured Lesbirel after 75 minutes and he sent a great ball to Reeve who rounded the keeper to put Guernsey three ahead. Three minutes later Pasquire made a fabulous save from a Blondel piledriver but the ball rebounded to Rowe who hammered it past him. Four minutes from time substitute McMillan created a chance for Fallaize to score number five making the final score Alderney-0, Guernsey-5.

Alderney: A. Pasquire, Benfield, P. Turner (c), T. Pasquire, Maurice, Greenslade, P. Newton, Coquelin, A. Greatbanks,Bohan, F. Keachie. Sub: B. Farnham.

Guernsey: C. Hamon, J. Reid, P. Blondel, G. Rowe, M. Marquand, D. Lesbirel, C. Hargreaves, N. Thoume, C. Fallaize, N. Le Page, C. Reeve.
 Subs: A. Pollock, A. McMillan.
Goalscorers: Reeve (2), Le Page, Rowe, Fallaize.

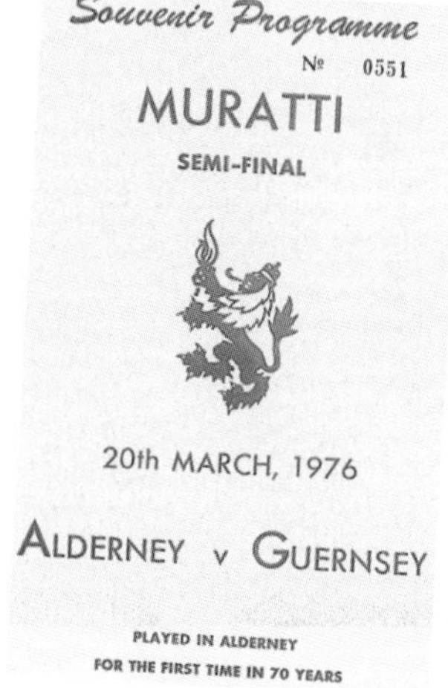

MURATTI FINAL.
8 May 1976, Springfield Stadium, Jersey.

Jersey -3, Guernsey -1.

Jersey had selected 4 new caps in Jimmy Murphy and Brent Pitman of First Tower, Peter Fleury (St. Peter) and Archie Baillie (St. Ouen). Guernsey had selected an experienced side for this Muratti match at Springfield.

The scene was set for this Muratti match in the opening seconds when Fleury and Blondel clashed head on ensuring that this would be a typical cup-tie. It was Guernsey who opened the scoring in the 21st minute when Fallaize took a throw in on the right; Le Page flicked the ball neatly to Reeve and from 15 yards he fired in a searing left-footer that gave Mathews no chance. Jersey replied with young Pitman forcing Froome into a great save sending the ball for a corner. From this kick the ball came out to Alan Pitman and the left back lobbed it hopefully goalwards from 20 yards, the ball slid from Froome's hands, over his shoulder and into the net for 1-1. The game now swung Jersey's way and Guegan should have put the visitors ahead at half time but Thoume cleared the ball out of the goal-mouth to leave the score Jersey-1, Guernsey-1.

Jersey began the second half in command and could have gone ahead but for a timely intervention by Johnny Reid. With 13 minutes from time Jersey did take the lead. Alan Pitman took a free kick on Jersey's left and swung the ball for his younger brother, Brent,

Reeve opens the scoring for Guernsey.

to head home at the far post. Guernsey immediately brought on John Loveridge in an attempt to save the game and from a Reid free kick Reeve came close. In the 82nd minute a low cross from Brent Pitman eluded Froome and it was chipped into the net by Guegan to make the final score Jersey-3, Guernsey-1.

Jersey: D. Mathews, D. A' Court, J. Carter, M. Mathews, A. Pitman, J. Murphy, S. Harzo, B. Pitman, P. Fleury, A. Baillie, A. Guegan.
Subs: D. Cooper, B. O'Boyle.
Goalscorers: A. Pitman, B. Pitman, Guegan.

Guernsey: R. Froome, J. Reid, P. Blondel, G. Rowe, A. Pollock, D. Lesbirel, C. Hargreaves, N. Thoume, C. Fallaize, N. Le Page, C. Reeve.
Sub: J. Loveridge.
Goalscorer: Reeve.

This was an excellent and well merited victory for Jersey and it was a proud Dixie A' Court that received the Muratti Vase from Guernsey's Lieut-Gov.

A'Court receiving the Muratti Vase.

Alderney squad.

1 9 7 7

MURATTI SEMI-FINAL.
26 March 1977, Mount Hale, Alderney.

Alderney -0, Jersey -3.

For the first time in their Muratti history Alderney entertained Jersey at Mount Hale. Alderney included the young Nigel Rose who, at 14 years and 11 months, was the youngest ever Muratti player. In total Alderney fielded six new caps in their young team. Jersey included Kerr Cameron (St. Peter) and Micky Cooper (Oaklands) for their first caps.

There was a crowd of around 300 for this historic Muratti match at Mount Hale and they saw Jersey taking only two minutes to score against their young and inexperienced opponents. Alderney keeper Alan Pasquire had the ball in his possession but let it slip and Rory Crick pounced on it and passed to Appleyard who transferred it to Brent Pitman who scored easily. A couple of minutes later Crick had a 'goal' disallowed by referee Trustum, then Nick Rizzuto tested Breuilly in the Jersey goal with a fine free kick. In the 20th minute Dave Cooper sent the ball through to Brent Pitman who in turn set up Crick who hit the ball off the left hand post to put Jersey 2-0 up. Crick had another 'goal' disallowed seven minutes later. Alderney responded with a breakaway by Albert Greatbanks, followed by a shot by Paul Rose that went wide, but the half time arrived with the score Alderney-0, Jersey-2.

Jersey continued on top in the second half but had an early scare when Mick Maurice came close. Jersey then had a third 'goal' disallowed when a Kerr Cameron header found the net, but the score was cancelled. Alderney again went on the attack and Frank Keachie fired in the shot of the match which caused Breuilly to launch himself to the top right hand corner to deflect the ball clear. Jersey came close when Jackie Murphy fed Archie Baillie, but his shot narrowly missed. As the game neared its end Jersey scored a third in the 85th minute when Baillie picked up a Cameron pass to shoot the ball under Pasquire's body into the net. This completed the scoring and the final result was Alderney-0, Jersey-3.

Alderney: A. Pasquire, N. Rose, J. Maurice, M. Richardson, P. Newton,
              A. Greatbanks, F. Keachie, P. Rose, N. Rizzuto, M. Maurice, Bunn.
              Subs: Allcroft, Poynter.

Jersey: B. Breuilly, M. Mathews, M. Cooper, D. Cooper, A. Pitman, J. Murphy,
              K. Cameron, A. Baillie, R. Crick, B. Pitman, E. Appleyard.
              Goalscorers: B. Pitman, Crick, Baillie

This was an excellent performance by the young Alderney team whose average age was 22. The man of the match for the home side was Frank Keachie, although young Nigel Rose had an excellent game. Jersey were worthy winners and their coach, Harry Proffitt, was quite happy with the result and performance.

MURATTI FINAL.
9 May 1977, The Cycling Grounds, Guernsey.

Guernsey -1, Jersey -5.

Guernsey goalkeeper, Dave Jones, was the fourth different goalkeeper that the selectors had chosen in the last four Muratti matches. The two new caps for Guernsey were Dave Jones and Alan Bougourd both of Vale Rec. There were no new caps in the Jersey line-up.

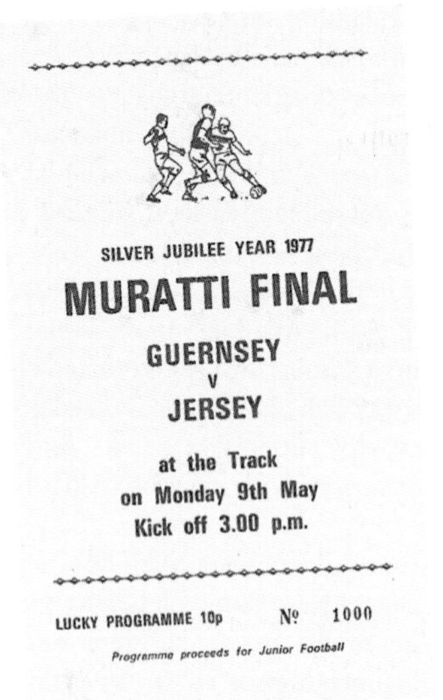

In the lead up to the Muratti Vase final Guernsey had an excellent 3-0 victory against Wokingham Town. It was thought that, following his two goals against Cambridge United and his excellent display against Fulham, that young Craig Allen (Rangers) would appear in the Guernsey side but the selectors did not consider him because, due to his Junior Muratti commitments, he was not available for the final trials against the Marines and Wokingham. Jersey's preparations for this match had gone well and they also recorded an excellent 3-0 win over Wokingham Town although Harry Proffitt, the selector/coach, was not very impressed with the side that was sent over.. There was a late change in the referee when the original official, Jack Taylor, was unable to officiate. The FA then named Mr. J.F. Bent of Hemel Hempstead as his replacement but he was fog bound on his way to Guernsey and with his

Appleyard, A. Pitman, Murphy, Breuilly, M. Cooper,
A'Court, B. Pitman, Crick, Mathews (c), D. Cooper, Fleury
Jersey. - 1977.

Jersey celebrates their opening goal.

non-arrival the senior linesman, Denis Hinsley of Jersey took charge. This was the first time that a Channel Islander had refereed a Muratti Final since Herbie Le Messurier of Guernsey took charge of the 1905 Final in Jersey.

Colin Hargreaves (Guernsey) and 'Mo' Mathews (Jersey) led their teams onto a very wet Cycling Grounds to contest the Silver Jubilee Muratti final. Guernsey had an early opportunity in the 8th minute to take the lead when Gleeson, receiving a pass from Graham, cleverly hooked it over his head into the Jersey goalmouth and the visiting defence just managed to prevent Fallaize from converting. Jersey, however, were shaping as the mote purposeful side and after 11 minutes they were in front. The home defence made two attempts to clear Eddie Appleyard's right wing corner and the ball dropped out to Brent Pitman who chipped it well over the packed goalmouth and out of keeper Jones' reach and into the net.

Just over two minutes later there was panic in the Guernsey defence following a Jersey free kick. Peter Blondel, in attempting to clear, hooked the ball against Jones' right hand post and it rebounded out to Peter Fleury who duly scored Jersey's second. Guernsey nearly pulled one back through Dave Lesbirel in the 17th minute but were denied by the brilliance of Breuilly. Gleeson, in the centre, skilfully laid on a chance for Lesbirel but Breuilly, springing to his left, turned his fine shot away. Crick and Fleury both went close for the visitors before Guernsey reduced the arrears in the 28th minute. Graham took a free kick and slipped the ball to Peter Blondel who found a gap in the Jersey wall and cracked the ball low into the net, beating Breuilly's dive to his right. This goal lifted Guernsey and the home supporters were cheering following a piece of 'Titch' Bougourd magic that had the Jersey defence on edge. Jersey restored their two goal lead in the 35th minute when Brent Pitman found his brother, Alan, overlapping down the left wing. The full back had all the time he needed to measure his cross and Fleury had time to slam home his shot. Guernsey once again responded and Breuilly had to be quick to clear from the feet of both Bougourd and Gleeson; he then held a long range drive from Martyn Loveridge and then saved from a Graham free kick at the second attempt. Half time score was Guernsey-1, Jersey-3.

Guernsey began the second half well and Gleeson saw his header from a Graham corner being tipped onto the bar by Breuilly. In the 62nd minute Gleeson sent a fine pass to Bougourd and he neatly beat Dave Cooper but mis-hit his shot with Breuilly at his mercy. Bougourd and Fallaize both had good chances to score but were unable to connect properly. The Jersey defence were coping very well with the Guernsey attacks and Dixie A'Court, along with Cooper, was very much in control. In the 66th minute Guernsey paid the price for their misses when Alan Pitman took a free kick 30 yards out and the ball swerved over Jones and into the net for the fourth Jersey goal. Fallaize and Lesbirel both had chances to score but it was Jersey who completed the scoring in the 88th minute when Brent Pitman scored from a Jackie Murphy cross to make the final score Guernsey-1, Jersey-5.

Guernsey: D. Jones, M. Loveridge, P. Blondel, C. Hargreaves (c), M. Marquand, D. Lesbirel, N. Thoume, L. Graham, A .Bougourd, C. Fallaize, K. Gleeson. Sub: R. Blondel.
Goalscorer: P. Blondel.

Jersey: B. Breuilly, D. A'Court, M. Cooper, D. Cooper, A. Pitman, J. Murphy, R. Crick, M. Mathews, E. Appleyard, P. Fleury, B. Pitman.
Goalscorers: B. Pitman (2), Fleury (2), A. Pitman.

A disconsolate Art Le Page, the Guernsey coach, felt that his team had been humiliated by a Jersey team that was quicker and more mobile. Best for Guernsey were captain Colin Hargreaves and Kevin Gleeson. Jersey's coach, Harry Proffitt, was delighted with an excellent team performance, with Rory Crick and the Pitman brothers, Alan and Brent, particularly outstanding. Jersey were understandably jubilant and it was skipper Mo Mathews who collected the Muratti Vase.

The jubilant Jersey team with the Muratti Vase.

Jersey manager, Harry Proffitt, holds the Muratti Vase.

1 9 7 8

MURATTI SEMI-FINAL.
March 1978, The Cycling Grounds, Guernsey.

Guernsey -12, Alderney -0.

Alderney had selected young Dale Blanchard (Vale Rec) for his first cap. Dale was in the running to be selected by Guernsey for their Junior Muratti team but was unsuccessful this year.

Bunn, Mortimer, Pasquire, Paul Rose, Nigel Rose, Blanchard, Greatbanks, Richardson, Allcroft, Maurice, Rizutto, Martel, Dupont, Butel.

Guernsey included Brian Knight (Vale Rec) for his first cap as well as selecting him as captain. Knight had joined Reading as an apprentice but signed as a professional in November 1964. He played in the first team three times in 1964/65 and just once the following season although he also played for the 'A' team in 1965/66. He left Reading to join Crawley Town before moving to Guernsey. They also included Craig Allen who became one of the small band of players to gain Senior and Junior Muratti caps in the same season. Other first caps were Colin Le Page (Rangers) and Rodney Webb (St. Martins).

Bunn, Mortimer, Pasquire, Paul Rose, Nigel Rose, Blanchard, Greatbanks, Richardson,
Allcroft, Maurice, Rizutto, Martel, Dupont, Butel.
Alderney.

Brian Knight (Guernsey) and Martin Richardson (Alderney) led their teams onto the Cycling Grounds in front of a small crowd of 353 for what was to be a difficult game for the visitors. Guernsey immediately took control and the Alderney goal survived some very narrow escapes before Webb opened the scoring in 15 minutes with a shot that Pasquire seemed to have turned over the bar, but the ball went behind him. Craig Allen then scored in the 21st and 27th minutes before Webb took a pass from Colin Le Page to make it 4-0 after 40 minutes. Alderney were a little shaken as half time came with the score Guernsey-4, Alderney-0.

Brian Knight.

Three minutes into the second half Webb scored his hat-trick from a Graham corner and five minutes later Allen ran through to score his third and Guernsey's fifth goal. Webb then raced through from a Froome clearance to make it 7-0 and then substitute Le Gallez headed in the eighth as Guernsey kept up the pressure on the shell-shocked Alderney team. Webb then laid on a further two goals for Allen and then Graham scored with a cross-shot for goal number 11. Graham then crossed in for Fallaize to score number 12 for a new Muratti record. The final score was Guernsey-12, Alderney-0.

Guernsey: R. Froome, J. Reid, P. Blondel, C. Hargreaves, M. Loveridge, C. Le Page, B. Knight (c),L. Graham, R. Webb, N. Le Page, C. Allen.
Subs: C. Fallaize, K. Le Gallez.
Goalscorers: Allen (5), Webb (4), Le Gallez, Fallaize, Graham.

Alderney: A. Pasquire, N. Rose, M. Richardson (c), H. Allcroft, D. Blanchard, J. Maurice, A. Greatbanks, P. Rose, N. Butel, N. Rizzuto, P. Bunn.
Subs: Mortimer, J. Martel.

Craig Allen had set a new individual scoring record for a Guernsey player in a Muratti match by scoring five goals. Although Billy Bohan, the Alderney coach, was bitterly disappointed with the result he stated that he thought that Guernsey had brought together a very good team.

It was announced that Mr. F. Cleal, who played eleven times for Guernsey between the years 1908-1914 had died on Monday 10th April 1978 aged 90.

Loveridge, Froome, Chester, N. Le Page, Allen, Le Gallez, Sebire, C. Le Page,
Fallaize, Hargreaves, Graham, Webb, Blondel, Reid.
Guernsey.

MURATTI FINAL.
9 May 1978, Springfield Stadium, Jersey.

Jersey -0, Guernsey -2.

Le Page (far left) crashed the ball past Mathews.

Jersey selectors had chosen an experienced side for their match with Guernsey with only Peter Vincenti (St. Paul's) being a new cap although A. Williams came on as substitute to win his first cap. Guernsey's had one new cap in goalkeeper Dave Chester of Rangers.

The Guernsey midfield were quick to take control of the game at Springfield with Fallaize, Knight and Graham starting to dominate that area and Rodney Webb giving the Jersey defence some anxious moments. Despite this early Guernsey dominance it was not until the 30th minute that they came close to scoring when Allen, coming through on the left, created a chance for himself, but, as he prepared to shoot, the ball got away from him and the chance was gone. Guernsey's opening goal, however, was only delayed and it came in the 37th minute. The Jersey defence made a poor attempt to clear their lines and the ball was headed back into the goalmouth by Webb, and Nigel Le Page held off a challenge to smash the ball low past Dave Mathews.

Three minutes later and the visiting fans were once again celebrating when Fallaize beat his man and sent over a great low ball which Nigel Le Page prodded home for goal number two. Guernsey continued to pressurise the Jersey defence with Graham, Fallaize, Le Page and Webb all coming close. The only real reply came from chances by Vincenti and A' Court which were dealt with by keeper Dave Chester. Half time arrived with the score Jersey-0, Guernsey-2.

The second half began with Crick finding the net but the 'goal' was ruled offside by linesman Satchwell. Although Jersey came more into the game the strong Guernsey defence and midfield were never really troubled. An injured Craig Allen was replaced by Colin Le Page after 55 minutes and he nearly scored when he crashed in a terrific shot that was brilliantly saved by Mathews at the expense of a corner. Graham came close with a great shot that went past the post followed by a Fallaize attempt that hit the same post. Webb was then sent away by an excellent pass from Nigel Le Page but the Jersey defence recovered well to clear. As the game neared its end Jersey had their best chance when Mick Cooper fired his shot over the bar. There was no more scoring and the game ended Jersey-0, Guernsey-2.

Jersey: D. Mathews, D.A'Court, M. Cooper, A. Pitman, J. Murphy, P. Vincenti, M. Mathews, P. Fleury, R. Crick, B. Pitman. Subs: A. Guegan, A. Williams.

Guernsey: D. Chester, C. Hargreaves, P. Blondel, K. Le Gallez, M. Loveridge, C. Fallaize, B. Knight (c), L. Graham, C. Allen, N. Le Page, R. Webb
Sub: C. Le Page.
Goal scorer: N. Le Page (2).

This was a superb team effort by Guernsey who never allowed Jersey to get into the game and Harry Proffitt, the Jersey coach, conceded that the visitors competed harder and were the better team. The Muratti Vase was presented to skipper Brian Knight by the Bailiff of Jersey Sir Frank Ereaut. Knight said that he was absolutely delighted to have been involved with ,and skippered, such a team. He also added a word of praise for those players who did not get on and took their disappointment like sportsmen.

Skipper Brian Knight and goal-scorer Nigel Le Page with the Muratti Vase.

1 9 7 9

MURATTI SEMI-FINAL.
27 March 1979, Springfield Stadium, Jersey.

Jersey -8, Alderney -0.

Following their heavy defeat the previous year the Alderney selectors picked three new caps in their team for their match against Jersey at Springfield and included Ian. McFarlane, John Malloy and Nigel Dupont. They have lost the services of Norman Butel who is currently out of action with an ankle injury.

The teams came out at Springfield in front of a crowd of 500 to contest this Muratti semi-final. As the match began Alderney were under immediate pressure and held out until the 9th minute when Jersey went ahead with Brent Pitman rising on the edge of the penalty area to head a free kick from his brother, Alan, into the top right hand corner of the net. Jersey came close to increasing this lead on a number of occasions but the good goalkeeping of Pasquire kept them out until the 29th minute when Mo Mathews, from a Brent Pitman pass, squeezed a low shot just inside the left hand post. Straight from the kick off Jersey gained a right wing corner and from Mathew's kick Alan Pitman headed in number three. Pasquire then had a brilliant save from a Mathews header to prevent Jersey going even further ahead but a minute before half time he was beaten by Brent Pitman who converted a cross from Cunningham. Half time, Jersey-4, Alderney-0.

Jersey continued the scoring within 5 minutes of the second half. Pasquire got down to make a great save from a 25 yard blast by A'Court but was unable to hold the ball and Fleury slipped it into the net. The Alderney defence held out, with Pasquire particularly busy, until near the end when Fleury scored number six after a ball by Ian Corfield was not cleared. Fleury again scored after a header by Alan Williams was cleared off the line and then Brent Pitman completed his hat-trick from a free kick to make the final score Jersey-8, Alderney-0.

Jersey: D. Mathews, I. Corfield,
A. Williams, M. Cooper, A. Pitman,\
J. Murphy, D. A'Court, M. Mathews,
A. Cunningham, P. Fleury, B. Pitman.
Sub: Martin, Herbert.
Goalscorers: Fleury (3), B. Pitman (3),
A. Pitman, M. Mathews.

Alderney: A. Pasquire, N. Rose,
M. Richardson, F. Keachie, P. Rose,
Greenslade, N. Rizzuto, A. Greatbanks,
 I. McFarlane, Dupont, J. Malloy.
Sub: M. Maurice, Mortimer.

Peter Fleury's Muratti Cap.

Referee Robinson congratulates the JEP's Bill Custard who was reporting on his 52nd Muratti.

Kevin Le Gallez (Guernsey) greets Alan Pitman (Jersey) as referee Robinson looks on.

MURATTI FINAL.
9 May 1979, The Cycling Grounds, Guernsey.

Guernsey-5, Jersey-0.

Bill Custard, the sports reporter for the Jersey Evening Post, was reporting on his last Muratti match. This was to be his 52nd Muratti and he was congratulated by referee Robinson prior to the match.

Guernsey selected an experienced side with only one new cap in Willie Kennedy of St. Martins. Jersey also had only one new cap in their team with A. Herbert (St. Paul's) making his debut.

Guernsey began the match very well and took the lead after five minutes. Willie Kennedy fired in a shot that Mathews did well to push round the post. Webb took the corner from the left and Le Gallez rose high to head the ball home. This was the start Guernsey were

Guernsey open the scoring through Le Gallez.

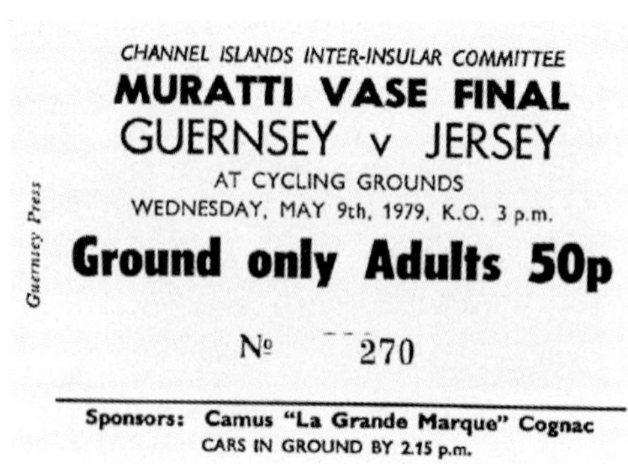

hoping for and they were so much on top that it was 20 minutes before Froome had to make a save. Peter Blondel then came close when he received a long throw in from Fallaize only to shoot straight at Mathews. Jersey stepped up the pace and Rory Crick came close to equalising and then Froome had to rush out as Brent Pitman chased through on a long ball from A'Court. Guernsey then went further ahead in the 34th minute when Le Gallez picked up a loose Jersey clearance and sent a beautiful pass to Kennedy, unmarked on the right, who hammered a hard low shot into the far side of the net. Jersey retaliated and a Williams header had beaten Froome but Hargreaves was covering the line and headed clear. With five minutes remaining of the half, Blondel took a free kick 50 yards from the Jersey goal and sent the ball right down the centre. Mathews came out but Fallaize leapt with him and got his head to the ball to make the half time score Guernsey-3, Jersey-0.

Early in the second half Blondel took another free kick and Webb's shot was partially cleared, Fallaize picked up the loose ball and swept into the box where he was brought down by Williams.

Referee Robinson was in an excellent position and had no hesitation in awarding a penalty. Blondel stepped up and sent the ball past Mathews' left for Guernsey's fourth goal. Jersey responded and Froome did well to put a Jackie Murphy corner over the bar and then Brent Pitman saw his header flash narrowly over. The final goal came when Le Gallez received a pass from Hargreaves and sent the ball into the Jersey centre. Mathews raced out to claim it before Webb but he lost the ball and Webb slipped the ball into the net to make the final score Guernsey-5, Jersey-0.

Guernsey: R. Froome, K. Allen, P. Blondel, R. Depres, C. Hargreaves, C. Fallaize, K. Le Gallez, M. Loveridge, W. Kennedy, N. Le Page, R. Webb.
Sub: A. Le Page, C. Le Page.
Goalscorers: Fallaize, Blondel (pen), Le Gallez, Kennedy, Webb.

Jersey: D. Mathews, D. A'Court, A. Williams, H. Herbert, A. Pitman (c), J. Murphy, M. Mathews, A. Cunningham, R. Crick, P. Fleury, B. Pitman.
Sub: G. Pinel, M. Cooper.

This was a superb performance by Guernsey and the local press stated that it avenged the 1977 result. The Muratti Vase was presented to the victorious Kevin Le Gallez by Guernsey's Lieutenant-Governor Vice Admiral Sir John Martin. The Jersey coach, Harry Proffitt, was very disappointed in his own team's performance but was full of praise for the home side. This was Guernsey's first home victory for 10 years.

This victory gave Guernsey a 31-30 lead in Muratti victories with Jersey.

During this decade both Guernsey and Jersey won five Muratti Vase Finals apiece. The overall score was now Guernsey 31 wins, Jersey 30 wins and Alderney 1 win. The Vase was shared in 1937.

Le Gallez receives the Muratti Vase from Guernsey's Lieut-Governor.

13
1980 - 1989

Alderney supporters.

1 9 8 0

MURATTI SEMI-FINAL.
29 March 1980, Mount Hale, Alderney.

Alderney -0, Guernsey -5.

Alderney had two new caps in their starting line up in Patrick Burland and Peter Walters with Arthur Jupp on the bench. Guernsey had one new cap for their match with Alderney at Mount Hale and he was Colin Bourgaize of North. This was the 60th anniversary of Alderney's Muratti victory of 1920 and Billy Bohan returned as goalkeeper as well as being selected as the team captain. Alderney coach, Dave Hugman, and Guernsey coach, Jim Cooley, were confident of an exciting match. The Guernsey team were based at the Sea View Hotel and held a practice match on the beach before the match.

Guernsey began the match with the strong wind at their backs which helped to give them an early advantage. Bohan was quickly brought into action and he made a superb save from a Fallaize header. In the 17th minute the Guernsey skipper, Kevin Le Gallez, gained possession on the left after a thrust by Fallaize and crossed in for Bougourd to whip in a fast header that gave Bohan no chance. The game became very even and both teams seemed to cancel each other out with no one getting on top. Alderney had a double escape in the 41st minute when first the bar and then Frank Keachie on the line prevented Graham from scoring. A minute later, however, a shot by Fallaize flashed home off Bohan's knees and inside the keeper's left hand post. Less than a minute after that Alderney lost the ball from the restart and, from a few yards inside their half, Fallaize, spotting the keeper out of his goal, fired in a shot that went in under the bar with Bohan scrambling backwards. With one minute remaining of the half Bougourd centred the ball for Willie Kennedy to finish off well and make the half time score Alderney-0, Guernsey-4.

As the second half began Fallaize went down Guernsey's right and turned to cross left footed for Kennedy to head home for his second goal to put Guernsey 5-0 ahead. Chris Hamon was then called into action when he rose well to keep out Malloy's great effort. The game swung to the other end and Bohan had a brilliant double save from Le Gallez; Blondel, Rowe, Colin Le Page and Graham all went close but the Alderney defence held out. In the last minute substitute Webb missed an easy chance but the game ended Alderney-0, Guernsey-5.

Alderney: W. Bohan (c), P. Burland, T. Pasquire, F. Keachie, H. Allcroft, A. Greatbanks, P. Rose, P. Cunningham, P. Walters, N. Rizzuto, P. Bunn. Sub: J. Malloy, A. Jupp.

Guernsey: C. Hamon, C. Bourgaize, P. Blondel, G. Rowe, A. Pollock, C. Le Page, K. Le Gallez (c), L. Graham, W. Kennedy, C. Fallaize, A. Bougourd. Sub: N. Le Page, R. Webb. Goalscorers: Bougourd, Fallaize (2), Kennedy (2).

The final result was a little hard on Alderney with three of the goals coming in a three minute spell before half time. The Guernsey coach, Jim Cooley, felt that his team had played well in patches. Dave Hugman, the Alderney coach, could draw encouragement from the performance, particularly young Patrick Burland on his debut.

Fallaize whips the ball past Bohan for Guernsey's second.

Alderney.

MURATTI FINAL.
9 May 1980, Springfield Stadium, Jersey.

Jersey -1, Guernsey -2. aet.

Jersey selected five new caps for their match with Guernsey in Peter Jones (First Tower), Charlie Lumsden (Oaklands), Colin McLeod (First Tower), Neil Livesey (Wanderers) and Steve Dewhurst (Oaklands). Guernsey's only new cap was Roy Brehaut of North.

Jersey began the match the sharpest pushing Guernsey onto the defence with fast aggressive football and almost scored in the 2nd minute when a McLeod drive just cleared the bar. Ron Depres hit his own bar as he chipped the ball back when put under pressure by Dewhurst two minutes later. Vincenti was causing Guernsey all sorts of problems especially when he combined with Dewhurst and McLeod. Guernsey managed to survive this onslaught and thought that they had scored in the 22nd minute when Kennedy sent the ball into the goalmouth which resulted in Breuilly rushing out to clear from Fallaize, and Nigel Le Page cracked the loose ball into the net. Referee Midgley, however, disallowed this goal after consulting his linesman, Mo Le Var. Three minutes later Vincenti sent in a great ball through the middle of the Guernsey defence and Hamon did well to stop young Livesey from scoring. The ball broke to Dewhurst who, from the left, swept it into the net just inside Hamon's left hand post to put Jersey 1-0 ahead. Guernsey then regained their shape and began to pressurise the home defence and Breuilly was forced into an acrobatic tip-over from a Le Gallez hook. Le Gallez then saw his header crash off the bar and, following a Brehaut free kick, Rowe then fired his shot inches over the bar from a Blondel free-kick to leave the half time score Jersey-1, Guernsey-0.

The second half began with Livesey, and then Pinel, threatening Hamon's goal but Guernsey settled and within five minutes they had equalised when Brehaut took a cut back pass from the right by-line from Fallaize and hammered the ball past Breuilly.

Jersey then put a lot of pressure on the Guernsey defence with Le Gallez clearing off his own line and McLeod saw his shot crash off the Guernsey bar as they tried to regain the lead. The tempo of the match was increased and in the 63rd minute a brilliant run and cross by Pitman found Vincenti, and his header was blocked on the line by Blondel and the ball was grabbed by Hamon. Vincenti then went in on Hamon and this resulted in a flare up with players tumbling into the net. After team-mates had managed to restrain the pair, Vincenti had a bleeding mouth and Blondel a cut on the back of his head. Referee Neil Midgley firstly sent off Vincenti and then Blondel to make them the first players to be sent off in a Muratti match. As things calmed down Jersey appeared to have taken the lead when Livesey scored from a Peter Jones cross but this 'goal' was disallowed as Hamon had been fouled and at the end of regulation time the score was Jersey-1, Guernsey-1.

The first real chance in extra time fell to Jersey but Brent Pitman's effort did not trouble Hamon. In the 11th minute Chris Hamon sent a long ball down the middle which was headed on by Lesbirel and then Fallaize for Willie Kennedy to chip it past Breuilly's left hand to put Guernsey 2-1 ahead. The remainder of the match was very even, and there was no more scoring and the result was Jersey-1, Guernsey-2.

Breuilly is beaten by Brehaut's shot for Guernsey's equalising goal.

Kevin Le Gallez with the Muratti Vase.

Jersey: B. Breuilly, P. Jones, D. A'Court, A. Herbert, A. Pitman, G. Pinel, Lumsden, McLeod, N. Livesey, S. Dewhurst, P. Vincenti.
Sub: B. Pitman, R. Crick.
Goalscorer: Dewhurst.

Guernsey: C. Hamon, G. Rowe, P. Blondel, R. Depres, A. Pollock, R. Brehaut, K. Le Gallez (c), D. Lesbirel, W. Kennedy, N. Le Page, C. Fallaize.
Sub: C. Bourgaize, A. Bougourd.
Goalscorers: Brehaut, Kennedy.

This was a tight and tense match and Jersey could consider themselves unlucky to have finished up losers. The Guernsey coach, Jim Cooley, conceded that his side had experienced a series of escapes and that the home team had not enjoyed the breaks.

As the Muratti Vase was being presented to Kevin Le Gallez by Jersey's Lieut-Gov, Sir Peter Whiteley, a gang of spectators were shouting obscenities much to the embarrassment of all those present.

1 9 8 1

MURATTI SEMI-FINAL.
21 March 1981, Mount Hale, Alderney.

Alderney -0, Jersey -5.

Once again Alderney's preparations suffered when they lost the services of Frank Keachie due to a fractured collar bone. Trevor Pasquire travelled from Nottingham to replace him in the team. Alderney player/coach, Billy Bohan was prepared for a hard fought match and although skipper Paul Rose was declared fit it was reported that he had a cracked rib. Jersey had four new caps in Keith Le Cornu (St. Peter), Mel Hales (First Tower), Peter Lock (St. Paul's) and Paul Harzo (St. Paul's) and it was noted that Barry Breuilly, in the Jersey goal, equalled the 19 caps won by Guernsey's Gerve Brazier.

Jersey began the match with the advantage of the stiff breeze at a windswept Mount Hale. The visitors were encamped in the Alderney half and immediately put Keeper Billy Bohan under severe pressure.

After nine minutes he pulled off a tremendous save by leaping, twisting and tipping over an attempt by Brent Pitman. A minute later, however, Jersey took the lead when Lock set up Rory Crick and his mis-hit shot wrong-footed Bohan and entered the net. Five minutes later Le Cornu set up Lock and he chipped in goal number two and a little later Brent Pitman scored when he collected a low ball from the left that eluded the Alderney defence. Alderney then suffered a blow when they lost the services of Peter Cunningham after 20 minutes due to a pulled calf muscle. Despite the scoreline the Alderney defence were performing well under the onslaught with Bohan, Pasquire, Richardson and young Paddy Burland performing heroics for the home side. Half time arrived with the score Alderney-0, Jersey-3.

Alderney took advantage of the wind to put some pressure on the Jersey defence and Breuilly was called into action when he saved a wind-assisted drive from the centre circle by Trevor Pasquire.

Referee Trevor Savident was suffering from Achilles tendon trouble most of the game and just after half-time he swapped roles with John Rolph, running the line on Alderney's behalf. Savident, however, had to give up running the line and he was replaced by the Alderney trainer, Louie Dupont. Paul Bunn then just failed to get his head to a cross ball and the chance was gone. Bert Greatbanks thought that he had put Bunn into a scoring position but substitute linesman, Louie Dupont, raised his flag for offside. Jersey withstood this push by Alderney and substitute Andy Cunningham completed the scoring with his two goals in the last 15 minutes to make the final score Alderney-0, Jersey-5.

Billy Bohan cuts out a Jersey cross.

Peter Vincenti jumps between Alderney's Pasquire and Richardson.

The Alderney team with three loyal supporters.

Alderney: W. Bohan, P. Burland, Pasquire, M. Richardson , Aldcroft, McFarlane,
              P. Newton, P. Rose (c), P. Cunningham, P. Bunn, Turner.
              Subs: A. Greatbanks, Malloy.

Jersey: B. Breuilly, P. Jones, M. Hales, A. Herbert, P. Harzo, K. Le Cornu,
              D. A'Court, R. Crick, B. Pitman, P. Lock, P. Vincenti.
              Subs: K. Cameron, A. Cunningham.
              Goalscorers: Crick, Lock, Pitman, Cunningham (2).

Alderney FA's new chief, Peter Cunningham, had nothing but praise for his team saying that he thought they had given a very good performance. Best for Alderney were man-of-the-match Billy Bohan, Pasquire, Richardson and Burland. The Jersey officials were not all that happy with their side's performance. Coach, Peter Heald, commented that they appeared to miss Peter Taylor and found it difficult to cope with the windy conditions. Best for Jersey were new cap Keith Le Cornu and substitute Cunningham.

MURATTI FINAL.
4 May 1981, The Cycling Grounds, Guernsey.

Guernsey -1, Jersey -4.

Jersey included Barry Breuilly (First Tower) in goal for his 20th cap, a record for a goal-keeper and they also selected Peter Taylor (St. Paul's) for his first cap. Guernsey selected Colin McKane and Andy Rowe, both of North, for their first caps. Guernsey went into this

Peter Vincenti jumps between Alderney's Pasquire and Richardson.

Alan Herbert receives the Muratti Vase from Sir Peter Le Cheminant.

match without the services of Peter Blondel who had been disciplined by the Guernsey Football Association.

Jersey had the advantage of the stiff breeze that was blowing down the pitch but they were finding it difficult to use it to their advantage. With this wind dominating play it was not until the 40th minute that a genuine chance was created. A huge throw in by Fallaize from the left touchline was headed in by Andy Rowe and was well punched clear by Breuilly. Jersey appeared to be coping with the conditions better but despite forcing a series of corners they were not particularly dangerous.

With two minutes remaining in the half Jersey scored when Le Cornu crossed the ball in from their right wing and Peter Taylor broke away from Glyn Smith and leapt in at the near post to loop a header that curled over Chris Hamon. This goal stunned Guernsey but straight from the kick off Jersey won possession and from all of 25 yards Keith Le Cornu sent in a swerving left foot shot that went into the top left hand corner of Hamon's net to make the half time score Guernsey-0, Jersey-2.

Guernsey came out fighting for the second half and in the first minute Willie Kennedy found Andy Rowe who sent in a left foot shot that was saved by Breuilly. Fallaize then headed a Le Gallez free kick just wide of the opposite post. Jersey then began to establish superiority in the mid-field and Hamon saved his team when he blocked a shot by Vincenti as he worked his way through the home defence. Alan Herbert, the Jersey captain, then sent in a fast cross that Le Cornu just failed to connect with. Guernsey sent on Roy Brehaut for Kennedy in an attempt to get back into the game and, from a Le Gallez cross, he shot just outside of the Jersey post. The visitors were looking very confident and with ten minutes remaining they scored again when Lock was sent clear on the left by a Cunningham pass and he returned the ball to Cunningham to rifle his shot past the helpless Hamon.

Jersey Goalscorers Andy Cunningham, Keith Le Cornu, Peter Lock and Peter Taylor.

Jersey pressed on and Hamon did well to turn another Cunningham shot over the bar. Then, following a free kick on Jersey's left, the ball reached Crick on the opposite side of the field and he sent it back across the face of the goal for Lock to turn it in from close range. Guernsey scored a consolation goal three minutes from time when substitute Tony Tostevin cut the ball past Breuilly from the right to make the final score Guernsey-1, Jersey-4.

Guernsey: C. Hamon, C. Bourgaize, C. McKane, G. Rowe, A. Pollock, G. Smith, K. Le Gallez (c), C. Fallaize, W. Kennedy, A. Rowe, R. Webb.
Sub: R. Brehaut, A. Tostevin
Goalscorer: Tostevin.

Jersey: B. Breuilly, P. Jones, D. A'Court, A. Herbert (c), P. Harzo, K. Le Cornu, R. Crick, P. Taylor, A. Cunningham, P. Lock, P. Vincenti.
Sub: B. Pitman, K. Cameron.
Goalscorers: Taylor, Le Cornu, Lock, Cunningham.

This was a thoroughly professional display by Jersey and they outthought and outplayed the home side in most departments. Alan Herbert collected the Muratti Vase from Guernsey's Lieut-Governor, Sir Peter Le Cheminant, and he later described it as the best moment of his career.

FIFA referee, Pat Partridge said that he enjoyed the match because the players allowed the game to flow. The windy conditions, he added, ensured that there were mistakes but both teams tried hard to entertain. Jubilant Jersey coach, Peter Head, said that he always thought that his side would play better against the wind and that Rory Crick was their best player.

1 9 8 2

MURATTI SEMI-FINAL.
24 March 1982, Corbet Field, Guernsey.

Guernsey -5, Alderney -1.

For the first time in Muratti history a Guernsey home match was not played at the Cycling Grounds when, on 24 March 1982, Guernsey hosted Alderney at the Corbet Field.

Guernsey coach Jim Cooley was confident of a home victory with a team that included Chris Dyer, Mark and Kevin Le Tissier for their first caps. The Alderney preparations were upset when Nottingham based striker, Trevor Pasquire had to withdraw due to an injured ankle but they had Alan Davies who was gaining his first cap. The Alderney team arrived in Guernsey on Wednesday 23 March and were based in the White Gables Hotel, Forest.

It took the home side a little time to settle and it was not until the 10th minute that they took the lead when following some skilful play by Colin Le Page he set up Alan Bougourd who scored easily. The Alderney defence was well marshalled by Scot Frank Keachie, ably supported by Billy Bohan and Peter Cunningham. Mid-way through the first half Keachie dashed up-field and fired in a shot that just went over the bar. Just before half-time, however, Alderney lost a controversial goal. Guernsey were awarded a rather harsh indirect free-kick for obstruction just inside the penalty box. The ball was passed to Kevin Le Tissier and he slipped it into the right-hand corner of the net. The Alderney defence complained that as Le Tissier shot there were two Guernsey players in an offside position. Referee Dave Billingham waived away their protests and the half ended Guernsey-2, Alderney-0.

Within six minutes of the second half Guernsey increased their lead when Colin Fallaize scored following some good work by Lawrence Graham and Kevin Le Tissier. Graham was

Kevin Le Tissier scores goal number two.

again involved as he set up Fallaize for his second and Guernsey's fourth goal. Bohan came to Alderney's rescue with a brave save from Kevin Le Tissier and then had some luck when a Bougourd shot rebounded off the inside of the post and into his hands. As the game wore on Bohan unfortunately gave away a penalty when he grabbed Bougourd, and Graham stepped up to score. Alderney's main moment of the match came in the 74th minute when, following a Paddy Burland corner, John Maloy headed brilliantly past Chris Hamon. This goal appeared to upset the Guernsey defence and they seemed to panic when Alderney broke into the attack. The game settled down and the whistle arrived with the score Guernsey-5, Alderney-1.

Guernsey: C. Hamon, J. Reid, A. Le Page, K. Le Gallez, C. Hargreaves, C. Le Page, C. Dyer, L. Graham, A. Bougourd, C. Fallaize, K. Le Tissier.
Subs: M. Le Tissier, R. Loaring.
Goalscorers: Bougourd, K. Le Tissier, Fallaize (2), Graham (pen).

Alderney: W. Bohan, P. Burland, M. Richardson, A. Davies, F. Keachie, P. Cunningham, N. Rizzuto, I. McFarlane, P. Newton, N. Dupont, J. Maloy.
Subs: A. Greatbanks, Rose.
Goalscorer: Maloy.

Alderney's Charlie Dupont was very disappointed with the final score and felt that they did not deserve a 5-1 beating. Jim Cooley was full of praise for the Alderney side saying that it was one of the best that Guernsey had played. The match ball, donated by a well-known local sports personality who wished to remain anonymous, was presented to John Maloy. Maloy's goal was the first scored by Alderney against Guernsey for 20 years and the first since Frank Keachie's against Jersey in 1975. This was not a very convincing per-formance by Guernsey who were best served by Alan 'Tich' Bougourd, Colin Le Page and, in the second half, Lawrence Graham. It was also felt that Guernsey would have to improve for their match against Jersey. Following this match a buffet disco was held at the White Gables Hotel in honour of the Alderney team. This had been organised by the Guernsey selectors.

MURATTI FINAL.
9 May 1982, Springfield Stadium, Jersey.

Jersey -2, Guernsey -1.

Jersey had four new caps in their line up in Martin Le Blancq (First Tower), Tommy Mogan (St. Paul's), Paul Duffy (St. Paul's) and Gary Westwood (First Tower). Martin Le Blancq had returned to Jersey after a spell as a semi-pro with Oxford City. Jersey's prepa-rations were enhanced by St. Pauls' victory against the semi-professionals of Wimbourne Town in the final of the Dorset Senior Cup followed three days later by the 2-0 victory over Vale Rec in the Upton. It was no surprise that there were five St. Pauls players in Jersey's final team. The referee for the match was Keith Hackett (Sheffield) who refereed

Gary Westwood, Paul Duffy, Martin Le Blancq, Rory Crick (c), Tommy Mogan,
Keith Le Cornu, Steve Dewhurst, Peter Vincenti, Peter Taylor, Peter Lock, Dixie A'Court.

the 1981 FA Cup Final between Tottenham Hotspur and Manchester City.

The early exchanges were very tight, Jersey adopted a man-for-man marking system with Tommy Mogan assigned to Colin Fallaize and Dixie A'Court policing Kevin Le Tissier. This system appeared to work and soon the Jersey midfield was on top. Jersey nearly took the lead after 8 minutes when Steve Dewhurst sent in a great cross-field ball that was collected by Keith Le Cornu, in a lot of space, on the right side but he was denied by a fine Chris Hamon save. Guernsey found it difficult to get in to the game but it was not until the 21st minute that Jersey made their superiority pay. Under no real pressure Mark Le Tissier attempted a pass back to Hamon but instead the ball found Pete Lock. Lock was taken by surprise and although his shot was not well hit it still slipped past Hamon's left hand and into the net. Jersey remained in control and increased their lead in the 38th minute when, following a Le Cornu corner, Mark Le Tissier headed the ball out only to see it cannon off Rory Crick's head and into the back of the net. As half time approached Lock was denied through a superb tackle by Le Gallez and at half time the score was Jersey-2, Guernsey-0.

Under pressure from Le Tissier, Dixie A'Court slides the ball past Le Blancq.

The second half began with a penetrating run by Andy Le Page in the opening minute. He sent in an excellent cross which was not collected by a Guernsey forward and the chance was lost. In the 49th minute Bougourd and Fallaize combined to set up a Guernsey attack. Kevin Le Tissier put Jersey's A'Court under severe pressure and this resulted in him putting the ball past his own keeper to make the score 2-1.

This goal gave Guernsey a great lift and Colin Le Page brought Le Blancq to his knees with a fine drive and moments later Le Blancq brought off a superb save from Bougourd. Guernsey had gained the midfield advantage through Colin Le Page and Chris Dyer as they strove in search of an equaliser. It nearly came when Bougourd received a pass from Kevin Le Tissier and cut inside his marker to send in a shot from just inside the penalty area. The ball was curling just under the bar when Le Blancq touched it over with a fantastic save. With nine minutes remaining Hamon saved well to prevent Dewhurst converting an A'Court cross into the net. The game ended with Jersey defending their slender lead and the match ended Jersey-2, Guernsey-1.

Jersey: M. Le Blancq, D. A'Court, T. Mogan, P. Duffy, G. Westwood, K. Le Cornu, R. Crick (c), P. Taylor, P. Vincenti, P. Lock, S. Dewhurst.
Subs: McLeod, Gammon.
Goalscorers: Lock, Crick.

Guernsey: C. Hamon, A. Le Page, K. Le Gallez (c), M. Le Tissier, C. Hargreaves, C. Le Page, C. Dyer, L. Graham, A. Bougourd, K. Le Tissier, C. Fallaize.
Sub: J. Reid.
Goalscorer: og.

After the game Guernsey's Lieut-Governer, Sir Peter Le Cheminant, presented the Muratti Vase to the victorious Jersey skipper Rory Crick.

Jersey coach, Peter Heald, conceded that his side had won the game on their first half performance but added that they had showed great character in the second half as Guernsey put them under considerable pressure. On his return from Jersey, Guernsey coach Jim Cooley was critical of the fact that no GFA official had accompanied the squad. It was also pointed out that the GFA flag was forgotten and was not flying from the Springfield mast on Sunday afternoon.

Jersey skipper, Rory Crick receives the Muratti Vase from Sir Peter le Cheminant.

1 9 8 3

MURATTI SEMI-FINAL.
9 April 1983 – Springfield Stadium, Jersey.

Jersey -6, Alderney -1.

Jersey's form going into this match was unimpressive following a 1-0 win over Southern Amateurs League side Lloyds Bank. Carberry scored the winning goal seconds from the finish. Jersey dominated from start to finish and should have won more convincingly. They were still confident, however, in progressing to the final. They included three new caps in their starting line-up with Jim Wylie (Jersey Scottish), Neville Davidson (St. Paul's) and Paul Carberry (First Tower). Alderney announced that 38-year-old goalkeeper Billy Bohan would be playing up front. Bohan had gained his first Muratti cap as a 16-year-old in 1961 as an outfield player. Bohan had originally asked not to be selected but relented as he had been in training for the London Marathon (along with team mate Martin Richardson).

Trevor Pasquire was travelling in from his home in Nottingham arriving on the morning of the match. Alderney included three new caps in goalkeeper Derek Oakman and Steve Davies, both of Alderney Athletics, and Peter Concanen of Northern Belles.

As expected Jersey were immediately on the attack but found a sturdy Alderney defence that was well marshalled by Trevor Pasquire ably supported by Oakman. Peter Concanen was also very impressive and he showed a willingness to run at and take on opponents. Alderney managed to control the Jersey attacks until the 20th minute when Paul Carberry cut in along the right and turned the ball back for Peter Taylor to open the scoring. Taylor and Vincenti then combined to lay on a goal for Lock and then Carberry set up chances for Vincenti and Rory Crick which they both dispatched past the helpless Oakman. Carberry then ran a long ball around the keeper to score number five and Lock was in the act of heading in number six when referee Rolph blew for half time leaving the score Jersey-5, Alderney-0.

Rory Crick crashes in Jersey's fourth goal past a despairing Derek Oakman.

Early in the second half Concanen created a chance for Paul Newton and later he collected a Burland pass to fire in a shot that Le Blancq saved. Jersey seemed to have lost their sense of urgency and at times seemed to overplay the ball as well as finding Oakman in excellent form. Alderney's special moment came in the 76th minute when Paddy Burland crossed in a ball that found Bohan just inside the penalty area on Alderney's left, he slipped as he shot but the ball went in low beyond Le Blancq just inside the far post. As the game was nearing its end Jersey substitute Dewhurst completed the scoring with an unstoppable shot for goal number 6. Taylor had the ball in the net twice but both scores were ruled off side and the final result was Jersey-6, Alderney-1.

Jersey: M. Le Blancq, D. A'Court, J. Wylie, P. Duffy, G. Westwood, N. Davidson, R. Crick, P. Taylor, P. Carberry, P. Lock, P. Vincenti.
Sub: S. Dewhurst, P. Harzo.
Goalscorers: Taylor, Lock, Vincenti, Crick Carberry, Dewhurst.

Alderney: D. Oakman, N. Rose, F. Keachie, M. Richardson, T. Pasquire, A. Davies, P. Burland, P. Concanen, S. Davies, P. Newton, W. Bohan.
Sub: I. McFarlane, A. Greatbanks, M. Cocquelin.
Goalscorer: W. Bohan.

Peter Heald, the Jersey manager felt that the game had been won through their first half performance. The Alderney coach, George Dale, was very pleased with the effort his team put in and felt that the score flattered Jersey. After the game JFA president, John Sherry paid tribute to Bohan and Oakman and presented them with association ties and named the keeper as his man-of-the-match.

MURATTI FINAL.
2 May 1983 – The Cycling Grounds, Guernsey.

Guernsey -2, Jersey -1.

Guernsey's manager, Harold Allen, included Dale Blanchard (Vale Rec) in their starting line-up for his first senior Guernsey cap. Dale played for Alderney against Guernsey in the 1978 Muratti semi-final. They also included Neil Laine and Carl Le Tissier of Vale Rec as well as Neil Hunter (Rangers) for their first caps. As both of their goalkeepers, Chris Hamon and Jon Dorey were nursing injuries Guernsey called Nigel Pinsard (North) into the squad. Chris Hamon was injured during Guernsey's 7-1 defeat by an FA XI. Peter Blondel returned to the side after two years and was installed as captain.

Dale Blanchard.

Jersey Muratti squad.

Rather surprisingly Jersey decided not to select Brent Pitman for the squad. Pitman had scored a hat-trick in First Tower's 4-2 Upton victory against Vale Rec. The Jersey side was an experienced one with only Neville Davidson making his debut.

It was announced that there would be a Muratti man-of-the-match trophy presented after this game. It was to be called the 'Ossie Eloury Memorial Trophy'. The trophy was donated by Magpies Football Club in memory of the late Mr. Ossie Eloury who was president at the time of his death on 28 December 1982. The winner of the award was to be decided by a panel of three - one representative from each of the JFA, GFA, or AFA, depending on who was in the final and they would be joined by a representative of the Magpies. This year's panel consisted of Dick Parker (JFA), Graham Skuse (GFA) and Nino Orengo (Magpies).

Kevin Le Tissier scores Guernsey's second goal.

The game was only one minute old when referee Downey booked Blondel for a foul on Peter Lock. The game was very tight with Jersey just edging the opening exchanges and had three chances to go ahead from crosses by Dewhurst but were unable to convert any of them due to some fine defending by goalkeeper Hamon and full back Hargreaves. After 20 minutes, however, Guernsey opened the scoring when Blondel took a free kick and sent the ball down the right for Le Page to centre. The ball beat both Vincenti and A'Court and Hunter grasped his opportunity to control and shoot past the helpless Le Blancq. Just before half time Jersey lost the services of the influential Peter Taylor due to a head gash and he was replaced by Peter Fleury. Guernsey had a chance to increase their lead when Laine broke through and played a quick one-two with Kevin Le Tissier but he was unlucky with his final header. Half time arrived with the score Guernsey-1, Jersey-0.

There was an explosive start to the second half when Colin Le Page fed Kevin Le Tissier who left Gary Westwood trailing and he cut in from the right to beat Martin Le Blancq with a glorious right foot shot into the far top corner for 2-0.

Five minutes after that score Jersey opened their account when another Steve Dewhurst centre from the left saw substitute Fleury come in between two defenders for a near post header that Hamon touched but couldn't divert. This goal gave Jersey a great lift and Fleury shot just inches wide from a Dewhurst pass. The game was now very even with occasional chances at both ends but Guernsey nearly increased their slender lead in the closing minutes when a Hargreaves-Bougourd- Falla move presented Bougourd with a chance which went awry. The final score was Guernsey-2, Jersey-1.

Guernsey: C. Hamon, C. Hargreaves, K. Le Gallez, P. Blondel (c), D. Blanchard, C. Le Page, C. Dyer, N. Laine, C. Le Tissier, N. Hunter, K. Le Tissier.
Sub: A. Bougourd, N. Falla.
Goalscorers: Hunter, K. Le Tissier.

Jersey: M. Le Blancq, P. Harzo, D. A'Court, P. Duffy, G. Westwood, N. Davidson, R. Crick (c), P. Taylor, P. Vincenti, P. Lock, S. Dewhurst.
Sub: P. Fleury, P. Carberry.
Goalscorer: Fleury.

Peter Blondel received the Muratti Vase from the Lieutenant-Governor of Guernsey, Sir Peter Le Cheminant.

This was a hard fought victory for Guernsey and JFA president, John Sherry, thought that the home side were just that bit better.

The first presentation of the Ossie Eloury Memorial Award for the Man-of-the-Match went to Guernsey captain; Peter Blondel. He received the trophy form the Lieutenant Governor of Jersey, General Sir Peter Whitley.

Guernsey coach, Harold Allen, felt that his team were superb and scored two excellent goals. The disappointed Jersey manager, Peter Heald, felt that the turning point was the loss of Peter Taylor followed by the second Guernsey goal. This was to be his last Muratti in charge of the Jersey team.

Unfortunately there was some crowd trouble before; during and after the match but at no time was the game in danger. A police spokesman said that the trouble was contained rea-sonably well during the game but at half-time an attempt was made by the rival supporters to meet head on but this was thwarted by the police, some of them with dogs. The trouble boiled over again after the match where three youths had to jump into the harbour to evade a large group of Guernsey youths. The main trouble was in St. Peter Port where around 600 youths were involved in scuffles from around 5.00pm until the boat for Jersey left at 6.30pm. The day ended with 50 arrests and 19 of the youths appeared in Guernsey's Magistrate Court on Tuesday morning. The remainder appeared at later Court sittings.

The victorious Guernsey team with the Muratti Vase.

Peter Blondel with the Ossie Eloury Trophy.

1 9 8 4

MURATTI SEMI-FINAL.
31 March 1984, Mount Hale, Alderney.

Alderney -0, Guernsey -6.

Former AFA president, Frank Bond, back home for 12 months after some years in Australia had donated a silver trophy for the Alderney Man-of-the-Match. Alderney selected Dave Mitchell, formally of North, and Stan Parry for their first caps. Guernsey's Mark Culverwell gained his senior and junior Muratti caps in the same season. Dave Mahoney (North) gained his first cap and Daryl Tapp (Vale Rec) was on the substitute's bench hoping for his first cap. Mahoney had only just qualified for Guernsey and, he used to play for Jersey Scottish although he himself is English.

History was made as this was the first Guernsey Muratti side to have been selected by one person namely, Harold Allen, the Guernsey manager.

It was reported in the Press that if Guernsey won the match in Alderney then players selected for the Muratti Vase Final in Jersey on Liberation Day would have to fall in with the travel and accommodation arrangements made by the GFA secretary. Anyone not prepared to do so would have no option but to withdraw from the squad. This tough line had been adopted by the GFA following complaints from secretary Graham Skuse. He had made all the arrangements for the trip to Alderney after contacting the players only to receive a number of requests for changes. He had to alter the arrangements five times.

Both teams were introduced to CI Inter-Insular Committee president, Les De La Mare, prior to the match.

Alderney.

18 year-old Culverwell, far left, scores Guernsey's third goal.

Very soon after the start the Alderney keeper, Oakman, was in action when he first tipped over an angled drive from Fallaize followed by a fine deflecting save from a Carl Le Tissier shot. Guernsey had an escape after 9 minutes when Stan Perry just failed to control a cross from Iain McFarlane with Hamon at his mercy and the scoring chance was gone. Three minutes later Guernsey went ahead when Hargreaves fed Graham who crossed in for young Mark Culverwell, racing up the centre, to volley past the helpless Oakman. The Alderney keeper had another good stop from Le Tissier, but in the 27th minute he had no chance when Fallaize neatly flicked in a pass from Culverwell for goal number two. The home side then created some chances with the Guernsey goal experiencing a few anxious moments when Parry just failed to get his head to a cross that came in from the right. Guernsey weathered the storm and as half time approached they increased their lead when Culverwell leapt in to convert an in swinging Graham corner to make the half time score Alderney-0, Guernsey-3.

Early in the second half Hamon had to rush out to block Parry as Alderney tried to get back in the game, but eight minutes later it was Guernsey who scored. Graham received a pass from Le Tissier and he scored off the inside of the post. Le Tissier himself fired a spectacular fifth goal after 68 minutes and seven minutes later Neil Laine flicked on a Blondel free kick for Chris Dyer to left foot goal number six. Oakman then produced another great save to prevent Culverwell completing his hat-trick. Alderney's 39 year-old skipper, Billy Bohan, brought Hamon to his knees with a fine effort and Steve Davies and Dave Mitchell both made commendable efforts but the match ended Alderney-0, Guernsey-6.

Alderney: D. Oakman, P. Burland, M. Richardson, T. Pasquire, H. Aldcroft, W. Bohan (c), P. Concannon, D. Mitchell, S. Perry, I. McFarlane, S. Davies.
Sub: N. Rose, T. Bohan.

Guernsey: C. Hamon, P. Blondel (c), K. Le Gallez, C. Hargreaves, D. Mahoney, M. Culverwell, C. Dyer, N. Laine, C. Le Tissier, L. Graham, C. Fallaize.
Sub: D. Martel, D. Tapp.
Goalscorers: Culverwell (2), Dyer, C. Le Tissier, Graham, Fallaize.

Alderney were, in the end, outclassed by Guernsey but they had good performances from Paddy Burland, Derek Oakman, Martin Richardson and the classy Dave Mitchell.

Following the match, the Guernsey contingent and visiting Jersey officials, including coach Jimmy Reeves, enjoyed magnificent hospitality from the Alderney FA at Guernsey's headquarters the Sea View Hotel. Rothmans helped sponsor the match and CI manager Ian Cameron was warmly thanked. The Alderney FA were delighted to receive a cheque for £100 from a former Alderney player now resident in the UK. The Guernsey players and officials stayed overnight and were entertained at a Muratti Dance by the Alderney FA at the Sea View Hotel.

The Frank Bond Alderney Man-of-the-Match Trophy was presented to Paddy Burland.

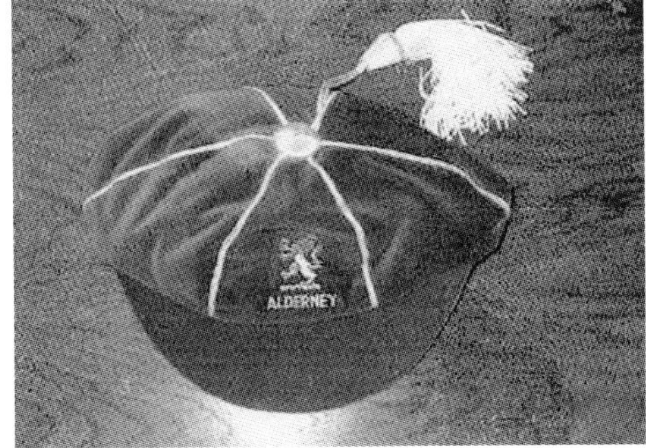

Dave Mitchell's Alderney Muratti Cap.

Derek Oakman produces another fine save.

MURATTI FINAL.
9 May 1984, Springfield Stadium, Jersey.

Jersey -6, Guernsey -2 aet.

Jersey caused a surprise by including veteran goalkeeper Barry Breuilly (St. Ouen) in their squad. Jamie Carney (First Tower), Billy Richardson (St. Paul's), Denis Corrigan (Springfield) and Jerry Guest (St. Peter) all made their debuts for Jersey. Jersey's preparations had not gone well and they lost against St. Mary's College, Twickenham by 4-2. This College team had drawn 2-2 with the Junior Island team the day before. Their new manager/coach, Jimmy Reeves was confident of a victory and this was backed up by the fact that Jersey teams had won the Upton, Wheway and Jeremie Cups in a triumphant end to their club season. The Guernsey squad had lost the services of Kevin Le Tissier, Neil Hunter, Colin Le Page and Andy Le Page but manager Harold Allen was still confident of securing a win as he selected a team with plenty of Muratti experience. The referee for the match is Trevor Spencer and he comes to the game with vast experience including running the line for the European Cup semi-final in Lisbon between Benfica and Ajax. Last year he was on the line for the EUFA Cup semi-final between Anderlecht and Bohemians Prague.

There was a fast start to the Muratti at Springfield when early on Fallaize narrowly failed to convert a chance laid on by Carl Le Tissier which was followed in the third minute by a goal for Jersey. A slip by Mark Le Tissier let Jerry Guest away on Jersey's right and he sent in a cross that a leaping Brent Pitman sent flashing past Chris Hamon. Seven minutes later Jersey struck again. A Paul Carberry corner from the right found Vincenti at the near post. Hamon played his header onto the bar but Guest was there to poke home the rebound for 2-0. Guernsey gradually settled and a Kevin Le Gallez shot from 18 yards fully tested Breuilly. In the 29th minute Dyer took a pass from Laine and crossed in for Le Gallez and his knock down was put in the net by Fallaize as Vincenti tried to block.

Fallaize fires in Guernsey's first goal despite the close attention by Vincenti.

Vincenti blasts in Jersey's third goal from the spot.

Fleury (14) races through to score Jersey's fourth goal.

Hat-trick hero Peter Fleury.

Almost immediately Hamon had to make a great stop, with his legs, to prevent Pitman restoring Jersey's two goal lead. Guernsey were, however, playing with great determination and equalised two minutes from half time when a Fallaize cross from the right was slammed home from close in by Le Gallez. Half time arrived in a pulsating match with the score Jersey-2, Guernsey-2.

The second half began very even with no side gaining the upper hand. Midway through the half Guernsey had the misfortune to lose the services of Blondel due to injury. The closest attempt in the second period fell to the visitors in the 83rd minute when a ball from Laine was flicked on to Fallaize and his effort rebounded away off Breuilly's right hand post. With two minutes remaining Laine sent in a drive that went just wide and at full time the score was Jersey-2, Guernsey-2.

The first period of extra time was very even with both defences in control with the main chance falling to Guest in the 101st minute but he miscued his shot. Just before half-time Jersey replaced Brent Pitman with Peter Fleury and when the whistle blew the score remained Jersey-2, Guernsey-2.

It was not until the second half that the game really burst into life again. In the 111th minute Le Gallez was adjudged to have tripped Dewhurst inside the box and referee Spencer had no hesitation in awarding a penalty. Vincenti stepped up and put the spot kick away to Hamon's left to put Jersey 3-2 ahead.

Some of the Guernsey players appeared to be suffering from cramp as Jersey began to up the pace and a minute later substitute Fleury collected a ball that was chipped through to him and raced past Le Gallez and Mahoney to send a right footed shot round the helpless Hamon.

He then leapt to meet a right-wing cross to power in a header into the net off Dyer and finally he was on hand to score from the rebound after Hamon had stopped a Dewhurst shot. This sensational 10-minute Fleury hat-trick in extra time stunned Guernsey and made the final score Jersey-6, Guernsey-2.

Jersey: M. Le Blancq, J. Carney, W. Richardson, P. Duffy (C), G. Westwood, D. Corrigan, P. Vincenti, P. Carberry, J. Guest, S. Dewhurst, B. Pitman.
Sub: P. Fleury, P. Harzo.
Goalscorers: Pitman, Guest, Vincenti (pen), Fleury (3).

Guernsey: C. Hamon, P. Blondel (c), K. Le Gallez, C. Hargreaves, D. Mahoney, M. Le Tissier, N. Laine, L. Graham, C. Dyer, C. Le Tissier, C. Fallaize.
Sub: A. Bougourd, M. Culverwell.
Goalscorers: Le Gallez, Fallaize.

The Ossie Eloury Memorial Trophy was presented to Jersey's Jerry Guest.

Jersey's manager, Jimmy Reeves, thought that his side had lost the initiative after surrendering a two-goal lead but showed great character to go on and win the match. He felt that Billy Richardson and Jamie Carney were superb along with hat-tick hero Peter Fleury. Guernsey's manager, Harold Allen, was understandably disappointed with the result although he praised his side for coming back so strongly from being two goals down. Referee Trevor Spencer refused to comment on his penalty decision other than to say it was for tripping.

GFA secretary, Graham Skuse, sportingly fills the Muratti Vase with champagne for the jubilant Jersey players.

1 9 8 5

MURATTI SEMI-FINAL.
23 March 1985, Mount Hale, Alderney.

Alderney -0, Jersey -5.

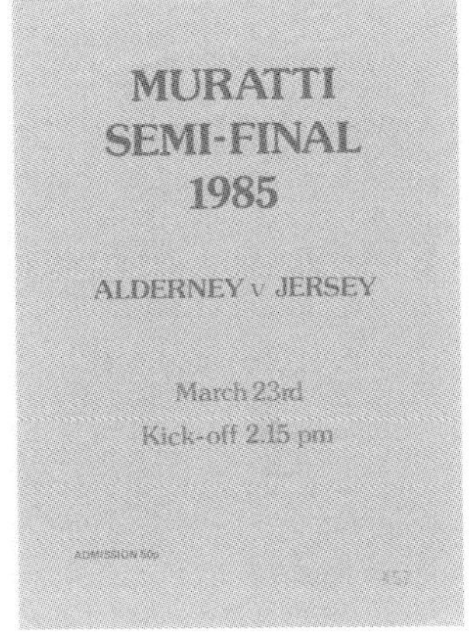

The visitors had two new caps for their match with Alderney, with Steve Kean (St. Paul's) and Neil McCarthy (Springfield) making their debuts in the competition.

Jersey began the match with a strong wind at their backs and were pressing forward from the start. They scored after 15 minutes when a corner kick by Steve Dewhurst was flicked on by Rory Crick at the near post and Neil Livesey came in to head past Oakman. The visitors' second goal came from an Alderney mistake when a Mick Coquelin free-kick was hit straight at Dewhurst and from all of 30 yards he drove the ball home. Two minutes later Denis Corrigan took the ball up the by-line and crossed in for Neil McCarthy to score number three. Jersey then had the misfortune to lose the services of centre back Billy Richardson who limped off after 26 minutes with a suspected fractured instep and he was replaced by Paul Harzo with Dixie A'Court moving in to the middle. Despite this change Jersey continued to push forward and they scored a fourth goal after 31 minutes when Gary Westwood hit a long ball down the left to Livesey and he turned quickly and crashed the ball into the net. Alderney tried to hit back before the interval when Dave Mitchell put Dave Bunn through but Steve Kean rushed out of his goal to thwart him leaving the half time score Alderney-0, Jersey-4.

The second half was a lot quieter with very few chances. Dewhurst came close but saw his effort come off the post. With only seconds remaining substitute Tony Salaun took the ball in his stride, went round a couple of defenders and crashed a great shot into the net to make the final score Alderney-0, Jersey-5.

Alderney: D. Oakman, P. Burland, M. Richardson, P. Cunningham (c), Coquelin, T. Bohan, F. Keachie, S. Davies, D. Mitchell, MacFarlane, D. Bunn. Sub: W. Bohan.

Jersey: S. Kean, D. A'Court, P. Duffy, W. Richardson, G. Westwood, D. Corrigan, P. Vincenti, R. Crick, N. Livesey, N. McCarthy, S. Dewhurst. Sub: P. Harzo, A. Salaun. Goalscorers: Livesey (2), Dewhurst, McCarthy, Salaun.

Despite this defeat Alderney could take comfort in fine performances from Peter Cunningham, Steve Davies and Paddy Burland.

MURATTI FINAL.
6 May 1985, The Cycling Grounds, Guernsey.

Guernsey -4, Jersey -3.

For the first time in Muratti history Guernsey selected three brothers for the final against Jersey. Mark and Carl Le Tissier play for Vale Rec and their brother, Kevin, plays for North. Also included in the team is their Uncle Peter Blondel and Peter's brother, Tony, is Guernsey's assistant manager. Guernsey has included one new cap in their starting line-up in Leon Smith of Rangers. Leon used to play for Jersey Wanderers. There were some doubts over the fitness of Kevin Le Tissier and Neil Hunter has been brought into the squad. On the Sunday prior to the match an injury prevented young Gary de Carteret making his Muratti debut and was replaced by Mark Culverwell. Guernsey's preparation for this match has been good with them winning five and drawing two of their eight representative matches with their only defeat being the 5-0 loss to Tottenham Hotspur. Jersey had lost the services of Paul Duffy of Springfield as he broke his leg in a Dylon Cup game playing for Thistle against Regent. They have selected one new cap in Nicky Thomas of Wanderers.

The game was only six minutes old when Jersey's young Nicky Thomas brought down Carl Le Tissier just outside the box on Guernsey's right. Le Tissier took the kick himself and crossed over for Smith to bullet a header past Kean in the Jersey goal to give Guernsey an early lead. Nine minutes later Fallaize took a long throw in near the left corner flag. As defenders and forwards leapt for it, it came off a head and landed for Kevin Le Tissier who quickly controlled it and fired it into the net past the helpless Kean. As Guernsey remained on the attack they scored again in the 21st minute when Fallaize controlled a ball from Colin Le Page, with his head, and, although under pressure, shot past a despairing Kean for goal number three. Guernsey were now well on top but Jersey gave them a warning when

Steve Dewhurst hit a drive that smashed back off Froome's crossbar. The keeper then had to make a great save to tip over a Crick header following a Brent Pitman cross. Jersey thought that they had scored when Vincenti leapt with Froome to head home a cross by Dewhurst only for it to be disallowed by referee Burden for a foul on the keeper. Fallaize then came close to scoring just before Jersey opened their account. Neil Livesey broke away from Mark Le Tissier after a long ball from Dewhurst and, just inside the penalty area, was brought down by Blondel. Vincenti took the kick and beat Froome on his right to make the half time score Guernsey-3, Jersey-1.

Jersey began the second half on top and scored again after eight minutes. Billy Richardson took a free kick and Vincenti's header beat Froome but Smith headed off the line only for Crick to head it back into the net to make the score 3-2. The visitors continued to push on and would have equalised but for a Colin Le Page goal-line clearance. Guernsey brought on Hunter for Culverwell in an effort to revive their flagging side but it was Jersey who scored again in the 72nd minute. Jersey won another free kick on the edge of the box and the ball was tapped to Dewhurst and, as his low drive came out of Froome's hands, Pitman was there to fire it in for the equaliser. Jersey were now well and truly in control and Dewhurst had a couple of chances to put the visitors in the lead. The game was moving towards extra time when Fallaize had a header pushed out by Kean, Carl Le Tissier retrieved the ball from Guernsey's right and crossed in for Fallaize to give Kean no chance with a header to end this remarkable game Guernsey-4, Jersey-3.

This was a truly sensational Muratti with Guernsey surrendering a 3-0 lead before Fallaize scored the winner in injury time.

The celebrations when Fallaize scored the late winner for Guernsey.

Guernsey: R. Froome, C. Hargreaves, P. Blondel (c), L. Smith, M. Le Tissier,
             M. Culverwell, C. Dyer, C. Le Page, K. Le Tissier, C. Fallaize,
             C. Le Tissier.
             Sub: A. Le Page, N. Hunter.
             Goalscorers: Smith, K. Le Tissier, Fallaize (2).

Jersey: S. Kean, D. A'Court, N. Thomas, W. Richardson, P. Harzo, D. Corrigan,
             P. Vincenti, R. Crick, N. Livesey, B. Pitman, S. Dewhurst.
             Goalscorers: Vincenti (pen), Crick, Pitman.

Peter Blondel received the Muratti Vase from Guernsey's Lieut-Governor, Sir Peter Le Cheminant. The Ossie Eloury Memorial Trophy was awarded to Mark Le Tissier.

It was a tremendous day for one Guernsey family with Mark Le Tissier winning the Ossie Eloury Memorial Trophy and his brothers Carl and Kevin staring in the team that also had uncle Peter Blondel as captain as well as uncle Tony Blondel acting as assistant manager. It was quite a day for the family.

Guernsey manager, Harold Allen, said that it was a tremendous game with a great fight

Peter Blondel proudly shows off the Muratti Vase.

back by Jersey after a superb opening 20 minutes from his side. Jersey coach, Jimmy Reeves, thought that his team were very unlucky to lose the match after getting back to 3-3.

Tony Blondel, Mark, Carl and Kevin Le Tissier and Peter Blondel.

Bunn, Rushbury, Quinain, Richardson, Aldcroft, Oakman, Cosheril, Rose, Quanten, Maloy.
Bohan, Dickens, Mitchell, Concanen, Chadwick.
Alderney - 1986.

1 9 8 6

MURATTI SEMI-FINAL.
9 April 1986, The Corbet Field, Guernsey.

Guernsey -7, Alderney -0.

For the second time Guernsey hosted a Muratti match away from the Cycling Grounds when the game against Alderney was played at the Corbet Field on 9 April 1986, Guernsey's new manager. Tony Blondel, had selected two new caps in Tony Russo and Martin Gallienne as well as having goalkeeper Jon Dorey on the substitutes bench awaiting his first cap.

Guernsey had an explosive start to the match and took the lead after just two minutes when left-back Mark Le Tissier, up in support of the attack, scored off the foot of the far post. Only three minutes later, Hunter moved onto a pass from Fallaize to knock the ball past the advancing Derek Oakman and into the net. Seconds later Hunter headed on to Fallaize who fired a left foot shot past the helpless Oakman to make the score 3-0 after only six minutes. It might have been four in eight minutes when Fallaize and Hunter rose for a Le Tissier cross for the ball to come back off the crossbar. Alderney tried to respond to this whirlwind start with Dave Mitchell displaying his craft in the midfield as the visitors tightened things up. As the half neared its end Hunter rounded Oakman only to see his shot cleared by Martin Richardson. In the last minute Hunter again broke through and curved a right footed shot around Oakman for goal number four. Alderney were pleased to hear the half time whistle with the score Guernsey-4, Alderney-0.

Hunter slides the ball past Oakman for Guernsey's second goal.

Alderney replaced the injured Mitchell with Andrew Cosheril for the second half. Guernsey began the second period as they did the first with a goal in two minutes when Hunter pulled away from Richardson on the right wing and squared the ball to Fallaize who unleashed another unstoppable drive. After 56 minutes Guernsey were awarded a penalty when referee Daniels decided that Hunter had been fouled by Oakman and captain Blondel made it 6-0 from the spot. Alderney improved slightly when Paul Bunn make a couple of determined runs at the home defence and Quinain twice broke away clear, only to be pulled up for offside. It was Fallaize, however, who completed the scoring in the 72nd minute when he put away the rebound from a Culverwell shot. Gallienne and Russo both made determined efforts to increase Guernsey's lead and it was just before the end when substitute Bougourd blasted his shot against the bar and the match ended Guernsey-7, Alderney-0.

Guernsey: C. Hamon, G. Smith, P. Blondel (c), M. Le Tissier, L. Smith, T. Russo, M. Culverwell, C. Dyer, M. Gallienne, C. Fallaize, N. Hunter.
Sub: J. Dorey, A. Bougourd.
Goalscorers: Blondel (pen), Le Tissier, Fallaize (3), Hunter (2).

Alderney: D. Oakman, T. Bohan, M. Richardson, P. Quanten, H. Aldcroft, P. Concanen, P. Rose, D. Mitchell, P. Bunn, G. Rushbury, R. Quinain.
Sub: S. Chadwick, A. Cosheril.

Alderney's coach was very disappointed with his side's disastrous start to the game but praised his players for the way they fought hard to redeem it. Tony Blondel was pleased with the way his team played particularly new caps Toni Russo and Martin Gallienne.

MURATTI FINAL.
9 May 1986, Springfield Stadium, Jersey.

Jersey -3, Guernsey -2.

Jersey had four new caps in their starting line-up in Andy Campbell (Springfield), Shaun A'Court (Wanderers), John Corrigan (Le Masuriers) and Colin Le Moignan (Wanderers). Rory Crick (First Tower) captained a side that showed six changes from the side that lost 4-3 against Guernsey last year. Jersey manager, Jimmy Reeves, broke his leg playing in the de la Salle College (Beeches) parents' v teachers friendly on Sunday 27 April and was not at the Muratti. First Tower's Alan Pitman took over the coaching duties for the match.

Guernsey's side showed three changes from the team that started against Alderney with Dave Mahoney (Sylvans) in for Leon Smith, new cap Mick Marley (Vale Rec) for Toni Russo and Kevin Le Tissier (North) for Martin Gallienne. Gary de Carteret, who lost out on his first cap the previous year due to injury, was on the substitutes bench. Guernsey's preparations had gone well with only one defeat in 6 representative matches, their only reverse coming in the 4-3 defeat at the hands of a Crystal Palace XI at Mitcham and new coach, Tony Blondel, was looking forward to a close contest.

Jersey had the ideal start to the match as they went ahead within four minutes of the kick-off when, from a build up on the right, Neil Livesey found Colin Le Moignan in the middle of the penalty area and he had time to control that ball and slip it into the net. Guernsey replied straight from the kick off when a long ball out of defence by Blondel found Kevin Le Tissier on the right wing and he left the Jersey rearguard standing as he cut in and beat Le Blancq with a searing low shot into the far side of the goal. Eleven minutes later Jersey regained the lead when Guernsey's Glyn Smith fouled Livesey and, with the visitors' defence in disarray, Dewhurst took the kick that beat both Livesey and Hamon to go in by the left hand post. The game became more even although the exchanges were far from inspiring. Jersey's Vincenti and Taylor both went close as did a Colin Fallaize header from a Hunter cross. Guernsey nearly equalised when Le Blancq couldn't hold a Le Tissier shot but they were unable to capitalise on the loose ball and the half ended Jersey-2, Guernsey-1.

Hunter, Gallienne, Leon Smith, Hamon, Culverwell, de Carteret, Mark Le Tissier, Blondel, Fallaize, Russo, Bougourd, Mahoney, Glyn Smith, Marley, Dyer, Kevin Le Tissier.

As the second half began Jersey came close in the first minute when Hamon did well to thwart Le Moignan and parry a blast by Vincenti with Dewhurst firing his shot over the bar. Seconds later Marley fed Le Tissier and his shot forced a fine save out of Le Blancq. The tension in the game was beginning to boil over, and it looked as though both sides were going to be reduced to 10 men when Jersey skipper Rory Crick and Guernsey's Mark Culverwell were involved in a right scrap in front of the dignitaries in the stand, but referee James contented himself with a booking for the pair of them. Guernsey began to stretch the game and equalised in the 51st minute when Hunter held off a challenge as he drove down the left hand side of the Jersey penalty area and, after almost reaching the bye-line, spun and crashed a diagonal shot behind Le Blancq as Harzo tried in vain to block the effort.

The game was flowing from end to end with Fallaize coming close followed by Dewhurst missing a good chance on Jersey counter attack. With five minutes remaining Dewhurst went down in the penalty area following a challenge by the onrushing Hamon but referee Mick James allowed play to continue and the ball broke to substitute Tony Salaun on the left, and he fired in a shot that took a slight deflection and soared into the far side of Hamon's net. Guernsey then pushed on in search of a third equaliser with Dyer sending a pass to Kevin Le Tissier but Le Blancq pulled off a good save from his shot and as the final whistle sounded Hunter was shaping up for a shot leaving the final score Jersey-3, Guernsey-2.

Jersey:	M. Le Blancq, Campbell, S. A' Court, P. Harzo, D. Corrigan, R. Crick, P. Vincenti, P. Taylor, C. Le Moignan, N. Livesey, S. Dewhurst. Sub: A. Salaun. Goalscorers: Le Moignan, Dewhurst, Salaun.
Guernsey:	C. Hamon, G. Smith, P. Blondel (c), D. Mahoney, M. Le Tissier, M. Marley, C. Dyer, M. Culverwell, K. Le Tissier, C. Fallaize, N. Hunter. Sub: A. Bougourd, G. de Carteret. Goalscorers: Le Tissier, Hunter.

Hunter fires in Guernsey's second goal as Harzo slides in.

Jersey celebrate their Muratti Vase triumph.

This was a typical Muratti match and JFA president, John Sherry, said that he thought that it was a hard fought game and there should not have been a loser. The Ossie Eloury Memorial Trophy was won by Jersey's Paul Harzo.

Following the return to Guernsey the team and officials had a dinner at the Villette Hotel, St. Martins.

1 9 8 7

MURATTI SEMI-FINAL.
17 March 1987, Springfield Stadium, Jersey.

Jersey -10 Alderney -0.

Jersey prepared for their match with an Alderney side that included Jersey born Andy Wright, a former St. Clements player, for his first cap. They also had Maxie Mackay, Mark Treais and Darren Braby making their debuts. On the substitute's bench they had two 15-year olds in Damien Walker and Mark Mullay. Braby, Walker and Mullay were all products of St. Anne's School team. There was a doubt who would be keeping goal for Alderney with both Derek Oakman and Billy Bohan in contention. Bohan was reported to have said that as he is in his 40's it might be a retrograde step for him to return, however, he was selected.

As the match began Alderney were first into the attack but Jersey quickly assumed control of the game and the visitors were soon defending in depth as they withstood some severe pressure. Jersey opened the scoring after 11 minutes when Peter Vincenti met a Lawlor free-kick and sent in a powerful header past the Alderney keeper. The home side swarmed into the attack and scored four more goals to make the half time score Jersey-5, Alderny-0.

In the second half Alderney very rarely got into the Jersey penalty area and Carlyon in the Jersey goal did not have a save to make. Alderney sent on their two young substitutes, Walker and Mullay, but the match continued to be played mainly in the visitors half. Jersey scored a further five goals ending up with Vincenti and Lawlor scoring hat-tricks, Dewhurst scoring twice and Livesey and Petulla scoring once. It was a relieved Alderney team who left the field with the score Jersey-10, Alderney-0.

Jersey: S. Carlyon, S. Olliver, P. Harzo, S. A'Court, J. Corrigan, A. Lawler, P. Vincenti, P. Carberry, N. Livesey, R. Weir, S. Dewhurst.
Subs: S. Petulla, Le Cornu.
Goalscorers: Vincenti (3), Lawler (3), Dewhurst (2), Livesey, Petulla.

Alderney: W. Bohan, A. Wright, Mackay, P. Burland, P. Bunn, P. Concanen, P. Rose, M. Treais, D. Brady, G. Rushbury, I. MacFarlane.
Subs: D. Walker, M. Mulley.

This was a comprehensive Jersey victory and it was felt that if they had stepped up the pace they might have surpassed their record 11-0 score against Alderney. The Alderney manager, John Maloy, was undaunted saying that this was the strongest team Alderney had fielded for a few years and he felt that the score flattered Jersey. The average age of this young Alderney side was 20.

MURATTI FINAL.
9 May 1987, The Cycling Grounds, Guernsey.

Guernsey -3, Jersey -4. aet.

Guernsey selected Dave Podmore of Belgrave Wanderers for his first Muratti cap for the match against Jersey at the Cycling Grounds. Jersey made wholesale changes to last year's winning team with nine of that starting line-up missing. They included Graeme Le Saux who joined the small band of players who had been selected for the Senior and Junior Muratti in the same season. The referee for this match was Alan Gunn (Burgess Hill) who'd been on the Football League list since 1976 and become a FIFA referee the previous year. He was linesman in the 1986 FA Cup Final as well as being on television when he refereed Arsenal v Tottenham Hotspur and Everton v Watford that season.

Reeves (manager), Davidson, Le Cornu, Le Saux, Carlyon, Le Moignan, Livesey, Duffy, A'Court.
Fraser, Salaun, Carpenter, Richardson, Dewhurst, Daly.
Jersey.

For the opening 30 minutes there was not much between the teams although Carlyon did have one splendid save from Hunter as he shot on the turn. In the 32nd minute, however, Guernsey opened the scoring. Dave Podmore put over the third of three consecutive corners and Chris Dyer nodded the ball down to Blondel and he in turn relayed it to Hunter who rammed it home from close range.

A few minutes before half time Hunter scooped over another chance following a Blondel free-kick. Jersey came close when Dewhurst collected the ball and fired in a shot that went only inches wide. Jersey equalised as the half neared its end when Steve Dewhurst got behind the Guernsey defence to collect a fine cross ball from Daly and delicately lift it over

Hunter raises his hand to salute his first goal.

Carlyon saves as Fallaize looks on.

over Dorey from the left. On the stroke of half time Kevin Le Tissier collected a clearance from Carlyon only to send his shot over the bar, and the half time score remained Guernsey-1, Jersey-1.

Early in the second half Dorey had to be alert to clear from Livesey who went for a Dewhurst cross to try and give Jersey the lead. Guernsey then took control and through Hunter maintained an advantage. As this pressure mounted Kevin Le Tissier set up Hunter and his first time right-footed shot fled into the top right hand corner of the net for a quite superb goal. In the 73rd minute Hunter received a throw in and cut in from the right to blast home his third goal for 3-1. Two minutes later Salaun raced through the Guernsey defence on the Jersey right and sent in a cross for Dewhurst to volley home at the far post for 3-2. There were good chances at both ends when, with a few minutes remaining, Kevin Le Tissier broke into the Jersey penalty area and as he tried to go round Carlyon the keeper stretched out and grabbed the ball. With only two minutes remaining Tony Salaun was on the spot to convert a pass from substitute Colin Le Moignan to tie up the scores at Guernsey-3, Jersey-3.

  At the start of extra time Steve Carlyon pulled off a magnificent save to deny a goal-bound shot from Kevin Le Tissier. Jersey were now in complete control and Daly hammered a shot against the bar as Guernsey were pushed back. Five minutes later Jersey went ahead for the first time when a fine through ball by young Graeme Le Saux from his own half reached Tommy Daly who duly found the net. The half-time score was Guernsey-3, Jersey-4.

Guernsey switched Peter Blondel into the attack in the second period of extra time and came close but Blondel's header from a Marley free-kick did not have the power to beat Carlyon. This was the last real scoring effort and the game ended Guernsey-3, Jersey-4.

Guernsey: J. Dorey, D. Blanchard, P. Blondel (c), D. Mahoney, M. Marley,
C. Le Tissier, C. Fallaize, C. Dyer, D. Podmore, K. Le Tissier, N. Hunter.
Sub: M. Culverwell, G. de Carteret.
Goalscorer: Hunter (3).

Jersey: S. Carlyon, D. A'Court, W. Richardson, P. Duffy, D. Le Saux, N. Davidson,
G. Fraser, A. Salaun, A. Daly, N. Livesey, S. Dewhurst.
Sub: K. Le Cornu, C. Le Moignan.
Goalscorers: Dewhurst (2), Salaun, Daly.

This was a truly remarkable match with plenty of excitement and incident. Young Steve Carlyon was a star for Jersey with a string of outstanding saves to deny Guernsey. Jersey's manager, Jimmy Reeves, said that he was a very proud man following this result. He also added that he thought that Neil Hunter was unlucky not to get the man-of-the-match award. It was to be young Graeme Le Saux's last Muratti as he was moving to England to pursue a career in professional football. Guernsey manager, Tony Blondel, was very disappointed especially after losing a 3-1 lead. He felt that the turning point was the Carlyon save from Kevin Le Tissier that prevented Guernsey going 4-2 ahead.

1 9 8 8

MURATTI SEMI-FINAL.
26 March 1988, Mount Hale, Alderney.

Alderney -1, Guernsey -5.

Alderney had selected goalkeeper Mark Randall and Gary Coenen for their first Muratti caps. Guernsey had two new caps in their squad in Gary Fitchet and M. Tullier. Guernsey also had a new captain in Chris Dyer (Vale Rec) and Alderney was led by Peter Concanen.

Alderney started well in their match at Mount Hale producing some good football. In the 12th minute the home side was awarded a penalty by referee McCreanney when de Carteret was deemed to have clipped Coenen's ankle. Rushbury took the kick and aimed it at the bottom left hand corner but Froome brought off a diving save.

Froome saving Rushbury's penalty.

Alderney were performing very well and were ably marshalled by their inspiring captain, Peter Concanen. Mark Treais came very close to scoring with a long range shot but soon afterwards, in the 32nd minute, Guernsey scored. Le Gallez brought the ball out of defence and fed Culverwell who in turn found Bougourd with a raking pass and he finished the move by beating keeper Mark Randall. Hunter then set up a chance for Bougourd following a mis-kick by Randall but the keeper managed to scramble back to block the shot. Then, in the last minute of the half, Gary Coenen miskicked a golden opportunity right in front of goal to leave the half time score Alderney-0, Guernsey-1.

Guernsey began to step up the pace in the second half and Randall twice had to save at the feet of Bougourd in the opening minutes. In the 56th minute this pressure paid off for the visiting side when they scored their second goal. Chris Dyer took a throw in and the ball was headed on by Gallienne to Bougourd who headed past Randall. Two minutes later Alderney reduced the arrears when Coenen crossed in from the right for Cornishman Mark Treais to throw himself at the ball and head home just inside Froome's right hand post. This was the first Muratti goal scored by Alderney on home soil as well as being the first goal since Billy Bohan scored against Jersey five years ago.

Guernsey replied immediately. The ball broke loose as Dyer challenged Randall for a cross and, after Le Tissier had failed to connect, Gallienne drove it into the net for 3-1. Disaster struck Alderney two minutes later when Paul Bunn had the misfortune to turn the ball past his own keeper with Dyer closing in to make sure it crossed the line. Bougourd headed a Hunter cross wide and Culverwell went close for the visitors when he sent in a header from a Le Tissier corner only for the ball to be cleared off the Alderney line, before, in the last minute, Le Tissier scored to make the final score Alderney-1 Guernsey-5.

Alderney: M. Randall, P. Bunn, Mackay, P. Concanen (c), P. Rose, P. Burland, A. Wright, M. Treais, D. Mitchell, G. Coenen, G. Rushbury. Sub: Cosheril. Goalscorer: Treais.

Guernsey: R. Froome, M. Marley, G. de Carteret, K. Le Gallez, G. Fitchet, M. Culverwell, C. Dyer (c), M. Gallienne, A. Bougourd, N. Hunter, C. Le Tissier. Sub: D. Blanchard, M. Tullier. Goalscorers: Bougourd (2), Gallienne, Dyer, Le Tissier.

Mark Treais (centre) flies in to head past Froome for Alderney's historic goal.

This was a very encouraging performance by Alderney and with a bit of luck may have had more than one goal to celebrate. Their first half performance was excellent and it was only in the second half that Guernsey pressed home their advantage. With Mark Treais scoring the first Alderney Muratti goal on home soil he raised £150 for the forthcoming Telethon event as six public houses had each offered to donate £25 for any home goal scored.

MURATTI FINAL.
2 May 1988, Springfield Stadium, Jersey.

Jersey -0, Guernsey -1.

Jersey had selected three new caps in O'Neill, Andy Barker and John Warren. The Guernsey team which although was not universally accepted, all had Muratti experience.

Guernsey had a dream start to the Muratti at Springfield when they took the lead after only three minutes. Gary de Carteret passed to Carl Le Tissier and as he took a return pass in the penalty area he was fouled by Shaun A'Court. The referee, David Hutchison, had no hesitation in pointing to the spot and Carl Le Tissier sent Carlyon the wrong way as he slotted it into bottom left hand corner.

Jersey responded to this setback with some fine attacking play orchestrated by new cap Andy Barker in the midfield but they found the Guernsey defence in turn well organised by Le Gallez and Tapp although Hamon was relieved to see a fast shot by Barker clear the crossbar. Likewise the Jersey defence were allowing Guernsey few opportunities to increase their lead by keeping a tight rein on Hunter and Bougourd. The home side came close, however, and Hamon had to be alert when he saved, at full stretch, a header by John Warren as Jersey strove for the equaliser. There was no more scoring and the half ended Jersey-0, Guernsey-1.

The second half began with the play confined mainly to the midfield although Jersey felt that they should have been awarded a penalty when Tony Lawlor went down in the box but the referee was unimpressed. Tony Salaun then beat two men and crossed well from the left and Peter Taylor was foiled by Chris Hamon's feet. Guernsey came close to increasing their lead in the 68th minute when a Hunter pass sent Le Tissier clear but he put his shot

Carl Le Tissier's third minute penalty.

wide of the right hand post with Carlyon at his mercy. Two minutes later Le Tissier fired in a free-kick from outside the box but the ball cannoned back off the opposite post and de Carteret slammed the rebound over the bar. As the game neared its end it was the Guernsey supporters who were whistling for the referee to end the game several minutes before he did so with the final score Jersey-0, Guernsey-1.

Jersey: S. Carlyon, O'Neill, S. A'Court, W. Richardson, D. Corrigan, P. Taylor, A. Barker, A. Salaun, A. Lawlor, P. Fleury, J. Warren.
Sub: K. Le Cornu, C. Le Moignan.

Guernsey: C. Hamon, K. Le Gallez, P. Blondel, D. Blanchard, M. Marley, C. Dyer (c), G. de Carteret, D. Tapp, A. Bougourd, N. Hunter, C. Le Tissier.
Sub: M. Culverwell, M. Tullier.
Goalscorer: Le Tissier (pen).

It was an emotional Tony Blondel, the Guernsey Coach, who hugged and thanked his players for this Muratti victory and the Jersey Coach, Jimmy Reeves, although disappointed in the result praised the Guernsey performance. The Ossie Eloury Memorial Trophy went to Kevin Le Gallez.

It was new captain, Chris Dyer, who proudly received the Muratti Vase from Jersey's Lieut- Gov Sir William Pillar.

Chris Dyer and the Guernsey team with the Muratti Vase.

Alderney team and the match officials.

1 9 8 9

MURATTI SEMI-FINAL.
18 March 1989, Mount Hale, Alderney.

Alderney -0, Jersey -4.

Alderney's preparations for their Muratti match with Jersey went well and in their annual Baker Cup match with Rangers they had a very credible 0-0 draw. Their one problem was with Mark Treais who had just returned from a long holiday and had not played any football since January. Player/Coach Billy Bohan decided to select him after some discussions with him. Jersey's starting side included three new caps in Martin Stratford (Wanderers), Bill Begbie (St. Paul's) and Willie O'Malley (Jersey Scottish).

The game started in difficult windy conditions with Alderney having the benefit of the breeze. Alderney used this to their advantage and came close from two early free-kicks just outside the penalty area. The first one came when Mark Treais fired in a shot that was saved by Steve Carlyon and from the second, full-back Paul Bunn drove his shot over the bar. It was Jersey, however, who took the lead in the 13th minute when Lawlor collected the ball from a throw-in and cut in from the right to blast in a shot that gave Bohan no chance. Lawlor came close again but this time Bohan saved his header. Mid-way through the half Alderney came close to equalising when, from a corner, Ian McFarlane fired in a fine goal-bound header but Carlyon dived to his right to smother the ball on the line. Two minutes from half time Jersey struck again when from a Gavin Frazer free-kick Andy Barker sent in a header which carried over an out-of-position Bohan to make the half time score Alderney-0, Jersey-2.

Early in the second half Tony Salaun nearly increased Jersey's lead when he saw his shot crash against the bar as the visitors strove on in search of more goals. In the 54th minute Neil Livesey took a pass from Willie O'Malley and played the ball across to Frazer. Livesey took the return ball and squeezed it past Bohan at the near post for Jersey's 3rd goal. Alderney replied with a fine Concanen run down the left and he set up McFarlane for a good shot but Jersey were now in control of the match. The visitors had two goals disallowed before they registered their fourth goal. Steve Kilshaw came on for his first cap and replaced O'Malley and he was immediately involved in the action. From a Frazer corner Kilshaw sent in a header that was blocked on the line only for Livesey to rush in and fire home the rebound. Dave Mitchell, who was a doubtful starter due to injury, was replaced by Nick Rizzuto but the match played out with the final score Alderney-0, Jersey-4.

Alderney: W. Bohan, S. Parilla, P. Concanen, J. Maxwell, P. Bunn, P. Burland, M. Treais, A. Wright, D. Mitchell, G. Rushbury, I. MacFarlane.
Sub: N. Rizzuto.

Jersey: S. Carlyon, M. Stratford, G. Le Cornu, A. Barker, W. Begbie, S. A'Court, A. Lawler, G. Fraser, N. Livesey, W. O'Malley, A. Salaun.
Sub: S. Kilshaw.
Goalscorers: Lawlor, Livesey (2), Barker.

Alderney were disappointed with their performance. Their coach, Billy Bohan, said that they could play a lot better. Best for Alderney were Peter Concanen, Mark Treais, Ian McFarlane and their man-of- the-match Andy Wright. Jimmy Reeves, the Jersey coach, was very impressed with this Alderney team.

It was announced by Billy Bohan that the Alderney team was to remain in the Guernsey Railway League and not apply for promotion to the Jackson League.

MURATTI FINAL.
1 May 1989, The Cycling Grounds, Guernsey.

Guernsey -0, Jersey -4.

1989 FOOTBALL FESTIVAL
25th April - 1st May
featuring the
MURATTI VASE FINAL
GUERNSEY v. JERSEY
In the presence of
The Lt. Governor of Guernsey, Lieutenant-General Sir Alexander Boswell, K.C.B., C.B.E.
The Lt. Governor of Jersey, Admiral Sir William Pillar
Sir Charles Frossard, Bailiff of Guernsey
at the Cycling Ground on Monday, 1st May. Kick-off 3.00 p.m.
· · · · · · and the · · · · · ·
PORTSMOUTH TROPHY
NORTHERNERS' A.C.
(Rediffusion Youth Division One Champions, Guernsey)
v
ST. OUEN F.C.
(Jersey Rediffusion Junior League, First Division Champions)
at the Cycling Ground on Saturday, 29th April. Kick-off 3.00 p.m.
· · · · · · and the · · · · · ·
CHANNEL ISLANDS END-OF-SEASON
YOUTH TOURNAMENT
featuring
FIRST TOWER UNITED F.C.
GUERNSEY ROVERS A.C.
JERSEY WANDERERS F.C.
VALE RECREATION F.C.
at Port Soif and the Corbet Field,
on Tuesday 25th April, Saturday 29th April and Sunday 30th April.

OFFICIAL PROGRAMME 50p

Guernsey Manager Tony Blondel selected what, in some quarters, was considered to be a controversial side that included eight of the Priaulx Championship winning Vale Rec team. It also included two new caps in young 19-year-old Grant Chalmers (North) and Ian Ozanne (Vale Rec). Guernsey had played six games in the lead up to this match winning three and losing three. Jersey were forced to make a late change to their side when skipper Keith Le Cornu (St. Peter) withdrew due to ligament trouble and Dave Coleman (Wanderers) was drafted in for his first cap with Bill Begbie (St. Paul's) taking over as captain. Jersey's preparation for this game had gone well with them only conceding one goal in five unbeaten games.

Guernsey began the match well and nearly went ahead in the 8th minute when Kevin Le Tissier raced in after a faulty pass back; Steve Carlyon was able only to partially

O'Malley, Kilshaw, Begbie, G. Le Cornu, A'Court, Barker, Carlyon, Warren, Thomas.
Stratford, K. Le Cornu, Fraser, Lawlor, Salaun.
Jersey.

clear from his feet and Neil Hunter smashed in a shot that came back off the post and the relieved Jersey defence cleared. In the 13th minute a Willie O'Malley shot was deflected for a corner and from a Fraser kick O'Malley flicked it to Lawlor who headed it past Hamon for 1-0 to Jersey. Two minutes later Le Tissier just failed to nudge the ball past Carlyon as the keeper rushed out to challenge. Carlyon then held a fierce left-footed drive by Hunter two minutes later. As Guernsey pushed on for an equaliser Jersey broke with Lawlor and he fired in past Hamon to put the visitors 2-0 ahead. Jersey now looked threatening every time they attacked down the right and the confidence of a two-goal lead allowed them to pass the ball around in style. Carlyon again thwarted Le Tissier as he ran on to a through ball from Bougourd. Jersey then underlined their superiority with a third goal after 33 minutes. Lawlor took a pass from Barker on the right and centred hard and low across the box; Tony Salaun whipped the ball back from the opposite side for Fraser to volley into the net. At half time the score was Guernsey-0, Jersey-3.

  Guernsey tightened up a little in the second half and ten minutes after the start they had to replace the struggling Neil Hunter with Gary de Carteret but Jersey were still in control and increased their lead in the 58th minute when a Fraser free-kick from the right found Shaun A'Court in the penalty area and he crashed the ball past Hamon for goal number four. Le Tissier finally had the ball in the Jersey net but he clearly used a hand to convert Hunter's cross. Le Tissier then passed to Bougourd who let the ball run onto de Carteret but his shot flew straight to Carlyon. Jersey replaced Steve Kilshaw with John Warren as they remained firmly in control. As Jersey pushed on in search of a fifth goal it took a couple of tremendous saves from Hamon, from Lawlor and substitute John Warren, to prevent a score and the match ended Guernsey-0, Jersey-4.

The Jersey defence holds firm as Carlyon saves from Hunter (11).

Guernsey: C. Hamon, D. Blanchard, I. Ozanne, K. Le Gallez, M. Marley, C. Dyer (c),
              N. Laine, G. Chalmers, K. Le Tissier, N. Hunter, A. Bougourd.
              Sub: G. Smith, G. de Carteret.

Jersey: S. Carlyon, M. Stratford, S. A'Court, W. Begbie (c), D. Coleman,
              A. Lawlor, A. Barker, G. Fraser, A. Salaun, S. Kilshaw, W. O'Malley.
              Sub: N. Thomas, J. Warren.
              Goalscorers: Lawlor (2), Fraser, A'Court.

Bill Begbie with the Muratti Vase.

This was a superb performance by Jersey as they recorded their biggest win at the Cycling Grounds for 12 years. Guernsey were disappointing although they did have some good performances from young Chalmers and Ian Ozanne. Tony Blondel announced that he would not be seeking re-election to the post of Guernsey manager.

The Muratti Vase was presented to Jersey's proud skipper Bill Begbie.

The Ossie Eloury Memorial Trophy was won by Jersey's Tony Lawlor.

During this decade Jersey recorded 6 wins and Guernsey 4. Jersey now had 36 Muratti Vase wins and Guernsey 35 wins and Alderney 1 win. The Muratti Vase was shared in 1937.

14

1990 - 1999

1 9 9 0

MURATTI SEMI-FINAL.
31 March 1990, The Cycling Grounds, Guernsey.

Guernsey -4, Alderney -0.

Alan Le Prevost was elected as the new Guernsey manager to be assisted by Coach Laurie Carre.

The Guernsey side included two new caps in goalkeeper Steve Ingrouille (North) and Neil Elmy. Alderney's new coach was Mick Price who had played at a semi-professional level with a number of west of England non-league clubs. Alderney included five new caps in their line-up with 18-year-old goalkeeper Nick Carre, Mathew Stubbs, John Stretton, Paul Walsh and Kevin Fairbrother all making their debuts.

As the match began it became apparent that Alderney coach, Mike Price, had his side well organised defensively. They began with five men at the back and four in midfield and they

Alan Le Prevost and Laurie Carre.

were competing with tremendous spirit. After 20 minutes Guernsey skipper Dyer was denied a goal when he headed in a cross by Chalmers, only to see Carre tipping the ball over the bar. Kevin Le Tissier came close to scoring after receiving a pass from his brother Carl but it was not until the 37th minute that Guernsey broke the deadlock. Kevin Le Tissier broke through the Alderney defence and sent in a powerful shot that Carre could only parry and Chris Dyer pounced to put away the rebound. Two minutes later Guernsey increased their lead when, following a Carl Le Tissier free-kick, Leon Smith headed home just inside Carre's right hand post. In the 42nd minute Martin Gallienne picked up a Kevin Le Tissier cross only to fire his shot against the bar. In the dying seconds of the first half Kevin Le Tissier latched onto a weak Alderney goal-kick and smashed the ball into the net only for referee Des Jegou to blow for half time as the ball was in flight leaving, the half time score Guernsey-2, Alderney-0.

Alderney began the brightest in the second half and in the 42nd minute Rushbury hooked wide from a Paddy Burland cross. From the resultant goal-kick the ball was worked to Carl Le Tissier who crossed for his brother Kevin to hammer in from the far post. Alderney replied a minute later when a Rushbury shot from long-range came close. The visitors again came close when in the 57th minute Guernsey keeper, Ingrouille, was forced to handle outside the box to prevent Rushbury getting hold of a long ball. Rushbury took the free-kick and his chip shot caused Ingrouille to pull off a fine save by pushing the ball over the bar. Guernsey soon reasserted themselves and in the 71st minute Carl Le Tissier's left wing corner was flicked on for Kevin Le Tissier to head in goal number four. Chalmers then came close as he took the ball round Carre but he lost control and the chance was gone. Guernsey sent on Martin Gauvain and Tony Vance for their first caps for the closing minutes of the match. As the game neared its end Carl Le Tissier hit the top of the bar with a free-kick and then Gallienne missed from close range as the match ended Guernsey-4, Alderney-0.

Kevin Le Tissier scores Guernsey's fourth goal.

Guernsey: S. Ingrouille, M. Marley, I. Ozanne, D. Tapp, L. Smith, R. Elmy,
               G. Chalmers, C. Dyer (c), M. Gallienne, C. Le Tissier, K. Le Tissier.
               Subs: M. Gauvain, A. Vance.
               Goalscorers: Dyer, Smith, K. Le Tissier (2).

Alderney: N. Carre, J. Maxwell, P. Bunn, M. Stubbs, J. Stretton, A. Wright,
               P. Burland, P. Walsh, M. Treais, K. Fairbrother, G. Rushbury.
               Sub: A. Cosheril.

Guernsey manager Alan Le Prevost was quite pleased with his side's performance. Alderney's coach, Mick Price felt that if his side could have kept the score at 0-0 until half time who knows what would have happened. He thought that his side fought well and did their Island proud.

The Alderney man-of-the-match was Paul Bunn and he was chosen by Guernsey's manager, Tony Blondel.

MURATTI FINAL.
7 May 1990 – Springfield Stadium, Jersey.

Jersey -2, Guernsey -1.

Guernsey manager, Alan Le Prevost, selected the same side that beat Alderney in the semi-final and felt that Jersey would have to improve on their recent performance against Windsor and Eton to be able to defeat his side. There was some doubt as to whether Jersey's Tony Lawlor would play today. He was sent off playing for St. Paul's against Le Masurier's in the Carnaby Jeremie Cup in February but the Disciplinary Committee did not hear the case until 14 April and at that meeting Lawlor was suspended even though he maintains he did not commit the offence. Lawlor appealed against the decision but the JFA Council would not hear the appeal until that day.

The game had only been in progress for ten minutes when, following a midfield tussle with two Guernsey players, Jersey striker Steve Kilshaw was badly injured. The game was held up for 10 minutes pending the arrival of an ambulance that took him to hospital with a suspected fracture of the right leg. He was replaced by Dougie Ross and after he had been on only a matter of moments he hooked in a shot that went off over the top of the bar. After 31 minutes Mick Marley conceded a free-kick outside his penalty area on Jersey's right and, when Stratford knocked it into the goalmouth, Ross sent a header flashing past Ingrouille to put Jersey 1-0 ahead. Guernsey were finding it difficult to make an impression on the game and their attacking moves, which aimed balls at Kevin Le Tissier, were easily cleared by an impressive Shaun A'Court and a capable Steve Carlyon in the Jersey goal and the half ended Jersey-1, Guernsey-0.

Alan Le Prevost, the new Guernsey manager, replaced Daryl Tapp, who was unwell, with Mark Bisson and switched Martin Gallienne to central defence. Early in the second half both Kevin and Carl Le Tissier were booked but it was from a Guernsey free-kick that nearly brought the visitors a goal. Carl Le Tissier took the kick from some 30 yards and he sent a crashing drive that was superbly held by Carlyon as he sprang to his right.

A minute later Ingrouille dived to the foot of his left hand post to turn round a Ross shot that appeared destined for the net. The game quickly turned to the other end and Jersey had a lucky escape when a Carl Le Tissier corner was headed onto the bar by Dyer and collected by Carlyon. The home side responded and Ingrouille was again called into action when he saved from Tony Lawlor. The game now was fast and furious and in the 72nd minute substitute Vance broke away on the right and was brought down by Barker just inside the box. Carl Le Tissier, for the second successive Springfield Muratti, stepped up and beat Carlyon with a shot low to his right for Guernsey's equaliser. The visitors were now pushing on looking for the winner and once again Carlyon came to Jersey's rescue when Dyer sent in a great header from a Vance corner he leapt to the top right hand corner to turn the ball round. A minute later Grant Chalmers came very close to scoring as Guernsey maintained their momentum. The game appeared to be edging to extra time when, with 38 seconds remaining, right back Martyn Stratford crossed a long low ball from just inside the touchline; Andy Barker collected the ball on the far side of the Guernsey penalty area and, skipping round a challenge, pulled the ball back across the face of the goal for Carberry to nip in and force it past Ingrouille and into the net. There was no time for a Guernsey recovery and the match ended Jersey-2, Guernsey-1.

Jersey: S. Carlyon, M. Stratford, S. A'Court, W. Begbie, D. Corrigan, A. Lawlor,
      A. Barker, P. Carberry, A. Salaun, J. Murray, S. Kilshaw.
      Sub: D. Ross.
      Goal scorers: Ross, Carberry.

Guernsey: S. Ingrouille, L. Smith, I. Ozanne, M. Marley, D. Tapp, R. Elmy,
      C. Dyer (c), G. Chalmers, M. Gallienne, C. Le Tissier, K. Le Tissier.
      Sub: A. Vance, M. Bisson.
      Goal scorer: C. Le Tissier (pen).

The Ossie Eloury Memorial Trophy was presented to new cap John Murray of Jersey.

Jimmy Reeves, the Jersey manager, was delighted with this victory and praised Guernsey for their second half performance although he felt that his side should have scored more goals in the first half when they were well on top. Alan Le Prevost was stunned at losing to such a late goal but felt that his team had not played in the first half and appeared to freeze. On the second half performance he said that they deserved to take the game to extra-time.

Steve Carlyon saves from a Carl Le Tissier free-kick.

Jersey celebrate with the Muratti Vase.

Alderney squad.

1 9 9 1

MURATTI SEMI-FINAL.
23 March 1991, Mount Hale, Alderney.

Alderney -1, Jersey -4.

Peter Concanen returned to the Alderney side but coach Mike Price announced that Paul Bunn was ruled out due to injury. Charlie Binet, Jersey FA chairman and Jersey coach, Jimmy Reeves were very unhappy prior to this match. An injury sustained in a Ryco Trust Sunday Soccer League match had ruled out Tony Lawlor (St. Paul's) and he was replaced by Paul Bouteloup (First Tower). Players had been warned that if they were unfit for a schedule practice match on Monday 18 March they would be left out of the side to play Alderney. They also lost the services of central defender Ricky Muddyman (Sporting Academics) due to a toe injury and he was replaced by Bill Begbie. This was to have been Muddyman's Muratti debut. Mr Binet was pleased with the Jersey squad's build up and was quoted as saying 'I know its only Alderney we are playing against, but anything can happen.' Jersey had selected three new caps for this match in Steve Coutanche (First Tower), Adam Greig (St. Paul's) and Chris Hamon (St. Peter).

As the match began Carre, in the Alderney goal was very quickly into the action with a magnificent reflex save from Chris Hamon. Three minutes later Alderney broke and over-lapping full-back, John Stretton, shot past the oncoming Carlyon only to see Paul Duffy clear on the line. Adam Greig then produced a jinking run for Jersey but fired his shot against the post. Alderney responded and a lapse by Duffy let in Kevin Gentle for a shot that extended Carlyon who did well to save to his right. It had been a lively opening spell with Alderney holding their own but in the 26th minute Jersey took the lead when Steve Coutanche cut in from the left and pulled the ball back for Hamon to score at the near post. The game remained very tight and at half time the score was Alderney-0, Jersey-1.

Jersey went two up in the second minute of the second half when, from a Paul Carberry right-wing corner, Shaun A'Court back-headed the ball over the line at the near post despite

James Maxwell's brave attempt to clear. Alderney struck back two minutes later when, from Alderney's only corner of the match, Begbie failed to cut the ball out and Andy Wright smashed in an unstoppable shot past Steve Carlyon. The match again became very even and it was not until the 67th minute that Jersey regained a two-goal advantage when Greig headed in a Coutanche cross past Carre. Jersey sent on substitute goalkeeper Richard Herbert as well as Tommy Querns and it was from a Herbert goal kick that Hamon set up the final goal for Greig. Alderney coach was on a substitute but the final result was Alderney-1, Jersey-4.

Alderney: N. Carre, D. Walker, J. Maxwell, P. Concanen, J. Stretton, A. Wright, K. Gentle, G. Rushbury, I. MacFarlane, P. Burland, M. Price.
Sub: P. Bunn, H. Aldcroft, A. Adamson.
Goalscorer: Wright.

Jersey: S. Carlyon, P. Duffy, A. Salaun, S. Coutanche, A. Greig, W. Begbie, P. Bouteloup, A. Barker, P. Carberry, C. Hamon, S. A'Court.
Sub: T. Querns, R. Herbert.
Goalscorers: Hamon, A'Court, Greig (2).

Jimmy Reeve, the Jersey coach, was not very impressed with the condition of the Mount Hale pitch and said that someone could get badly injured he was, however, full of praise for Alderney. Best for Jersey was midfielder Andy Barker. The goal that Andy Wright scored for Alderney was the first home goal scored against Jersey and only the 18th to be scored against them.

Jersey official, Tommy De Feu, selected goalkeeper, Nick Carre, as Alderney's man-of-the-match. Best for Alderney were Carre, Concanen and young Damien Walker.

A report in the Alderney Journal commented on the famous Alderney Muratti team of 1920 and the fact that the cap worn by Sam Allen (landlord of the Divers) was on display under a glass dome in the bar.

MURATTI FINAL.
6 May 1991 – Cycling Grounds, Guernsey.

Guernsey-3, Jersey-0.

Guernsey's Craig Allen (Rangers) returned to the squad for the first time since 1978. He had come back from America where he played in the professional indoor soccer tournaments. Guernsey's preparations for this final had gone very well with them winning two and drawing three of their five matches. Their finest victory was the 1-0 win against Wycombe Wanderers at the Cycling Grounds on Easter Monday. Guernsey had two new caps in their line-up with Mick Ogier (Belgrave Wanderers) and Lee Luscombe (St. Martin's) making their Muratti debuts. Jersey's preparations included their winning all five of their games including the 4-1 victory against Alderney. They had unfortunately lost the services of Tony Lawlor through injury and Adam Greig through suspension. Prior to the match commencing, the crowd were entertained by the band of the Dorset and Wiltshire Regiment. In attendance at the game were the Lieut-Governors of both islands and their ladies and the Bailiff and Lady Frossard.

Jersey started the quickest and, after four minutes, nearly capitalised on a misunderstanding in the Guernsey defence that resulted in Ingrouille punching the ball clear from outside his area. Baker took the resultant free-kick and sent the ball round the six-man wall and it crashed off the bar. Referee Saville ordered the kick to be retaken and Paul Carberry tamely hit his shot into the wall. Steve Carlyon was called on to make the first save of the match after 11 minutes as he easily collected Chris Dyer's 30 yard shot then a minute later Ingrouille made a fine save diving to his right to thwart Jersey's Chris Hamon. Tony Salaun came close with a 35 yard shot before Guernsey gradually began to pull things together and after 23 minutes Muddyman had to clear off his line after a Guernsey free-kick following a foul on Luscombe just outside the box. Less than a minute later Carl Le Tissier struck when he collected the ball on the right, went past a couple of defenders, before striking in a superb left-foot shot past Carlyon's right hand post to put the home side 1-0 ahead. Jersey replied three minutes later when, from a free-kick on the left edge of Guernsey's penalty area, John Murray hit his header against Ingrouille's right hand post and Bill Begbie collected the rebound but from only eight yards could only send his shot high over the bar. Jersey had to reorganise their side when Begbie had to limp off to be replaced by Paul Bouteloup. Guernsey were beginning to assert themselves and Luscombe came close twice when he headed a Chalmers cross just wide and then as he raced past the Jersey defence from an Ingrouille clearance he fired his shot over the bar. Half time score was Guernsey-1, Jersey-0.

Two minutes into the second half Vance was injured in a tackle with Muddyman and soon after had to leave the field being replaced by Craig Allen. Allen was quickly into the game and set up a goal chance for Luscombe who was denied by a brave save by Carlyon and as the ball ran away from him he had to be quick to deny Allen. Jersey were now being pushed deeper into defence but following a quick breakout Ingrouille had to be sharp to make a great clutching save to cut out a dangerous cross by Murray. On the hour mark as the play revolved around the Jersey goal Carlyon came quickly off his line to make a fine

L. Carre (coach), Ingrouille, de Carteret, Coutanche, Tapp, Dyer, Luscombe, Allen, Le Tissier, A. Le Prevost (manager).
Bisson, Chalmers, Marley, Vance, Ogier, Gauvain, Exall.
Guernsey squad.

Lee Luscombe watches his shot hit the post.

blocking save to deny Chalmers and then Le Tissier set up Luscombe but his shot failed to hit the target. As the game seemed to be pulling away from Jersey they had their hopes raised when Shaun A'Court sent in a glancing header that Ingrouille saved low to his left. In the 74th minute Guernsey struck again when Luscombe outpaced Querns and hit a left foot shot that struck the base of Carlyon's left hand post and the unfortunate Bouteloup rushing in to clear ran the ball over his own line. Guernsey continued to create chances through Allen and Chalmers but it was not until the 90th minute that once again Luscombe raced away from the Jersey defence to crash a great shot wide of Carlyon to make the final score Guernsey-3, Jersey-0.

Guernsey: S. Ingrouille, M. Gauvain, D. Tapp, C. Dyer (c), M. Marley, M. Ogier, G. de Carteret, G. Chalmers, C. Le Tissier, L. Luscombe, A. Vance. Sub: C. Allen. Goal scorers: C. Le Tissier, og. , Luscombe.

Jersey: S. Carlyon, R. Muddyman, W. Begbie, S. A'Court (c), A. Querns, S. Coutanche, P. Carberry, A. Barker, A. Salaun, J. Murray, C. Hamon. Subs: P. Bouteloup, J. Warren.

This was a superb team performance by Guernsey and gave them a thoroughly deserved victory. It was a double celebration with Grant Chalmers being awarded the Ossie Eloury Memorial Trophy.

Sir John Sutton with Chris Dyer.

Chris Dyer was presented with the coveted Muratti Vase by Jersey's Lieut-Governor Field Marshal Sir John Sutton. Sir John, although disappointed with the result, said that it was a clean match and that Guernsey had played very well. Jersey coach, Jimmy Reeves, was a very disappointed man as this was to be his last Muratti in charge.

In this match when Micky Ogier gained his first cap it was surprising to note that he was the first Ogier to be capped at senior Muratti level in the history of the competition.

Rex Bennet, the Evening Press chief football writer who had reported on virtually every Muratti match since the war, was unwell and unable to attend this match.

The victorious Guernsey team show off the Muratti Vase.

John Arlott OBE (1914 – 1991).

On 14 December 1991 John Arlott OBE died. He was probably the most famous commentator to report on the Muratti as he gave live radio broadcasts in the 1950's. He was born in Basingstoke, Hampshire on 25 February 1914. He was a BBC radio cricket commentator of unparalleled descriptive powers as well as being the writer, co-author or editor of some eighty books. He retired from the BBC in 1980 and moved to Alderney.

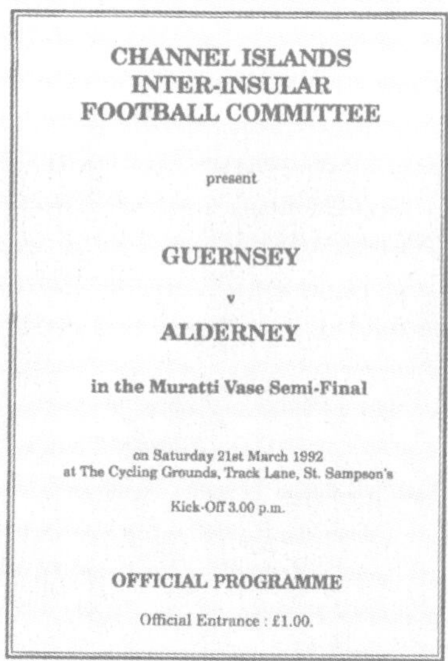

CHANNEL ISLANDS
INTER-INSULAR
FOOTBALL COMMITTEE

present

GUERNSEY

v

ALDERNEY

in the Muratti Vase Semi-Final

on Saturday 21st March 1992
at The Cycling Grounds, Track Lane, St. Sampson's

Kick-Off 3.00 p.m.

OFFICIAL PROGRAMME

Official Entrance : £1.00.

1 9 9 2

MURATTI SEMI-FINAL.
21 March 1992, The Cycling Grounds, Guernsey.

Guernsey -9, Alderney -1.

Guernsey had chosen Tony Vance for this match despite him playing for Enfield in the Diadora League this season although still on Sylvans' books. He was eligible because he was not under contract to Enfield and does not receive playing fees. Alderney were concerned after losing the services of central defender, John Stretton, who began a period of suspension. The Alderney FA queried the decision to ban him from representing them in the Muratti competition but the Inter-Insular Committee ruled that he was not eligible to play. Alderney also lost the services of Paul Bunn due to a long term injury. Alderney's coaches, Mike Price and Billy Bohan, were confident of a good result as they had been playing well as a team in Guernsey's Railway League.

Alderney won the toss and rather surprisingly chose to play against the wind. The game was only three minutes old when Guernsey took the lead when the Alderney defence failed to clear a Vance cross and, from the edge of the box, Kevin Le Tissier scored with a shot into the bottom left hand corner as Craig Allen dummied the ball. Only two minutes later Allen put Guernsey two up as Vance crossed in from a short left-wing corner by Carl Le Tissier. Seconds later Kevin Le Tissier set up Vance for goal number three. The Guernsey pressure was incessant and but for some fine goalkeeping by Carre and the woodwork on a couple of occasions the score would have been greater. Alderney held out until the last five minutes of the half when Dyer headed home a Carl Le Tissier right-wing corner and then Chalmers and Vance set up another goal for Le Tissier. In between these goals Dyer almost handed Alderney a goal when his faulty back-pass found Kevin Gentle but he was quickly closed down by Gary De Carteret. The half time score was Guernsey-5, Alderney-0.

The second half began as the first ended and very soon Allen had hit the woodwork fol-

A happy group of Alderney supporters.

Craig Allen scoring Guernsey's second goal.

lowing a brilliant run by Chalmers and a pass from Kevin Le Tissier. Kevin Le Tissier soon made it 6-0 from a through ball from his brother, Carl, and a minute later a repeat move let in Kevin to score number 7. In a rare Alderney attack Ian Drillot had to dash out to clear from Kevin Gentle. Seconds later Chalmers scored again for Guernsey from a Carl Le Tissier free-kick. In the 65th minute Guernsey received a shock when, after Wright had knocked down an Ian MacFarlane free-kick, Fairbrother threw himself forward at the far post to score for Alderney although there was a slight suspicion that it was a hand rather than his head that had put the ball in the net. This goal brought out the biggest cheer of the afternoon. Guernsey regained their 8-goal advantage when Mark Bisson, receiving from substitute Exall, came in from the right to set up Kevin Le Tissier for his fifth goal in the 78th minute. Kevin Le Tissier nearly scored his 6th but his header came off the post. In the dying minutes Carre did well to prevent Exall and then Kevin Le Tissier from adding to the total leaving the final score Guernsey-9, Alderney-1.

Guernsey: I. Drillot, D. Tapp, C. Dyer (c), G. de Carteret, M. Marley, M. Bisson, G. Chalmers, C. Le Tissier, C. Allen, K. Le Tissier, A. Vance.
Subs: A. Exall, R. Gallienne.
Goalscorers: K. Le Tissier (5), C. Allen, Vance, Dyer, Chalmers.

Alderney: N. Carre, P. Burland, P. Concanen, J. Maxwell, M. Price, I. MacFarlane, A. Wright (c), D. Walker, K. Fairbrother, G. Rushbury, K. Gentle.
Sub: H. Aldcroft.
Goalscorer: Fairbrother.

Following the game Billy Bohan stated that Alderney had the worst possible start to the game and overall did not do themselves justice. In scoring five goals Kevin Le Tissier equalled Craig Allen's five goal performance of 1978.

It was reported in the Press of Saturday 28 March that Aurigny Nomads would be applying for promotion to the Jackson League. Matt Walker, the Aurigny Nomads secretary, said that they could only play in both the Railway and Jackson Leagues with the help of Alderney's other team, the Colts, who only play friendlies. He added that their ultimate aim was to play in the Priaulx League. The Aurigny Nomads had an excellent 1991-92 season by winning the Railway League Championship as well as the Rouget Cup.

MURATTI FINAL.
4 May 1992, Springfield Stadium, Jersey.

Jersey -2, Guernsey -3. aet.

Jersey had a new coach in former Muratti player Peter Vincenti. Peter gained 12 Muratti caps between 1978 to 1987 scoring 6 goals and winning 4 Muratti medals. He had chosen two new caps in Gary Lightbody and P. Grierson along with Simon Le Rougetel on the substitute's bench. Guernsey had chosen an experienced starting line-up but had two players on the substitute's bench who would gain their first caps in Stuart Polson (North) and Adrian Exall (Vale Rec). In attendance at Springfield were Sir John Sutton, Lieut-Governor of Jersey, and Sir Michael Wilkins, Lieut-Governor of Guernsey, and the Bailiff of Jersey, Sir Peter Crill, and their ladies.

It was a fine sunny day at Springfield and the thrills began early as within five minutes Carlyon had to plunge to the foot of his right hand post to save a shot from Vance. Two minutes later, however, it was Jersey who took the lead when Barker played the ball from the centre to Carberry on the left and, as he crossed, Livesey dived in to score past Ingrouille. Twice more Livesey threatened the visitor's goal as Jersey took control with Guernsey struggling to get into the game. The match was 30 minutes old before Guernsey threatened when Carl Le Tissier sent Chalmers clear and he crossed for Kevin Le Tissier to hit a shot that was saved by Carlyon. The Jersey keeper did very well soon afterwards to hold a Carl Le Tissier drive following a fine touchline drive

by Vance. A minute later Carl Le Tissier conceded a free-kick following a foul on Livesey and Murphy's kick led to Barker increasing Jersey's lead as he took advantage of defensive uncertainty in the visitors defence. As half time approached Guernsey rallied and Carlyon managed to save at the feet of Kevin Le Tissier. The game entered injury time and a sparkling run by Allen let in Kevin Le Tissier and, after rounding the keeper, scored an important goal to make the half time score Jersey-2, Guernsey-1.

Guernsey made a tactical switch at half-time when they pulled Mark Bisson out of the midfield to play at right back and reverted to the sweeper system that had served them well all season. However it was Jersey that made the more impressive start to the second half with Lawlor coming close to restoring the home side's two goal advantage. Guernsey responded and won a series of free-kicks, one of which led to a close-in chance for Vance but he was thwarted by Carlyon. With 17 minutes remaining Guernsey equalised with a

Kevin Le Tissier appears to use his hand for Guernsey's equalising goal as Carlyon rushes out.

Vance crashes home Guernsey's winning goal.

controversial score. Allen sent a ball into the Jersey defence and Kevin Le Tissier went up with Bouteloup and appeared to use his hand to tip the ball over the onrushing Carlyon and into the net.

The game became very even and could have gone either way but Guernsey had an escape when Mick Marley cleared off the line following a corner. Livesey then did well to keep the ball in play on the right touchline and get a cross in which saw Ingrouille rush out and clear from substitute Hamon and the match ended Jersey-2, Guernsey-2.

Guernsey gained the advantage eight minutes into extra time when, following a brilliant run by Allen from the left in which he slipped three or four tackles, he set up Tony Vance who created some space and scored with a great rising shot.

Jersey again came back and de Carteret cleared a Muddyman header from under the bar and then Ingrouille tipped over a fine shot-on-the-turn by Carberry. The first period of extra-time ended Jersey-2, Guernsey-3.

In the second period of extra time Ingrouille again came to Guernsey's rescue when he turned aside a blast by Barker. As the game neared its end Guernsey missed a great chance to increase their slender lead when Chalmers, put through by Allen, flicked the ball over the bar and the match ended Jersey-2, Guernsey-3.

Jersey: S. Carlyon, R. Muddyman, P. Bouteloup, W. Begbie, J. Murray, A. Lawlor, A. Barker, G. Lightbody, P. Grierson, N. Livesey, P. Carberry.
Sub: S. Le Rougetel, C. Hamon.
Goalscorers: Livesey, Barker.

Guernsey: S. Ingrouille, D. Tapp, C. Dyer (c), G. de Carteret, M. Marley, C. Le Tissier, G. Chalmers, M. Bisson, K. Le Tissier, C. Allen, A. Vance.
Sub: S. Polson, A. Exall.
Goalscorers: K. Le Tissier (2), Vance.

This was a tremendous fight back by Guernsey although their equalising goal was very controversial. Although it looked like a hand ball the chairman of Jersey's selectors, Charlie Binet, said that the better side had won. Jersey's new coach, Peter Vincenti, felt that his team should never have lost after gaining a two-goal advantage but although they played well in the first half they were hustled out of it by Guernsey. Alan Le Prevost said that the half time changes were required because the team was looking lethargic and he felt that they had to stabilise things. He felt that Guernsey looked more solid from the start of the second half.

It was interesting to note that an unruly spectator was ejected from Springfield during the match by a police officer by the name of Barry Breuilly. Barry was Jersey's Muratti goalkeeper from 1966-1981 gaining 20 caps and seven winners' medals.

Chris Dyer receives the Muratti Vase.

1 9 9 3

MURATTI SEMI-FINAL.
20 March 1993-Mount Hale, Alderney.

Alderney -0, Guernsey -10.

Alderney had two new caps in their side in Jamie Sugden and Hatcher as well as having Clem Sugden on the substitute's bench. They were, however, without the services of Peter Concanen and John Stretton. Guernsey had two new caps on the substitute's bench in Geraint ap Sion (Vale Rec) and Paul Nobes (Sylvans). Paul Nobes was to win his first senior cap just before earning his second junior cap. Guernsey was led out onto Mount Hale by mascot Ross Yeates for this Muratti match.

Guernsey were rather slow to take command and took the lead only after 10 minutes when Dyer headed back a Carl Le Tissier free-kick from the far post and Kevin Le Tissier set up Craig Allen who hooked a shot onto the underside of the bar and bounced into the net. Five minutes later Carl Le Tissier sent over a corner kick and Allen scored again after a Dyer header had been blocked.

Guernsey kept up the pressure and Micky Ogier came in from the left and cut back for Allen to complete his hat-trick after 29 minutes and nine minutes later Ogier supplied a through ball for Kevin Le Tissier to score number four, although Carre got a touch to the

Craig Allen beats the Alderney defence to score his second goal.

ball. A minute later a four man Guernsey move ended with Kevin Le Tissier scoring after Carre had saved from Allen. Although stunned by these reverses Alderney kept battling and in the 42nd minute they won a corner which was taken by Rushbury, and Drillot did well to claim the ball in the air under pressure from Mark Treais. Half time arrived with the score Alderney-0, Guernsey-5.

Alderney made a promising start to the second half setting up some serious attacks. They had replaced Hatcher and Cosheril with Robert Bohan and Clem Sugden and were making some positive headway but in the 63rd minute Allen struck with two goals in a minute.

As the pressure on the Alderney defence continued Carre denied Kevin Le Tissier with a tip-over save and then Guernsey sent on ap Sion and Paul Nobes in place of Daryl Tapp and Tony Vance. The Alderney defence were finding it difficult to cope with the incisive

Allen scoring his fourth goal.

play of Allen and in the 69th minute he disposed a defender and ran in to score goal number eight and nine minutes later a Carl Le Tissier corner was headed back by Dyer to Allen to head in number nine. With four minutes remaining Kevin Le Tissier sent in a goal-bound shot which was cleared by Alderney skipper, Andy Wright, by using his hand and referee Browne had no hesitation in awarding a penalty. Kevin Le Tissier took the kick which was well saved by Carre, but ap Sion rushed in and scored from the rebound to make the final score Alderney-0, Guernsey-10.

Alderney: N. Carre, P. Burland, A. Wright (c), MacFarlane, J. Sugden, Maxwell, M. Treais, Gentle, G. Rushbury, Hatcher, A. Cosheril.
Sub: R. Bohan, C. Sugden.

Guernsey: I. Drillot, G. de Carteret, M. Gauvain, D. Tapp, C. Dyer (c), M. Marley, C. Le Tissier, M. Ogier, A. Vance, K. Le Tissier, C. Allen.
Sub: G. ap Sion, P. Nobes.
Goal scorers: C. Allen (7), K. Le Tissier (2), ap Sion.

This was a match in which Craig Allen re-wrote the record book by scoring 7 goals in a single Muratti match beating the previous record of five goals. The Alderney coach, Alan Adamson, felt that, despite the result, his team had played better than when they lost 9-1 to Jersey last year and was full of praise for Jamie Sugden, keeper Carre and Andy Cosheril. Guernsey manager, Alan Le Prevost, although happy with the result was not satisfied with the slow start to each half.

It was announced in the Press of Monday 22nd March that Bill Custard of the Jersey Evening Post had sadly died aged 78. Rex Bennet wrote a moving tribute to his old friend and colleague in the Press of 27th March. As well as being Jersey's leading sports reporter he was an Evening Press correspondent for many years. He was born in South Africa of an English father and moved to Jersey before the Second World War. He specialised in covering football, cricket and boxing for the Jersey Evening Post from the late 1940's until his retirement in 1979.

In the run up to the 1993 Muratti Vase Final Guernsey's first 'Fanzine' was published and it was entitled 'The Hand of Le Tissier' It was billed as '100% Unofficial' and included items such as the worst Muratti teams ever (the entire Jersey selection was Peter Vincenti). The publication was very quickly banned by the officials and only a few survive. The title related to the controversial Kevin Le Tissier goal at Springfield in 1992.

Rex Bennet & Bill Custard.

MURATTI FINAL.
3 May 1993, The Cycling Grounds, Guernsey.

Guernsey -1, Jersey -2.

Bill Robilliard, secretary of the CI Inter-Insular Football Committee revealed that the Guernsey and Jersey Bailiffs as well as both Lieutenant-Governors and their ladies would be attending the Muratti Vase final. Mr. Robilliard had been contacted by Sir Peter Crill, the Jersey Bailiff, to say he would be attending. Guernsey's Bailiff, Mr. Graham Dorey, will be attending as a patron of the GFA as is the Lieutenant-Governor.

Guernsey's coach, Alan Le Prevost, was confident of a victory despite the fact that Guernsey had lost 3-1 to the Air Naval Command, 7-1 to Southampton and 4-0 against the Royal Navy. Jersey had beaten an RAF XI 3-0 during their Muratti build-up.

The Guernsey Scout Band entertained the crowd of around 3,000 as the teams came onto the field. Guernsey were captained by Chris Dyer who came out with Ross Yeates, the team mascot, and Jersey were led out by skipper Andy Barker.

The first opening of the match came when Craig Allen from the right bye-line found Chris Dyer just outside the six-yard box but his goal-bound shot was brilliantly saved by Steve Carlyon in the Jersey goal. Jersey responded and de Freitas sent in a cross that Andy Barker headed just over, then de Freitas was again involved with a Jersey attack when his left-foot shot from the right produced a great one-handed save from Ingrouille. Ingrouille again came to Guernsey's rescue when he once again foiled de Freitas. There were chances at both ends with Kevin Le Tissier putting two shots over the bar before, in the 27th minute, Jersey took the lead. The visitors broke through the centre and Ingrouille did well

Kevin Le Tissier fires home Guernsey' equaliser past a despairing Muddyman.

to foil de Freitas but the ball broke to Greig and he forced it over the line with Kellett following it in. Guernsey responded three minutes later when Carl Le Tissier sent a glorious ball to his brother Kevin who turned inside from the right wing to crash a low left-foot shot past Carlyon's left hand.

Guernsey went all out for a second goal but had an escape in the 37th minute when de Freitas fired just wide from 30 yards. A minute later Jersey regained the lead when Greig received a pass from Barker and slipped the ball past Tapp as he raced into the box only for Tapp to hit him with his shoulder. Referee Brian Hill had no hesitation in pointing to the spot and Paul Harzo beat Steve Ingrouille to his right. Half-time arrived with the score Guernsey-1, Jersey-2.

The second half began with a Carl Le Tissier free-kick on the edge of the penalty area being blocked by the Jersey wall then Kevin Le Tissier, on a pass from Carl, had his shot deflected over the bar. Guernsey continued to press and Tony Vance set up Craig Allen but his shot came off the bar and this was followed by Ogier feeding Carl Le Tissier but his cross-shot was brilliantly tipped over by Carlyon. An excellent move involving Ogier, Kevin Le Tissier and Vance resulted in another magnificent save by Carlyon and as the ball broke to Martin Gauvain he fired his shot over. De Freitas relieved this Guernsey pressure at times and Jersey managed to hold out leaving the final result Guernsey-1, Jersey-2.

Guernsey: S. Ingrouille, G. de Carteret, M. Gauvain, D. Tapp, C. Dyer (c), M. Marley, C. Le Tissier, M. Ogier, A. Vance, K. Le Tissier, C. Allen.
Sub: A. Exall.
Goalscorer: K. Le Tissier.

Jersey: S. Carlyon, M. Stratford, R. Muddyman, P. Harzo, S. Kirkpatrick, S. Petulla, A. Barker (c), J. Kellett, P. Greirson, N. de Freitas, A. Greig.
Subs: M. Forbes, M. McKenna.
Goalscorers: Greig, Harzo (pen).

The Muratti Vase was presented to the Jersey captain, Andy Barker, by Guernsey's Lieutenant-Governor. The Ossie Eloury Memorial Trophy was presented to Nelio de Freitas. The panel consisted of John Brehaut, Junior Island coach, a representative from the JFA along with a Magpies representative.

Although de Freitas was awarded the man-of-the-match trophy it was felt by the Guernsey team, as well as some of the Jersey side, de Freitas included, that the trophy should have gone to goalkeeper Steve Carlyon. It was agreed that Carlyon had thwarted Guernsey on a number of occasions with a series of truly magnificent saves. Retiring Guernsey coach, Alan Le Prevost, shook his head in disbelief at some of the saves. Best for Guernsey were Gary de Carteret and Micky Ogier.

Barker receiving the Muratti Vase.

1 9 9 4

Graeme Le Saux (Blackburn Rovers) gained his first full England cap against Denmark at Wembley Stadium on 9 March 1994. He becomes the first Channel Island footballer to win an England cap as well as being the only Muratti player to play in a full international match. He won one Muratti cap in Jersey's dramatic 4-3 win against Guernsey at the Track on 9 May 1987.

Graeme Le Saux (Jersey & England).

Matthew Le Tissier (Southampton) became the first Guernsey player to gain a full England cap when he came on as a substitute after 67 minutes in the same game.

MURATTI SEMI-FINAL.
19 March 1994 – Springfield Stadium, Jersey.

Jersey -18, Alderney -0.

Jersey had five new caps in their side with Craig Ferey, Trevor le Maistre (St. Peter), Ian Daley (St. Pauls), Craig Morton (Jersey Scottish) and Jerry O'Shea (First Tower). Alderney were without the services of Paddy Burland and young full-back Angus MacDonald took his place to gain his first cap. M. Lee was also making his debut for Alderney as well as substitute Sebire.

Alderney opened up brightly against Jersey at Springfield and produced an eight-man passing move which was repulsed by the home side. The visitors were soon under severe pressure and the match became a goal procession as Jersey re-wrote the Muratti scoring book with wave after wave of attacks. Alderney had no answer as they were overrun, and incredibly when half-time arrived the score was Jersey -8, Alderney-0.

The second half was one of torment for Alderney as Jersey continued to score at will and found the net a further 10 times. Jersey's control and passing in the wet conditions was markedly superior and shots rained in on the unlucky Carre, who had difficulty in holding the greasy ball all afternoon. Alderney enjoyed only one real scoring chance and that did not arrive until late in the game which finally ended Jersey-18, Alderney-0.

Jersey: S. Carlyon, R. Muddyman, C. Ferey, T. le Maistre, I. Daly, A. Barker, C. Morton, N. de Freitas, P. Carberry, J. O'Shea, S. Petulla.
Sub: N. de Jesus, Steigenberger.
Goal scorers: Petulla (5), O'Shea (5), de Freitas (3), Carberry (2), Le Maistre, Muddyman, Steigenberger.

Alderney: N. Carre, A. MacDonald, J. Maxwell, A. Wright, M. Treais, W. White, P. Concanen, Lee, C. Sugden, G. Rushbury, K. Gentle.
Sub: Sebire.

This was an overwhelming victory for Jersey as they comprehensively re-wrote the Muratti scoring record book. Although Simon Petulla and Jerry O'Shea (both of First Tower) scored five goals apiece, remarkably no player beat Craig Allen's score of seven goals in a Muratti match.

Alderney's most impressive players were their Jersey born captain Andy Wright and young full-back Angus MacDonald in what was a depressing result for them.

On Thursday 24 March 1994 the Guernsey Evening Press published a rather cutting cartoon by 'Wakky' that referred to Jersey's record Muratti score.

Alderney team.

MURATTI FINAL.
2 May 1994- Springfield Stadium, Jersey.

Jersey -3, Guernsey -1.

The Guernsey side had a new manager in Colin Fallaize as well as four new caps in goal-keeper Glyn Ridley from Vale Rec and John Nobes, Joel Avery and Mark Coutanche all from Sylvans. John Nobes was winning his first senior cap in the same season he won a junior cap.

The first half started quietly with very few chances at either end. Chalmers was shaping up well for Guernsey and his skilful play was causing some concern to the home defence. New cap John Nobes was playing well in the heart of the visitors' defence and, along with Mick Marley, were protecting goalkeeper Ridley effectively. The game sparked into life when a run by Micky Ogier on the right set up Tony Vance who, as he ran into the box, appeared to be brought down, but referee Alcock waived away the Guernsey protests. The only two goal chances in the half were created by Jersey and the best one was from a Barker corner kick that was headed over by Petulla much to his annoyance. Jersey slightly edged the half but the score remained Jersey-0, Guernsey-0.

Guernsey started the second half more in control and came close on two occasions one of which was when Chalmers combined with Le Tissier but the move came to nothing. Nine minutes into the half Coutanche was fouled on the left touchline and Chalmers sent in a cross into the Jersey area, Bouteloup attempted to head clear but only succeeded in nod-ding it down to Kevin Le Tissier who instantly hammered it past Carlyon to put Guernsey 1-0 ahead.

Kevin Le Tissier hammers the ball past Carlyon.

Vance was only inches away from scoring moments later and then on 58 minutes Le Tissier burst through the centre on a long ball and fired in a shot that Carlyon brilliantly got his fingers to, preventing a certain goal. This magnificent save was the turning point in the match and two minutes later Jersey were level, when a 25 yard swerving shot by Nick de Jesus appeared to hit a bump and shot into the net between the keeper, Glyn Ridley, and his left hand post. Fourteen minutes later Jersey went ahead when, following a left-wing corner by de Jesus, Ridley was put under a lot of pressure by Muddyman and the Jersey forwards and despite two attempts to clear the ball fell to Petulla who scored from close quarters. With nine minutes remaining de Freitas sent a pass to substitute Daley and as he entered the penalty area he was brought down by Joel Avery. Referee Alcock immediately pointed to the spot and Petulla fired his shot beyond the reach of Ridley's right hand. Guernsey responded and again there were appeals for a penalty when it seemed that Le Tissier had been brought down but again the referee was unimpressed and the match ended Jersey-3, Guernsey-1.

Jersey: S. Carlyon, P. Harzo, R. Muddyman, T. le Maistre, P. Bouteloup, C. Morton, N. de Jesus, A. Barker, P. Carberry, N. de Freitas, S. Petulla.
Sub: I. Daley, M. Stratford.
Goal scorers: De Jesus, Petulla (2, 1 pen).

Guernsey: G. Ridley, M. Marley, J. Nobes, J. Avery, M. Coutanche, M. Ogier, G. Chalmers, C. Dyer (c), M. Bisson, K. Le Tissier, A. Vance.
Sub: A. Exall, D. Yeates
Goal scorer: K. Le Tissier.

The adjudicators for the Ossie Eloury Memorial Trophy were Ian Golding and Charlie Binet of Jersey, and Guernsey's Keith Parkin and they selected two-goal Simon Petulla of Jersey.

Alderney.

1 9 9 5

MURATTI SEMI-FINAL.
18 March 1995, Mount Hale, Alderney.

Alderney -1, Jersey -7.

Alderney had included 15-year old William Benfield as one of their substitutes for their match against Jersey. Jersey also included a junior player as one of their substitutes in Ross Peebles. Ross was also eligible for Jersey's junior Muratti team and could join the small band of Jersey players to play in both Junior and Senior Muratti matches in the same season. Jersey also included Lee de St. Croix for his first cap.

After a rather quiet start Jersey took the lead after 10 minutes when debutant Lee de St. Croix scored and seven minutes later Andy Barker headed in the second for the visitors. It appeared as if Jersey were preparing to run up a major score early on and may have done but for the excellent play of the Alderney goalkeeper, Alan Adamson. Alderney managed to withstand this pressure and surprised Jersey by reducing the arrears after 26 minutes. Referee Geoff Carre ruled that keeper Steve Carlyon had picked up a back-pass and awarded a free-kick to Alderney. Mark Treais took the kick and saw his low shot deflected into the Jersey net past Carlyon. The game continued to be tight and at half-time the score was Alderney-1, Jersey-2.

Two minutes into the second half Jersey were awarded a corner and as Yozalde Santos' cross came over and appeared to be punched into the net by Adamson. Soon after this goal Santos was tripped in the Alderney penalty area and Nelio de Freitas scored from the spot kick. Adam Greig, who earlier had missed a few good chances for Jersey, scored number five before substitute Michael Steigenberger came on to score two more goals. Young

William Benfield made a good impression when he came on and set up a late chance for Mark Treais and in the closing moments Treais, James Maxwell and Damien Walker all came close to giving Alderney a second goal, but the final result was Alderney-1, Jersey-7.

Alderney: A. Adamson, A. MacDonald, A. Wright, K. Gentle, W. White, J. Maxwell, M. Treais, M. Lee, D. Walker, J. Williamson, G. Rushbury.
Sub: W. Benfield.
Goalscorer: Treais.

Jersey: S. Carlyon, M. Stratford, R. Muddyman, C. Ferey, N. de Freitas, A. Barker, J. O'Shea, C. Morton, L. de St. Croix, A. Greig, Y. Santos.
Subs: M. Steigenberger, R. Peebles.
Goalscorers: de St. Croix, Barker, de Freitas (pen), Greig, Steigenberger (2), og.

After the game Peter Vincenti, Jersey's manager, praised Alderney for their excellent performance on a good Mount Hale surface. When young William Benfield came on as a substitute for Alderney it was believed that, at 15 years and 35 days, he becomes the youngest ever Muratti player. The previous youngest player was Alderney's Freddie Odoire who gained his first Muratti cap in 1934 aged 15 years and 9 months.

The Guernsey Press cartoonist, Wakky, comments on the Muratti Sponsor.

MURATTI FINAL.
30 April 1995, The Cycling Grounds, Guernsey.

Guernsey -1, Jersey -2.

Guernsey manager, Colin Fallaize, selected only one new cap in his starting line-up with David Gilman of Sylvans winning his first cap. Tony Fitton (North) would make his debut from the substitute's bench. Peter Vincenti had chosen an experienced Muratti team.

The first half was a rather dull affair with very few scoring chances created as both teams appeared to be cancelling each other out. The first clear attempt on goal did not arrive until the 24th minute when, from a left wing Daley corner, Drillot flew to his left hand side and tipped a Steigenberger header over the bar. From the resulting corner Drillot again did well to keep out de St. Croix's effort. Guernsey's best effort came when Vance set up Chalmers but he sliced his shot well wide. Half time arrived with the score Guernsey-0, Jersey-0.

The second half sparked into life in the 61st minute when Grant Chalmers fired in a wonderful volley that beat Carlyon on his right and into the top corner, to put Guernsey 1-0 ahead.

The home team now battled to retain their lead but the game changed with what was to be an inspired substitution when, with 33 minutes remaining, Yozalde Santos came on. His pace and running began to seriously trouble the Guernsey defence and his running was giving the front men more space. Jersey benefited from this space when Ian Daley sent in a fine cross to pick out Greig at the far post and he

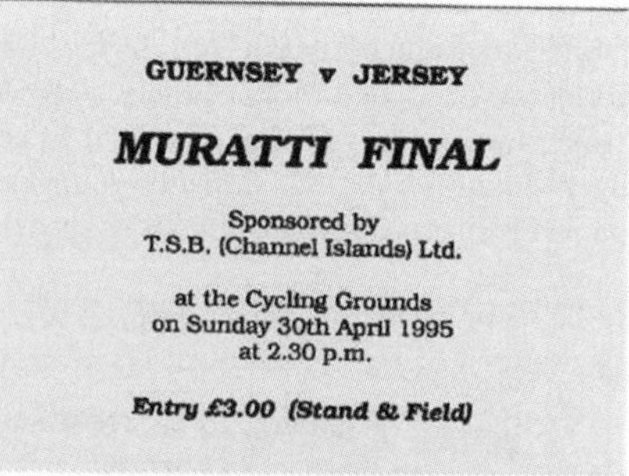

Guernsey Muratti squad.
M. Ogier, Fitton, Dyer, Ozanne, Drillot, J. Nobes, Chalmers, Coutanche, P. Nobes.
Marley, Bisson, Gilman, Colin Fallaize, S. Ogier, Avery, Vance.

Carlyon is beaten by Chalmers' shot.

lashed a right foot shot across Drillot and into the net to bring the scores level. Six minutes later Jersey took the lead when Muddyman launched a long ball out to the right from deep on the left towards Santos. Although Santos' initial attempt was blocked the ball found its way back to him and despite three Guernsey defenders on the line he curled in a superb left foot shot from 15 yards and into the far corner. Guernsey reorganised their side bringing on Tony Fitton for his first cap in an attempt to save the game but nearly went even further behind when with three minutes to go Drillot made a great tip over save from Greig. In the final minute Vance went down from a challenge from Muddyman but referee Willard waived away the Guernsey claims and the game ended Guernsey-1, Jersey-2,

Guernsey: I. Drillot, D. Gillman, M. Marley, J. Nobes, C. Dyer (c), M. Coutanche, M. Ogier, M. Bisson, G. Chalmers, P. Nobes, A. Vance.
Sub: J. Avery, A. Fitton.
Goal scorer: Vance.

Jersey: S. Carlyon, M. Stratford, T. le Maistre, R. Muddyman, I. Daley, L. de St. Croix, J. Kellett, A. Barker (c), C. Morton, M. Steigenberger, R. Peebles.
Sub: Y. Santos, J. O'Shea.
Goal scorer: Greig, Santos.

The Ossie Eloury Memorial Trophy was presented to Jersey's Ricky Muddyman (pictured above left), whilst The Muratti Vase was presented to Andy Barker by Guernsey's Lieut-Governor Sir John Coward.

1 9 9 6

MURATTI SEMI-FINAL.
16 March 1996, Mount Hale, Alderney.

Alderney -0, Guernsey -2.

Alderney had two new caps in their line up with Damien Walker and Nigel Jarvis making their debuts. It was also announced that the former Elizabeth College striker, Jim Williamson would take his place up front for Alderney. Alderney player/manager, Alan Adamson, who will be the reserve goalkeeper and defender, was expecting a very tough game. Colin Fallaize, Guernsey manager, axed Martin Gauvain (Sylvans) from the squad when he was informed that he would not be available for the preparation for a possible Muratti Final. Mr. Fallaize said that it was very disappointing but he had no choice after the Sylvans player told him that he would be away from the island for the entire week leading up to the Final on 6 May only returning on the evening of 5 May. His place in the match against Alderney was taken by Mick Marley (Vale Rec). Paul de Garis (Sylvans) would be making his Muratti debut and Steve Ogier (Belgrave W.) would gain his first cap by coming on as a substitute late in the second half. There was some concern over the condition of the Mount Hale pitch and there was evidence of a number of potholes especially down the wings.

Guernsey started the quickest and was soon on top. They would have opened the scoring but for a superb save by keeper Carre from a Kevin Le Tissier header. He was then called into action from the resultant corner as Vance's shot hit the crossbar. Alderney then settled into the game and, on 20 minutes, new cap Andrew Davies played a quick on-two with Damien Walker but put his shot wide of the post. Moments later de Garis in the Guernsey goal had to hang onto a low bobbling shot by Nigel Jarvis. The Guernsey defence came under more pressure and on 27 minutes Jarvis again was close when he evaded two challenges only to drag his left foot shot wide of the far post. Vance came close for the visitors followed by a sliced shot by Walker but in the 38th minute the deadlock was finally broken. An Adie Exall shot was blocked on the edge of the box and the ball flew up just above waist height. Le Tissier latched onto the ball and crashed an unstoppable volley into the top right-hand corner. Despite this reverse Alderney continued to battle well and at half time the score was Alderney-0, Guernsey-1.

The second half was only nine minutes old when Guernsey grabbed their second goal. They won a corner and Vance crossed the ball in, Carre appeared to flap at it and allowed Le Tissier to send a powerful downward header into the net. Le Tissier should have completed his hat-trick on the hour but he blazed his shot over from six yards. Two minutes later Le Tissier limped off to be replaced by Matt Falla, who was gaining his first cap, and then Lee Renouf replaced a hobbling John Nobes. Seven minutes later James Maxwell should have scored for Alderney but he missed his chance from 14 yards out when in plenty of space. Steve Ogier came on late in the game to gain his first Muratti cap. This was the last main chance and the game ended Alderney-0, Guernsey-2.

Two-goal Le Tissier is foiled by Nick Carre.

Steve Ogier.

Alderney: N. Carre, A. Davies, A. Wright, K. Gentle (c), P. Concanen, K. Fairbrother, D. Walker, M. Treais, J. Maxwell, N. Jarvis, J. Williamson.
Subs: Harvey, Battrick, S. Benfield.

Guernsey: P. De Garis, G. de Carteret, J. Nobes, C. Dyer (c), M. Marley, P. Nobes, R. Elmy, J. Avery, K. Le Tissier, A. Exall, A. Vance.
Subs: M. Falla, L. Renouf, S. Ogier.
Goalscorer: Le Tissier (2).

  This was not a satisfactory performance by Guernsey and it was left to Kevin Le Tissier to save their blushes with two goals. Rodney Elmy had an excellent game in the midfield. Alderney had some early chances to take the initiative but finally paid the price for not capitalising on them.

  It was announced in the Press of 4 May that 76-year old Harold Le Poidevin had died. Harold, a stylish, elegant defender and always cool under pressure, won four Muratti caps between 1948 and 1951. He captained Guernsey when they defeated Jersey 3-1 after extra-time in the 1951 Muratti Vase Final in front of a record crowd of 12,692. He was a true gentleman both off and on the field and renowned for his sportsmanship. The news of his passing, after a lengthy illness, will have saddened all who knew, liked and respected him.

MURATTI FINAL.
6 May 1996, St. Peter's F.C., Jersey.

Jersey -0, Guernsey -0. aet.

  Jersey had an injury concern over the former Exeter professional, Mark Brown, as he had slight tear of a knee ligament but he did in fact make his Muratti debut coming off the substitute's bench. The one new cap in Jersey's starting line-up was Damon Pih of Jersey Scottish. Guernsey would give Muratti debuts to Ashley Smith (Port City) and Mike de la Haye (North). Referee, Steve Dunne, refereed the FA Cup quarter-final match at Old Trafford between Manchester United and Southampton.

There was a strong wind blowing down the pitch at St. Peter's as Jersey and Guernsey prepared for the Muratti Vase final. Guernsey began the match with the wind at their backs but Jersey looked the stronger with their defence coping easily with the visitor's attacks. After 11 minutes Jersey should have gone ahead when Ian Daley's left wing cross cleared Mick Marley and found Adam Greig unmarked only 10 yards from goal. He controlled the ball well but he delayed and allowed Paul Nobes to slide in for a great saving tackle and the ball was cleared. Three minutes later Greig mis-kicked after a Nelio de Freitas pull back found him in space close in. Soon after this Mick Marley had to go off due to a knee injury and he was replaced by his Vale Rec teammate, Daryl Yeates. Jersey continued to make scoring chances and midway through the half de Garis threw out a left hand to touch Craig Morton's

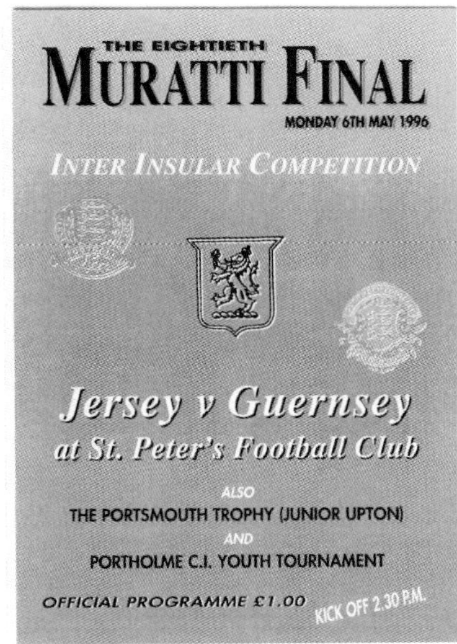

25 yard shot round for a corner. Guernsey broke up-field and Smith fed Vance who in turn found Le Tissier and the alert Carlyon managed to beat away his 18 yard snap shot. With 10 minutes remaining Carlyon again denied Le Tissier when he saved his tame far post header from a Vance cross. As the half neared its end de Freitas went close with a long range shot followed by a fine le Maistre header that went just over leaving the half time score Jersey-0, Guernsey-0.

As the second half started de Garis had to be sharp as he saved from Greig and five minutes later he tipped over Greig's header on a Hamon cross. With 20 minutes remaining both teams rang the changes with Guernsey's Smith taken off for Adie Exall, and Peter Vincenti putting on Mark McKenna for Damon Pih. Paul Nobes began to venture further forward

Carlyon saving with Le Tissier close by.

A tight midfield struggle.

with some sparkling runs but the home defence were able to mass behind the ball to clear the danger. Jersey again went on the offensive and Morton could only blaze his shot over following good work by Ian Daley on the right. There was five minutes remaining when Vance latched on to a Paul Nobes pass and nicked it past Carlyon but then lost possession and with Nobes and Le Tissier disputing who should attempt a shot the chance was gone with the final score Jersey-0, Guernsey-0.

Half way through the first period of extra time Yeates had Carlyon stretching to tip over and five minutes later a totally unmarked Le Tissier waited in vain for a pass from Exall who finally lost the ball following a Muddyman tackle. Mark Coutanche, who came on for Vance, released the nippy Exall and his shot from a tight angle beat Carlyon as well as the goalmouth. The half-time score was Jersey-0, Guernsey-0.

Three minutes into the second period John Nobes appeared to use his hand to block the ball but referee Steve Dunne was unimpressed and waived away the Jersey protests. With nine minutes remaining Dyer chased a long ball from Muddyman back towards his goal with Steigenberger right behind him. As de Garis came out to collect, Dyer touched the ball and it looped over the keeper and ricocheted off the post and into the arms of a grateful de Garis much to the relief of Dyer. There was no scoring and the match ended Jersey-0, Guernsey-0.

Jersey: S. Carlyon, T. le Maistre, C. Morton, R. Muddyman, C. Ferey, I. Daley, D. Pih, A. Barker (c), A. Greig, C. Hamon, N. de Freitas.
Sub: M. McKenna, M. Brown, M. Steigenberger.

Guernsey: P. de Garis, J. Avery, J. Nobes, C. Dyer (c), M. Marley, P. Nobes, M. de la Haye, M. Culverwell, A. Vance, K. Le Tissier, A. Smith.
Sub: D. Yeates, A. Exall, M. Coutanche.

This was the first draw for 21 years and only the second 0-0 draw in the history of the Muratti competition, the other being at the Cycling Grounds in 1955. This was to have been Chris Dyer's last Muratti appearance but now he was looking forward to the replay before his retirement. The replay was scheduled for Sunday 19 May at the Cycling Grounds.

MURATTI FINAL-REPLAY.
19 May 1996, The Cycling Grounds, Guernsey.

Guernsey -0, Jersey -1.

Once again there was Muratti controversy but this time it occurred before a ball was kicked in the replay. Jersey manager, Peter Vincenti, raised the temperature following a live broadcast on Radio Jersey where he told the listeners that his players were carrying 'above the waist injuries' from the first game and that he was disappointed to be coming back to Guernsey as he and his players had better things to do. The Guernsey manager, Colin Fallaize, on the other hand raised a few eyebrows with his squad selection for this match. On a lighter note Darren Duquemin, the Muratti Programme editor, couldn't believe his eyes when he opened the programme to find out that Guernsey skipper, Chris Dyer, had apparently been transferred to St. Martin's. It was later announced that this had been a genuine typing error.

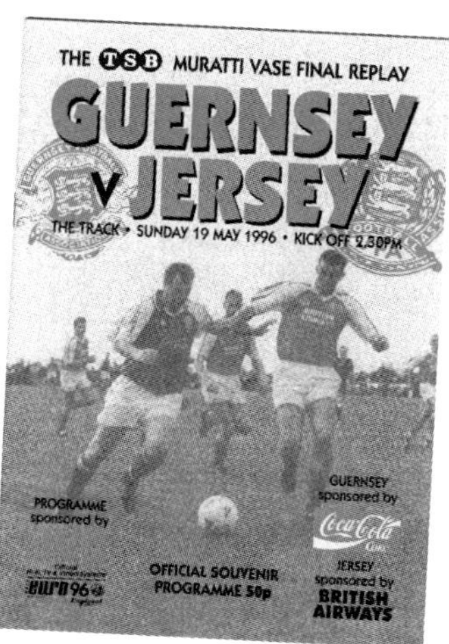

Guernsey started the brightest with Grant Chalmers proving a handful for the Jersey defence and Barker was booked for a rather hefty tackle on him after only 70 seconds. Guernsey continued to force the play with Chalmers using his skill and speed in an attempt to create an opening and he came close himself when he looped a header just over. He then freed Exall down the right and Carlyon had to dive low to his left to save his stinging shot. On the 15 minute mark Paul Nobes hooked in a left wing cross that caused Ferey some concern and he sliced his clearance over his own crossbar under severe pressure from Culverwell.

Unfortunately for Guernsey they lost Chalmers after 22 minutes when he had to leave the field injured and was replaced by Craig Allen. The main area of play was in the midfield with Culverwell and de la Haye prominent for the home side with Daley impressive for Jersey. The visitors were finding it difficult to create any scoring chances but with seven minutes to go de Freitas, coming down the right, set up Martin Cassidy but he fell over the ball in the six yard box. A minute later a Mike de la Haye corner found Dyer, free 10

Ferey slices the ball past Carlyon and over the bar with Culverwell pressurising.

Carlyon foils Craig Allen

yards, out and he powered a header that Steve Carlyon had to palm away at full stretch. Just before the interval Jersey's Chris Hamon had de Garis scrambling across his goal to cover a 30 yard snap shot leaving the half time score Guernsey-0, Jersey-0.

Ten minutes into the second half a quick Jersey break set up a chance for de Freitas but he was thwarted by a superb covering tackle by Coutanche. The visitors were now beginning to push Guernsey back and de Freitas screwed his shot wide on 56 minutes, and four minutes later Barker volleyed a difficult shot wide.

Guernsey appeared to have survived this period of pressure but in the 71st minute a seemingly harmless cross field ball from the left was allowed to run and de Freitas got goal-side of his marker to shoot under the advancing de Garis to put Jersey 1-0 ahead. Guernsey responded and Culverwell was robbed by Ferey at the expense of a corner and from this corner Culverwell headed just over. Guernsey sent on Kevin Le Tissier for Culverwell, as they began to push forward in search of an equaliser Le Tissier quickly created a chance for himself but he put his shot wide under Barker's challenge. This opened up the game and it nearly allowed Hamon to score but he put his shot wide and moments later a de Garis block tackle denied Barker at the edge of the box. A scramble in the visitor's area in the last minute ended when an offside decision was given and the final result was Guernsey-0, Jersey-1.

Guernsey: P. de Garis, J. Avery, J. Nobes, C. Dyer (c), D. Yeates, M. Coutanche, M. de la Haye, M. Culverwell, G. Chalmers, P. Nobes, A. Exall.
Sub: C. Allen, K. Le Tissier, M. Gauvain.

Jersey: S. Carlyon, T. le Maistre, C. Morton, R. Muddyman, C. Ferey, I. Daley, M. Cassidy, A. Greig, A. Barker (c),C. Hamon, N. de Freitas.
Sub: M. Steigenberger, M. Brown, J. Kellett.
Goalscorer: De Freitas.

The Muratti Vase was presented to the Jersey captain, Andy Barker, by Sir John Coward.

Chris Dyer, the Guernsey captain since 1990, announced his retirement from senior football. Chris had won 24 successive Muratti caps winning five medals and scoring 4 goals. He was an inspirational captain and one of the greats of Muratti history.

Guernsey captain Chris Dyer.

Jersey celebrate with the Muratti Vase.

Muratti captains and officials.

1 9 9 7

MURATTI SEMI-FINAL.
22 March 1997, Mount Hale, Alderney.

Alderney -0, Guernsey -6.

Alderney started with an experienced side with two of their substitutes, Peter Tugby and A. Stone, the only new caps. Guernsey gave Muratti debuts to Leighton Chainey and Mark Ogier as well as having Steve Brehaut and R. Jones winning their first caps from the substitute's bench.

The conditions at Mount Hale were perfect for Alderney's match against Guernsey as new captain John Nobes led out his side. The game was only two minutes old when a long throw in into the Alderney area by Paul Nobes was not taken cleanly by Nick Carre and new cap Mark Ogier stabbed the ball home to give the visitors an ideal start. Alderney responded with Nigel Jarvis to the forefront but he was finding it difficult to compete with the Guernsey midfield. The Guernsey defence ably coped with the Alderney attack and this allowed Gauvain and Coutanche to stretch the game down the wings. Kevin Gentle was superb in the centre of the overworked Alderney defence although at times his challenges on young Mark Ogier required some repair work by Guernsey physio, Pete Lawlor. In the 24th minute Guernsey went further ahead when another long throw in by Paul Nobes found Kevin Le Tissier and, from five yards out, fired it home.

Alderney settled down following these reverses and Jim Williamson hammered in a shot that Drillot shepherded out of play and moments later Alderney's James Maxwell hit the side netting with his shot. As the half neared its end Le Tissier headed over from 6 yards and Martin Gauvain saw his rasping shot hit the Alderney crossbar. The half time score remained Alderney-0, Guernsey-2.

Guernsey continued on top in the second half giving the Alderney defence of White, Concanen and Gentle a torrid time. This pressure paid off and Le Tissier rose to meet a through ball by Chainey to find the bottom corner of the net for goal number three. The fourth goal was all about Le Tissier as he made room for himself at the edge of the area and guided a 20 yard shot into the top right hand corner. Alderney's Jarvis tried to emulate this but his long range effort was fractionally wide. Mark Ogier added a fifth goal when he dived to head home a cross by Gauvain into the top right of the goal. With five minutes remaining Alderney came close to scoring but Drillot made a superb save from Peter Tugby to keep his goal intact. Just on the final whistle, substitute Matt Falla, slipped the ball under Carre to make the final score Alderney-0, Guernsey-6.

Alderney: N. Carre, P. Concanen, K. Gentle, W. White, A. Wright, A. Davies, K. Fairbrother, N. Jarvis, J. Maxwell, M. Treais, J. Williamson.
Sub: P. Tugby, A. Stone, A. Adamson.

Guernsey: I. Drillot, R. Elmy, M. Gauvain, J. Nobes (c), M. Coutanche, L. Chainey, G. Chalmers, Mick Ogier, P. Nobes, K. Le Tissier, Mark Ogier.
Sub: S. Brehaut, M. Falla, R. Jones.
Goalscorers: Le Tissier (3), Mark Ogier (2), Falla.

Carre is put under pressure by the Guernsey attack.

Journalist Rex Bennet, 65, died on 31 March 1997 after a short illness.

Rex began his career in 1946 at 'The Star and Gazette' in the Bordage and joined the 'Press' when it bought the 'Star' in 1951. He remained the Island's top sports writer until his retirement from the 'Press' in 1995. He covered the Muratti for many years along with his great friend, the late Bill Custard, from Jersey. He joined the 'Guernsey Globe' and wrote 'Rex in the Frame' for them. Tributes came in from all Press and sporting areas from both colleagues and friends.

MURATTI FINAL.
5 May 1997, The Cycling Grounds, Guernsey.

Guernsey -2, Jersey -1.

In a move to increase the gate for the forthcoming Muratti Vase Final the Guernsey Press ran a 'Let's Pack the Track' campaign. This campaign was similar to one that was used in 1909 when the Press advert called on 10,000 spectators to cheer on the Green and White. The attendance on that day was 6,200.

Guernsey suffered a blow before the kick-off when Grant Chalmers was ruled out with an ankle injury and was replaced by Steve Brehaut (Sylvans). The Guernsey starting line-up had nine Sylvans players as they strove to win the Muratti Vase for the first time since 1992.

The opening of the game was poor and no one was given much time to settle on the ball. There were very few chances in a game and the occasion seemed to get to most of the players who showed little of their normal skill and control. Guernsey had the first chance when, from a free-kick, Paul Nobes sent a curling ball into the Jersey area for his brother John to head into the side netting as he came in on the back post. Jersey's response was when Chris Hamon broke clean through and was prevented from scoring when Ian Drillot quickly charged off his line. The first half appeared to be drifting to a 0-0 scoreline when, in the 43rd minute Jersey opened up from defence and a clever header by Hamon sent Yazalde Santos rushing down the right wing. He crossed it over and it hit Joel Avery's outstretched boot and sliced over Drillot's head and as Martin Gauvain tried to clear he steered it into the net. Both teams trooped off after a disappointing half ended Guernsey-0, Jersey-1.

Guernsey began the second half a little better and had a stroke of good fortune after five minutes. Carlyon lost his footing when taking a goal kick and Coutanche's header back into the danger area was misjudged by the keeper and it bounced over his head for Exall to have a simple task of taping it in. The main battle was now situated in the midfield as Ogier began to get the upper hand on Jersey's skipper, Barker. It was Barker who came close in the 78th minute when his dangerous header was well smothered by Drillot as the Jersey forwards awaited a mistake by him. With 19 minutes remaining coach Colin Fallaize sent on Muratti veteran Kevin Le Tissier in an attempt to win the game. With four minutes to go Paul Nobes sent in a trademark long throw in which Jan Renouf flicked on to Steve Brehaut and from eight yards he volleyed into the bottom corner of the net.

It looked as though Guernsey had scored again in the 90th minute through Le Tissier but referee Reed adjudged that Paul Nobes had overrun the ball. There was no more scoring and the game ended Guernsey-2, Jersey-1.

Guernsey: I. Drillot, R. Elmy, M. Gauvain, J. Nobes (c), J. Avery, M. Coutanche, M. Ogier, S. Brehaut, J. Renouf, P. Nobes, A. Exall.
Sub: K. Le Tissier.
Goalscorers: Exall, Brehaut.

Jersey: S. Carlyon, A. Salaun, I. Daly, R. Lumsden, C. Ferey, C. Morton, J. Kellett, A. Barker, J. Reilly, C. Hamon, Y. Santos.
Subs: Ross Crick, D. Pih, N. de Freitas.
Goalscorer: og.

It was a jubilant John Nobes (pictured), Guernsey's youngest ever captain at 21, who received the Muratti Vase.

The winner of the Ossie Eloury Memorial Trophy was Guernsey's Micky Ogier.

Jan Renouf celebrates Steve Brehaut's winning goal.

Guernsey celebrates their Muratti Vase victory.

It was announced that former Jersey manager, Jimmy Reeves, died at the end of August 1997. Jimmy was a very successful manager not only of the Jersey Muratti team but also of St. Paul's, Wanderers and Le Masuriers. He later became President of Magpies.

1 9 9 8

MURATTI SEMI-FINAL.
14 March 1998, Mount Hale, Alderney.

Alderney -0, Jersey -2.

Jersey's coach, Peter Vincenti vowed to give youth a chance in the forthcoming Muratti match against Alderney. Their team included only four survivors from the previous year's team that lost 2-1. Former Bristol City professional, Lee De St. Croix (St. Peter) was elected captain. They had lost the services of goalkeeper Steve Carlyon (Rozel Rover) due to injury and included four new caps in Sean McDonald (First Tower) in goal, Robbie Fernandez (Portuguese Club), Craig Culkin (Jersey Scottish), and Lee Bramley (Rozel Rovers) in their line-up.

Alderney's squad included eight players who appeared against Guernsey 1997. Joint Alderney managers/coaches, Alan Adamson and James Maxwell announced that 19-year old William Benfield would captain their side. It is believed that he is the youngest ever Muratti captain. Benfield had nine months with Peterborough's Youth team in season 1996/97. Alderney also included his brother, 15 year-old Simon Benfield as one of their substitutes.

The conditions at Mount Hale were good although the pitch was a little bumpy. Right from the kick-off Alderney's defence was put to the test as Jersey quickly put them under pressure. Bramley and Morton missed good chances before Bramley was set up by some excellent wing play by Steve Coutanche but his shot hit the side of Alderney's goal. Yozalde Santos followed this up with a fine bicycle kick that went over the crossbar. The Jersey forwards were being frustrated by the tight Alderney defence but it was an error by a home defender that gave Jersey their opening. Mike Lee was adjudged to have pushed

Alderney.

Sean McDonald (Jersey).

William and Simon Benfield.

Craig Culkin in the box and referee Ted Teed had no hesitation in awarding a penalty and Lee Bramley stepped up to put Jersey1-0 ahead. Alderney responded with two half-chances that never really troubled McDonald and the half ended Alderney-0, Jersey-1.

Nick Carre in the Alderney goal was quickly in action in the second half as he produced a super one-handed save from Lee De St Croix. The Jersey pressure continued but the home defence, well marshalled by Nigel Jarvis, continued to block the shots as they guarded Carre's goal. It was not until midway through the second half that Jersey increased their lead when Culkin's screwed shot found substitute Jimmy Reilly and he hammered the ball home giving Carre no chance. Alderney nearly pulled one back when an Andrew Davis long range shot from near the half-way line had McDonald scrambling backwards to push the ball away. Alderney again came close when a superb volley by William Benfield was heading for the top corner before it struck Fernandez on the head. Dougie Ross could consider himself unlucky as two of his efforts were ruled out, one for offside and the second for apparently fouling the goalkeeper. In the closing stages of the match there appeared to be a handball in the Alderney penalty area that was not spotted by the linesman, Paul Southcott and the game ended Alderney-0, Jersey-2.

Alderney: N. Carre, A. Davies, W. Benfield (c), N. Jarvis, M. Lee, K. Gentle, K. Fairbrother, M. Treais, J. Williamson, G. Rushbury, P. Tugby.
Subs: R. Bohan, J. Maxwell, S. Benfield.

Jersey: S. McDonald, R. Muddyman, C. Ferey, R. Fernandez, C. Culkin, S. Coutanche, Y. Santos, L. de St. Croix (c), C. Morton, D. Ross, L. Bramley.
Subs: J. Reilly, G. Lightbody, C. Dummond.
Goalscorers: Bramley (pen), Reilly.

Alderney's Nigel Jarvis gets up to clear.

Alderney's joint coach, Alan Adamson was very pleased with the performance of his side saying that they did everything that was asked of them and came close to scoring on a couple of occasions. Peter Vincenti, Jersey manager, said that he was not disappointed with the result. He added that it was Alderney's day and if they had scored it would have been reward for their effort. Simon Benfield became one of the youngest ever Muratti players at 15 years 272 days when he came on as a substitute for Alderney.

MURATTI FINAL.
4 May 1998, Springfield Stadium, Jersey.

Jersey -2, Guernsey -0.

Guernsey had a new manager in Phil Corbet and as he prepared to lead his side into his first Muratti it was announced that this would be Jersey manager Peter Vincenti's last Muratti in charge. Guernsey was creating a little Muratti history when they included ten Sylvans players in their starting line-up with only Mark Bisson of Rangers not with the St. Peter's side.

Guernsey were quietly confident as they came out onto a sunny Springfield to play Jersey. They had performed well on tour and included 10 of the Upton winning Sylvans side. Jersey were first to threaten as in the 2nd minute Damon Pih sent in a volley that looped high and wide. The visitors then began to play well and came very close to an early lead when Lee Renouf saw his shot brilliantly saved by Carlyon in the Jersey goal. For the first half hour the game was very even

The rival managers-Vincenti (Jersey) and Corbet (Guernsey).

with not a lot of goalmouth incident and Joel Avery in the Guernsey defence dealing with any danger that came his way. With four minutes to half time Craig Culkin miscued his shot and, as it went down Jersey's right, it was picked up by Lee de St. Croix, he beat Coutanche, and sent in a low left footed cross which skidded under Potter's boot and Riley slipped it in from 8 yards to give Jersey a crucial goal. Guernsey appeared to lose their composure and nearly lost a second goal when Michael Steigenberger beat the offside trap and tipped the ball past the advancing Drillot but Renouf had tracked back and cleared the danger and as half time arrived the score was Jersey-1, Guernsey-0.

Jersey came out for the second half full of confidence with Yazalde Santos causing a lot of problems for the Guernsey defence especially down the left wing. The visitors were finding it very difficult to maintain any sustained pressure and brought on Kevin Le Tissier, winning his 20th cap, and Mark Ogier for Adie Exall and Mark Bisson in an attempt to change things round but it was Jersey who scored again in the 72nd minute. Santos gave Craig Morton a short pass and as he entered the penalty area he was tripped by John Nobes and referee Neale Barry had no hesitation in awarding a penalty. Ricky Muddyman stepped up and sent Drillot the wrong way as he fired his shot to the keeper's left for a well deserved second goal. Jersey were now in complete command and knocked the ball around as they ran down the clock to win comfortably leaving the final score Jersey-2, Guernsey-0.

Jersey: S. Carlyon, T. Le Maistre, C. Ferey, R. Muddyman, L. de St. Croix, Y. Santos, D. Pih, C. Culkin, C. Morton, M. Steigenberger, J. Reilly.
Subs: L. Bramley, P. Crompton, D. Ross.
Goalscorers: Reilly, Muddyman (pen).

Guernsey: I. Drillot, J. Avery, M. Gauvain, J. Nobes (c), I. Potter, M. Coutanche, L. Renouf, M. Bisson, A. Vance, A. Exall, P. Nobes.
Subs: K. Le Tissier, Mark Ogier, M. Smith.

Muddyman crashes the penalty past Drillot for Jersey's second goal.

Ricky Muddyman was awarded the Ossie Eloury Man-of-the Match trophy. Peter Vincenti said that it was nice to go out with a win in front of a home crowd. He felt that although there were a lot of good Jersey performances during the match, Ricky Muddyman was head and shoulders above anyone else. Phil Corbet, Guernsey coach, was very disappointed with his team's performance especially in the second half.

As Peter Vincenti bade farewell to the Jersey manager's job, he left with a superb record. In 12 Muratti matches at under-21 and senior level since 1992 he had been on the losing side just twice – the dramatic penalty shoot-out at Springfield in 1996 and the previous year's 2-1 senior defeat in Guernsey. He also led Jersey to the Island Games Football Gold Medal in Jersey in 1997.

1 9 9 9

MURATTI SEMI-FINAL.
27 March 1999, Mount Hale, Alderney.

Alderney -0, Guernsey -1.

Alderney included Dale Blanchard (Vale Rec) in their team to play Guernsey in the Muratti-Semi Final at Mount Hale. Dale made his Alderney debut as a 16-year old in 1978; he then won three caps for Guernsey between 1987-1989. He qualified for Alderney as his mother was born in the northern isle. He is believed to be only the second player to play for two islands in Senior Muratti matches, the first being A. Yates (Athletics and Caesareans) who played for Guernsey in 1907 and Jersey in 1909. Alderney included four players who were not resident in the island namely Nigel Jarvis, Kevin Fairbrother, Andrew Davies and Jim Williamson. Also in the squad were 16-year old Simon Benfield and 17-year old substitute Michael Bohan. Alderney were lead out by their mascot, 3-year old Ciaran Higgs. In attendance was Muratti veteran, Denis Jones, who played for Alderney

Alderney

between 1953 – 1963 before retiring at the age of 40. Denis made his annual visit from Burnley. Guernsey included six new caps in their starting line-up in goalkeeper Jody Bisson (Vale Rec), Ryan Tippett (Rovers), Matt Falla (Vale Rec), Ross Cameron (North), Kevin Gilligan (St. Martins) and Youth 2 player Matt Warren. On the substitutes bench is Youth 2 player, Chris Chamberlain.

Guernsey's build up for this match included a fine 5-3 victory against the Royal Navy as well as gaining their first win in the South-West Counties Championship by defeating Wiltshire 2-0.

There was a strong wind at Mount Hale as Alderney and Guernsey contested the Norman-Piette Muratti Semi-final. The game was just three minutes old when skipper John Nobes should have opened the scoring but put his header straight at Alderney keeper Carre. On 14 minutes Guernsey again came close but Ryan Tippett's header found Carre and the chance was gone. The Alderney defence were coping very well with the Guernsey attack with Nigel Jarvis, Simon Benfield and Dale Blanchard being particularly effective. Alderney's best offensive work usually stemmed from Jim Williamson and this encouraged the size-able Alderney support who cheered every move. The deadlock was nearly broken when in the 27th minute Martin Gauvain nearly scored when he shot from the top right of the penalty area only to see Carre pulling off an athletic save and tipping the ball away. Alderney's best effort came when John Nobes rose to head clear but luckily for Guernsey his back-header drifted clear much to the relief of the stranded Bisson. An eventful half ended Alderney-0, Guernsey-0.

Guernsey began the second half with the advantage of the wind and after 8 minutes opened the scoring. Martin Gauvain's free-kick from well inside his own half was helped along by the strong wind and found young Matt Warren and he fired the ball into the roof of the net. Alderney responded to this setback with Jarvis pushing up to support Rushbury and Treais and they began to pressurise Guernsey. As the game progressed Mark Ogier had a clear chance for Guernsey but was denied by an excellent save by Carre and this was followed by a good tackle by Nobes halting a run by Jarvis. The atmosphere was building up and the play was becoming more physical as Alderney's confidence increased. As the game wore on Alderney's joint coach (and substitute) Alan Adamson was dismissed from the touchline by referee Charlie Tostevin after linesman, Roy Bougourd highlighted some foul language. The game remained very tight and after around 12 minutes of injury time the referee Charlie Tostevin blew his whistle with the score Alderney-0, Guernsey-1.

Alderney: N. Carre, S. Benfield, D. Blanchard, K. Gentle, N. Jarvis, J. Maxwell, K. Fairbrother, A. Davies, J. Williamson, G. Rushbury, M. Treais. Subs: M. Bohan, P. Tugby.

Guernsey: J. Bisson, M. de la Haye, J. Nobes (c), S. Polson, R. Cameron, M. Warren, K. Gilligan, M. Gauvain, M. Falla, J. Renouf, R. Tippett. Subs: Mark Ogier, C. Chamberlain. Goalscorer: Warren.

Alderney's joint player/coach, James Maxwell was very pleased with his side's disciplined performance. When Alan Adamson was sent off for Alderney he became only the third player to be dismissed in a Muratti match as well as being the first player to be sent-off before coming on to the pitch. Kevin Gentle was full of praise for the performance of Alderney's two young players Simon Benfield (16) and Michael Bohan (17). Guernsey's coach, Phil Corbet, was very relieved and commented that this was always a tricky fixture but the result was the important thing. He was disappointed with his side's finishing although he was full of praise for Alderney.

It was reported that Jersey's Andy Barker (St. Paul's) was sent off for the first time in his career in the Collins Cup match against Rangers. There was a possibility that due to this he may miss the Muratti Vase Final in May.

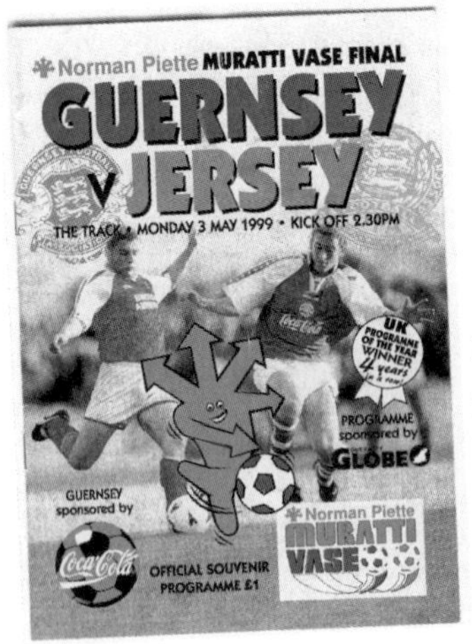

MURATTI FINAL.
3 May 1999, The Cycling Grounds, Guernsey.

Guernsey -2, Jersey -0 aet.

Jersey had a new manager in Welshman Kevin MacCarthy, succeeding Scotsman Peter Vincenti. Jersey selected four new caps in Craig Grant (Rozel Rovers), David Brodie (St. Brelade), Paul Docherty (St. Martin) and Andy Essler (Jersey Scottish) for their visit to Guernsey. Jersey had a strong Scottish football connection with Grant having had spells with Aberdeen and Montrose, Brodie with Queens Park (scoring on his debut), Essler was a professional with

Dumbarton and Dougie Ross was a semi-professional with Caledonian Thistle. Guernsey selected one new cap in their starting line-up in Matt Le Cras (Sylvans) with one of their substitutes, Dale Garland (Rangers) as yet uncapped.

Jersey started the brightest at the Cycling Grounds with Lee Bramley coming close after only three minutes. Guernsey replied but they were denied by some fine defending by Paul Docherty, Muddyman and Ferry. In the 13th minute Drillot in the Guernsey goal did well to punch clear an Andy Barker free-kick whilst under pressure and five minutes later Docherty was denied by a superb tackle by Stuart Polson. As the half wore on neither goalkeeper was being tested and in the 37th minute a De St. Croix centre was headed over by Ross. There was not much between the teams as half time approached and Jersey were forced into a change when Andy Essler came off with a calf injury and was replaced by Yozalde Santos. Half time arrived with the score Guernsey-0, Jersey-0.

Jersey's new Manager, Kevin McCarthy.

The second half was nine minutes old when a clash between Matt Le Cras and Steve Carlyon resulted in Carlyon receiving treatment. Le Cras was cautioned for this challenge by referee Peter Jones when the visitors felt that it merited a more severe punishment.

Shortly after this incident Andy Barker did well to block a goal-bound effort from Ryan Tippett and then Docherty fired his shot over the bar as the play swung from end to end. Jersey then came close when Drillot made two block saves from Ross and then pulled off the save of the game when a low corner kick by Barker in the 69th minute was played to Santos and he drilled in a low shot through a group of players for Drillot to pounce and palm the ball away. The injured Carlyon had not recovered from Le Cras' earlier challenge and was replaced by Sean McDonald and Guernsey replaced Gilligan by Tony Vance. The introduction of Vance livened up Guernsey and Lee Renouf slipped a fine through ball to Vance but his shot went agonisingly wide. Substitute McDonald in the Jersey goal was

Carlyon clutches the ball after bravely diving at the feet of Guernsey's Matt Le Cras.

Le Cras celebrates scoring the opening goal.

quickly called into action and he saved well at the foot of the post. In the final minute of the game Docherty and Bramley combined well to set up Reilly but he put his shot wide leaving the score Guernsey-0, Jersey-0.

The first chance of extra-time fell to Reilly but he put his snap-shot over the bar. Both sides were pushing on for the all-important opening goal but the defences were in command and the first half of extra-time ended with the score Guernsey-0, Jersey-0.

Two minutes into the second period Guernsey made the break-through when clearing up a Guernsey attack Muddyman attempted to play the ball round Matt Warren but the ball struck Warren and rebounded behind Muddyman. Warren raced onto the ball and sent a cross into the middle of the penalty area, for Le Cras to nip in front of Ferey, and hooked the ball past McDonald.

Jersey came close to equalising when a Barker cross found Ferey but he put his header wide. Eight minutes later Guernsey doubled their lead when a long clearance from Guernsey's half bounced in front of Ferey and Le Cras won the ball and raced into the Jersey goal and sent a powerful drive past McDonald. This goal completed the scoring and the final result was Guernsey-2, Jersey-0.

Guernsey: I. Drillot, M. Gauvain, J. Nobes (c), S. Polson, M. de la Haye, K. Gilligan, L. Renouf, J. Renouf, M. Warren, R. Tippett, M. le Cras.
Subs: A. Vance, D. Garland, M. Falla.
Goalscorer: Le Cras (2).

Jersey: S. Carlyon, C. Ferey, R. Muddyman, C. Grant, Le de St. Croix, A. Barker, D. Brodie, P. Docherty, A. Essler, D. Ross, L. Bramley.
Subs: S. McDonald, Y. Santos, J. Reilly.

Jersey manager Kevin MacCarthy was very disappointed saying that two costly errors cost them the game. Understandably Guernsey coach, Phil Corbet was delighted at the victory although he conceded that Jersey had caused them a lot of problems early in the game.

Magpies' Ian Solomon selected Matt Le Cras as the Ossie Eloury Memorial Trophy winner. He stated that three players were in the running Le Cras, David Brodie and Stuart Polson but he chose Le Cras as goals win matches and he took his two chances well.

In this decade Jersey recorded 6 wins and Guernsey 4 wins. Jersey now have 42 Muratti Vase wins, Guernsey 39 and Alderney 1 win. The Muratti Vase was shared in 1937.

15

2000 - 2004

2 0 0 0

The proposed development of Footes Lane as the new home of the Muratti came under fire from Deputy Harold Allen. Harold, former Rangers and Island coach (as well as being a former president of Rangers), suggested that while he supported the initiatives of looking into the feasibility of a sports stadium at Footes Lane he believed that it had to stand alone for athletics and be viable without the support of the Guernsey Football Association.

Harold Allen is backing the Track.

He added that the home of Guernsey football must be the Track with its long history and influence it has had on the local game for more than a century. He stated that the GFA has had for a decade permission to develop their headquarters at the Track, but finding the finance to do so had always been the problem. The Track was crying out for major redevelopment and has the area that would allow a new stadium incorporating an indoor sports hall and purpose built headquarters for the GFA. He said that the Island Games Organising Committee, together with Recreation, Tourist Board and the GFA should at least examine the option and talk to the Amalgamated Football Club. This debate is sure to continue as the 2003 Island Games approaches.

MURATTI SEMI-FINAL.
25 March 2000, Mount Hale, Alderney.

Alderney -0, Jersey -10.

Jersey had included two new caps in their starting line-up against Alderney in Paul Duxbury (Rozel Rovers) and Paddy O'Toole (Jersey Scottish).

The conditions at Mount Hale were windy but Jersey immediately imposed themselves on what could have been a tricky fixture as they opened the scoring after 5 minutes when a

Alderney's Muratti mascot.

fine lofted pass was left by Santos and Reilly scored from seven yards. A minute later Docherty picked up an under-hit back pass to score number two. Alderney's only worthwhile effort came when Michael Bohan kept his balance and slipped between two Jersey defenders to send in a powerfully driven shot which went high and wide of Carlyon's goal. In the 20th minute Alderney had the misfortune to lose the services of their captain, Nigel Jarvis, through injury. In the 23rd minute Carre saved brilliantly from Reilly only to see Brodie putting the rebound into the net for 3-0. Ten minutes later it was goal number four when Santos cut in from the left to send a shot low into the corner from 16 yards. In 38 minutes Gentle was adjudged to have fouled Brodie in the box and Muddyman stepped up to score number five to make the half time score Alderney-0, Jersey-5.

The second half was a repeat of the first with Carre producing heroics to keep the score down but in 53 minutes Jersey increased their lead when a good build up by Reilly and Brodie set up a chance for Docherty and he side-footed the ball home from six yards. Six minutes later Brodie went on a fine probing run and was unceremoniously brought down for the games

Yazalde Santos pulls away from the Alderney defence.

second penalty which Muddyman converted. Just after the hour mark Reilly curled in a pass that was met by Docherty to complete his hat-trick. In 67 minutes Carre went for a Santos corner kick and, under severe pressure by the Jersey attack, punched the ball into his own net. In the 73rd minute a great run by substitute Salaun set up Reilly and his cross was met by Docherty who hooked in Jersey's tenth goal. Barry Hardisty replaced Santos for his first Muratti cap and nearly marked it with a goal but Carre brought off a superb save to push the shot round the post. Jersey put on Barker in place of O'Toole but the commitment of the visitors never waned and the final result was Alderney-0, Jersey-10.

Alderney: N. Carre. S. Benfield, G. Rushbury, K. Gentle, N. Jarvis, J. Maxwell, A. Davies, D. Blanchard, R. Heathcote, J. Williamson, M. Bohan.
Subs: A. Stone, R. Bohan, T. McCormack.

Jersey: S. Carlyon, R. Muddyman, C. Ferey, C. Grant, L.de St. Croix, P.O'Toole, D. Brodie, P. Duxbury, P. Docherty, J. Reilly, Y. Santos.
Subs: A. Barker, A. Salaun, B. Hardy.
Goalscorers: Docherty (4), Muddyman (2 pens), Brodie, Santos, Reilly, og.

Kevin McCarthy, the Jersey manager, was delighted with his team's effort over the 90 minutes and selected four-goal Paul Docherty as his man-of-the-match. It was felt that despite loosing 10 goals Alderney keeper Carre had had an excellent game and but for him Jersey could have bettered their 18-0 victory of 1988. Following the match McCarthy confessed that he was a little worried that he could have become the first Jersey manager to lose against Alderney and it was nice to settle the nerves with a couple of early goals. Alderney FA's president, Billy Bohan, thought that Jersey were a very good side and that they had (unfortunately) caught them on a good day. Alderney's player/manager, James Maxwell, agreed that it was a devastating blow to lose the services of their influential captain, Nigel Jarvis, after only 20 minutes but conceded that Jersey were an excellent side and he took them to beat Guernsey in the final.

A 'Wakky' view on the Muratti.

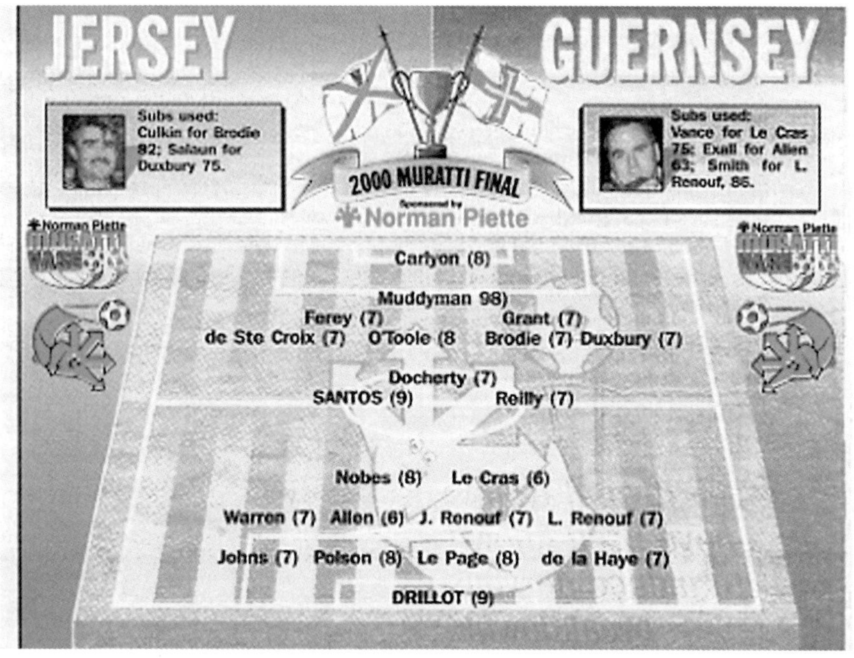

MURATTI FINAL.
1 May 2000, Springfield Stadium, Jersey.

Jersey -1, Guernsey -0.

Ryan Tippett had to withdraw from Guernsey's Muratti squad as he had not recovered from the hamstring injury he received in Guernsey's 3-1 victory over ASSA Vallee du Dropt in France. Adie Exall was called into the squad. The visitors had three new caps in their starting line-up in Matt Le Page (Vale Rec), Luke Allen (St. Martins) and Simon Johns (North). All of Jersey's players had Muratti experience. Steve Carlyon won his 21st Muratti cap for Jersey to make him the most-capped goalkeeper in Muratti history.

There were more than 2,000 spectators at Springfield when Ricky Muddyman (Jersey) and Jan Renouf (Guernsey) led their teams onto the field. After a quiet opening the first chance fell to Guernsey when, after 7 minutes, a Paul Nobes throw-in forced Muddyman into a headed clearance that fell to Jan Renouf but he fired his shot wide of the right hand post. Jersey responded a minute later when Paul Docherty slipped the ball to David Brodie only for Mike de la Haye to clear. Guernsey again came close when, from a goal-kick, Carlyon sent the ball to Paul Nobes who lobbed the ball back but Matt Le Cras squandered the chance. The visitors were slightly on top and could have opened the scoring but Jan Renouf headed a de la Haye cross wide of the post. The play then swung into the Guernsey area and Drillot had to be alert to save, at the second attempt, from Paul Duxbury as he latched onto a de St. Croix cross. Jersey came more into the game and after 18 minutes

Muddyman crashes home the penalty.

produced two good goal scoring chances. Paddy O'Toole worked a fine one-two with de St. Croix and lobbed his shot inches over Drillot's bar from around 30 yards. A minute later David Brodie knocked a free-kick square to Muddyman and his superb shot crashed off the right hand post from 35 yards. The decisive moment came after 28 minutes when Santos picked up a loose ball and ran at the Guernsey defence, he beat three defenders and as he entered the penalty area was brought down by Polson. Referee Bennett had no hesitation in awarding a penalty and Jersey skipper, Muddyman, stepped up and drove the ball past Drillot's left hand post to put the home side ahead. The game was moving on at an exciting pace and following a corner Docherty diverted a goal-bound shot by team mate Reilly over the bar. Le Cras and Nobes then combined to set up Warren but his shot was taken by Carlyon and at half time the score was Jersey-1, Guernsey-0.

The second half began with Guernsey winning a free-kick and Warren curled his kick round the wall for Carlyon to save easily. In the 54th minute de St. Croix sent a defence splitting ball to Reilly but Drillot rushed out to save with his right knee. The high pace was maintained and a mix up between Ferey and Muddyman allowed Le Cras to run clean through the middle but an excellent tackle by Grant saved the day for Jersey. Drillot then had to spread himself to deny Reilly following a neat one-two with Docherty. Just after the

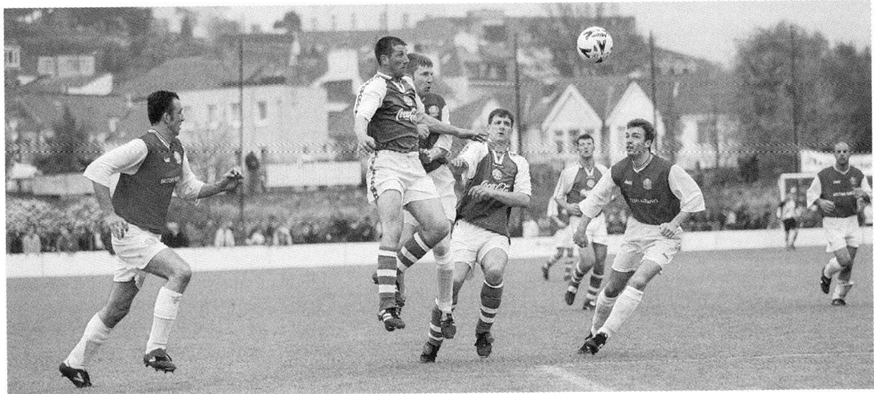

Exall fires in a header.

The Jersey defence close down Matt Le Cras.

Warren congratulates Jersey skipper, Muddyman.

hour mark Guernsey replaced Allen with Exall to form a three man forward line and it almost paid dividends immediately as the ball bounced in and around the Jersey penalty area before being cleared.

Guernsey should have equalised following an excellent move from their own goal-line. Warren took the ball from a stumbling Santos on the goal-line and sent a long pass to Exall on the half-way line. He quickly sent Nobes down the left and he fed Le Cras but he could only hook the ball over the bar from five yards.

Guernsey then had a scare when Drillot fumbled a shot by Reilly and, as Docherty latched onto the loose ball, the keeper dived bravely at his feet. As Guernsey pushed on for the equaliser it was Carlyon who came to Jersey's rescue when he pulled off two great saves in stoppage time. He turned away an Exall shot for a corner then, seconds before the final whistle, he saved at full stretch from substitute Tony Vance. Jersey were relieved to hear the final whistle with the score Jersey-1, Guernsey-0.

Jersey:	S. Carlyon, R. Muddyman (c), C. Ferey, C. Grant, L. de St. Croix, P. O'Toole, D. Brodie, P. Duxbury, P. Docherty, Y. Santos, J. Reilly.
Subs: C. Culkin, A. Salaun.
Goalscorer: Muddyman (pen).

Guernsey:	I. Drillot, M. de la Haye, S. Johns, S. Polson, M. Le Page, L. Allen, L. Renouf, J. Renouf (c), M. Warren, M. Le Cras, P. Nobes.
Subs: A. Vance, A. Exall, M. Smith.

This was an excellent Muratti Vase final that could have gone either way. Guernsey had chances to score in the first 10-15 minutes as Jersey were rather slow in starting, with Carlyon, winning his 21st cap, rather hesitant. Jersey's defence was superb and Carlyon made up for his shaky start with two great saves at the end. Jersey now lead the series 43-39. The Ossie Eloury Memorial award went to Jersey's Yozalde Santos.

It was announced in the press on 22 November 2000 that Jersey goalkeeper, Steve Carlyon, (pictured) was retiring from football. He had played in 21 Muratti matches winning 9 winners medals in a Muratti career that spanned 13 years. He was first capped against Alderney on 17 March 1987. Two ex-island managers, Colin Fallaize and Alan Le Prevost, both regarded Steve Carlyon as the greatest Jersey goal-keeper of all time.

2 0 0 1

MURATTI SEMI-FINAL.
24 March 2001, Mount Hale, Alderney.

Alderney -0, Guernsey -6.

Guernsey travelled to Mount Hale for their Muratti Vase match against Alderney expect-ing a hard fought game. Alderney included 15-year old Steve Concannon in their starting line-up. Steve is the son of former Alderney Muratti player Peter Concanen and is a

Steve Concanen.

Torquay United and Blackpool trialist. He plays his club foot-ball in Guernsey for St. Martin's Youth two side and it was hoped that he might play in the same Muratti team as his father but Peter had to decline due to a groin injury.

Two other Alderney players, Alan Patterson and Aiden Farrell, gained their first caps when they came on as substi-tutes. Alderney were led by goalkeeper Nick Carre and Guernsey, by John Nobes.

The opening exchanges were close although Guernsey should have taken the lead after just three minutes when Paul Nobes put Chamberlain down the right and his right foot shot narrowly cleared the bar. Three minutes later Smith rose to meet Chris Chamberlain's left footed cross but he sent his header straight at keeper Carre. Guernsey continued with this pressure and, after ten minutes, forced a series of corners. Carre tipped a Chamberlain corner onto the post then from the second corner Ryan Tippett's shot on the turn was collect-ed by Carre. Chamberlain then played a short corner to Paul Nobes and he curled a cross into the box and it was met by Smith who hammered it into the roof of the net from 8 yards.

Referee Le Cornu prepares to send off Jarvis.

Alderney were not fazed by this score and, although most of their shots were from long range, a James Maxwell effort from 25 yards just cleared Bisson's bar. As the Alderney defence continued to contain the Guernsey attacks Bisson had to be alert to save from a Steve Concanen 30 yard drive on 21 minutes. Guernsey then came close with a Stuart Polson header on 32 minutes which went wide. Just before half time there was an incident that had a major affect on the result when Alderney's Nigel Jarvis and Guernsey's Luke Allen were jostling for position and, in the penalty area, Jarvis appeared to lash out with his right hand catching Allen in the face. Referee Le Cornu had an unobstructed view of the incident and sent Jarvis off as well as awarding a penalty to Guernsey.

Ryan Tippett stepped up and slotted the ball home past Nick Carre's right. At half time the score was Alderney-0, Guernsey-2.

The second half was very comfortable for Guernsey as they had a two goal lead and a man advantage. Twelve minutes into the half John Nobes headed a Chris Chamberlain cross into the net and six minutes later Smith and Tippett combined to set up Simon Johns, and his fierce left foot volley was goal number four. Tippett then found Smith near the penalty spot and his shot came off his shin and past Carre's left.

With 20 minutes remaining North Junior Muratti midfielder, Gavin Le Page, came on and almost scored with a 35 yard shot that went just wide. Guernsey nearly scored when substitute Shaun Kelling's effort was ruled out for offside and it was left to Guernsey's third substitute, Matt Falla, to complete the scoring with a curling right foot free-kick into Carre's right hand corner to make the final score Alderney-0, Guernsey-6.

Richard Heathcote and Micky Smith challenge for the ball.

Alderney: N. Carre (c), A. Davies, R. Heathcote, K. Gentle, J. Maxwell, A. Stone, S. Concanen, N. Jarvis, M. Treais, Rushbury, M. Bohan.
Sub: A. Patterson, R. Bohan, A. Farrell.

Guernsey: J. Bisson, M. Wilson, J. Nobes (c), S. Polson, S. Johns, C. Chamberlain, M. Warren, L. Allen, M. Smith, R. Tippett, P. Nobes.
Sub: M. Falla, G. Le Page, S. Kelling.
Goalscorers: Smith, Tippett (pen), J. Nobes, Johns, Falla.

Although this was a comprehensive win for Guernsey in the end the sending off of Jarvis was a major turning point. Jarvis became the third player to be sent off in a Muratti match as well as being the first Alderney player to receive his marching orders in the competition. The referee, Le Cornu, was given a hard time by sections of the home supporters and it was announced later that Alderney Football Association president, Billy Bohan, faced disciplinary action by the Inter-Insular Committee following the match. On a more positive note Alderney's Bavaria Nomads went on to win the Rouget Cup by defeating Vale Rec in the final.

Billy Bohan, Alderney FA President.

MURATTI FINAL.
7 May 2001, The Cycling Grounds, Guernsey.

Guernsey -4, Jersey -1.

Guernsey selected an experienced team for their match with only Gavin Le Page, who came on as a substitute, gaining his first cap and joined the small band of players who have gained Junior and Senior caps in the same season. Jersey made changes in their line-up and included six uncapped players in their squad of 18. There were three new caps in the starting line-up in Darren Toudic (St. Paul's) in goal, Mark Ray (St. Paul's) and Gary Freeman (St. Peter). John Rutter (First Tower) was to come on as a substitute to gain his first cap.

The match started in the usual Muratti fashion, fast and furious, with neither team taking

Bisson clears under severe pressure.

Toudic saving Falla's penalty.

control of the game. Guernsey began to get hold of the game and scored in 17 minutes following a series of corners. Kevin Gilligan played a short corner to Paul Nobes whose neat back heel return to him resulted in a lovely cross that was headed home by Matt Falla. Falla went close minutes later when his half volley was well taken by Darren Toudic to his right.

Jersey's response came when a Ricky Muddyman free kick found Jimmy Reilly in space but John Nobes quickly closed him down. As the half neared its end Ryan Tippett shaped up for a shot but he was foiled by a last ditch tackle by Craig Ferey and the half time score remained Guernsey-1, Jersey-0.

The first chance of the second half fell to Guernsey when, following a Paul Nobes free-kick, Toudic saved well for the visitors. In the 57th minute it was disaster for Jersey when, following a two footed lunge at Mark Warren, Mark Ray was sent off by referee Rob Styles to become only the fourth player to be sent off in a Muratti match. On the hour Jersey sent on Dave Brodie to try and pep up their performance but it was Guernsey who increased their lead three minutes later. Stuart Polson placed a free-kick into the Jersey area and Falla nipped in behind a motionless defence to crash a low shot into the right corner. Jersey reduced the arrears in the 68th minute when a Santos free-kick was only partially cleared by Jody Bisson in the Guernsey goal and Barry Hardisty was on hand to whip the ball back for Freeman to score. Guernsey again pushed on to the attack and as Paul Nobes made inroads on the Jersey goal he was brought down in the penalty area. Matt Falla came up and took the kick only to see Toudic dive to his right to produce a fine save.

A minute later, however, Guernsey did score when substitute Micky Smith took a ball from Simon Johns' throw in and turned to hit a half-volley past the stranded Toudic for 3-1. Guernsey then sent on Junior Muratti player Gavin Le Page and he scored when Tippett crossed over from the left for Falla, positioned at the far post, to head it back for Le Page to scramble it home. This was the last score making the final result Guerney-4, Jersey-1.

Gavin Le Page turns away after scoring the fourth goal.

Guernsey: J. Bisson, I. Potter, J. Nobes (c), S. Polson, S. Johns, J. Renouf, K. Gilligan, M. Warren, M. Falla, R. Tippett, P. Nobes.
Sub: M. Smith, G. Le Page, L. Allen.
Goalscorers: Falla (2), Smith, Le Page.

Jersey: D. Toudic, R. Muddyman (c), L. De St. Croix, C. Ferey, P. Duxbury, B. Hardisty, M. Ray, P. O'Toole, Y. Santos, G. Freeman, J. Reilly.
Sub: J. Rutter, C. Grant, D. Brodie.
Goalscorer: Freeman.

This was Guernsey's biggest winning margin against Jersey for 11 years and it was a truly merited victory. It was a very disappointing display by the Jersey side and was encapsulated by the Jersey Evening Post's headline 'Red shirts-Red card-Red-faces'.

In the Island Games held in the Isle of Man Jersey were successful in winning the Football Bronze Medal.

In October 2001 it was announced that the Muratti Vase had a new sponsor in Cherry Godfrey Finance. The Channel Islands based company have agreed a four-year deal worth £40,000 – the biggest sponsorship in the 96-year history of the competition. Alec Le Noury, the President of the GFA, and Charlie Tostevin, President of the JFA, were joined by Roy Parrack, representing the Alderney FA and David Cherry, managing director, at the signing of the agreement.

Guernsey celebrates winning the Muratti Vase.

Roy Parrack, Charlie Tostevin, David Cherry and Alec Le Noury.

2 0 0 2

The Guernsey Press on Saturday 9 February reported that it may be possible for Southampton legend, Matt Le Tissier, to play for Guernsey in the Muratti in 2003. Matt's contract with Southampton was to expire at the end of June and the former England international was not ruling out returning to pull on a Guernsey shirt. He said that he had not really thought about it but he supposed that it could happen. Guernsey Football Association secretary, Dave Dorey, revealed that Matt would be eligible as long as he was not under professional contract, as he is a native of Guernsey.

Matt Le Tissier.

Jersey announced that they had selected Ron Harris as their new manager. Ron 'Chopper' Harris was a hard-tackling half back for Chelsea having signed professional forms in November 1961. He was a former Chelsea captain making around 350 appearances for the first team. He skippered Chelsea to an FA Cup victory, against Leeds United after a replay, in 1970.

Ron Harris in his playing days.

MURATTI SEMI-FINAL.
9 March 2002, Mount Hale, Alderney.

Alderney -1, Jersey -2.

Jersey had seven new caps in their starting line-up with Jamie Brewster (St. Peter), James Hayward (First Tower), David Lloyd (Trinity), Peter Edwards (Trinity), Bradley Vowden (First Tower), Darren Swanson (Trinity), and Danny Craven (St. Ouen). Two of their substitutes, Stuart Andre (St. Paul's) and Lee Harvey (Jersey Scottish) would also make their debuts during the game. Andre, who came on as a substitute, joins the small band of players who have won Junior and Senior caps in the same season. The Jersey Evening Post were very confident of an easy victory against Alderney despite the wholesale changes in the Jersey squad and felt that it would be a case of a damage limitation exercise for Alderney. Jersey manager Ron Harris was confident that his side could match Jersey's last visit to Mount Hale when they won 10-0. Alderney had a new cap in Jason Atkins as well as substitute Liam Davey (St. Martins).

In almost gale force conditions on a bumpy Mount Hale pitch in front of a crowd of 300 Jersey started nervously. Once Jersey settled to the conditions, however, they began to control the game and took the lead after 14 minutes when Paul Duxbury hooked the ball home after Darren Swanson had flicked on a corner.

The wind played a key role throughout the match and when Bradley Vowden fired in a 35 yard shot from the left, the ball soared into the top right hand corner giving Alderney keeper Nick Carre no chance. Jersey almost made it 3-0 but David Lloyd saw his header thump back off the crossbar and at half time the score remained Alderney-0, Jersey-2.

Jersey began the second half facing a strong wind as they prepared for an Alderney assault. They managed to contain the home attack that had Michael Bohan and Andrew Davies ably supporting lone striker, Kevin Gentle, until 20 minutes from time.

Kevin Gentle was fouled just to the left of the Jersey penalty area and Nigel Jarvis sent the kick into the area for Mark Treais to rise unchallenged and head home at the back post. This was Treais' third Muratti goal and the first scored by Alderney since 1995 (also scored by Treais). It made for an exiting last 20 minutes but the Jersey defence held out comfortably to make the final score Alderney-1, Jersey-2.

Paul Duxbury (far right) opens the scoring for Jersey.

Mark Treais (6) heads home Alderney's goal.

Alderney: N. Carre, A. Farrell, J. Maxwell, N. Jarvis, R. Bohan, S. Concanen,
J. Atkins, M. Treais, M. Bohan, A. Davies, K. Gentle.
Subs: P. Tugby, S. Benfield, L. Davey.
Goalscorer: Treais.

Jersey: J. Brewster, J. Hayward, C. Grant (c), D. Lloyd, P. Duxbury, P. Edwards,
B. Vowden, D. Swanson, Y. Santos, D. Craven, Ross Crick.
Subs: S. Andre, L. Harvey.
Goalscorers: Duxbury, Vowden.

After the match Ron Harris, the Jersey manager, said that he was disappointed that his side only won 2-1 but he added that a win is a win. Understandably Alderney were delighted with their performance and pleased that they had run Jersey so close.

It was announced in the Guernsey Press of 30 April that Stan Noel, Guernsey football's oldest Muratti player, had passed away. Stan won 10 Muratti caps during the 1920's winning three Muratti medals. He was born in January 1899 and played all his football for the North. He was handicapped at scratch by the Royal Guernsey Golf Club and was Island Champion in 1934 and won nearly all local Open Competitions at one time or another. He entered the English Amateur Golf Championships in 1935, 1936 and 1937. In 1929 Stan starred for Guernsey in their famous 7-1 victory against Jersey at Westmount in the Muratti semi-final by scoring three goals. In those days when the Muratti was played in Jersey the scores were put on a board outside the Evening Press office. Stan recalled 'Though my father was not a football fan, I remember him telling me how he stood in Smith Street and was so proud when my name went up.' Stan Noel was a true football gentleman and will be sadly missed.

MURATTI FINAL.
6 May 2002, Springfield Stadium, Jersey.

Jersey -2, Guernsey -1.

Jersey's Ross Crick (First Tower) was a doubt for the match as he had limped out of an island training session on the Wednesday with a groin strain but he recovered in time to take his place. Guernsey's Matt Falla (St. Martins) had an injury prone season but took his place in the starting line-up. Both Springfield goalmouths were re-turfed on 1 May in preparation for the game.

Craig Grant (Jersey) and John Nobes (Guernsey) led their teams out onto Springfield in front of a crowd of more than 3,000 in what was Ron Harris' first Muratti Vase final in charge of the home team.

The early part of the game was very open and for the first 15 minutes Guernsey, although enjoying the greater possession, were finding it difficult to create any genuine chances. During this period Jersey looked the more menacing with both Lee Harvey and Gary

Jersey Muratti squad.

Freeman engineering two half chances for the home side. Harvey's positive runs through the midfield were causing Guernsey a lot of problems and Freeman's link-up play with Ross Crick was very dangerous. Crick was inches away from connecting with a cross and Peter Edwards had a close range effort blocked. Freeman thought he had opened the scoring for Jersey but he was adjudged to have used his hand. On chances created Guernsey could consider themselves rather lucky to go in at half time with the score Jersey-0, Guernsey-0.

Guernsey began the second half more composed and two early chances fell to them through Gavin Le Page and a Matt Falla shot that went inches wide, but their play lacked that final cutting edge. With 20 minutes remaining it was Jersey who took the lead. Edwards was not closed down in the middle of the park and he sent a lovely ball to the

C. Gontier (G), referee M. Dean, M. Le Cornu (J).

A dejected Bisson turns away as Jersey celebrate their winning goal.

right for James Hayward and his drilled cross found an unmarked Gary Freeman powering in at the far post to slot the ball home. Guernsey responded in the 76th minute by bringing on Tony Vance and Danny Bisson and three minutes later the substitutions paid off. Vance started a run straight at a concerned Jersey defence and he sent in a brilliant shot that flew past Brewster to bring the scores level. The game was now very tight and it was looking as if extra-time would be required when, in the third minute of injury time, Harvey received the ball 35 yards from goal and he moved forward sending in a crisp left-foot drive that deflected off John Nobes' head and past a startled Jody Bisson.

In the final minute of the match Peter Edwards was sent off for a second bookable offence, for what looked like a tired challenge, to become the fifth player in Muratti history to receive his marching orders. Seconds later the match ended Jersey-2, Guernsey-1.

Jersey: J. Brewster, S. Andre, C. Grant (c), D. Lloyd, J. Hayward, B. Vowden, P. Duxbury, P. Edwards, L. Harvey, Ross Crick, G. Freeman.
Sub: B. Hardisty.
Goalscorers: Freeman, Harvey.

Guernsey: J. Bisson, J. Avery, J. Nobes (c), S. Polson, I. Potter, G. Le Page, J. Renouf, M. Warren, M. Falla, P. Nobes, R. Tippett.
Subs: A. Vance, D. Bisson.
Goalscorer: Vance.

The Ossie Eloury Memorial Trophy was presented to Peter Edwards of Jersey. The Muratti Vase was presented to Jersey skipper, Craig Grant. The Jersey manager, Ron Harris, felt that his side deserved to win, although it was an evenly-balanced game he felt that Jersey did more going forward. He also praised the home support and he added that his players had responded to them. Phil Corbet, the Guernsey manager, although very dis-appointed agreed that it had been a good football match.

Craig Grant and Jamie Brewster celebrate with the Muratti Vase - 2002.

2 0 0 3

It was announced in February 2003 that Ron Harris had resigned as Jersey manager apparently due to disagreements with the Jersey Football Association. He was in charge of the Jersey team for only two Muratti matches, winning both.

Ron Harris with the Muratti Vase.

Dave Matthews was selected as the Jersey manager for a two-match trial. Dave was a goalkeeper who won 6 Muratti caps from 1975 to 1979 winning one Muratti medal. Following this trial a decision would be made as to the new long-term manager.

There was an historic meeting of the Guernsey Football Association held on Thursday 13 March and it was decided that the Muratti Vase Final on 5 May 2003 would be played at the Osmond

Priaulx Memorial Field, Foote's Lane. The GFA's council delegates voted in favour of an executive recommendation to stage this year's Muratti Vase Final at Osmond Priaulx Memorial Field, Foote's Lane. They were apparently given little choice after GFA chief executive, Dave Dorey, said that council was 'faced with the option of Foote's Lane or Jersey.' This broke nearly 100 years of Muratti football tradition at the Cycling Grounds and this would be only the third Muratti match in Guernsey not to be played at there. The first was the semi-final match between Guernsey and Alderney that was played at the Corbet Field on 24 March 1982. The match on 5 May, however, would be the first Muratti Final in Guernsey not to be played at the Cycling Grounds. It was also agreed that the centenary Muratti Final of 2005 would also be played at Foote's Lane.

Dave Matthews.

Foote's Lane – Future Muratti venue?

MURATTI SEMI-FINAL.
22 March 2003, Mount Hale, Alderney.

Alderney -1, Guernsey -4.

There was some doubt whether Steve Concanen (St. Martin's) would play for Alderney in this match but after some discussions he lined up against Guernsey, winning his third cap. Alderney also included Mark Ault for his first cap but they lost the services of Liam Davey (St. Martin's) and playmaker Nigel Jarvis. Guernsey coach, Phil Corbet had a massive selection dilemma as he decided who to partner Ryan Tippett up front. He had lost the services of Matt Falla and Neil Clegg due to injury. Matt Warren was also a slight doubt as he had had to pull out of Guernsey's trip to Gloucester the previous weekend. The Guernsey squad included Darren Martin who would be gaining his first cap.

There were around 300 spectators at Mount Hale as Alderney and Guernsey contested the Muratti Vase semi-final. Although Guernsey had the advantage of the wind they started nervously and their football was very edgy as they struggled to find any sort of rhythm. In trying to take advantage of the wind they resorted to sending in long balls that proved very unproductive. It was not until the 25th minute when Tony Vance, winning his 16th cap, broke down the left and when inside the box he appeared to be brought down by a James Maxwell challenge. Referee Bradshaw immediately awarded a penalty. Ryan Tippett stepped up but saw his kick well saved by Nick Carre in the Alderney goal to keep the score at 0-0.

With a third of the match gone Alderney were apparently containing Guernsey but the visitors soon opened the scoring when Brehaut met a long throw-in and sent in a strong header that looped over Carre from 12 yards. Alderney began to put the Guernsey defence under some pressure but after 37 minutes following a quick break out Guernsey increased their lead when Chamberlain converted a low cross into the net past a wrong-footed Carre. There was no more scoring and at half time the score read Alderney-0, Guernsey-2.

Steve Concanen.

Player manager Kevin Gentle with Alderney's mascot, Shannon Clarke (7).

Ryan Tippett had his 25th minute penalty saved by Carre.

Michael Bohan.

Five minutes into the second half Guernsey scored again through a Danny Bisson header and in the 64th minute Ryan Tippett took advantage of a defensive lapse to fire in number four. Guernsey was threatening to score many more but in the 67th minute the Alderney defence broke up an attack by sending the ball up-field. Michael Bohan raced after the ball and as Polson hit his hurried clearance against the Alderney player, Bohan steadied himself and as he drew Bisson to the edge of the 18 yard box he curled a beautiful shot past the keeper and inside the far post. The goal was greeted like a Muratti winner by the enthusiastic crowd and it appeared to unsettle Guernsey and the final 25 minutes were very even. Carre was again called into action on a number of occasions and pulled off two brilliant saves as the match ended Alderney-1, Guernsey-4.

Alderney: N. Carre, S. Concanen, M. Bohan, S. Benfield, P. Tugby (c). A. Patterson, R. Bohan, J. Atkins, A. Stone, J. Maxwell, K. Gentle.
Subs: M. Treais, M. Ault, W. Benfield.
Goalscorer: M. Bohan.

Guernsey: J. Bisson, M. Wilson, J. Nobes (c), S. Polson, S. Johns, C. Chamberlain, S. Brehaut, G. Le Page, A. Vance, R. Tippett, D. Bisson.
Subs: D. Martin, M. Warren, M. Le Cras.
Goalscorers: Brehaut, Chamberlain, Bisson, Tippett.

Alderney's player/coach, Kevin Gentle, was delighted with his team's performance and commented on their drive and passion. The goal by Michael Bohan was the first against Guernsey since 1992 and the Alderney man-of-the-match award went to keeper Nick Carre. Phil Corbet, the Guernsey coach, was quietly happy with the result and could now prepare for the final against Jersey.

As part of their Muratti preparations Guernsey travelled to France to play ASSA Vallee du Dropt and defeated the semi-professional French team 2-0. There followed a shock

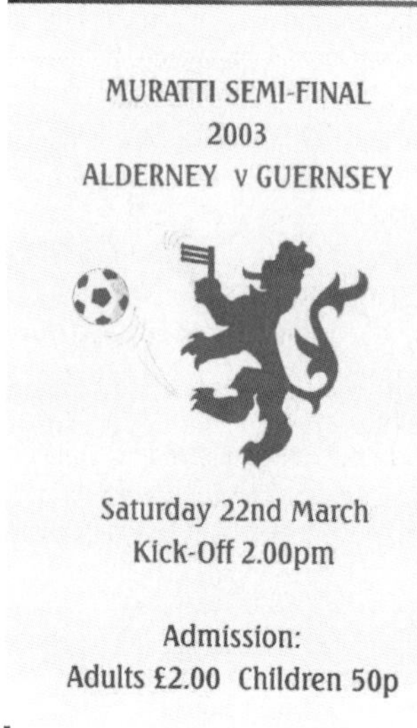

Nick Carre

announcement that Coach Phil Corbet had tendered his resignation with immediate effect on Easter Saturday. This unexpected move came after six years in the position and less than two weeks before the Muratti Vase Final against Jersey. GFA President, Alec Le Noury, accepted the resignation 'with regret' while Guernsey were in the South of France. The GFA refused to release the full details behind Phil Corbet's resignation, they said that he had quit for 'personal reasons'.

Phil Corbet.

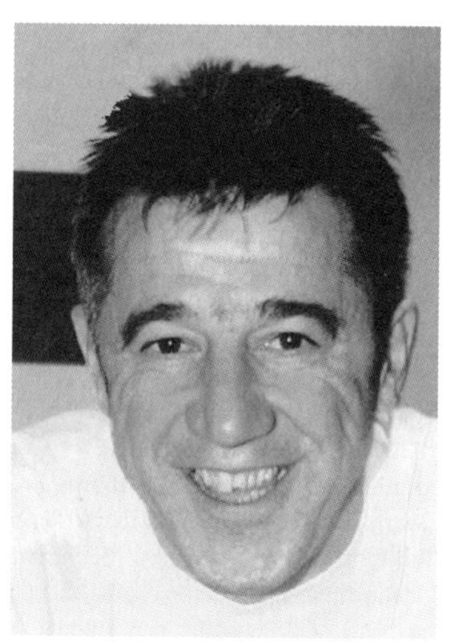

Colin Fallaize.

Phil Corbet was Guernsey's longest serving island coach taking over the post in 1997. He won the Muratti Vase in 1999 and 2001. In 2001 he led Guernsey to the gold medal in the Island Games. Assistant coach, Colin Fallaize, took charge of Guernsey for the match against the Army in Aldershot on Monday 28 April and the Muratti Vase Final on 5 May. Colin played in 19 Muratti matches between 1975 and 1987, scoring 16 goals as well as winning five medals. He became the first ex-Muratti player to take charge of Guernsey's team. A long-term appointment would not be made until the annual meeting in July.

A report appeared in the Jersey Evening Post of 24 April that stated that former Jersey manager, Ron Harris, had expressed a keen interest in taking over from retired Guernsey coach, Phil Corbet. He allegedly said that if Guernsey wanted him then it was up to them to contact him. He would certainly consider the position but he would not do it with the same conditions as he had with Jersey. Guernsey would have to pay his travel and accommodation costs. There was no official comment from the Guernsey authorities but the general feeling among the football public was that Ron Harris would not be the next Guernsey manager.

The Guernsey Press of 25 April announced the death of Len Duquemin on 20 April in London. Known both in London and Guernsey as 'The Duke' Len played more than 274 times for Tottenham Hotspur, scoring 114 goals in a sparkling 13 year career with them. Len's finest footballing moment was scoring the goal that ultimately clinched the Football League championship for the Spurs in season 1950-51. When he left Spurs he joined amateurs Bedford Town and won a Southern League championship medal with them. He was born Leonard Stanley at Cobo on 17 July 1924. He was one of 10 children and all the brothers represented Guernsey at various levels. There was talk of him possibly playing for Guernsey in the 1946 Peace Cup match against Jersey, but it never transpired. Len Duquemin – A true Guernseyman.

MURATTI FINAL.
5 May 2003, Osmond Priaulx Memorial Field, Foote's Lane, Guernsey.

Guernsey -3, Jersey -3. aet.

In the build up to the Muratti Final Colin Fallaize broke with recent tradition by announcing his team early. Included in the side was Tony Vance (Sylvans) who would be gaining his 16th cap. It was also announced that Tony would be Guernsey's assistant coach for this match. Jersey's manager, Dave Mathews, named his side on the day of the game and caused a surprise by leaving Yazalde Santos (Jersey Scottish) on the substitute's bench. He included Peter Edwards and David Le Roux, both of Upton winners, Trinity, who looked set to start suspensions that day but these were delayed as they had asked for personal hearings with the Jersey Disciplinary Committee. The Jersey starting line-up included four new caps with Tim Crowell (St. Peter), John Fitzmaurice (Trinity), Charlie Smith (Scottish) and David Le Roux making their debuts. Chris Andrews on the substitute's bench would also make his debut. Bradley Vowden (First Tower) would captain the Jersey side with John Nobes (Sylvans) leading Guernsey. Bradley would be following in his father's footsteps by not only playing for Jersey but also captaining the side. Bradley's father was Mo Vowden who captained Jersey in 1969. The guests at the match would be the Lieutenant- Governor of Guernsey, Lieutenant General Sir John Foley KCB, OBE, MC, The Bailiff of Guernsey, Sir de Vic Carey and the Bailiff of Jersey, Sir Philip Baihache.

A crowd of 4,500 packed into the new Foote's Lane venue to witness the first Guernsey Muratti Final not to be played at the Cycling Grounds. There were around 760 spectators in the impressive Garenne Stand.

Tim Crowell (left) powers his header past Bisson for Jersey's first equaliser.

Guernsey almost took the lead after just three minutes when Ian Potter forced his way down the right and sent in a lovely cross that Simon Johns missed by an inch. They maintained the upper hand and in the 9th minute Chris Chamberlain slipped past two Jersey defenders and laid on a good chance for Danny Bisson who found his goal-bound shot blocked. This early pressure continued and Chamberlain came close with a near post header. In the 17th minute Guernsey took the lead when, following a short corner, Simon Johns received the ball and floated it over to John Nobes on Jersey's left. He was unchallenged as he headed it back across the goal and Danny Bisson stooped low to head home. Jersey then stepped up the pace and pushed the Guernsey midfield back and a minute later Charlie Smith saw his cracking shot flash past the post. Jersey won a corner on Guernsey's left and Charlie Smith's cross was flicked on by Bradley Vowden to Tim Crowell and he headed in from six yards past a despairing Bisson. As the game picked up pace it appeared as if both defences were vulnerable as chances were created at both ends. Guernsey again were gain-

ing the upper hand but were unable to capitalise on the chances that were being created and at half time the score was Guernsey-1, Jersey-1.

The second half began well for Guernsey and they came close to scoring within 90 seconds of the start when Bisson latched onto a long punt from defence but could not take full advantage and the chance was gone. Jersey then created an excellent chance in the 57th minute when Peter Edwards set up John Fitzmaurice who sent

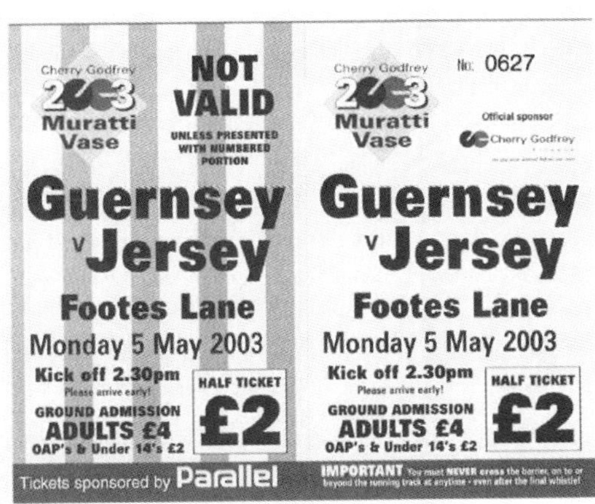

in an excellent cross for Gary Freeman and his header was brilliantly saved by Bison. The Guernsey keeper then pulled of a couple of fine saves as Jersey started to get on top and was fortunate to see a shot come off the bar and to safety. Bisson then pulled off a magnificent save from a superb shot by Paul Duxbury and then Guernsey suffered a setback as skipper John Nobes limped off injured, the result of an innocent clash with Yazalde Santos earlier. There was no more scoring and the 90 minutes ended Guernsey-1, Jersey-1.

The early part of extra-time was relatively quiet until the 9th minute when Ryan Tippet took the ball down the right, beat his defender and crossed in for Tony Vance to head in from close range to put Guernsey 2-1 ahead.

Both sides then appeared to cancel each other out and the first period of extra-time ended Guernsey-2, Jersey-1.

Guernsey was maintaining their slight edge in the second half with their defence coping well with Jersey's attacks and with eight minutes remaining they increased their lead. Paul Nobes produced some trickery on Jersey's right and slipped round the defender to set up Ryan Tippett to score number three with a left-foot shot. Tippett again came close but his shot from his left was well saved by Brewster. Jersey then broke away and a cross by Gary Freeman on Guernsey's left found Santos in some space and he slotted it home from close-in to make the score 3-2. From the kick-off Guernsey lost possession and it was returned into their own half. Chris Andrews received the ball and, as the seconds ticked away, burst forward through the Guernsey defence and, after getting a lucky bounce off Stuart Polson, found himself in the Guernsey penalty area and coolly hammered home the equaliser past a helpless Bisson. Jersey's two goals in quick succession completed the scoring and the match ended Guernsey-3, Jersey-3.

Guernsey: J. Bisson, S. Johns, S. Polson, J. Nobes (c), I. Potter, A. Vance, S. Brehaut, M. Warren, C. Chamberlain, R. Tippett, D. Bisson.
Subs: P. Nobes, M. Wilson, G. Le Page.
Goalscorers: Bisson, Vance, Tippett.

Tony Vance celebrates scoring Guernsey's second goal.

Chris Andrews celebrates his dramatic late equaliser.

Jersey: J. Brewster, T. Crowell, D. Lloyd, Lee de St. Croix, J. Fitzmaurice, B. Vowden (c), P. Edwards, C. Smith, P. Duxbury, G. Freeman, D. Le Roux.
Subs: Y. Santos, C. Andrews, M. Ray.
Goalscorers: Crowell, Santos, C. Andrews.

This was a remarkable finish to a good game which came alive in extra-time. The Guernsey camp were very disappointed at giving away a two-goal advantage with so little time left but Jersey must be congratulated for the way they fought to the end. Guernsey manager, Colin Fallaize, stated that when you have got yourselves two goals up with not a lot of time left you would think that it was a good position to be in. He said that they now have to roll their sleeves up and hopefully finish the job in Jersey. Dave Mathews, the Jersey manager, said that he was feeling fantastic and that it was a great match. He added that to come back from 3-1 down showed great character and that he was very confident about Jersey's chances at Springfield.

The Jersey evening Post produced this cartoon following an unfortunate incident at Footes Lane when a Jerseyman streaked across the park during extra-time. It turned out that the streaker was an ex- Jersey Junior Muratti player. He was later arrested, charged and found guilty in the Guernsey Court.

The replay was scheduled for Springfield Stadium on Sunday 18 May.

'It's bad enough when they whip off their shirts after scoring but this is a bit OTT!'

MURATTI FINAL REPLAY.
18 May 2003, Springfield Stadium, Jersey.

Jersey -1, Guernsey -0.

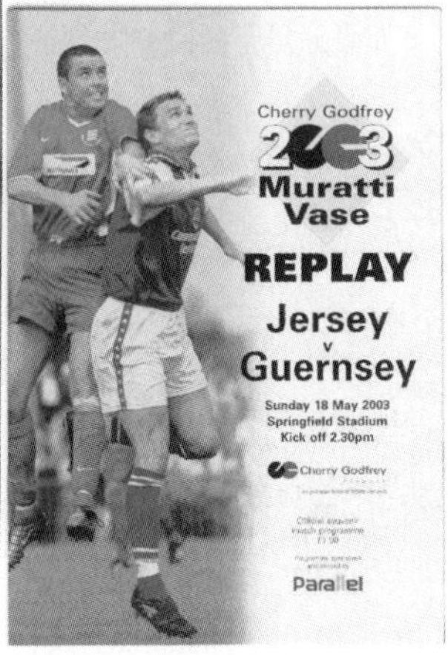

Jersey made four changes to their starting line-up for this replay with James Hayward (First Tower), Ryan Lumsden (Jersey Scottish), Mark Ray (St. Paul's) and Ross Crick coming in for Tim Crowell, Lee de St Croix, Paul Duxbury and Dave le Roux. Guernsey made one change with Michael Wilson (Northerners) replacing the injured John Nobes of Sylvans and Stuart Polson (Northerners) took over the captaincy.

It was announced that for the first time there would be two Ossie Eloury man-of-the-match awards and they would be presented after the match. One would be for the first match that took place at Footes Lane on 5 May and the second for this replay. The adjudicator was Magpies stalwart Dave Le Var and both recipients would have their name engraved on the trophy and be kept for six months.

At a rain soaked Springfield in front of a crowd of around 2,000 Guernsey took the early initiative by putting the home defence under pressure and winning three free-kicks in the first five minutes but they failed to trouble Brewster in the Jersey goal. Steve Brehaut came very close to opening the scoring when he latched onto a Chamberlain free-kick but sent his header just wide. David Lloyd then came to Jersey's rescue when his timely interception prevented Tippett bursting clear. Jersey replied when skipper Vowden side footed a Smith cross goalwards only to see his effort hit a Guernsey defender. The wet surface was continuing to affect the play and it was not until the 36th minute that there was a shot on target when Danny Bisson's shot was well held by Brewster. Just before the break a fine Guernsey move resulted in Warren moving in front of his marker and firing in a twisting header that was put over the bar by Brewster and at half time the score was Jersey-0, Guernsey-0.

Simon Johns' miscue crashes past the unfortunate Bisson as Peter Edwards (7) celebrates.

Jersey captain Vowden celebrates with the Muratti Vase.

For the second half Freeman had to go off with a rib injury and he was replaced by Dave le Roux. The second half began with Jersey missing a potential chance when Smith decided on a shot rather than a pass and then they had a let-off when Brewster took a goal kick which was charged down by Tippett but the ball went wide. Tippett and Warren both got behind their markers to put dangerous balls into Jersey's penalty area but in each case no one was in a position to convert. Jersey then broke away and Vowden flicked a ball out to Ray on the left and he put it into the Guernsey area. Ross Crick turned it on and as Simon Johns attempted to clear he crashed it into his own net to give Jersey the lead.

Guernsey responded and after Lumsden denied Warren, Chamberlain went down in the Jersey penalty area under a challenge by Lloyd but Premiership referee Clive Wilks, well up with play, turned down Guernsey's claim for a penalty. Guernsey brought on Paul Nobes for Danny Bisson but it was Chamberlain who set up Vance who could only lift his effort over the crossbar. Jersey appeared to sit back and as Guernsey pushed on, Hayward, Lloyd and Lumsden all made good blocks to keep the visitors out, and at full time the score was Jersey -1, Guernsey-0.

Jersey:	J. Brewster, J. Hayward, Lumsden, Lloyd, J. Fitzmaurice, C. Smith, P. Edwards, B. Vowden (c), M. Ray, G. Freeman, R. Crick.
	Subs: D. Le Roux.
	Goalscorer: og.
Guernsey:	J. Bisson, I. Potter, S. Polson (c), M. Wilson, S. Johns, C. Chamberlain, M. Warren, S. Brehaut, A. Vance, R. Tippett, D. Bisson.
	Subs: P. Nobes, M. Le Cras.

Stuart Polson.

Jersey FA President with the successful coaching staff.

The Ossie Eloury Man-of–the Match awards were made after the game and for the first time there were two awards, with Stuart Polson (Guernsey) winning for the first match in Guernsey and Lumsden (Jersey) winning for his performance in the replay.

Dave Mathews, the Jersey manager, was delighted with the result saying that his team worked hard today and in the two weeks between the games. He paid tribute to both teams who played well in difficult conditions. The Guernsey manager, Colin Fallaize, was not happy with his team's performance but was looking forward to the Island Games.

2002/2003 was a very successful season for Jersey with then annexing the Muratti Vase as well as the ladies, U-21 and U-18 trophies.

Guernsey put the massive disappointment of the Muratti Vase behind them to begin their preparations for the forthcoming Nat West Island Games and were worthy winners of the Gold medal at Foote's Lane on 4 July.

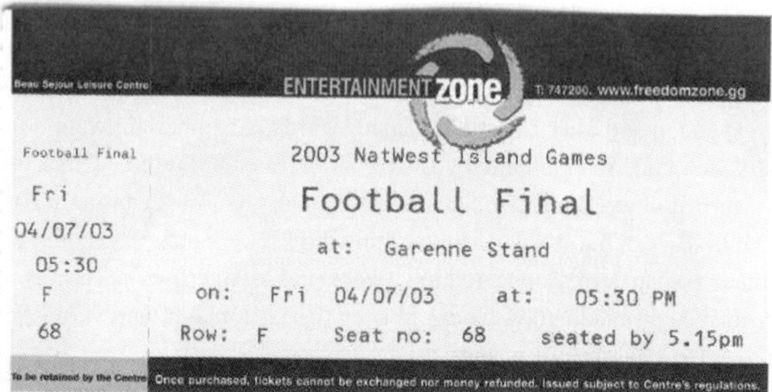

Following the success in retaining the football Gold medal Colin Fallaize announced his retirement as manager and he was replaced by Steve Ogier, who had resigned as St. Martin's manager. Steve selected Paul Ockleford as his assistant.

There was some disquiet amongst a lot of Guernsey fans at the decision to hold future Muratti matches at Footes Lane. The feeling was that the venue lacked the special atmosphere of the Track. The GFA, however, were adamant that their decision would not be reversed. A petition to return to the Track was organised by Nigel Gavet and local fans

Steve Ogier.

Paul Ockleford.

signed in their hundreds including some high-profile names such as current and ex-Muratti players and managers. Details of the future redevelopment of the Track were soon to be released by the officials of the Amalgamated Football Club.

Guernsey's assistant coach, Paul Ockleford, moved to Guernsey in 1995 after a non-league playing career with Dorchester and Weymouth. He joined Rangers as a player and soon after began studying for his Uefa Coaching Licences.

The news in the local Press that apparently the Guernsey economy was performing better than Jersey's prompted cartoonist Peewee to produce this cartoon on 5 September:

The Track.

Bill Farmer, one of Guernsey's first professional footballers, died peacefully on 16 September 2003 at the King Edward Hospital aged 78. He played in goal for Belgrave Wanderers in 72 games as well as gaining five Muratti caps between 1948-1951 winning two Muratti medals. He signed for Nottingham Forest in 1953 and made 58 appearances for them over the following three years. Bill was born in Jersey and latterly lived in the Vale

It was reported in the Press of 10 September that the campaign to take big football matches back to the Track had received a major boost when plans to redevelop the old stadium were being considered by the Island Development Committee. Project director, former Guernsey manager, Harold Allen, was confident that the IDC would support the Amalgamated Sports and Football Club's application to re-establish the Track as the premier football ground in Guernsey. The Amalgamated has split the plans into three sections.
Block A, on the site of the current grandstand would feature a new stand seating over 500 spectators, a presentation podium and state-of –the-art changing facilities.
Block B, at the eastern end of the ground, would include a sports hall with viewing gallery and a disaster recovery section to let out to outside businesses.
Block C, at the western end of the ground, would feature a single storey gymnasium.
Mr. Allen has not yet investigated ways of paying for the proposed development as he is waiting for permission to be granted.

Graeme Mourant, former president of both the Jersey Football Association (1991-1994) and the Jersey Football Combination (1980-1988), died at the Jersey Hospice on Wednesday 26 November 2003. The 73-year-old retired Customs Officer represented Jersey in the 1947 and 1948 Junior Muratti before playing in the senior Muratti in 1951. He gained 11 Muratti caps winning six medals. In his last appearance he captained Jersey to a 2-1 victory over Guernsey at Springfield in 1962.

2 0 0 4

MURATTI SEMI-FINAL.
6 March 2004, Mount Hale, Alderney.

Alderney -0, Jersey -4.

Alderney Manager, Alan Adamson, was preparing for a very tough game against Jersey as many of the established players had retired and they would be relying on a group of young players. Alderney, however, came into this game following the experience in competing in the NatWest Island Games in Guernsey the year before. They would be without young Steve Concannen, as he would be in the Guernsey squad, and Andrew Stone. They were, however, boosted by the appearance of the experienced Kevin Gentle, who would win his 13th cap.

Jersey announced that Sean McDonald, their goalkeeping coach, would be on standby for a position on the substitutes' bench as their first choice goalkeeper, Jimmy Styles (Wanderers), picked up an injury during squad training. Casey Hickling took over in goal, winning his first Muratti cap. Jersey Manager, Dave Matthews, conceded that the match would be very tricky and that he did not want to create a bit of history by being the first Jersey manager to lose to Alderney. Chris McNabb (Jersey Scottish) and John Beatson (St. Paul's) were to gain their first caps in this match.

Alderney began the match with the sun at their backs and immediately began working hard to close down their opponents. Although Jersey started positively there was edginess about their play and they appeared to be put out of their stride by the combative play of Alderney who gave the Jersey forwards little time to dwell on the ball. Jersey took the lead after 30 minutes play following a rather fortunate free-kick. Impressive Dave Brodie took

Kevin Gentle.

the kick and fed Chris Andrews who in turn sent in a low cross that was hit home by Ross Crick, with keeper Paul Williams helpless.

Minutes later Andrews appeared to have been tripped inside Alderney's penalty area but referee Andy Priaulx waved away Jersey's protests. Jersey continued to press and scored their second four minutes later when the irrepressible Brodie slipped the ball to Andrews and as he slipped his markers he crashed a 12 yard shot past Williams' despairing left hand. This goal seemed to settle Jersey with both debutant Lee Bradshaw and Dave Le Roux heading good chances just past the Alderney post, and the half ended Alderney-0, Jersey-2.

Alderney started the second half brightly and came close to opening their account but the chances went past. Although competing well, the game was slipping away from Alderney and it was no surprise when Jersey added a third goal on the hour mark. Andrews passed to Crick who controlled well and held off the defence before feeding the ball back to Chris McNabb to fire in a 20-yard shot inside Williams' left-hand post. The final goal came in the 71st minute when McNabb came close to scoring his second, but his effort was diverted across goal by the onrushing Williams and Le Roux had a simple tap-in from five metres to make the final score Alderney -0, Jersey-4.

Alderney: P. Williams, S. Benfield, J. Atkins, R. Bohan, K. Gentle, M. Bohan, W. Benfield (c), J. Vizard, M. Aldcroft, A. Lawrence, L. Davey.
Subs: J. Walker, E. Phelan, M. Sebire.

Jersey: C. Hickling, J. Hayward, R. Lumsden, L. Bradshaw, J. Beatson, C. Andrews (c), D. Brodie, C. McNabb, C. Hamon, R. Crick, D. Le Roux.
Subs: G. McConnell, J. Reilly.
Goalscorers: Crick, Andrews, McNabb, Le Roux.

Ross Crick opens the scoring For Jersey.

After the game both Managers expressed their pleasure in the performances of their respective teams. Alan Adamson stated that he could not have asked more from his team as they had played well and worked really hard. Dave Matthews put his team's performance down to excellent preparation as well as the team having the correct attitude. In a game that was played in an excellent spirit a major highlight was when an Alderney player went down following a robust challenge and the Jersey players called for the ball to be put out. Le Roux did not hear the call and sent in a shot that hit Williams on the legs. The ball broke to Crick with the goal at his mercy, but he quickly sent the ball out for a throw-in so that the Alderney player could receive treatment.

Alderney Football Association President, Billy Bohan, was standing down from his position at the end of the season. He gained 21 Muratti caps from 1969-1989, both in goal as well as outfield, scoring 1 goal. He served Alderney as a player, coach, as well as President for over 35 years.

As both Jersey and Guernsey were preparing for the 2004 Muratti Vase Final the Guernsey Press looked back 50 years to the 1954 Final that became known as the 'Micky Brassell' Final following his four goals on his Muratti debut as Guernsey defeated Jersey 5-3 at Springfield on 6 May 1954. It would appear that the football prediction made in February 1937 proved to be very accurate.

Chris Andrews prepares to fire in a shot.

Alderney.
M. Bohan, Lawrence, S. Benfield, R. Bohan, Gentle, W. Benfield (c).
Atkins, Aldcroft, Vizard, Williams (son Jack), Davey.

Micky Brassell.

MURATTI FINAL.
3 May 2004, Springfield Stadium, Jersey.

Jersey -3, Guernsey -0.

Guernsey selected Joby Bourgaize (Belgrave Wanderers) for his first senior cap adding himto the small group of players who have gained Senior and Junior caps in the same season. Steve Concanen (St. Martins), by being selected by Guernsey for the first time, became only the third player to play Senior Muratti for two different islands. Steve has three caps for Alderney (2001-2003). Guernsey's third new cap was Jon Veron (North). Jersey Manager, Dave Matthews, believed that the crowd could spur his team on to victory. He selected an experienced team with only goalkeeper Jimmy Styles (Wanderers) gaining his first cap.

Prior to the commencement of the match a minutes silence was observed to mark the passing of John Martel who died on 27 April 2004 aged 90. John Martel gained 12 Muratti caps between 1934-1947. He was one of the small band of players who played Muratti football before and after the Second World War. He won 5 Muratti medals and scored 3 goals. He captained Guernsey in the first Muratti after the war in 1947 and he acted as linesman in the 1955 Muratti Vase Final and replay. He played his club football for Rangers. He was widely accepted as Guernsey's outstanding inside-forward during the 1930's.

Guernsey started the match well and had the first real chance through Jon Veron but his shot was well blocked by Jersey's Craig Ferey. Jersey's response appeared to be a shoot-on-sight policy although their early efforts were way off the mark. It was a typical Muratti beginning to the game with both teams appearing somewhat nervous and taking a little time to settle. Matt Warren opened up the game when he sent an excellent pass down Guernsey's right where Dave Rihoy latched onto it but as he attempted to pull the ball back Paul Duxbury did very well to make up ground and cut out the cross. Guernsey continued with this early pressure and Jan Renouf found himself unmarked from a corner but he sent his header straight at Jimmy Styles in the home goal. Jersey's first real chance came after 15 minutes when Chris Hamon fired in a shot from the left that Bisson could not hold, Ged McConnell sent in a goal

John Martel.

S .Ingrouille T. Duff, Renouf, Bourgaize, de Garis, Heaume, Bisson, Polson, Potter, B .Duff, P. Ockleford S. Ogier (coach).
Concanen, Warren, Coutanche, Veron, Tippett, Le Page, Brehaut, Johns, Rihoy.
Guernsey Muratti squad.

bound shot that was scrambled clear. Veron was proving a danger to the Jersey defence and only a superb tackle by Ryan Lumsden prevented him from racing clear of the defence. Jersey began to settle down and play a more controlled game with more accurate passing as David Brodie took charge of the midfield. It was from a Brodie pass that Chris Andrews was set up in the 23rd minute and he cut in from the right, through a couple of challenges, to slip the ball to Ross Crick. Crick's right foot shot came back off the post but he was the first to react and he scored with his left from close range from the rebound to put Jersey 1-0 ahead. Almost immediately Renouf came very close but his low effort was well saved by Styles. Jersey were now playing a confident brand of football and could have gone 2-0 two minutes later when Hayward sent a high ball into the Guernsey area and it was headed

Ian Potter brings down David Le Roux for Jersey's penalty.

clear by Concanen and then Bourgaize. The ball broke to Brodie who passed to Hamon on Jersey's left and his cross found Crick in space but his close-in header was well saved by Bisson. A minute later Bisson again saved Guernsey with a superb block save from David Le Roux. Warren then picked up the ball and sent an excellent pass through to Ryan Tippett but his left foot shot was well saved by Styles for a corner. It seemed that Guernsey would be going in at the break only 1-0 down when, on the stroke of half time, Brodie gave the ball to Le Roux and as he turned inside Ian Potter, the Guernsey defender stuck out a leg to bring him down inside the box and referee Howard Webb had no hesitation in awarding a penalty. Ross Crick stepped up and crashed his shot into the left hand corner of the net as Bisson dived the other way to make the half time score Jersey-2, Guernsey-0.

The second half began with Jersey still dominant as they comfortably restricted Guernsey's efforts. Brodie was in control in the middle of the park and most of Jersey's moves were instigated by him. Early in the second half Brodie once again found a lot of space and as he drove into the Guernsey half he sent a fine pass through to Crick and his quick shot found the net, but unfortunately for Jersey the linesman already had his flag up for offside. Jersey continued to press and Duxbury fed Hamon but his shot was blocked and as he cut in again he was fouled by Concanen. Brodie took the kick and curled the ball over the Guernsey wall onto the top of the crossbar and over for a goalkick. As the game progressed Guernsey became less and less of a threat and it was no surprise when Jersey increased their lead in the 68th minute. A Guernsey move broke down and Brodie collected the ball and passed to Andrews who was free down Jersey's right. His long cross was played back into the box by Hamon to Crick but he was quickly closed down by the Guernsey defence. He slipped the ball back out to Hamon and his fine cross was headed home by Ged McConnell from 6 yards for 3-0. The game was drawing to an end and it was apparent that Jersey was more likely to increase their lead rather than Guernsey being able to reduce the arrears and at full time the score was Jersey-3, Guernsey-0.

Jersey:	J. Styles, J. Hayward, C. Ferey, R. Lumsden, P. Duxbury, C. Andrews (c), D. Brodie, G. McConnell, C. Hamon, R. Crick, D. Le Roux.
	Subs: C. McNabb, J. Reilly.
	Goalscorers: Crick (2-1 pen), McConnell.
Guernsey:	J. Bisson, S. Concanen, S. Polson (c), I. Potter, S. Johns, J. Bourgaize, J. Renouf, M. Warren, D. Rihoy, R. Tippett, J. Veron.
	Subs: S. Brehaut, T. Duff.

Jersey celebrates winning the Muratti Vase.

Jersey's victorious Muratti squad.
McDonald, Le Roux, Grant, Crick, Ferey, Brewster, Dave Matthews, Styles, Hayward, Hamon, Andrews, Lumsden, Toudic.
Swanson, McConnell, McNabb, Brodie, Beatson, Reilly, Duxbury, Bradshaw.

This was an emphatic victory for a fine Jersey team and their manager, Dave Matthews, was delighted not only with the victory but also with the excellent football played by his side. Ross Crick put a disappointing Upton behind him by capping an excellent scoring season by notching his 59th and 60th goals in the match. Steve Ogier, Guernsey's manager, was very disappointed with the result but was full of praise for the Jersey side.

The Ossie Eloury Memorial Trophy was presented to David Brodie just before the Muratti Vase was presented to Chris Andrews by Guernsey's Lieut- Governor, Lieutenant General Sir John Foley, amidst great cheers from the jubilant Jersey team and their supporters.

The weekend was a special one for the Matthews family. Dave managed the victorious Muratti team on Monday 4 May the day after his brother, Mo, managed the Jersey Ladies to a 4-1 victory over Guernsey. In goal for Jersey ladies was Dave's daughter, Krystle.

A report appeared in the Guernsey Press of 22 July 2004 concerning a petition to return the Muratti matches to the Cycling Grounds (the Track). The main complaint is that there is a lack of atmosphere at Footes Lane due to the fact that standing spectators are being kept so far away from the action. The petition was recently handed over to the GFA by James Gavet on behalf of his late father, Nigel. The petition has been signed by 850 local football fans. This petition plus letters expressing differing views will be discussed at the council

Dave and Krystle Matthews.

meeting on 2 September. A letter from Rangers Football Club was received by the Guernsey Football Association in June requesting that future Muratti matches be played at the Track. The GFA secretary, Matt Fallaize, stated that it was decided to contact interested parties such as the Sports Commission, Steve Ogier (Island manager), Culture and Leisure, sponsors and the Amalgamated committee, asking for their views by the middle of July. Other council members were asked to submit their views of having a properly informed decision on the whole subject at the council meeting on 2 September. The last Muratti match to be

Darren Duquemin.

played at the Track was the final on 7 May 2001 when Guernsey defeated Jersey 4-1.

On 23 July Darren Duquemin, representing match sponsor Cherry Godfrey Finance, said that exciting developments, which would be unveiled the following month, should reduce the clamour for the game to go back to the Track. 'Cherry Godfrey would be revealing their plans for the centenary game to football officials on 26 August' said Duquemin. 'Plans to get spectators close to the action would be unveiled then'. He was confident that their proposals would make for a memorable occasion that would be remembered for years to come. They wished to make it the perfect celebration of the Muratti centenary.

Plans were unveiled on 26 August to make Foote's Lane into a 5,000 all-seater stadium for the 2005 Centenary Cherry Godfrey Muratti final. In a presentation open to all interested parties at Beau Sejour, the sponsor's marketing representative, Darren Duquemin, revealed the proposals to put temporary stands and have fans 'on top of the action'. The organisers are looking to put approximately 800 seats behind each goal, 2,400 opposite the Garenne Stand and 400 next to the stand, which itself seats 700 spectators. There is also the possibility of erecting a large screen at either end of the pitch. It was also revealed that the cost of the project would not be funded by the Guernsey Football Association or the paying public.

Although Cherry Godfrey has an exclusive sponsorship deal for the Muratti they are prepared to invite additional sponsors to make all the proposals happen. It was pointed out, however, that Foote's Lane would be the only venue where these plans could be put into operation because money would not be found to carry out this work at the Track. The final decision on where the Centenary Muratti Vase final would be played fell to the GFA clubs.

Part of the Muratti crowd behind the barriers off the running track.

Muratti Vase Final 2005?

At a GFA Council Meeting on Thursday 2 September 2004 the clubs voted 12-2 in favour of holding the 2005 Muratti Final at Footes Lane. Preparations could now go ahead for the Centenary Muratti Vase Final on 2 May 2005.

At the end of the first century of Muratti football Jersey had taken a substantial lead in the series with 46 wins with Guernsey on 40 wins and Alderney with 1 win. The Muratti Vase was shared by Guernsey and Jersey in 1937. As 2005 approached I believe that the origina-tors of the competition could look with pride at what they have given to Channel Island sport. These games have been about players, match officials and spectators. There have been around 1,000 players who have been fortunate enough to gain a Muratti Cap. Nearly 550 match officials have been used over the years and they, along with an estimated 700,000 spectators, have witnessed close on 800 goals. There has been controversy, excite-ment, happiness and sadness with games throwing up heroes and villains. There have been great games (and not-so-great games) as well as a host of players, and officials, who could grace any football stage.

The first Muratti century has left a lasting football legacy that, I am sure, will be success-fully built on by the Muratti into the next century. The name 'Muratti is now synonymous with any inter-island competition but to paraphrase a comment that has appeared in many Muratti Vase programmes

'There is only one Muratti and you have been reading about it.'

ALDERNEY'S MURATTI RESULTS

Year					VENUE	ALDERNEY GOALSCORERS
1905	Alderney	0	Guernsey	6	Guernsey	
1906	Alderney	0	Guernsey	1	Guernsey	
1907	Alderney	1	Jersey	2 aet.	Guernsey	F. Quinain.
1908	Alderney	0	Guernsey	3	Jersey	
1909	Alderney	0	Guernsey	2	Jersey	
1910	Alderney	1	Jersey	7	Jersey	Vagg.
1911	Alderney	1	Guernsey	2	Guernsey	og.
1912	Alderney	0	Guernsey	4	Guernsey	
1913	Alderney	2	Jersey	5 aet.	Guernsey	Quinain, Cleale.
1914	Alderney	0	Guernsey	4	Jersey	
1920	Alderney	1	Guernsey	0	Jersey	Lihou.
1921	Alderney	0	Jersey	2	Jersey	
1922	Alderney	0	Guernsey	8	Guernsey	
1923	Alderney	2	Guernsey	3	Guernsey	J. Baker, T. Baker.
1924	Alderney	0	Jersey	1	Jersey	
1925	Alderney	0	Guernsey	3	Jersey	
1926	Alderney	1	Jersey	7	Jersey	Hammond.
1927	Alderney	0	Jersey	3	Jersey	
1928	Alderney	0	Guernsey	4	Guernsey	
1929	Alderney	0	Guernsey	5	Guernsey	
1930	Alderney	2	Jersey	3	Guernsey	S. Newton, Randall.
1931	Alderney	0	Guernsey	1	Jersey	
1932	Alderney	2	Guernsey	4	Jersey	J. Newton, McLernon.
1933	Alderney	0	Jersey	6	Guernsey	
1934	Alderney	0	Guernsey	3	Guernsey	
1935	Alderney	0	Guernsey	5	Guernsey	
1936	Alderney	0	Jersey	9	Jersey	
1937	Alderney	1	Guernsey	4	Guernsey	F. Odoir.
1938	Alderney	1	Guernsey	3	Jersey	G. Burness.
1939	Alderney	1	Jersey	2	Jersey	H. Simon.
1948	Alderney	0	Guernsey	3	Guernsey	
1949	Alderney	0	Jersey	9	Jersey	
1950	Alderney	1	Guernsey	3	Guernsey	Ron Fever (pen).
1951	Alderney	1	Jersey	8	Jersey	Noel Mignot.
1952	Alderney	2	Guernsey	7	Guernsey	Venton, Noel Mignot.
1953	Alderney	0	Jersey	4	Jersey	
1954	Alderney	1	Guernsey	2	Guernsey	N. Mignot.
1955	Alderney	0	Jersey	3	Jersey	
1956	Alderney	0	Guernsey	4	Guernsey	
1957	Alderney	1	Jersey	7	Jersey	Peter Moore.
1958	Alderney	2	Guernsey	8	Guernsey	Peter Moore (2) (1 pen).
1959	Alderney	0	Jersey	6	Jersey	
1960	Alderney	1	Guernsey	5	Guernsey	Barry Venton (pen).
1961	Alderney	2	Jersey	4	Jersey	Dupont, Albert Randall.
1962	Alderney	1	Guernsey	6	Guernsey	Clarke.
1963	Alderney	0	Jersey	6	Jersey	
1964	Alderney	0	Guernsey	3	Guernsey	
1965	Alderney	0	Jersey	8	Jersey	
1966	Alderney	0	Guernsey	10	Guernsey	
1967	Alderney	1	Jersey	3	Jersey	M. Smith.
1968	Alderney	0	Guernsey	2	Guernsey	
1969	Alderney	0	Jersey	5	Jersey	
1970	Alderney	0	Guernsey	4	Guernsey	
1971	Alderney	0	Jersey	11	Jersey	
1972	Alderney	0	Guernsey	5	Guernsey	
1973	Alderney	1	Jersey	6	Jersey	Louie Farnham.

Year	Team 1	Score	Team 2	Score	Venue	Scorer
1974	Alderney	0	Guernsey	6	Guernsey	
1975	Alderney	1	Jersey	3	Jersey	Frank Keachie.
1976	Alderney	0	Guernsey	5	Alderney	
1977	Alderney	0	Jersey	3	Alderney	
1978	Alderney	0	Guernsey	12	Guernsey	
1979	Alderney	0	Jersey	8	Jersey	
1980	Alderney	0	Guernsey	5	Alderney	
1981	Alderney	0	Jersey	5	Jersey	
1982	Alderney	1	Guernsey	5	Guernsey	John Maloy.
1983	Alderney	1	Jersey	6	Jersey	Billy Bohan.
1984	Alderney	0	Guernsey	6	Alderney	
1985	Alderney	0	Jersey	5	Alderney	
1986	Alderney	0	Guernsey	7	Guernsey	
1987	Alderney	0*	Jersey	10	Jersey	
1988	Alderney	1	Guernsey	5	Alderney	Mark Treais.
1989	Alderney	0	Jersey	4	Alderney	
1990	Alderney	0	Guernsey	4	Guernsey	
1991	Alderney	1	Jersey	4	Alderney	Andy Wright.
1992	Alderney	1	Guernsey	9	Guernsey	Kevin Fairbrother.
1993	Alderney	0	Guernsey	10	Alderney	
1994	Alderney	0	Jersey	18	Jersey	
1995	Alderney	1	Jersey	7	Alderney	Mark Treais.
1996	Alderney	0	Guernsey	2	Alderney	
1997	Alderney	0	Guernsey	6	Alderney	
1998	Alderney	0	Jersey	2	Alderney	
1999	Alderney	0	Guernsey	1	Alderney	
2000	Alderney	0	Jersey	10	Alderney	
2001	Alderney	0	Guernsey	6	Alderney	
2002	Alderney	1	Jersey	2	Alderney	Mark Treais.
2003	Alderney	1	Guernsey	4	Alderney	Michael Bohan.
2004	Alderney	0	Jersey	4	Alderney	

GUERNSEY'S MURATTI RESULTS

Year	Team 1	Score	Team 2	Score	Venue	Guernsey Goalscorers
1905	Guernsey	6	Alderney	0	Guernsey	Heaume (3), Crews (2), Jackson.
	Guernsey	1	Jersey	0	Jersey	F. Stranger.
1906	Guernsey	2	Jersey	1	Jersey	Cotton (2).
	Guernsey	1	Alderney	0	Guernsey	Cotton.
1907	Guernsey	3	Jersey	2 aet.	Jersey	F.G. Mockler, J. Leadbeater, T. Holland.
1908	Guernsey	3	Alderney	0	Jersey	V.Cooper, J. Leadbeater, F.G. Mockler.
	Guernsey	0	Jersey	4	Guernsey	
1909	Guernsey	3	Jersey	0	Guernsey	T. Zabiela, F.Duquemin, A.H.P. Davey.
	Guernsey	2	Alderney	0	Jersey	J. Leadbeater, F. Cleale.
1910	Guernsey	2	Jersey	3	Guernsey	R. Chapple (2).
1911	Guernsey	2	Alderney	1	Guernsey	R.Chapple, A.H.P. Davey.
	Guernsey	1	Jersey	4	Jersey	W. Bird.
1912	Guernsey	3	Jersey	3	Jersey	H. Stranger (2), F. Cleale.
	Guernsey	5	Jersey	2	Jersey	H. Stranger (2), A.Yates, F. Cleale (2).
	Guernsey	4	Alderney	0	Guernsey	T. Zabiela (2), A. Yates, F. Cleale.
1913	Guernsey	4	Jersey	2	Jersey	F. Cleale, H. Stranger (2), A. Yates.

Year	Home		Away		Venue	Scorers
1914	Guernsey	4	Alderney	0	Jersey	H.E.K. Stranger (2), Blicq, F. Cleale.
	Guernsey	2	Jersey	1	Guernsey	F. Cleale, Blicq.
1920	Guernsey	1	Jersey	0	Guernsey	W. Warr.
	Guernsey	0	Alderney	1	Jersey	
1921	Guernsey	0	Jersey	1	Guernsey	
1922	Guernsey	8	Alderney	0	Guernsey	F. Jeffreys, H. Cumber (4), HC Chapell (2), F. Rich.
	Guernsey	2	Jersey	1	Jersey	H. Chapell (2).
1923	Guernsey	1	Jersey	0	Jersey	H. Cumber.
	Guernsey	3	Alderney	2	Guernsey	H. Chapell, W. Warr, F. Rich.
1924	Guernsey	0	Jersey	1	Jersey	
1925	Guernsey	3	Alderney	0	Jersey	S.A. Noel (3).
	Guernsey	2	Jersey	1	Guernsey	S.A. Noel (2).
1926	Guernsey	1	Jersey	5	Guernsey	H.C. Chapell.
1927	Guernsey	1	Jersey	0	Guernsey	W. Barrasin.
1928	Guernsey	4	Alderney	0	Guernsey	W. Warr, H. Dorey, W. Down, S.A. Noel.
	Guernsey	1	Jersey	2 aet.	Jersey	H. Dorey.
1929	Guernsey	7	Jersey	1	Jersey	D. Mauger, S.A. Noel(3), W. Barrasin (3).
	Guernsey	5	Alderney	0	Guernsey	C.Solway,L.Purdy, W.Barrasin(2), S.A.Noel.
1930	Guernsey	3	Jersey	2	Jersey	J.S. Brookes, W. Warr, H. Dorey.
1931	Guernsey	1	Alderney	0	Jersey	W.C. Freeman.
	Guernsey	2	Jersey	4	Guernsey	H. Dorey (2).
1932	Guernsey	2	Jersey	0	Guernsey	H. Dorey, W. Warr (pen).
	Guernsey	4	Alderney	2	Jersey	H. Dorey (2), D. Mauger, M. Brassel.
1933	Guernsey	4	Jersey	1 aet.	Guernsey	D. Mauger,H. Dorey (3)
1934	Guernsey	3	Alderney	0	Guernsey	T. le Prevost, W. Friess, J A Martel.
	Guernsey	1	Jersey	0	Jersey	A.E. Broadrib.
1935	Guernsey	1	Jersey	0	Jersey	T. le Prevost.
	Guernsey	5	Alderney	0	Guernsey	J.J Brookes,T.le Prevost(2), M.Brassel, og.
1936	Guernsey	2	Jersey	1	Guernsey	H. Duquemin, H. Dorey.
1937	Guernsey	4	Alderney	1	Guernsey	H. Dorey (2), D. Mauger, J.A. Martel.
	Guernsey	2	Jersey	2 aet.	Jersey	H. Duquemin, A.E. Broadrib.
	Guernsey	3	Jersey	3 aet.	Guernsey	W. Allen (2), W. Crocker.
1938	Guernsey	4	Jersey	3	Guernsey	W. Crocker, H. Duquemin (2), T. le Prevost.
	Guernsey	3	Alderney	1	Jersey	H. Marley, J.A. Martel, T. le Prevost.
1939	Guernsey	0	Jersey	1	Guernsey	
1947	Guernsey	1	Jersey	3	Guernsey	T. le Prevost.
1948	Guernsey	3	Alderney	0	Guernsey	S. de la Mare, A. Hunter, L. Collins.
	Guernsey	3	Jersey	6	Jersey	H. Falla (2), V. Tostevin.
1949	Guernsey	1	Jersey	2	Guernsey	G. Buckingham.
1950	Guernsey	3	Alderney	1	Guernsey	K. Tayler (2), A.M. Hunter.
	Guernsey	2	Jersey	0	Jersey	L.J. Robilliard, A.M. Hunter.
1951	Guernsey	3	Jersey	1 aet.	Guernsey	R. Robilliard, A.M. Hunter, L. Collins.
1952	Guernsey	7	Alderney	2	Guernsey	H. Falla, J. le Maitre, W. le Page(2), L. Collins (3).
	Guernsey	3	Jersey	1	Jersey	W. le Page (2), J. le Maitre.

Year						
1953	Guernsey	0	Jersey	2	Guernsey	
1954	Guernsey	2	Alderney	1	Guernsey	H. Falla, A.M. Hunter.
	Guernsey	5	Jersey	3	Jersey	M. Brassel (4), A.M. Hunter.
1955	Guernsey	0	Jersey	0 aet.	Guernsey	
	Guernsey	0	Jersey	1	Jersey	
1956	Guernsey	4	Alderney	0	Guernsey	R. Harvey (2), D. Meechem, L. Collins.
	Guernsey	1	Jersey	2	Jersey	D. Meechem.
1957	Guernsey	6	Jersey	4	Guernsey	L. Robilliard (2), L. Collins (2), J. Eker, V. Tostevin.
1958	Guernsey	8	Alderney	2	Guernsey	R. Harvey (3), D. Meechem (2), A. Hamon, og (2).
	Guernsey	1	Jersey	2	Jersey	A. Sandrey (pen).
1959	Guernsey	2	Jersey	3	Guernsey	L. Duquemin, og.
1960	Guernsey	5	Alderney	1	Guernsey	N. le Cheminant (2), L.Arnold (2), L. Collins.
	Guernsey	1	Jersey	5	Jersey	L. Arnold.
1961	Guernsey	1	Jersey	2	Guernsey	C. Renouf.
1962	Guernsey	6	Alderney	1	Guernsey	M. Wylie (2), A. Hamon (2), J. Brehaut, J. Mahy.
	Guernsey	1	Jersey	2	Jersey	B. Mahy.
1963	Guernsey	1	Jersey	4	Guernsey	L. Collins.
1964	Guernsey	3	Alderney	0	Guernsey	C. Renouf (2), M. le Tissier.
	Guernsey	0	Jersey	1	Jersey	
1965	Guernsey	2	Jersey	4	Guernsey	J. Loveridge, A. Williams.
1966	Guernsey	10	Alderney	0	Guernsey	J. Loveridge (4), Eldridge (3), W. Torode, Conway, A. Pugh.
	Guernsey	1	Jersey	1 aet.	Jersey	J. Loveridge.
	Guernsey	3	Jersey	1	Guernsey	J. Loveridge (3)
1967	Guernsey	1	Jersey	3 aet.	Guernsey	K. Giles.
1968	Guernsey	2	Alderney	0	Guernsey	M. Duncan, C. Renouf.
	Guernsey	1	Jersey	2	Jersey	J. Loveridge.
1969	Guernsey	2	Jersey	1	Guernsey	M. Girard (pen), C. Renouf.
1970	Guernsey	4	Alderney	0	Guernsey	J.Loveridge, H.Davey, W.Torode, A.le Page.
	Guernsey	0	Jersey	2	Jersey	
1971	Guernsey	0	Jersey	1	Guernsey	
1972	Guernsey	5	Alderney	0	Guernsey	J. Loveridge (2), C. Reeve, H. Davey, D. Lesbirel.
	Guernsey	3	Jersey	0 aet.	Jersey	C. Reeve, K. Giles, W. Torode,
1973	Guernsey	1	Jersey	4	Guernsey	C. Reeve.
1974	Guernsey	6	Alderney	0	Guernsey	R. Blondel (4),C. Reeve (2).
	Guernsey	2	Jersey	1 aet.	Jersey	R. Blondel (2).
1975	Guernsey	2	Jersey	2 aet.	Guernsey	C. Fallaize, C. Reeve.
	Guernsey	3	Jersey	2	Jersey	N. le Page, D. Lesbirel (pen), C. Fallaize.
1976	Guernsey	5	Alderney	0	Alderney	C.Reeve (2),N.le Page, G Rowe, C.Fallaize.
	Guernsey	1	Jersey	3	Jersey	C. Reeve.
1977	Guernsey	1	Jersey	5	Guernsey	P. Blondel.
1978	Guernsey	12	Alderney	0	Guernsey	C. Allen (5), R. Webb (4), K. le Gallez, C. Fallaize, L. Graham.
	Guernsey	2	Jersey	0	Jersey	N. Le Page (2).

1979	Guernsey	5	Jersey	0	Guernsey	C.Fallaize, P.Blondel(pen), K. LeGallez, W. Kennedy, R. Webb.
1980	Guernsey	5	Alderney	0	Alderney	A. Bougourd,C.Fallaize (2), W. Kennedy (2).
	Guernsey	2	Jersey	1 aet.	Jersey	R. Brehaut, N. le Page.
1981	Guernsey	1	Jersey	4	Guernsey	T. Tostevin.
1982	Guernsey	5	Alderney	1	Guernsey	A. Bougourd, K. Le Tissier, C.Fallaize (2), L. Graham (pen).
	Guernsey	1	Jersey	2	Jersey	og.
1983	Guernsey	2	Jersey	1	Guernsey	N. Hunter, K. Le Tissier.
1984	Guernsey	6	Alderney	0	Alderney	M.Culverwell (2), C. Dyer, C.LeTissier, L. Graham, C. Fallaize.
	Guernsey	2	Jersey	6 aet.	Jersey	K. Le Gallez, C. Fallaize.
1985	Guernsey	4	Jersey	3	Guernsey	L. Smith, K. LeTissier, C. Fallaize (2).
1986	Guernsey	7	Alderney	0	Guernsey	P. Blondel (pen), M. LeTissier, C. Fallaize (3), N. Hunter (2).
	Guernsey	2	Jersey	3	Jersey	K. LeTissier, N. Hunter.
1987	Guernsey	3	Jersey	4 aet.	Guernsey	N. Hunter (3)
1988	Guernsey	5	Alderney	1	Alderney	C. Dyer, M.Gallienne, A. Bougourd (2), C. Le Tissier.
	Guernsey	1	Jersey	0	Jersey	C. LeTissier (pen).
1989	Guernsey	0	Jersey	4	Guernsey	
1990	Guernsey	4	Alderney	0	Guernsey	K. LeTissier (2), C. Dyer, L. Smith.
	Guernsey	1	Jersey	2	Jersey	C. LeTissier (pen).
1991	Guernsey	3	Jersey	0	Guernsey	C. Le Tissier, L. Luscombe, og.
1992	Guernsey	9	Alderney	1	Guernsey	K. le Tissier (5), C. Allen, A. Vance, C. Dyer, G. Chalmers.
	Guernsey	3	Jersey	2	Jersey	K. Le Tissier (2), A. Vance.
1993	Guernsey	10	Alderney	0	Alderney	C. Allen (7), K. Le Tissier (2), G. apSion.
	Guernsey	1	Jersey	2	Guernsey	K. Le Tissier.
1994	Guernsey	1	Jersey	3	Jersey	K. Le Tissier.
1995	Guernsey	1	Jersey	2	Guernsey	G. Chalmers.
1996	Guernsey	2	Alderney	0	Alderney	K. Le Tissier. (2).
	Guernsey	0	Jersey	0	Jersey	
	Guernsey	0	Jersey	1	Guernsey	
1997	Guernsey	6	Alderney	0	Alderney	K. Le Tissier (3), Mark Ogier (2), M. Falla.
	Guernsey	2	Jersey	1	Guernsey	S. Brehaut, A. Exall.
1998	Guernsey	0	Jersey	2	Jersey	
1999	Guernsey	1	Alderney	0	Alderney	M. Warren.
	Guernsey	2	Jersey	0 aet.	Guernsey	M. Le Cras (2).
2000	Guernsey	0	Jersey	1	Jersey	
2001	Guernsey	6	Alderney	0	Alderney	M. Smith (2), R. Tippett (pen.), J. Nobes, S. Johns, M. Falla.
	Guernsey	4	Jersey	1	Guernsey	M. Falla (2), M. Smith, G. Le Page.
2002	Guernsey	1	Jersey	2	Jersey	A. Vance.
2003	Guernsey	4	Alderney	1	Alderney	S. Brehaut, C. Chamberlain, D. Bisson R. Tippett.
	Guernsey	3	Jersey	3 aet	Guernsey	D. Bisson, A. Vance, R. Tippett.
	Guernsey	0	Jersey	1	Jersey	
2004	Guernsey	0	Jersey	3	Jersey	

JERSEY'S MURATTI RESULTS

Year					VENUE	GUERNSEY GOALSCORERS
1905	Jersey	0	Guernsey	1	Jersey	
1906	Jersey	1	Guernsey	2	Jersey	Voison.
1907	Jersey	2	Alderney	1 aet.	Guernsey	Poiter, le Page.
	Jersey	2	Guernsey	3 aet.	Jersey	Poingdestre, Cole.
1908	Jersey	4	Guernsey	0	Guernsey	Grimster (3), W. Fox.
1909	Jersey	0	Guernsey	3	Guernsey	
1910	Jersey	7	Alderney	1	Jersey	Cartwright(4), Chapman, Wheway(2).
	Jersey	3	Guernsey	2	Guernsey	Chapman (2), Wheway.
1911	Jersey	4	Guernsey	1	Jersey	Wheway (2), Sonnen, Honeycombe.
1912	Jersey	3	Guernsey	3	Jersey	Stratford (2),Sonnen.
	Jersey	2	Guernsey	5	Jersey	Stent, G.S. Fox.
1913	Jersey	5	Alderney	2 aet.	Guernsey	Moyse, Wheway (2), Kennedy, Beasley.
	Jersey	2	Guernsey	4	Jersey	Goldsmith, Whitworth.
1914	Jersey	1	Guernsey	2	Guernsey	Goldsmith.
1920	Jersey	0	Guernsey	1	Guernsey	
1921	Jersey	2	Alderney	0	Jersey	Stent, Stewart.
	Jersey	1	Guernsey	0	Guernsey	Kemp (pen).
1922	Jersey	1	Guernsey	2	Jersey	Beech (pen).
1923	Jersey	0	Guernsey	1	Jersey	
1924	Jersey	1	Alderney	0	Jersey	Le Masurier.
	Jersey	1	Guernsey	0	Jersey	Le Masurier.
1925	Jersey	1	Guernsey	2	Guernsey	Garnettt.
1926	Jersey	5	Guernsey	1	Guernsey	Owen, Marett, St. George (2). og.
	Jersey	7	Alderney	1	Jersey	Garnett (3), Owen (3), St. George.
1927	Jersey	3	Alderney	0	Jersey	St. George, Garnett, Marett.
	Jersey	0	Guernsey	1	Guernsey	
1928	Jersey	2	Guernsey	1 aet.	Jersey	Folliott (2).
1929	Jersey	1	Guernsey	7	Jersey	Rouxin.
1930	Jersey	3	Alderney	2	Guernsey	Le Feuvre (2), Garnett.
	Jersey	2	Guernsey	3	Jersey	Garnett, Carpenter.
1931	Jersey	4	Guernsey	2	Guernsey	Carpenter,Le Feuvre, Garnettt, Pincott.
1932	Jersey	0	Guernsey	2	Guernsey	
1933	Jersey	6	Alderney	0	Jersey	Carpenter (3), Boyd (2), Cox.
	Jersey	1	Guernsey	4 aet.	Guernsey	Boyd.
1934	Jersey	0	Guernsey	1	Jersey	
1935	Jersey	0	Guernsey	1	Jersey	
1936	Jersey	9	Alderney	0	Jersey	Morris,J.Gamblin, A.F.Davenport. Galway (3), Berry, og. Benest.
	Jersey	1	Guernsey	2	Guernsey	Hurel.
1937	Jersey	2	Guernsey	2 aet.	Jersey	E. Chevalier, C. Dale.
	Jersey	3	Guernsey	3 aet.	Guernsey	E. Chevalier, Benest, J. Lees.
1938	Jersey	3	Guernsey	4	Guernsey	J. Lees (2), E. Chevalier.
1939	Jersey	2	Alderney	1	Jersey	E.R. Gould, J. Drew.
	Jersey	1	Guernsey	0	Guernsey	F.Leamen.
1947	Jersey	3	Guernsey	1	Guernsey	G. le Maistre (3)
1948	Jersey	6	Guernsey	3	Jersey	J. Sherry, R. Hart, G.le Maistre (3), R. Pamplin.
1949	Jersey	9	Alderney	0	Jersey	S. Davies, J.Drew (2), C St. George, G.le Maistre (3), R.Pamplin,R.White.
	Jersey	2	Guernsey	1	Guernsey	J. Drew, R. White.

Year		Score		Score	Venue	Scorers
1950	Jersey	0	Guernsey	2	Jersey	
1951	Jersey	8	Alderney	1	Jersey	Sherry (2), Belhomme (2), White (2), G. le Maistre, R. Pamplin.
	Jersey	1	Guernsey	3 aet.	Guernsey	R. Jones.
1952	Jersey	1	Guernsey	3	Jersey	G. le Maistre.
1953	Jersey	4	Alderney	0	Jersey	R. Pamplin, G. le Maistre (2) le Gallais.
	Jersey	2	Guernsey	0	Guernsey	R. de Gruchy, G. le Maistre.
1954	Jersey	3	Guernsey	5	Jersey	G. le Maistre (2),de Gruchy.
1955	Jersey	3	Alderney	0	Jersey	G. le Maistre (2), Noel.
	Jersey	0	Guernsey	0 aet.	Guernsey	
	Jersey	1	Guernsey	0	Jersey	de Gruchy.
1956	Jersey	2	Guernsey	1	Jersey	G. le Maistre (2).
1957	Jersey	7	Alderney	1	Jersey	D. Parker (5), de Gruchy (2).
	Jersey	4	Guernsey	6	Guernsey	de Gruchy, G. le Maistre (2) D. Parker.
1958	Jersey	2	Guernsey	1	Jersey	Harben, de Gruchy.
1959	Jersey	6	Alderney	0	Jersey	D. Parker (3), de Gruchy (2), Harben.
	Jersey	3	Guernsey	2	Guernsey	de Gruchy (2), G. le Maistre.
1960	Jersey	5	Guernsey	1	Jersey	D. Parker (2), de Gruchy (2) G. le Maistre.
1961	Jersey	4	Alderney	2	Jersey	D. Parker (2), Venton, G. Mourant.
	Jersey	2	Guernsey	1	Guernsey	D. Parker, D.Gorin.
1962	Jersey	2	Guernsey	1	Jersey	D. Parker (2).
1963	Jersey	6	Alderney	0	Jersey	D. Parker (2), D. Cronin, Megaw, Venton, og.
	Jersey	4	Guernsey	1	Guernsey	D. Cronin, Ryan, D. Gorin (2).
1964	Jersey	1	Guernsey	0	Jersey	Nash Venton.
1965	Jersey	8	Alderney	0	Jersey	D. Parker (2), J. Ruellan (4), A. Venton, D. Cronin.
	Jersey	4	Guernsey	2	Guernsey	D. Cronin, D. Parker, J. Ruellan, A. Venton.
1966	Jersey	1	Guernsey	1 aet.	Jersey	J. Wilson.
	Jersey	1	Guernsey	3	Guernsey	og.
1967	Jersey	3	Alderney	1	Jersey	D. Cooper, P. Rowan, D. Cronin.
	Jersey	3	Guernsey	1 aet.	Guernsey	P. Rowan, J. Ruellan, D. Cooper.
1968	Jersey	2	Guernsey	1	Jersey	J. Ruellan (2).
1969	Jersey	5	Alderney	0	Jersey	T. Brown, H. Proffitt, J. Ruellan, A. Bone, og.
	Jersey	1	Guernsey	2	Guernsey	I. Watts.
1970	Jersey	2	Guernsey	0	Jersey	J. Ruellan, og.
1971	Jersey	11	Alderney	0	Jersey	J. Ruellan (2), B. O'Boyle (4), B. Thorpe, R. Marett, og (3).
	Jersey	1	Guernsey	0	Guernsey	J. Ruellan.
1972	Jersey	0	Guernsey	3	Jersey	
1973	Jersey	6	Alderney	1	Jersey	D. Huson (3), Seater (2), R. Crick.
	Jersey	4	Guernsey	1	Guernsey	Benest (2),J.Carter (pen.), P.Sands.
1974	Jersey	1	Guernsey	2 aet.	Jersey	Falle.
1975	Jersey	3	Alderney	1	Jersey	R. Pollock (2), R. Harbin.
	Jersey	2	Guernsey	2 aet.	Guernsey	E. Appleyard, R. Harbin.
	Jersey	2	Guernsey	3 aet.	Jersey	J. James, R. Harbin.
1976	Jersey	3	Guernsey	1	Jersey	A. Pitman, B. Pitman, A. Guegin.
1977	Jersey	3	Alderney	0	Alderney	B. Pitman, R.Crick, Baillie.
	Jersey	5	Guernsey	1	Guernsey	B.Pitman(2),P.Fleury(2), A. Pitman.
1978	Jersey	0	Guernsey	2	Jersey	

Year						Scorers
1979	Jersey	8	Alderney	0	Jersey	P. Feury (3), B. Pitman (3), A. Pitman, M. Mathews.
	Jersey	0	Guernsey	5	Guernsey	
1980	Jersey	1	Guernsey	2 aet.	Jersey	S. Dewhurst.
1981	Jersey	5	Alderney	0	Jersey	R. Crick, B. Pitman, P. Lock, Cunningham (2).
	Jersey	4	Guernsey	1	Guernsey	P.Taylor, K.leCornu, Cunningham, P. Lock.
1982	Jersey	2	Guernsey	1	Jersey	P. Lock, R. Crick.
1983	Jersey	6	Alderney	1	Jersey	P. Taylor, P. Carberry, P. Lock,R. Crick, P. Vincenti, S. Dewhurst.
	Jersey	1	Guernsey	2	Guernsey	P. Fleury.
1984	Jersey	6	Guernsey	2 aet.	Jersey	B.Pitman, J. Guest, P.Vincenti, P. Fleury (3).
1985	Jersey	5	Alderney	0	Alderney	N. Livesey (2), S. Dewhurst MacCarthy, A. Salaun.
	Jersey	3	Guernsey	4	Guernsey	P. Vincenti (pen), R.Crick,B.Pitman.
1986	Jersey	3	Guernsey	2	Jersey	C.le Moignan, S.Dewhurst, A.Salaun.
1987	Jersey	10	Alderney	0	Jersey	P. Vincenti (3), A. Lawlor (3), S. Dewhurst (2), N. Livesey, S. Petula.
	Jersey	4	Guernsey	3 aet.	Guernsey	S.Dewhurst(2), A.Salaun, T.Daly.
1988	Jersey	0	Guernsey	1	Jersey	
1989	Jersey	4	Alderney	0	Alderney	N. Livesey (2) A.Barker, A. Lawlor.
	Jersey	4	Guernsey	0	Guernsey	A.Lawlor(2),G.Fraser, S.A'Court.
1990	Jersey	2	Guernsey	1	Jersey	D. Ross, P. Carberry.
1991	Jersey	4	Alderney	1	Alderney	C. Hamon, A'Court, A. Greig (2).
	Jersey	0	Guernsey	3	Guernsey	
1992	Jersey	2	Guernsey	3	Jersey	N.Liversey, A. Barker.
1993	Jersey	2	Guernsey	1	Guernsey	A. Greig, P. Harzo.
1994	Jersey	18	Alderney	0	Jersey	S.Petulla (5), J.O'Shea (5), N. de Freitas (3), P. Carberry (2), T. leMaistre, R. Muddyman, M. Steigenberger.
	Jersey	3	Guernsey	1	Jersey	S. de Jesus, S. Petulla (2).
1995	Jersey	7	Alderney	1	Alderney	L. de St. Croix, A. Barker, N. de Freitas(pen), A. Greig, M. Steigenberger (2), og.
	Jersey	2	Guernsey	1	Guernsey	A. Greig Y. Santos.
1996	Jersey	0	Guernsey	0 aet.	Jersey	
	Jersey	1	Guernsey	0	Guernsey	N. de Frietas.
1997	Jersey	1	Guernsey	2	Guernsey	og.
1998	Jersey	2	Alderney	0	Alderney	L. Bramley (pen), J. Reilly.
	Jersey	2	Guernsey	0	Jersey	J. Reilly, R. Muddyman (pen).
1999	Jersey	0	Guernsey	2 aet.	Guernsey	
2000	Jersey	10	Alderney	0	Alderney	Docherty (4), R.Muddyman (2 pens.) Brodie, Santos, Reilly, og.
	Jersey	1	Guernsey	0	Jersey	R. Muddyman (pen).
2001	Jersey	1	Guernsey	4	Guernsey	G. Freeman.
2002	Jersey	2	Alderney	1	Alderney	P. Duxbury, B. Vowden.
	Jersey	2	Guernsey	1	Jersey	G. Freeman, L. Harvey.
2003	Jersey	3	Guernsey	3 aet.	Guernsey	
	Jersey	1	Guernsey	0	Jersey	og.
2004	Jersey	4	Alderney	0	Alderney	R.Crick, C.Andrews, C.McNabb, D.Le Roux.
	Jersey	3	Guernsey	0	Jersey	R. Crick (2-1 pen), G. McConnel.

MATCH OFFICIALS

Date.	Match.	Referee.	Linesmen.
1905	Guernsey v Alderney.	Mr. H.E. le Messurier (Guernsey).	J. le Maitre, J. Coward.
	Jersey v Guernsey.	Mr. H.E. le Messurier (Guernsey).	A. Reed (J),J. Le Quesne (G).
1906	Jersey v Guernsey.	Mr. G. Wagstaffe Simmons.	Ben Hayden (J), J. Torode (G).
	Guernsey v Alderney.	Mr. G. Wagstaffe Simmons.	J. Torode (G), J. le Maitre (A).
1907	Alderney v Jersey.	T.S. Mellanby (Ryde,Isle of Wight.)	R. Norris (J), F. Mourant(G).
	Jersey v Guernsey.	Mr. G.H. Muir.	B. Hayden (J), F. Mourant (G).
1908	Alderney v Guernsey.	M. Bromley.	C. Cleal (A), J. Duffey (G).
	Guernsey v Jersey.	Mr. R. Pook (Portsmouth).	W.le Messurier(G), E.Rattenburgh(J).
1909	Guernsey v Jersey.	Mr. R. Dommett.	H.le Messurier (G), A. Gould (J).
	Alderney v Guernsey.	A. Humby (Southampton.)	Cleale (A), J. Duffey (G).
1910	Jersey v Alderney.	S.H. Todd (Portsmouth).	A.J. Carter (J), F.W. Mourant (G).
	Guernsey v Jersey.	Mr. R. Pook (Portsmouth).	Coward (G), R.W. Norris (J).
1911	Guernsey v Alderney.	L.J. Duncan (Bournmouth.)	C.J. Rawlinson (G), C. Batiste (A).
	Jersey v Guernsey.	Mr. G.J. Ross.	F.C. Godbolt (J), A.A. Allain (G).
1912	Jersey v Guernsey.	Mr. G.L. Miller (Norfolk.)	
	Jersey v Guernsey.	Mr. G.L. Miller (Norfolk.)	
	Guernsey v Alderney.	L.J. Duncan (Bournmouth.)	C.J.Rawlinson (G), T.S. Mellanby.
1913	Alderney v Jersey.	J.W. Haxwell.	Henson (A), Carter (J).
	Jersey v Guernsey.	Mr. L. J. Duncan (Bournmouth).	
1914	Alderney v Guernsey.	J.W. Haxell (Bournmouth.)	
	Guernsey v Jersey.	Mr. L. J. Duncan (Bournmouth.)	
1920	Guernsey v Jersey.	Mr. L. J. Duncan (Bournmouth.)	C.J.H. Rawlinson(G), J.E. Coombes(J).
	Alderney v Guernsey.	R. Pook (Portsmouth).	C. Batiste (A), T. Zabiela (G).
1921	Jersey v Alderney.	A.C. Rogers (Parkston).	C. Batiste (A),
	Guernsey v Jersey.	Mr. T. C. Morris (Weymouth.).	H.le Messurier (G), C. Kent (J).
1922	Guernsey v Alderney.	S. Stollery (Hampshire FA.)	S. Collins (G), C. Batiste (A).
	Jersey v Guernsey.	Capt. A.J. Prince Cox.	
1923	Jersey v Guernsey.	R.C. Wildig.	J. Coombes (J), J. Chapple (G).
	Guernsey v Alderney.	G. Partridge (Portsmouth.)	H. le Messuier (G), C. Batiste (A).
1924	Alderney v Jersey.	R.C. Winton (Sussex)	C. Batiste (A), L. Burke (J).
	Jersey v Guernsey.	F. Tolfree.	P.A. Tatum (J), J. Chapple (G).
1925	Alderney v Guernsey.	W. Musther (London.)	A. Hensen (A), W.J. Adlam (G).
	Guernsey v Jersey.	J.T. Howcroft (Bolton).	T.H. Zabiela (G), H.A. Journeaux (J) .
1926	Guernsey v Jersey.	W. Musther (Sunderland).	
	Jersey v Alderney.	S.A. Donaldson.	A.V. Ingram (J), A. Henson (A).
1927	Jersey v Alderney.	F.H. Rowlands.	D.D. Pallot (J), A. Henson (A).
	Guernsey v Jersey.	W.J. Lewington.	A.B. Pugh (G), A.V. Ingram (J).
1928	Guernsey v Alderney.	S.F. Rouse (Herts.).	W.H. Crews (G), A. Henson (A).
	Jersey v Guernsey.	H.P. Morley.	A. Garnier (J), A.F. Foster (G).
1929	Jersey v Guernsey.	W. Musther.	H.A. Journeaux (J), G. Keyho (G).
	Guernsey v Alderney.	H.E. Edwards (London).	H. Webley (G), W.R. Hammond (A).
1930	Alderney v Jersey.	W. Radley (London).	W.R. Hammond (A), Falle (J).
	Jersey v Guernsey.	A. J. Jewell (London).	
1931	Alderney v Guernsey.	J.C. Battison (Essex).	J.A. Hammond (A), T.H. Zabiela (G).
	Guernsey v Jersey.	S.A. Donaldson.	G. Keyho (G), P.J. Cabot (J).
1932	Guernsey v Jersey.	S.F. Rouse (Hemel Hempstead).	C.F.Halstead(G),Capt.G.Clover-Price(J).
	Alderney v Guernsey.	C.W. Durham (Wealdsdone.)	W. Hammond (A), L. Purdy (G).
1933	Jersey v Alderney.	A. West.	J. Nolan (J), W. Hammond (A).
	Guernsey v Jersey.	Rev. C.V. Clibben.	H. le Messurier (G),A.E. Marret (J).
1934	Guernsey v Alderney.	H.N. Mee.	T.H. Zabiela (G), J. Hammond (A).
	Jersey v Guernsey.	R.G. Rudd.	S.J. Audrain (J), W. Finnegan (G).
1935	Jersey v Guernsey.	L.E. Gibbs (Reading).	A.E. Marret. (J), N.F. Ozard (G).
	Guernsey v Alderney.	A.J. Jewell (London.)	H. Trustum (G), J.R. Hammond (A).
1936	Jersey v Alderney.	Dr. A.W. Barton (Repton).	C.M. le Cras (J), A. Henson (A).
	Guernsey v Jersey.	Capt. Hamilton Jones.	T.H. Zabiela (G), G.A. Nolan (J).
1937	Guernsey v Alderney.	Dr. A.W. Barton (Repton).	V.J. Clark (G), J.F. Hammond (A).
	Jersey v Guernsey.	A.A Horwood (Surrey.)	J.B. Vance (J), H. Martel (G).
	Guernsey v Jersey.	A.A Horwood (Surrey.)	H.A. Martel (G), C.M. le Cras (J).
1938	Guernsey v Jersey.	H.N. Mee.	

Year	Match	Referee	Players
	Alderney v Guernsey.	P.V.S. Reed.	H.L. Renouf (G), A. Henson (A).
1939	Alderney v Jersey.	C.E. Argent.	
	Guernsey v Jersey.	J.M. Wiltshire.	V.J. Clark(G), S.A. Goodrich (J).
1947	Guernsey v Jersey.	G. Reader (Southampton).	F. Prout (G).
1948	Guernsey v Alderney.	W. Ling.	E. Field (G), J. Hammond (A).
	Jersey v Guernsey.	C.J. Barrick (Northants).	G.F. Bowden (J), C. Wood (G).
1949	Jersey v Alderney.	A. Peacock.	G. Greaves (J), J. Hammond (A).
	Guernsey v Jersey.	V. Rae (London).	S.W. Tranfield (G), A. Labbe (J).
1950	Guernsey v Alderney.	A.C. Williams.	J.A. Martel (G), J. Hammond (A).
	Jersey v Guernsey.	R.J. Burgess.	H. Hamon (G).
1951	Jersey v Alderney.	A.H. Blythe(London).	W.Le Vote (J).
	Guernsey v Jersey.	A.H. Bond (Fulham).	R.G. Warr (G), J. Payne (J).
1952	Guernsey v Alderney.	L.A.M. Mackay (Fulham).	E.J. Bichard (G), J.F. Hammond (A).
	Jersey v Guernsey.	W.E. Dellow (Croydon).	C.J. Dupre (J), H.E. Trustum (G).
1953	Jersey v Alderney.	F.S. Fiander (Loudwater, Bucks).	S. Guy (J), J. Hammond (A).
	Guernsey v Jersey.	A.W. Smith (Aldershot).	H. Bisson (G), C. Lesbirel (J).
1954	Guernsey v Alderney.	H. Ball (Worcester).	W. Allen (G), J. Hammond (A).
	Jersey v Guernsey.	B.M. Griffiths(Newport).	F. Proudley (J), F.J. Bichard (G).
1955	Jersey v Alderney.	J.C. Pollard.	
	Guernsey v Jersey.	N. Taylor (Westbury).	J.A. Martel (G), A.G.D. Wood (J).
	Jersey v Guernsey.	N. Taylor (Westbury).	A.G.D. Wood (J), J.A. Martel (G),
1956	Guernsey v Alderney.	B.A.E. Buckle (Peterborough).	H. Hamon (G), H Le Cheminant.
	Jersey v Guernsey.	J. Williams (Nottingham).	J. Le Pennec (J), W. Wakeford (G)
1957	Jersey v Alderney.	L. Callaghan (Merthyr, Wales).	Bro. David (J), O. Riou (A).
	Guernsey v Jersey.	E.S. Oxley(Pontefract.)	W. Robilliard (G), R.E Troy (J)
1958	Guernsey v Alderney.	J.W. Hunt (Emsworth).	J.A. Martel (G), P. Bond (A).
	Jersey v Guernsey.	K. Howley.	E. Smith (J), G. Solway (G).
1959	Jersey v Alderney.	J.A. Martel (Guernsey).	S. Gallichan (J), F. Bond (A).
	Guernsey v Jersey.	J. Husband (Surrey).	H. Le Cheminant (G), G. Asselin (J).
1960	Guernsey v Alderney.	S. Proudley (Jersey).	J. Savident (G), W. Wakeford (J).
	Jersey v Guernsey.	G.W. Pullin.	S.E. Guy (J), E.J. Bichard (G).
1961	Jersey v Alderney.	H. le Cheminant.	N. Allo (J), G. Bohan (A).
	Guernsey v Jersey.	W. Clements (West Bromwich).	G. Solway (G), S. Gallichan (J).
1962	Guernsey v Alderney.	R.E. Troy (Jersey).	T Creber (G), J. Dupont (A).
	Jersey v Guernsey.	J.V. Stringer (Liverpool).	A. Single (J), L. Smith (G).
1963	Jersey v Alderney.	L. Smith (Guernsey).	
	Guernsey v Jersey.	D.W. Smith (Stonehouse, Glos.).	R. Trustum (G), R. Hope (J).
1964	Guernsey v Alderney.	A.G.D. Wood (Jersey).	L. Ingrouille, W. Wakeford.
	Jersey v Guernsey.	E. Crawford (Doncaster).	R. Pyman (J), V. Ozard (G).
1965	Jersey v Alderney.	M.W. Robilliard (Guernsey).	S.G. Blondel (J), A. Le Breton (A).
	Guernsey v Jersey.	G.D. Roper (Cambridge).	D. Cherry (G), L. Mauger (J).
1966	Guernsey v Alderney.	S. Guy (Jersey).	
	Jersey v Guernsey.	E.T. Jennings (Worcester).	S.G. Blondel (J), Savidet(G).
	Guernsey v Jersey.	E.T. Jennings (Worcester).	J. Savident (G), S.G. Blondel (J).
1967	Jersey v Alderney.	A.L. Lambourne (Guernsey.)	
	Guernsey v Jersey.	P. Bye Bedford).	T. Creber (G), C. Poree (J).
1968	Guernsey v Alderney.	J. Le Pemec (J).	L. Hudson (G), G. Bohan (A).
	Jersey v Guernsey.	K. Dagnall (Bolton).	H. Sawyer (J), W. Robilliard (G).
1969	Jersey v Alderney.	G.T. Solway (G).	C. Poree (J), I. Nutter (J).
	Guernsey v Jersey.	D. Corbett (Wolverhampton).	G. Ogier (G), B. Ahier (J).
1970	Guernsey v Alderney.	R. Pyman (Jersey).	R. Trustum (G), D. Solway(A).
	Jersey v Guernsey.	R. Tinkler (Boston).	R. Parker (J), L. Ingrouille (G).
1971	Jersey v Alderney.	J. Savident (Guernsey).	B. Ahier (J), D. Solway (A).
	Guernsey v Jersey.	N. Burtenshaw (Great Yarmouth).	V. Ozard (G), D Le Breton (J).
1972	Guernsey v Alderney.	B. Ahier (Jersey).	R. West (G), D. Solway (A).
	Jersey v Guernsey.	E.D. Wallace (Swindon)..	P. Tomlinson (J), L. Hudson (G).
1973	Jersey v Alderney.	D. Cherry (Guernsey).	R. Parker (J), M. Allo.
	Guernsey v Jersey.	H. Hackney (Barnsley).	C. Harkins (G), A. Le Cornu (J).
1974	Guernsey v Alderney.	A. Le Breton (Jersey).	T. Savident (G), R. Mauger.
	Jersey v Guernsey.	B.J.Homewood (Sudbury-on-Thames).	J.Rolph (G), I. Nutter (J).
1975	Jersey v Alderney.	R. Trustum (Guernsey).	R. Parker (J), A. Le Cornu (J).
	Guernsey v Jersey.	K. Burns (Dudley).	D. Trustum (G), R. Coppell (J).
	Jersey v Guernsey.	K. Burns (Dudley).	R. Coppell (J), D. Trustum (G).

Year	Match		
1976	Alderney v Guernsey.	R. Parker (Jersey).	G. Ogier (G), M. Wherry (G).
	Jersey v Guernsey.	R. Challis (Tonbridge, Kent).	M. Allo (J), W. De La Mare (G).
1977	Alderney v Jersey.	D. Trustum (Guernsey).	S. Jeffreys (A), A. Moignard (J).
	Guernsey v Jersey.	D. Hinsley (Jersey.)	A. Richings (G), W. De La Mare (G).
1978	Guernsey v Alderney.	I. Nutter (Jersey).	I. Chipperfield (G), S. Jeffreys (G).
	Jersey v Guernsey.	J.E. Bent (Hemel Hempstead.)	R. Satchwell (J), G. Skuse (G).
1979	Jersey v Alderney.	G. Ogier (Guernsey).	R. Coppell (J),J. Penney.
	Guernsey v Jersey.	Mr. A. Robinson (Portsmouth).	A. Blondel (G), A. Moignard (J).
1980	Alderney v Guernsey.	A. Le Cornu (Jersey).	A. Phillips (A), W. Robilliard (G).
	Jersey v Guernsey.	N. Midgley (Salford.)	M. le Var (J), T. Savident. (G).
1981	Alderney v Jersey.	T. Savident (Guernsey) J. Rolph (A).	J. Rolph (A), G. Esnouf (J), L. Dupont (A)
	Guernsey v Jersey.	P. Partridge (Durham).	J. Martel (G), D. Billingham (J).
1982	Guernsey v Alderney.	D. Billingham (Jersey).	A. Richings (G), M. Vaudin (A).
	Jersey v Guernsey.	K. Hackett (Sheffield).	K. McCreanney (J), I.Chipperfield (G).
1983	Jersey v Alderney.	J. Rolph (G).	M. Le Var (J), M. Vaudin. (A).
	Guernsey v Jersey.	C. Downey (Hounslow.)	K. Brouard (G), D. Jegou (J).
1984	Alderney v Guernsey..	A. Phillips. (Jersey.)	G. Skuse (G), J. Martel (A).
	Jersey v Guernsey.	T. Spencer. (Salisbury.)	G. Esnouf (J), M. Vaudin (G).
1985	Alderney v Jersey.	A. Richings (Guernsey.)	D. Jegou (J), E. Graham (G).
	Guernsey v Jersey.	L.F. Burnett (Poole.)	A. Langlois (G), A. Phillips. (J).
1986	Alderney v Guernsey.	P. Daniel (Jersey.)	J. Rolfe. (G), T. Savident (G).
	Jersey v Guernsey.	M. James (Horsham.)	C. Tostevin (J), E. Graham (G).
1987	Jersey v Alderney.	K. Brouard (Guernsey).	P. Daniel (J), L. Rondel (J).
	Guernsey v Jersey.	A. Gunn (Burgess Hill.)	R. Bougourd (G), R. Richardson (J).
1988	Alderney v Guernsey.	K. Mc Creanney. (Jersey).	M. Walker (A), C. Tapp (G).
	Jersey v Guernsey.	D. Hutchinson (Oxford.)	D. Ferguson (J), G. Ogier (G).
1989	Alderney v Jersey.	E. Graham. (Guernsey.)	M. Walker, D. Bisson (J).
	Guernsey v Jersey.	R. Groves (Weston-Super-Mare.)	C. Tapp (G), D. Bisson (J).
1990	Guernsey v Alderney.	D. Jegou (Jersey).	T. Savident (G), P. Southcott (A).
	Jersey v Guernsey.	A. Ward (London.)	P. Daniel (J), K. Priaulx (G).
1991	Alderney v Jersey.	R. Bougourd (Guernsey.)	
	Guernsey v Jersey.	A. Seville. (Birmingham.)	K. Seeds (G), M. Blampied (J).
1992	Guernsey v Alderney.	G. Esnouf (Jersey.)	D.Burtenshaw (G), S. Freear (G).
	Jersey v Guernsey.	K. Morton (Bury St. Edmunds.)	C. Browne (J), R. Bougourd (G).
1993	Alderney v Guernsey.	C. Browne (Jersey.)	P. Southcott (A), T. Savident (G).
	Guernsey v Jersey.	B. Hill (Market Harborough.)	T. Savident (G), A. Bradshaw (J).
1994	Jersey v Alderney.	K. Priaulx (Guernsey.)	R. Richardson (J), P. Southcott (A).
	Jersey v Guernsey.	P. Alcock (Redhill.)	B. Youd (J), A. Richings (G).
1995	Alderney v Jersey.	G. Carre (Guernsey).	
	Guernsey v Jersey.	G. Willard (Worthing.)	S. Frear (G), C. Hansford (J).
1996	Alderney v Guernsey.	A. Bradshaw (Jersey).	P. Soutcott (A), A. Sarre (G).
	Jersey v Guernsey.	S. Dunne (Leicester.)	C. Gouyette (J), G. Ogier (G).
	Guernsey v Jersey.	M. Bodenham (Cornwall).	G. Ogier (G), E. Graham (G).
1997	Alderney v Guernsey.	R. Richardson (Jersey.)	P. Southcott (A), K. Seeds (G).
	Guernsey v Jersey.	M. Reed (Birminham.)	E. Teed (G), R. Barry (J).
1998	Alderney v Jersey.	E.Teed (Guernsey.)	S. Landick (J), P. Southcott (A).
	Jersey v Guernsey.	N. Barry (Boston).	B. Breuilly (J), E. Graham (G).
1999	Alderney v Guernsey.	C. Tostevin (Jersey).	P. Southcott (A), R. Bougourd (G).
	Guernsey v Jersey.	P. Jones (Loughborough.)	G. Carre (G), S. Landick (J).
2000	Alderney v Jersey.		P. Southcott (A)
	Jersey v Guernsey.	S. Bennett (Orpington).	R. Stockton (J), A. Sarre (G).
2001	Alderney v Guernsey.	M. Le Cornu (Jersey.)	P. Southcott (A), A. Sarre (G).
	Guernsey v Jersey.	R. Styles.	R. Bougourd (G), C. Brown (J).
2002	Alderney v Jersey.	K. Seeds (Guernsey).	P. Southcott (A), A. Bradshaw (J).
	Jersey v Guernsey.	M. Dean.	M.Le Cornu (J), C. Gontier (G).
2003	Alderney v Guernsey.	A. Bradshaw (Jersey).	P. Southcott (A), E. Teed (G).
	Guernsey v Jersey.	J. Winter	M. Walsh (G), S. Landick (J).
	Jersey v Guernsey.	C. Wilkes.	S. Landick (J), M. Walsh (G).
2004	Alderney v Jersey.	A. Priaulx (Guernsey).	P. Southcott (A), A. Cox (G).
	Jersey v Guernsey.	H. Webb (Rotherham).	C. Gouyette (J), K. Seeds (G).

ALDERNEY APPEARANCES

	Name.	Club.	Caps.	Goals.	Muratti Career.
1	W. Bohan.	Alderney Athletics.	20	1	1961-1989.
2	J. Harrington.	Alderney Athletics, Northern Belles.	15		1948-1967.
3	K. Gentle.	Bavaria Nomads.	14		1991-2004.
4	J. Maxwell.	Bavaria Nomads.	14		1989-2003.
5	M. Treais.	Bavaria Nomads.	14	3	1987-2003.
6	J. Newton.	Sylvans.	13	1	1921-1935.
7	P. Burland.	Aurigny Nomads.	12		1980-1993.
8	G. Rushbury.	Aurigny Nomads.	12		1986-2001.
9	N. Carre.		12		1990-2003.
10	P. Concanen.	Northern Belles.	11		1983-1997.
11	L. Farnham.	Rangers.	11	1	1966-1976.
12	W. Hammond.	Northern Belles.	11		1948-1963.
13	P. Moore.	Northern Belles.	11	3	1950-1960.
14	S. Newton.	Sylvans.	11	1	1924-1934.
15	A. Wright.	Aurigny Nomads.	11	1	1987-1997.
16	P. Bunn.		10		1977-1990.
17	I. McFarlane.	Aurigny Nomads.	10		1979-1993.
18	J. Mannion.	Beeches.	10		1953-1963.
19	P. Turner.	Northern Belles.	10		1967-1976.
20	B. Venton.	St. Paul's, First Tower, Oaklands.	10	1	1950-1962.
21	D. Bate-Jones.	Burnley Highways.	9		1954-1964.
22	D. Clark.	Northern Belles.	9	1	1956-1968.
23	F. Keachi.		9	1	1973-1985.
24	H. Newton.		9		1925-1933.
25	F. Odoir.	Alderney Athletics.	9	1	1934-1950.
26	M. Richardson.		9		1977-1986.
27	J. Catts.		8		1905-1914.
28	H. Cleale.		8	1	1905-1913.
29	A. Greatbanks.		8		1976-1983.
30	J. Hammond.		8	1	1920-1929.
31	L. Jacques.		8		1906-1914.
32	W. McLernon.	Rangers.	8	1	1920-1927.
33	P. Rose.		8		1977-1988.
34	S. Benfield.	Bavaria Nomads.	7		1996-2004.
35	G. Chappelhow.	Garrison RA.	7		1928-1934.
36	W. Cauvain.	Northern Belles.	7		1948-1955.
37	N. Mignot.	Cowes, Isle of Wight.	7	2	1948-1955.
38	Pasquire.		7		1922-1930.
39	F. Quinain.		7	2	1906-1914.
40	J. Simon.	Belgrave W., Guernsey Athletics.	7		1950-1956.
41	N. Simon.	Belgrave W.	7		1935-1950.
42	R. Venton.	Pirelli Southampton.	7	1	1950-1959.
43	H. Allcroft.	(Aldcroft ?)	6		1977-1986.
44	Allen.		6		1920-1933
45	J. Allen.		6		1906-1911.
46	T. Baker.		6	1	1921-1926.
47	Batiste.		6		1906-1914.
48	A. Burgess.		6		1909-1914.
49	M. Bohan	Bavaria Nomads.	6	1	1999-2004.
50	R. Bohan.	Bavaria Nomads.	6		1998-2004.
51	P. Catts.		6		1931-1939.
52	A. Davies.	Bavaria Nomads.	6		1996-2002.

53	C.J. Dupont.		6		1962-1972.
54	C. Dupont.	Guernsey Athletics.	6	1	1956-1968.
55	K. Farebrother.		6	1	1990-1999.
56	P. Greenslade.	Rovers, Rangers.	6		1972-1979.
57	A. Henson.		6		1905-1912.
58	N. Jarvis.		6		1996-2002.
59	Jennings.	see G. Jennings.	6		1920-1932.
60	P. Newton.	Rovers.	6		1975-1983.
61	Parmentier.		6		1924-1929.
62	A. Benfield.		5		1969-1976.
63	F. Bond.	Northern Belles.	5		1949-1954.
64	J. Carpenter.	Alderney Athletics.	5		1963-1968.
65	J. Gamblin.		5		1909-1914.
66	M. Mapp.	Alderney Athletics, North.	5		1956-1966.
67	Maurice.		5		1970-1976.
68	D. Mitchell.		5		1984-1989.
69	T. Olliver.		5		1920-1924.
70	K. Oselton.		5		1910-1914.
71	A. Pasquire.		5		1975-1979.
72	A. Randall.	Penquins, Northern Belles.	5	1	1957-1962.
73	C. Randall.	Rangers.	5		1970-1974.
74	N. Rizzuto.		5		1977-1982.
75	N. Rose.		5		1977-1984.
76	J. Rose.		5		1927-1931.
77	P. Tugby.	Bavaria Nomads.	5		1997-2003.
78	J. Williamson.		5		1995-1999.
79	A.L. Allen.	Alderney Athletics.	4		1934-1937.
80	P. Allen		4		1937-1948.
81	R. Audoir.		4		1963-1966.
82	Barker.		4		1929-1933.
83	D. Baron.		4		1972-1975.
84	R. Brehaut.		4		1936-1939.
85	J. Cadoret.	Northern Belles.	4		1963-1968.
86	D. Coquelin.	Centrals.	4		1972-1976.
87	P. Cunningham.		4		1980-1985.
88	A. Cosheril.		4		1986-1993.
89	D. Hugman.		4		1964-1972.
90	J. Malloy.		4	1	1979-1982.
91	E. le Maitre.		4		1905-1908.
92	D. Oakman.	Alderney Athletics.	4		1983-1986.
93	W. Roberts.	RAF, Wales.	4		1964-1969.
94	D. Walker.		4		1987-1996.
95	J. Atkins.	Bavaria Nomads.	3		2002-2004.
96	Attewell		3		1920-1922.
97	H. Attewell		3		1912-1914.
98	J. Baker.		3	1	1921-1924.
99	A. Barker.		3		1961-1963.
100	J. Barker.		3		1969-1974.
101	W. Benfield.		3		1995-2004.
102	G. Bohan.	Alderney Athletics.	3		1956-1965.
103	T. Bohan.		3		1984-1986.
104	P. Bond	Northern Belles.	3		1960-1962.
105	J. Buckle.		3		1921-1923.
106	G. Burness.		3	1	1936-1938.
107	W. Caplain.		3		1909-1913.
108	J. Catts.		3		1920-1922.

No.	Name	Club			Years
109	S. Concanen.	Bavaria Nomads, St. Martins..	3		2001-2003.
110	Duplain.		3		1931-1939.
111	J. Dupont.		3		1969-1972.
112	K. Duquemin.	Sylvans.	3		1953-1959.
113	Gadie.		3		1923-1926.
114	J. Goasdoue.	BEA Manchester.	3		1966-1968.
115	G. Jennings.		3		1934-1936.
116	L. McLean.	Royal Navy.	3		1948-1952.
117	M. Lee.		3		1994-1998.
118	L. McLernon.		3		1925-1927.
119	W. Mc Lernon.		3		1910-1914.
120	McLernon.		3		1930-1932.
121	J. Lihou.		3		1910-1912.
122	R.J. O'Neill.		3		1938-1948.
123	J. Pasquire.	Vale Rec., Rangers.	3		1955-1957.
124	T. Pasquire.	Rangers.	3		1974-1976.
125	E. Picot.	RAF Calshot.	3		1934-1937.
126	F. Pike.		3		1920-1922.
127	H. Quinain.		3		1937-1939.
128	Randall.		3	1	1930-1933.
129	C.J. Richards.		3		1938-1949.
130	A. Stone		3		1997-2003.
131	R. Stower.		3		1968-1970.
132	J. Simon.	Rangers.	3		1969-1971.
133	W. White.		3		1994-1997.
134	A. Adamson.		2		1995-1997.
135	H. Allen		2		1938-1939.
136	A. Barker		2		1949-1951.
137	M. Baker.	Northern Belles.	2		1960-1967.
138	Baker.		2		1929-1930.
139	Bideau.		2		1923-1924.
140	D. Blanchard.	Vale Rec.	2		1978-1999.
141	C. Brookes.		2		1907-1911.
142	G. Cartwright.	Penquins.	2		1958-1959.
143	R. Crook.		2		1973-1974.
144	Davies		2		1984-1985.
145	L. Davey.	Bavaria Nomads, St. Martins.	2		2002-2004
146	A. Mc Donald.		2		1994-1995.
147	A. Dupont.	Penquins, Alderney Athletics.	2		1959-1961.
148	J. Dupont.	Penquins.	2		1958-1960.
149	Dupont.		2		1979-1982.
150	A. Farrell.	Bavaria Nomads.	2		2001-2002.
151	R. Fever.		2	1	1950-1951.
152	Henson.		2		1932-1933.
153	Mackay.		2		1987-1988.
154	H. le Maitre.		2		1907-1908.
155	Jas le Maitre.		2		1906-1908.
156	J. le Maitre.		2		1905-1906.
157	R. Mapp	Alderney Athletics.	2		1959-1963.
158	M. Maurice.		2		1977-1979.
159	J. Maurice.		2		1977-1978.
160	G. Miller.		2		1938-1939.
161	Mortimer.		2		1978-1979.
162	B. Newton.		2		1923-1924.
163	E. Odoir.		2		1934-1935.
164	A. Patterson.	Bavaria Nomads.	2		2001-2003.

165	J. Petite.		2		1905-1906.
166	Pasquire.	Vale Rec.	2		1972-1973.
167	Pasquire.		2		1980-1981.
168	T. Pasquire.		2		1983-1984.
169	H. Pike.		2		1934-1935.
170	M. Price.		2		1991-1992.
171	O. Riou.		2		1935-1938.
172	R. Riou.		2		1936-1937.
173	T. Simon.	RAF Gosport.	2		1935-1936.
174	Simon.		2		1928-1934.
175	C. Smith.		2		1908-1909.
176	M. Smith.	Belgrave W., Guernsey Athletics.	2	1	1967-1968.
177	P. Sowden		2		1971-1974.
178	J. Stretton.	Aurigny Nomads.	2		1990-1991.
179	C. Sugden.		2		1993-1994.
180	Vague.		2		1949-1952.
181	Willey.		2		1928-1930.
182	Aldcroft.		1		1992
183	Aldcroft.		1		2004
184	P. Allen.		1		1934
185	T. Allen.		1		1905
186	Anquetil.		1		1933
187	M. Ault.		1		2003
188	T. Baker.		1		1914
189	Baker.		1		1913
190	Baker.		1		1920
191	A. Barker.		1		1936
192	W. Barker.		1		1936
193	Barrett.		1		1970
194	Battrick.		1		1996
195	W. Birmingham.		1		1953
196	G. Bohan.		1		1962
197	L. Bohan.		1		1937
198	Bohan.		1		1993
199	D. Braby.		1		1987
200	N. Butel.		1		1978
201	Caplain.		1		1928
202	Carre.		1		1957
203	Carre.		1		1966
204	G. Cauvain.	Northern Belles.	1		1958
205	M. Cauvain.		1		1971
206	S. Chadwick.		1		1986
207	R. Chivers.		1		1969
208	J. Clark.		1		1965
209	M. Coquelin.	Guernsey Police.	1		1983
210	J. Coen.	Penguins.	1		1960
211	J. Coenen.(Coen?)		1		1964
212	Coenen.		1		1988
213	B. Collenette.		1		1914
214	P. Collenette.		1		1925
215	Cunningham.		1		1972
216	A. Davies.		1		1983
217	S. Davies.	Alderney Athletics.	1		1983
218	Davies		1		1982
219	C.A. Dupont.		1		1971
220	C. Dupont (1).		1		1964

221	C. Dupont (2).		1		1964
222	C. Dupont jnr.		1		1956
223	C. Dupont		1		1965
224	J. Dupont.		1		1965
225	Gadie.		1		1920
226	J. Gamblin.		1		1908
227	T. Gaudion.		1		1905
228	W. Greenslade.		1		1955
229	Harvey.		1		1996
230	Hatcher.		1		1993
231	R. Heathcote.	Bavaria Nomads.	1		2001
232	P. McIlroy.		1		1908
233	E. Jones.		1		1927
234	Jupp.		1		1980
235	A. Lawrence.		1		2004
236	D. Mc Leod.		1		1951
237	Mc Lernon.		1		1929
238	Lihou.		1	1	1920
239	Machon.		1		1970
240	Maiorano.		1		1973
241	J.H. le Maitre.		1		1907
242	J. le Maitre.		1		1905
243	J. Martel.		1		1978
244	E. Martyn.		1		1922
245	H. Mesney.		1		1952
246	Mesney.		1		1928
247	A. Mignot.		1		1948
248	R. Mignot.		1		1948
249	M. Mullay.		1		1987
250	A. Newman.		1		1927
251	J. Ogden.		1		1927
252	Odoir.		1		1932
253	Olliver.		1		1910
254	S. Parilla.		1		1989
255	Parry.		1		1984
256	A. Pasquire.(J?)	VOBA.	1		1952
257	B. Phelan.		1		2004
258	Poynter.		1		1977
259	A. Price.		1		1907
260	P. Quanten.		1		1986
261	R. Quinain.		1		1986
262	Randall.		1		1988
263	Redhead.		1		1926
264	G. Rennel.		1		1965
265	W. Roberts.		1		1953
266	Roberts.		1		1949
267	Roberts.		1		1973
268	Robilliard.		1		1966
269	A. Rose.		1		1955
270	Rose.		1		1982
271	M. Sebire.		1		2004
272	Sebire.		1		1910
273	Sebire.		1		1994
274	H. Simon.		1	1	1939
275	L. Simon.		1		1949
276	Smart.		1		1974

			Caps	Goals	Year
277	Stevens.		1		1975
278	Stubbs.		1		1990
279	J. Sugden.		1		1993
280	W. Tarrant.		1		1935
281	Turner.		1		1981
282	Vagg.		1	1	1910
283	C. Vague.		1		1911
284	H. le Vallee.		1		1905
285	W.J. le Vallee.		1		1905
286	le Vallee.		1		1909
287	Venton.		1		1949
288	J. Vizard		1		2004
289	J. Walker.		1		2004
290	Waller	Penquins.	1		1957
291	Walsh.		1		1990
292	Walters.		1		1980
293	P. Williams.		1		2004

GUERNSEY APPEARANCES

	Name.	Club.	Caps.	Goals.	Muratti Career.
1	L. Collins.	Belgrave W.,North.	25	10	1947-1964.
2	C. Dyer.	Vale Rec.	24	4	1982-1996.
3	P. Blondel	Vale Rec.	20	3	1973-1988.
4	K. Le Tissier.	Vale Rec.North, Rovers, Bels.	20	22	1982-1998.
5	C. Brazier.	St. Martins.	19		1962-1975.
6	C. Falliaze.	North, St. Martins.	19	16	1975-1987.
7	A. Vance.	Sylvans, Enfield.	18	4	1990-2003.
8	D. Mauger.	North.	17	4	1927-1939.
9	C. Renouf.	St. Martins.	17	5	1961-1974.
10	W. Warr.	North.	17	5	1920-1932.
11	P. Bougourd.	North.	16		1925-1937.
12	J. Loveridge.	St. Martins.	16	13	1963-1976.
13	M. Marley.	Vale Rec.	16		1986-1996.
14	M. Carre.	Rangers, Centrals.	15		1948-1957.
15	W.H. Down.	Rangers.	15	1	1923-1933.
16	W.C. Freeman.	Rangers.	15	1	1930-1939.
17	L. Graham.	Sylvans,St.Martins, Vale Rec.	15	3	1971-1984.
18	R. Harvey.	Vale Rec, North, Athletics.	15	5	1956-1968.
19	J. Mahy.	North.	15		1906-1914.
20	D. Mechem.	Sylvans.	15		1931-1939.
21	W. Barrasin.	North.	14	6	1927-1936.
22	K. Le Gallez.	St. Martins.	14	3	1978-1989.
23	P. Nobes.	Sylvans.	14		1993-2004.
24	D. Lesbirel.	Belgrave W.,Vale Rec.	14	2	1968-1980.
25	L.J. Robilliard.	Belgrave. W.	14	3	1947-1958.
26	C. Le Tissier.	Vale Rec, Rangers.	14	5	1983-1993.
27	V. Tostevin.	Belgrave W.	14	2	1948-1958.
28	C. Hamon.	Belgrave W., Vale Rec.	13		1976-1989.
29	A.M. Hunter.	St. Martins, Rangers.	13	6	1948-1956.
30	J. Nobes.	Sylvans.	13	1	1994-2003.
31	A. Bougourd.	Vale Rec.	12	4	1977-1989.
32	H. Dorey.	North, First Tower.	12	14	1927-1937
33	H. Falla.	Rangers.	12	4	1948-1955.
34	H. de Garis.	Rangers.	12		1932-1938.

35	C. Hargreaves.	Vale Rec.	12		1976-1985.
36	J.A. Martel.	Rangers.	12	3	1934-1947.
37	E. Sauvage.	North.	12		1939-1955.
38	R (D?). Vaudin.	Rangers.	12		1954-1961.
39	G. de Carteret	Belgrave W.	11		1986-1996.
40	F.Cleal.	North.	11	8	1908-1914.
41	N. Le Page.	Vale Rec., Rangers.	11	5	1974-1980.
42	S. Polson.	North.	11		1992-2004.
43	L. Purdy.	North.	11	1	1920-1929.
44	W. Torode.	St. Martins.	11	3	1966-1972.
45	G. Chalmers.	North, Sylvans.	10	2	1989-1997.
46	H.C. Chapell.	Rangers.	10	6	1920-1926.
47	M. Culverwell.	St. Martins.	10	2	1984-1996.
48	L. Duquemin.	North.	10	1	1956-1965.
49	A. Exall.	Vale Rec., Sylvans.	10	1	1992-2000.
50	M. Gauvain.	North, Sylvans.	10		1990-1999.
51	W. Huelin.	Belgrave W.	10		1927-1937.
52	S.A. Noel.	North.	10	10	1921-1929.
53	Art Le Page	Centrals, Vale Rec.	10	1	1968-1974.
54	C. Reeve.	Belgrave W.	10	9	1970-1976.
55	M. Warren.	Sylvans.	10		1999-2004.
56	T. Waterman.	Belgrave W.	10		1905-1912.
57	T. Zabiela.	Rangers.	10	3	1908-1912.
58	J. Aubert	Belgrave W.	9		1905-1920.
59	A. Benstead.	North.	9		1905-1911.
60	R.S. Chapple.	Belgrave W.	9	3	1910-1914.
61	S.C. Chapple.	Belgrave W.	9		1920-1926.
62	M. Duncan.	St. Martins.	9	1	1966-1970.
63	J. Herpe.	St. Martins.	9		1966-1974.
64	G. Rowe.	Vale Rec.,St. Martins.	9	1	1973-1981.
65	D. Tapp.	Vale Rec.	9		1984-1993.
66	E.J. Warren.	Rangers.	9		1931-1939.
67	C. Allen.	Rangers.	8	13	1978-1996.
68	J. Avery.	Sylvans.	8		1994-2002.
69	J. Bisson.	Vale Rec.	8		1999-2004.
70	F. Dorey.	North.	8		1911-1914.
71	I. Drillot.	North, Sylvans.	8		1992-2000.
72	F.(J). Duquemin*.	Belgrave W.	8	1	1906-1914.
73	N. Hunter.	St. Martins.	8	7	1983-1989.
74	F. Lanyon.	Rangers.	8		1909-1914.
75	J.A. Lewis.	Rangers.	8		1929-1935.
76	D (B?). Mechem.	North.	8	4	1954-1962.
77	C. Le Page.	Rangers.	8		1978-1985.
78	T.J. Le Prevost.	Rangers.	8	7	1934-1947.
79	F. Stranger.	North.	8	1	1905-1910.
80	R.Tippett.	Rovers, St. Martins,Sylvans.	8	3	1999-2004.
81	P. F. Watson.	North.	8		1921-1925.
82	A.E. Broadrib.	North.	7	2	1934-1938.
83	A. Le Cheminant.	North.	7		1920-1924.
84	M. Coutanche.	Sylvans.	7		1994-1998.
85	M. Falla.	Vale Rec., St. Martins.	7	4	1996-2002.
86	K. Giles.	Vale Rec.	7	2	1966-1972.
87	S. Johns.	North.	7		2000-2004.
88	Mick Ogier.	Belgrave W., Vale Rec.	7		1991-1997.
89	A. Pollock.	Belgrave W.,North.	7		1975-1981.
90	J. Renouf.	Sylvans, St. Martins.	7		1997-2004.

91	C. Solway.	North.	7	1	1927-1931.
92	K. Allen.	St. Martins.	6		1972-1979
93	M. Bisson.	North.	6		1990-1998.
94	R. Brehaut.	Belgrave W.(Sylvans?)	6		1957-1965.
95	S. Brehaut.	Sylvans.	6	2	1997-2004.
96	K. Carter.	Rangers.	6		1949-1956.
97	W. Crews.	Belgrave W.	6	2	1905-1909.
98	W. Crocker.	Rangers.	6	2	1937-1939.
99	H. Davey.	St. Martins.	6	2	1966-1972.
100	H. Duquemin.	North, First Tower.	6	4	1936-1939.
101	R. Froome.	St. Martins.	6		1975-1988.
102	Mark Le Tissier.	Vale Rec.	6	1	1982-1986.
103	M. Loveridge.	St. Martins.	6		1975-1979.
104	M. Marquand.	Vale Rec.	6		1974-1977.
105	J. Murray.	North.	6		1954-1956.
106	W.G. Le Page.	Rangers.	6	4	1949-1955.
107	I. Potter.	Sylvans.	6		1998-2004.
108	R. Robilliard.	North.	6	1	1948-1953.
109	H.E.K. Stranger.	North.	6	8	1912-1914.
110	J. Beach	North.	5		1921-1924.
111	F.C. Bird.	North.	5		1929-1931.
112	D. Blanchard.	Vale Rec.	5		1983-1989.
113	G. Brehaut.	North.	5		1961-1967.
114	A.H.P. Davey.		5	2	1908-1911.
115	A. Eldridge.	Vale Rec.Belgrave W.	5	3	1964-1966.
116	R. Elmy.	North.	5		1990-1997.
117	W. Farmer.	Belgrave W.	5		1948-1951.
118	M. Girard.	North, Sylvans.	5	1	1969-1972.
119	A. Hamon.	Vale Rec. (Athletics)	5	3	1958-1966.
120	M.de la Haye.	Sylvans.	5		1996-2000.
121	R. Hemery.	Belgrave W.	5		1965-1971.
122	S. Ingrouille.	North.	5		1990-1993.
123	N. Jeffreys.	Rangers,Vale Rec.	5		1964-1969.
124	J. Leadbeater.	North.	5	3	1907-1909.
125	J. le Maitre.	Rangers, Belgrave W.	5	2	1950-1953.
126	J. Mahy.	North.	5	1	1959-1963.
127	B. Meechem.	North.	5		1958-1962.
128	G. Le Page.	North.	5	1	2001-2003.
129	C. Purdy.	Belgrave W.	5		1911-1921.
130	J. Reid.	Vale Rec.	5		1976-1982.
131	F. Rich.		5	2	1922-1924.
132	A. Sandrey.	Rangers.	5	1	1956-1960.
133	E. Thorne.	Athletics.	5		1905-1907.
134	R. Webb.	St. Martins.	5	5	1978-1981.
135	L. Arnold.	Rangers.	4	3	1959-1961.
136	D. Bisson.	Vale Rec.	4	2	2002-2003.
137	A.S. Blicq.	Rangers.	4	2	1914-1920.
138	M.J. Brassel.	Rangers.	4	2	1932-1935.
139	M. Brassel.	Belgrave W., Rangers.	4	4	1954-1957.
140	J.S. Brookes.	Rangers.	4	1	1930-1933.
141	H. Cumber.	North.	4	5	1922-1925.
142	V. Cooper.	Athletics.	4	1	1907-1911.
143	M. le Cras.	Sylvans.	4	2	1999-2003.
144	R. Depres.	Belgrave W., Rangers.	4		1975-1980.
145	S. Ephgrave.	Rangers.	4		1949-1953.
146	N. Froome.	VOBA, Rangers.	4		1947-1955.

147	M. Gallienne.	Belgrave W.	4	1	1986-1990.
148	B.Hill.	North.	4		1958-1963.
149	T. Holland.	North.	4	1	1907-1911.
150	S. Jackson.	Rangers.	4	1	1905-1906.
151	W. Kennedy.	St. Martins.	4	3	1979-1981.
152	N. Laine.	Vale Rec.	4	2	1983-1989.
153	D. Mahoney.	North.	4		1984-1987.
154	B. Mahy.	North.	4	1	1961-1963.
155	J. Martel.	St. Martins.	4		1964-1967.
156	R.O. Martin.	Rangers.	4		1958-1960.
157	Andy le Page.	Rangers.	4		1979-1985.
158	H. Le Poidevin.	North.	4		1948-1951.
159	A. Pugh.	St. Martins.	4		1965-1970.
160	L. Renouf.	Sylvans, St. Martins.	4		1996-2000.
161	L. Rich.	Rangers.	4		1920-1923.
162	L. Smith.	Rangers,Vale Rec.	4	2	1985-1990.
163	M. Smith.	St. Martins.	4	3	1998-2001.
164	G. Symons.		4		1923-1925.
165	Marcus le Tissier.	Belgrave W.	4	1	1964-1968.
166	M. Wilson.	North.	4		2001-2003.
167	A. Yates.	Athletics.	4	3	1907-1913.
168	L. Allen.	St. Martins.	3		2000-2001.
169	A. Bannister.	St. Martins.	3		1969-1970.
170	D. Batiste.	Belgrave W.	3		1959-1960.
171	R. Blondel.	Vale Rec.	3	6	1974-1977.
172	C. Bourgaize.	North.	3		1980-1981.
173	R. Brache.	St. Martins.	3		1963-1964.
174	J. Brehaut.	North.	3	1	1962-1964.
175	C. Chamberlain.	Vale Rec.	3	1	1999-2003.
176	S. Collins.	Athletics.	3		1925-1926.
177	Falla.	North.	3		1913-1914.
178	P. de Garis.	Sylvans.	3		1996
179	K. Gleeson.	Vale Rec.	3		1974-1977.
180	K. Gilligan.	St. Martins.	3		1999-2001.
181	J. Hartland.	Belgrave W.	3		1947-1948.
182	J. Hebdon.	North.	3		1912
183	A. Helyer.		3		1929-1931.
184	A. de Jersey.	North.	3		1971-1976.
185	A. Leadbeater.		3		1927-1928.
186	R. Leale.		3		1913-1914.
187	A.le Maitre.	Rangers.	3		1933-1936.
188	J. Meager.		3		1925-1926.
189	J. le Messurier.	Rangers.	3		1956-1960.
190	F.G. Mockler.	Athletics.	3	2	1907-1908.
191	Mark Ogier.	Belgrave W.	3	2	1997-1999.
192	I. Ozanne.	Vale Rec.	3		1989-1990.
193	E. Parry.	Rangers.	3		1907-1908.
194	R.W. Podger.	Belgrave W.	3		1905-1906.
195	G. Smith.	Belgrave W.	3		1981-1986.
196	J. Smith.		3		1923-1924.
197	N.Thoume.	St. Martins.	3		1976-1977.
198	A.E. Tooley.	Athletics.	3		1912
199	D. Trustum.	Vale Rec.	3		1957-1959.
200	D. Yeates.	Vale Rec.	3		1994-1996.
201	R. Bannister.	Belgrave W.	2		1971-1972.
202	F.C. Bevan.		2		1928

	Name	Club			Year
203	F. Bird.		2		1926-1927.
204	B. Bishop.	Athletics.	2		1960-1962.
205	R. Brehaut.	North.	2	1	1980-1981.
206	R. Brown.	North.	2		1920
207	M. Cotter.	Vale Rec.	2		1975
208	S. Cotton.	Athletics.	2	3	1906
209	B.Curtis.		2		1920
210	R. Diamond.	Belgrave W.	2		1959-1960.
211	J. Dorey.	Sylvans.	2		1986-1987.
212	L. Eker.	North.	2	1	1957-1963.
213	M. Falla.	Vale Rec.	2		1973-1974.
214	W. Froome.		2		1909
215	S. Hands.		2		1905
216	G. Heaume.	Athletics.	2	3	1905
217	J. Hickman.	Belgrave W.	2		1922-1924.
218	F. Jeffreys.		2	1	1922
219	H. Keyho.	Belgrave W.	2		1920-1925.
220	B. Knight.	Vale Rec.	2		1978
221	F. Maguire.	Belgrave W.	2		1906
222	H. Marley.	North.	2	1	1938
223	R. McAvoy.	Rangers.	2		1920
224	D. Martel.	Rangers.	2		1922
225	J. McCarthy.	Rangers.	2		1934-1936.
226	F. Mellanby.	Belgrave W., Centrals.	2		1947-1954.
227	P. Mellor.	Vale Rec.	2		1968
228	A. McMillan.	Sylvans.	2		1971-1976.
229	J. Newbury.	Belgrave W.	2		1905
230	L. Pasquire.	Belgrave W.	2		1958-1960.
231	J.J. Richardson.		2		1925
232	F.E. Robins.	Rangers.	2		1931
233	W. Searle.		2		1914
234	P. Smith.		2		1909
235	H. Trustum.	North.	2		1928
236	M. Tullier.	St. Martins.	2		1988
237	W. Warr.	VOBA.	2		1949-1951.
238	E. Zabiela.	Rangers.	2		1911
239	P. Allen.	Rangers.	1		1910
240	W. Allen.	North.	1	2	1937
241	R. Anthony.	Belgrave W.	1		1974
242	G. ApSion.	Rangers.	1	1	1993
243	R. Barrasin.	North.	1		1953
244	W. Bird.	Athletics.	1	1	1911
245	R. Body.	Rangers.	1		1958
246	J. Booth.	St. Martins.	1		1967
247	C. Bougourd.		1		1926
248	J. Bourgaize.	Belgrave W.	1		2004
249	J.J. Brookes.		1	1	1935
250	G. Buckingham.	St. Martins.	1	1	1949
251	R. Cameron.	North.	1		1999
252	R. Carre.	Belgrave W.	1		1948
253	L. Chainey.	Belgrave W.	1		1997
254	R. Chapple.	Belgrave W.	1		1921*
255	N. le Cheminant.	Sylvans.	1	2	1960
256	D. Chester.	Rangers.	1		1978
257	D.B. Collenette.	North.	1		1937
258	S. Concanen	St. Martins.	1		2004

No.	Name	Club			Year
259	A. Conway.	Rangers.	1	1	1966
260	C.M. Douch.	Rangers.	1		1921
261	T. Duff.	North.	1		2004
262	W. Dunn.		1		1920
263	J.H. Duquemin.	North.	1		1937
264	N. Falla.	Rovers.	1		1983
265	G. Fitchet.	St. Martins.	1		1988
266	A. Fitton.	North.	1		1995
267	H. Finn.	North.	1		1947
268	J. Forsey.	St. Martins.	1		1965
269	W. Freiss.	North.	1	1	1934
270	R. Gallienne.	Sylvans.	1		1992
271	D. Garland.	Rangers.	1		1999
272	D. Gilman.	Sylvans.	1		1995
273	B. Gorvel.	St. Martins.	1		1968
274	L. Howlett.	Belgrave W.	1		1953
275	K. Jeffreys.		1		1975
276	D. Jones.	Vale Rec.	1		1977
277	R. Jones.	Vale Rec.	1		1997
278	S. Kelling.		1		2002
279	A.C. Leadbeater.	North.	1		1933
280	S. le Lievre.		1		1939
281	R. Loaring.	Sylvans.	1		1982
282	C. Loveridge.	North.	1		1973
283	L. Luscombe.	St. Martins.	1	1	1991
284	S. de la Mare.	St. Martins.	1	1	1948
285	G. Mahy.	Vale Rec.	1		1969
286	R. Mahy.	North.	1		1952
287	D. Martel.	St. Martins.	1		1984
288	D. Martin	North.	1		2003
289	A.W. Maunder.	Rangers.	1		1913
290	C. McKane.	North.	1		1981
291	N. Millman.	Vale Rec.	1		1974
292	J. Murray.	North.	1		1961
293	R. Oakley.	Rangers.	1		1950
294	S. Ogier.	Belgrave W.	1		1996
295	M. le Page.	Vale Rec.	1		2000
296	L. Perriam.	North.	1		1947
297	D. Podmore.	Belgrave W.	1		1987
298	E. Purchas.	Athletics.	1		1910
299	G. Ridley.	Vale Rec.	1		1994
300	D. Rihoy.	North.	1		2004
301	Rihoy.		1		1905
302	B. Robson.	Belgrave W.	1		1973
303	A. Rowe.	North.	1		1981
304	T. Russo.		1		1986
305	A. Smith.	Port City.	1		1996
306	E.J. Smith.	St. Martins.	1		1956
307	G. Smith.	St. Martins.	1		1989
308	L. Smith.	Belgrave W.	1		1933
309	Spiller.		1		1926
310	P. Stranger.	Athletics.	1		1922
311	A. Taylor.	St. Martins.	1		1973
312	G. Taylor.	Rangers.	1		1939
313	K. Taylor.	Vale Rec.	1	2	1950
314	G. Tolcher.	North.	1		1952

			Caps	Goals	Year
315	A. Toms.		1		1930
316	T. Tostevin.	North.	1	1	1981
317	V. Tostevin.	Belgrave W.	1		1962
318	J. Tostevin.	Progressives.	1		1912
319	H. Tozer.	Rangers/Belgrave W.?	1		1934
320	B. Tullier.	St. Martins.	1		1968
321	J. Veron	North.	1		2004
322	G. West.	R.G.A.	1		1910
323	W. Whare.	St. Martins.	1		1947
324	F. Wilcocks.	North.	1		1957
325	A. Williams.	St. Martins.	1	1	1965
326	M. Wylie.	Athletics.	1	2	1962

JERSEY APPEARANCES

	Name.	Club	Caps.	Goals.	Muratti Career.
1	A. Venton.	Oaklands, Wanderers.	23	5	1957-1973.
2	S. Carlyon.	Wanderers,First Tower,Rozel Rovers.	21		1987-2000.
3	R. Crick.	First Tower.	21	6	1971-1986.
4	G. le Maistre.	St. Paul's, First Tower.	21	24	1947-1960.
5	B. Breuilly.	First Tower,Oaklands,St Paul's, St.Ouen.	20		1966-1981.
6	D. A' Court.	Magpies, St. Peter, First Tower.	19		1973-1987.
7	A. Barker.	St. Paul's, Magpies.	17	3	1988-2000.
8	D. de Gruchy.	Beeches.	16	13	1952-1962.
9	D. Parker.	Wanderers, Oaklands.	16	21	1957-1968.
10	R. Jones.	St. Paul's, Magpies.	15	1	1947-1956.
11	R. Muddyman.	Oaklands,1st.Tower.St.Paul's,Sp. Acs.Wands.	15	5	1991-2001.
12	D. Pitman.	Oaklands, St. Paul's, Wanderers.	15		1948-1961.
13	J. Ruellan.	Georgetown.	14	13	1963-1971.
14	D. Crenan.	Magpies, Oaklands.	13		1957-1965.
15	T. Garnier.		13		1912-1926.
16	D. Lempriere.	Magpies, Wanderers.	13		1954-1962.
17	G. Newton.	Beeches.	13		1953-1961.
18	W.C. Beasley.	Wanderers.	12	1	1910-1922.
19	F. Davis.		12		1922-1932.
20	C. Ferey.	St. Paul's.	12		1994-2004.
21	A. Pitman.	First Tower.	12	3	1973-1980.
22	P. Vincenti.	St. Paul's.	12	6	1978-1987.
23	M. Vowden.	Wanderers.	12		1963-1969.
24	A.E. Garnet.	Wanderers.	11	8	1925-1932.
25	P. Harzo.	St. Paul's.	11	1	1981-1994.
26	F.H. le Marquand.	Wanderers.	11		1952-1961.
27	M. Mathews.	First Tower.	11	1	1972-1979.
28	G. Mourant.	Beeches.	11	1	1951-1962.
29	B. Pitman	First Tower.	11	10	1976-1985.
30	Y. Santos.	Jersey Scottish.	11	2	1995-2003.
31	P. Carberry.	FirstTower,St.Paul's,Sport.Accad.,Jsy Scott.	10	4	1983-1994.
32	D. Cronin.	Beeches, Wanderers, First Tower.	10	5	1963-1968.
33	S. Dewhurst.	Oaklands, First Tower.	10	8	1980-1987
34	D. Henstridge.	Wanderers.	10		1962-1968.
35	M. le Louarn.	Georgetown.	10		1965-1971.
36	H. Proffitt.	Oaklands.	10	1	1964-1971.
37	A. Salaun.	Wanderers.	10	3	1985-1997.
38	H.V. Benest.	YMCA.	9	2	1929-1937.
39	P. Fleury.	St. Peter.	9	9	1976-1988.
40	C.S. Freeman.	Wanderers.	9		1927-1937.
41	C. Morton.	Jersey Scottish.	9		1994-1998.

42	J. Reilly.	Jersey Scottish.	9	3	1997-2004.
43	G. le Riche.	Magpies, St. Paul's.	9		1934-1949.
44	B. Thorp.	Georgetown.	9	1	1967-1972.
45	R. White.	Magpies.	9	4	1947-1954.
46	S. A' Court.	Wanderers.	8	2	1986-1991.
47	A.F. Davenport.	YMCA.	8	1	1934-1939.
48	J. Drew.	First Tower.	8	4	1938-1950.
49	N. Livesey.	Wanderers, St. Paul's, Sporting Acs.	8	6	1980-1992.
50	G.A. Malzard.	YMCA.	8		1932-1937.
51	A. Marett.	Wanderers.	8	2	1920-1927.
52	R. Megaw.	Oaklands.	8	1	1960-1966.
53	G.W. Scoones.	Wanderers.	8		1909-1914.
54	L. de St. Croix.	St. Peter.	8	1	1995-2001.
55	J. Sherry.	Beeches.	8	3	1947-1954.
56	F. Wheway.		8	7	1910-1914.
57	G. Arthur.	Wanderers, First Tower.	7		1948-1954.
58	J. Coppin.	Rangers, Wanderers.	7		1906-1912.
59	P. Duffy.	St. Paul's, Springfield.	7		1982-1991.
60	P. Duxbury.	Rozel Rovers.	7	1	2000-2004.
61	Folliot.		7	2	1925-1929.
62	N. de Freitas.	Portuguese.	7	5	1993-1997.
63	E. Hurel.		7	1	1927-1936.
64	W. Millow.	Western United.	7		1907-1914.
65	S.V. Nobes.	First Tower.	7		1936-1939.
66	R. Pamplin.	Wanderers.	7	4	1948-1953.
67	Parker.		7		1924-1927.
68	D. Poingdestre.(P?)	St. Paul's	7		1948-1953.
69	G. Quarry.	Beeches.	7		1955-1958.
70	M. Stratford.	Wanderers, First Tower.	7		1989-1995.
71	W. Begbie.	St. Paul's.	6		1989-1992.
72	D. Blake.	Old Victorians.	6		1971-1975.
73	B. O' Boyle.	Wanderers	6	4	1970-1976.
74	D. Brodie.	Jersey Scottish.	6	1	1999-2004.
75	G.H. Carpenter.		6	5	1929-1933.
76	K. le Cornu.	St. Peter.	6	1	1981-1988.
77	D. Corrigan.	Springfield, Jersey Scottish.	6		1984-1990.
78	Ross Crick.	First Tower.	6	3	1997-2004.
79	I. Daly.	St. Paul's, Magpies.	6		1994-1997.
80	C. Dingle.	Wanderers.	6		1952-1961.
81	C. Grant.	Rozel Rovers, First Tower.	6		1999-2002.
82	A. Greig.	St. Paul's, Jersey Scottish.	6	5	1991-1996.
83	C. Hamon.	St. Peter.	6	1	1991-1997.
84	C.A. Harben.		6		1927-1932.
85	M. Harben.	Beeches.	6	2	1953-1959.
86	D. Huson.	First Tower.	6	3	1970-1973.
87	G. Huson.	St. Paul's.	6		1921-1926.
88	A. Lawlor.	St. Paul's.	6	6	1987-1992.
89	T. le Maistre.	St. Peter.	6	1	1994-1998.
90	D. Mathews.	Georgetown, First Tower.	6		1975-1979.
91	J. Murphy.	First Tower.	6		1976-1979.
92	H. le Roux.	Beeches.	6		1953-1957.
93	M. Steigenberger.	First Tower.	6	3	1994-1998.
94	R.R. Stevens.	Wanderers.	6		1905-1910.
95	P. Taylor.	St. Paul's, First Tower.	6	2	1981-1988.
96	White.		6		1925-1931
97	M. lo Blancq.	First Tower.	5		1982-1986
98	H. Boyd.	YMCA.	5	3	1930-1935.
99	W.G. Chapman.	Wanderers.	5	3	1905-1911.
100	E. Le Chevalier.	Magpies.	5	3	1937-1939.

101	M. Cooper.	Oaklands.	5		1977-1979.
102	J.A. Cummins.		5		1930-1933.
103	C. St. George.	National Rovers.	5	4	1920-1927.
104	J. Hayward.	First Tower.	5		2002-2004.
105	A. Herbert.	St. Paul's.	5		1979-1981.
106	Journeux.	YMCA.	5		1921-1924.
107	P. Lock.	St. Paul's.	5	4	1981-1983.
108	O' Neil.*		5		1921-1930.
109	J.M. Poingdestre.	Rangers.	5	1	1906-1910.
110	A. Reed.	Wanderers.	5		1908-1912.
111	D. Renouf.	Oxenford House, Wanderers.	5		1905-1912.
112	Riley.		5		1922-1925.
113	W. Richardson.	St. Paul's.	5		1984-1988.
114	P. Sands.	First Tower.	5	1	1969-1973.
115	T.J. Thornton.	Wanderers.	5		1906-1909.
116	G. Westwood.	First Tower.	5		1982-1985.
117	J. Whitworth.	Wanderers.	5	1	1911-1913.
118	E. Appleyard.	Oaklands, First Tower.	4	1	1975-1977.
119	Barker.		4		1925-1927.
120	P. Berry.	First Tower.	4		1932-1938.
121	P. Bouteloup.	First Tower.	4		1991-1994.
122	A.W. Burtenshaw.	First Tower.	4		1931-1933.
123	J. Brewster.	St. Peter.	4		2002-2003.
124	J. Carter.	First Tower.	4	1	1973-1976.
125	D. Cooper.	First Tower.	4		1976-1978.
126	A. Cunningham.	Oaklands.	4	3	1979-1981.
127	G. Davies.	YMCA.	4		1921-1924.
128	S. Davies.	Wanderers.	4	1	1939-1949.
129	P. Edwards.	Trinity.	4		2002-2003.
130	E.F. le Feuvre.		4	3	1930-1933.
131	G.S. Fox.		4		1908-1912.
132	G. Freeman	St. Peter.	4	2	2001-2003.
133	R. le Gallais.(W?)	First Tower, Magpies.	4	1	1952-1957.
134	A. Galway.	Wanderers, St. Paul's.	4	3	1935-1938.
135	C. St. George.	First Tower.	4	1	1949-1951.
136	J. Kellett.	First Tower.	4		1993-1997.
137	J.E. Lees.	Wanderers.	4	3	1937-1939.
138	D. Lloyd.	Trinity.	4		2002-2003.
139	R. Lumsden.	Jersey Scottish.	4		1997-2004.
140	le Masurier.		4	2	1923-1925.
141	Medder.	St. Paul's.	4		1921-1923.
142	G.M. le Page.	Wanderers.	4	1	1905-1907.
143	S. Petulla.	First Tower.	4	8	1987-1994.
144	S. Pirouet.	First Tower, Wanderers.	4		1972-1975.
145	W. Poingdestre.		4		1922-1924.
146	D. Ross.	Jersey Scottish, Rozel Rovers..	4	1	1990-1999.
147	D. Le Roux.	Trinity.	4	1	2003-2004.
148	L. Selkirk.	First Tower.	4		1968-1973.
149	H. Stent.		4	1	1912-1914.
150	E. Stent.	Wanderers.	4	1	1920-1922.
151	Stuart.	National Rovers.	4	1	1920-1923.
152	Sonnen.		4	2	1911-1914.
153	R. Spink.	Georgetown.	4		1970-1972.
154	B. Vowden.	First Tower.	4	1	2002-2003.
155	I. Watts.	St. Paul's.	4	1	1967-1969.
156					
157	R. Ballstone.	St. Paul's.	3		1955
158	K. Billot.	St. Paul's, St. Peter.	3		1974-1975.
159	L. Bramley.	Rozel Rovers.	3	1	1998-1999.

160	T. Browne.	Beeches.	3	1	1969-1970.
161	K. Cameron.	St. Peter.	3		1977-1981.
162	S. Cartwright.		3	4	1909-1910
163	R. Craydon.	Magpies, First Tower.	3		1965-1969.
164	S. Coutanche.	First Tower.	3		1991-1998.
165	C. Culkin.	Jersey Scottish.	3		1998-2000.
166	D. Crowell.	St. Paul's.	3		1947-1951.
167	C.J. Dale.	First Tower.	3		1937-1938.
168	N. Davidson.	St. Paul's.	3		1983-1987.
169	P. Docherty.	St. Martin.	3	4	1999-2000.
170	G. Fraser.	Magpies, St. Peter.	3	1	1987-1989.
171	M. Freeman.	Wanderers.	3		1950-1952.
172	J. Gamblin.	St. Paul's.	3	1	1936-1939.
173	H.F. le Gresley.	YMCA.	3		1931-1935.
174	A. Guegan.	First Tower, St. Peter.	3	1	1975-1978.
175	D. Gorin.	First Tower.	3	3	1961-1963.
176	R. Harbin.	First Tower.	3	3	1975
177	S. Harzo.	Beeches.	3		1975-1976.
178	A. H. Honeycombe.	Rangers.	3	1	1905-1911.
179	J. James.	St. Paul's.	3	1	1975
180	P. Jones.	First Tower.	3		1980-1981.
181	C. Kent.	First Tower.	3		1938-1939.
182	S. Kilshaw.	Le Masuriers.	3		1989-1990.
183	Labey.	Wanderers.	3		1906-1907.
184	J. Lazel.	First Tower.	3		1947-1949.
185	T.S.Mellanby.		3		1910-1911.
186	R (D?). Mauger.	St. Paul's, Oaklands.	3		1951-1958.
187	C. le Moignan.	Wanderers.	3	1	1986-1988.
188	G.E. Morris.	St. Paul's.	3	1	1935-1936.
189	M. Murray.	Le Masuriers, Wanderers.	3		1990-1992.
190	J. Newson.		3		1912-1913.
191	P. Osment.	Wanderers.	3		1964-1965.
192	E. Pettiquin.	St. Luke's, Caesareans.	3		1905-1907.
193	D. Pih.	Jersey Scottish.	3		1996-1998.
194	M. Ray.	St. Paul's.	3		2001-2003.
195	A. Romano.	Caesareans.	3		1913-1914.
196	D. Rouille.	Beeches.	3		1962-1963.
197	J. O'Shea.	First Tower.	3	5	1994-1995.
198	B. Smith.	YMCA.	3		1921-1923.
199	P.O' Toole.	Jersey Scottish.	3		2000-2001
200	J. Warren.	Wanderers.	3		1988-1991.
201	A. Williams.	Oaklands, St. Peter.	3		1978-1979.
202	Allchin.		2		1930
203	S. Andre.	St. Paul's.	2		2002
204	C. Andrews	Wanderers.	2	1	2003-2004.
205	McAvoy.		2		1928-1929.
206	A. Baillie	St. Ouen.	2	1	1976-1977.
207	Bailey.		2		1910-1911.
208	B. Beckett.	First Tower.	2		1966
209	F. Belhomme.	Samaritans.	2	2	1951
210	Benest.	Old Victorians.	2	2	1972-1973.
211	J. Berry.	St. Paul's.	2	1	1936
212	J. Blake.	National Rovers, First Tower.	2		1920-1923.
213	C. le Blancq.		2		1908-1909.
214	A. Bone.	Magpies.	2	1	1969
215	T. Browne.	Beeches.	2		1960-1962
216	M. Brown.	Jersey Scottish.	2		1996
217	Carter.		2		1928-1929.
218	Cole.	Caesareans.	2	1	1907

219	P. O'Connor.		2		1934-1935.
220	G. McConnell	Jersey Scottish.	2	1	2004
221	D.Cooper.	First Tower.	2	2	1967
222	S. de la Cour.	St. Luke's, Wanderers.	2		1905-1907.
223	S. McDonald.		2		1998-1999.
224	O. Eloury.	Magpies, First Tower.	2		1954-1955.
225	J. Fitzmaurice.		2		2003
226	W. Fox.		2	1	1908-1909.
227	Gamblin.	St. Paul's.	2		1933
228	Goldsmith.		2	2	1913-1914.
229	W. Golding.	S. Luke's, Caesareans.	2		1905-1906
230	E.R. Gould.	Wanderers.	2	1	1939
231	P. Grierson.	St. Pauls, Le Masuriers.	2		1992-1993.
232	C. Hamon.	Wanderers.	2		2004
233	T. Hamon.		2		1935-1937.
234	B. Hardisty.	St. Peter.	2		2001-2002.
235	R. Hart.	Wanderers.	2	1	1948-1950.
236	L. Harvey.	Jersey Scottish.	2	1	2002
237	W. Hitchcock.		2		1933
238	N. de Jesus.	St. Peter.	2	1	1994
239	S. Kean.	St. Paul's.	2		1985
240	P. Kemp.	Wanderers.	2	1	1920-1921.
241	M. McKenna.	Jersey Scottish.	2		1993-1996.
242	P. McLaughlin.	Magpies.	2		1966
243	C. Mc Leod.	First Tower.	2		1980-1982.
244	G. Lightbody.	Wanderers.	2		1992-1998.
245	W. O'Malley.	Jersey Scottish.	2		1989
246	Marriot.		2		1926
247	C. Martin.		2		1930
248	C. Mauger.		2		1924
249	Moyse.		2	1	1913
250	C. McNabb	Jersey Scottish.	2	1	2004
251	*B. O'Neill.	Wanderers.	2		1933-1934.
252	Newington.		2		1928-1929.
253	T. Noel.	Magpies.	2	1	1953-1955.
254	Owen.		2	4	1926
255	A. Petra.	Wanderers.	2		1934-1937.
256	P. Poiter.	Caesareans.	2	1	1907
257	G. Pinel.	Beeches.	2		1979-1980.
258	A. Querns.	Jersey Scottish.	2		1991
259	J. Roberts.	Magpies.	2		1973-1974.
260	P. Rowan.	Georgetown.	2	2	1967
261	A. Salaun.		2		2000
262	M. Seater.	Magpies.	2	2	1973-1974.
263	C. Smith.		2		2003
264	Stratford.		2	2	1912
265	N. Thomas.	Wanderers.	2		1985-1989.
266	Thornton.		2		1927
267	W. le Vaillant.		2		1908-1909.
268	A. Voisin.	Caesareans.	2	1	1906-1907.
269	E. Alexandre.	Caesareans.	1		1907
270	Baillie.		1		1973
271	J. Beatson.	St. Paul's.	1		2004
272	Beech.		1	1	1922
273	Blacklock.	Wanderers.	1		1972
274	P.H. Boomer.	Caesareans.	1		1905
275	L.M. Bourke.		1		1913
276	L. Bradshaw.		1		2004
277	R. Brown.		1		1920

278	A. Browne.	Magpies.	1		1952
279	V. Bourgoise.	Army.	1		1972
280	A. Campbell.	Sprinfield.	1		1986
281	J. Carney.	First Tower.	1		1984
282	R. Carter.		1		1909
283	MacCarthy.		1	1	1985
284	M. Cassidy.	Jersey Scottish.	1		1996
285	F. le Cocq.	Royal Welsh Fusiliers.	1		1924
286	Coleman.		1		1989
287	I. Corfield.	Oaklands.	1		1979
288	J. Corrigan.	Le Masuriers.	1		1987
289	Corley.		1		1956
290	G. le Cornu.	St. Paul's.	1		1989
291	S. le Cornu.		1		1963
292	R. Coutanche.	St. Paul's.	1		1974
293	E. Cox.	YMCA.	1	1	1933
294	D. Craven.	St. Ouen.	1		2002
295	P. Crompton.	Rozel Rovers.	1		1998
296	T. Crowell		1		2003
297	T. Daly.	Le Masuriers.	1	1	1987
298	P.O. Dart.		1		1908
299	W. Dauny.	First Tower.	1		1937
300	McDermott.		1		1922
301	Dingle.		1		1933
302	L. Dolbel.	Wanderers.	1		1974
303	C. Dummond.		1		1998
304	Dundas.		1		1977
305	R. Dunford.	Georgetown.	1		1975
306	Elliot.		1		1930
307	A. Essler.	Jersey Scottish.	1		1999
308	H. Falle.	St. Paul's.	1	1	1974
309	Fenn.		1		1925
310	D. Ferey.	St. Paul's.	1		1964
311	R. Fernandez.		1		1998
312	M. Forbes.	Jersey Scottish.	1		1993
313	Fox.	Western United.	1		1907
314	R. Galway.	Oaklands.	1		1963
315	M. Gamblin.	St. Paul's.	1		1939
316	Gammon.		1		1982
317	Godrich.		1		1927
318	Golding.		1		1934
319	Golding.		1		1968
320	P. Gosling.	Beeches.	1		1947
321	P. Gosling.	Beeches.	1		1957
322	H.F. de Gresley.		1		1928
323	J.W. de Gresley.		1		1928
324	F. Grimster.		1	3	1908
325	J. Griffiths.	Magpies.	1		1973
326	R. de Gruchy.		1		1953
327	J. Guest.	St. Peter.	1	1	1984
328	R. Harben.	Beeches.	1		1962
329	S. Haines.		1		1932
330	B. Hardy.		1		2000
331	M. Hales.	First Tower.	1		1981
332	Hefford.		1		1930
333	C. Hickling.		1		2004
334	Hocquard.		1		1929
335	Holmes.		1		1923
336	H. Hughes.	Magpies.	1		1938

337	D.M. Jones.	Wanderers.	1		1906
338	D. Jones.	National Rovers.	1		1920
339	D. Jones.	Wanderers.	1		1974
340	M. Keites.	Georgetown.	1		1964
341	G. Kennedy.		1	1	1913
342	Knight.	Magpies.	1		1947
343	S. Kirkpatrick.	Jersey Scottish.	1		1993
344	Kitcher.		1		1921
345	F. Leamon.	Mertonians.	1	1	1939
346	C. Lumsden.	Oaklands.	1		1980
347	Mahrer.	Oaklands.	1		1963
348	R. Marett.		1	1	1971
349	H.G. Marie.	Wanderers.	1		1935
350	A.G. Marshall	Wanderers.	1		1920
351	H. Martin.	First Tower.	1		1979
352	Morgan.	St. Paul's.	1		1982
353	T.F. Mulholland.	Wanderers.	1		1905
354	O'Neill.		1		1988
355	N.T. Noel.	St. Paul's.	1		1935
356	S. Olliver.	St. Peter.	1		1987
357	le Page.		1		1913
358	R. Peebles.	Jersey Scottish.	1		1995
359	Picot.		1		1923
360	Pincott.		1	1	1931
361	Poree.	First Tower.	1		1952
362	W. Poingdestre.		1		1914
363	R. Pollock.		1	2	1975
364	S. le Rougetel.	St. Peter.	1		1992
365	Rouxin.		1	1	1929
366	Rowan.		1		1973
367	J. Rutter.	First Tower.	1		2001
368	M. Ryan.	Wanderers.	1	1	1963
369	J. Salsac.	Magpies.	1		1955
370	G. le Saux.	St. Paul's.	1		1987
371	P. Scott.	Oaklands.	1		1968
372	E. Smith.	Magpies.	1		1936
373	G.L. Smith.	First Tower.	1		1937
374	Smith.	First Tower.	1		1947
375	E.J. Stephens.		1		1932
376	J. Styles.	Wanderers.	1		2004
377	D. Swanson.	Trinity.	1		2002
378	Soudain.		1		1934
379	A.J. Syvret.	Wanderers.	1		1936
380	Thomas.	First Tower.	1		1952
381	D. Tredant.		1		1955
382	D. Toudic.	St. Paul's.	1		2001
383	Troy.		1		1927
384	F. Vardon.	First Tower.	1		1937
385	W. Vardon.	Gorey.	1		1906
386	Vauden.		1		1956
387	E. Vibert.	Georgetown.	1		1961
388	H. Watts.		1		1935
389	R. Weir.	St. Paul's.	1		1987
390	H. Weir.	Wanderers.	1		1905
391	Wellman.		1		1914
392	J. Wilson.	Magpies.	1	1	1966
393	J. Wylie.	Jersey Scottish.	1		1983
394	A. Yates.	Caesareans.	1		1909

MURATTI GOALSCORERS

2004.

The first Muratti goal was scored by G. Heaume (Guernsey) against Alderney at the Track on 17 April 1905. A silver medal with a gold centre was presented to him after the match to commemorate this feat.

The top Muratti goal scorer is Graeme Le Maistre (Jersey) who scored 24 Muratti goals in his 21 games. In second place is Kevin Le Tissier (Guernsey) who scored 22 Muratti goals in 20 appearances.

The most individual goals scored in a single Muratti match is 7 scored by Craig Allen (Guernsey) against Alderney in a 10-0 victory in 1993. There have been five occasions where an individual scorer has scored five goals.

D. Parker (Jersey) v Alderney in 1957. Jersey-7, Alderney-1.

C. Allen (Guernsey) v Alderney in 1978. Guernsey-12, Alderney-0.

K. Le Tissier (Guernsey) v Alderney in 1992. Guernsey-9, Alderney-1.

S. Petulla (Jersey) v Alderney in 1994. Jersey-18, Alderney-0.

J. O'Shea (Jersey) v Alderney in 1994. Jersey-18, Alderney 0.

The record score for a Muratti is the 18-0 victory by Jersey over Alderney in 1994.

Mickey Brassel (Guernsey) scored 4 goals on his Muratti debut against Jersey in 1954. Guernsey won 5-3 at Springfield. No Jersey player has scored more than 3 goals against Guernsey in a match. Fred Grimster was the first Jersey player to score a hat trick against Guernsey in the 4-0 win at the Track in 1908. Graeme Le Maistre (Jersey) is the only player to score a hat trick in three successive Muratti matches. He scored three goals against Guernsey in the 1947 final and again in the 1948 final. He made it a hat trick of hat tricks when he scored three against Alderney in 1949.

F. Cleale (Guernsey) is the only player to score in 6 successive Muratti matches between 1912 and 1914. Graeme Le Maistre scored in 5 successive Muratti matches between 1952 and 1955. David Parker (Jersey) repeated this feat between 1960 and 1963.

Guernsey holds the record of scoring in 27 successive Muratti matches between 1955 and 1971. Jersey scored in 26 successive Muratti matches between 1955 and 1971.

Jersey has scored 399 goals in Muratti matches, conceding 187. Guernsey have scored 388 goals and conceded 201. Alderney have scored 39 goals and conceded 438.

Guernsey have went 4 successive Muratti matches without conceding a goal between 1934 and 1935. They repeated this feat between 1978 and 1980. Jersey have went 3 successive Muratti matches without conceding a goal in 1950. They repeated this feat between 1970 and 1971.

There have only been two no-score draws in the 178 Muratti matches. The first was in 1955 when Guernsey and Jersey drew 0-0 at the Track. The second 0-0 draw occurred between Jersey and Guernsey in Jersey in 1996.

MURATTI PENALTY KICKS

The first penalty kick awarded in a Muratti match was for Guernsey against Jersey in the Final of 1910. Benstead took and missed the penalty.

	Date.	Match.	Penalty taker.	Successful.
1	1910	Jersey-3, Guernsey-2.	A. Benstead (G)	No.
2	1921	Jersey-2, Alderney-0 (aet).	Beasley (J).	No.
3		Guernsey-0, Jersey-1.	Kemp (J).	Yes.
4	1922	Jersey-1, Guernsey-2.	Beech (J).	Yes.
5	1928	Jersey-2, Guernsey-1 (aet).	Dorey (G).	No.
6	1932	Guernsey-1, Jersey-0.	W. Warr (G).	Yes.
7	1933	Guernsey-4, Jersey-1 (aet).	Carpenter (J).	No.
8	1936	Jersey-9, Alderney-0.	G.A. Malzard (J).	No.
9	1950	Guernsey-3, Alderney-1.	R. Fever (A).	Yes.
10	1958	Guernsey-8, Alderney-2.	L. Collins (G).	No.
11		Guernsey-8, Alderney-2.	P. Moore (A).	Yes.
12		Jersey-2, Guernsey-1.	A. Sandrey (G).	Yes.
13	1960	Guernsey-5, Alderney-1.	B. Venton (A).	Yes.
14	1969	Guernsey-2, Jersey-1.	M. Girard (G).	Yes.
15	1973	Guernsey-1, Jersey-4.	J. Carter (J).	Yes.
16	1975	Jersey-2, Guernsey-3.	D. Lesbirel (G).	Yes.
17	1979	Guernsey-5, Jersey-0.	P. Blondel (G).	Yes.
18	1982	Guernsey-5, Alderney-1	L. Graham (G).	Yes.
19	1985	Guernsey-4, Jersey-3.	P. Vincenti (J).	Yes.
20	1986	Guernsey-7, Alderney-0.	P. Blondel (G).	Yes.
21	1988	Alderney-1 Guernsey-5.	G. Rushbury (A).	No.
22		Jersey-0, Guernsey-1.	C. Le Tissier (G)	Yes.
23	1990	Jersey-2, Guernsey-1.	C. Le Tissier (G)	Yes.
24	1993	Alderney-0, Guernsey-10.	K. Le Tissier (G).	No.
25		Guernsey-1, Jersey-2.	P. Harzo (J).	Yes.
26	1994	Jersey-18, Alderney-0.	S. Petulla (J).	Yes.
27		Jersey-18, Alderney-0.	S. Petulla (J).	Yes.
28	1994	Jersey-3, Guernsey-1.	S. Petulla (J).	Yes.
29	1995	Alderney-1, Jersey-7.	N. de Frietas (J).	Yes.
30	1998	Alderney-0, Jersey-2.	L. Bramley (J).	Yes.
31		Jersey-2, Guernsey-0.	R. Muddyman (J).	Yes.
32	2000	Alderney-0, Jersey-10.	R. Muddyman (J).	Yes.
33		Alderney-0, Jersey-10.	R. Muddyman (J).	Yes.
34		Jersey-1, Guernsey-0	R. Muddyman (J).	Yes.
35	2001	Alderney-0, Guernsey-6.	R. Tippett (G).	Yes.
36		Guernsey-4, Jersey-1.	M. Falla (G).	No.
37	2003	Alderney-1, Guernsey-4.	R. Tippett (G).	No.
38	2004	Jersey-3, Guernsey-0.	R. Crick (J).	Yes.

MISCELLANEOUS

BEST-EVER POST WAR MURATTI TEAMS.

Football, it is said, is all about opinions. Supporters can apparently all see the same incident but report it in various different ways all with varying emphasis. They also look at players in this way and can spend hours (of pleasure?) discussing the abilities of their favourite teams and players. The Muratti is no different and if asked for their 'Best-Ever' teams the discussions could go on for ever. Although supporters will no doubt disagree with the respective 'Best-Ever' teams of Alderney, Guernsey and Jersey I do not think that they will disagree with the pedigrees of the players who have selected their teams. Billy Bohan (20 caps and 1 goal) selected his Alderney squad and team, Colin Renouf (17 caps and 5 goals) produced his Guernsey team and Graeme Le Maistre (21 caps and 24 goals) selected his Jersey side. The one proviso was that they should be in the final line-up as well as acting as captain.

ALDERNEY.
Billy initially selected a short-listed squad of players before deciding on his final team. His squad consisted of W. Bohan, F. Bond, P. Burland, N. Rose, D. Jones, M. Mapp, J. Harrington, W. Cauvain, P. Turner, D. Clark, J.C. Dupont (Mullo), P. Concanon, A. Barker, J. Maxwell, J. Mannion, N. Jarvis, T. Pasquire, Buster Hammond, M. Treais, P. Moore.

Billy Bohan (c).

Patrick Burland   Peter Turner.
Joe Harrington   Walter Cauvain.

Alan Barker   James Maxwell.

Peter Concanon   Nigel Jarvis

Peter Moore   Mark Treais.

GUERNSEY.

Colin Renouf had an equally difficult task in selecting his team and his series of articles that appeared in the Guernsey Press in December-January of 2001/2 caused a lot of discussion in the island. He short listed five players for each position before finally deciding on the following Guernsey team:

Colin Gervaise-Brazier.

Art Le Page Colin. Renouf (c) Richard Harvey John Herpe.

Dave Lesbirel Jack Martel Les Collins.

Craig Allen John Loveridge Kevin Le Tissier.

JERSEY.

Graeme Le Maistre agreed that he had played alongside some wonderful players in his distinguished Muratti career and agreed with Billy Bohan and Colin Renouf that it was not an easy task to choose his finest eleven but he finally selected the following Jersey team:

Bram Le Rich.

Dennis Crowel   Dempsey Poingdestre.

Doug Pitman Reg Jones John Sherry

Tubby White Taffy Pamplin

Tot De Gruchy Graeme Le Maistre (c) Johnny Drew.

There is no doubt that this is a wonderful collection of Muratti players all of whom would grace a Muratti team of any generation.

PLAYERS OF THE DECADE.

	Alderney	Guernsey.	Jersey.
1905-1910	J. Catts (8)	F. Stranger (8-1)	R. Stevens (6).
1910-1914	F. Quanain (7-2).	F. Cleal (11-8).	F. Wheway (8-7)
1920-1930	J. Hammond (8-1).	H. Dorey (12-14)	C. St George (5-4).
1930-1939	F. Audoir (9-1).	D. Mechem (15).	E. Le Feuvre (4-3)
1947-1950	W. Hammond (11).	M. Carre (15)	R. Jones (15-1).
1950-1960	P. Moore (11-3)	L. Collins (25-10).	G. Le Maistre (21-24)
1960-1970	W. Bohan (20-1).	C. Renouf (17-5).	J. Ruellan (14-13)
1970-1980	F. Keachie (9-1).	P. Blondel (20-3).	R. Crick (21-6)
1980-1990	P. Burland (12).	K. Le Tissier (20-22).	N. Livesey (8-6).
1990-2000	N. Carre (12).	A. Vance (18-4).	S. Carlyon (21).
2000-2005	M. Treais.	M. Warren.	Y. Santos.

OSSIE ELOURY MEMORIAL TROPHY

Year	Player	Team	Year	Player	Team
1983	P. Blondel.	Guernsey.	1994	S. Petulla.	Jersey.
1984	J. Guest.	Jersey.	1995	R. Muddyman.	Jersey.
1985	M. le Tissier.	Guernsey.	1996	A. Barker.	Jersey.
1986	P. Harzo.	Jersey.	1997	M.Ogier.	Guernsey.
1987	W. Richardson.	Jersey.	1998	R. Muddyman.	Jersey.
1988	K. le Gallez.	Guernsey.	1999	M.le Cras.	Guernsey.
1989	T. Lawlor.	Jersey.	2000	Y. Santos.	Jersey.
1990	J. Murray.	Jersey.	2001	M. Falla.	Guernsey.
1991	G. Chalmers.	Guernsey.	2002	P. Edwards.	Jersey.
1992	G. Chalmers.	Guernsey.	2003	S. Polson.	Guernsey.
1993	N. de Freitas.	Jersey.		R. Lumsden.	Jersey.
			2004	D. Brodie	Jersey.

DISSMISALS

When you consider the passion that has been generated by the Muratti since 1905, it may be surprising to note that there have been very few sending off's. The first were in the Muratti Final of 1980 when, at Springfield, Peter Vincenti (Jersey) and Peter Blondel (Guernsey) received their marching orders. On 27 March 1999 Alan Adamson, Alderney's joint coach and substitute, was dismissed from the touchline by referee Charlie Tostevin. He is the only player to be sent-off during a Muratti match before coming onto the pitch.

The following players have been sent off in Muratti matches:

Peter Vincenti (Jersey). Jersey v Guernsey - Springfield, Jersey.1980.
Peter Blondel (Guernsey). Jersey v Guernsey – Springfield, Jersey. 1980.
Alan Adamson (Alderney). Alderney v Guernsey – Mount Hale.1999.
Nigel Jarvis (Alderney). Alderney v Guernsey – Mount Hale, Alderney. 2001.
Mark Ray (Jersey). Guernsey v Jersey – The Cycling Grounds, Guernsey. 2001.
Peter Edwards (Jersey). Jersey v Guernsey – Springfield, Jersey. 2002.

Supporting Local Football

Norman Piette are proud to have sponsored the Muratti during the 1999/2000/2001 seasons.

We are also proud to have sponsored the Guernsey Football Leagues and the Stranger Cup competition. Our commitment to the sport continues with the sponsorship of Vale Rec FC until 2009.

Norman Piette

Guernsey's leading builders' merchant

Norman Piette, Bulwer Avenue, St Sampson

Telephone: 245801   Facsimile: 248542

Email: sales@norman-piette.com

Web: www.norman-piette.com

Acknowledgements

In deciding to undertake the task of writing the history of the Muratti Vase competition my love and enthusiasm for the wonderful game of football took me a long way. My Glasgow upbringing in the great Celtic/Rangers rivalry gave me an understanding of the passions that a local derby can arouse. My move to Guernsey in 1975 introduced me to a similar rivalry, this time between footballing islands. Initially I felt that I could possibly complete a book on the Muratti on my own but I quickly realised that it would have been devoid of the true local flavour that you can only get from speaking to the people to whom these matches mean so much. During my research I was fortunate enough to meet and talk to many fine people who managed to give me a glimpse of their very special view of these matches and I am truly indebted to them for their help.

The sponsorship of the book by Credit Suisse was greatly appreciated and thanks should go to Mr. Albert Good and his support of local football.

The assistance I received from the staff at the Guernsey Press was immense. There were long meetings (and even longer phone calls) with Nigel Baudains and when things were looking dark his enthusiasm gave me a great lift. The quality of the enhancement work on the very many photographs that was done by Mike Steadman and Brian Green of the Press was a credit to their professionalism (and patience). My main contact with The Jersey Evening Post was Jan Hadley and I really appreciated all the work she done in finding some long lost photographs. I am also indebted to the Guernsey Press and Jersey Evening Post for waiving the copyright on all their photographs, a truly magnificent gesture. For the main body of the research I was fortunate enough to meet and work with the excellent staff at the Priaulx Library. I spent countless hours in the Library and always found the staff very helpful and understanding. At an early stage I had decided to include details on the referees and officials who took part in these matches and I got a great deal of information from Graham Skuse (Guernsey Football Association- Referees' Officer). Richard Heaume (Guernsey Occupation Museum) gave me a lot of information and photographs that related to the inter-island matches that took part in the Laufen Internment Camp during the occupation of the Channel Islands. Pat Fitzgerald, Secretary of the Bury & District Amateur Football League, also assisted in finding out details of the two matches that took part in the UK in 1942 between Guernsey and Jersey footballers based in Bury and Stockport. John Treleven was very helpful in filling in some team and referee details as well as finding the 1922 Muratti programme.

I had meetings with many people who gave me some excellent information as well as access to their Muratti possessions and some of them were Mrs Janet Browning (Ginger Solway), Harry Attewell (Alderney Peace Cup photograph as well as his father's Alderney Cap and 1920 winner's medal), John Parsons, Martell Maides (1910 postcards), the Guernsey Museum (1912 Guernsey Muratti team), the Alderney Journal for their Alderney Muratti photographs, Mrs. Le Vasseur (1905 photograph of James Henry Le Maitre of Alderney), Nigel Rose (access to his Muratti project for school), Billy Bohan, Kevin Gentle, Keith Webster, 'Buster' Hammond, Mrs. Le Poidevin and many more. I could not have completed the book without their help. Numerous Muratti players from each of the islands gave me valuable guidance and suggestions during my research and I hope that they enjoy the finished product.

I also received a lot of encouragement from Dave Dorey, Matt Fallaize, Dave Nussbaumer, Darren Duquemin and the late Nigel Gavey. Their quiet words from time to time kept me positive when my progress seemed to slow down. I believe that they all felt part of the process and it was reassuring to know that I was not alone in my endeavours.

Special thanks should also go to Tony Williams who guided me through some of the highs and lows. Having played, and scored, in a Muratti Final he could easily remember his feelings for the day. His professional experience in publishing matters was put to good use.

I appreciate all the help I received in producing this book and if I have missed anyone out then I apologise. I was not fortunate enough (or good enough) to have played in a Muratti match my only involvement being with the stewarding, gate money collecting or programme selling but even if I was only on the edge of the real action I quickly felt the tension and excitement of the day. I hope when you read this history some of your happier memories will come flooding back and make you realise that you have been part of something very special. Long may it continue.

DEDICATION

This book is dedicated to my long-suffering family. My wife, Margaret who, along with Jeremy, Raymond, Jacqueline and David, has been very patient with me over the years as my research notes grew and grew. They can now have their dining room, spare room and living room back.

NOTE

I have tried not to include any personal comments throughout the book but any opinions that have been expressed will be mine and not from any of the Football Associations. Any mistakes and omissions are my responsibility and I apologise for any errors that appear.